The
Lin Piao
Affair

EDITED BY MICHAEL Y. M. KAU

The Lin Piao Affair

POWER POLITICS

AND MILITARY COUP

INTERNATIONAL ARTS AND SCIENCES PRESS, INC., WHITE PLAINS, N.Y.   iasp

To my parents, V.O.P.

"Comrade Lin Piao has consistently held high the great red banner of Mao Tse-tung Thought and has most loyally and resolutely carried out and defended Comrade Mao Tse-tung's proletarian revolutionary line. Comrade Lin Piao is Comrade Mao Tse-tung's close comrade-in-arms and successor."

THE CONSTITUTION OF THE
COMMUNIST PARTY OF CHINA,
ADOPTED APRIL 14, 1969

"During and after the Ninth Congress, Lin Piao continued with his conspiracy and sabotage in spite of the admonishments, rebuffs, and efforts to save him by Chairman Mao and the Party's Central Committee. He went further to start a counterrevolutionary coup d'etat ... in a wild attempt to assassinate our great leader Chairman Mao and set up a rival central committee."

CHOU EN-LAI'S POLITICAL REPORT
TO THE TENTH PARTY CONGRESS,
AUGUST 24, 1973

Contents

Preface

If the drama of Mao Tse-tung's tireless striving for the ideal of continuing the revolution and transforming Chinese society is fascinating to the Western student of Chinese politics, the collateral struggle over policy and power is probably even more so. One recent development in this saga is of course the startling rise and fall of Lin Piao, the minister of defense and official successor-designate to Mao up until his mysterious death on September 13, 1971.

The Ninth Congress of the Chinese Communist Party, held in 1969, officially proclaimed Lin Piao to be "Comrade Mao Tse-tung's close comrade-in-arms and successor." Lin and the army under his command were praised for having consistently held high the great red banner of Mao Tse-tung thought and for having most loyally and resolutely carried out and defended Mao's proletarian revolutionary line. Yet, at the Tenth Party Congress, a scant four years later, Lin was publicly labeled "the bourgeois careerist, conspirator, double-dealer, renegade and traitor" and stood accused of having engineered a military coup d'etat in an attempt to split the Party, assassinate Mao, and restore capitalism in China. Even his death was unusually dramatic. He was reported to have died in a plane crash in Mongolia in an attempt to escape to the Soviet Union after his coup plot was aborted.

Indeed, the dramatic development of the Lin Piao affair, together with the great political turmoil of the Cultural Revolution, challenges many of the theories and assumptions about the patterns and processes of the Chinese political system which Western scholars had formulated prior to 1966. More specifi-

cally, Lin Piao's military coup attempt raises serious questions
about the civil-military relationship and the tradition of the
multifunctionality of the Red Army in China. The Maoist model
of army-building calls for the military to perform a wide variety of nonmilitary tasks, while insisting that the civilian Party
control of the army be maintained. In Mao's own words, the
army should function not only as a "fighting force" but also as
a "working force"; and "the Party commands the gun and the
gun shall never be allowed to command the Party."

This book focuses on the background events and politics of
Lin Piao's abortive military coup and its aftermath. The book
is also concerned with the broad critical questions concerning
the role of the military in the Chinese Communist political system, which has been under strain since the mid-1960s, the escalation of power politics triggered by the Cultural Revolution,
and the crisis of political succession now confronting the aging
Mao.

The Editor's Introduction presents a reconstruction and critical analysis of the Lin Piao affair based on sources and information gathered inside and outside China. Since no definitive
work on a case as intriguing as that of Lin's can be undertaken
without unrestricted access to all relevant documents and evidence in China and, more importantly, since this fact is
not likely to change for the foreseeable future, this volume
also assembles a wide range of important source materials
crucial to an understanding of the case. They include "top-
secret" Party documents, Red Guard publications, press and
secret criticisms of Lin, as well as a comprehensive collection
of Lin's own speeches and instructions from the 1965-1970
period. It is hoped that by making this set of important materials readily available in a single volume to students of Chinese
politics, this book will stimulate more interest and further research on the perplexing case of Lin Piao. The value of the
materials contained here transcends the Lin Piao affair itself,
however. They offer most revealing information about and
valuable insights into many other important questions of the
past two decades, ranging from factional politics to Mao's

authoritarian rule, from the disputes over economic and military priorities to the controversies over the role of individuals in history.

Although the secret Party documents gathered in this volume are collected from sources outside China (Hong Kong, Taiwan, and Japan), their authenticity has fortunately been confirmed consistently by Peking's official statements, informal conversations with cadres inside China, Red Guard reports, and a wide range of corroborating known facts. In order to compensate for possibly deliberate distortions and fabrications of Lin's ideological and policy stances present in the official version of the case, a comprehensive collection of fifty-one speeches, statements and instructions given by Lin between 1966 and 1970 is included. This gives Lin the opportunity to speak out in his own defense.

This volume owes its initial conception to the interests and insights into the significance of materials related to the Lin affair conveyed to me by some members of the Advisory Committee of the journal Chinese Law and Government, which I edit. Their encouragement and assistance resulted first in the publication of some of the documents in the journal, and later convinced me of the usefulness of producing this volume.

In the process of research and preparation of this volume for publication, I have received valuable advice, bibliographical help, and moral support from many scholars and librarians in this country. I am particularly indebted to A. Doak Barnett, Thomas P. Bernstein, Pao-min Chang, Parris H. Chang, King C. Chen, Philip E. Ginsburg, John W. Lewis, Victor H. Li, John T. Ma, Susan H. Marsh, Suzanne Ogden, Michel Oksenberg, Pierre M. Perrolle, Lucian W. Pye, James D. Seymour, Christopher J. Szymanski, Tang Tsou, Ezra F. Vogel, Richard Williams, Lea E. Williams, Eugene Wu, and P. K. Yu.

I wish especially to acknowledge the generosity of Thomas W. Robinson, Council on Foreign Relations, in making available to me his manuscript on Lin Piao, which was an invaluable aid in my research.

During my recent research trip to China, Hong Kong, and

Japan (1973-74), my work was greatly facilitated by the gracious assistance and cooperation rendered by Steve S. K. Chin, David Dean, Likhit Dhiravegin, Etō Shinkichi, Loren Fessler, B. Michael Frolic, Galen W. Fox, Wever Gim, William Hsu, Ichiko Chūzō, Kawamura Yoshio, Joseph Lelyveld, Sidney Liu, William L. Parish, Jr., Tai Kuo-hui, John J. Taylor, Ting Wang, Tokuda Noriyuki, Byron S. J. Weng, Martin K. Whyte, and Caroline A. Yang.

Research grants awarded by the Social Science Research Council and the Fulbright-Hays Program have enabled me to devote myself to research and writing during the academic year 1973-74. Their support is gratefully acknowledged. However, the analysis and opinions presented in this volume, needless to say, are strictly my own.

The superb editorial support and moral encouragement given by Douglas Merwin, China Publications Editor, and Fred Ablin, Editorial Director, both of International Arts and Sciences Press, were most invaluable, and I thank them.

My wife and our children are, as always, delighted that the ordeal of this project has finally come to an end.

M. Y. M. K.

Providence, R. I.
May 1974

Introduction

The Cultural Revolution and Lin Piao's abortive military coup
have probably been the most significant and dramatic developments in the political system of China since the Communists
seized power in 1949. In the context of these colossal political
upheavals, the downfall of Liu Shao-ch'i in the sixties and the
purge of Lin Piao in the seventies are particularly challenging
and fascinating for the student of Chinese politics. Liu and Lin
were different in many ways with respect to their political orientations and career backgrounds, yet they had one thing in
common: Each was officially designated by Mao at one point
as his successor, the man to be entrusted with the future of
China's continuing revolution; yet each was subsequently found
to be a "revisionist" and "sham Marxist." Each was at one
stage of his political career regarded as the most loyal follower
of Chairman Mao and the best pupil of Mao Tse-tung thought;
yet each allegedly became a "traitor" and "careerist" who
plotted against his leader. (1)

What are the factors that contributed to such a perplexing
development? Was it caused by the "struggle between two
lines" over policy and ideological matters, as the Maoists
would argue? Or was it prompted by other variables such as
the power struggle, the quest for political security, and the
anxiety over the uncertainties of political succession? It is
hoped that a close examination of the case of Lin Piao will
shed some light on these important questions.

The Rise of Lin Piao and His Army

Even before the nationwide Communist victory in 1949, Lin's

brilliant military career had already made him well known. (2)
Some highlights of his early career are worth noting. (3) He
was appointed commander of the Communist-led First Army
Corps as early as 1931, when he was only twenty-four years
old. Later, between 1934 and 1936, he took part in the historic
Long March side by side with Chairman Mao. During the Yenan
period he served as president of the prestigious Anti-Japanese
Military and Political University. In the last stage of the Civil
War in the late 1940s, the Fourth Field Army under his command scored a series of impressive victories from Northeast
to Central China. In the early 1950s he was reported to have
commanded the Chinese "Volunteers" in the Korean War.
However, owing to poor health, he became relatively inactive
politically throughout the fifties.

But Lin's big political advance came immediately after the
stormy Lushan Politburo Conference (July 2-August 1, 1959)
and the Eighth Plenum of the Eighth Central Committee (August 2-16, 1959), when P'eng Te-huai openly challenged Mao
on the issues of the Great Leap Forward and the commune
movement. P'eng was purged as minister of national defense,
and Lin was appointed to replace him. (4) From then on, Lin
became identified as the foremost student of Mao's thought, the
Chairman's most loyal follower, and the man who had faithfully
put into effect the Maoist line of army-building.

In retrospect, there is no doubt that Lin deserved that reputation and honor. (5) No sooner had he resumed control of
the People's Liberation Army (PLA) in 1959 then he began to
overhaul and reinvigorate the entire Party structure within the
military and to reestablish the priority of Party control and
leadership in the army in accordance with the "political work
system" model advocated by Mao. The revived "political
work system" was soon applied to mobilizing the army to carry
out a series of mass movements designed to strengthen and
politicize the PLA. As vividly revealed in the secret military
journal Bulletin of Activities (Kung-tso t'ung-hsün) (6), it was
clearly at Lin's personal initiative and under his close guidance
that "Give Prominence to Politics," "Living Study and Applica-

tion of Mao Tse-tung Thought," "Four Firsts," "Three-Eight Work Style," "Five-Good Company," "Five-Good Soldier," and other such slogans became fully animated in the early 1960s and were vigorously applied in the army's daily life. (7)

By 1962, when the process of internal overhaul and reinvigoration had been completed, the army began to turn outward, exerting conspicuous influence in society at large. Army heroes like Wang Chieh, Lei Feng, and Mai Hsien-te were, one after another, hailed as revolutionary models for the whole nation to emulate. People all over the country were mobilized from 1964 on to take part in the "Learn from the PLA" movement. (8) Between 1964 and 1966 the organizational structure of the army's "political work system" was introduced into schools, enterprises, factories, and even Party organs throughout the nation, and large numbers of army cadres and demobilized servicemen, in a particularly notable way, were transferred to man the newly organized "political work departments" in all sectors of civilian life. (9)

The power and influence of the military grew still further during the Cultural Revolution. As the regular Party apparatus and state bureaucracy were paralyzed by the Red Guards' violent assaults to seize power from the "power-holders" and "capitalist-roaders," the military emerged from early 1967 on as the "mainstay of the dictatorship of the proletariat." (10) Mao finally called on the military to intervene to impose military control and maintain law and order when chaos and armed conflict among factions and groups seriously threatened the state. (11) Since then, the army's formidable influence and presence have been maintained in every walk of life through the nationwide "three-support and two-military" campaigns (i.e., support the broad masses of the Left, support industry, and support agriculture; and carry out military control and military training). (12)

The influence of the army was even formally institutionalized when military representatives came to dominate the composition of the provisional organs of power (known as revolutionary committees), taking the form of the "three-way alliance" of the

military, the revolutionary masses, and the revolutionary
cadres. Later, in the reorganized Party committees, the military continued to play the most dominant organizational role. (13)

It was also during the Cultural Revolution that Lin Piao
reached the peak of his political career. Described in August
1966 as Mao's "close comrade-in-arms" and sole vice chairman
of the Central Committee of the Party, by 1969, without precedence in Party history, Lin was officially proclaimed as
Chairman Mao's successor in the new Party Constitution (approved at the Ninth Party Congress, April 1-24, 1959). The
Constitution explicitly stated:

> Comrade Lin Piao has consistently held high the great red
> banner of Mao Tse-tung thought and has most loyally and
> resolutely carried out and defended Comrade Mao Tse-
> tung's proletarian revolutionary line. Comrade Lin Piao
> is Comrade Mao Tse-tung's close comrade-in-arms and
> successor. (14)

The Making of a Military Coup

As Lin's prestige and influence reached a pinnacle in the
political arena and his army rapidly expanded its power and
dominance in every sector of society, tensions began to emerge
between Mao and Lin and between the military and the civilian
leadership. Each side appears to have increasingly perceived
the other as the competitor for power and influence. (15) An
abrupt turning point in this tense relationship occurred during
the Second Plenum of the Ninth Central Committee held at
Lushan, August 23 to September 6, 1970. At this meeting some
specific disagreements between Mao and Lin came to light.
Mao was apparently shocked by the unexpected "surprise attack"
launched to challenge his authority between August 23 and 25
by Ch'en Po-ta and seven top military leaders, probably acting
on Lin's initiative. (16) The gist of the surprise attack was an
attempt to reverse Mao's previous instruction of March 1970
that preparations be made for convening the Fourth National

People's Congress and that in the new state constitution a state chairmanship should not be provided for. The incident apparently prompted Mao to reevaluate Lin's loyalties and policy orientations. Mao was later to describe the events at the Lushan Plenum as "a struggle between two headquarters." (17)

The struggle that followed the Lushan confrontation may be broadly divided into two stages. In the first stage, from September 1970 to January 1971, Mao maneuvered rapidly in an attempt to break up Lin's power bases in the Central Committee, the Military Affairs Commission (MAC), and the Peking Military Region by taking three preemptive measures. In Mao's own words:

> One was to throw stones, one was to mix in sand, and the third was to dig up the cornerstone. I criticized the material Ch'en Po-ta had used to deceive many people, and I commented on reports of the Thirty-Eighth Army and of the Tsinan Military Region on opposing arrogance and complacency. I also made critical comments on a document of the long forum of the Military Affairs Commission which didn't criticize Ch'en at all. My method was to get hold of these stones and give critical comments, and then let everyone discuss them — this was throwing stones. When dirt is too tightly packed, no air can get through, but if a little sand is mixed in, air can circulate. When work groups of the Military Affairs Commission did not have enough people mixed in, more were added — this is called mixing in sand. Reorganizing the Peking Military Region is called digging up the cornerstone. (18)

Indeed, on September 15, 1970, Mao issued "A Letter to the Whole Party" demanding the launching of a "Criticize Ch'en [Po-ta] Rectification Campaign," obviously aimed indirectly at Lin and his followers within the Central Committee. Next, he convened the Enlarged Politburo Conference at Peitaiho (also known as the North China Conference) in December, insisting on open criticism and self-criticism for the seven "big

generals," Lin's key supporters in the MAC. And finally, in
late January 1971, Mao successfully reorganized the high command of the Peking Military Region by transferring the Thirty-
Eighth Army, a unit loyal to Lin, out of Peking and by relieving
both the commander, Chen Wei-shan, and the second political
commissar, Li Hsüeh-feng, who were known to be Lin's followers. (19)

The second stage of the struggle is characterized by Lin's
desperate countermaneuvering for political survival from
February until his death on September 13, 1971. Obviously
gravely alarmed by Mao's ultimate aim, Lin began to search
for a way out, and in late February he decided to resort to the
desperate alternative of organizing a military coup against
Mao. Lin's son, Lin Li-kuo, then deputy director of operations
of the Air Force, was, logically, chosen to direct the secret
organizing and planning. A number of top military leaders who
were close followers of Lin such as Huang Yung-sheng (chief
of staff), Wu Fa-hsien (commander-in-chief of the Air Force),
Li Tso-p'eng (first political commissar of the Navy) and Ch'iu
Hui-tso (director of the General Logistics Department) seem to
have been involved in the plot from the early stages of preparation. From March 22 through March 24 an outline plan for a
military coup called "Project 571" (the number, read "wu-
ch'i-i" in Chinese, is a homonym for "armed uprising") was
drafted in the Shanghai area. The strategy called for a quick
strike and occupation of the Shanghai-Nanking area and then
extension of control to the Peking and Canton areas through coordinated action with other units of the armed forces. (20) A
specific contingency plan called for the assassination of Mao
on September 12 by bombing his train while he was on an inspection tour in the Hangchow and Shanghai areas. However,
Lin's daughter, Lin Tou-tou, revealed the plot to Chou En-lai,
just in time to warn Mao of the imminent strike. (21)

On hearing of the foiling of the coup attempt, Lin, his wife,
Yeh Ch'ün, and Lin Li-kuo boarded an Air Force Trident jet,
No. 256, at Peitaiho and took off in an attempt to escape to the
Soviet Union. But the plane crashed in a forced landing near

Undur Khan, Mongolia, at 2:30 a.m. on September 13, and all nine persons aboard were burned to death. (22) The key co-conspirators, notably Ch'en Po-ta, Huang Yung-sheng, Wu Fa-hsien, Li Tso-p'eng, and Ch'iu Hui-tso, were immediately arrested and dismissed from office. An ad hoc investigation team was formed by the Central Committee to look into the conspiracy and other secret activities of the Lin-Ch'en group. (23) The team concluded its work by submitting for action its final investigation and recommendation report to the Central Committee on July 10, 1973, prior to the opening of the Tenth Party Congress. (24)

The Context of Struggle: Policy Differences

The abrupt downfall of Lin Piao from the pyramid of power, surrounded by a cloud of mysterious intrigue and conspiracy, caused a great shock both inside and outside China. Even his death was startling in a way that no student of Chinese Communist politics would have ever expected. For three years after his death, without his name being mentioned, he was attacked as a "political swindler like Liu Shao-ch'i," a "traitor," and an "ambitious careerist." He was accused of having secretly plotted to assassinate Mao, to split the Party, and to seize power through a military coup d'etat. In addition, he was alleged to have committed a wide variety of ideological and policy errors.

Since the Tenth Party Congress of August 1973, Lin has been publicly identified by name as "the bourgeois careerist, conspirator, double-dealer, renegade, and traitor." (25) A nation-wide campaign to "criticize Lin and Confucius" was launched soon thereafter designed to totally discredit Lin as a Confucius of the modern age, an agent of the slave-owning landlord-bour-geois class, and a counterrevolutionary plotting to restore the "rites" of capitalism. (26)

The "crimes" Lin is alleged to have committed seem to fall into two broad categories: (1) Lin's deviations from the policy and line set by Mao and the Party, and (2) his personal ambition

and drive for power through conspiracy and military coup d'etat
against Mao and the Party. The documentation of the case to
date, however, does not convincingly support the argument that
the attempted coup by Lin against Mao was prompted chiefly by
a profound divergence in policy orientation between the two.
The thrust of the case instead appears mainly to have been the
power struggle among the key individual political actors and
competing institutional forces led by Mao and Lin respectively.
However, policy divergences seem to have played a role which
provided an ideological and policy context for power struggle and thus facilitated the generation of a military coup,
even if the coup itself may have actually been triggered by
other causes.

Policy differences between Mao and Lin may be inferred
from two separate sets of documents: the alleged plot outline
and the criticisms of Lin Piao. The plot documents are particularly revealing on policy divergence because the conspirators
had articulated their policy stands in order to justify their action against the existing leadership. (27) Their attacks on Mao
range from his poor management of economic policy and foreign
affairs to his periodic purges of cadres and his theory of continuing the revolution.

In the outline of "Project 571" the economy is described as
stagnant, the standard of living as falling, and the masses as
dissatisfied. The peasants lacked food and were short of clothing, while the workers felt exploited because their wages had
been frozen. The "571" plot called for a policy of " a prosperous people and a strong country" to replace "a prosperous
country but an impoverished people" and for making people
"happy with their homes and content with their work."

Further evidence of Lin's dissatisfaction with economic
policy may be inferred from the accusation that Lin attempted
to "overturn the three agenda items of the Second Plenary Session
of the Ninth Central Committee." (28) It is not entirely clear
what the exact nature of the three agenda items was, but the
Second Plenum communiqué suggests that one was the State
Council Report on the National Planning Conference and the
National Economic Plan for 1970. (29) Moreover, at the Tenth

Party Congress, convened in August 1973, Lin was formally accused of having produced for the Ninth Party Congress, held in April 1969, in collaboration with Ch'en Po-ta, a draft political report that stressed the priority of economic production over the task of continuing the revolution and class struggle. (30) Indeed, such accusations against Lin are consistent with the theme emphasized in the current campaign of "criticizing Lin Piao and Confucius," which identifies Lin as a representative of the capitalist-landlord class and a reactionary Rightist, rather than a "Leftist" as he was sometimes branded in the press before 1973. (31)

The foreign policy line of the conspirators was not very explicit, but several points suggest that there may have been an appreciable difference between Mao and Lin on the most important foreign policy issue of the sixties, namely, the attitude toward the potential security threat posed by the Soviet Union. The "Project 571" outline does state that the conspirators would have the support of the Soviet Union. It is possible that "illicit relations" or at least some tacit agreements existed between the conspirators in China and individuals in the Soviet Union. This was not necessarily the case, however. Indeed, Soviet support would most likely be available to any faction plotting against Mao regardless of whether or not any prearrangements had been made. Lin's alleged attempt to escape to the Soviet Union on September 13, 1971, is indicative of, at least, the plotters' perception of the likely Soviet attitude toward a coup against Mao. More significantly, the plot outline states that the "confrontation between China and the Soviet Union is giving the Soviet Union a hard time." This would suggest that in Lin's view the Soviet Union was at least as much on the defensive as China. From the accusation that Lin neglected the policy of military training and preparedness we may infer that Lin also perceived the Soviet threat as being less serious than Mao's assessment of it. This possibility is reinforced by the fact that a second agenda item of the 1970 Lushan Plenum which Lin sought to overturn appears to have been a report of the MAC on "Strengthening the Work for Preparedness Against War." (32)

The most vehement expressions of dissatisfaction in the "Project 571" outline are related to the method of periodic rectification and purge campaigns and in particular to Mao's leadership style. Mao's theory of continuing the revolution and class struggle was denounced as being nothing more than Trotsky's theory of permanent revolution. The conspirators objected to Mao's "merry-go-round" style of engaging successive groups in political struggle. The Lin group attacked:

> Their socialism is, in essence, social fascism. They have turned China's state machine into a kind of meat grinder for mutual slaughter and strife, and they have made the Party and the whole country's political life into a patriarchal life of the feudal, dictatorial, and autocratic type. (33)

As to Mao himself, the conspirators felt:

> He abuses the trust and status given him by the Chinese people. In an historical sense he is going backward — actually he has become a contemporary Ch'in Shih-huang [the First Emperor of the Ch'in dynasty].... He is not a true Marxist-Leninist, but rather one who follows the way of Confucius and Mencius, one who dons Marxist-Leninist clothes but implements the laws of Ch'in Shih-huang. He is the biggest feudal despot in Chinese history. (34)

The close associates of Mao were described as "corrupt, muddled, and incompetent, opposed by the masses and deserted by their followers":

> A small gang of officials have become remorseless and despotic; moreover they control military power and make enemies on all sides. Their heads are swelling and they overestimate themselves. (35)

On the whole, these criticisms of Mao are closer to personal

attacks than to clearly argued policy differences. Furthermore,
these criticisms were made when Lin and his supporters were
already under fire. The reason behind Lin's opposition to
"merry-go-round" revolutionary struggle was undoubtedly his
realization that he was the next target. In this light it is not
difficult to see why the attacks became so personal and bitter.
From Lin's perspective, as explicitly stated in the plot outline,
"the coup [by Mao] is presently developing in a way that will
benefit the pen [civilian forces]." (36) Such a statement shows
that the plotters perceived the conflicts very much in terms
not only of the personal animosity and distrust between Mao
and Lin but also of the power relationship between the Party
and the army.

    On the subject of military policy, the plot outline itself does
not reveal any policy dispute. In the Maoists' charges made
against him, however, Lin is accused of having turned the PLA
into a "cultural [wen-hua] army," engaging only in civil [wen]
training and neglecting military training. (37) It should be
noted that the balance between military and political work, like
the balance between "democracy" and "centralism," for instance,
is a delicate one, difficult to assess, particularly as it is subject to change with shifting objective conditions. Given the difficulty of evaluating the "correct" balance, disagreement with
Mao is a likely occurrence.

    It is possible, as mentioned earlier, that the cause of Lin's
deviation of giving greater emphasis to political work at the
expense of military training was related to a difference between the two men in assessing the military threat of the Soviet
Union. Lin may have disagreed with Mao on the necessity of
stepping up military training because he did not see the great
urgency that a Soviet threat would entail. It is also possible
that he viewed the issue in terms of the balance of power between two competing groups within the PLA: A policy shift
toward more military training might work in favor of those
generals who wanted to further professionalize the army and
withdraw the military from political involvement, which in the
context of his ambition for and ascendance to power, Lin was

not prepared to adopt. Considering the political developments of the sixties in China, it is highly unlikely that Lin would have been able to carry out such a thorough reorganization and politicization of the army for as long as ten years if Mao had truly disagreed with him on basic policy matters. (38)

The Thrust of Struggle: Power and Security

If the cause of the attempted military coup by Lin Piao against Mao cannot be satisfactorily explained in terms of policy divergence and dispute between Mao and Lin, it can be viewed more fruitfully in terms of struggle for power and quest for political security and survival. This is not to say that it should be assumed that all political actors in China always seek to maximize their power and security to the extent of resorting to a coup d'etat. The development of the Lin Piao affair seems to have resulted from a rather special power relationship at the top in the late 1960s and from a peculiar process of the escalation of power struggle that developed from the Cultural Revolution. In historical retrospect, the record is clear that before and during the Cultural Revolution Mao cultivated Lin and his army to support him in his struggle to regain the power he had lost to Liu Shao-ch'i. But at the same time Mao also created a dilemma for himself: Lin and the military expanded their power far beyond what Mao had anticipated at the outset. Under such circumstances, Mao became overly sensitive to and jealous of his precarious authority, status, and power under the shadow of the increasingly powerful military and Lin Piao. (39)

In retrospect again, there is little doubt that since 1959, Lin and the army under his command had consciously and systematically taken advantage of Mao's setbacks to expand their power and activity into every sector of society. Organizationally, as discussed earlier, they infused the army into the administrative and leadership structure from the top echelons down to the production units. This infusion took place in three steps. (40) First, between 1964 and 1966 the organizational structure of the army's "political work system" was introduced into schools, factories, enterprises, and even Party organs throughout the nation. Large numbers of army cadres and ex-army personnel were transferred to their newly organized "political work departments" in virtually all sectors of civilian life. Second, during the Cultural Revolution the military emerged as the "mainstay of the dictatorship of the proletariat," and the military representatives became legitimate and prominent partners of the "three-way alliances" of the "provisional organs of power" ("revolutionary committees," which were formed at the provincial level between January 31, 1967, and September 5, 1968). Finally, as the reconstruction of the Party began after the Ninth Party Congress (provincial-level Party committees were reestablished between November 24, 1970, and August 19, 1971), the dominant position of the army persisted. As shown in the table below, the representation of the PLA in the provincial Party committee leadership was even greater than in the earlier provincial revolutionary committees. Statistically, the power of the Army clearly surpassed other institutions such as the Party and the state bureaucracy.

To Mao, the excessive expansion of the power of the military constituted a gross violation of the fundamental principle of military line that he had advocated since 1929: "The Party commands the gun, and the gun must never be allowed to command the Party." (41) Even worse, the growing power and arrogance of the PLA posed a serious threat to the status and strength of the Party and state which he represented. By the late 1960s, therefore, the relationship between the Party and the army, between Mao and Lin, began to change from the traditional bonds of "the Party in command" to a new situation of rivalry and competition.

As revealed in the "top-secret" documents of the Central Committee, Mao complained bitterly during his inspection tour to the provinces in September 1971:

> Local Party committees had already been established, and
> they should have exercised unified leadership. Wasn't it
> just confusing if matters already decided upon by local

Military Representation in
the New Power Structure, 1969-71

Organization	Total Membership (number)	Military Representation (number)	%
Politburo [1]	25	13	52
Central Committee [2]			
Full members	170	64	38
Alternate members	109	41	38
Provincial Revolutionary Committee [3]			
Chairmen	29	21	72
Vice chairmen	250	90	36
Provincial Party Committee [4]			
First secretaries	29	22	74
All secretaries	158	95	60

Sources:
1) Issues & Studies VIII: 1 (October 1971), 23-27.
2) Tsu-kuo No. 89 (August 1971), 9-11.
3) Chung-kung yen-chiu VI: 7 (July 1972), 2.
4) Tsu-kuo No. 100 (July 1972), 7-8.
Also, Derek J. Waller, "Elite Composition and Revolutionary Change in Communist China, 1965-1969," paper presented at the Association for Asian Studies Meeting, 1972; Donald W. Klein and Lois B. Hager, "The Ninth Central Committee," The China Quarterly, No. 45 (January-March 1971), 37-56. These data are also reported in Ying-mao Kau, "The Case Against Lin Piao," Chinese Law and Government, V:3-4 (Fall-Winter 1972-73), 8.

Party committees were still taken to army Party committees for discussion? (<u>42</u>)

Mao clearly perceived that the army was reluctant to relinquish
its political power and administrative authority and restore
them to the Party committees even after the Party was being
rebuilt at the local levels. Moreover, as Mao put it, the army
also became "arrogant and complacent," and the tradition of
giving emphasis to the mass-line style of leadership was dis-
regarded. Mao's great dissatisfaction with the army was clearly
reflected in his strong demands in 1969-71 to carry out campaigns requiring "the PLA to learn also from the people of the
whole nation," and the army to observe strictly the Three Main
Rules of Discipline and the Eight Points for Attention. (<u>43</u>)

Although the development of the power and working relationship between the Party and the army since the Cultural Revolution was definitely not to Mao's liking, Mao and Lin appear to
have managed to maintain with restraints their symbiotic relations and tensions without open confrontation. Yet, the strains
in their relationship erupted dramatically at the Second Plenum
of the Ninth Central Committee in September 1970 over the
issue of state chairmanship in the new draft state constitution
which was then under discussion. It was to the conflict over
this particular question that the chain of events leading to the
coup attempt can be traced.

After Lin's formal designation as the successor-to-be at the
Ninth Party Congress in 1969, his followers apparently began
to initiate definitive measures to consolidate his newly gained
status in order to ensure an orderly and predictable political
succession when Mao passed from the scene. (<u>44</u>) To Lin and
his followers, to minimize the ambiguities in succession was
a way to maximize their political security and guarantee the
nation's continued stability. It was probably with that blend of
spirit and motives that Lin's followers, acting against Mao's previous instruction, reopened the issue of creating a state chairmanship in revising the state constitution at the Lushan Plenum of
August 1970. But Mao's reaction was immediate and outraged:

> Do not establish a state chairman and I will not be state
> chairman — I said this six times — and each time was just
> one sentence wasn't it? Even if there had been six thousand
> sentences they wouldn't listen. My words aren't even worth
> half a sentence; they aren't worth anything. (45)

Mao apparently quickly concluded that Lin wanted to occupy
that position himself for reasons of personal political ambition.
Mao said: "A certain person was very anxious to become State
Chairman, to split the Party and to seize power." (46)

What also particularly irked Mao was the way in which Lin
attempted to promote his own status and ideas. Political style
and work methods seem to have been as important in Mao's
mind as policy. Evidence of this is the strong wording used by
Mao in his August 1971 accusations and the more recent campaign calling for all political opposition to be "open and aboveboard" and not to "intrigue or conspire." (47) The method Lin
adopted at the Lushan Plenum was probably one not very different from the Western style of politics, e.g., lobbying and
caucusing behind closed doors before an open meeting. But to
Mao this type of behavior was totally unacceptable:

> At that [1970 Lushan] conference they engaged in surprise
> attacks and underground activities. Why weren't they brave
> enough to come out in the open? It was obvious they were
> up to no good. First they concealed things, then they
> launched a surprise attack.... Their coup didn't just last a
> day-and-a-half, but went on for two-and-a-half days, from
> August 23 and 24 to noon on the twenty-fifth. They cer-
> tainly had a purpose in doing all that! (48)

The incident apparently crystallized Mao's sense of the adverse
political situation surrounding him. He even perceived it as a
definite indication that the PLA was not being completely loyal
to him. Mao bluntly asked: "He [Lin] also said that the People's Liberation Army was founded and led by me, but personally commanded by Lin — why can't the founder also command?" (49)

In fact Mao cast the entire plenum in the extreme context of a
"struggle between two lines" and explicitly ranked Lin with his
principal enemies from Ch'en Tu-hsiu, Wang Ming, and Chang
Kuo-t'ao to P'eng Te-huai and Liu Shao-ch'i. (50)
After the plenum, however, Mao did indicate that the current
case differed from the nine previous major struggles in the history of the Party: The opposition had not yet been dealt with
conclusively and still had the opportunity to rehabilitate itself:

> What should we do with these people? We must still adopt
> the policy of education, that is, "learn from past mistakes
> to avoid future ones" and "cure the sickness to save the
> patient." We still want to protect Lin. No matter who one
> is, if one makes mistakes and ignores unity and line it is
> never a good thing. When I return to Peking I will again
> seek them out to talk things over. If they won't come
> to me, I'll go to them. Some can probably be saved, some
> not — we must observe their actions. (51)

This was the reason, according to Mao, that the plenum decided,
contrary to normal practice, to postpone an official "summing
up" at the end of the session, thereby leaving the door of mercy
and reconciliation ajar for Lin and his associates.
Attempting to become state chairman was not Lin Piao's only
effort to ensure his political security and guarantee his succession, however. Lin also promoted the "theory of genius." (52)
The theoretical issue is that of the role of individuals (heroes
or geniuses) in the historical process. The theory of genius
supports the importance of individuals such as Mao Tse-tung
and by implication denigrates the historical role of the masses
and of leadership organizations such as the Party. (53) The
practical issue, however, involves the symbolic manipulation
or "deification" of Mao Tse-tung. Whatever Lin's motives may
have been for elevating the status of Mao and his works before
and during the Cultural Revolution, the motives surely took on
a new dimension following his official designation as Mao's successor in 1969. Since an explicit line of succession had been

made between Mao and Lin, and since Lin had established himself as "the best pupil of Mao Tse-tung thought," Lin could
only stand to gain from increasing the symbolic charisma and
legitimacy of his predecessor-to-be. Mao asserted that this
was indeed the true motive of Lin: "He wanted to build me up
but in fact I don't know who he had in mind — the truth is that
he built himself up." (54) Furthermore, the "theory of genius"
underscores the importance of having a single dominant political leader. If this theory gained widespread acceptance, it
would clearly give legitimacy to one-man succession by Lin
Piao rather than to the formation of a collective leadership.

According to Mao, Lin also relied on factional loyalties to
build up his personal and organizational kingdom and split the
Party. This was widely practiced in key organizations such as
the MAC, the military region and district commands, and provincial Party committees and became evermore conspicuous
particularly after the purge of Chief of Staff Yang Ch'eng-wu
in March 1968. At the Lushan Plenum of 1970 Lin Piao had
apparently even won the support of Ch'en Po-ta, the foremost
ideologue of the nation and Mao's closest associate for over
thirty years, although the precise nature of their complicity
remains obscure. (55) As a special case of personal loyalty
Mao singled out the role played by Lin's wife, Yeh Ch'ün: "I
have never approved of one's wife heading the administrative
office of one's work unit. At Lin Piao's place, Yeh Ch'ün is the
director of the administrative office." (56)

One of Mao's major concerns with the building up of personal
loyalties was that it would generate mountaintopism, an independent kingdom, and factionalism within the Party and army. (57)
In speaking to local Party leaders during his inspection tour in
1971, Mao accused Lin of having attempted to split the Party,
and he demanded that "the Party must be unified, must be put
in order." (58) He also called for a campaign to study the
spirit of the "Internationale" with a special stress on the subject of Party unity:

The "Internationale" tells us to unite and march into

tomorrow.... To study Marxism is to emphasize unity
not splittism! We have sung the "Internationale" for fifty
years, yet some people in our Party have tried to split
the Party ten times. (59)

The Plan for Action: "Project 571"

In spite of his gesture of mercy and possible reconciliation
offered at the Lushan Plenum of 1970, Mao proceeded to put
his preemptive measures into action immediately after the
session. The Lin Piao loyalists were quick to see themselves
and the army as the potential targets of Mao's political maneuvering. At the time of its drafting, March 22-24, 1971, the
outline of "Project 571" assessed the situation as follows:

> [B-52, a code name for Mao, and his handful of dictators]
> not only incite cadres to struggle against cadres, and the
> masses to struggle against the masses, but they also in-
> cite the armed forces to struggle against the armed forces
> and Party members against Party members. They are the
> greatest advocates of armed struggle in China.
> They manufacture contradictions and splits in order to
> attain their goal of divide and rule, destroying each group
> in turn and maintaining their ruling position.
> ...Today he uses this force to attack that force; to-
> morrow he uses that force to attack this force. Today he
> uses sweet words and honeyed talk to those whom he
> entices, and tomorrow he puts them to death for some
> fabricated crimes. Those who are his guests today will
> be his prisoners tomorrow.
> Looking back at the history of the past few decades, do
> you see anyone whom he had supported initially who has not
> finally been handed a political death sentence? (60)

Given this outlook, the conspirators saw no possibility of pla-
cating Mao's anger and reversing their adversities without a
confrontation. They also realized that their fate would not be

decided by Mao alone and that they could not avoid a head-on
clash with the "civilian forces" which were determined to de-
prive the army of its newly gained power and status. As they
put it, "a new power struggle cannot be avoided; if we do not
seize control of revolutionary leadership, it will fall into the
hands of others."

In discussing the timing of the coup, the conspirators presented an even more desperate view of the predicament they
found themselves in:

> Both we and the enemy are riding a tiger from which it is
> hard to dismount.... This is a life-or-death struggle —
> either we devour them or they devour us. Strategically,
> there are two critical moments: one is when we have com-
> pleted our preparations and are able to devour them; one
> is when the enemy has opened his mouth to devour us and
> we are in critical danger; at this point we must burn our
> bridges behind us whether or not we are prepared. (61)

It is in this frame of mind that the group went ahead with its
planning. The architects of "Project 571" were apparently convinced of the general feasibility of a coup in spite of certain
difficulties. They were aware of the possibility that the timing
of the coup might have to be a bit premature under the pressure
of Mao's attacks. Indeed, they stated that "at present the preparation of our strength is still not adequate." (62) However,
as the months between March and September 1971 went by, the
problem of the lack of preparedness presumably was greatly
diminished. But the conspirators found that other obstacles to
launching a military takeover remained formidable; these were
(1) the tight security surrounding Mao, (2) the lack of unity
among military units, and (3) the defensive measures already
taken by Mao.

To overcome the problem of security it was vaguely proposed
that the "palace" could be encircled and that a high-level meeting could be used "to get all [Mao and key Central Committee
members] in the net at once." The plot document also mentions

such gruesome means as the use of poison gas, assassination, car accidents, kidnapping, and a new type of weapon code-named "543."

To the conspirators, the lack of military unity was another serious problem. From the experiences of the Cultural Revolution, most notably the Wuhan incident of July 1967, it was clear that when pressed for commitment various military units did not necessarily have unified loyalties and that such complexities in fact often made it difficult to refer to "the military" as though it were an undifferentiated corporate body. In the words of the "Project 571" plan, "because of B-52's divide and rule policy, the army's internal contradictions are fairly complex, which makes it difficult to form a united force which we can control." Mao Tse-tung's preemptive actions following the 1970 Lushan Plenum revealed that some military elements were clearly loyal to him. Through the tactics of "mixing in sand," Mao added military men loyal to him to work groups of the Military Affairs Commission, which were packed by Lin's followers. He also "dug up the cornerstone" of the opposition by reorganizing the Peking Military Region in January 1971, removing commanders and units loyal to Lin Piao and replacing them with loyalists of his own. (63) The conspirators were keenly aware of such moves, which appear to have effectively thwarted their initial plan to seize power through the control of the capital, Peking.

This left Lin with the alternative of seizing power "over the whole nation" by using the highly mobile (and also highly reliable) Air Force. Indeed, the architects of the plot included key Air Force figures such as Lin Piao's own son, Lin Li-kuo (deputy director of the Air Force Operations Department), Yü Hsin-yeh (deputy director of the Air Force Political Department), Li Wei-hsin (deputy director of the Secretariat of the Political Department of the Fourth Air Force Group), and Chou Yü-ch'ih (deputy director of the Air Force Political Department). Listed as basic supporting units in the coup plan were the Fourth and Fifth Air Force Groups controlled by Wang Wei-kuo (political commissar of the Fourth Air Force

Group stationed in Nanking), Ch'en Li-yün (political commissar
of the Fifth Air Force Group stationed in Chekiang), and Chiang
T'eng-chiao (political commissar of the Air Force Unit of the
Nanking Military Region).

Support for Lin was not restricted to the Air Force alone.
Other reliable military units named included the Shanghai,
Peking, and Canton "Fleets" (code name for pro-Lin forces):
the Ninth and the Eighteenth Divisions, the Twenty-first Tank
Regiment, the Thirty-fourth Division, and civilian aviation.
In addition, auxiliary support was expected from the Twentieth
and the Thirty-eighth armies, the Administrative Office of the
MAC, the Scientific and Technological Commission of the Ministry of Defense, and finally, unidentified forces of the Soviet
Union. It is also known from the criticism campaign which
followed the Second Plenum that Lin was supported by such
major figures as the chief of the general staff (Huang Yung-
sheng), the Air Force commander-in-chief (Wu Fa-hsien), the
first political commissar of the Navy (Li Tso-p'eng), the director general of the Logistics Department (Ch'iu Hui-tso), and
the director of the Administrative Office of the MAC (Lin's
own wife, Yeh Ch'ün). The military support Lin Piao was
ready to muster was obviously considerable.

One specific plan of action called for seizing power in
Shanghai militarily, capturing Chang Ch'un-ch'iao (first secretary of the Shanghai Party Committee and loyal to Mao) and
criticizing him politically. Military control would then be extended to Nanking, Chekiang, and Kiangsi and eventually to the
entire country, with the seizure and maintenance of strict control over radio stations and communications links. Public support was to be generated by "attacking B-52's forces while
waving B-52's flag" and by offering amnesty to all those "who
in the past have been persecuted by B-52 on fabricated charges."

From the point of view of military seizure of power, the coup
plan looked highly feasible. The more difficult task would have
been that of establishing a basis of legitmacy for political rule
and an effective administrative control following the military
takeover. Historically, since the years of the revolutionary

movement, the PLA had been serving as a "working force" in
a broad range of nonmilitary activity. Moreover, after Lin
Piao assumed command in 1959, and especially during the Cultural Revolution, the military had systematically infused itself
into all levels of the Party and state organizations and economic
enterprises. Aside from its extensive organizational skills and
administrative experience, the PLA as a whole also enjoyed
tremendous prestige and popularity because of its historical
role and its close ties with the masses. (64) In view of this, it
seems that as an institution the PLA had both the popular acceptance and the capacity to assume political rule. There were
indeed the important precedents that the PLA had at least twice
effectively exercised such political rule in the name of "military
control": first, during the takeover from the Nationalists in
the late 1940s, and then, during the chaotic years of the Cultural Revolution in the 1960s.

A question which is far more difficult to deal with, however,
involves the potential leadership role and legitimacy of Lin
Piao himself. Lin of course had already benefited from his
designation as Mao's successor. He could hardly have hoped
for more in the way of legitimate status, particularly as reinforced by his dissemination of the "theory of genius." Nevertheless, one cannot overlook the fact that the coup would have
been directed against the existing legitimate and charismatic
leader and would have been very difficult to justify regardless
of the popular images of the PLA and of Lin Piao. It is not
surprising, therefore, that the conspirators showed great concern about the "blind faith" of the masses in Chairman Mao. (65)
The plot outline specifically instructed: "attack B-52's forces
while waving B-52's flag in order to soften public opinion."
And in reference to the planned capture of Chang Ch'un-ch'iao,
the outline called for "bringing into play all the instruments of
public opinion to publicize his traitorous crimes." (66) Success
in implementing legitimate rule immediately following the coup
clearly hinged more on justifying the removal from power of
Lin's opponents than on building up authority for Lin Piao,
whose prestige was already assured. And the most difficult

problem of all, of course, would have been the disposition of
the hitherto infallible leader, Mao Tse-tung, whom the masses
worshiped with "blind faith." The worries and preoccupations
of this kind are clearly reflected in the conversations of the
plotters in their planning sessions. According to the confession
of Li Wei-hsin after the foiling of the coup attempt, a key conspirator was reported to have argued:

> There are ways of doing it, such as placing the Chairman
> under house arrest for the purpose of negotiation. [We]
> can get rid of the Chairman while placing the blame on
> somebody else. Send for Wang Tung-hsing and Chang
> Ch'un-ch'iao and get rid of them first. Then just say that
> they are in collusion with Wang, Kuang, Ch'i [ultra-
> Leftists] or so-and-so in an attempt to murder the Chair-
> man. Or get a few prisoners to be the scapegoats. By that
> time, since the chief [Lin Piao] would have the supreme
> power, he could come out to make some statements and
> take care of the whole situation. (67)

In Conclusion: The Coup Attempt and Its Aftermath

The mysteries surrounding Lin's coup attempt will probably
never be completely reconstructed and understood. A careful reading of all the available documentation on the case,
however, conveys a distinct impression that, policy and ideological diverence and tensions notwithstanding, the thrust
of the life-and-death struggle was most likely triggered by
the struggle for power and security between Mao and Lin
and between the Party and the army. Its major impetus flowed
from the chain of actions and reactions, challenges and re-
sponses which stemmed from the dynamics of the balancing
and struggle for power. In the absence of a well-defined or
institutionalized process of political succession, the successor-
designate was forced to consolidate his power base, and such
efforts ran counter to Mao's jealously guarded authority and
style of operation. Having aroused Mao's anger and suspicions

with regard to his loyalty, Lin saw no alternative but to attempt by force and conspiracy to seize power for his own survival.

In this chain of events, the incident over the issue of the state chairmanship at the 1970 Lushan Plenum apparently constitutes the watershed from which the tensions between Mao and Lin made a "dialectical leap" from the realm of policy disputes to that of personal distrust and hostility, and from the domain of reconcilable "nonantagonistic" contradictions to that of irreconcilable "antagonistic" struggle.

In this regard, it should be pointed out, Lin's coup and assassination attempts were basically "reactive" and "defensive" in nature. He resorted to them in the spring of 1971 mainly in response to Mao's successful preemptive moves to corner him and eliminate him. No available sources to date suggest that Lin premeditated a coup and assassination as his chosen method to seek power and succession before 1970. It may therefore be argued that had Mao not assumed such an "antagonistic" posture of struggle following the 1970 Lushan Plenum, it is doubtful that Lin would have gone so far as to take the ultimate step of coup d'etat.

It is interesting to note that the major political struggles between "two headquarters" among the top leadership in China since 1949 appear to fall into two broad categories: One stems primarily from power struggle, and the other emerges from disputes over basic line and policy matters. The cases of Kao Kang and Jao Shu-shih typify the former, while those of P'eng Te-huai and Liu Shao-ch'i exemplify the latter. In the first category, as personal ambitions and power considerations are dominant, the struggle tends to be extremely bitter and violent and to culminate in the physical death of the opponents. In the second, since they are disputes over abstract principles and policies, they are likely to be more impersonal and less violent, and victims are generally given a chance to repent and rectify themselves. The latter approach is generally in line with the official recognition of the legitimacy of "inner-Party struggle" and Mao's well-known policy of "curing the sickness to save the patient" when dealing with cadres who make mistakes. (68)

The case of Lin Piao, however, falls into the first category,
and the more lenient approach of "nonantagonistic" struggle
did not apply. Thus Lin came to a violent death. The Lin Piao
affair, however, did not end with his death and the arrest of his
followers in September 1971. Since that time there have been
ongoing political campaigns aimed at thoroughly discrediting
Lin and resolving various problems triggered by the crisis.

The downfall of leading political figures in China has usually
entailed extensive buildups of a case against such individuals,
including some rewriting of history and the presentation of evidence which sometimes reaches far into the past. The attack
on Lin is no exception. It is said now that Lin all along had
been a reactionary follower of Confucius and a counterrevolutionary, plotting to restore the "rites" of capitalism to the
state. (69) His pessimistic and conservative attitude toward
the revolutionary movement was detected by Chairman Mao
as early as 1930. (70) Moreover, the Party has also circulated
a private letter Mao is purported to have written to his wife
Chiang Ch'ing on July 8, 1966, expressing his serious doubt
about Lin's ideological purity and loyalty to the Party. (71)

In conjunction with the vehement attacks on Lin's personal
greed for power and fame, the ongoing nationwide campaigns to
"criticize Lin Piao and Confucius," launched after the Tenth
Party Congress of August 1973, have also greatly expanded and
magnified Lin's "sinister crimes" into a broad array of ideological and policy matters. The long list of his deviations ranges
from idealist apriorism to "inspiration-ism," and from sabotaging the educational revolution to undermining Mao's cadre
policy. (72) The orchestration of accusations against Lin in
line and policy, many of which are poorly substantiated and
uncomprehensible, seems to be aimed mainly at raising the
level of criticisms from the rather uninspiring level of power
struggle to the more acceptable plane of ideological and policy
disputes, thus justifying Mao's purge of Lin with the noble cause
of struggle for continuing the revolution. It is not surprising,
therefore, to find that Lin is now condemned as an "out-and-out
Rightist," and not a "Leftist," as he was regarded during and

immediately after the Cultural Revolution. At most, he was
"Left in form but Right in essence." (73)

One problem of great importance clearly discernible in the
aftermath of Lin's coup attempt concerns the role of the military in China's political system under the Communist leadership. The Maoist doctrine of army-building, as emphasized
earlier, involves two basic principles: The military should
function not only as a "fighting force" but also as a "working
force"; and "the Party commands the gun." (74) In essence,
this means that the PLA should participate in political, economic, cultural, and other work outside the barracks, but that
such work should be done only under the leadership of the Party.
The military should never be allowed to dominate the Party or
exercise direct control over society. The crisis of Lin's attempted coup clearly taught Mao the lesson that an excessive
expansion of the role of the military could lead the army to
overstep the bounds of its authority and upset the correct pattern of civil-military relationship that he favored. (75)

The energetic campaigns launched after the Ninth Party Congress to reinforce the Party's "centralized leadership" (i-yüan-
hua ling-tao) and to rectify the army's style of work clearly
reflect Mao's sense of urgency that the military was moving
in the wrong direction. (76) Some specific corrective measures
taken by Mao since 1969 are noteworthy. The Party reconstruction movement that was begun in 1969 demanded an end
to the abnormal phenomenon of "military control," replacing
it with the Party committee's collective leadership and unified
leadership. At the same time, the weight of military representation in Party committees and revolutionary committees
at various levels was gradually reduced, and the military was
asked to withdraw from direct involvement in administrative
and managerial control. (77) Within the PLA, as stated in a
major article in Red Flag, "military consolidation and training
and political consolidation and training should be given equal
time." (78) It was further pointed out that "politics must be in
command of and lead military affairs, but it cannot replace
military affairs." (79)

To combat the "arrogance and complacency" of armymen
entrenched in their new positions of power inside and outside
the barracks, the Party also reissued the Three Main Rules of
Discipline and the Eight Points for Attention of the old Red
Army and singled them out as "important teaching materials
for education in ideology and political line." (80) The tenor of
the educational campaign gave disciplinary matters the highest
priority, demanding that the armymen "obey [Party] orders in
all actions." (81)

To be sure, the efforts to redefine the limits of the Army's
activity, to restore the proper "mix" between military and
political work in the Army, and to reimpose the traditional work
style on the armymen have shown considerable success since
the Ninth Party Congress. Yet the general influence and power
of the PLA is still highly visible today. In the Tenth Central
Committee elected in August 1973, for example, over one quarter of the membership still comprises military men. (82) Hence
the problems of controlling the military, which involve such
sensitive and complex questions as power distribution and organizational coordination on a large scale, are likely to persist
for some time beyond the demise of Lin Piao.

Another extremely important and intricate legacy of the
Lin Piao affair concerns the problem of political opposition.
The authoritarian Chinese system is by nature intolerant of
political opposition, and the aging Mao, with his formidable
charisma and preoccupation with continuing the revolution, has
undoubtedly compounded the problem. The coup attempt organized by Lin shows clearly that Mao's opponents included
not only those close personal associates of Lin's but also military leaders who had developed vested interests in the growing
status and power of the army.

Immediately after the fall of Lin, at least 32 key generals
occupying top posts (chief-of-staff, commanders or deputy commanders, and political commissars or deputy political commissars) in the three general departments, two services, and
eight arms of the PLA at the national level were arrested and
dismissed. At the local levels of the military region and the

military district, more than 25 commanders and political commissars had been removed by early 1973. (83) According to one source, as many as 130 ranking military leaders at various levels, who were close associates of Lin's, may have been removed from active duty. (84) In the same period, a total of 48 top provincial-level Party secretaries and deputy secretaries appear to have been removed from their posts. Among them were 35 military commanders and political commissars, representing 73 percent of those removed at this particular level. The removal of these military leaders reduced the proportion of PLA representation in the provincial Party committees from 60 percent in August 1971 to about 46 percent by 1972 (61 out of 132 provincial secretaries). In contrast, the proportion of Party representation increased from 35 percent to 48 percent in the same period. (85) The overwhelming majority of these purged leaders were clearly Lin's close followers since the days of the Fourth Field Army. In the Tenth Central Committee elected in August 1973, for instance, the number of former Fourth Field Army leaders dropped from a previous record high of 41 to 27. (86)

The decline of the power and status of the military as a whole after Lin's abortive coup is clearly reflected in the overall drop of military representation in the Tenth Central Committee. (87) Of the 195 full members and 124 alternate members, the PLA now accounts for only 29 percent and 23 percent respectively. In contrast with its strength of 38 percent (for both full and alternate members) achieved in the Ninth Central Committee formed in April 1969, there was a drop of over 10 percent. While only 17 Party cadres of the Ninth Central Committee failed to get reelected to the Tenth Central Committee, the figure for the military leaders was 52, amounting to a casualty rate of 76 percent of the military representatives in the Ninth Central Committee. In the 25-member Politburo, the loss of military representation was even sharper between 1969 and 1973, when it fell from 52 percent to 20 percent. The unprecedented large-scale reshuffle of top military commanders and political commissars in eight out of China's eleven military

regions in January of this year is just another example of Mao's
determination to further weaken the power base of the PLA and
his opponents and to put them under tighter control of the
Party. (88)

These impressive moves of purge and rectification by Mao,
however, by no means signify a complete victory for the Party
and the conclusion of a cleanup of the opposition within the political system. The ongoing movement to "criticize Lin Piao
and Confucius," as revealed by Chou En-lai at the Tenth Party
Congress, is only the beginning of a stepped-up, concerted effort to thoroughly weed out the Lin clique and its poisonous
influence in China. (89)

Periodic campaigns against opposition inside and outside the
Party, often accomplished at a considerable cost to political
stability, have long been a familiar political phenomenon in
China's revolutionary society. (90) In theory, Mao holds the
view that "inner-Party struggle" has a legitimate place in the
political process and that "political opposition" has a positive
role to play in the sense that the determination of correct political line requires a process of dialectical confrontation of
alternatives. But the struggle should be carried out according
to the formula of "unity-criticism-unity." (91) A recent article
in the Party organ Red Flag states:

> During the prolonged struggle the fine style of criticism
> and self-criticism has been formed in our Party, and it
> has become the main weapon with which to uphold truth,
> rectify mistakes, resolve intra-Party contradictions, and
> achieve unity of the whole Party. (92)

Opposition aimed at creating permanent schisms and splitting
the Party cannot be tolerated.

It should be noted, however, that Mao's theory of continuing
revolution also asserts:

> For a long time to come, there will still be two-line strug-
> gles within the Party, reflecting [class] contradictions,

and such struggles will occur ten, twenty or thirty times. Lin Piaos will appear again and so will persons like Wang Ming, Liu Shao-ch'i, P'eng Te-huai and Kao Kang. This is something independent of man's will. (93)

Since class and political struggles are inevitable, as Wang Hung-wen pointed out at the Tenth Party Congress, "a true Communist must act without any selfish considerations and dare to go against the tide, fearing neither removal from his post, expulsion from the Party, imprisonment, divorce nor guillotine." (94) The big question remains, of course, of how to uphold "unity" and "dare to go against the tide" at the same time, and how to distinguish the "antagonistic" from the non-antagonistic" contradictions in practice. (95) The extent to which these ambiguous and contradictory principles can be effectively operationalized and coordinated to generate sufficient political dynamics within the boundary set by the theory for constructive purposes continues to be a crucial question of political institutionalization in Mao's revolutionary society.

The last, but not the least, problem of far-reaching significance left in the legacy of Lin Piao's purge, of course, is the crisis of political succession. In one sense the Cultural Revolution attempted to create a generation of political successors and solve the problem of succession to Mao himself. (96) In the course of the Cultural Revolution Lin Piao did emerge as Mao's successor, and his position was formalized by the 1969 Party Constitution. But the Lin Piao affair again frustrated Mao's attempt at choosing his own successor after his painful experience with Liu Shao-ch'i, and once more threw open the urgent problem of political succession. Mao's attempted solution to the problem has proved to be an unviable one. Naming a successor clearly had disastrous consequences in the intra-elite political behavior. It comes as no surprise, therefore, that since the Lin incident the question of succession has been re-evaluated. Mao's present views on the question seem to be that no single individual should succeed him. Thus, in addressing the Tenth Party Congress in August 1973, Wang Hung-wen formally declared that the tasks of the Party in training "successors" are to train "not just one or two persons, but millions" in the course of mass struggles. (97) "Ruling by the voice of one man alone" was denounced as "a manifestation of the ideological style of the bourgeoisie." (98) This new position is apparent as well in Mao's repudiation of the "theory of genius." The campaign for education in ideology and political line following the fall of Lin Piao stressed that:

> The emergence of such [proletarian] heroes is precisely a manifestation of the making of history by the masses....
> Heroes in various periods are those who come to the fore to answer the needs of the struggles of the masses....
> Every time history presents a new task of struggle, heroes who lead the masses in it are bound to emerge. (99)

The expectation that a successor could arise from the process of mass struggles is apparently based on Mao's unfailing faith in the masses and their role in history which he developed during the revolutionary movement. This hope, moreover, is at present probably the only viable alternative to his previous attempt, which proved fruitless and disastrous. It remains unclear, however, how the new approach of "mass struggle" can be put into practice without seriously disrupting the political stability and organizational effectiveness that are indispensable for China's continuing development. Whatever approach he may eventually choose to follow, Mao is, for the time being at least, settling for the noncommittal and safe formula of "combining the old, the middle-aged, and the young in leading bodies at all levels." (100) This new form of "three-way alliance" also serves the timely need of replacing the old formula of the "three-way alliance" of military representatives, Party and administrative cadres, and representatives of mass organizations, which must now become defunct if the military is to withdraw from active participation in politics and administration. It is possible, however, that the current approach is merely a temporary measure for the purpose of buying time until another successor can be found. The question, then, remains whether Mao at his advanced age of eighty-one can afford to wait any longer and whether he will once more run into another Liu Shao-ch'i or Lin Piao.

THE DOCUMENTS

The documents presented in this volume are organized into five chronological sections. We begin in Section I with a comprehensive biography of Lin Piao that presents a detailed account of his life and career up to 1969. The "top-secret" Party documents in Section II deal in depth with the nature and scope of Lin's errors and "crimes" as well as with evidence of his attempts to engineer a military coup and assassinate Mao. Sections III and IV assemble a wide range of press criticisms, secret denunciations, and official reports released in conjunction with the waves of nationwide campaigns to "criticize Lin Piao" started in 1970. The criticism campaigns not only provided further details on the Lin clique's ambitions and double-dealing in its quest for power but also elevated the plane of criticism to Lin's ideological and policy deviations. Before the Tenth Party Congress of August 1973, Lin was identified in the public press as a "political swindler like Liu Shao-ch'i" without mentioning his name. But at the Tenth Party Congress his name was formally revealed. Since then, the campaigns have been intensified from the stage of "criticizing Lin Piao" to that of "criticizing Lin Piao and Confucius." The final section, Section V, is a comprehensive collection of Lin's own speeches, writings, messages and instructions from 1965 to 1970, covering the most crucial period of his political rise to and fall from the pinnacle of power. The materials in this section are also arranged chronologically.

All the source materials gathered and edited for this volume, except Selection 21, originated in China. All the originals are translated and published here as they have become available to us. Roughly one half of the materials presented in

this volume are either labeled as "top-secret" documents
of the Central and local Party organizations or are drawn from
semisecret Red Guard publications. The other half comprises official reports or articles published in various Party
newspapers and journals. In either case, the sources are fully
cited in each selection.

The two selections which comprise Section I include a lengthy
biography of Lin Piao published in June 1969, and an official
explanation why Lin was designated as Mao's successor at
the Ninth Party Congress. The biography provides a great
deal of hitherto little-known detail on Lin's family background and early life. Presumably it purports to be Lin's
official biography, and as such similar to that of Mao written by Edgar Snow. (101) But, more importantly, it attempts to explain why Lin was the "most faithful follower"
of Chairman Mao and the "best pupil" of Mao's thought.
Lin's military record and contributions to the revolution
are greatly glorified. It is even explicitly suggested that
on many occasions in the history of the Party, Mao owed
his life and career to Lin's unselfish dedication to him.

The eleven selections comprising Section II are all "top-
secret" Party documents issued by the Central Committee for
restricted circulation among the high-level cadres. The documents include Mao's own account of the origin and cause of
his disputes with Lin and the army, the original text of Lin's
coup plan, "Project 571," as well as a wide range of evidence —
records, reports, and confessions — related to the Lin Piao
affair.

Selection 3, commonly known as Document No. 12, provides
the essence of Mao's talks to local Party and military leaders
during his inspection tour (mid-August through September 12,
1971) just prior to the coup strike scheduled by Lin. The talks,
typical of Mao's blunt and earthy style, spell out in detail Lin's
policy and line deviations and give Mao's version of what happened during the Lushan Plenum and its aftermath. The talks
and his inspection tour seem to represent an effort by Mao, in
going down to local levels, to drum up support, as he had done

in previous struggles, for a final showdown with Lin and
his associates. (102) Selection 9 is a translation of the
complete text of the "Project 571" coup plan. The exceptionally poor style of writing and choice of words would
seem to suggest the Project was either drafted in a great
hurry or done by lesser leaders of little literary ability.
As for Selection 10, elaborate additional material and docu-
mentary evidence was presented by the Central Committee
to substantiate its charges on Lin's conspiratorial activities
and coup attempt. The complete text of the document in
its original Chinese version was reported to be over 100
pages. So far, unfortunately, we have only the listing of the
titles of the exhibits. (103)

Selection 11 is an especially revealing document on the issue
of Mao's insistence that no state chairman be provided for
under the revised state Constitution. The document also reveals how Mao's instructions were handled in the Central Committee and provides a succinct picture of the policymaking
process at the top of China's political system. Selection 12 is
the Final Report submitted to the Central Committee by the
Ad Hoc Team responsible for investigating the Lin Piao affair.
Aside from presenting a summing-up of the case, the Report
also looked into Lin's past "counterrevolutionary activities"
and made recommendations for punishments for Lin and other
key plotters.

In September 1972, approximately a year after the Lin Piao
incident, Mao released a private letter he was supposed to
have written to his wife, Chiang Ch'ing, on July 8, 1966. The
letter, which is included in this volume as Selection 13, not only
sheds important new light on the intricate relations between
Mao and Lin but also lays fresh ground for controversy, speculation, and reinterpretation of the entire process and history
of the Cultural Revolution. According to the letter, Mao had
sensed serious problems and errors in Lin's leadership style
and policy line as early as May 1966, even before the drive of
the Cultural Revolution was intensified. Referring to Lin as
"my friend," Mao was particularly disturbed by and skeptical

of Lin's manipulation of the personality cult, emphasis on the theory of "genius," promotion of the "magic power" of the Little Red Books, and dwelling on the theme of "political coup." Mao confided to his wife, "I was driven by them to join the rebels of the Liangshan Mountain. It seems that I have to concur with them. It is the first time in my life that I unwillingly concur with others on major questions. I have to do things against my own will." (104) If both the date and the contents of the letter are genuine, as they are purported to be, we will have to do a lot of rethinking of our knowledge of the political process of China.

According to Taiwan and Hong Kong sources, additional documents of the Central Committee related to Lin Piao's plot and his purge include the following:

> Chung-fa, 1971, Nos. 65, 68, 77
> (Charges on Lin Piao's conspiracy for state chairman-
> ship and military coup)
> Chung-fa, 1972, No. 3
> (Part I of the materials on the Lin-Ch'en coup).

Unfortunately, no texts of these documents are yet available. (105)

Section III consists of five representative articles selected from the official Party organs specifying and criticizing Lin Piao's crimes without mentioning his name. In keeping with common practice in China, individual names are usually not mentioned in the initial stage of a purge involving top leaders. (106) This method usually serves a number of tactical purposes. It can serve as a preliminary test of the strength of opponents, avoid a premature rush into a head-on clash with key opponents, prepare the necessary momentum to bring about a big campaign and above all offer a chance to opponents to repent and surrender. While such indirect censure as "political swindler like Liu Shao-ch'i" or "ambitious careerist" is consistently used in these articles, the intent and contents of the criticism are unmistakably clear.

In regard to the distortion of Mao's "five requirements" for revolutionary successors (107) and the theory of "genius," as elaborated in Selections 14, 15 and 18, the articles leave no doubt that Lin was the target of criticism. It was Lin who openly suggested the modification of the "five requirements" at the Eleventh Plenum of the Eighth Central Committee on August 1, 1966, and it was he who popularized the altered form put forth as the "three criteria" for cultivating cadres during the Cultural Revolution. To quote Lin's own words:

> In the light of the five requirements for the cultivation of successors to the cause of proletarian revolution set forth by Chairman Mao, we have proposed three criteria, to which the Chairman has agreed: (1) Do they hold high the red banner of Mao Tse-tung thought? Those who fail to do so shall be dismissed from office. (2) Do they engage in political and ideological work? Those who disrupt it and the Great Cultural Revolution are to be dismissed. (3) Are they enthusiastic about the revolution? Those who are entirely devoid of such enthusiasm are to be dismissed.
> These three criteria are consistent with the five requirements set forth by the Chairman. We must select, promote, and employ cadres in accordance with Chairman Mao's five requirements and these three criteria, especially the first one. (108)

The theory of "genius" was also beyond doubt originated by Lin Piao. It was Lin who first expounded that theory in his major speech at the Enlarged Meeting of the Politburo on May 18, 1966, and later publicized the theme throughout the Cultural Revolution. According to Lin,

> Chairman Mao's sayings, works, and revolutionary practice have shown that he is a great proletarian genius. Some people don't admit genius, but this is not Marxist. . . . Dialectical materialism pervades Mao Tse-tung thought, and Chairman Mao has creatively applied and developed Marxism-Leninism; he is unparalleled in the present world. Marx and Engels were geniuses of the nineteenth

century; Lenin and Comrade Mao Tse-tung are the geniuses
of the twentieth century. (109)

Although names are never specifically mentioned in the repudi-
ations, all the words and phrases singled out for criticism can
be traced to Lin's writings or speeches. (110)
   The other articles selected in Section III, it should be noted,
take up and elaborate on virtually every major point of Mao's
criticisms as set forth in the secret documents. Selection 16,
for example, echoes Mao's charges that Lin had split the Party,
conspired to seize power, and betrayed the country to foreign
powers. In Selection 17, we see a full elaboration of Mao's
criticisms of Lin's errors of line in promoting "the gun to command the Party," pursuing the one-sided policy of "Learn from
the PLA," and turning the PLA into a "cultural army." Selections 15 and 17 amplify Mao's specific demands, first voiced
during his inspection tour in August and September 1971, that
campaigns be launched for education in ideology and political
line and for correction of the deviations of "arrogance and complacency" in army-building.
   These selections represent only a minute fraction of the public criticism of Lin in the press. For a complete survey, one
should go over the three major Party organs (Red Flag, People's Daily, and Liberation Army Daily) from November 1, 1971.
For example, several articles in Red Flag, Nos. 1-2, and
People's Daily, February 5-10, 1972, focus on the revised revolutionary opera On the Docks. The big publicity campaign
and the theme of the opera are apparently aimed at the Lin
case: the villain of the opera betrayed the Party and conspired
to flee to foreign countries. (111)
   Selections 19-22, which comprise Section IV, show the further
deepening, expansion, and progress of the campaigns against
Lin Piao since 1973. A number of new and important trends
are discernible from these documents. First, the campaigns
have moved from the stage of "criticism without mentioning
the name" to that of "open criticism by name." Second, the
movement has expanded from involvement of only high-level

cadres to that of the broad masses throughout the nation. Third, the focus of criticism has been extended from the realm of power struggle to that of ideological and policy disputes. Fourth, the documentation and denunciation of Lin's crimes and errors have gone beyond the conspiracy for military coup and assassination itself to the historical past of his career. And last and most recently, the nature of the campaigns has switched from "Criticize Lin Piao and Rectify the Work Style" to the combination of "Criticize Lin Piao and Criticize Confucius."

The important secret speech given to a restricted audience of high-level local cadres in the Kunming Military Region by Wang Pi-ch'eng, commander and Party secretary of the region, is most revealing of the intricate process of organizational preparation and issue articulation with which the campaign against Lin was built up and conducted (see Selection 19). The speech also discloses a clear picture of China's dual-channel political communications. In 1972, while the public was left groping in the dark about the elusive shadows of "swindler like Liu Shao-ch'i" and the abstract debates over the "five requirements" versus the "three criteria," detailed information concerning the Lin affair was already being transmitted downward level by level to cadres to educate and prepare them for the launching of a mass campaign.

The detailed, public indictments of Lin's "counterrevolutionary crimes" by Chou En-lai at the Tenth Party Congress and by the official press, which are included here as Selections 20 and 21, mark a major effort to broaden the focus of criticism from the realm of power struggle to that of ideological and policy matters, on the one hand, and to nail Lin down as a "Rightist," "capitalist-roader" and "revisionist" like his predecessors Liu Shao-ch'i, P'eng Te-huai and others, on the other. An editorial in the Liaoning Daily is particularly explicit in this regard:

The revisionist line of swindlers like Liu Shao-ch'i mirrors the wishes of the overthrown landlord and bourgeois

classes at home and the imperialists, revisionists, and
reactionaries abroad for a counterrevolutionary comeback.
It is out-and-out opposed to the proletarian dictatorship
and the revolution. In short, it is the revisionist line and
the Right opportunist line.

Swindlers like Liu Shao-ch'i, in their attempts to carry
out their counterrevolutionary consipiracies, have employed
some tricks which were "Left" in form but Right in essence
at times on certain issues to fan up ultra-Leftist sentiments. They appeared to be ultra-"Left," but we could
easily perceive their ultra-Rightist essence through the
capricious and vacillating tricks and certain ultra-"Leftist"
utterances of such swindlers. (112)

The efforts to link Lin Piao with Confucius, the sage dead
for almost 2,500 years, in the current "Criticize Lin Piao and
Confucius" campaign seem uncomprehensible to many observ-
ers of the Chinese scene. Whether or not Lin did use such
words of Confucius as "restrain oneself and restore the rites"
and others at some time in his life is probably irrelevant and
insignificant — by tradition, everybody still does that in China
even today. The relevant question to ask is: If the Maoist
policy is to shift the anti-Lin campaigns from the realm of
power struggle to the plane of line and policy disputes, who
better than Confucius can fulfill the role of popular symbol of
political and social conservatism and serve as a negative example of what Mao ideologically and politically stands for in
China? By associating Lin with Confucius, the Maoist leadership seems to hope to make easier the difficult task of educating the masses to understand why Lin and his coconspirators
were reactionary villains who had to be purged.

There is no doubt that the "true nature" of the Lin Piao affair, the historical significance of his role in China's continuing
revolution, and/or whatever errors of line and policy he might
have committed will be subject to further reevaluations and
reinterpretations by the Chinese leadership as the pendulum of
revolutionary politics in China continues to swing between Left

and Right. (113) It is possible that we may even find the entire history of the affair rewritten in the future. One can be sure, however, no matter which way the official emphasis may turn, that no objective and balanced inquiry into the Lin Piao affair and the politics of ideological and power struggles since the Cultural Revolution is possible without a close examination of Lin's own writings, statements, and instructions. Therefore we have included in the last section of this volume a comprehensive collection of fifty-one of Lin's public as well as secret speeches and instructions which we have been able to gather outside of China to date.

CHRONOLOGY OF LIN PIAO'S CAREER
AND COUP ATTEMPT

To help the reader keep track of Lin's career in the "twists and turns" of the Communist movement and the political struggles in China, we are providing below a chronology of the highlights of Lin's political and military career up to 1966, and a more detailed listing of important events since that time related to Lin's dramatic rise and fall in China's political arena. (114)

1907 Born in Hupei Province on October 7 to a working class family.
1921 Studied at Kung-chin Middle School in Wuchang (1921-25); actively involved in Communist movement.
1925 Joined the Socialist Youth League.
1926 Entered the fourth class of the Whampao Military Academy; served as platoon leader in Yeh T'ing's Independent Regiment in the Northern Expedition.
1927 Became a CCP member and company commander; participated in the Nanchang Uprising of August 1.
1928 Joined the forces led by Mao, Chu Te, and Ch'en I at Chingkangshan; promoted from battalion commander to regimental commander under Chu Te.
1929 Commander of the Fourth Army at the age of twenty-two.
1931 Ranking member of the Central Executive Committee of

the Kiangsi Soviets and of the Revolutionary Military
Commission; commander of the First Army Corps at
the age of twenty-four.

1934   Took part in the Long March, commanding the First
Army Corps (1934-35).

1935   Supported Mao at the Tsunyi Conference; appointed deputy
commander of the Northward March Vanguard Detach-
ment under P'eng Te-huai.

1936   President of Anti-Japanese Military and Political University (known as K'angta) in Yenan.

1937   Commander of the 115th Division of the Eighth Route
Army.

1938   Wounded in action and went to the Soviet Union for
treatment; remained there until January 1942.

1942   Vice president of the Central Party School headed by
Mao.

1945   Elected to the Seventh Central Committee (CC) of the
Party.

1946   Commander and political commissar of the Northeast
Democratic Allied Force; secretary of the Central
Committee's Northeast Bureau; president of the
Northeast Military and Political University.

1948   Commander and political commissar of the Fourth Field
Army; commander of the Peking-Tientsin Front.

1949   Commander of the Central China Military Region; chairman of the Central-South Military and Administrative
Committee; member of the Central People's Government Council (1949-1954).

1950   First secretary of the Central Committee's Central-
South Bureau; elected to the Politburo at the Third
Plenum of the Seventh CC; reportedly commanded the
Chinese "Volunteers" in the Korean War.

1954   Vice premier of the State Council and vice chairman of
the National Defense Council (September 1954-
September 1971).

1956   Elected to the Politburo of the Eighth CC in September,
ranking ninth.

(Politically inactive, 1951-1957).

1958   Elected vice chairman of the CC and member of the
       Standing Committee of the Politburo, ranking sixth,
       at the Second Session of the Eighth Party Congress.

1959   Appointed defense minister after P'eng Te-huai's dis-
       missal at the Eighth Plenum at Lushan (September
       1959-September 1971); began reorganizing Party
       apparatus in the PLA and stressing priority of politi-
       cal training in army-building.

1960   "Resolution on Strengthening Political and Ideological
       Work in the Army" adopted by the Enlarged Military
       Affairs Commission (MAC) Conference on October 20;
       campaign to "give prominence to Mao's thought"
       intensified.

1961   Selected Readings of Mao Tse-tung published by the PLA
       General Political Work Department.

1962   First in a series of campaigns to emulate PLA heroes
       such as Wang Chieh (and later Lei Feng, 1963-1964,
       Mai Hsien-teh, 1966-1967, etc.) launched; the Social-
       ist Education Campaign initiated by Mao at the Tenth
       CC Plenum in September.

1963   "The PLA Political Work Regulations" issued on
       March 27.

1964   Campaign to "Learn from the PLA" intensified in
       February; "political work departments" introduced
       into nonmilitary organizations (1964-65).

1965   Campaign for "the living study and application of Mao's
       thought" stepped up in the spring; "Long Live the
       Victory of People's War" published in September;
       attacks on the "Three-Household Village" began in
       November; Lin criticized Lo Jui-ch'ing, chief of
       staff, at the Politburo Standing Committee meeting
       in Shanghai in December.

1966   Apr.   Hanchow Conference of the Standing Committee
               of the Politburo convened.
       May   Lin led formal attacks on P'eng Chen, Lu Ting-i,
               Lo Jui-ch'ing, and Yang Shan-k'un and ex-

pounded on the theory of "genius" at the Enlarged Meeting of the Politburo, May 4-18;
Lin deployed the Thirty-eighth Army, loyal to
him, to garrison the Peking area in May-July.

June   Mao stayed in seclusion away from Peking.

July   Mao wrote to Chiang Ch'ing on July 8 expressing
doubt about Lin's ideological purity and political loyalty; Mao returned to Peking on July 18.

Aug.   Eleventh Plenum of the Eighth CC, August 1-12,
adopted "Decision Concerning the Great Proletarian Cultural Revolution"; Lin elected sole
vice chairman of the CC; proposed the "three
criteria" for revolutionary successors based
on Mao's "five requirements" during the
session;

Red Guards emerged in major cities;

Lin appeared beside Mao as his "close comrade-
in-arms" at eight mass rallies in Peking from
August 18 to November 26.

Nov.   Chiang Ch'ing, Mao's wife, appointed advisor to
the PLA Cultural Revolution Group on November 28.

1967 Jan.   Red Guards began to seize power from "capitalist-
roaders"; PLA ordered to intervene in support
of the Left; first revolutionary committees
based on "three-way alliance" organized (in
Shansi) with the military as the core; the MAC
declared as headquarters of the Cultural Revolution; the PLA became the "mainstay of the
proletarian dictatorship."

Feb.   "February Adverse Current" led by T'an Chen-
lin opposing the purge of the Liu-Teng group.

Mar.   "Three-support and two-military" campaign
stepped up.

May   "Left adventurism" led by Wang Li, Kuang Feng
and Ch'i Pen-yü emerged.

July   The Wuhan Incident took place on July 21.

| | Sept. | The ultra-Leftist "May 16 Regiment" purged; Mao called for "Revolutionary Great Alliance" and criticized factionalism. |

Sept.   The ultra-Leftist "May 16 Regiment" purged; Mao called for "Revolutionary Great Alliance" and criticized factionalism.

1968 Jan.   PLA instructed "to support the Left, but not any faction."

Feb.   "Support the Army" campaign stepped up.

Mar.   Lin announced the dismissal of Yang Ch'en-wu, Yu Li-chin, and Fu Ch'ung-pi for their role in the "February Adverse Current" on March 4; Huang Yung-sheng appointed chief of staff on March 22.

July   "Worker-Peasant Mao Tse-tung Thought Propaganda Teams" organized to control factional fights; the role of the Red Guards declined.

Aug.   "Struggle-Criticism-Transformation" campaign intensified.

Oct.   Liu Shao-ch'i officially expelled from the Party at the Twelfth CC Plenum, October 13-31.

1969 Jan.   "Purify class ranks" movement stepped up.

Mar.   PLA's "arrogance and complacency" criticized.

Apr.   The Ninth National Party Congress, called on April 1-24 in Peking, adopted the new Party Constitution and elected the CC (170 full and 109 alternate members, dominated by the army); Lin and Ch'en Po-ta's earlier draft of Political Report rejected by Mao; Lin delivered the revised Political Report on April 1 and was designated in the Constitution as Mao's "successor."

Politburo (21 full and 4 alternate members) and its Standing Committee (5 members: Mao, Lin, Chou En-lai, Ch'en Po-ta, K'ang Sheng) elected at the First Plenum of the Ninth CC, April 28; Lin elected sole vice chairman.

July   "Centralized leadership" of the Party stressed.

Oct.   Criticism of the "ultra-Left" May 16 Group stepped up.

Dec.   The CC Cultural Revolution Group disappeared from the press.

1970 Mar.   Mao instructed that preparation be made for the Fourth National People's Congress and revision of the state Constitution and proposed that no state chairman be provided for.

July   Committee on Revision of the State Constitution formed on July 12 with Mao as chairman and Lin as vice chairman.

Aug.   Second Plenum of the Ninth CC met August 23-September 6 at Lushan and "basically" approved the draft revision of the state Constitution; Lin made a speech without advance consultation and knowledge of Mao on August 23; "five generals" (Huang Yung-sheng, Wu Fa-hsien, Yeh Ch'ün, Li Tso-p'eng, Ch'iu Hui-tso) made a "surprise attack" on August 23-25, attempting to reverse Mao's instruction on omission of the office of state chairman. Mao issued his 700-word "Some Opinions of Mine."

Sept.   Mao issued on September 15 "A Letter to the Whole Party" calling for a "Criticize Ch'en [Po-ta] and Rectify the Work Style" campaign; campaign for "Education in Ideology and Political Line" launched.

Oct.   Press campaign intensified to strengthen the spirit, unity, and unified leadership of the Party.

Nov.   The first provincial Party committee formed in Hunan on November 24.

Dec.   Enlarged Politburo Conference called at Peitaiho (North China Conference) demanding that key leaders of the MAC repudiate Ch'en; Mao told Edgar Snow that the personality cult had gone too far.

1971 Jan.   The leadership of the Peking Military Region reshuffled; Lin's supporters Cheng Wei-shan and

Li Hsüeh-feng removed as commander and second political commissar, respectively. Lin's Thirty-eighth Army reassigned out of the Peking area.

Feb.   Lin and Yeh Ch'ün went to Soochow and instructed their son Lin Li-kuo to direct the planning and organizing of a military coup.

Mar.   Lin Li-kuo called first meeting of key plotters in Shanghai on March 20; the coup plan "Project 571" drafted March 22-24. Starting in March, the press, without mentioning his name, criticized Ch'en Po-ta as a "sham Marxist."

Apr.   A meeting of ninety-nine top central and regional military leaders presided over by Chou En-lai to criticize Ch'en Po-ta and "seven generals."

June   Lin's last public appearance, June 3, meeting Ceaucescu of Rumania with Mao.

July   Lin took a field trip on July 23 checking on the coup preparation in the name of an "inspection tour."

Aug.   Mao took an inspection tour of provinces from mid-August through September 12. En route he discussed "ten great struggles between lines" in Party history, specified Lin's policy mistakes, and disclosed Lin's "surprise attack" at the Second CC Plenum.

Sept. Order to put the coup plan into effect was issued by Lin on September 8.

A contingency coup plan called for the assassination of Mao by bombing his train traveling from Hangchow to Shanghai on September 12; the plot was revealed to Chou En-lai.

An emergency meeting of top-level Mao supporters called at the People's Great Hall in Peking throughout the night of September 12; Chou En-lai's previously scheduled interview with visiting Japanese Diet members for the same day unexpectedly canceled.

The Chinese Air Force Trident jet No. 256
crashed at 2:30 a.m., September 13, near
Undur Khan, Mongolia. All nine persons
aboard, including Lin Piao, Yeh Ch'ün and
Lin Li-kuo, were burned to death. All flights
in China grounded for fifty-eight hours,
September 13-15.

Oct.   The traditional October 1 National Day celebra-
tion canceled.

Magazines and books containing Lin's pictures or
writings quietly recalled from bookstores.

Nov.   Red Flag began to criticize Lin without mentioning
his name; press campaign against "political
swindler like Liu Shao-ch'i," and "conspirator"
stepped up from November 1.

Dec.   Foreign diplomats advised by the Chinese Foreign
Ministry not to mention Lin in their messages;
"the PLA Must Learn from the People" campaign intensified in all military districts; discipline and military training in the army emphasized.

1972   Jan.   "Criticize Revisionism and Rectify the Work Style"
movement intensified; the theory of "genius"
repudiated; and the need for the Party's unified
leadership further stressed.

1973   July   The CC Ad Hoc Team concluded investigation of
the Lin Piao affair and recommended on
July 10 that Lin, Ch'en Po-ta, and other key
conspirators be expelled from the Party.

Aug.   Tenth Party Congress held in Peking, August 24-
29; adopted the new Party Constitution and
elected the Tenth CC (195 full and 124 alternate members); in Chou En-lai's Political
Report, Lin was for the first time publicly
identified by name as "the bourgeois careerist,
conspirator, double-dealer, renegade, and
traitor."

First Plenum of the 10th CC met on August 30 and
elected Chou En-lai, Wang Hung-wen, K'ang
Sheng, Yeh Chien-ying and Li Te-sheng as
vice chairmen, a 25-member Politburo (21 full
and 4 alternate members) and a 9-member
Standing Committee of the Politburo.

Sept.   "Criticize Revisionism and Rectify the Work Style"
movement converted into the "Criticize Lin
and Rectify the Work Style" movement; the
campaign "to study the documents of the Tenth
Party Congress" launched.

Oct.   Campaigns to organize urban militia started.

1974 Jan.   Reshuffling of military commanders in 8 out of
China's 11 military regions announced on
January 1.

Feb.   "Criticize Lin and Rectify the Work Style" movement converted into the "Criticize Lin and
Confucius" campaign and intensified throughout
the nation.

Notes

1) Portions of the analysis contained in this Introduction are
drawn from the editor's previous works, "The Case Against
Lin Piao," Chinese Law and Government, V: 3-4 (Fall-Winter
1972-73), 3-30; coauthor with Pierre M. Perrolle, "The Politics of Lin Piao's Abortive Military Coup," Asian Survey,
XIV: 6 (June 1974), 558-577.

2) For an excellent study of Lin's career before 1949, see
Thomas W. Robinson, A Politico-Military Biography of Lin
Piao, Part I, 1907-1949 (Santa Monica, Calif.: Rand, 1971);
see also Martin Ebon, Lin Piao: The Life and Writing of
China's New Ruler (New York: Stein & Day, 1970).

3) This portion of the discussion is based mainly on Selection 1 of this volume.

4) For the history and politics of the PLA, see Ying-mao
Kau et al., The Political Work System of the Chinese Commu-

nist Military (Providence: East Asian Language and Area Cen-
ter, Brown University, 1971); Ellis Joffe, Party and Army
(Cambridge: Harvard University Press, 1965); John Gittings,
The Role of the Chinese Army (London: Oxford University
Press, 1967); and William Whitson, The Chinese High Command
(New York: Praeger, 1973).

   5) For the details on the role of the PLA in the sixties sum-
marized in this portion of the discussion, see Ying-mao Kau,
ed., The People's Liberation Army and China's Nation-Building
(White Plains, N. Y.: International Arts and Sciences Press,
1973), Introduction. Recent articles on the PLA include
Ralph L. Powell "The Increasing Power of Lin Piao and the
Party-Soldiers, 1959-1966," The China Quarterly, No. 34,
(April-June 1966); William Whitson, "The Field Army in
Chinese Communist Military Politics," The China Quarterly,
No. 37, (January-March 1969); Jürgen Domes, "The Role of
Military in the Formation of Revolutionary Committees, 1967-
1968," The China Quarterly, No. 44 (October-December 1970);
Thomas W. Robinson, "The Wuhan Incident: Local Strife and
Provincial Rebellion During the Cultural Revolution,"
The China Quarterly, No. 47 (July-September 1971); Harvey
Nelsen, "Military Forces in the Cultural Revolution," The China
Quarterly, No. 51 (July-September 1972); Parris H. Chang,
"Regional Military Power: The Aftermath of the Cultural
Revolution," Asian Survey, XII: 12 (December 1972); and
William L. Parish, Jr., "Factions in Chinese Military Politics,"
The China Quarterly, No. 56 (October-December 1973).

   6) The issues available in the West covering the period
January-August 1961 were completely translated in J. Chester
Cheng, ed., The Politics of the Chinese Red Army (Stanford:
Hoover Institution, 1965).

   7) The "Four Firsts" mean: the human factor first in handling the relationship between men and weapons, political work
first in handling the relationship between various kind of work
and political work, ideological work first within political work,
and living ideology first within ideological work. The "Three-
Eight Work Style" refers to three phrases and eight characters

enunciated by Mao: "a firm and correct political direction, a
persevering and simple style of work, and flexible strategy and
tactics;" and "unity, intensity, solemnity, and liveliness." The
"Four Goods" stress "good in political and ideological work,
good in the 'three-eight work style,' good in military training,
and good in management of army livelihood." The "Five Goods"
emphasize "good in political ideology, good in military techniques, good in the 'three-eight work style,' good in carrying
out assigned tasks, and good in physical training."

8) Their significance is well elaborated in "The Whole
Country Must Learn from the PLA," Jen-min jih-pao, [People's
Daily], February 1, 1964; The Diary of Wang Chieh (Peking:
Foreign Languages Press, 1967).

9) Chalmers Johnson, "Lin Piao and His Role in Chinese
Society," Current Scene, IV: 13-14 (July 1966); and Ralph L.
Powell, "Commissars in the Economy," Asian Survey, V: 3
(March 1965), 125-138.

10) The theme was elaborated in Hung-ch'i [Red Flag],
No. 14 (1967), and Peking Review, No. 36 (September 1, 1967),
5-7.

11) See "Decision Concerning the PLA's Resolute Support
of the Revolutionary Masses of the Left," issued jointly by the
four major central organs, Chinese Law and Government,
IV: 3-4 (Fall-Winter 1971), 325-327.

12) The campaign amounts to an effort to impose military
control and discipline for law and order. A revealing article
may be found in "New Contributions to the Consolidation of the
Dictatorship of the Proletariat Made by the Three-Support and
Two-Military Personnel of the PLA," Kuang-ming jih-pao
[Bright Daily], July 28, 1970.

13) The phenomenon and its statistical significance will be
treated in depth later in this Introduction.

14) For the full text of the Constitution see Peking Review,
No. 18 (April 30, 1969), 36-39.

15) The phenomena will be dealt with in detail later in the
discussion of the thrust of the struggle. See also William
Whitson, ed., The Military and Political Power in China in the

1970's (New York: Praeger, 1972).

16) These military leaders were Huang Yung-sheng, Wu
Fa-hsien, Yeh Ch'ün, Li Tso-p'eng, Ch'iu Hui-tso, Li Hsüeh-
feng, and Cheng Wei-shan. See "Mao chu-hsi tsai wai-ti hsün-
shih ch'i-chien t'ung yen-t'u ko-ti fu-tse t'ung-chih ti t'an-hua
chi-yao" [Summary of Chairman Mao's Talks to Responsible
Local Comrades During His Tour of Inspection], commonly
known as Document No. 12 (1972) of the Central Committee of
the Chinese Communist Party. The document is Selection 3 in
this volume.

17) Ibid.

18) Ibid.

19) Based on Selections 3-11 in this volume. For a detailed
study of the military personnel movement, see Chiang I-shan,
"The PLA Before and After the Downfall of Lin Piao (in
Chinese)," Tsu-kuo (China Monthly, Hong Kong), No. 101
(August 1972), 13-16.

20) Based on Selection 9. Other sources of information on
the plot include Mao's interviews with Sri Lanka Premier
Bandaranaike on June 28, 1972, and French Foreign Minister
Maurice Shuman on July 10, 1972. See also The New York
Times, October 12, 1972, for Chou En-lai's account of Lin's
escape in his interview with representatives of the American
Society of Newspaper Editors; Hsüan Mo, "An Analysis of the
Joint Anti-Mao Activities Led by Lin Piao and Ch'en Po-ta
(in Chinese)," Chung-kung yen-chiu [Studies on Chinese Com-
munism, Taipei] VI: 7 (July 1972), 4-14; and Chi P'eng, "A
Study of the Coup d'Etat Guidelines of the Lin Piao Group (in
Chinese)," Chung-kung yen-chiu VI: 6 (June 1972), 5-8.

21) For a sensationalized detailed account of the events,
see a report by the Australian reporter Wilfred Burchett in
the Guardian (New York), August 29, 1973; translated into
Chinese in Ch'i-shih nien-tai [The Seventies, Hong Kong],
No. 45 (October 1973), 40-42. The contingency plan was also
mentioned in Chung-fa, 1971, No. 60 — Selection 5.

22) Ibid. Travelers to China in early 1972 also reported
hearing a similar account; see "Traveler Relates Version of

Lin Piao's Plot and Death," Translations on the People's Republic of China, No. 183 (JPRS, 55638; April 5, 1972), 1-3; "Death of Lin Piao's Fate Revealed," ibid., No. 179 (JPRS, 55376; March 7, 1972), 1-3.

23) Based on Chung-fa, 1971, No. 62 — Selection 7. See also Chung-fa, 1973, No. 34 — Selection 12.

24) For the text, see Selection 12.

25) See Chou En-lai's Political Report — Selection 20.

26) See, for example, Selection 22.

27) Unless otherwise noted, this section of the discussion is based primarily on Selections 9-10.

28) See Selection 10.

29) For the text of the communiqué, see Peking Review, No. 37 (September 11, 1970), 5-7.

30) Chou En-lai's Political Report — Selection 20.

31) See Selection 22.

32) See note 29 above; also Philip Bridgham, "The Fall of Lin Piao," The China Quarterly, No. 55 (July-September 1973), 427-499. The accusation on his "illicit contacts" in betraying the Party is particularly revealing in Chi P'ing, "Ch'iang-wo she-hui chu-i shih-ch'i ch'ieh-chi tou-cheng ti kuei-lü" [Grasp the Law of Class Struggle in the Socialist Period] Hung-ch'i [Red Flag], No. 8 (August 1, 1972), 6-10.

33) Selection 9.

34) Ibid.

35) Ibid.

36) Ibid.

37) Selection 3.

38) Ying-mao Kau, ed., The People's Liberation Army and China's Nation-Building, Introduction.

39) For an elaboration, see ibid.

40) For a detailed analysis of the structural relationship between the Party and the army, see Ying-mao Kau et al., The Political Work System of the Chinese Communist Military.

41) Mao Tse-tung, Selected Works of Mao Tse-tung (Peking: Foreign Languages Press, 1961-1965), Vol. II, p. 224.

42) See Selection 3.

43) See, for example, "Learn Humbly from the Masses," Hung-ch'i [Red Flag], No. 4 (April 1, 1971); translated in Selections from China Mainland Magazines, No. 704 (1971); also Selection 15.

44) See Selections 3-12.

45) Selection 3.

46) Ibid.

47) See, for example, Selection 16.

48) Selection 3.

49) Ibid.

50) Ibid.

51) Ibid.

52) See, for example, Lin's May 18, 1966, speech (Selection 28).

53) Selection 18.

54) Selection 3.

55) It is likely that Ch'en threw his support to Lin in exchange for the latter's protection from attack on him for his Leftist leadership during the Cultural Revolution. Lin naturally welcomed his support for strengthening his own power base. Hsüan Mo, "Lin Piao Ch'en Po-ta lien-ho fan-Mao ti fen-hsi" [An Analysis of the Lin Piao-Ch'en Po-ta Alliance Against Mao]. Chung-kung yen-chiu (Studies on Chinese Communism), VI: 7 (July 1972), 4-15.

56) Selection 3. This certainly raises the question of how Mao views the role of his own wife, Chiang Ch'ing.

57) For excellent analyses, see William Whitson, op. cit., and William L. Parish, Jr., op. cit.

58) Selection 3.

59) Ibid.

60) Selection 9.

61) Ibid.

62) Unless specified otherwise, this portion of the discussion is based on Selection 9.

63) Selection 3.

64) For an elaboration, see Ying-mao Kau, ed., The People's Liberation Army and China's Nation-Building.

65) Selection 9.

66) Ibid.

67) Ibid.

68) See, for example, Liu Shao-ch'i, On Inner-Party Struggle (Peking: Foreign Languages Press, n.d.); and Mao Tsetung, Selected Works of Mao Tse-tung, Vol. III, p. 50.

69) See, for example, "Criticize 'Restraining Oneself and Restoring the Rites,'" Peking Review, No. 9 (March 1, 1974), 7-8; also Selection 22.

70) Shih Chih-chien, "A Forceful Criticism of Lin Piao's Right-Deviationist Pessimism: Notes on Studying 'A Single Spark Can Start a Prairie Fire,'" Peking Review, No. 2 (January 11, 1974), 7-9.

71) For the text, see Selection 13.

72) See Selection 21.

73) Liaoning Radio Broadcast, January 5, 1973; quoted in China News Summary, No. 453 (January 25, 1973), p. 5.

74) Mao Tse-tung, Selected Works of Mao Tse-tung, Vol. II, p. 224; Vol. IV, p. 337.

75) For more discussion, see Ying-mao Kau, ed., The People's Liberation Army and China's Nation-Building, Introduction, xix-lxxvi.

76) "Tsung-chieh chia-ch'iang tang ti ling-tao ti ching-yen" [Sum up Experience in Strengthening Party Leadership], Hung-ch'i [Red Flag], No. 13 (December 1, 1971), 4-6.

77) "T'uan-chieh ch'i-lai cheng-ch'ü keng-ta ti sheng-li" [Unite to Win Still Greater Victories], 1972 New Year's Day joint editorial by Jen-min jih-pao [People's Daily] and Hung-ch'i [Red Flag], No. 1 (January 1, 1972), 5-11. The editorial also appeared in English in Peking Review, No. 1 (January 7, 1972), 8-11.

78) "An-chao Mao-chu-hsi chien-chün lu-hsien chua-chin chün-shih hsün-lien" [Grasp Military Training According to Chairman Mao's Line of Army-Building], Hung-ch'i [Red Flag], No. 5 (May 1, 1972), 32-34. See Selection 17.

79) Ibid.

80) Selection 15. The Three Main Rules and the Eight Points are in the Selected Works of Mao Tse-tung, Vol. IV, pp. 155-156.

81) Ibid.

lxxiv THE LIN PIAO AFFAIR

82) Twenty-seven percent to be exact. More analysis of elite changes is presented in the last portion of this Introduction.

83) Chang Ching-wen, "Mao's Purge of Lin Piao's Faction," Issues & Studies, IX: 7 (April 1973), 19-27.

84) Free China Weekly, April 12, 1973.

85) Data taken from Ying-mao Kau, "The Case Against Lin Piao"; Parris H. Chang, "Mao Tse-tung and His Generals," a paper given at the Annual Meeting of the Association for Asian Studies, April 1973, p. 5; Chiang I-shan, "Lin Piao tao-t'ai ch'ien-hou ti jen-min chieh-fang-chun" [The PLA Before and After the Downfall of Lin Piao] Tsu-kuo [China Monthly], No. 101 (August 1972), 13-16.

86) Chang Ching-wen, op. cit.

87) Data discussed in this portion are based on the authors' computation. For comparable analysis, with slightly different results, see Fang Chün-kuei, "Chung-kung shih-chieh chung-yang wei-yüan-hui ti fen-hsi" [An Analysis of the Tenth Central Committee of the Chinese Communist Party], Chung-kung yen-chiu [Studies in Chinese Communism], VII: 9 (September 1973), 16-27; "Chung-kung shih-chieh chung-wei-hui ch'eng-yüan chien-chieh" [A Brief Survey of the Membership of the Tenth Central Committee of the Chinese Communist Party], Chung-Hua yüeh-pao [The China Monthly], No. 697 (October 1, 1973), 28-34. A modified version of these two articles appears in English in Chinese Law and Government, VII: 1-2 (Spring-Summer 1974).

88) For details, see Chu Wen-lin, "Personnel Changes in Peiping's First-Level Military Regions," Issues & Studies, X: 5 (February 1974), 10-17.

89) Chou En-lai's Political Report — Selection 20.

90) For a study of the cyclical campaigns, see Ying-mao Kau, "Patterns of Recruitment and Mobility of Urban Cadres," in John W. Lewis, ed., The City in Communist China (Stanford: Stanford University Press, 1971), pp. 91-121.

91) Mao Tse-tung, On the Correct Handling of Contradictions Among the People (Peking: Foreign Languages Press, 1960).

92) Ch'i Yung-hung, "Chin i-pu chin-ch'iang tang ti i-yüan-hua ling-tao," Hung-ch'i [Red Flag], No. 1 (January 1, 1972), 38-43.

93) Chou En-lai's Political Report — Selection 20.

94) Wang Hung-wen, "Report on the Revision of the Party Constitution," Peking Review, Nos. 35-36 (September 7, 1973), 29-33 (hereafter cited as "Report on the Constitution, 1973").

95) These important theoretical concepts are expounded by Mao Tse-tung in his On the Correct Handling of Contradictions Among the People.

96) On this aspect of the Cultural Revolution, see Robert Jay Lifton, Revolutionary Immortality (New York: Random House, 1968).

97) Wang Hung-wen, "Report on the Constitution, 1973."

98) Selection 14.

99) Selection 15.

100) Wang Hung-wen, "Report on the Constitution, 1973."

101) Edgar Snow, Red Star Over China (New York: Grove Press, 1961), pp. 121-258.

102) The method used during the 1960s has been well analyzed in Parris Chang, "Research Notes on the Changing Loci of Decision in the CCP," The China Quarterly, No. 44 (October-December 1970), 169-194.

103) See the editor's source note for the selection.

104) Selection 13.

105) They are cited in Hsüan Mo., op. cit. (note 20 above); Chao Ts'ung, "My View on Factional Struggle Within the CCP (in Chinese)," Tsu-kuo (China Monthly, Hong Kong), No. 99 (June 1972), 19-25; Chung Hua-min, "An Analysis of the Lin Piao Case (in Chinese)," ibid., No. 102 (September 1972), 2-8.

106) For example, Liu Shao-ch'i, former chairman of the state, was attacked as "China's Khrushchev" for two years; and Ch'en Po-ta was initially identified as a "sham Marxist" in the press.

107) The "five requirements" were first proposed by Mao in 1964 in China's polemics with the Soviet Union. They were slightly modified in wording and placed in the Ninth Congress

Constitution as the formal requirements for the Party member:

(1) Study and apply Marxism-Leninism-Mao Tse-tung Thought in a living way; (2) Work for the interests of the vast majority of the people of China and the world; (3) Be able at uniting with the great majority, including those who have wrongly opposed them but are sincerely correcting their mistakes; however, special vigilance must be maintained against careerists, conspirators and double-dealers so as to prevent such bad elements from usurping the leadership of the Party and the state at any level and guarantee that the leadership of the Party and the state always remains in the hands of Marxist revolutionaries; (4) Consult with the masses when matters arise; (5) Be bold in making criticism and self-criticism.

108) Lin Piao's speech of August 1, 1966 (Selection 29).

109) See Lin's address of May 18, 1966 (Selection 28).

110) More discussions on the issue may be found in Hai Feng, "Communist China's Party Affairs in 1971 (in Chinese)," Tsu-kuo (China Monthly, Hong Kong), No. 100 (July 1972), 2-11.

111) For the text of the opera, see "Hai kang," Hung-ch'i [Red Flag], No. 2 (February 1, 1972), 22-48.

112) Quoted in China News Summary, No. 453 (January 25, 1973), p. 5.

113) For the pattern of pendulum swing in Chinese politics, see Ying-mao Kau, "Patterns of Recruitment and Mobility of Urban Cadres."

114) Main sources used for compiling this chronology include: Selection 1; Chung-kuo wen-t'i yen-chiu chung-hsin, comp., Lin Piao chuan-chi [A Special Collection on Lin Piao] (Hong Kong: Tzu-lien, 1970); Chung-kung jen-ming lu [Directory of Chinese Communist Leaders] (Taipei: Institute for International Relations, 1967); Thomas W. Robinson, A Politico-Military Biography of Lin Piao (Santa Monica: Rand, 1971); Donald Klein et al., Biographic Dictionary of Communist China (Cambridge: Harvard University Press, 1971); and Union Re-

search Institute, Who's Who in Communist China (Hong Kong:
Union Research Institute, 1966). The events related to the
coup attempt are based primarily on Selections 3-13, the secret
documents of the Central Committee contained in this volume.

The
Lin Piao
Affair

I Lin Piao: Chairman Mao's Close Comrade-in-Arms and Successor

1

CHAIRMAN MAO'S SUCCESSOR:
DEPUTY SUPREME COMMANDER LIN PIAO*

The Constitution of the Communist Party of China unanimously adopted by the Ninth National Congress of the Communist Party of China has explicitly stipulated that Comrade Lin
Piao is the successor to the great leader Chairman Mao. This
is a great victory for the Great Proletarian Cultural Revolution,
a great victory for Marxism-Leninism-Mao Tse-tung Thought.
Vice Chairman Lin is the long-tested, outstanding leader of our
Party, the closest comrade-in-arms and best pupil of Chairman
Mao, and our deputy supreme commander. He has consistently
been loyal to and most steadfastly stands on the side of Chairman Mao's revolutionary line. He has most courageously defended Mao Tse-tung thought and has made outstanding contributions to the cause of the Party. Vice Chairman Lin holds
highest the red banner of Mao Tse-tung thought and is a brilliant model in the creative study and application of Mao Tse-
tung thought. We must follow the brilliant example of Vice
Chairman Lin and forever be loyal to Chairman Mao, Mao Tse-
tung thought and Chairman Mao's proletarian revolutionary line.

---

*Mao chu-hsi ti chieh-pan-jen: Lin Piao fu-t'ung-shuai (n.p.,
June 1969). This pamphlet was apparently prepared as the
official biography of Lin Piao after he had been formally designated as the successor to Chairman Mao at the Ninth Party Congress of April 1969. It provides a great deal of rarely known information about Lin's early life and family background, in addition to
a detailed official account of his special achievements and contributions to the revolution as well as his faithful support and devotion
to Chairman Mao before his abortive military coup.

A Revolutionary Family and a Red Native Place

On the first day of the eleventh month of the lunar calendar
in the year 1907, our respected and beloved Vice Chairman Lin
Piao was born to a poverty-stricken family of Lin-chia-ta-wan
at the foot of Pai-yang Hill in the Hui-lung mountainous area,
Huang-kang hsien, Hupei Province.

Lin-chia-ta-wan is located in a hilly section of Huang-kang
hsien. Before liberation, this area was densely populated, and
most of the broad masses of the laboring people led the life of
handicraftsmen or weavers. Under the oppression of the warlords, life was very poor and difficult. In normal years Comrade Lin Piao's family of nine tilled land (equivalent to 2.25
mou) that could yield only nine piculs of grain, and after the
payment of taxes and levies, not much of the grain harvested
was left. His father and elder brothers depended mainly on
weaving to feed the young and the old of the entire family.
Owing to poverty, the family painfully betrothed one of Comrade
Lin Piao's younger sisters as a child-bride to a family in the
vicinity.

The area of Lin-chia-ta-wan was one of the earliest bases
of operations in Hupei Province at the time of the founding of
our Party. The people there had a glorious revolutionary tradition, and they made outstanding contributions to the cause of
the liberation of the Chinese people. Comrade Lin Piao's
family was one of the families among these people.

In his early years, Lin Ming-ch'ing, Comrade Lin Piao's
father, worked as a shop assistant in a grocery store and a
bookkeeper onboard a small ferry boat. After he was out of
work, he took up weaving at home. He was a man of integrity
and honesty and hated the old society intensely. He constantly
spoke out against the injustices inflicted on the poverty-
stricken peasants.

Comrade Lin Piao's mother always cherished labor. She
worked hard and led a plain life. Although her own family was
needy, she was most willing to give relief to the poor people.
She not only loved and was good at educating her own children

but also treated the poor children of the area as her own. All
this greatly influenced the shaping of Comrade Lin Piao's noble
qualities.

Comrade Lin Piao's father was most sympathetic and sup-
portive of the revolutionary activities that developed in the
area. He and other members of the family energetically supported the revolutionary activities in which Comrade Lin Piao
participated in his early years. After joining the revolution,
Comrade Lin Piao never came home to see his people, but his
mother never complained. On one occasion, Comrade Lin
Piao's father was arrested by Lung Sha, commander of the
puppet Peace Preservation Corps, on the pretext of his being
a "family member of the Communist bandits." He was asked
to disclose the secrets of the revolutionary activities in the
locality, but the old man stood firm before the ferocious enemy
and did not tell anything. Later, he was rescued by the local
masses.

Comrade Lin Piao's four brothers took part in the revolution
at different times. Lin Ch'ing-fu, Comrade Lin Piao's older
brother, joined the local militia led by our Party during the
War of Resistance Against Japan and served as commander of
the Sixth Column. After liberation he worked at the Provincial
Museum of Culture and History. He died of illness in 1959.
Lin's third younger brother, Lin Yü-chü (now called Lin Ch'eng),
took part in the revolution in 1944. He is now working in the
Tuberculosis Hospital of Tientsin Municipality. Lin Hsiang-
jung, Lin's fourth younger brother, went to Yenan to study at
Resist Japan Military and Political University [K'angta] in
May 1938. During the War of Liberation he served as political
commissar in a certain regiment of the First Field Army. He
gloriously sacrificed his life in the battle for the liberation of
T'ai-yüan in 1949.

Comrade Lin Piao's two cousins, Lin Yü-nan and Lin Yü-ying
(also known as Chang Hao), were excellent leading cadres of our
Party. Both sacrificed their precious lives at different times
for the revolutionary cause of the Chinese people. Martyr Lin
Yü-nan was one of the founders of the Hupei Communist Group.

As early as 1917 Comrade Lin Yü-nan went to the Soviet Union and accepted the truth of Leninism. In 1920 he organized a Communist Group at Pa-tou-wan, which is behind Lin-chia-wan-tzu (the place where Comrade Lin Piao was born), thus laying the foundation for the founding of our Party in the Huang-kang area. During the great revolution, Comrade Lin Yü-nan devoted himself for a long time to the workers' movement. He served as secretary general and an executive committee member of the All-China Federation of Trade Unions, director of the Wuhan Regional Office of the Secretariat of the All-China Federation of Trade Unions, and a member of the Party Central Committee. Later he was betrayed by a renegade and was arrested. In 1931 he gloriously died for the cause, together with Li Ch'iu-shih and twenty-four other comrades at Lung-hua, Shanghai.

Lin Yü-ying, that is, Martyr Chang Hao (also known as Lin Chung-tan), led the labor movement in the early period of his career and was a leader of the trade union movement. He served at different times as chairman of the All-China Federation of Trade Unions, member of the Central Committee of the Communist Party of China, secretary of the Wuhan Municipal Party Committee, secretary of the Hupei Provincial Party Committee, political commissar of the 129th Division of the Eighth Route Army, and principal of the Yenan Workers' University. He was arrested and imprisoned on a number of occasions in Shanghai and in the three Northeast Provinces, but he remained gallant and upright under the cruel torture of the enemy. In 1942 Comrade Chang Hao died of illness in Yenan. After his death, our great leader Chairman Mao came in person to pay his last respects, and he wrote a funeral ode for the deceased. When Comrade K'ang Sheng gave the eulogy on the life of Martyr Chang Hao, he gave the highest appraisal of the revolutionary life of Martyr Chang Hao.

Comrade Lin Piao's family was a revolutionary family, and his native place was a red native place. Under the long and cruel rule of Chiang Kai-shek and the Japanese bandits, the heroic people of Lin-chia-ta-wan dared to struggle and did not surrender. This revolutionary spirit is precisely the most precious quality of the Chinese people. After liberation, the people of Lin-chia-ta-wan, together with the broad masses all over the country, marched forward in big strides along the bright road of collectivization under the guidance of Chairman Mao's revolutionary line. They established the Hui-lung People's Commune and quickly transformed their poor and blank look. After the outbreak of the Great Cultural Revolution, the revolutionary masses there renamed the Hui-lung Commune of the hilly Hui-lung area as the Red Guard Commune of the hilly Red Guard area. This revolutionized name has most appropriately manifested the revolutionary tradition of the heroic people of Lin-chia-ta-wan. It also has conveyed to the full extent their determination to respond to Comrade Lin Piao's call, their perpetual loyalty to Chairman Mao and his proletarian revolutionary line, and their revolutionary red heart for defending until death the great thought of Mao Tse-tung.

Militant Childhood and Glorious Youth: Studying for the Revolution and Rebelling Against the Old World

Comrade Lin Piao's original name was Lin Yü-jung. He spent one year in a traditional private school when he was nine years old. In 1919 Comrade Lin Yü-nan founded Chun-hsin School at Pa-tou-wan, and Comrade Lin Piao went to study in that school.

Chun-hsin School was a center of local revolutionary activities. In 1920 Ch'en T'an-ch'iu and Lin Yü-nan formed at Pa-tou-wan a Communist group (at that time it was called the Marxism-Leninism Study Group, and Lin Yü-ying, Hu Liang-yin, and other comrades were also members of the group), and Chun-hsin School was turned into a place for the Communist Group to propagate revolutionary truth and to shelter revolutionary activities. Comrade Hu Liang-yin, the principal of the school, was one of the earliest founders of the Party organization at the Huang-kang area, and he was an outstanding member of our Party. During the great revolution, he served as

secretary of the Huang-kang Hsien Party Committee, and when
the Kuomintang and the Communist Party formed the first
united front, he served as a member of the Standing Committee
of the Huang-kang Hsien Party Headquarters. The underground
Party members led by him joined the "August 1" Nanchang Uprising. During the period of agrarian revolution, Comrade Hu
Liang-yin sacrificed his life in Honan.

When Chun-hsin School was first founded, there were only
ten or so pupils. The number increased to more than twenty
in 1921, and most of them were children of poverty-stricken
peasants. The school was free. Funds for running the school
were raised by the revolutionary organizations led by Yün Tai-
ying, Ch'en T'an-ch'iu, and Lin Yü-nan. The form of education
and the content of lessons taught were different from the old-
style education under the old school system, where the Four
Books and the Five Classics were read mechanically.

From the time Comrade Lin Piao studied in this school at
the age of twelve or thirteen, he received revolutionary en-
lightenment and education under the influence of these revolutionary comrades, and he joined the "Social Welfare Society"
organized by Comrade Yün Tai-ying in Hupei.

Ever since his childhood, Comrade Lin Piao has had profound
class feelings for the laboring people. When dealing with comrades and the working people, "he bowed his head and willingly
served the children like an ox." But he was "cruelly defying,"
extremely hostile, and thoroughly rebellious to the reactionary
rule of the old society. When he was in primary school, under
the influence and education of Hu Liang-yin and other comrades
he learned that there were poor people and rich people in society and why the poor people were oppressed by the rich people. He intensely hated the old society in which the rich people
oppressed and exploited the poor people. He once performed
together with other students a play called "The Nine-Headed
Snake." This play portrayed how the landlords ruthlessly exploited and oppressed the tenant-peasants and how they tightly
coiled around the tenant-peasants like a poisonous snake; the
play thus profoundly exposed the crimes of the landlord class.

Comrade Lin Piao also took part in some "modern plays" that made propaganda for the refusal of women to bind their feet and for the equality of men and women, and against superstition and the twenty-one articles of national betrayal concluded by the warlords. These plays were warmly welcomed by the masses of the peasants.

Comrade Lin Piao received education in materialism in school, and he did not believe in gods and ghosts. He and some other students once pulled down with a rope the clay idol in an ancient temple next door to Chun-hsin School and threw it into a pond. In the old society in which the people were benumbed by the rule of feudal superstition, he did this at the risk of his life. However, Comrade Lin Piao dared to break the bounds of the feudal teaching of propriety, and this showed his great hatred of the feudal teaching of propriety in the old society.

Comrade Lin Piao also greatly detested the bad habits of the old society such as playing cards and gambling. Advising his young friends not to contaminate themselves with such habits, he organized them to carry out proper literary and artistic activities.

Since the age of twelve or thirteen, Comrade Lin Piao had begun to show his revolutionary spirit of daring to rebel against the old society.

In search of revolutionary truth, Comrade Lin Piao was eager to move to broader horizons. In the autumn of 1921 he passed the entrance examination for Kung-chin Middle School in Wuchang. This middle school was one of the centers of revolutionary activities in Wuchang. Ch'en T'an-ch'iu and many comrades taught in this school. Comrade Lin Piao was among the students of the first class in this school.

Comrade Lin Piao had by then learned even more revolutionary truths. Seeing that the warlords were at war with each other year after year and that the people were unable to make a living at that time, he harbored unsurpassed anger against the old society. He had a deep understanding of the oppression and exploitation suffered by the working people in China, and he showed boundless sympathy for the riots which occurred in many places at that time. He made up his mind to join the revolution and work for the emancipation of the broad masses of the distressed laboring people in China.

At Kung-chin Middle School, Comrade Lin Piao was very concerned with national affairs and participated actively in student movements. To sabotage the student movement in this school, Hsiao Yüeh-nan, chieftain of the local reactionary warlords, sent secret agents to Kung-chin School to join the Student Union. When Comrade Lin Piao discovered these secret agents, he fearlessly waged a face-to-face struggle against them, rebutted them into silence, and intimidated them into running away in embarrassment.

When he participated in revolutionary activities in the school, Comrade Lin Piao was already beginning to show his outstanding genius for organization. Although he did not assume any post in the school, no revolutionary organizations formed and no political activities carried out in the school were excluded from Comrade Lin Piao's strong organizational work. Comrade Lin Piao was one of the founders of the "Kung-chin Library," which was formed by Class II of Kung-chin Middle School under the guidance of revolutionary teachers. This organization led the students to read progressive books and publications, magazines, and newspapers published after the "May Fourth" movement and played a positive role in leading the students to participate in revolutionary activities. Comrade Lin Piao and some other revolutionary students also organized the "New Village of Self-Government," which was responsible for leading the student movement.

Comrade Lin Piao actively mobilized and helped students around him to participate in revolutionary activities. His fellow villager and schoolmate Lin Shih-chih thought about nothing but study, so that he could invent or create things in the future. Comrade Lin Piao frankly told Lin Shih-chih: "To study dead books alone offers no solution to the question of bread. If problems are not solved politically, it is impossible for the individual to create or invent things." He mobilized him to pay attention to politics. In order to help his fellow students make progress, Comrade Lin Piao regularly gave them progressive books and publications. Led by Comrade Lin Piao, more than thirty out of the forty-odd students of Class II of

Kung-chin Middle School became concerned with national affairs and participated actively in revolutionary activities inside
and outside the school.

Comrade Lin Piao did not merely participate in the revolutionary activities of the school. He also clearly understood
that in order to overthrow the reactionary rule the masses
must be mobilized. He therefore often went out of the school
gate into society and mingled with the workers and peasants
to propagate revolution, to expose the old society as well as
the exploitation and oppression of the laboring people by the
reactionary ruling classes, and to awaken the masses to seek
emancipation with revolutionary means and to create their own
happy life. Comrade Lin Piao once put it clearly to Lin Shih-
chih: "We must make those who want revolution understand
revolution and believe in revolution."

Because of the role he played in the student movement and
the outstanding ability he demonstrated, Comrade Lin Piao enjoyed a very high prestige in the school. Those progressive
teachers and students who knew him well all admired him very
much. He once represented students of Wuhan at the National
Conference of the Student Unions convened in Shanghai. When
the "May 30" movement erupted in 1925, Comrade Lin Piao
was an active organizer of the student demonstration and strike
in Wuhan.

The student movement at Kung-chin Middle School organized
by some revolutionary teachers and Comrade Lin Piao surged
ahead in a big way, and the school became one of the headquarters of the revolutionary intellectuals and Marxist-Leninist
activists in Hupei. The student movement at this school gave
great impetus to the overall student movement in Wuhan.

In 1919 Chairman Mao grandly wrote in the inaugural an-
nouncement of the Hsiang-chiang Review [Hsiang-chiang p'ing-
lun]: "Don't be afraid of what ? Don't be afraid of Heaven, of
ghosts, of the dead, of bureaucrats, of warlords, and of capitalists." Comrade Lin Piao took practical action himself to put
Chairman Mao's martial statement into practice. Comrade
Lin Piao's fearless spirit of daring to make revolution and

rebellion under the dark rule of the reactionaries set a glorious model for us proletarian revolutionaries.

The Excellent Qualities of
Modesty, Diligence, and Frugality

Comrade Lin Piao has since his childhood developed and cultivated an unusual character and excellent qualities. He generally did not like to talk too much. In work he was serious and down-to-earth and applied himself with total devotion. He spoke in a leisurely manner and dealt with things without hurry or emotion. He was slow to speak until he understood the situation. When other people put forth different points of view and argued violently, he modestly listened to all sides, analyzed them, and explained his own correct view with patience and care to other people in a sensible and reasonable manner.

Comrade Lin Piao studied assiduously, diligently, and consistently. He opposed mechanical study and advocated combining study with practice. He consistently maintained that useful articles should be read carefully and repeatedly until the main points were remembered. Sometimes, in order to read a lesson carefully, he would skip a meal and would not give up until the whole lesson was remembered and comprehended. When he felt tired from reading, he would tie sand bags to his legs and climb in the mountains to reinvigorate himself and temper himself physically.

The students of Kung-chin Middle School came from all parts of the country. Some were rich and some were poor. Some rich students were particular about their food and clothing. However, Comrade Lin Piao, deeply aware of the sufferings of the laboring people, always maintained the habit of leading a diligent, frugal, and simple life and never spent one penny unnecessarily. When he was studying at Kung-chin Middle School, he was forced to cease studying for half a year in 1923 because of his family's poverty and his inability to pay school fees, and he worked as a substitute teacher in a school for workers' children outside the Ts'ao-k'ou Gate in Wuchang.

This school was at first privately funded by some senior middle-school students in Wuchang and was rather short of funds, so Comrade Lin Piao mobilized the students to reclaim land and grow vegetables to supplement the school's expenditures. The frugal and simple life style of Comrade Lin Piao was well known throughout the school.

In 1925 Comrade Lin Piao graduated from Kung-chin Middle School. Out of his concern for his son and anxiety over the poverty of his family, his father hoped that Comrade Lin Piao would choose teaching as his profession. However, Comrade Lin Piao had by then become an eighteen-year-old young man with a far-sighted political viewpoint and a revolutionary ambition, so he genially declined his father's suggestion. He said: "At present the country is facing tremendous disasters and difficulties because the warlords are at war with each other and everything is in chaos. I want to join the army and work for national salvation and social reforms." He also said: "There cannot be peace in China without thirty years of revolution." His father understood Comrade Lin Piao's state of mind and supported his taking the revolutionary road. In January 1926, with the approval of the Party organization, he was recommended to study at the Whampoa Military Academy.

Advancing as a Vanguard of the Northern Expedition and Raising the Flag at the Nanchang Uprising: A Young Commander in the "Iron Army"

In January 1926 Comrade Lin Piao brought revolutionary ambition and determination to the center of the great Revolution — Kwangtung. He studied at the Whampoa Military Academy as a student of the fourth class of the Academy. From that time on, he changed his name to Lin Piao.

Soon afterward, the Northern expedition began, and Comrade Lin Piao served as a probationary platoon commander in Yeh T'ing's Independent Regiment.

The Yeh T'ing Independent Regiment was a revolutionary force under the direct leadership of the Communist Party of

China organized with members of the Communist Party and
the Communist Youth League as its backbone. It was a brave
and excellent fighting force, and it also upheld strict discipline.
In May 1926 this regiment advanced into Hunan as the vanguard
of the Northern Expeditionary forces. Throughout the Northern
Expeditionary War, the Independent Regiment spearheaded
every battle as the vanguard force of the Northern Expeditionary Army. In the Battles of Ting-szu-ch'iao and Ho-sheng-
ch'iao, the Independent Regiment routed Wu P'ei-fu's troops.
In the Wuchang campaign, the Independent Regiment was the
first to ascend She Mountain and forced its way into Wuchang City to wipe out the 20,000-strong enemy defenders there.
Because of its splendid combat record in the Northern Expeditionary War, the Yeh T'ing Independent Regiment won the glorious title of the "Iron Army."

As a young commander in the "Iron Army," Comrade Lin
Piao fought from Kwangtung to Honan. In fierce battles he
stormed and breached the enemy citadels with bravery and
presence of mind. Hard working and good at learning, he demonstrated his firm revolutionary determination and exceptional
competence in commanding. A military genius of the proletariat quickly grew to maturity through the practice of the
revolutionary war and was prepared to meet the storms of a
still greater class struggle.

Raising the Red Banner at the Nanchang Uprising and Achieving a Remarkable Record at the Battle of Lai-yang

While the Northern Expeditionary War was advancing in triumph in 1927, the young Communist Party of China was attacked
by the enemy from within and without the revolutionary camp.
Chiang Kai-shek openly rebelled against the revolution and
launched the "April 12" counterrevolutionary coup to carry
out a bloody massacre of the Communists and the Chinese people. The Right capitulationist line was actively pursued by
Ch'en Tu-hsiu and Liu Shao-ch'i. This brought about a setback
of the heroic great revolution and allowed White Terror to over-
shadow the whole country.

At this life-and-death juncture of the Chinese Revolution, our great leader Chairman Mao, with his outstanding Marxist-Leninist genius, surveyed the revolutionary situation at home and abroad, analyzed the concrete conditions of the Chinese revolution, and pointed out that the use of revolutionary armed forces to wipe out the counterrevolutionary armed forces was the one and only correct road that could save China. The proletarian revolutionaries headed by Chairman Mao thus overcame Ch'en Tu-hsiu's Right capitulationist line and held high the great banner of armed revolution.

Guided by the great red banner of Mao Tse-tung thought, the "August 1" Nanchang Uprising fired the first shot against the Kuomintang reactionaries.

In accordance with Chairman Mao's proletarian revolutionary line, in 1927 Comrade Lin Piao firmly adhered to the correct road of armed struggle, took part in the Nanchang Uprising, and went with the armed forces to the vicinity of I-ch'ang in Hunan to engage in guerrilla warfare. The armed forces were then reorganized as the First Division of the Workers and Peasants' Red Army of China, and Comrade Lin Piao served as commander of the Second Company of the First Battalion. This young company commander of the Red Army demonstrated his extraordinary military talent in the Red Army. In the famous Battle of Lai-yang, with a company of men under his command and fighting in close coordination with more than 3,000 peasant self-defense forces and red guard forces, he defeated in a single stroke a division of the invading Kuomintang forces and victoriously occupied Lai-yang city, thus performing a brilliant feat of arms by beating a far bigger force with a small force under conditions in which the balance of strength was distinctly in favor of the enemy.

In the middle of March 1928, alarmed by the revolutionary storm whipped up by the First Division of our Workers and Peasants' Red Army in Hunan, the Kuomintang reactionaries and the warlords of Hunan, Kwangtung, and Kwangsi continuously sent troops to carry out suppression. A division under warlord Hu Tsung-to of Kwangsi invaded Lai-yang. At that time only the divisional headquarters and two battalions of the

First Division of the Workers and Peasants' Red Army were stationed at Lai-yang, while the First and Second Battalions were stationed in the countryside. Because the invading enemy forces were powerful and we were outnumbered, our troops temporarily pulled out of Lai-yang to await an opportunity for action.

The Second Company of the First Battalion under the command of Comrade Lin Piao was then stationed in a town ninety li northeast of the city. When he received an order from the divisional headquarters telling him to converge his forces on Lai-yang city, Comrade Lin Piao quickly assembled his troops and also mobilized more than 1,000 local red guard forces to march toward Lai-yang city. On the evening of the following day, the Second Company had rushed to Ao-shan-miao, 30 li northeast of Lai-yang city, and learned that the hsien town had been occupied by the enemy. At that time the local people all wanted to fight in coordination with the Red Army to recover Lai-yang city.

Having analyzed the situation calmly, Comrade Lin Piao held that although the enemy had one division of men, they were Kwangsi troops, and having just arrived at Lai-yang, they were unfamiliar with the terrain. Although we had only one company, we were supported by the militia, and the morale of the armymen and militiamen was high. Furthermore, it was evening, so we could take the enemy by surprise. Comrade Lin Piao therefore resolutely made up his mind to attack Lai-yang. He deployed more than 1,000 red guard forces and about 2,000 men from the peasants' self-defense force of Ao-shan-miao to attack from the east, south, and west flanks and make lots of noise to confuse the enemy. At the opportune moment, the Second Company would serve as the shock brigade and launch a surprise attack on the enemy from the high land north of the city.

The enemy actually thought that a big force of the Red Army was counterattacking, and abandoned the city and beat a hasty retreat. The Red Army took advantage of the enemy confusion and, after a night of fighting, shattered the enemy division and

put it to rout. The city of Lai-yang was liberated once again.
In the flush of victory the Red Second Company pursued the
enemy to Tsao-shih and wiped out another big band of armed
landlords.

The Battle of Lai-yang inspired all Hunan. In this battle,
Comrade Lin Piao put into practice Chairman Mao's great
strategic thought of people's war by relying on the strength of
the masses to the full extent and beat the enemy by surprise
with his fearless revolutionary spirit of daring to struggle and
win and with his outstanding art of military command.

After the Battle of Lai-yang, Comrade Lin Piao was promoted
to commander of the First Battalion of the First Division of the
Red Army.

Climbing up the Towering Ching-kang Mountains

As early as the "August 7" conference of the Party, the great
leader Chairman Mao had put forward the wise assertion that
"political power grows out of the barrel of a gun." The grand
old man himself personally launched and led the world renowned
Autumn Harvest Uprising, and marched on the Ching-kang
Mountains to build the first people's army of an entirely new
type in the world and to establish the red cradle of the proletarian revolution — the Ching-kang Mountains revolutionary
base.

In April 1928 Comrade Lin Piao, with boundless faith in and
boundless adoration and fervent love for Chairman Mao, resolutely made his way up the Ching-kang Mountains and came to
the side of the great leader Chairman Mao. From that time on,
Comrade Lin Piao has always followed Chairman Mao, actively
and assiduously studied Mao Tse-tung thought, and become
Chairman Mao's closest comrade-in-arms and best pupil.

After Comrade Lin Piao led his troops to the Ching-kang
Mountains, his forces were merged with the Red Army there
to form the Red Fourth Army with Chairman Mao as the Party
representative. Comrade Lin Piao at first served as commander of the First Battalion of the Twenty-eighth Regiment of the

Red Fourth Army, but soon afterward he was promoted to commander of the Twenty-eighth Regiment. In the arduous struggle
to establish and defend the Ching-kang Mountains base, Comrade Lin Piao rendered immortal meritorious service.

During the famous Battle of Ch'i-chi-ling, he led the heroic
Twenty-eighth Regiment to smash three enemy regiments invading the base. In the course of pursuit they wiped out another
enemy regiment and thus destroyed Chiang Kai-shek's "encirclement and extermination" campaign.

In the Ching-kang Mountains, Comrade Lin Piao seized every
opportunity to eagerly study Chairman Mao's writings. Sometimes he even studied them on horseback. Therefore he comprehended most profoundly and applied most creatively Mao
Tse-tung thought.

On one occasion, all the commanders and fighters of the
Twenty-eighth Regiment were discussing the question of establishing the Lo-hsiao Mountain base at a meeting where
Chairman Mao was present. At the meeting a violent dispute
developed. Some people did not attach importance to the building of bases, and they advocated roving from place to place.
Comrade Lin Piao firmly opposed this kind of "roving bandit
mentality." He categorically said: "Our army is called the
Workers and Peasants' Red Army and is an army that will
serve the people to the end. We not only must fight but also
must carry out mass work and production. Ours is a fighting
force as well as a work force and production force. We must
go everywhere to make propaganda among the masses, to arm
the masses, and to help the masses establish their revolutionary political power. Therefore we should firmly believe that
the strategic principle advanced by Comrade Mao Tse-tung is
absolutely correct. This is the one and only correct road that
will lead the Chinese revolution to victory...." Comrade Lin
Piao's profound comprehension and penetrating exposition of
Chairman Mao's brilliant thought concerning the "occupation
of territory by the armed forces of the workers and peasants"
won the praise of all the comrades present. At that time
Chairman Mao nodded his head and looked up and down at the

heroic posture of Comrade Lin Piao with approving eyes.

In another battle, the Thirty-first Regiment was defeated, and Chairman Mao and Comrade Lin Piao led troops to come to its rescue. When the enemy counterattacked, Comrade Lin Piao promptly let the Thirty-first Regiment take a rest; he himself led the Twenty-eighth Regiment to intercept the enemy, and they returned in victory. Chairman Mao praised Comrade Lin Piao saying: "Lin Piao is not only a man of ability but also a general of talent. A person like him is capable of keeping the whole situation in mind, and our armed forces will need such a person to lead them in the future."

Boundlessly Loyal to Chairman Mao: Braving the Adverse Wind and the Stormy Waves

During the Second Revolutionary Civil War, a violent struggle between two lines emerged within the Party over the question of whether or not to persist in protracted, arduous armed struggle and to establish and consolidate the revolutionary bases in rural areas.

Under the White Terror, with "the foe surrounding us in thousands of circles," Chairman Mao insisted on mobilizing the peasant masses to carry out the agrarian reform in depth and to strive to establish revolutionary bases, while at the same time adopting the "policy of advancing in waves" to enlarge the base area. In January 1929 Chairman Mao led the Red Fourth Army to open up bases in southern Kiangsi and western Fukien. "Red flags leap over the Ting River and turn downward to Lung-yen and Shang-hang." The moving scene of "people very busy dividing land and holdings" emerged wherever the Red Army fought.

However, the "Left" opportunists frenziedly opposed Chairman Mao's correct line and attacked the "policy of advancing in waves" as "conservatism." In August 1928 they forced part of the Red Army to make an adventurous move into southern Hunan. This brought about the "August defeat" in the Hunan-Kiangsi area. In June 1929, at the Seventh Party Congress of

the Red Fourth Army held in Lung-yen, Fukien, they eased
Chairman Mao out of the Red Fourth Army, sending him to
work on the Special Party Committee in western Fukien.

In this difficult hour Comrade Lin Piao stepped forward and
steadfastly stood by Chairman Mao. On the one hand he firmly
adhered to Chairman Mao's revolutionary line and strengthened
the building of bases. On the other he sent one battalion of men
to western Fukien to protect Chairman Mao.

At the Eighth Party Congress of the Red Fourth Army held
at Shang-hang, Comrade Lin Piao and the broad masses of
commanders and fighters unanimously demanded the return of
Chairman Mao to lead the Red Fourth Army. However, the
"Left" and Right opportunists suppressed Comrade Lin Piao's
correct view and once again ousted Chairman Mao, thus causing
the Red Fourth Army to suffer a series of defeats.

Bloodshed and futile sacrifice aroused a strong dissatisfaction with the "Left" and Right opportunists among the broad
masses of commanders and fighters. At the critical moment
the great helmsman Chairman Mao returned to the Red Fourth
Army. In December 1929 Chairman Mao presided over the
important Ku-t'ien Conference and personally drafted the resolution of the Ku-t'ien Conference, "On Correcting Mistaken
Ideas in the Party," which most scientifically summed up the
struggle between two lines at the early stage of the building of
the Red Fourth Army and the base areas. The resolution not
only clearly pointed out the orientation of Party and army-
building for the Red Army but also established our basic line
for the construction of the Party and the army. It was of
epochal significance in the history of our Party and Army.

The resolution of the Ku-t'ien Conference was first implemented by Comrade Lin Piao's troops. Comrade Lin Piao
resolutely opposed P'eng Te-huai's "roving bandit mentality"
and "warlord mentality." He conscientiously carried out
Chairman Mao's correct military line of "the Party commands
the gun."

In June 1930 the Red Fourth Army provided the basis for a
merger with the Red Third Army and the Red Tenth Army to

form the First Army Corps of the Workers and Peasants' Red Army of China. Comrade Lin Piao was appointed commander of the Red Fourth Army of the First Army Corps. The Party Central Committee then was under control of Li Li-san's "Left" opportunists. They frenziedly opposed Chairman Mao's revolutionary line and erroneously engineered general uprisings in big and medium-sized cities all over the country; this forced the Red Army to attack Changsha on two occasions, and both attacks failed.

During the second attack against Changsha, individualist careerist P'eng Te-huai, an agent of Li Li-san, stooped so low as to write a letter to Comrade Lin Piao in a vain attempt to win him over. However, Comrade Lin Piao stood firm and was boundlessly loyal to Chairman Mao. He promptly handed over the letter to Chairman Mao and thus completely smashed P'eng Te-huai's conspiracy. Chairman Mao firmly opposed the attack on Changsha. When the Red Army had failed to take the city after a prolonged attack, Chairman Mao patiently persuaded some of the Red Army cadres to pull back their troops from Changsha. Following this, he ordered the Red Army "to cross the great pass with red flags fluttering in the wind" and sent "100,000 workers and peasants to take Chi-an," thus opening up a great area in western Fukien and eastern Hunan.

In 1931 our Party was for the third time controlled by the "Left-deviationist" line, this time represented by Wang Ming. Wang Ming was even more frantically opposed to Chairman Mao. At the Party representative conference of the base area convened in November at Jui-chin (i.e., the South Kiangsi Conference), they relieved Chairman Mao of his duties as vice chairman of the Military Affairs Commission of the Central Committee and intended to turn the post over to their trusted pawn P'eng Te-huai. However, Chairman Mao continued to sternly criticize and repudiate P'eng Te-huai's erroneous proposal to attack Kan-chou and mapped out a wise plan for an assault on Chang-chou in southern Fukien. Before the battle was fought, Chairman Mao wisely decided to appoint Comrade Lin Piao as commander of the First Army Corps. Lin Piao, who was then only twenty-four years old, thus became a "young general" and Chairman Mao's most able lieutenant. Led by Chairman Mao and Comrade Lin Piao, the First Red Army Corps marched to southern Fukien, took Chang-chou, and won a series of important victories.

But Wang Ming firmly clung to his reactionary stand and was impervious to reason. At the Work Conference of the Central Committee held in August 1932 at Ning-tu, he opposed across-the-board what he called "Mao Tse-tung's opportunism and guerrilla-ism." He also relieved Chairman Mao of all his duties in the Party, the government, and the army.

When Wang Ming and his like attacked and persecuted the wisest and greatest supreme commander Chairman Mao, brave comrade Lin Piao feared neither encirclement and attack nor pressure. He steadfastly stood beside Chairman Mao like a green pine erect in a storm, acting as a militant and strong bodyguard, intercepting the attack of the enemy. He boundlessly adored Chairman Mao, the genius leader of our Party. Cherishing unsurpassed faith in Chairman Mao, he cried with deep feeling from the bottom of his heart: "The Chinese revolution cannot be separated from Comrade Mao Tse-tung!"

Comrade Lin Piao not only steadfastly stood beside Chairman Mao in the struggle between two lines but also firmly adhered to Chairman Mao's military line and made great contributions to the struggle for consolidating and enlarging the base areas of the Party Center.

In the first violent struggle against "encirclement and extermination" at the end of 1930, the Red Fourth Army led by Comrade Lin Piao faithfully carried out Chairman Mao's operational policy of "resorting to active defense, luring the enemy deep into our net, concentrating our forces, and smashing the enemy one by one." In the Battle of Lung-kang, fighting in coordination with friendly forces, it wiped out more than 10,000 enemy troops and captured alive their front field commander Chang Hui-tsan. "Round mist-filled Lung-kang blurred a thousand peaks, as in unison all shouted: Far away at the front they have captured Chang Hui-tsan." This was written by

Chairman Mao in praise of this battle.

In June 1932 Chiang Kai-shek launched the fourth "encirclement and extermination" campaign against the base areas of
the Party Center. In accordance with Chairman Mao's strategic thought, Comrade Lin Piao went on adopting the operational
policy of making noise in the east while attacking in the west,
ambushing the enemy with army corps and concentrating a
superior force to encircle and wipe out the enemy. In the
Battle of Huang-po, we wiped out the Fifty-second Division and
Fifty-ninth Division of the enemy army, thus laying the foundation for victory in the fourth counter-"encirclement and extermination" campaign.

Because "Left" opportunist Wang Ming ousted and persecuted
Chairman Mao, the great supreme commander of the Red Army,
the fifth counter-"encirclement and extermination" campaign
failed. Thus the Red Army made an important shift in strategy
and began its Long March of 25,000 li, which is world renowned.

Those Who Did Not Reach the Great Wall
Were Not True Men

When the Long March was about to begin, Wang Ming, P'eng
Te-huai, and their like, harboring a sinister design, wanted to
leave Chairman Mao in Kiangsi. Actually they wanted to hand
him over to the enemy. Because Comrade Lin Piao and the
broad masses of commanders and fighters waged a firm struggle against this evil plot, the scheme of Wang Ming and company did not materialize.

At the beginning of the Long March, Wang Ming and other
opportunists adopted the escapist policy of moving the household on a large scale, thus bringing heavy losses to the Red
Army. "Raising their heads and seeing the Dipper, the Red
Armymen think of Mao Tse-tung." In January 1935, the epochal
Tsun-yi Conference was convened. At this great turning point
in history, Comrade Lin Piao most loyally supported Chairman
Mao and waged a sharp struggle against Wang Ming, Po Ku, and
their like.

"The Red Army fears not the trial of a distant march; to
them a thousand mountains, ten thousand rivers, are nothing."
After the Tsun-yi Conference Chairman Mao himself served
concurrently as political commissar to the Red First Army
Corps under the command of Comrade Lin Piao. Chairman
Mao was constantly on the move with the Red First Army
Corps. He attended the meetings of the Red First Army Corps
and gave many concrete instructions. Under the direct leadership and solicitude of Chairman Mao, the Red First Army
Corps was the shock brigade which cleared the way through
mountains and rivers in the Long March. In a series of battles
that included the return of forces to Tsun-yi, the breakthrough
at the Wu River, the forced crossing of the Chin-sha River and
the capture of the Lu-ting Bridge, the heroic Red First Army
Corps performed immortal feats of arms.

In June 1935 the Red Army had conquered the snow-covered
mountains and was advancing toward the vast grasslands.
Chairman Mao and the Party Central Committee entrusted the
task of clearing the way across the grasslands to Comrade Lin
Piao's Red First Army Corps. Although Comrade Lin Piao
was sick then, he went deep among the rank and file to show
his concern for the fighters, and he also went to the front in
person to observe the enemy. When assigning tasks to comrades of the advance regiment, he especially emphasized: "No
matter how difficult the grasslands may be, we must walk
through. This is a very important step for carrying out the
decision of the Party Central Committee to go to the North to
fight against the Japanese, and Chairman Mao is very concerned about this action. . . ." On the days when grain supplies
ran out, Comrade Lin Piao himself suggested ideas and methods, and he even risked poisoning to taste the wild plants himself. In those hard days Comrade Lin Piao was boundlessly
loyal to Chairman Mao's revolutionary line, thus setting a
magnificent example for the broad masses of fighters of the
Red Army.

On the second day of the march into the grasslands, Chang
Kuo-t'ao, obstinately clinging to escapism, shamelessly lured

the soldiers to go southward to Szechwan to feed on rice. He
also dispatched two army units in an attempt to stop the Red
First Field Army from continuing with the march northward.
Outraged, Comrade Lin Piao ordered the First Army to deploy
in a line and mount more than ten machine guns. A thundering
order was issued: "Anybody who dares to stand in the way will
be mercilessly destroyed!" Chang Kuo-t'ao was scared to
death and immediately pulled back his troops.

After Comrade Lin Piao led the heroic troops across the
vast grasslands, he went to the front line in person to assume
command, and broke through the last dangerous pass of the
Long March — the hazardous natural barrier of La-tzu-k'ou.
Under the wise leadership of the great supreme commander
Chairman Mao, the Red Army won a complete victory in the
Long March of 25,000 li.

Wiping Out the Japanese Bandits at the P'ing-hsing Pass

After the outbreak of the War of Resistance Against Japan,
Chairman Mao, a great and far-seeing Marxist-Leninist genius,
scientifically analyzed the situation at home and abroad and
laid down the most correct line for launching a general war of
resistance. However, Wang Ming, Liu Shao-ch'i, P'eng Te-
huai, and their like were desperately opposed to Chairman
Mao's correct line and echoed the cry of the Kuomintang diehards: "A war of resistance will fail," and "Fighting continuously will lead to the downfall of the country." They desperately advertised the capitulationist line of "unified command,"
"unified organization," and "unified operations" and put forward
the reactionary slogans of "all through the united front" and
"all following the line of the united front."

In order to smash the capitulationist note of the Kuomintang
diehards and the Right opportunists within the Party, Chairman
Mao instructed Comrade Lin Piao: "The most urgent question
of the moment is to win a big battle and deal a heavy blow to
the frenzied enemy so as to arouse people, boost morale, and
usher in the War of Resistance in North China." Comrade Lin

Piao closely followed Chairman Mao's great strategic plan and actively carried out preparatory mobilization. He said: "It is necessary to fight the first battle well, fire the first shot loud, and fight a great battle of annihilation. This is the hope of the people all over the country as well as the hope of the Party Central Committee and Chairman Mao." Comrade Lin Piao led the heroic 115th Division to the front in the night, and in accordance with the principle of "independence and autonomy," he smashed the conspiracy of the Kuomintang reactionaries who attempted to wipe out our army through the hands of the Japanese bandits.

On September 25, 1937, the Battle of the P'ing-hsing Pass, which won resounding fame throughout China and the world, began. After a day of fearless fighting, our 115th Division completely wiped out more than 3,000 men of the Itagaki Regiment, which the Japanese bandits described as the "flower of the army," and won the first great victory in the War of Resistance.

The great victory of the P'ing-hsing Pass greatly boosted the morale of the Chinese people and greatly deflated the arrogance of the so-called invincible "Imperial Army." It gave the Kuomintang reactionaries and such people as Wang Ming and Liu Shao-ch'i a resounding slap in the face. Chairman Mao highly praised this great victory, saying that the Battle of P'ing-hsing Pass showed the indomitable spirit and the heroic and magnificent fighting strength of the Chinese people.

Faithful to the Educational Cause of the Party

On the eve of the outbreak of the War of Resistance Against Japan, the political situation of the whole country was at the point of transition from the Revolutionary Civil War to the War of Resistance Against Japan. Chairman Mao pointed out that this turning-point was not easily transversed and that the most important link was to study afresh and retrain the cadres. On June 1, 1936, because Chairman Mao was directly concerned with the matter, the Chinese People's Resist-Japan Military and Political University [K'angta] came into being to meet the needs of the great War of Resistance Against Japan.

Our great leader Chairman Mao selected his close comrade-in-arms Comrade Lin Piao to serve as president of Resist Japan University. He also personally laid down for Resist Japan University the most correct educational policy: "To cultivate a firm and correct political orientation, and industrious and simple style of work, and flexible strategy and tactics." Chairman Mao also personally wrote the motto, "Be united, alert, earnest and lively," for Resist Japan University.

Vainly attempting to run Resist Japan University as a "school of the united front," Wang Ming and his like made every effort to advertise that "the Three People's Principles are the banner of unity for resistance against Japan." The old-time counter-revolutionary Liu Shao-ch'i desperately wanted to peddle his sinister term "Self-Cultivation" at Resist Japan University.

Our great helmsman Chairman Mao clearly pointed out that Resist Japan University was not a school of the united front but a cadre school of the Eighth Route Army under the leadership of the Party. Comrade Lin Piao faithfully and thoroughly carried out Chairman Mao's series of instructions concerning Resist Japan University and ran Resist Japan University as a great red school of Mao Tse-tung thought. The basic textbooks used in Resist Japan University were Chairman Mao's works, such as "Problems of Strategy in China's Revolutionary War," "On Tactics Against Japanese Imperialism," "On Contradiction," "On Practice," and so on.

Chairman Mao wrote an inscription for Resist Japan University: "Be faithful to the educational cause of the Party." Comrade Lin Piao was boundlessly loyal to Chairman Mao's thought on education. He regarded class struggle and the struggle between two lines as the principal subjects for Resist Japan University and laid down for the university the basic educational principles "link theory with practice" and "less but better." Comrade Lin Piao also integrated the educated youths with the worker-peasant masses and regarded hard struggle as a chief subject for Resist Japan University.

In the short course of nine years Resist Japan University trained for our Party more than 100,000 revolutionary cadres, thus making a great contribution to the cause of the liberation of the Chinese people. Chairman Mao praised Resist Japan University as the most revolutionary, most progressive, and most capable school in the fight for the liberation of the nation and society.

In March 1938 Comrade Lin Piao was wounded in action, whereupon Chairman Mao sent him to the Soviet Union for recuperation. During his recuperation, despite the fact that he was not fully recovered, Comrade Lin Piao demonstrated his noble proletarian internationalism by participating in the war of self-defense of the Soviet Union, and performed immortal feats of arms and won the high praises of Comrade Stalin.

In February 1942 Comrade Lin Piao returned to China from the Soviet Union. During the rectification campaign in the Liberated Areas, Comrade Lin Piao steadfastly stood beside Chairman Mao and waged a firm and stern struggle against the "Left" and Right opportunists. He called on the whole Party to rally closely around Chairman Mao, saying, "Great is the Party of the Soviet Union and great is the Soviet Union today because the Party of the Soviet Union rallies around Stalin. The Party of China should rally around Comrade Mao Tse-tung so that we may build a great Party of China and a great new democratic China." Comrade Lin Piao also called on the whole Party: "Be loyal to our nation, be loyal to our Party, be loyal to our great leader!"

At that time Chang Wen-t'ien and others like him in the Central Party School obstinately clung to the opportunist stand. They feigned compliance with the rectification campaign but resisted and opposed Chairman Mao's instructions. Because of this, the Central Committee decided to reorganize the leading body of the Party School. Chairman Mao himself served as principal of the school, and he selected his close comrade-in-arms Comrade Lin Piao to serve as vice principal.

From the end of 1942 to July 1943, Comrade Lin Piao was in Chungking to take part in negotiations between the Kuomintang and the Communist Party. Together with our respected and beloved Premier Chou, he waged a tit-for-tat struggle against the Kuomintang reactionaries. At the Seventh Party Congress in April 1945, Comrade Lin Piao was elected a member of the Central Committee. On August 9, 1945, Chairman Mao issued the order to engage in "the last round with the Japanese invaders." He sent Comrade Lin Piao to lead an army 100,000 strong to the Northeast theater of war, which defeated the Japanese Kanto Army. On August 14 Japanese imperialism surrendered unconditionally.

Sweeping Away the Enemy Forces Like Rolling Up a Mat

Following the surrender of the Japanese bandits, China entered the period of the Third Revolutionary Civil War, in which a decisive battle over two kinds of destiny and future was fought. At the crucial moment marking the approach of the ultimate victory of the Chinese revolution, a sharp and violent struggle between the proletarian revolutionary line represented by Chairman Mao and the bourgeois reactionary line represented by Liu Shao-ch'i was launched over a series of fundamental questions — whether or not, and if so, how we should seize political power throughout the country.

Confronted with Chiang Kai-shek's political swindle of false "peace negotiations" but genuine civil war, Chairman Mao opportunely exposed Chiang Kai-shek's counterrevolutionary plot to the whole Party and the people of the whole country and put forward the clarion call: "Give tit for tat and dispute every inch of ground." He also clearly pointed out: "At present Chiang Kai-shek is in the process of sharpening his blade, and because of this we too must sharpen our blade." "The arms of the people — every rifle and every bullet — must be preserved and cannot be handed over." Chairman Mao called on the whole Party: "The rights already won by the people can never be given up lightly and must be defended by fighting." China's Khrushchev, Liu Shao-ch'i, sang a tune that ran counter to Chairman Mao's. At the grave point of the approach of a nationwide civil

war, Liu vociferously advertised the reactionary fallacy that
"China has entered the new stage of peace and democracy," in
a vain attempt to liquidate the People's armed forces, give up
the Chinese revolution, and hand over to the Kuomintang the
fruits of victory which the Chinese people had shed their blood
to win. He also advertised that "the principal form of struggle
of the Chinese revolution has now been turned from armed
struggle into unarmed struggle," and he wanted to liquidate the
leadership of the Party over the people's armed forces. In
order to achieve his sinister aim, Liu Shao-ch'i, taking advantage of the opportunity while Chairman Mao was away in Chungking for talks and he was in charge of the routine work of the
Central Committee, sent his trusted man P'eng Chen in August
1945 to the Northeast Bureau to serve as first secretary. After
his arrival in the Northeast, P'eng Chen made every effort to
disseminate the "peaceful atmosphere" with such nonsense as
our Party's "policy toward Chiang Kai-shek is still one of
washing his face, and not one of beheading."

Comrade Lin Piao, who was then commander-in-chief of the
Democratic Allied Forces of the Northeast, firmly carried out
Chairman Mao's correct policy and waged an uncompromising
struggle against Liu Shao-ch'i and P'eng Chen's capitulationist
line. Comrade Lin Piao sharply pointed out: "There is basically no such word as peace in Chiang Kai-shek's mind. He only
makes use of it occasionally to peddle his swindle." "Chiang
Kai-shek's policy of national betrayal is a foregone conclusion."
In February 1946, at the Mei-ho-k'ou Conference of the Northeast Bureau, Comrade Lin Piao sternly criticized and repudiated the "thought of peace" of the Northeast Bureau under the
control of P'eng Chen. P'eng Chen blatantly declared: "The
Northeast Bureau has not given the cadres any thought of
peace." Giving tit for tat, Comrade Lin Piao pointed out: "But
neither has it given the cadres any thought of war." In February 1947, at a mass work conference in the Northeast, Comrade Lin Piao delivered a special talk on the question of whether "the policy of washing his face" or "the policy of beheading"
should be adopted toward Chiang Kai-shek. He said, "A

revolutionary struggle is a life-and-death struggle. When dealing with Chiang Kai-shek, we should think in terms of 'defeating him,' 'crushing him,' 'suppressing him,' 'striking him down' and 'wiping him out.'" This directive of Comrade Lin Piao's, which glittered with the radiance of Mao Tse-tung thought, strongly criticized and repudiated Liu Shao-ch'i and P'eng Chen's capitulationist fallacy, greatly heightened the revolutionary vigilance of the cadres and the masses of the Northeast, and guaranteed politically a great victory in the Northeast theater of war.

In order to cover up his political capitulationism, P'eng Chen adopted military adventurism.

In December 1945 Chairman Mao issued the great call for "building secure base areas in the Northeast." He instructed our army to "keep away from the main communication lines but occupy their two flanks," to concentrate on work in the medium-sized and small cities situated farther away from the occupied centers of the Kuomintang and in the broad rural areas, to go deep among the masses to mobilize them, and to accumulate strength and prepare to counterattack. This was the one and only correct path for winning victory in the whole country under the condition that the enemy was strong and we were weak at the early stage of the War of Liberation. However, P'eng Chen preached the "particularity of the Northeast," obstinately opposed Chairman Mao's instruction, desperately clung to the cities, and advanced the ultra-"Left" slogans of "hold off the enemy outside Shanghaikuan," "defend Changchun to the last ditch," "defend Ma-te-li to the last ditch," etc. He refused to carry out Chairman Mao's correct policy of shifting positions on our own initiative to avoid losses, thus bringing undue losses to our army at Szu-p'ing. P'eng Chen also wanted to attack Shenyang. After these adventurist policies failed, he jumped from one extreme to the other and adopted an escapist policy. As a result our army had to retreat from Shenyang to north of Harbin. Under these unfavorable conditions, Comrade Lin Piao came forward. He firmly carried out Chairman Mao's wise instruction — "Keep away from

the main communication lines but occupy their two flanks" —
and sent 15,000 cadres to the countryside to launch a penetrating mass movement for agrarian reform and the removal of
traitors. Comrade Lin Piao called on the cadres to "remove
their leather shoes, put away their leather briefcases, put on
peasant clothing, and eat sorghum." He also set an example
for them by constantly finding time to go deep into the countryside to eat and live together with the poor and lower-middle
peasants and to learn about their suffering. Because of this,
the 200,000 bandits in the service of Chiang Kai-shek were
annihilated, and the base areas in the rear were established
and consolidated in northern Manchuria in a very short time.
Because Comrade Lin Piao put a timely end to P'eng Chen's
erroneous decisions — "Attack Shenyang," "defend Changchun
to the last ditch" — and moved our armed forces to north of
the Sungari River and to eastern, western and northern Manchuria to avoid the brunt of the superior enemy forces, he
smashed P'eng Chen's military adventurism and escapism.
Because Comrade Lin Piao resolutely defended and carried
out Chairman Mao's revolutionary line, he was ruthlessly attacked and persecuted by Liu Shao-ch'i, P'eng Chen, and company. Backed by Liu Shao-ch'i, P'eng Chen ganged up with his
"sworn brothers" and frenziedly opposed Comrade Lin Piao.
Old-time opportunist Li Li-san even wickedly called for "the
reorganization of the command headquarters" in a vain attempt
to oust Comrade Lin Piao. Chairman Mao saw through their
conspiracy just in time. In June 1946 Chairman Mao dismissed
P'eng Chen from office and appointed Comrade Lin Piao as
first secretary of the Northeast Bureau. This was a great victory for Chairman Mao's revolutionary line. From then on,
earthshaking changes took place in the Northeast theater of
war under the guidance of Chairman Mao's revolutionary line
and the direct command of Comrade Lin Piao.

Chairman Mao said, "All the guiding principles of military
operations grow out of the one basic principle: to strive to the
utmost to preserve one's own strength and destroy that of the
enemy." Comrade Lin Piao superbly mastered this brilliant

concept and creatively put forward the tactics of "one point, two areas," the "three-three system," and "be fast in four respects and slow in one respect." He also assumed personal command over the training of troops. These tactics were enormously effective in the War of Liberation. Comrade Lin Piao paid special attention to grasping political and ideological work in the armed forces. He energetically launched the "two recollections, three checkups" movement and actively strengthened military training on the basis of class education. Because of this, the fighting strength of our army was quickly raised. As Comrade Lin Piao correctly carried out Chairman Mao's revolutionary line the base areas of the Northeast were consolidated and developed, and the emancipated peasants whipped up a high tide in supporting the front and joining the army. The Northeast People's Liberation Army quickly grew from an army of several hundred thousand men into an invincible, mighty army one million strong in twelve columns.

In the second half of 1947 Chairman Mao issued to the whole army the great call for "a nationwide counteroffensive." Comrade Lin Piao at once led his heroic troops to launch a large-scale autumn general offensive and a winter offensive.

After several months of bitter and difficult fighting, eighteen big cities, including Szu-p'ing, Ying-k'ou and Kirin were captured. More than 300,000 enemy troops were wiped out, and the army of the Chiang Kai-shek bandits in the Northeast pulled back into the few isolated cities of Changchun, Chin-chou and Shenyang to await their doom. Chairman Mao had high praise for the large-scale winter offensive that lasted several scores of days. He said that by braving the frigid weather of thirty degrees below zero to wipe out most of the enemy forces and to capture the well-known cities in the winter offensive, our Northeast Field Army had won resounding fame throughout the country.

In September 1948 Chairman Mao decided to launch a nationwide strategic offensive from the Northeast theater of war, and he proposed the arduous task of liberating the entire Northeast and completely wiping out the enemy forces there. Chairman

Mao instructed Comrade Lin Piao "to ignore the enemy forces
in Changchun and Shenyang," and he pointed out that "when attacking Chin-chou, preparations should be made to wipe out the
enemy reinforcements coming from Changchun and Shenyang
to the aid of Chin-chou." Comrade Lin Piao brilliantly implemented Chairman Mao's wise directive and adopted the tactics
of making noise in the east while attacking in the west. He employed a small number of his troops to continue the encirclement and attack of Changchun and Shenyang so as to give the
enemy the false impression that the attack was aimed at Changchun, but at the same time he violently attacked Chin-chou with
heavy forces and also fought spirited battles of interception at
Hei-shan and T'a-shan. Under the correct command of Comrade Lin Piao, our army needed only thirty-one hours to wipe
out completely the 100,000 enemy defenders of Chin-chou and
to capture alive Fan Han-chieh, "deputy commander-in-chief
of the Communist Suppression Command in the Northeast."
During the Liaoning-Shenyang campaign, Chiang Kai-shek, the
public enemy, assumed command in person. He changed his
chief commander three times and was furious with frustration,
but all to no avail. The Liaoning-Shenyang campaign started
on September 12 in the Chin-chou area, and after fifty-two
days of fierce fighting, 470,000 of Chiang's bandit troops in the
Northeast were wiped out. From then on, the Northeast came
back into the hands of the people.

The great victory of the Liaoning-Shenyang campaign brought
about a basic change in the balance of power between the enemy
and ourselves. Chairman Mao said: "The military situation in
China has now come to a new turning point.... The People's
Liberation Army has already become superior not only in
quality but also in numbers. This signifies the approach of the
success of the Chinese revolution and of peace in China." This
was a great victory for Chairman Mao's military line as well
as the result of Comrade Lin Piao's faithful implementation
of Chairman Mao's great strategic policy.

In November 1948 the forces led by Comrade Lin Piao were
reorganized into the Fourth Field Army with Comrade Lin Piao

as commander. Immediately after the reorganization, the
Fourth Field Army rushed through Shanhaikuan into China
proper, according to Chairman Mao's instruction. Comrade
Lin Piao himself directed the renowned Peking-Tientsin campaign and the liberation war in North China, thus laying the
foundation for the liberation of the whole country.

In order to protect half of the country and win time to
catch their breath, the United States-Chiang reactionaries
hoisted the torn banner of "peace negotiations." Liu Shao-ch'i
also took advantage of this and jumped forward crying: "The
present situation is developing too fast." "Rather than too fast,
it is better to be a bit slower." He vainly attempted to stop the
advance of the wheel of history. Our great helmsman Chairman
Mao then issued to the people of the whole country the great
call "Carry the Revolution Through to the End." Comrade Lin
Piao closely followed Chairman Mao's great strategic plan and
clearly pointed out that "the 'peace' which the Kuomintang reactionaries are playing with today is being advanced under the
condition that their armed forces have been almost completely
annihilated in the thoroughly wicked civil war which they themselves launched"; it is for the purpose of "winning time to catch
their breath militarily so that they may regroup their forces
for a counterattack." In April 1949 Comrade Lin Piao held
talks in Peking with the Kuomintang Nanking Government on
behalf of the Communist Party. In the course of the negotiations he resolutely smashed the "peace" conspiracy of the
Chiang bandits and gave traitor Liu Shao-ch'i a slap in the face.

"Over Chung-shan swept a storm, headlong; our mighty army,
a million strong, has crossed the Great River." After Chairman Mao issued the "Order to the Army for Nationwide Advance," Comrade Lin Piao led the heroic Fourth Field Army
southward in May of 1949. The Fourth Field Army fought its
way across the Yangtze River, and with the speed of lightning,
headed straight for Hupei, Hunan, Kwangtung and Kwangsi; it
captured Wuhan, fought in Canton, and captured Kweilin and
Nanning. In April 1950 the heroic Fourth Field Army under
the command of Comrade Lin Piao defeated warships with

wooden junks, crossed the stormy Hainan Strait, and hoisted
the Five-Star Flag over the Five-Finger Mountains, thus liberating Hainan Island and performing a feat unprecedented in the
military history of China and other countries as well.

Our respected and beloved Vice Chairman Lin closely followed the great supreme commander Chairman Mao to fight in
the north and in the south. From the Ch'ang-pai Mountains in
the northeast, he fought all the way to the Five-Fingers Mountains on Hainan Island, carrying all before him. He thus performed great, immortal feats of arms for the cause of the liberation of the Chinese people.

Only Heroes Can Expel Tigers and Leopards, No Brave Men Are Afraid of Wild Bears

"Now the cock has crowed and all under heaven is bright."
On October 1, 1949, the People's Republic of China was established. Since the founding of the People's Republic the violent
struggle between the proletarian headquarters headed by Chairman Mao and the bourgeois headquarters headed by Liu Shao-
ch'i had been constantly revolving around the basic question of
whether or not the proletarian dictatorship should be consolidated and whether or not the proletarian revolution should be
carried through to the end. In this struggle, Comrade Lin Piao
at all times stood firmly beside Chairman Mao to wage struggle
most resolutely against Liu Shao-ch'i. Teng Hsiao-p'ing, and
a handful of capitalists within the Party.

At the Second Plenum of the Seventh Central Committee,
Chairman Mao clearly pointed out that after the liberation of
China the contradictions between the working class and the
bourgeoisie were the basic contradictions in China and that
capitalism must be gradually abolished in the cities and the
countryside. But as soon as the session concluded, Liu Shao-
ch'i cried out for "the consolidation of the new democratic
order." He frenziedly undermined agrarian reform in the
countryside, supported the rich peasants, shielded the landlords, and developed capitalism in the countryside. Giving

tit for tat, Comrade Lin Piao advocated that the mopping up of
the bandits and the suppression of the despots in the countryside and the agrarian reform movement must be carried
through to the end. He waged a determined struggle against
Liu Shao-ch'i's conspiracy to undermine agrarian reform and
rural work.

When socialist transformation was gradually gaining depth,
the Kao Kang and Jao Shu-shih anti-Party clique, working in
collusion with P'eng Te-huai, were so daring that they openly
wrote a letter calling on Chairman Mao "to take a rest," so
that they might "take a turn at assuming command," in a vain
attempt to usurp the leadership of the Party Central Committee.
Comrade Lin Piao steadfastly stood beside Chairman Mao and
completely smashed the anti-Party conspiracy of the Kao Kang
and Jao Shu-shih clique, thus performing immortal deeds of
merit in defending Chairman Mao and Chairman Mao's revolutionary line.

During the three years of temporary difficulties in the economy, the Liu-Teng sinister headquarters worked in coordination with Soviet revisionist Khrushchev, imperialism, and the
reactionaries of all countries to create counterrevolutionary
public opinion and promote capitalist restoration activities on
a large scale. They viciously attacked the Three Red Flags
and vociferously advertised the "three freedoms and one guarantee" and the "three harmonies and one reduction." At the
Enlarged Central Committee Work Conference in January 1962,
Liu Shao-ch'i came forward in person to make a vicious attack
against Chairman Mao. He said that the three difficult years
were "30 percent owing to natural calamities and 70 percent
owing to man-made evils." He also openly tried to reverse
the verdict on P'eng Te-huai.

Precisely at the crucial moment Liu Shao-ch'i was attempting to change the course of the revolution, Comrade Lin Piao
held high the great red banner of Mao Tse-tung thought and
stood forth to defend resolutely the Three Red Flags. He declared: "The Three Red Flags put forward by our Party in
recent years — the General Line, the Great Leap Forward,

and the People's Commune — are correct. They reflect the realities of life and are the product of the development of the Chinese revolution, the creation of the people and the Party." He pointed out: "Work was carried out successfully in the past because Chairman Mao's thought was not interfered with. Whenever Chairman Mao's thought was interfered with or not respected, troubles would emerge. The history of the past few decades is history of this kind. In times of difficulty, therefore, it is all the more necessary for the Party to unite and follow Chairman Mao closely. Only in this way can the Party proceed from victory to victory, and can the country make a turn for the better." Comrade Lin Piao's heroic struggle effectively hit back at the frenzied attack of Liu Shao-ch'i's capitalist restoration and made enormous contributions to the steadfast and triumphal advance along the path of Chairman Mao's revolutionary line.

In 1963 Chairman Mao issued the great call for carrying out the socialist education movement in the countryside. At that time Liu Shao-ch'i jumped out again to openly oppose Chairman Mao's revolutionary line. He frenziedly carried out the bourgeois reactionary line which was "Left" in form but Right in essence. He actively peddled Wang Kuang-mei's so-called "T'ao-yüan experience" in a vain attempt to undermine the socialist education movement in the countryside. With specific reference to this situation, Comrade Lin Piao wrote a letter to Chairman Mao declaring that he would firmly implement and carry out Chairman Mao's supreme directive regarding the "four clean-ups" campaign; moreover he decided to broadly propagandize the directive within the Army. Comrade Lin Piao once again heroically defended Chairman Mao's revolutionary line.

During this Great Proletarian Cultural Revolution Comrade Lin Piao stood beside Chairman Mao with unsurpassed steadfastness and made outstanding contributions toward the complete destruction of the Liu-Teng bourgeois sinister headquarters. Under Chairman Mao's intimate solicitude, in February 1966 Comrade Lin Piao entrusted Comrade Chiang Ch'ing with the task of convening a forum on literature and art in the armed forces, and published the "Summary of the Forum." This summary held high the great red banner of Mao Tse-tung thought and gave P'eng Chen's February "Outline Report" tit for tat. Using Mao Tse-tung thought to answer many important questions of the Great Cultural Revolution in the socialist period, it not only was of great current significance but also of far-reaching historical significance. Over the course of the Great Cultural Revolution, Chairman Mao and Comrade Lin Piao jointly received the mighty army of the Great Cultural Revolution — 11 million strong — on eight occasions. On many occasions Comrade Lin Piao made important speeches on holding high the great red banner of Mao Tse-tung thought and made enormous contributions to the triumphant development of the Great Proletarian Cultural Revolution.

The achievements of Comrade Lin Piao's heroic struggle were especially salient in his resolute struggle against the agents of Liu Shao-ch'i and Teng Hsiao-p'ing in the army, such as P'eng Te-huai, Lo Jui-ch'ing, and their like, and in his running our army as a great school thoroughly red with Mao Tse-tung thought.

The struggle between the two lines in the army constantly revolved around some fundamental question — whether or not the great red banner of Mao Tse-tung thought should be held high, whether political affairs or military affairs should come first, whether the Party should command the gun or the gun should command the Party.

Chairman Mao said, "Our principle is that the Party commands the gun, and the gun must never be allowed to command the Party." However, P'eng Te-huai frenziedly opposed Chairman Mao's line of army-building. He vociferously advertised the "theory of the army over the Party," and made every effort to peddle the bourgeois and revisionist contraband of "modernization" and "regularization" in a vain attempt to temper with and change the nature of our army at its roots, thus turning the army into their tool for restoring capitalism.

At the enlarged conference of the Military Affairs Commission held in May and June 1958, with special reference to the complete set of revisionist contraband peddled by P'eng Te-huai, Comrade Lin Piao sternly pointed out: "Ours is an army in the service of politics, and we must use politics to guide military affairs and routine work. Some people say that only foreign things are scientific. This is wrong.... Don't just relish things of foreign origin and regard things of Chinese origin as 'country bumpkins.' We have things of Chairman Mao's; we don't have to learn theirs!"

At the Lushan Conference in 1959 Chairman Mao and the Party Central Committee dismissed P'eng Te-huai from office and decided to put Comrade Lin Piao, Chairman Mao's close comrade-in-arms, in charge of work at the Military Affairs Commission. This wise decision smashed P'eng Te-huai's plot to usurp power in the army. In September 1959 Comrade Lin Piao personally convened an enlarged meeting of the Military Affairs Commission in which he angrily exposed, criticized, and repudiated P'eng Te-huai's sinister crimes. In October of the same year he wrote an article entitled "Hold High the Red Banner of the General Line and Mao Tse-tung's Military Thought and March Forward in Big Strides," which further criticized and repudiated P'eng Te-huai's bourgeois military line comprehensively and in-depth and defended Chairman Mao's military line.

"A thunderstorm burst over the earth, and the demon rose from a heap of white bones." Precisely at the time Comrade Lin Piao held high the great red banner of Mao Tse-tung thought and ran the People's Liberation Army as a great school thoroughly red with Mao Tse-tung thought, Lo Jui-ch'ing, another agent of the Liu-Teng sinister headquarters in the army, also jumped out. He inherited the mantle of P'eng Te-huai, frenziedly opposed Chairman Mao's proletarian line of army-building and the living study and application of Chairman Mao's writings, and wantonly peddled a set of revisionist contraband: "military affairs are politics," and "equal attention should be paid to military affairs and politics." Lo Jui-ch'ing was so daring that he arbitrarily decided in January 1964 to hold a big all-PLA contest of military skills behind the back of Chairman Mao and Comrade Lin Piao. He attempted to make the contest of military skills prevail over everything else and hence to abolish proletarian politics and usurp power at its roots in the army.

In the nick of time Comrade Lin Piao exposed Lo Jui-ch'ing's big conspiracy in holding the "big contest of military skills." He sternly pointed out that this was aimed at "battering politics" and that "if it were allowed to follow its own course without being rectified, the consequences would be unmanageable." He categorically pointed out that "this evil wind must be checked." At the end of 1964 Comrade Lin Piao gave an instruction on bringing politics to the fore. He called on the whole army to bring politics to the fore and put political work above all other kinds of work in our army. However, Lo Jui-ch'ing feigned compliance. He even doubled his efforts in demanding that Comrade Lin Piao "make way for the talent" and "hand over power" and continually and obstinately carried out his bourgeois line of army-building. Seeing that Chairman Mao had directly expressed his concern, Comrade Lin Piao decisively exposed Lo Jui-ch'ing's plot to oppose the Party and usurp power in the army at the Shanghai Conference held in December 1965. Afterward, at the meeting of the Central Committee Work Group in March 1966, Comrade Lin Piao again smashed the big conspiracy of Liu Shao-ch'i, Teng Hsiao-p'ing and P'eng Chen, who attempted to shield Lo Jui-ch'ing. He sternly pointed out: "The principle and sternness of the Party must be upheld." "We certainly must give a factual account of Lo Jui-ch'ing's crimes and express the indignation of those comrades present." In this way the "time bomb" which Liu and Teng had buried in our army was finally unearthed and removed.

Since Comrade Lin Piao took charge of the work of the Military Affairs Commission of the Central Committee, he held high the great red banner of Mao Tse-tung thought and creatively put forward a series of policies, principles, and important measures for strengthening the ideological revolutionization of our army, such as "making living study and application of Chairman Mao's works," "giving prominence to proletarian politics," "implementing the four firsts," "energetically promoting the three-eight work style," "launching the four-good company movement," and so on. In May 1965 military ranks were abolished in the Chinese People's Liberation Army directly commanded by Comrade Lin Piao. This great and wise measure further strengthened the proletarianization and militancy of our army.

Our Japanese friends praised Comrade Lin Piao as "the first marshal in the world who removed his own epaulet himself." They praised the troops under the command of Chairman Mao and Comrade Lin Piao as "the most revolutionary troops in the world." In September of the same year, Comrade Lin Piao published an article entitled "Long Live the Victory of People's War." This article most systematically and incisively expounded Chairman Mao's brilliant thought concerning people's war and made the most essential and most fundamental war preparation for the revolutionary people all over the world to smash the imperialist war blackmail.

During the historically unprecedented Great Proletarian Cultural Revolution Comrade Lin Piao also called on the People's Liberation army to "hold high the great red banner of Mao Tse-tung thought and render new meritorious service in the Great Cultural Revolution Movement." In the course of carrying out the glorious task of "three supports and two military" [supporting industry, agriculture, and the Left; exercising military control and military training], there emerged numerous heroic fighters such as Ts'ai Yung-hsiang and Li Wen-chung and model collectives such as the "Heroic Fourth Platoon." The Liberation Army is worthy to be called the strong pillar of proletarian dictatorship in China and the indestructible Great Wall of iron and steel.

Chairman Mao highly praised Comrade Lin Piao for his great contributions to army-building. The great leader Chairman Mao pointed out: "The four firsts are good because they are original. After Comrade Lin Piao put forward the four firsts and the three-eight work style, the ideological-political

work and the military work of the Liberation Army has made
greater development and become more concrete and theorized
than in the past. Chairman Mao also called on "the whole
country to learn from the People's Liberation Army."

Sailing the Seas Depends on the Helmsman, Making Revolution Depends on Mao Tse-tung Thought

Comrade Lin Piao is Chairman Mao's close comrade-in-
arms and best pupil. He boundlessly cherishes and adores,
and is boundlessly faithful and loyal to Chairman Mao and Mao
Tse-tung thought.

Back in the days of the Ching-kang Mountains, Comrade Lin
Piao had thirstily and hungrily studied Chairman Mao's writings. Sometimes he studied even on horseback. During the
Second Revolutionary Civil War, Comrade Lin Piao declared:
"Mao Tse-tung thought must be taken as the yardstick for
everything. No matter when, no matter what the problem, we
must have strong and undoubting faith in Chairman Mao's
thought and instructions."

Over the past several decades Comrade Lin Piao has always
struck back at those who attacked Chairman Mao, Mao Tse-
tung thought and Chairman Mao's revolutionary line, no matter
what quarter they came from. He pointed out: Chairman Mao
is the most outstanding leader of the proletariat of the contemporary era and the greatest genius of the contemporary era.
It took China several thousand years and the world several
hundred years to bring forth a genius such as Chairman Mao.
Chairman Mao is the Lenin of the contemporary era, the representative of our era. He also pointed out: Mao Tse-tung thought
is the highest and most lively form of Marxism-Leninism of
the contemporary era, the strongest ideological weapon against
revisionism and dogmatism. Mao Tse-tung thought is the
guiding principle of the whole Party, the whole army, and the
whole country. Anyone who opposes Chairman Mao and Mao
Tse-tung thought will be punished by the whole Party and denounced by the whole country!

Comrade Lin Piao has most wisely, most vigorously, and most conscientiously led and organized the movement for the broad popularization of Mao Tse-tung thought, and he has made the greatest and most outstanding contributions to the direct mastery of Marxism-Leninism-Mao Tse-tung Thought by the workers, peasants, and soldiers.

Long before the nationwide victory was won, Comrade Lin Piao had told us: "What is of great significance to us is that we must make efforts to study and arm our own heads with Marxism-Leninism-Mao Tse-tung Thought." After the liberation of the whole country, especially after Comrade Lin Piao took charge of the work of the Military Affairs Commission, he held even higher the great red banner of Mao Tse-tung thought, launched energetic mass movements for the living study and application of Chairman Mao's writings, and expanded them all over the country and the world.

In 1960 Comrade Lin Piao himself presided over the enlarged conference of the Military Affairs Commission and formulated the "Decision on Strengthening Political-Ideological Work in the Armed Forces." To the whole Party, the whole army and the people of the whole country he issued the great call: "Study Chairman Mao's writings, follow his teachings, and act according to his instructions."

In January 1961, in his "Instruction on Strengthening Political and Ideological Work in the Armed Forces," Comrade Lin Piao again put forward the most advanced and effective method for the study of Chairman Mao's writings: "It is necessary to study with problems in mind, conduct living study and application, integrate study with application, study first what is urgent to yield prompt results and exert oneself in 'application.'"

During the stormy Great Proletarian Cultural Revolution, Comrade Lin Piao went a step further and called on the whole Party, the whole army, and the people of the whole country to push the mass movement for the living study and application of Chairman Mao's works to a new stage. On December 16, 1966, he wrote the Foreword to the second edition of Quotations from Chairman Mao. He also instructed the people of the whole country "to study the 'three constantly-read articles' as mottos." In recent years our respected and beloved Vice Chairman Lin also issued to us the great call, "Sailing the seas depends on the helmsman, making revolution depends on Mao Tse-tung thought." He instructed that we should organize study courses in Mao Tse-tung thought with Chairman Mao's teaching "combat self, criticize revisionism," as the key link.

Our respected and beloved deputy supreme commander Lin has encouraged the broad and powerful mass movement for the living study and application of Chairman Mao's writings throughout the country. This movement is now being pushed further, from China out to the whole world, and an unprecedented favorable situation has emerged in the international Communist movement. This is Deputy Supreme Commander Lin's most outstanding and greatest contribution to revolution in China and the world. This immortal achievement of his will be entered on the glorious historical records of the International Communist movement as an epochal great event.

From the rather incomplete account presented here, it can be seen that our respected and beloved Deputy Supreme Commander Lin, in the past few decades as though in a single day, has been boundlessly loyal to Chairman Mao, Mao Tse-tung thought, and Chairman Mao's revolutionary line. He has followed most closely the great leader Chairman Mao and has held highest the great red banner of Mao Tse-tung thought. We must follow the radiant example of Deputy Supreme Commander Lin and forever be loyal to the great leader Chairman Mao, the splendidly brilliant Mao Tse-tung thought, and Chairman Mao's proletarian revolutionary line.

2

A GLORIOUS PRODUCT, A GREAT DEVELOPMENT
(Excerpts)*

The new draft Constitution of the Party was drawn up under
the leadership of the great leader Chairman Mao after four
rounds of earnest discussion and revision — both from the upper levels down and from the lower levels up — and with the
views and suggestions of the vast revolutionary masses assembled and incorporated.... What are the outstanding features
of the new Party Constitution? [Among other features] the new
Party Constitution expressly designates Comrade Lin Piao as
Chairman Mao's successor.

The new Constitution specifically provides: "Comrade Lin
Piao has consistently held high the great red banner of Mao
Tse-tung thought and has most loyally and resolutely carried
out and defended Comrade Mao Tse-tung's proletarian revolutionary line. Comrade Lin Piao is Comrade Mao Tse-tung's
close comrade-in-arms and successor." This is the most in-
disputable conclusion, one naturally drawn from Comrade Lin
Piao's experience in waging revolutionary struggles for more
than forty years, and it is completely supported by facts.

---

*"Kuang-hui ti chieh-ching wei-ta ti fa-chan (chieh-lu)."
Excerpts of Hsüeh-hsi Chung-kuo kung-ch'an-tang chang-ch'eng
chiang-hua ts'ai-liao [Discussion Materials for the Study of
the Constitution of the Chinese Communist Party] (n. p., 1969);
reprinted in Yüan Jui, comp., Lin Piao shih-chien yüan-shih
wen-chien hui-pien [A Compilation of Original Documents on
the Lin Piao Affair] (Taipei: Chung-kuo ta-lu yen-chiu-so,
1973), pp. 1-5.

This provision has gained the enthusiastic support of the whole
Party, army, and people. It also has won the support of the
revolutionary peoples around the world. Not only is it a boundless blessing to us to have our great leader Chairman Mao, the
greatest Marxist-Leninist in the contemporary era, but we also
feel extremely blessed to have Vice Chairman Lin, the univer-
sally recognized successor to Chairman Mao.

Comrade Lin Piao has consistently held high the great red
banner of Mao Tse-tung thought and has most loyally and
courageously carried out and defended Chairman Mao's proletarian revolutionary line. Comrade Lin Piao has studied Mao
Tse-tung thought most thoroughly, applied it most ably, and
carried it out most resolutely. As early as forty years ago
Comrade Lin Piao was already the close comrade-in-arms of
the great leader Chairman Mao. Comrade Lin Piao was a model
example of those who, after the failure of the Nanchang Uprising,
took their units to the Chingkang Mountains and accepted
Chairman Mao's leadership. Since then, Comrade Lin Piao
has always followed Chairman Mao closely, defended Chairman
Mao's proletarian revolutionary line, and made outstanding
contributions to the Chinese people's revolutionary war and
revolutionary enterprises. In the three struggles against "Left"
opportunism during the period of the Third Revolutionary Civil
War, in the struggle against the Right opportunist line represented by Wang Ming during the War of Resistance against
Japan, in the struggle against the Right opportunist line of
Liu Shao-ch'i and P'eng Chen during the War of Liberation
period, and in the struggle against the anti-Party alliance of
P'eng Te-huai, Kao Kang and Jao Shu-shih after the liberation
of the whole nation, Comrade Lin Piao has always stood steadfastly in the forefront of struggle under the immediate leadership of Chairman Mao.

After taking charge of the Military Affairs Commission,
Comrade Lin Piao propagated Chairman Mao's thought on army-
building as developed at the Ku-t'ien Conference by introducing
the "four-firsts," the "three-eight work style," the "four-good
company," and the "five-good fighter," as well as by reempha-

sizing the Three Main Rules of Discipline and the Eight Points
for Attention, thus promoting our army to become a big,
thoroughly red school of Mao Tse-tung thought. Comrade Lin
Piao effectively propagated Mao Tse-tung thought by declaring:
"Always keep in mind the class struggle; always keep in mind
the proletarian dictatorship; always remember to give prominence to politics; and always remember to hold high the great
red banner of Mao Tse-tung thought." As a result of his suggestion, Quotations from Chairman Mao was first published in
the army in 1961, and was quickly circulated to the entire nation and even the entire world. That was one of the most important measures taken during the preparatory stage of the
Great Proletarian Cultural Revolution. This red book of wisdom has popularized the Marxism-Leninism developed by
Chairman Mao and spread Mao Tse-tung thought to an unprecedented extent among the whole Chinese people and even
among the revolutionary peoples of the whole world. It has
armed ideologically millions upon millions of revolutionary
masses. It is the most powerful mobilization of public opinion
in support of the Great Proletarian Cultural Revolution and
has exerted far-reaching influence.

Toward the end of 1965, after Chairman Mao had launched
the criticism of the play Hai Jui Leaves Office, Comrade Lin
Piao uncovered the counterrevolutionary conspiracy of Lo Jui-
ch'ing to oppose the Party and the army. By his suggestion,
Comrade Chiang Ch'ing was entrusted to preside over the
Forum on Literature and Art in the Armed Forces to provide
a sharp contrast to P'eng Chen's "February Outline"; the summary of the Forum was also publicized. All this has powerfully
propelled the Great Cultural Revolution forward. On May 18,
1966, Comrade Lin Piao made an important speech at the enlarged meeting of the Politburo and expounded the "Circular"
of May 16, 1966, drawn up personally by the Chairman, and announced: "At any time and under any circumstances, whoever
opposes Chairman Mao and Mao Tse-tung thought should be denounced by the whole Party and punished by the whole nation."
This important statement of Comrade Lin Piao has held high

the great red banner of Mao Tse-tung thought and thereby become the rallying cry of the Great Proletarian Cultural Revolution.

During the past three years of the Great Proletarian Cultural
Revolution, Comrade Lin Piao has made important talks at
many crucial junctures, for example, in August 1966 at the
Work Conference of the Central Committee after the conclusion
of the Eleventh Plenum of the Eighth Central Committee, in
October 1966 at the Work Conference of the Central Committee,
in December 1966 at the Industrial Conference, in March 1967
at the Cadres Conference of the Army Level and Above, on
March 24, 1968, at the Meeting for Exposing the Problem Concerning [Yang Ch'eng-wu], and in October 1968 at the Enlarged
Twelfth Plenum of the Central Committee. In accordance with
the series of most recent instructions of Chairman Mao, Lin
Piao thoroughly exposed the counterrevolutionary revisionist
line represented by Liu Shao-ch'i, severely criticized the adverse currents and evil winds from both the Right and the
extreme "Left" aimed at reversing verdicts already pronounced,
and kept firmly on course the direction of the Great Proletarian
Cultural Revolution set forth by Chairman Mao. All these
speeches made by Comrade Lin Piao have won the support and
praise of our great leader Chairman Mao and have become the
combat orders of the proletarian headquarters, which is headed
by Chairman Mao with Vice Chairman Lin as the deputy head,
for millions upon millions of the revolutionary people across
the country and particularly for the People's Liberation Army,
which is personally created and led by Chairman Mao and immediately commanded by Vice Chairman Lin in performing its
"three-support" and "two-military" tasks.

Comrade Lin Piao is the closest comrade-in-arms, the best
student, and the most ideal successor of Chairman Mao. The
new Party Constitution's specific provision that Comrade Lin
Piao is Chairman Mao's successor is a great event that will
affect the future and the destiny of our Party and state. It is
also a great event that will affect the future and the destiny of
world revolution. It provides the fundamental guarantee that

our Party and state will never change their color, that Mao Tse-tung thought will be faithfully adhered to in the process of pursuing socialist revolution and socialist construction, and that the revolutionary direction pointed out by Chairman Mao will always be followed in the victorious march forward.

II Power Struggle and Military Coup: ''Top-Secret'' Documents

3

SUMMARY OF CHAIRMAN MAO'S TALKS
TO RESPONSIBLE LOCAL COMRADES
DURING HIS TOUR OF INSPECTION*
(Mid-August to September 12, 1971)

Top-Secret Document

Document of the Central Committee of the
Chinese Communist Party, Chung-fa, 1972, No. 12.

Chairman Mao's Instruction: Approved.

I. Notice of the Central Committee of the Chinese Communist Party

To the Party committees of each province, municipality [directly under the Central Government], autonomous region; Party committees of each military region, provincial military district, and field army; Party committees of each general department of the Military Affairs Commission and each service branch; leading groups of each department and ministry under the Central Committee and the State Council; and core groups of the Party:

---

*"Mao chu-hsi tsai wai-ti hsün-shih ch'i-chien t'ung yen-t'u ko-ti fu-tse t'ung-chih ti t'an-hua chi-yao." Commonly known as Document No. 12 (1972) of the Central Committee of the Chinese Communist Party.

This translation is based on the Chinese text released by Chung-yang jih-pao [Central Daily, Taipei], August 10, 1972.

In 1971, from the middle of August until September 12, our
great leader Chairman Mao undertook a tour of inspection and
engaged in many important talks en route to responsible comrades. Many units have asked that these talks of Chairman Mao
be edited and published. On the basis of notes taken from Chairman Mao's talks in various places, the Central Committee has
compiled a comprehensive summary. It is now printed and distributed to you. Please transmit its contents to the whole Party,
the whole army, and the people of the nation, in accordance with
the scope stipulated by the Document Chung-fa, 1972, No. 3.

The chief concerns of Chairman Mao's talks are the struggles between lines; in his talks he summarized the ten struggles
between lines during the fifty years of our Party. He also set
forth the three fundamental principles, "We must practice Marxism and not revisionism; unite, don't split; be open and aboveboard, don't intrigue and conspire." He clearly pointed out that
the struggle at the 1970 Lushan Conference was a struggle between two roads, between two headquarters; and he repeatedly
emphasized that we must adopt toward cadres who have made
mistakes the policy of "learning from past mistakes to avoid
future ones, and curing the sickness to save the patient."

Chairman Mao's talks constitute a programmatic document
for conducting education in ideology and political line and for
strengthening Party- and army-building, and they are a powerful weapon for smashing the anti-Party Lin-Ch'en clique. The
whole Party, the whole army, and the people of the whole nation
must conscientiously study Chairman Mao's talks in order to
promote further the great revolutionary criticism of the Lin-
Ch'en anti-Party clique, and in order to carry through to the
end the struggle to smash the Lin-Ch'en anti-Party clique.

Central Committee of the
Chinese Communist Party
March 17, 1972

II. Summary of Chairman Mao's Talks to
Responsible Local Comrades
During His Tour of Inspection
(Mid-August to September 12, 1971)

(Chairman Mao said): I hope you will practice Marxism and
not revisionism; unite, and don't split; be open and aboveboard,
and don't intrigue and conspire.

Whether or not a line is ideologically and politically correct
decides everything. If the Party's line is correct, then we will
get everything: if there are no men, we will get men; if there
are no guns, we will get guns; if we do not hold power, we will
get power. If our line is incorrect, even if we have [these
things], we can lose them. The line is the key link; once it is
grasped, everything falls into place.

Our Party has a history of fifty years, and we have had ten
big struggles over line. During these ten struggles over line,
there have been those who wanted to split our Party, but none
of them were successful. This problem is worth scrutiny. The
only way to explain why this big a country with this many people does not split is to say that the hearts of the people, the
hearts of those in the Party, would not approve of it. Historically
speaking, there is hope for this Party of ours.

It began with Ch'en Tu-hsiu's right opportunism. After the
"August 7" Conference in 1927, he and people like Liu Jen-ching
and P'eng Shu-chih organized a "Leninist left-wing opposition
clique." Eighty-one people published a statement in order to
split our Party, but they did not succeed, and they fled to the
Trotskyites.

Subsequently it was Ch'ü Ch'iu-pai who made a mistake in
line. In Hunan they seized a small pamphlet which had in it
statements of mine like "political power grows out of the barrel
of a gun." They got very excited and asked how political power
could grow out of the barrel of a gun. Then they fired me as
alternate member of the Politburo. Afterward Ch'ü Ch'iu-
pai was arrested by the KMT; he wrote "Unnecessary Words"
and voluntarily turned traitor.

After the Sixth National Party Congress in 1928, Li Li-san's
star rose with arrogance. From June to September 1930 he
promoted the Li-san line for over three months. He advocated
attacking the big cities and achieving victory first in one or
several provinces. I didn't approve of his method. At the Third
Plenum of the Sixth Central Committee, Li Li-san was deposed.

From 1930 to 1931 the Lo Chang-lung Rightist clique established a separate Central Committee in an attempt to split the
Party, but they also failed.

Wang Ming's line lasted the longest. He began his sectarianism in Moscow, where he organized the "twenty-eight Bolshe-
viks." Relying on the strength of the Third International, they
seized power in the Party for four years. At the Fourth Plenum
of the Sixth Central Committee, which he convened in Shanghai,
Wang Ming published a small pamphlet entitled "Struggle to Increasingly Bolshevize the Chinese Communist Party," in which
he criticized Li Li-san for not being "Left" enough. He couldn't
be comfortable until the base areas were done away with, and
essentially that's just what he did. During the four years from
1931 to 1934 I had no right to speak in the Central Committee.
The Tsunyi Conference of January 1935 rectified Wang Ming's
erroneous line, and he was ousted.

In the course of the Long March, after the First and Fourth
Armies had joined up, Chang Kuo-t'ao tried to split the Party
by establishing another separate Central Committee, but he
failed. When the Red Army, which had numbered 300,000 before
the Long March, reached northern Shensi, there were only
25,000 left. Of the 80,000 from the Central Soviet Area, only
8,000 managed to get to northern Shensi. Chang Kuo-t'ao's
split line was that he didn't want to go to northern Shensi. If
we hadn't gone to northern Shensi then, there simply would
have been no way out. This was a question of political line. At
that time our line was the correct one. If we hadn't gone to
northern Shensi, how could we have got to the Northern China
Area, the Eastern China Area, the Central China Area, and the
Manchurian Area? How could we have established so many
base areas during the War of Resistance Against Japan? When

we arrived in northern Shensi, Chang Kuo-t'ao fled.

After we achieved a nationwide victory, Kao Kang and Jao Shu-shih formed an anti-Party alliance in order to seize power, but they failed.

At the Lushan Conference of 1959, P'eng Te-huai maintained contacts with foreign countries and tried to seize power. Huang K'o-ch'eng, Chang Wen-t'ien, and Chou Hsiao-chou also popped up in opposition to the Party. They set up a military club, but never talked about military affairs; rather, they said things like "the communes were set up too early," "the gain didn't make up for the loss," etc. P'eng Te-huai even wrote a letter, which amounted to an open challenge to seize power, but he did not succeed.

Liu Shao-ch'i and his company also tried to split the Party, but they didn't make it either.

That was followed by the struggle at the 1970 Lushan Conference. At that conference they engaged in surprise attacks and underground activities. Why weren't they brave enough to come out in the open? It was obvious they were up to no good. First they concealed things, then they launched a surprise attack. They deceived three of the five standing members* and the majority of comrades in the Politburo, except for the big generals. The big generals, including Huang Yung-sheng, Wu Fa-hsien, Yeh Ch'ün, Li Tso-p'eng, Ch'iu Hui-tso, and also Li Hsüeh-feng and Cheng Wei-shan, maintained airtight secrecy and suddenly launched a surprise attack. Their coup didn't just last a day-and-a-half, but went on for two-and-a-half days, from August 23 and 24 to noon on the twenty-fifth. They certainly had a purpose in doing all that! P'eng Te-huai set up his military club and issued a challenge, but they didn't even match up to P'eng; so you can see how base their style was.

I thought that their surprise attacks and underground activity were planned, organized, and programed. Their program was to set up a state chairman, advocate "genius," oppose the line set forth by the Ninth Party Congress, and overthrow the three

---

*Mao, Chou En-lai, and K'ang Sheng. — Editor.

items on the agenda of the Second Plenum of the Ninth Central
Committee. A certain person was very anxious to become state
chairman, to split the Party, and to seize power. The question
of genius was a theoretical one; they advocated idealist empiricism, saying that opposition to genius was opposition to me. I
am not a genius. I read Confucian books for six years and cap-
italistic books for seven years, and only began reading Marxism-Leninism in 1918 — how can I be a genius? How could I
have circled [for emphasis] those adverbs [ingeniously,
comprehensively, creatively] several times? The Party
Constitution of the Ninth Congress had already been decided on — why didn't they take a look at it? "Some Opinions
of Mine" was written after I had talked with some people and
done some investigation and research. It was meant to criticize
specifically the theory of genius. I certainly don't want to talk
about genius. Genius just means someone who is a little more
intelligent. Genius does not depend on one person or a few people; it depends on a party. Our Party is the vanguard of the proletariat. Genius depends on the mass line and on collective wisdom.

Comrade Lin Piao did not consult with me about or show me
that talk of his.* The reason that they didn't air their views
prior [to the meeting] was probably because they were so sure
of them, and it seemed they would succeed. But as soon as they
were told that it wouldn't be approved, they panicked. At first
their courage was enough to level Lushan [Lu Mountain] or stop
the earth's turning. But after a few days, they hastily recalled
the minutes.** If she was right, why did she recall them? This
is an indication of their lack of confidence and their fear.

The struggle at the 1959 Lushan Conference with P'eng
Te-huai was a struggle between two headquarters. The strug-

---

*This refers to Lin Piao's talk on August 23, 1970, during the
Second Plenum of the Ninth Central Committee. — Editor.
**This refers to the fact that Yeh Ch'ün personally recalled the
minutes of her speech before the Central-South Group during the
Second Plenum of the Ninth Central Committee. — Editor.

gle with Liu Shao-ch'i was also a struggle between two headquarters. The struggle at this Lushan Conference was again a struggle between two headquarters.

The struggle at Lushan this time, however, was different from the past nine times. In the previous nine times, conclusions were drawn. This time, to protect Vice Chairman Lin, no conclusions concerning individuals were reached. But, of course, he must take some of the responsibility. What should we do with these people?

We must still adopt the policy of education, that is, "learn from past mistakes to avoid future ones," and "cure the sickness to save the patient." We still want to protect Lin. No matter who one is, if one makes mistakes and ignores unity and line, it is never a good thing. When I return to Peking, I will again seek them out to talk things over. If they won't come to me, I'll go to them. Some can probably be saved; some not — we must observe their actions. There are two future possibilities: one is to reform; one is not to reform. Those who have made serious mistakes of principle, of line, and of direction, and who have been the leaders in this, will find it difficult to reform. Historically, did Ch'en Tu-hsiu reform? Did Ch'ü Ch'iu-pai, Li Li-san, Lo Chang-lung, Wang Ming, Chang Kuo-t'ao, Kao Kang, Jao Shu-shih, P'eng Te-huai, and Liu Shao-ch'i reform? They did not.

I have told Comrade Lin Piao that some things he said aren't particularly proper. For example, he said that the whole world only produces one genius every few hundred years, and China every few thousand years. That just doesn't square with the facts! Marx and Engels lived in the same era, and it wasn't even a hundred years until Lenin and Stalin; so how can you say it takes a few hundred years to produce one? China has had Ch'en Sheng, Wu Kuang, Hung Hsiu-ch'üan, Sun Chung-shan [Yat-sen]. How can you say it takes a few thousand years to produce one? As for such things as "apex" and "one sentence worth ten thousand sentences," don't you think that is a little too much? One sentence is one sentence — how can it be worth ten thousand? Do not establish a state chairman and I will not be state chairman — I said this six times — and each time was just one sentence, wasn't it? Even if there had been sixty thou-

sand sentences, they wouldn't listen. My words aren't even
worth half a sentence; they aren't worth anything. Only when
Ch'en Po-ta spoke to them was one sentence worth ten thousand.
In such talks about "going all out to build," he said he wanted
to build me up, but in fact I don't know who he had in mind —
the truth is that he built up himself. He also said that the People's Liberation Army was founded and led by me, but personally commanded by Lin — why can't the founder also command?
As to the founding, it wasn't by me alone.

On questions of line and principle, I always stand firmly. I
will not compromise on important questions of principle. After
the Lushan Conference, I adopted three methods. One was to
throw stones, one was to mix in sand, and the third was to dig
up the cornerstone. I criticized the material Ch'en Po-ta had
used to deceive many people, and I commented on reports of
the Thirty-Eighth Army and of the Tsinan Military District on
opposing arrogance and complacency. I also made critical comments on a document of the long forum of the Military Affairs
Commission, which didn't criticize Ch'en at all. My method was
to get hold of these stones and make critical comments, and
then let everyone discuss them — this was throwing stones.
When dirt is too tightly packed, no air can get through; but if a
little sand is mixed in, air can circulate. When work groups of
the Military Affairs Commission did not have enough people mixed
in, more were added — this is called mixing in sand. Reorganizing
the Peking Military Region is called digging up the cornerstone.

What do you think of the Lushan Conference? For instance,
what after all was the No. 6 Brief Bulletin of the North China
Group — revolutionary, semirevolutionary, or counterrevolutionary? I personally feel that it was a counterrevolutionary
bulletin. You all attended the ninety-nine-man conference* In

_____

*A conference called by the Chinese Communist Party in April
of 1971 to exchange results of the Criticize Ch'en Po-ta Rectification Campaign. Attending the conference were ninety-nine
responsible cadres from the central government, local government, and the armed forces. — Editor.

his summation, the premier gave the confessions of five big generals [Huang Yung-sheng, Wu Fa-hsien, Yeh Ch'ün, Li Tso-p'eng, Ch'iu Hui-tso]. He also made public the confessions of the two big generals Li Hsüeh-feng and Cheng Wei-shan, and everyone felt that the problem was solved. In fact, however, this Lushan affair was not over; the problem has not been solved. They wanted to cover it up and not even let cadres on the level of the directors of the general political departments of the General Staff Department know about it. How can that be permitted?

All of what I've said is just my own personal opinion — I'm just shooting the breeze with you. Do not draw any conclusions now; that's for the Central Committee to do.

(Chairman Mao said): We must be careful. First, the army must be careful; second, the various localities must also be careful. We should not be arrogant; as soon as that happens, mistakes are made. The army must be unified, must be put in order. I just don't believe that our army would rebel. I just don't believe that you, Huang Yung-sheng, could lead the Liberation Army to rebel. Each army includes divisions and regiments, and also command and political and logistics departments — if you order troops to do evil things, will they listen to you?

You must be concerned with military affairs: you can't just be a civilian official, but must also be a military official. Grasping military affairs means studying the line, rectifying incorrect styles, avoiding mountaintopism and sectarianism, and emphasizing unity. The army has always stressed strict discipline, and I agree. But in solving questions of ideology one can't use strict discipline; rather, fact and reasoning must be relied on.

I approved the document of the Canton Military Region on the "three supports and two militaries.* Above the endorse-

_____

*A report endorsed for distribution by the Central Committee of the Chinese Communist Party on August 20, 1971, entitled "A Summary of the Canton Military Region's Forum on the Political and Ideological Work of the Three Supports and Two Militaries." — Editor.

ment by the Central Committee, I wrote four characters, "study
conscientiously" [jen-chen hsüeh-hsi] in order to arouse everyone's attention. Local Party committees had already been established, and they should have exercised unified leadership.
Wasn't it just confusing if matters already decided upon by local
Party committees were still taken to army Party committees
for discussion?

In the past, our army's military training included the curricu-
lum of the basic system and method. The training from the individual to the battalion level took five to six months. Now we
only engage in civil [wen] training, and not military training.
Our army has become a cultural [wen-hua] army.

"One-good leads three goods." That one-good of yours might
lead correctly, and it might not. Also, what has been the effect
of those conferences of representatives of activists? The question is worth studying. Some are run well and some not. The
line is the chief problem. If the line is wrong, then the conference of representatives of activists will go poorly.

In industry, learn from Tach'ing; in agriculture, learn from
Tachai; the whole country should learn from the PLA. This is
not enough — it should be added that the PLA should learn from
the people of the whole nation.

(Chairman Mao said): Study the article by Lenin commemorating the twenty-fifth anniversary of the death of Eugene Pottier
[author of the "Internationale"], learn to sing the "Internationale" and "The Three Main Rules of Discipline and Eight Points
for Attention." Don't just sing them, but explain and understand
them and put them into practice. The words of the "Internationale" and the article by Lenin fully represent the Marxist
stand and viewpoint. What they say is that slaves should rise
up and struggle for truth, for there never has been a savior
and we cannot rely on gods or emperors. Our salvation must
rely entirely on ourselves. Who creates the human world? We,
the laboring masses do. At the time of the Lushan Conference, I wrote a 700-character article ["Some Opinions of
Mine"] which treated the problem of whether heroes create
history or slaves do. The "Internationale" tells us to

unite and march into tomorrow, for communism is bound to be realized. To study Marxism is to emphasize unity, not splittism! We have sung the "Internationale" for fifty years, yet some people in our Party have tried to split the Party ten times. I think this will probably happen ten, twenty, thirty more times — do you believe that? If you don't believe it, I do. When we reach communism there will be no more struggle? I don't believe it. When we reach communism we will still have struggle, only it will be between old and new, correct and incorrect? Ten thousand years from now, the incorrect will still be wrong, still unable to sustain itself.

As to "The Three Main Rules of Discipline and the Eight Points for Attention," "every single one must be kept clearly in mind," and "the people all over the country will support and welcome us." Now, however, it seems that some of them have not been kept clearly in mind, especially the first rule of discipline and the first and fifth points for attention. These articles have not been kept clearly in mind. If they can all be kept clearly in mind and serve as a guide for doing everything, how wonderful it will be! The first rule of discipline is "obey orders in all your actions; march in step to win victory." If we do not march in step, we cannot win victory. Next are the first and fifth points for attention: Be polite, not arrogant, toward the people, toward soldiers, and toward subordinates; resolutely eradicate the warlord's style. These are the key points. Without key points, there can be no policy. I hope "The Three Main Rules of Discipline and the Eight Points for Attention" will be used to educate soliders, cadres, the masses, Party members, and the people.

(Chairman Mao said): At the Lushan Conference I said that we should read books by Marx and Lenin. I hope that in the future you will read more books. High-level cadres did not even understand what materialism and idealism were. How could they? What can be done about the fact that books by Marx and Lenin are hard to understand? You can ask a teacher to help. You are all [Party] secretaries, but you can also be students. Every day, I myself am a student. Every day, I read two issues of Reference Materials so I can know something about international situations.

I have never approved of one's wife heading the Administrative Office of one's own work unit. At Lin Piao's place, Yeh Ch'ün is the director of the Administrative Office. When those four [Huang Yung-sheng, Wu Fa-hsien, Li Tso-p'eng, Ch'iu Hui-tso] asked for instructions from Lin Piao, they all had to go through her. In work one should rely on one's own effort — read reports yourself, endorse reports yourself. You shouldn't rely on secretaries and allow secretaries to get such enormous power. My secretary just handles receiving and dispatching — I sort documents myself, read them myself, and write necessary comments by myself to avoid mistakes.

(Chairman Mao said): The Great Cultural Revolution dragged out Liu Shao-ch'i, P'eng [Chen], Lo [Jui-ch'ing], Lu [Ting-i], and Yang [Shan-k'un]. That was a great accomplishment. There was also some loss. Some good cadres still have not been rehabilitated. The great majority of our cadres are good; only an extremely small minority are bad. Only one percent was liquidated, and even adding those whose status is still in doubt, the figure won't reach three percent. The bad ones should receive appropriate criticism, and the good ones should be commended. But there should be no flattery — what good is there in praising someone in his twenties as a "super genius"? At this Lushan Conference, some comrades were misled and deceived. The problem isn't with you; it's in Peking. And it's not important if there are mistakes, for our Party has a rule that if you make a mistake, you can examine yourself and be permitted to rectify your mistake.

You must grasp line education on ideology and politics. The policy is still to learn from past mistakes to avoid future ones, and to cure the sickness to save the patient. We must unite to win even greater victories.

4

CHAIRMAN MAO'S OPEN LETTER
TO THE WHOLE PARTY [1971]
(Abridged)*

Top-Secret Document

Document of the Central Committee of the
Chinese Communist Party, Chung-fa, 1971, No. 57

Chairman Mao's Instruction: Distribute Accordingly.

I. Notice of the Central Committee of the
Chinese Communist Party

Hereby issued to you is an open letter written by Chairman
Mao to the whole Party. It is hoped that upon receiving it you
will immediately organize reading, discussion, and transmission and report the results back to the central authorities.

Central Committee of the
Chinese Communist Party
September 14, 1971

*"Mao chu-hsi kei ch'üan-tang ti i-feng kung-k'ai hsin
(ta-yao)." Reprinted in Yüan Jui, comp., Lin Piao shih-chien
yüan-shih wen-chien hui-pien [A Compilation of Original
Documents on the Lin Piao Affair] (Taipei: Chung-kuo ta-lu
yen-chiu-so, 1973), pp. 21-22.

II. Chairman Mao's Open Letter
to the Whole Party (Abridged)

Ch'en Po-ta is a sham Marxist-Leninist. For a long time
Ch'en Po-ta has been arguing with me on the question of genius,
holding that a genius is born with natural talents rather than
deriving his talents from practice or from among the masses.
He wants me to recognize him as a genius, and in so doing he
covets nothing less than the chairmanship of the state. In my
opinion, he is a careerist. During the Second Plenum of the
Ninth Party Central Committee held in Lushan, Ch'en Po-ta
delivered a speech on genius and withdrew from the meeting
before it ended. For a long time he did not report to the Party
Central Committee on his work and was engaged in secret
maneuvers behind the scene and in splitting activities in the
Party Central Committee. With regard to his mistakes, the
Party has conducted criticism in good time. May I now propose:
The question of Ch'en Po-ta must be brought up before and
transmitted to the whole Party for criticism. This letter has
been shown to Comrade Lin Piao. Comrade Lin Piao basically
agrees with my suggestion.

Mao Tse-tung

5

COMMUNIQUÉ OF THE CENTRAL COMMITTEE OF THE
CHINESE COMMUNIST PARTY CONCERNING LIN PIAO'S
"SEPTEMBER 12" ANTI-PARTY INCIDENT (Abridged)*

Top-Secret Document

Document of the Central Committee of the
Chinese Communist Party, Chung-fa, 1971, No. 60

On September 12, when Chairman Mao was making an inspection tour in the South, Lin Piao took advantage of the opportunity and attempted to blow up the train in which Chairman Mao was riding near Shanghai in order to accomplish his objective of assassinating Chairman Mao. When the plot failed and was exposed, Lin Piao hurriedly left Peking on the afternoon of September 12 and boarded a British-made Trident jet military transport, with the intention of surrendering to the enemy and betraying his own country. After crossing the national border, his plane crashed near Undur Khan in Mongolia. Lin Piao, Yeh Ch'ün, Lin Li-kuo, and the pilot were all burned to death.

Lin Piao, by his act of surrendering to the enemy and betraying his own country, invited his own destruction. Yet his death could not redeem his crime, and his notoriety will last for ten thousand years to come. What has been most intolerable

---

*"Chung-kung chung-yang kuan-yü 'chiu-i-erh' Lin Piao p'an-tang shih-chien kung-pao (ta-yao)." Reprinted in Yüan Jui, comp., Lin Piao shih-chien yüan-shih wen-chien hui-pien [A Compilation of Original Documents on the Lin Piao Affair] (Taipei: Chung-kuo ta-lu yen-chiu-so, 1973), pp. 23-24.

is that Lin Piao stole a huge quantity of secret documents and foreign currencies and shot and wounded one of his long-time bodyguards. Lin Piao's sworn followers, Yü Hsin-yeh, Chou Yü-ch'ih and Ch'en Li-yün took off separately in two military helicopters in an attempt to escape from the country. They were intercepted by the Air Force units of the Peking Region. Yü Hsin-yeh and Chou Yü-ch'ih shot the pilots to death and then committed suicide. Ch'en Li-yün put up a fight and was seriously wounded. All the documents they had attempted to take with them aboard the two aircraft were recovered.

Lin [Tou-tou], daughter of Lin Piao, placed national interest above filial piety by refusing to escape with Lin Piao, and she reported the situation to the premier in time, which led to the foiling of her father's monstrous conspiracy. Lin [Tou-tou] has thus performed a great service to the Party and the state and helped the Party Central Committee smash a serious counterrevolutionary coup d'etat.

> Central Committee of the
> Chinese Communist Party
> September 18, 1971

6

COMMUNIQUÉ OF THE CENTRAL COMMITTEE OF THE
CHINESE COMMUNIST PARTY CONCERNING THE
LIN-CH'EN ANTI-PARTY CLIQUE (Abridged)*

Top-Secret Document

Document of the Central Committee of the
Chinese Communist Party, Chung-fa, 1971, No. 61

It was not with a sudden change of mind that Lin Piao took
the lead to organize a counterrevolutionary clique to oppose
the Party and Chairman Mao. As early as the land reform
period he already opposed Chairman Mao. During the period
of the War of Resistance Against Japan, he also made many
speeches of complaint against the Party. During the War of
Liberation period, he was engaged in building up an independent
kingdom in the northeastern region behind the back of the central authorities. After liberation and from the time he took
charge of the Military Affairs Commission, he did make certain
worthy contributions to the Party and the state. Therefore the
Party adhered to a policy of long-term assistance, education,
and cultivation toward him.

However, Lin Piao belittled such assistance, education, and
cultivation rendered by the Party. After the Ninth Party Con-

---

*"Chung-kung chung-yang kuan-yü Lin-Ch'en fan-tang chi-
t'uan ti kung-pao (ta-yao)." Reprinted in Yüan Jui, comp., Lin
Piao shih-chien yüan-shih wen-chien hui-pien [A Compilation
of Original Documents on the Lin Piao Affair] (Taipei: Chung-
kuo ta-lu yen-chiu-so, 1973), pp. 25-27.

71

gress, he colluded with Ch'en Po-ta and took the lead in organizing a counterrevolutionary clique in a wild attempt to
oppose the Central Committee, to split the Party, and to establish another mountaintop.

Under the shield of Lin Piao, Ch'en Po-ta at the Second
Plenum of the Ninth Party Central Committee jumped out
openly to oppose the Central Committee and refuted and rejected the resolution of the Central Committee not to establish
a state chairman. With the support of Huang Yung-sheng, Wu
Fa-hsien, Yeh Ch'ün, Li Tso-p'eng, and Ch'iu Hui-tso, the backbone elements of the clique, he wooed other members of the
Central Committee and engaged actively in splitting activities.

The Central Committee has already demanded that the errors
committed by Ch'en Po-ta be brought up within the whole Party
for open criticism. But Lin Piao expressed his opposition,
whereas Huang Yung-sheng, Wu Fa-hsien, Yeh Ch'ün, Li Tso-
p'eng, and Ch'iu Hui-tso all remained silent. As a result, the
Politburo of the Central Committee was unable to make a decision agreeing to criticize Ch'en Po-ta.

On the question of Ch'en Po-ta, Chairman Mao helped Lin
Piao and wanted him to maintain his own standpoint, so as not
to commit another series of mistakes. However, Lin Piao,
under the pretext of poor health, refused to report to work.
Huang Yung-sheng, Wu Fa-hsien, Yeh Ch'ün, Li Tso-p'eng, and
Ch'iu Hui-tso were all of the view that there was no need for
conducting self-examination. For this, the Central Committee
held the North China Conference and, with the exception of Lin
Piao, they finally made a halfhearted self-examination. Only
then was the essense of Ch'en Po-ta's case brought up for
criticism within the whole Party.

Nevertheless, after the North China Conference was concluded, Lin Piao, while not doing his regular work under the
pretext of poor health, held secret mettings with Ch'en Po-ta.
He also summoned Huang, Wu, Li, and Ch'iu many times to
hold black meetings in preparation for a counterrevolutionary
armed coup d'etat, with the intention of usurping the Party,
army and government and restoring capitalism in China.

Lin Piao and Yeh Ch'ün also sent Lin Li-kuo to Shanghai, Nanking, Hangchow, Canton, and other places to engage in counterrevolutionary liaison activities. Moreover, they illegally used foreign currencies of the state to purchase a large quantity of espionage equipment from Hong Kong and overseas and set up three fascist espionage organizations in Canton in a vain attempt to coordinate the armed coup.

The Central Committee considers the series of conspiracies plotted by the Lin-Ch'en anti-Party clique as a serious counter-revolutionary affair. The Central Committee hopes that Party organizations across the country thoroughly recognize this matter and go a step further to understand Chairman Mao's instructions on the nature of continuous contradictions and struggles within the Party and on never forgetting the class struggle, in order to smash any and all activities plotting to split the Party and to unite forever around the Party Central Committee headed by Chairman Mao.

Central Committee of the
Chinese Communist Party
1971

7

DECISION OF THE CENTRAL COMMITTEE OF THE
CHINESE COMMUNIST PARTY CONCERNING THE
LIN-CH'EN ANTI-PARTY CLIQUE (Abridged)*

Top-Secret Document

Document of the Central Committee of the
Chinese Communist Party, Chung-fa, 1971, No. 62

1. Resolved by the Central Committee of the Chinese Communist Party: An Ad Hoc Investigation Committee be formed
in the Central Committee of the Chinese Communist Party and
composed of Comrades Yeh Chien-ying, Chang Ch'un-ch'iao,
Li Te-sheng, Chi Teng-k'uei, Wang Tung-hsing, and Ch'en Hsi-
lien to conduct the investigation into the Lin Piao-Ch'en Po-ta
anti-Party clique.

2. Resolved by the Central Committee of the Chinese Communist Party: Ch'en Po-ta be stripped of all positions both
within and outside the Party and be arrested and brought before
the Ad Hoc Committee of the Central Committee of the Chinese
Communist Party for investigation. Also resolved by the Party
Central Committee: Huang Yung-sheng, Wu Fa-hsien, Li Tso-
p'eng, Ch'iu Hui-tso, etc., be dismissed from all their positions both within and outside the Party, made to repent and

---

*"Chung-kung chung-yang kuan-yü tui Lin-Ch'en fan-tang
chi-t'uan ti ch'u-li (ta-yao)." Reprinted in Yüan Jui, comp.,
Lin Piao shih-chien yüan-shih wen-chien hui-pien [A Compilation of Original Documents on the Lin Piao Affair] (Taipei:
Chung-kuo ta-lu yen-chiu-so, 1973), pp. 29-30.

recount their misconduct, and brought before the Ad Hoc Committee of the Central Committee for investigation. (Lin Piao and Yeh Ch'ün have already died.)

3. Resolved by the Central Committee of the Chinese Communist Party: Comrade Yeh Chien-ying be placed in charge of the daily routine of the Military Affairs Commission of the Central Committee.

4. The Central Committee of the Chinese Communist Party demands that the Party committees and revolutionary committees of various levels submit immediately to the central authorities all important materials or criminal evidence they have uncovered on the Lin Piao-Ch'en Po-ta anti-Party clique. Such materials should be brought by special messengers to Peking for Comrades Li Te-sheng and Chi Teng-k'uei of the Ad Hoc Committee of the Central Committee to handle. They in turn should make reports to the Central Committee.

Central Committee of the
Chinese Communist Party
1971

8

NOTICE OF THE CENTRAL COMMITTEE OF THE
CHINESE COMMUNIST PARTY CONCERNING THE
DISCARDING OF THE "FOUR-GOOD" AND "FIVE-
GOOD" MOVEMENTS AND THE TURNING IN TO
HIGHER AUTHORITIES OF THE EPITAPHS
AND PORTRAITS OF LIN PIAO (Abridged)*

Top-Secret Document

Document of the Central Committee of the
Chinese Communist Party, Chung-fa, 1971, No. 64

1. Resolved by the Central Committee of the Chinese Communist Party: Comparisons and competitions of the "four-
good" and "five-good" movements be discarded from 1972 on,
and the "Congress of Activists for Living Study and Application
of Chairman Mao's Works" as well as the "Meeting for Exchange of Experience on Studying Mao Tse-tung Thought" at
various levels be disbanded.

2. Resolved by the Central Committee of the Chinese Communist Party: Copies of the "Constitution of the Chinese Communist Party," "Documents of the Ninth Party Congress," and
"Long Live the Victory of the People's War" be turned in to the

---

*"Chung-kung chung-yang kuan-yü ch'e-hsiao 'ssu-hao wu-hao
yün-tung' ho shang-chiao Lin Piao t'i-tz'u hua-hsiang ti t'ung-
chih (ta-yao)." Reprinted in Yüan Jui, comp., Lin Piao shih-
chien yüan-shih wen-chien hui pien [A Compilation of Original
Documents on the Lin Piao Affair] (Taipei: Chung-kuo ta-lu
yen-chiu-so, 1973), p. 31.

central authorities for disposal. Other works about Lin Piao, as well as Lin Piao's epitaphs and portraits, be collected by the basic levels and submitted to the hsien [county] authorities for disposal.

Central Committee of the
Chinese Communist Party
November 1971

9

STRUGGLE TO SMASH THE LIN-CH'EN ANTI-PARTY
CLIQUE'S COUNTERREVOLUTIONARY COUP
(Materials, Part II)*

Top-Secret Document

Document of the Central Committee of the
Chinese Communist Party, Chung-fa, 1972, No. 4

Chairman Mao's Instruction: Distribute Accordingly.

I. Notice of the Central Committee of the Chinese Communist Party

To the Party committees of each province, municipality [directly under the Central Government], and autonomous region;
the Party committees of each military region, provincial military district, and field army; the Party Committees of each
general department of the Military Affairs Commission and
each service branch; the leading groups of each department,
ministry, and commission of the Central Committee and the
State Council; and the core groups of the Party:

---

*"Fen-ts'ui Lin-Ch'en fan-tang chi-t'uan fan-ke-ming cheng-
pien ti tou-cheng (ts'ai-liao chih erh)." The translation of this
selection is based on several sources from Taiwan. I. "Chung-
kung chung-yang t'ung-chih" is translated from a Xerox copy
of the original document obtained from Taipei; II. "Fan-ke-
ming cheng-pien kang-ling 'wu-i-ch'i kung-ch'eng chi-yao' ti
shuo-ming,'" Chung-yang jih-pao [Central Daily, Taipei],

We are now distributing to you "Struggle to Smash the Lin-Ch'en Anti-Party Clique's Counterrevolutionary Coup (Materials, Part II)," assembled by the Ad Hoc Group of the Central Committee. Please immediately arrange transmission and discussion in accordance with the spirit of Chung-fa, 1972, No. 3 document. The main emphasis of transmission and discussion is to criticize Lin Piao and company's counterrevolutionary program "Outline of 'Project 571.'" Transmission should be divided into two steps. The first is to transmit it among cadres, and the second, to the masses. Party committees at various levels, especially responsible Party cadres, should conscientiously read the documents and, using Marxism-Leninism-Mao Tsetung thought as weapons, criticize this counterrevolutionary program of Lin Piao line by line and paragraph by paragraph. Only in this way can the organization of transmission and discussion be done well and the broad masses led to develop even further the great struggle against the Lin-Ch'en anti-Party clique.

Central Committee of the
Chinese Communist Party
January 13, 1972

April 13, 1972; III. "Wu-i-ch'i kung-ch'eng chi-yao," Fei-ch'ing chuan-pao [Special Bulletin on Bandit Intelligence, Taipei], No. 5 (June 6, 1972), 1-9; IV. "Li Wei-hsin kung-tz'u," Chung-Hua yüeh-pao [China Monthly, Hong Kong], No. 696 (September 1973), 35 and 60. Excerpts and abridged versions of this document are widely circulated in the press and journals (Issues & Studies, Chung-kung yen-chiu, Fei-ch'ing yüeh-pao, China News Summary, Report on Mainland China, etc.). But as far as we can tell, this selection is the most complete text available to date. This document is often cited as Document No. 4 (1972) of the Central Committee.

II. Explanation of the Counterrevolutionary Program
"Outline of 'Project 571'"

After the Second Plenum of the Party's Ninth Central Committee [August 23-September 6, 1970], a Partywide rectification campaign to criticize Ch'en [Po-ta] was launched. At the
same time, education in ideology and political line was carried
out. Chairman Mao and the Party's Central Committee, following the principle of "learning from past mistakes to avoid future
ones" and "curing the sickness to save the patient," carried out
criticism and education about Lin Piao and Huang [Yung-sheng,
chief of the General Staff], Wu [Fa-hsien, Air Force command-
er-in-chief], Yeh [Ch'ün, Lin's wife and director of the Administrative Office of the Military Affairs Commission], Li
[Tso-p'eng, first political commissar of the Navy], and Ch'iu
[Hui-tso, director general of the Logistics Department]. Following this, a North China Conference was convened in December of 1970, and the Peking Military Region was reorganized
at the end of January 1971. This momentous measure dug out
the cornerstone of the "Lin-Ch'en anti-Party clique" and dealt
a blow to their scheme to launch a "counterrevolutionary coup"
in the capital and North China areas. However, "Lin Piao and
company stubbornly refuse to repent, and they hide in dark corners
plotting a new 'counterrevolutionary' scheme even more strenuously." In the latter half of February 1971, Lin Piao and Yeh
Ch'ün sent Lin Li-kuo [Lin Piao's son and deputy director of
the Air Force Operations Department] from Soochow to Shanghai to Hangchow in order to study and draw up plans for a coup
d'etat with others of the group. On March 18, Li-kuo brought
Yü Hsin-yeh [deputy director of the Air Force Political Depart-
ment] back to Shanghai from Hangchow. That evening, Li-kuo
told Yü and Li Wei-hsin [deputy director of the Secretariat of
the Fourth Group Political Department of the Air Force], who
was already in Shanghai, that a coup plan should be drafted under the current situation. Li-kuo then summoned Chou Yü-ch'ih
[deputy director of the Air Force Political Department] from

Peking, telling him, "Just now I briefed the viscountess [code name for Yeh Ch'ün] on our discussion in Hangchow.   She told me to pay attention to cover and security in Shanghai."*

On March 20 Lin Li-kuo called a meeting of Chou Yü-ch'ih, Yü Hsin-yeh, and Li Wei-hsin in Shanghai, telling them, "I have talked about this matter with the chief [Lin Piao], and he told me to go ahead and draft a plan." According to Lin Piao's wishes, Lin Li-kuo, Yü Hsin-yeh and others then wrote up a "coup program" from March 22 to 24, 1971. Lin Li-kuo called this "coup program" "An Outline of 'Project 571,'" because 571 [wu-ch'i-i] is a homonym for military uprising [wu (chuang) ch'i-i].

III. "Outline of 'Project 571' "

A. Possibility

After the Second Plenum of the Ninth Central Committee, the political situation has been unstable; the ruling group... [words unclear, as below] admits that the broad masses of the peasantry are oppressed, the economy is stagnant, the actual living standard of the masses, basic-level cadres, and soldiers... is falling, and the mood of dissatisfaction is spreading daily — people are angry but dare not speak; they are even to the point of daring not to be angry. The ruling group is corrupt, muddled, and incompetent — they are opposed by the masses and deserted by their followers.

1) A political crisis is in the making.

2) A struggle for power is in progress.

3) ... successors.

4) China is in the midst of a gradual, peacefully evolving political coup.

5) This kind of political coup is a familiar method of B-52

---

*The preceding four sentences from "On March 18" on are missing in the Chinese text released in the Central Daily of April 13, 1972. This portion of translation is taken from Report on Mainland China, No. 26 (June 26, 1972), 4. — Editor.

[code name for Mao].

6) They reenact one of their old tricks.

7) The coup is presently developing in a way that will benefit the pen [the civilian forces].

8) Therefore, we must use a violent, revolutionary coup to block this peacefully evolving counterrevolutionary gradual development. Otherwise, if we cannot use "Project 571" to stop this peaceful evolution, once they succeed, who knows how many heads will fall? Who knows how many years the Chinese revolution will be delayed?

9) A new power struggle cannot be avoided; if we do not seize control of revolutionary leadership, it will fall into the hands of others.

Our strengths:

Through several years of preparation our organizational, ideological and military level has risen considerably; we have a definite ideological and material foundation.

All over the country, only this strength of ours is emerging, rising, and flourishing daily.

Political power in the future will devolve on whoever gains revolutionary leadership.

What attitude will our "fleet" [code name for Lin's force] take in the future political revolution in China?

Seizing the leadership of the revolution means seizing political power in the future. Revolutionary leadership has historically devolved on our fleet.

Compared with "Project 571s" in other countries, our preparation and strength is much more complete, and our assurance of success is much greater.

Compared with that of the Soviets during the October Revolution, our strength is not small.

Our geographical maneuvering space is large.

The Air Force is highly mobile.

Comparatively speaking, it is easier for the Air Force to gain political power over the whole nation through a "571" than for each military district to divide up local control.

There are two possibilities: to seize national political power, or to have regional control.

B. Necessity and Inevitability

B-52 cannot enjoy good sense for long; within a few years he must hurriedly arrange for things after his death.

He is wary of us.

It is better to burn our bridges behind us rather than to sit and wait to be captured.

If we act first militarily and then politically, . . . will be greatly threatened.

The Trotskyist clique wielding the pen still willfully tampers with and distorts Marxism-Leninism, making it serve their private interests. They use false revolutionary rhetoric in place of Marxism-Leninism in order to deceive and mislead the thoughts of the Chinese people; at present, their theory of continuous revolution is, in fact, Trotsky's theory of permanent revolution.

The target of their revolution is, in fact, the Chinese people, and first in their way are the army and those who do not agree with them.

Their socialism is, in essence, social fascism. They have turned China's state machine into a kind of meat grinder for mutual slaughter and strife, and they have made the Party and whole country's political life into a patriarchal life of the feudal, dictatorial, and autocratic type.

Of course, we do not deny his historic role in unifying China; it was precisely because of this that during the revolution we gave him the status and support he deserved. Now, however, he abuses the trust and status given him by the Chinese people. In an historical sense he is going backward — actually, he has become a contemporary Ch'in Shih-huang.*

Owing to our responsibility to the Chinese people and to Chinese history, there is a limit to our waiting and our tolerance.

He is not a true Marxist-Leninist, but rather one who follows

---

*First Emperor of the Ch'in dynasty, 221-209 B.C., who was remembered in history as one of the most ruthless, ambitious, and able despots in China. — Editor.

the way of Confucius and Mencius, one who dons Marxist-Leninist clothes but implements the laws of Ch'in Shih-huang. He is
the biggest feudal despot in Chinese history.

C. Fundamental Conditions

Favorable conditions:
Domestic political contradictions are intensifying; crises
arise on all sides; the dictator is losing the trust of the
masses every day.
The ruling group is internally very unstable; the struggling for power, striving for advantage, scheming, and lock-
ing horns have almost reached a climax.
The army has been oppressed; its middle- and higher-level
cadres show no respect and are dissatisfied.
A small gang of polished men have become remorseless
and despotic; moreover, they control military power and
make enemies on all sides. Their heads are swelling, and
they overestimate themselves.
Cadres who were rejected and attacked in the course of the
protracted struggle within the Party and the Cultural Revolution are angry but dare not speak.
The peasants lack food and are short of clothing.
The sending of young intellectuals to the mountains and the
countryside is really a disguised form of labor reform.
During the early stages, the Red Guards were cheated and
used, and they served as cannon fodder; during the later
stages, they were suppressed and made into scapegoats.
Administrative cadres were retrenched and sent to "May
7" cadre schools, which amounted to their losing their
jobs. Workers (especially young workers) had their wages
frozen, which amounted to disguised exploitation.
Contradictions abroad are intensifying.
The confrontation between China and the Soviet Union is
giving the Soviet Union a hard time; our action will have
the support of the Soviet Union.
The most important condition: we have the prestige and

of our chief [Lin Piao] and the strength of the united fleet.
As to natural conditions: our large country provides much
room for maneuver and, in addition, the high mobility of
the Air Force will be helpful for surprise attacks, coordination, detour, and even retreat.
Difficulties:
At present, the preparation of our strength is still not adequate.
The blind faith of the masses in B-52 [code name for Mao]
personally is very deep.
Because of B-52's divide and rule policy, the army's internal contradictions are fairly complex, which makes it
difficult to form a united force which we can control.
The fact that B-52 lives in seclusion, rarely appears in public,
conceals his movements with mystery, and is guarded by tight
security poses certain difficulties for our actions.

D. Timing

Both we and the enemy are riding a tiger from which it is
difficult to dismount.

The present superficial and temporary balance will not last
long; the balance of contradictions is temporary and relative,
while imbalance is absolute.

This is a life-or-death struggle — either we devour them, or
they devour us.

Strategically, there are two critical moments:
One is when we have completed our preparations and are
able to devour them.
One is when the enemy has opened his mouth to devour us,
and we are in critical danger; at this point we must burn
our bridges behind us, whether or not we are prepared.
Tactical timing and methods:
When B-52 is in our hands and all of the enemy's main
battleships [key members of the Central Committee] are
in the palm of our hand; this is the type that all throw themselves into the net.
We should utilize high-level meetings and get them all in

the net at once.
First cut off their teeth and paws and create a fait
accompli.
Force B-52 to surrender.
The method of encircling the palace.
Use special means, such as poison gas, biological weapons,
bombs, "543"*, car accidents, assassination, kidnapping,
small urban guerilla bands.

E. Basic Strength and Potential Strength

Basic strength:
The united fleet and various branch fleets (Shanghai, Peking,
Canton).
The Fourth and Fifth Air Force Groups (backbone strength)
controlled by Wang [Wei-kuo, political commissar of the
Fourth Air Force Group Stationed in Nanking], Ch'en [Li-
yun, political commissar of the Fifth Air Force Group in
Chekiang], and Chiang [T'eng-chiao, political commissar
of the Air Force Unit of the Nanking Military Region]. The
Ninth Division and the Eighteenth Division.
The Twenty-First Tank Regiment.
Civilian aviation.
The Thirty-Fourth Division.
Auxilliary Strength:
Domestically, the Twentieth Army, the Thirty-Eighth Army,
and Huang [Yung-sheng's Administrative Group of the Mili-
tary Affairs Commission]. The Scientific and Technological
Commission of the Defense Ministry, Canton, Chengtu,
Wuhan, Kiangsu, Tsinan, Foochow, Hsinkiang, Sian.
Externally, the Soviet Union (secret negotiations).
Use Soviet forces to check various forces at home and
abroad.

---

*Taiwan intelligence sources indicate that "543" is a
new type of weapon recently developed in China. — Editor.

Temporary protection by the Soviet Union's nuclear umbrella.

F. Slogans and Program for Mobilizing the Masses

All army commanders, unite! The whole Party, unite! The people all over the country, unite! Down with the contemporary Ch'in Shih huang-ti, B-52! Overthrow the feudal dynasty which carries the placard of socialism and establish a socialist country which truly belongs to the proletariat and the laboring people!

Externally, true Marxism-Leninism all over the world, unite! Proletarians and oppressed peoples of the world, unite! Our external policy is to resolutely uphold the Five Principles of Peaceful Coexistence, recognize present diplomatic relations with various countries, and guarantee the safety of the personnel of various legations.

Follow the slogan "A Prosperous People and a Strong Country," instead of "A Prosperous Country but an Impoverished People," to make the people happy with their homes and content with their work, to give them enough to wear and eat, and genuinely to liberate them politically and economically. Use true Marxism-Leninism as our guiding ideology to establish true socialism and replace B-52's social fuedalism.

All of the country's workers, peasants, administrative cadres, and those in various enterprises and trades must stay at their posts, strive for production, protect state properties and documents, observe and maintain social order. For this reason, various districts, units, and departments are not permitted to carry out liaison among themselves. Military forces all over the country must obey the centralized, unified orders of the command headquarters, and must rigorously suppress counter-revolutionary revolts and all sabotage activities.

G. Essentials for Implementation

Three stages:

First, the preparatory stage: (1) Planning. (2) Forces and commanding groups: Chiang, Wang, Ch'en. Two sets of garrison systems: public, Li Sung-t'ing; secret, the responsibility of the Shanghai group — Officers Instruction Corps of the First Hsin-Hua Village. (Ground) training the troops of the Fourth and Fifth Groups. Work concerning the division directly under the Nanking Air Force Unit (the Tenth Division) is the responsibility of Chou Chien-p'ing. Win over the Twentieth Army (Chiang, Wang, Ch'en). (3) Logistic preparation: weapons to be allocated or self-manufactured. Communications equipment (including Project 012)*... vehicle control; locations of warehouses; main munitions dumps. (4) The guaranteeing of intelligence: grasp the three links — collection, analysis, and reporting.

The second stage, the stage of implementation. Another one is to coordinate first and then strike — when the top is coordinated, attack suddenly; one is to strike first and then coordinate; and a last one is to carry on both at the same time. Chang Ch'unch'iao [first secretary of Shanghai Party Committee and Mao's supporter] must be captured. Then immediately bring into play all the instruments of public opinion to publicize his traitorous crimes. In sum there are two guidelines: one is surprise attack; the second is once it is started, carry it through to the end.

The third stage: consolidate our battle front and broaden the battle achievements. (1) Consolidate militarily: exert all efforts to hold Shanghai, occupy the radio stations and telegraph office and communications, and cut off all links between Shanghai and the outside. Do our utmost to neutralize Nanking, but set up good defenses. Hold Chekiang, and Kiangsi and control the paratroopers and air transports. (2) Attack politically: a showdown at the top. Control the instruments of public opinion and broaden the political offensive. (3) Expand organizationally: expand the armed forces quickly. Coordinate with all sides.

---

*According to KMT sources, the project refers to a new radio transmission system set up by Lin Li-kuo. — Editor.

H. Policy and Strategy

Attack B-52's forces while waving B-52's flag, in order to soften
public opinion. Unite all forces which can be united, liberate the majority, and concentrate the attack on B-52 and his handful of dicta-
tors; liberate the majority and protect the majority. What they call
attacking a handful is nothing each time but concentrating their fire
power on a handful and destroying them one group at a time. Today
they use this group to attack that group; tomorrow they use that group
to attack this group. Today one small handful, tomorrow another;
added together, it becomes a big group. They not only incite cadres
to struggle against cadres, and the masses to struggle against the
masses, but they also incite the armed forces to struggle against
the armed forces, and Party members against Party members.
They are the greatest advocates of armed struggle in China.

They manufacture contradictions and splits in order to attain
their goal of divide and rule, destroying each group in turn and
maintaining their ruling position.

They know that launching an attack on everyone at the same
time is suicidal, so each time they use one force to attack another. Today he uses this force to attack that force; tomorrow he
uses that force to attack this force. Today he uses sweet words
and honeyed talk to those whom he entices, and tomorrow he
puts them to death for some fabricated crimes. Those who are
his guests today will be his prisoners tomorrow.

Looking back at the history of the past few decades, [do you see]
any one whom he had supported initially who has not finally been
handed a political death sentence?

Is there a single political force which has been able to work
with him from beginning to end? His former secretaries have
either committed suicide or been arrested. His few close com-
rades-in-arms or trusted aides have also been sent to prison
by him. Even his own son has been driven mad by him.

He is a paranoid and sadist. His philosophy of liquidating
people is either don't do it, or do it thoroughly. Everytime he
liquidates someone, he will put them to death before he desists;
once he hurts you, he will hurt you all the way; and he puts the

blame for all bad things on others.

Frankly speaking, all of those who have been forced from the scene in his merry-go-round style have in fact been made scapegoats for his own crimes.

In the past, publicity about B-52 arose out of historical necessity or concern for national unity or the need to resist foreign enemies or his fascist oppression or the lack of inside information about him.

To these comrades, we offer an historical materialist analysis and give pardon and protection; tho those who in the past have been persecuted by B-52 because of some fabricated charges, we offer political liberation without exception.

9. Security and Discipline

This project is absolutely top-secret, and disclosure to anyone is forbidden without authorization. Resolutely carry out all actions according to commands and display the "spirit of Edashima."* Be prepared to die for the cause if we don't succeed.

Those who leak secrets, fail in their responsibilities, waver, or turn traitor will be severely punished.

IV. Confession of Li Wei-hsin**

In February 1971 Lin Li-kuo, Lin Piao, and Yeh Ch'ün went to Soochow together. After that Lin Li-kuo went from Soochow to Hangchow. On March 18 Li-kuo and Yü Hsin-yeh arrived in Shanghai from Hangchow. That very evening Lin Li-kuo told

---

*Edashima is the place where the Japanese Navel Academy was located. The spirit of Edashima refers to the daring spirit of the traditional Japanese warriors. — Editor.

**Li was then deputy director, Secretariat, of the Political Department of the Fourth Air Force Group. This section of the document is taken from Chung-Hua yüeh-pao [China Monthly, Hong Kong], No. 696 (September 1973), 35 and 60. — Editor.

Hsin-yeh and me that under the current situation a coup plan should be considered. He wanted to summon Chou Yü-ch'ih from Peking immediately for consultation and at the same time asked Yü Hsin-yeh not to return to Peking for the time being, in order to take charge of this matter. Li-kuo added: "Just now I briefed the viscountess [code name for Yeh Ch'ün] on our discussion in Hangchow. She told me to pay attention to cover and security in Shanghai."

On March 20 Chou Yü-ch'ih arrived in Shanghai. That evening Li-kuo and Yü-ch'ih held a secret meeting. After it was over, they summoned Hsin-yeh. The next morning the three of them began to hold secret talks, and soon I was asked to join them. Li-kuo said, "On the basis of the current power distribution pattern in various regions [of the country], the words of the chief [Lin Piao] continue to have a definite influence. I have talked about this matter with the chief, and he told me to go ahead and draft a plan."

At that time, primarily the following issues were discussed:

1. To Study the Situation, Principally in Three Respects

a) Under the prevailing conditions, the power and influence of the chief were absolutely predominant, and there was a leaning to one side. Now was the best time to act. But such predominance might be weakened gradually.

b) Chang Ch'un-ch'iao was expanding his influence. After the Ninth Party Congress the situation across the nation had been basically stable, and during peacetime the activities and influence of the "civilians" are bound to expand.

c) According to the laws governing the development of things, a good trend can develop only to a certain point, and after that it will change and move toward the opposite direction. This is a rule of alternating developments.

Li-kuo also added: "This is what the Chairman [Mao] has been doing all the time. He always uses one faction at one time and another at another time, in order to strike a balance. The current trends indicate that he is using Chang Ch'un-ch'iao."

2. To Study the Issue of Lin Piao's Succession to Power — Three Possibilities Were Considered

a) The chief assumes power through peaceful transition. Yü-ch'ih said: "This will happend in about five or six years, maybe even sooner." Li-kuo said: "It might take more than five or six years. Even if it is five or six years, a lot of things could change, and nobody can predict that the chief will retain his present status that long. But a peaceful transition is the most ideal thing."

b) The chief is... [ousted from power by others]. Yü-ch'ih maintained that this was not likely, at least for the coming three years. Li-kuo said: "Nothing is predictable. The Chairman commands such high prestige that he need only utter one sentence to remove anybody he chooses." Hsin-yeh said: "The chief has been chosen by the Chairman himself." Li-kuo said: "Liu Shao-ch'i was also his own choice." He appreared to feel that Lin Piao could be removed any time, and [Lin Piao] wanted him to make active preparations for a counterrevolutionary coup. Then we read the March 16 article in Shanghai's Wen-hui pao. Li-kuo considered that article to be not casually written, and for that matter it should be taken as a signal — a step intended to prepare public opinion.

c) The chief assumes power ahead of time. Two methods were discussed: (1) To get rid of Chang Ch'un-ch'iao and his followers, while preserving the status of the chief. Then a peaceful transition. [Chang was considered as the most probable substitute for Lin Piao.] (2) To endanger the life of the Chairman himself. But they had to consider the high prestige enjoyed by the Chairman and therefore would try to avoid this as far as possible, lest it should be difficult to handle the political situation afterward. Yü-ch'ih said: "Of course this must be done, and there are ways of doing it, such as placing the Chairman under house arrest for the purpose of negotiation. [We] can get rid of the Chairman while placing the blame on somebody else. Send for Wang Tung-hsing and Chang Ch'un-ch'iao and get rid of them first. Then just say that they are in

collusion with Wang, Kuang, Ch'i or so-and-so in an attempt to
murder the Chairman. Or get a few prisoners to be the scapegoats. By that time, since the chief would have the supreme
power, he could come out to make some statements and take
care of the whole situation. Politically, however, the chief
would pay a very high price for resorting to this alternative."

3. To Study Methods — Striving for a Peaceful Transition, But Also Preparing for an Armed Uprising. Two Things Were to Be Done Immediately

a) To draft a plan.

b) To have the Fourth Air Force Group organize an Instruction Corps.

The "Plan":

We first searched for a code name. After thinking about it
for a long time, Li-kuo himself decided on "Project 571,"
"571" being a homonym for "armed uprising" [wu-chuang
ch'i-i].

As for the goals and contents of the plan, [Li-] kuo said:
"Have the Shanghai Group take the lead in the Instruction Corps
to get rid of Chang [Ch'un-ch'iao] and Yao [Wen-yüan]. Maybe
ask Wang Wei-kuo to invite Chang and Yao over, or have the
Garrison Commissioner Li Sung-t'ing take people to Chang's
residence." (At that moment, Lin Li-kuo asked me whether
Chang's residence was under the jurisdiction of the Garrison
Commission. I said I did not know. Lin Li-kuo asked me to
gather some information about it. I remember asking Commissioner Li Sung-t'ing about it. Li said that Chang's residence
was under our jurisdiction, since we sent the guards there and
shipped the daily supplies. I reported this back to Lin Li-kuo,
and in so doing I carried out counterrevolutionary activities
for their counterrevolutionary plan.)

Lin Li-kuo added: "After we have taken care of Chang and
Yao, let Wang Wei-kuo and Ch'en Li-yun, if necessary, draw
on part of the Nanking Air Force to control the situation in
Shanghai; then link other forces all over the country to issue

a declaration of support, and force the Central Committee to
express its support. If Hsü Shih-yu leads troops to interfere,
have Wang Wei-kuo and his group guard Shanghai and thus produce a stalemate which will lead to peace negotiations. The
worst outcome is to go to the mountains and carry on guerrilla
warfare in Chekiang first." Lin Li-kuo also said: "These problems were discussed with Ch'en Li-yün while I was in Hangchow. I think we will have Yü Hsin-yeh draw up the plan on the
basis of the framework developed at the Hangchow meeting."
I cannot remember the several different sections of the plan,
but it seems to have consisted of implementation preparations,
blueprints, and postcoup arrangements.

The Instruction Corps:

An Instruction Corps was to be organized on the pretext of
cultivating basic-level cadres. The Corps was to be made up
of about one hundred men who were able and could keep the
secret to be stationed at the First Hsin-Hua Village in Shanghai. The cadres of the Instruction Corps were very important
and had to be carefully selected. But to rely on this Instruction
Corps alone was not enough. It was necessary to control the
Shanghai group, and within the group, Ch'iu Cho-hsien and
Chiang Kuo-chang are the main targets. All the men in the
group, in ones or twos, were also expected to control a unit of
the Fourth Air Force Group, and everyone was to hold an official position in the unit he was assigned to control. In addition,
more vehicles and guns were to be provided to the Instruction
Corps in order to increase its mobility. As for rifles, Wang
Wei-kuo could be asked to prepare for their manufacture. In
military matters, the Instruction Corps was to learn more
skills, and politically, to cultivate a feeling of affection toward
the "chief" [Lin Piao] and the "deputy director" [Lin Li-kuo].

Lin Li-kuo also said: "At present, only the 'fleet,' Chiang
T'eng-chiao, Wang Wei-kuo, and Ch'en Li-yün know about the
"571" plan and the Instruction Corps. Some information may
be passed on to the Shanghai group."

The above describes the counterrevolutionary activities of
Lin Li-kuo in Shanghai during March. The following are some
other facts and clarifications.

1) I did not see the "571" plan after it was drafted. However, on September 11, 1971, Yü Hsin-yeh boasted that Lin Li-kuo had left the plan and a copy of examples of military uprising recently compiled by himself with the chief [Lin Piao] and the director [Yeh Ch'ün] at Peitaiho.

2) During July and August, while Yü Hsin-yeh was in Canton, he said to me: "At the criticize Ch'en rectification meeting, Lin Li-kuo was fairly nervous. He figured there were three possibilities for the meeting: first, just a general discussion; second, the rectification would reach as far as the administrative operations groups of the Military Affairs Commission; and third, the rectification would reach as far as the chief. At the meeting, Huang [Yung-sheng], Wu [Fa-hsien], Ch'iu [Hui-tso], Li [Tso-p'eng], and Yeh [Ch'ün] all criticized themselves. Moreover, because it was the Chairman [Mao] who approved their self-criticism, the director [Yeh Ch'ün] was extremely nervous and wanted to put "571" into action right away; she even discussed it with Huang Yung-sheng."

10

STRUGGLE TO SMASH THE
COUNTERREVOLUTIONARY COUP D'ETAT
OF THE LIN PIAO ANTI-PARTY CLIQUE
(Materials, Part III)*

Top-Secret Document

Document of the Central Committee of the
Chinese Communist Party Chung-fa, 1972, No. 24

Chairman Mao's Instruction: Approved for Issuance.

I. Notice of the Central Committee of the
Chinese Communist Party

To Party committees of provinces, municipalities, and autonomous regions; Party committees of military regions, military
districts, and field armies; Party committees of headquarters
of the Military Affairs Committee and service branches; leading groups of Party committees of ministries and commissions
of the State Council; and core groups of the Party:
Hereby issued to you is the document "Struggle to Smash the

---

*"Fen-ts'ui Lin Piao fan-tang chi-t'uan fan-ko-ming cheng-
pien ti tou-cheng (ts'ai-liao chih san)." Reprinted in Chung-kung
nien-pao [Yearbook on Chinese Communism], 1973, Section VII,
pp. 8-10. This translation is taken, with minor editorial
changes, from Nationalist sources, Report on Mainland China
(New York), No. 27 (October 18, 1972). According to Taiwan
sources, the original document contains over 100 pages in Chinese. Unfortunately, the complete text is not yet available outside China. What we have here are excerpts only.

Counterrevolutionary Coup d'Etat by the Lin Piao Anti-Party
Clique (Materials, Part III)," i.e., "Criminal Evidences of the
Counterrevolutionary Coup d'Etat by the Lin Piao Anti-Party
Clique," selected and compiled by an ad hoc committee of the
Party's Central Committee. You are required to organize circulation, reading and discussion, in accordance with the spirit of the
document Chung-fa, 1972, No. 3. When "Materials, Part III," is
being circulated and discussed at various localities, you should use
the "Summary of Chairman Mao's Talks to Responsible Local
Comrades During His Tour of Inspection (Mid-August to September 12, 1971)" as a weapon, penetratingly carry out a Criticize Lin
Rectification Movement, go one step further in exposing the crimes
of the Lin Piao anti-Party clique, and launch great revolutionary criticism to purge the Lin Piao anti-Party clique. Various
local Party committees, when circulating among the masses
Chairman Mao's important talks and Central Committee documents regarding the tenth struggle between the lines, adopted the
measures of summing up experiences gained from spot experi-
mentation, setting up study groups, cultivating core cadres on a
"spot" basis, then generally starting circulation, propaganda, and
teaching among the masses. These measures have been proven effective and should be adopted at this time in conveying this material to the masses. As for the translation of this Central Committee
document into the Mongolian, Tibetan, and Uighur languages, this
should be taken up by the nationalities publishing organizations.

Central Committee of the
Communist Party of China
July 2, 1972

II. Struggle to Smash the Counterrevolutionary
Coup d'Etat of the Lin Piao Anti-Party Clique
(Materials, Part III)

Foreword

The sinister goal of the Lin Piao anti-Party clique in launching

a counterrevolutionary coup d'etat was to divide our Party, to
seize the top power of the Party and the state by conspiratory
measures, . . . [words missing, as below] the line adopted
at the Ninth Party Congress, fundamentally change the Party's
basic line and policy during the historical stage of . . . socialism, overthrow the proletarian dictatorship, and restore
capitalism.   They wanted to revive the landlord-bourgeois
class that our Party, our army, and all people of our nation
under the leadership of Chairman Mao smashed with their
own hands.   Inside the country, they wanted to exercise a
landlord-comprador-bourgeois fascist dictatorship in alliance
with the landlords, rich peasants, counterrevolutionaries,   `
undesirables, and rightists; internationally, they wanted to
capitulate to the Soviet revisionist social-imperialism, to
join hands with the Soviet Union and the United States to
oppose China and communism.

The counterrevolutionary Lin Piao anti-Party clique is an
agent in our Party of the overthrown landlord-bourgeois
class of our country and of imperialists, revisionists, and
reactionaries.   Their policy line summarizes and reflects
the wishful thinking of class enemies inside and outside the
country who want to carry out a counterrevolutionary
comeback in China. Yet this plot of the Lin Piao anti-
Party clique to stage a counterrevolutionary comeback will
never succeed.   Under the leadership of Chairman Mao and
the Party Central Committee, our Party, army and people
have scored a great victory in smashing the counterrevolutionary coup by the Lin Piao anti-Party clique.   This is a
great victory for Mao Tse-tung's thought and Chairman
Mao's proletarian revolutionary line.   Following Chairman
Mao's instructions to "stress evidence, investigation, and research and strictly forbid duress," and to "stress evidence
rather than taking any confession lightly," we have carried
out investigation of a great quantity of evidence and have verified it.   On January 16, 1972, we published the counterrevolutionary directive "Outline of 'Project 571.'"   Now, a part of

the verified criminal evidence is hereby published.

Ad Hoc Committee of the
CCP Central Committee
June 26, 1972

A. Criminal Evidence of the Lin Piao Anti-Party Clique's
Launching of a Counterrevolutionary Coup During the
Second Plenary Session of the Ninth Central Committee

During the Second Plenary Session of the Party's Ninth
Central Committee in 1970, the Lin Piao anti-Party clique
carried out clandestine activities and went all out in their plots
and trickeries. Adopting such despicable methods as sneak attacks, fanning wind and lighting fire, fabricating rumors and
hoodwinking comrades, they launched a well-planned, organized,
and programed attack. Their anti-Party programs were: in-
augurate a state chairman, advocating "genius," opposing the
line adopted by the Ninth Party Congress, and overturning the
three agenda of the Second Plenary Session of the Ninth Central
Committee. Their sinister goal was an attempt to split our
Party and army, to seize power from Chairman Mao and from
the Party Central Committee. In essence, it was an out-and-
out counterrevolutionary coup d'etat that was smashed.

Appendixes:

1) A mobilization order issued by Lin Piao to launch a counterrevolutionary coup d'etat, and his anti-Party program.

2) Fanatic attacks on the Party Central Committee by the
Lin Piao anti-Party clique during the Second Plenary Session
of the Ninth Central committee.

3) Clandestine conspiratory activities of the Lin Piao anti-
Party clique during the Second Plenary Session of the Ninth
Central Committee.

B. Evidence Indicating the Lin Piao Anti-Party Clique's Preparations for Launching a Counterrevolutionary Armed Coup

Even before the Second Plenary Session of the Ninth Central

Committee, the Lin Piao anti-Party clique had started its anti-Party power-seizure conspiratory activities, with a view to overthrowing the Party's Central Committee with Chairman Mao as its leader. After the Plenary Session, the Lin Piao anti-Party clique, refusing to admit failure, rejected efforts by Chairman Mao and by the Party Central Committee to educate and salvage it, hid in dark corners . . . and concocted the program for a counterrevolutionary coup dubbed the "Outline of 'Project 571.'" They set up an extremely secret fascist intelligence organization, created public opinion, trained special agents, bought over cadres, imported from abroad large quantities of agent tools, established underground bases of operation, and made preparations in various fields for a counterrevolutionary armed coup.

Appendixes:

1) The so-called "Order No. 1" issued by Lin Piao.

2) Anti-Party activities of the Lin Piao-Huang [Yung-sheng]-Wu [Fa-hsien]-Yeh [Ch'ün]-Li [Tso-p'eng]-Ch'iu [Hui-tso] alliance.

3) Lin Piao's letter to Chou Yü-ch'ih and Liu Pei-feng* in his own handwriting.

4) Wu Fa-hsien's orders of appointment to Lin Li-kuo, Chou Yü-ch'ih and others.

5) Lin Piao's reactionary "Second Trip to the Ching-kang Mountains"** and its music score.

6) A record of the two-faced counterrevolutionary tricks by Lin Piao and Yeh Ch'ün.

7) Lin Piao's "July 23 Inspection Tour," which used "preparations for war" as a pretext but actually aimed at seizing Party power.

---

*Member, Ninth Central Committee; deputy secretary, Hupei Provincial Party Committee; vice chairman, Hupei Provincial Revolutionary Committee; first political commissar, Wuhan Military Region. — Editor.

**A poem by Lin Piao. The Ching-kang Mountains were the location of a Communist stronghold in Kiangsi Province during the early thirties. — Editor.

8) Black material incriminating Politburo comrades, fabricated by the Lin Piao anti-Party clique, and intelligence it collected for the purpose of launching a counterrevolutionary coup.

9) Information and data collected by Lin Piao and Yeh Ch'ün for studying the feasibility of a counterrevolutionary coup.

10) The counterrevolutionary guerrilla group "Little United Fleet" established by Chou Yü-ch'ih, under the direction of Lin Piao.

11) Original text of the "Information for Applicants for Party Membership" issued by the Shanghai Party Group.

12) Secret intelligence activities of the counterrevolutionary guerrilla group "Little United Fleet."

13) The so-called Three-Nation Quadripartite Conference secretly called by Lin Li-kuo in Shanghai.

14) Evidences indicating Yü Hsin-yeh's plan for preparing and carrying out the counterrevolutionary "Project 571" ahead of schedule (abridged).

15) Cajolery of Lin Piao by Chou Chih-ping.*

16) Counterrevolutionary public opinions created by the Lin Piao anti-Party clique for seizing Party power, and abridged version of Liu Yen-nien's confession of his anti-Party activities.

17) Evidences of a black meeting of the counterrevolutionary guerrilla group "Little United Fleet" (abridged version of the original minutes).

18) Secret counterrevolutionary bases set up by Lin Li-kuo and other members of the Lin Piao bandit group.

19) Large quantities of equipment and material indicating counterrevolutionary coup activities by the Lin Piao anti-Party clique, seized at various secret bases.

20) Training in the operation of the . . . aircraft, secretly carried out by Chou Yü-ch'ih.

21) Training in the operation of amphibious vehicles,

---

*Member, Ninth Central Committee; deputy secretary, Fukien Provincial Party Committee; political commissar, Foochow Military Region. — Editor.

secretly carried out by Lin Li-kuo.

C. Evidence Indicating the Lin Piao Anti-Party
   Clique's Attempts at Assassinating the Great
   Leader Chairman Mao, at Launching a
   Counterrevolutionary Coup Against the
   Party Central Committee, and at Turning
   Traitor and Escaping to an Enemy Country
   After Being Foiled

In September 1971 the Lin Piao anti-Party clique, in ac-
cordance with the counterrevolutionary directive "Project 571,"
launched a desperate counterrevolutionary armed coup. Under
Lin Piao's direct command, they tried in vain to assassinate
Chairman Mao when he was making an inspection tour of the
South, and at the same time murder Politburo comrades in
Peking, so as to seize the top power of the Party and the state.
After this counterrevolutionary plan went bankrupt, Lin Piao
then plotted to take Huang Yung-sheng, Wu Fa-hsien, Yeh Ch'ün,
Li Tso-p'eng, Ch'iu Hui-tso, and others to escape south to Canton and set up another central committee. However, actions
taken by Chairman Mao torpedoed this arrangement by the Lin
Piao anti-Party clique. Seeing his plot exposed and his fate
sealed, Lin Piao then took his wife, son, and a bunch of cohorts
and hastily fled to an enemy country, thus turning into a traitor
to the Party and the state. At 2:30 in the morning of September 13, 1971, the Trident jet, No. 256, in which Lin and others
took flight crashed near Undur Khan in Mongolia. All those on
board, including Lin Piao, Yeh Ch'ün, and Lin Li-kuo, were
burned to death. They died a renegade's and traitor's death,
which was by no means enough to compensate for their crimes.
As for Wu, Li, Ch'iu, and others, after Lin Piao's traitorous
escape to the enemy country, they destroyed most of their
criminal evidences in an attempt to cover up their own crimes.
   Appendixes:
   1) A counterrevolutionary order issued personally by Lin
Piao. This order, and a letter to Huang Yung-sheng in Lin

Piao's own handwriting, were carried by Chou Yü-ch'ih and Yü Hsin-yeh during their flight in a helicopter. When the helicopter was forced to land, Chou, attempting to destroy the evidence, tore these documents into pieces, which were later collected by responsible comrades at the site, pasted together, and restored. According to Chiang Teng-chiao, Hu Ping*, Li Wei-hsin, and more than ten others who participated in the counterrevolutionary coup and who had read this order themselves, the original text of the order to start a counterrevolutionary coup was: "Please act in accordance with the order conveyed by Comrades Li-kuo and Yü-ch'ih — Lin Piao."

2) Lin Piao's letter to Huang Yung-sheng in his own handwriting: "Comrade Yung-sheng: Miss you very much. Be optimistic at all times and take good care of yourself. If you have any problems, consult Comrade Wang Fei** in person. Salute — Lin Piao."

3) Wang Fei's confession in his own handwriting.

4) Numerous telephone contacts among Yeh, Huang, Wu, Li and Ch'iu on the eve of the counterrevolutionary armed coup by the Lin Piao anti-Party clique.

5) Code names for some chief figures of the counterrevolutionary coup, e.g., Chin-chung T'ung-ling for Chou Yü-ch'ih, Huang-hsiang a-fei for Wang Fei, and Ch'iu-tzu chiu-tzu for Liu Pei-feng, in Yeh Ch'ün's own handwriting.

6) Intelligence information sent to Yeh Ch'ün by Huang, Wu, Li, Ch'iu, and others

7) Records made by Chen Hung-chen regarding conspiratory activities by the Lin Piao anti-Party clique in plotting to assassinate Chairman Mao and Politburo comrades (photostat copy of original text); "map of Tiao-yü-t'ai"; "Sun Yung-sheng's chemical weapon"; [Some code words follow, which can be roughly translated as:] "No. 10 morning special express train

---

*Deputy director of the General Staff Department of the PLA Air Force Command. — Editor.

**Also deputy director of the General Staff Department of the Air Force Command. — Editor.

on a certain day in September in England"; "receive the political commissar at the four dragon gates"; "No. 16 special express train tomorrow, door short of a bar, Peking."

8) "Four links without a bar; ten powers attack" [appar-
ently code words] plotted by the Lin Piao anti-Party clique for
assassinating Chairman Mao.

9) Lu Ping's* confession in his own handwriting.

10) Chiang Teng-chiao's confession in his own handwriting.

11) "Topographical Map of Tiao-yü-t'ai"** secretly drawn by
the Lin Piao anti-Party clique for assassinating Politboro
comrades.

12) Wang Fei's confession in his own handwriting.

13) List of persons scheduled to flee south to Canton with
Lin Piao, Yeh Ch'ün, Huang, Wu, Li, and Ch'iu, as drawn by
Wang Fei at a black meeting.

14) Confession by Liu Chih in his own handwriting.

15) A telephone message scheduled to be sent to Wang Wei-
kuo by Lin Piao when his plane to Canton passed over Shanghai
(from Li Wei-hsin's diary).

16) Confession by Hu Ping in his own handwriting.

17) . . . [Missing]

18) Explanation by Li Tso-p'eng.

19) Large quantities of absolutely secret documents of our
Party and PLA that Lin Piao and Yeh Ch'ün planned to take
with them on their flight but later discarded.

20) Picture of Lin Piao and Yeh Ch'ün taken just before
their flight to an enemy country.

21) An account of how Lin Piao and Yeh Ch'ün made their
hasty escape.

---

*Director of the Operations Department and deputy director
of the General Staff Department of the PLA Air Force. — Editor.

**Tiao-yü-t'ai, known as the Senkaku Islands in Japanese,
is a tiny islet on the continental shelf between Taiwan and the
Ryukyus. It is said to be oil-rich and was the focal point of
disputes among China, Taiwan, and Japan in 1971, before it
was returned by the U. S. to Japanese control. — Editor.

22) Pictures showing the two fuel trucks rammed by Lin Piao's Trident jet No. 256 as it made a hasty takeoff, and fragments of the right wing of the plane after the collision.

23) Site of the Trident crash.

24) Helicopter used by Chou Yü-ch'ih and others in their escape attempt that was forced to land by our forces.

25) Part of criminal evidences indicating Lin Piao's betrayal of the Party and the state, seized from the helicopter.

26) Confession by Li Wei-hsin in his own handwriting.

11

NOTICE OF THE CENTRAL COMMITTEE OF
THE CHINESE COMMUNIST PARTY*
(September 12, 1970)

Document of the Central Committee of the
Chinese Communist Party, Chung-fa, 1970, No. 56

Chairman Mao's Instruction: Distribute Accordingly.

To the core groups of the Party in all provinces, municipalities [directly under the Central Government], and autonomous
regions; and to the Military Affairs Commission of the Central
Committee:
We are now distributing to you "The Draft Revision of the
Constitution of the People's Republic of China" basically passed
by the Second Plenum of the Ninth Central Committee of the CCP.
Please pass it on immediately to all factories and mines, communes, army units, administrative organs, schools, enterprises and business units, and basic-level leadership organs
in street organizations; broadly organize the masses to discuss it and make suggestions for revision.
"The Draft Revision of the Constitution of the People's Republic of China" is the continuation and development of the
1954 "Constitution of the People's Republic of China." The
1954 Constitution played a great, historic role in the struggle

*"Chung-kung chung-yang t'ung-chih." Chung-kung yen-chiu
[Studies on Chinese Communism], VI:2 (February 1972), 118-
120. A translation of the complete text of the draft revision of
the Constitution appears in Chinese Law and Government, VII:3
(Fall 1974).

to mobilize and unite the people all over the country, to construct a socialist country under the dictatorship of the proletariat, and to protect the homeland. In the excellent revolutionary situation at home and abroad, our great leader Chairman Mao, in March of 1970, suggested that we convene the Fourth People's Congress and revise the Constitution, and he also recommended that we not establish a state chairman.*

"The Draft Revision of the Constitution of the People's Republic of China" has been presented after repeated discussions over half a year by the whole Party, the whole army, and the broad masses of workers, peasants, and soldiers all over the country, under the leadership of our great leader Chairman Mao and his close comrade-in-arms Vice Chairman Lin; it is a joint product of the Party leadership and the broad masses. In March the Central Committee Politburo began making preparations for revising the Constitution. On July 12 the Committee for Drafting a Revision of the Constitution, under the CCP Central Committee, was set up with Chairman Mao as director and Vice Chairman Lin as vice director. The Central Committee Politburo and the Revision Committee, after carefully studying the opinions of the masses of workers, peasants, and soldiers of the whole country toward revision of the 1954 Constitution, proposed the "Draft Revision of the Constitution of the People's Republic of China" and submitted it for study to the Second Plenum of the Ninth Central Committee on August 23. On September 6 the Plenary Session basically passed this draft revision of the Constitution and decided to mobilize all the people of the country to discuss and revise it.

"The Draft Revision of the Constitution of the People's Republic of China" was formulated on the basis of Chairman Mao's great theory and practice regarding the concept of the state as the guiding thought. This draft revision of the Constitution clearly defines: the leadership position of our great leader Chairman Mao and his close comrade-in-arms Vice Chairman Lin; the leadership of the nation by the Chinese Communist

---

*Emphasis added by the editor.

Party; how Marxism-Leninism-Mao Tse-tung Thought is the
theoretical foundation to guide our thoughts and the guiding
compass for all our work in the country; social classes
under socialism, class contradictions, class struggle, proletarian dictatorship, and continuous revolution under the
dictatorship of the proletariat; and the great role of the
masses of the people and the people's party. Every attempt was made to make it simple, concise, easily compre-
hensible, and thus convenient for the masses to study and
apply. After everyone in the country discusses revisions
and after it is adopted by the Fourth People's Congress, it
will become the fighting program for mobilizing and uniting
the people to win new victories.

Discussing revisions of "The Draft Revision of the Constitution of the People's Republic of China" is a great event in the
political life of our nation. The key to doing this work well is
leadership. We hope that responsible comrades at all levels
will raise high the great banner of Mao Tse-tung thought, give
prominence to proletarian politics, and combine study of the
communiqué of the Second Plenum of the Ninth Central Committee with propagating to the masses this draft revision of
the Constitution, arousing them to express enthusiastically
their opinions on revision. The revolutionary committees of
each province, municipality, and autonomous region, and the
Military Affairs Commission of the Central Committee, please
gather the opinions of the masses and report them to the Central Committee at the end of September.

Central Committee of the
Chinese Communist Party
March 17, 1972

Enclosure: "Draft Revision of the Constitution of the People's Republic of China" (basically passed by the Second Plenum
of the Ninth Central Committee of the Communist Party of
China, September 6, 1970).

(This document may be printed and distributed to factories
and mines, communes, army units, administrative organs,

schools, enterprises and business units, and basic-level leadership organs of street organizations. It may be read to the revolutionary masses; but it should not be copied, posted, broadcast, or published in newspapers.)

12

REPORT ON THE INVESTIGATION OF THE
COUNTERREVOLUTIONARY CRIMES OF THE
LIN PIAO ANTI-PARTY CLIQUE*

Top-Secret Document

Document of the Central Committee of the
Chinese Communist Party, Chung-fa, 1973, No. 34

I. Notice of the Central Committee of the Chinese Communist Party

The Central Committee of the Chinese Communist Party
unanimously adopts and approves the "Report on the Investigation of the Counterrevolutionary Crimes of the Lin Piao Anti-
Party Clique" submitted by the Central Ad Hoc Team.

> Office of the Central Committee
> of the Chinese Communist Party
> Approved on August 20, 1973
> Issued on September 8, 1973

II. Report on the Investigation of the Counterrevolutionary Crimes of the Lin Piao Anti-Party Clique

After the Lin Piao anti-Party clique failed in their plot to

---

*"Kuan-yü Lin Piao fan-tang chi-t'uan fan-ko-ming tsui-hsing
ti shen-ch'a pao-kao." Released by Nationalist sources. This
translation is taken, with minor editorial changes, from Issues
& Studies, X: 6 (March 1974), 117-120.

launch a counterrevolutionary coup d'etat, Lin Piao, accompanied by Yeh Ch'ün, Lin Li-kuo, and several other diehards, hurriedly commandeered a plane to defect to the Soviet revisionists in betrayal of their Party and country. The plane carrying them crashed in the vicinity of Undur Khan in Mongolia. Lin Piao, Yeh Ch'ün, and the others aboard were killed, though as renegades and traitors they deserved a penalty worse than death.

Under the leadership of Chairman Mao and the Party's Central Committee, the whole Party, the whole army, and the people of the whole country, in their greatest proletarian indignation, have denounced Lin Piao, exposed and criticized the Lin Piao anti-Party clique's crimes, and have thus unfolded the movement to criticize Lin Piao and rectify the work style, a movement of great historical significance. Through the exposure efforts of the broad masses and investigations and studies conducted by the Central Ad Hoc Team, a large amount of criminal evidence against the Lin Piao anti-Party clique has been found. The "Materials on the Struggle for Smashing the Lin Piao Anti-Party Clique's Counterrevolutionary Coup d'Etat," Parts I, II and III, prepared and printed by the Central Ad Hoc Team, illustrates how the proletarian headquarters headed by Chairman Mao struggled against the bourgeois headquarters led by Lin Piao. These materials have penetrated Lin Piao's camouflage and deception and thoroughly exposed the true facts of Lin Piao's intrigue and conspiracy for practicing revisionism and splittism. These materials provide incriminating evidence of the Lin Piao anti-Party clique's secret plot to launch a counterrevolutionary coup d'etat in a wild attempt to assassinate our great leader Chairman Mao and overthrow the proletarian dictatorship. The careerist, conspirator, and counterrevolutionary double-dealer Lin Piao anti-Party clique is a counterrevolutionary treacherous group in betrayal of the Party and country.

1. The material evidence and witnesses which have been identified by the Central Ad Hoc Team based on their investigation and verification are:

a) As early as before the Ninth Congress was held Lin Piao

assembled his men for selfish purposes and together with his
wife, Yeh Ch'un, colluded with Ch'en Po-ta, Huang Yung-sheng,
Wu Fa-hsien, Li Tso-p'eng, Ch'iu Hui-tso, and others to form
a bourgeois headquarters with himself as the head. And through
his son Lin Li-kuo he surreptitiously established a counterrevolutionary intelligence organization called the "Joint Fleet."
The Lin Piao anti-Party clique is the proxy of landlords, rich
peasants, counterrevolutionaries, bad elements, and Rightists
at home and imperialism, revisionism, and reaction abroad.
The backbone of his clique is a handful of renegades, enemy
agents, Trotskyists, class opportunists, degenerates, and absolutely unrepentant persons in power taking the capitalist
road, who sneaked into our Party, and new counterrevolutionaries. They secretly plotted to launch a counterrevolutionary
coup d'etat in a wild attempt to overthrow the Party's Central
Committee headed by Chairman Mao.

  b) The Lin Piao anti-Party clique's surprise attack on the
Party at the Second Plenary Session of the Ninth Central Com-
mittee was premeditated. Under Lin Piao's direct command,
Ch'en Po-ta, Huang Yung-sheng, Wu Fa-hsien, Yeh Ch'ün, Li
Tso-p'eng, and Ch'iu Hui-tso secretly met many times before
and during the session and prepared successive treacherous
schemes for organized and programed attacks on the Party.
On August 22, 1970, Lin Piao delivered an anti-Party speech.
Later, on the morning of August 26, the counterrevolutionary
Briefing No. 6 prepared by Li Hsüeh-feng as directed by Lin
Piao and Ch'en Po-ta appeared, and they worked on it for two
and a half days. Their anti-Party program was to "set up a
chairman of the state" based on the idealist "theory of innate
genius" and to oppose the "Ninth Congress" line and overthrow
the three agenda of the Second Plenary Session of the Ninth
Central Committee. Anxious to become chairman of the state,
Lin Piao wanted to split the Party and seize power from Chairman Mao and the Central Committee. In nature his move was
a smashed counterrevolutionary coup d'etat.

  c) After the close of the Second Plenary Session of the Ninth
Central Committee, the Lin Piao anti-Party clique immediately

made preparations for their armed counterrevolutionary coup
d'etat. They drew up the plan for an armed counterrevolutionary coup d'etat entitled "Outline of Project 571" and stepped
up their treacherous activities in support of Lin Piao's counterrevolutionary coup d'etat in the fields of politics, military affairs, organization, and intelligence. On September 8, 1971,
Lin Piao issued an order for the armed counterrevolutionary
coup d'etat, and on September 10 he personally wrote a letter
to Huang Yung-sheng. Under the direct command of Lin Piao
the sworn followers of Lin Piao employed vicious means in a
wild attempt to assassinate Chairman Mao on his tour of inspection outside Peking and planned to murder the leading comrades of the Central Committee in Peking at the same time.
Their plot was aborted. Lin Piao again directed Wu Fa-hsien to
secretly arrange planes in order to flee to Canton with Huang
Yung-sheng, Wu Fa-hsien, Yeh Ch'ün, Li Tso-p'eng, Ch'iu
Hui-tso, and others. There he planned to establish a rival
Central Committee in a wild attempt to create a situation like
the so-called "North and South Kingdoms." Lin Piao also intended to collude with the Soviet revisionists to attack us simultaneously from the north and the south. However, all their
schemes were made thoroughly bankrupt.

   d) Lin Piao's betrayal of the Party and country had a historical background. He was brought up in a big landlord, capitalist family. After admission into the Party, his bourgeois
world outlook was never remolded. During the period of the
Agrarian Revolution, he was pessimistic and despaired of the
future of the Chinese revolution. During the fifth counteren-
circlement and suppression campaign in the central soviet
area, Lin Piao pursued Wang Ming's left opportunist line and
vigorously advocated abrupt attacks. After the Tsunyi Conference, at the critical juncture when Chairman Mao directed the
Red Army to move from resistance to victory, Lin Piao together
with P'eng Te-huai wanted to seize power from Chairman Mao.
In the early days of the Red Army's arrival in northern Shensi,
Lin Piao stubbornly insisted on himself leaving the main force
of the Red Army to engage in guerrilla operations in southern

Shensi and wanted to be independent of the Party. During the War of Resistance Against Japan, Lin Piao published anti-Party articles shamelessly eulogizing Chiang Kai-shek's Kuomintang. In the Liaoning-Shenyang and Peking-Tientsin Battles during the War of Liberation, Lin Piao repeatedly resisted Chairman Mao's strategic guidance and plans. Together with Liu Shao-ch'i he opposed Chairman Mao's wise decision to resist America and aid Korea and refused to be assigned to the Korean battlefield. Lin Piao was the behind-the-scene planner for Kao Kang and Jao Shu-shih's anti-Party alliance. In the early 1960s, when the whole country suffered from severe natural disasters, Lin Piao, taking advantage of the anti-Chinese countercurrent initiated by the Khrushchev renegade clique, opposed the Party's General Line, advocated the "fixing of output quotas based on the household" and wanted to compromise with the Soviet revisionists in defiance of our Party's efforts to expose and criticize Soviet revisionism. When he administered the routine work of the Central Committee Military Affairs Commission, Lin Piao cultivated and planted his close followers, assailed and betrayed revolutionary cadres, and strenuously carried out his bourgeois military line. He put forth the anti-Party and army-disrupting slogans of overthrowing "the armed Liu-Teng line" and "singling out the small handful from the army" to strike at the majority and protect the minority, undermined the Great Proletarian Cultural Revolution in a wild attempt to usurp Chairman Mao's position of commander-in-chief, drew up the erroneous theory that "the founder of the People's Liberation Army cannot command the army," and wildly urged that the army be put under his direct command. He opposed Chairman Mao's principle that "the Party commands the gun, and the gun must never be allowed to command the Party," hoping to basically alter the proletarian nature of our army. Toward the mistakes committed by Lin Piao in the past, Chairman Mao's Party Central has insistently adopted the policy of "learning from past mistakes to avoid future ones and curing the sickness to save the patient." Even after the Second Plenary Session of the Ninth Central

Committee, Chairman Mao still tried to save him through
benevolent and righteous education, giving him a chance for
repentance and self-correction. However, Lin Piao always
played counterrevolutionary double-dealing tricks on the Party.
He overtly obeyed but covertly disobeyed, said one thing but
thought another, and deceived the Party and the people. Finally
he cut himself off from the Party and the people.

2. The emergence of the Lin Piao anti-Party clique was an
acute manifestation of bitter class struggle at home and abroad.
The Great Proletarian Cultural Revolution was a great political
revolution in which the proletariat opposed the bourgeoisie and
all the other exploiting classes. This great revolution first
achieved a great victory in the smashing of the Liu Shao-ch'i
renegade clique. But the class enemies did not accept their
defeat willingly; they wanted to engage in a desperate struggle
before their death. Besides, the imperialists, especially the
Soviet social-imperialists, were tempted to subvert the proletarian dictatorship in our country at any time. Under these
conditions the Lin Piao anti-Party clique, acting as the representative of the class enemies at home and abroad lost their
patience and jumped out hurriedly. They were bound to jump
out as their behavior was determined by the nature of their
own class. Their sinister purpose was to thoroughly change
the Party's basic line and policy in the entire historical stage
of socialism, overthrow the proletarian dictatorship, and restore capitalism. They wildly attempted to resurrect the landlord bourgeoisie which had been overthrown personally by our
Party, our army and our people under the leadership of Chairman Mao. At home they wanted to unite with the landlords,
rich peasants, counterrevolutionaries, bad elements, and Rightists to practice the fascist dictatorship of the landlord bourgeoisie. Abroad they wanted to capitulate to the Soviet social-
imperialists and unite with them to oppose China, communism,
and revolution. However, this was only a treacherous scheme,
a wild attempt of a handful of Lin Piao's sworn followers which
was extremely feeble in nature and quite shameful; and therefore it could not make any markable achievement or significant

impact upon the whole situation. Hence, their defeat was pre-
destined and inevitable. Our Party is a long-tested, great,
glorious and correct party. Under the leadership of the Party's
Central Committee with Chairman Mao as the head, the whole
Party, whole army, and all the people have smashed the Lin
Piao anti-Party clique and gained a great victory for the Party's
Tenth line struggle. It is the heaviest blow dealt to the class
enemies at home and abroad, a great victory for the Great Pro-
letarian Cultural Revolution, and a great victory for Chairman
Mao's proletarian revolutionary line.

3. In view of the Lin Piao anti-Party clique's capital crimes
of launching a counterrevolutionary coup d'etat in betrayal of
the Party and country, the Central Ad Hoc Team proposes to
the Central Committee of the Party that:

a) the bourgeois careerist, conspirator, counterrevolutionary double-dealer, renegade, and traitor Lin Piao be
dismissed from the Party forever;

b) the Lin Piao anti-Party clique's key element, the
Kuomintang anti-Communist, Trotskyist renegade, enemy
agent and revisionist Ch'en Po-ta be dismissed from the
Party forever and removed from all his posts inside and
outside the Party;

c) the Lin Piao anti-Party clique's key element, alien
class element sneaking into the Party, enemy agent, renegade and traitor Yeh Ch'ün be dismissed from the Party
forever;

d) the Lin Piao anti-Party clique's key elements Huang
Yung-sheng, Wu Fa-hsien, Li Tso-p'eng, Ch'iu Hui-tso,
and Li Hsüeh-feng be dismissed from the Party forever
and removed from all their posts inside and outside the
Party.

We solicit the review and approval of the Central Committee.

The Central Ad Hoc Team
July 10, 1973

Appendices:

A. "Materials on the Struggle for Smashing the Lin Piao Anti-Party Clique's Counterrevolutionary Coup d'Etat," Parts I, II and III, prepared and printed by the Central Ad Hoc Team.

B. "The Report on the Investigation of the History of the Counterrevolutionary Crimes of the Kuomintang Anti-Communist, Trotskyist renegade, Enemy Agent and Revisionist Ch'en Po-ta."

Office of the Central Committee
of the Chinese Communist Party

13

MAO TSE-TUNG'S PRIVATE
LETTER TO CHIANG CH'ING*
(July 8, 1966)

Chiang Ch'ing:

Your letter of June 29 has been received. It is better for
you to stay there longer as suggested by Comrade Wei (1) and
Comrade Ch'en. (2) This month I shall have to give audience
to two foreign guests. I will tell you my schedule after the
audience. After I left Wulin on June 15, I stayed in a cave in
the west for some ten days. There the communications were
not very good. I arrived at Paiyun Huang Ho on June 28. Since
then, ten days have elapsed. Here I read materials every day;
it is interesting work. The situation changes from a great up-
heaval to a great peace once every seven or eight years. Ghosts

---

*"Mao Tse-tung chih Chiang Ch'ing ssu-han," an appendix to
the "top-secret" document Chung-fa, No. 25 (September 1972),
"Criticisms on Lin Piao's Works and Speeches," issued by the
Central Committee as study materials for the campaign against
Lin Piao. Aside from Mao's letter reprinted here, the docu-
ment includes five other titles: A Criticism of Lin Piao's
"China's Three Years' War for National Liberation, 1940"; A
Criticism of Lin Piao's "May 18, 1966, Address"; "On Short
Assault"; Mao's Instruction on A Small Glossary of Philosoph-
ical Terms; and Mao's Instruction on Chang Ch'un-ch'iao and
Yao Wen-yüan's "Concerning the Experience of Study." The
text of the letter was released by Taiwan sources and published
in Chung-yang jih-pao [Central Daily], November 4, 1972.
This translation, and notes, is taken, with permission, from
Issues & Studies, IX:4 (January 1973), 94-96.

monsters jumped out by themselves. Their destiny being decided by their own class, they had to jump out. The Central
urged me to publish the address of my friend [Lin Piao] (3),
and I have prepared to agree with it.

His address was devoted entirely to a political coup. There
has never been any address like his before. I was quite uneasy
at some of his thinking. I have never believed that the several
booklets I wrote would have so much supernatural power. Now,
after he exaggerated them, the whole nation has exaggerated
them just as Wang P'o bragged about the melons she sold. I
was driven by them to join the rebels of the Liangshan Mountain. (4) It seems that I have to concur with them. It is the
first time in my life that I unwillingly concur with others on
major questions. I have to do things against my own will! Yüan
Chi (5) of the Chin dynasty was opposed to Liu Pang. (6) Yüan
traveled from Loyang to Chengkao. A humble man as he was
became renowned because there were no heroes in the world
at that time. Lu Hsün had corrected his own articles. He and
I are of one mind; I like his straightforwardness. He said that
he "anatomized himself more strictly than others." After having
fallen down several times, I often do as he did. But our comrades often do not believe it. I have self-confidence but also
some doubt. I once said when I was in my teens that I believed I
could live two hundred years and sweep three thousand li. (7)
I was haughty in appearance and attitude. But somewhat I doubt
myself and always feel that when tigers are absent from the
mountain, the monkey there professes himself a king. I have
become such a king. But it does not mean eclecticism. In my
mind there is some air of tiger which is primary, and also some
air of monkey which is secondary. I once quoted Li Ku's letter (8)
to Huang Ch'iung (9) of the Han dynasty as saying, "A tall thing
is easy to break; a white thing is easy to stain. The white
snow in spring can hardly find its match; a high reputation is
difficult to live up to." The last two sentences refer exactly to
me. I have also read these passages at one of the standing committee meetings of the Central Politburo.

It is valuable to know oneself. At the Hangchow Conference (10) held in April this year, I expressed my opinion, which was different from that of my friend's [Lin Piao's]. I could do nothing else. In the conference held in May in Peking, he spoke in the same manner. The press spoke even more so, describing me as a god. In that situation, I could only go up to Liangshan. I guessed that their very intention was to strike the ghosts by the help of Chung K'uei. (11) I became Chung K'uei of the Communist Party as early as in the 1960s. Things always go toward the opposite side. The higher a thing is blown up, the more serious it is hurt at the fall. I am now prepared to be broken to pieces. This does not bother me. For the matter can never be destroyed; I may become pieces, that's all. There are more than one hundred parties (12) in the world. Most of the parties no longer believe in Marxism. Even Marx and Lenin have been smashed by them, much less we. I suggest that you should also pay attention to this problem and should not become dizzy with success. (13) You should remind yourself often of your weak points, shortcomings, and mistakes. On this I have talked with you numerous times, and I did so last April in Shanghai. The above seem to be black words. But don't the anti-Party elements say so? I feel that some methods of their presentation are not very appropriate; I mean the effect on me. What they want to do is overthrow our Party and myself. This is the difference between me and the black gang. These words cannot be made public at the present time since all the Leftists say so now. Publication of these words will mean pouring cold water on them, which helps the Rightists. Our current task is to overthrow a part of (it is not possible to overthrow all of) the Rightists in all the Party and throughout the country. We shall launch another movement for sweeping up the ghosts and monsters after seven or eight years, and will launch more of this movement later.

I cannot determine when we should publish these words, for the Leftists and the broad masses of people do not welcome my saying so. Maybe we should wait until I die when the Rightists come to power, and let them do the publication. The Rightists may attempt to use my words to hold high the black banner. By so doing, they would get behind the eight ball. In China, after the emperor was overthrown in 1911, reactionaries could not hold power long. If there arises an anticommunist rightist political coup in China, I am certain that it will not be peaceful, and very probably would be short-lived. For all revolutionaries, who represent the interest of 95 percent of the people, would not tolerate it. At that time, the Rightists may prevail for some time by using my words, but the Leftists may also organize some of my other words to overthrow the Rightists. The Cultural Revolution this time is a large-scale and serious maneuver. In some areas (such as Peking Municipality), the revolutionaries were resurrected overnight. Some units (such as Peking University and Tsinghua University) collasped quickly because of their involved and complicated ingredients. As a rule, where the Rightists are more rampant, the worse they will be defeated and the more vigorous the Leftists will be. This is a nationwide maneuver in which the Leftists, the Rightists, and the staggering fence-sitters will absorb useful lessons. The conclusion is, and still is: our future is bright, but the road before us is twisted.

Notes

1) Comrade Wei refers to Wei Wen-po, secretary of the CCP Shanghai Municipal Committee and concurrently secretary of the Eastern China Bureau of the CCP Central Committee during the Cultural Revolution.

2) Comrade Ch'en refers to Ch'en P'i-hsien, first secretary of the CCP Shanghai Municipal Committee, and concurrently secretary of the Eastern China Bureau of the CCP Central Committee and first political commissar of the Shanghai Garrison District Command. Both Wei Wen-po and Ch'en P'i-hsien were criticized, struggled against, and paraded by the Red Guards and rebels during the power-seizure struggle in January 1967.

3) The "friend" refers to Lin Piao, and the "address of my friend" to Lin Piao's address at the enlarged meeting of the CCP Central Politburo held on May 18, 1966. In the address, Lin dealt with the crisis of a possible political coup at the highest level of the Communist regime and Mao's efforts to put

the clamp on it. Lin also flattered Mao as being a "genius" of modern Marxism-Leninism and called for a mass movement for living study and application of Mao's works.

4) "Driven to join the Liangshan mountain rebels" — an old Chinese saying derived from the Chinese classic novel All Men Are Brothers. Most of the characters in this novel were good men originally, but later joined the bandits on Liangshan because of persecution by corrupt government officials.

5) Yüan Chi, one of the noted scholars in the Chin dynasty (265-419 A.D.).

6) Liu Pang, the first emperor of the Han dynasty (206 B.C.-220 A.D.).

7) Li — A unit of Chinese measure equal to about 600 meters.

8) Li Ku alias Tzu Chien, defense minister during the reign of Emperor Chung (145-146 A. D.).

9) Huang Ch'iung alias Shih Ying, a noted statesman during the reign of Emperor Shun (126-144 A.D.).

10) "Hangchow Conference" refers to the Enlarged Meeting of the Standing Committee, CCP Central Politburo, held in April-May 1966. The meeting was first presided over by Mao in Hangchow, and later removed to Peking and was chaired by Lin Piao. It was in these two conferences that the criticism in the press was transformed into actions. Resolutions adopted in the meeting included (1) rescinding the "February Outline" drafted by P'eng Chen and others, deactivating the five-man "Cultural Revolution Group" and establishing the "Central Cultural Revolution Group" under the Standing Committee, Central Politburo; (2) reorganizing the CCP Peking Municipal Committee and dismissing P'eng Chen and others from the Party offices; (3) reorganizing the Propaganda Department of the CCP Central Committee, dismissing Lu Ting-i and others from office, and reorganizing the People's Daily; and (4) determining the crimes of "counterrevolutionary revisionists" P'eng Chen, Lu Ting-i, Lo Jui-ch'ing, and Yang Shang k'un.

11) Chung K'uei, a character in Chinese legend, said to be a chin-shih that Emperor Hsüan Tsung (713-742 A.D.) met in his dream. According to the emperor, Chung K'uei had power to

repel ghosts and evil spirits. After he awoke, the emperor
ordered a painter to draw Chung K'uei's picture based on his
impression in the dream. The picture later was reproduced
and adopted by civilians who posted it on their doors on the eve
of the New Year to protect their houses against the invasion
of ghosts.

12) The "parties" here refers to Communist parties.

13) "Success" refers to the victory of the Cultural Revolution.

III "Swindler Like Liu Shao-ch'i": Press Criticism of Lin without Mentioning His Name

14

STRENGTHEN THE PROLETARIAN
PARTY SPIRIT*

Writing Group of the Liaoning Provincial
Committee of the Chinese Communist Party

After the Second Plenum of the Ninth Central Committee of
the Party, in accordance with Chairman Mao's instruction on
conducting education on ideology and political line, the whole
Party launched a campaign of criticizing revisionism and rectifying work style. This campaign is a further development
of socialist revolution and a continuation of the struggle between
two classes, two roads, and two lines in the Great Proletarian
Cultural Revolution. We Communist Party members, particularly the leading cadres of the Party, must conscientiously
study the works of Marx, Lenin, and Chairman Mao in the
course of the struggle, strive to transform our world outlook
in accordance with the five requirements that the new Party
Constitution stipulates each Communist Party member must
meet, firmly strengthen the Party spirit of the proletariat, fulfill various fighting tasks put forth by the Ninth National
Party Congress and the First and Second Plenums of the
Ninth Central Committee, and consolidate the proletarian
dictatorship.

The Great Leader Chairman Mao summed up the positive and

---

*Chung-kuo kung-ch'an-tang Liao-ning sheng wei-yüan-hui
hsieh-tso hsiao-tsu, "Chia-ch'iang wu-ch'an-chieh-chi tang-
hsing," Hung-ch'i [Red Flag], No. 12 (November 1, 1971), 14-18.

negative aspects of international historical experiences of the
dictatorship of the proletariat, and he set out the five requirements for successors to the revolutionary cause of the proletariat. On the basis of these five requirements, the new Party
Constitution stipulates the five basic demands on Communist
Party members. The demands require that we study and apply
Marxism-Leninism-Mao Tse-tung Thought in a living way,
work for the interests of the vast majority of people of China
and the world, be able to unite with the great majority, consult
with the masses when problems arise, and be bold in making
criticism and self-criticism. These five requirements point
out the political orientation, basic-goals work method, and
work style for Communist Party members. Collectively, they
embody the Party spirit of the proletariat and represent the
temperament and work style that each Communist Party member must cultivate.

There exists struggle between the two lines on the question
of whether or not to adhere persistently to the five requirements and the Party spirit of the proletariat. This kind of
struggle, in the last analysis, is a question of which class
world outlook should be used to transform the Party and the
world. To adhere firmly to the five requirements put forward
by Chairman Mao means to transform the Party and the world
according to the world outlook of the proletarian vanguard.
However, proceeding from the reactionary stand of the landlords and bourgeoisie, political swindlers like Liu Shao-ch'i
frenziedly opposed the principle of Marxist Party spirit. They
put out the sinister book On Self-Cultivation and the black "Six
Theories" to corrode and poison the Communist Party members, in a vain attempt to turn them into docile tools for promoting revisionism. They even used the trick of passing fish
eyes for pearls to wantonly distort and tamper with the five
requirements set forth by Chairman Mao. In their reactionary
articles, such as the sinister book On Self-Cultivation, swindlers like Liu Shao-ch'i dished out another set of the so-called
"standards" for Communist Party members and revolutionary
cadres, in which they did not even mention Marxism-Leninism

and the masses of the people. They fundamentally abandoned the theory of proletarian revolution and proletarian dictatorship and rejected the world outlook of dialectical materialism and historical materialism. Their aims were to transform our Party with the world outlook of the bourgeoisie and to carry out their sinister plots of capitalist restoration.

For a Communist Party member, the first and also the most important question is one of guiding ideology and political orientation. That is to say, one should "go in for Marxism-Leninism and not for revisionism." Marxism-Leninism-Mao Tse-tung Thought is the theoretical basis of our Party's guiding ideology. The fifty years of the history of our Party prove that our Party advances with one victory after another if we act in accordance with Marxism-Leninism-Mao Tse-tung Thought and march forward along Chairman Mao's proletarian revolutionary line. However, our Party suffers setbacks and defeats if we divorce ourselves from Marxism-Leninism-Mao Tse-tung Thought and run counter to Chairman Mao's revolutionary line. To determine whether or not a Communist Party member is imbued with the Party spirit, we should first of all see whether or not he holds fast to Marxism-Leninism-Mao Tse-tung Thought, applies dialectical materialism in observing and handling problems, transforms his subjective world while transforming the objective world, and unswervingly sides with Chairman Mao's revolutionary line in the course of the sharp and complicated class struggle and the struggle between the two lines. One cannot talk about enthusiasm in isolation from line and policy. If the line is erroneous, the greater "enthusiasm" one has, the more errors one is going to make. We should not talk about politics if we divorce ourselves from the Marxist world outlook and the proletarian world outlook. The reactionary viewpoint which opposes and distorts Marxism-Leninism-Mao Tse-tung Thought certainly cannot represent proletarian politics; it can only represent bourgeois politics and revisionist politics. Therefore, a Communist Party member must study hard and painstakingly implement Marxism-Leninism-Mao Tse-tung

Thought, in close association with the practice of revolutionary struggle and his own ideology, and armed with the proletarian world outlook. Only by so doing will it be possible for him to improve his ability to recognize and oppose Marxists and sham political swindlers such as Liu Shao-ch'i, and to wage effectively a resolute struggle against the class enemies inside and outside the Party.

Communist Party members "must work for the interests of the vast majority of the people, for the vast majority of the Chinese people, and for the interests of the vast majority of the world's people. They must not work for the interests of the minority; nor should they work for the exploiting classes, the bourgeoisie, the landlords, rich peasants, counterrevolutionaries, evil elements, and Rightists." To overthrow the bourgeoisie and all the exploiting classes, to continue persistently the revolution under the dictatorship of the proletariat, and to liberate all mankind are part of the profound revolutionary struggle. In this struggle, the proletariat must unite with the great majority of the people, and it must isolate to the greatest possible extent, and deal heavy blows at, the handful of enemies. It is not enough to rely only on the minority of people; it is imperative to unite with the majority of people. It is essential to "unite with the broad masses of people and cadres who comprise ninety-five percent of the total population." Therefore, any sectarian trend or any word or deed which undermines unity within the Party and the unity between the Party and the people is incompatible with the five requirements for the Communist Party member. If we do not unite with the masses of the people and cadres according to Chairman Mao's teachings, and if we build mountaintop strongholds, promote sectarianism, and introduce the bourgeois corrupting work style into our Party, that means we transform the Party and the world according to the bourgeois world outlook. Those who display bourgeois factionalism find it easy to confuse the enemies with ourselves and to "carry the sedan chair" and "blow the trumpet" for the bourgeois careerists and conspirators. It is dangerous to allow such trends to develop. To work

for the interests of the vast majority of the people of China and
the world and to dedicate our whole life to the struggle for the
liberation of all mankind, we Communist Party members must
always proceed from the interests of the whole Party in order
to strengthen unity within the Party and the ties between the
Party and the masses. We must never harm the revolutionary
cause or the interests of the Party for our own sake, for small
mountaintop strongholds, or for small groups.

Communist Party members must also maintain close ties
with the masses, consciously accept the masses' criticism and
supervision, and never isolate themselves from the masses.
They must learn the Marxist method of leadership — "from
the masses, to the masses" — and cultivate the democratic
work style of being good at listening to the opinions of the
masses. If we have shortcomings and errors, we must boldly
examine ourselves and resolutely overcome and correct them
in the course of practice. Just as Chairman Mao has repeatedly taught us, "[We] must sincerely conduct self-criticism
and resolutely overcome our own shortcomings and correct
our mistakes in our work." We must not regard ourselves as
always being correct; we must not hear only eulogies and refuse to listen to criticism. In particular, under the circumstances of victories, we must "remain humble and prudent and
guard against arrogance and rashness," and we must be alert
against corruption by bourgeois ideology. We must consciously
practice democratic centralism and safeguard the unified
leadership of the Party. Only by doing so will it be possible
to implement the line of unity for victory set at the Ninth
National Party Congress and to fulfill the various tasks of the
Party.

The five requirements stipulated in the Party Constitution
must be met by every Communist Party member. It is on
fundamental questions such as this that a Communist Party
member demonstrates his Party spirit and shows his attitude
toward the revolution. To distort or split up the five requirements constitutes an act of destroying the proletarian Party
spirit. Allowing theory to be divorced from practice, or applying

the five requirements to others and not to oneself, is also an expression of the impurity of Party spirit.

Unity of theory and practice has been a consistent ideological principle of our Party. If a Communist Party member recognizes the five requirements in words alone but never really follows them in practice, this simply indicates that though he has joined the Party organizationally, he has never joined the Party ideologically or completely. During the Rectification Movement in Yenan, Chairman Mao pointed out: "We must assert that the absence of a scientific attitude, that is, the absence of the Marxist-Leninist approach which unites theory and practice, means that Party spirit is either absent or deficient." Chairman Mao severely criticized this deficiency and said that to use such a bad bourgeois work style "to govern one's own conduct is to harm oneself, to teach it to others is to harm others, and to apply it to direct the revolution is to harm the revolution." Only by thoroughly criticizing and overcoming such bad work styles as divorcing words from deeds, acting one way externally and in another way internally, and detaching theory from practice will it be possible to truly grasp and apply the five requirements, strengthen the proletarian Party spirit, and achieve one victory after another in the cause of the Party.

To divorce theory from practice and to split the subjective from the objective constitute the idealist world outlook of the bourgeoisie and the source of the theory of knowledge of the "Left" and Right opportunist lines. Liu Shao-ch'i and other political swindlers like him are themselves a very sinister example of detaching theory from practice and splitting the subjective from the objective. Even though they repeatedly declared their "faith" in Marxism, they had never followed Marxism to conduct their work. They merely used Marxist phraseology as a decorated front to conceal their revisionism and to deceive and frighten others. We must be good at uncovering and resisting their tricks, and we must provide no market for such revisionist merchandise.

There are others who have lowered the requirements for Communists. They described the ideological style which ran

counter to the five requirements as "matters of little importance." This viewpoint is very wrong.

What are matters of little importance? And what are matters of great importance? These questions should be analyzed
on the basis of the Marxist-Leninist theory of class and dialectic. The five requirements put forward by Chairman Mao
are matters of great importance for Communists, since they
embody a high level of unity of proletarian world outlook and
methodology, a high level of unity of the universal truth of
Marxism-Leninism and the concrete practice of Chinese revolution, and the guiding principles for the conduct of Communists.
"To go in for Marxism-Leninism and not revisionism" is a
matter of the greatest importance. Liu Shao-ch'i and other
swindlers like him who betrayed the fundamental principles of
Marxism-Leninism-Mao Tse-tung Thought are renegades
against the proletariat. Idealism, individualism, arrogance,
complacency, ruling by the voice of one man alone, telling lies,
and divorcing oneself from the masses represent the ideological
style of the bourgeoisie. They seriously obstruct the implementation of the Party's correct line. If we do not resolutely
resist and overcome these wrong styles which are directly opposed to the five requirements, we will not be able to maintain
a realistic attitude and the revolutionary principles; nor will
we be able to uphold unity and correct political orientation on
the basis of the principles of Marxism-Leninism-Mao Tse-
tung Thought for achieving the goal of serving the great majority of the people of China and the whole world. How can the
question of ideological style be regarded as merely "a matter
of little importance"? Moreover, nothing is isolated, static,
and unchangeable. Some persons become politically degenerate because of the bad influence of the ideological style of the
bourgeoisie. Wrong ideological style has developed into serious errors in orientation and line. Therefore, under no circumstances should the ideological style violating the five requirements be regarded simply as "a matter of little importance." A Communist must constantly examine himself in
accordance with the five requirements, place strict demands

on himself, act resolutely on the five requirements, and temper himself to be a true advanced element of the proletariat.

During the Great Cultural Revolution, the criticism was made that Liu Shao-ch'i and other political swindlers like him opposed matters of great revolutionary significance of the proletariat under the pretense of "paying attention to important matters." When they called "attention to matters of great importance," they meant attention to serving their bourgeois headquarters, which opposed Chairman Mao's correct line. The "matters of little importance" which they said did not merit attention were precisely those questions of principle involving the distinction between the proletariat and the bourgeoisie, and between revolution and counterrevolution. In order to carry out such a revisionist organizational line, Liu Shao-ch'i and his company had to oppose, distort, and alter the five requirements, so as to negate the five requirements completely and to negate matters of revolutionary importance to the proletariat. The historical experiences of the struggle between the two lines have told us that the reason why they had to do so is because their aim was to recruit deserters and turncoats and gather a handful of bad elements to form a sinister clique in a vain attempt to undermine the dictatorship of the proletariat and to erode and disintegrate our Party. We must continue to launch revolutionary mass criticism against their shameless lies. We must use Marxism-Leninism-Mao Tse-tung Thought as the weapon which will thoroughly criticize their sinister revisionist trash and eliminate their pernicious influences. We must carry out an incessant struggle against any ideas or actions which run counter to the five requirements and which lower the Party's standard, so that our Party's Marxist-Leninist spirit and principles can be maintained, and our Party's fighting strengths can be enhanced continuously.

In expounding the five requirements for the successors to the cause of proletarian revolution, Chairman Mao contrasted each requirement to the negative example of Khrushchev's teaching and provided us an historical lesson. Moreover, Chairman Mao reminded the whole Party "to be vigilant against

individual careerists and conspirators like Khrushchev and to
prevent such bad persons from usurping the leadership of the
Party and state at all levels." The five requirements put forth
by Chairman Mao are the sharp weapons for distinguishing
genuine Marxism from sham Marxism.

Historically, all the sham Marxists appeared with masks.
They used Marxist phraseology to cover their anti-Marxist
words and deeds. Owing to the unprecedented consolidation of
the dictatorship of the proletariat in our country, to the increasing penetration of Mao Tse-tung thought into the heart
of the people, and to the highest prestige enjoyed by the great
leader Chairman Mao, those sham Marxists and bourgeois
careerists and schemers who had sneaked into the Party were
forced to use counterrevolutionary dual tactics to oppose Marxism-Leninism-Mao Tse-tung Thought. Otherwise, they could
not even last for a single day. Liu Shao-ch'i and other
political swindlers like him were precisely those revisionists
carrying the signboard of Marxism-Leninism whom Chairman
Mao criticized in expounding the five requirements. They were
bourgeois careerists and conspirators who tried to divide the
Party and counterrevolutionary double-dealers who played
tricks. They were also the Khrushchev-type persons against
whom Chairman Mao called on the whole Party to be vigilant.
Owing to their own exploiting class nature, they always violated,
distorted, and opposed in theory and in deeds the five requirements put forward by Chairman Mao; and here and there they
failed to cover up their tricks. So long as our Party members
and revolutionary people read and study conscientiously and
have a good grasp of Marxism, strengthen the Party spirit of
the proletariat, transform their own world outlook, and apply
the five requirements set forth by Chairman Mao, in contrast
with the words and deeds of those sham Marxists and political
swindlers, we will be able to see through their true characteristics, resist their erroneous line, and resolutely carry through
Chairman Mao's revolutionary line.

Socialist society continues through a rather long historical
period. Throughout this historical period, there exist classes,

class contradictions, and class struggle; there is still the struggle between the socialist road and the capitalist road; there is
the danger of capitalist restoration; and there is the threat of
subversion and aggression by imperialism and socialist imperialism. Chairman Mao emphatically pointed out in a talk in
October 1968: "We have won great victories. But the defeated
class will still struggle. These people are still around, and
this class still exists. Therefore, we cannot speak of final
victory, not even for decades." For this reason, we must never
forget class struggle and weaken our concept of class struggle.
We should see that class enemies at home and abroad fear and
hate the great victory of our Great Proletarian Cultural Revolution, the growing prosperity of our socialist fatherland, and
the excellent domestic and international situations. Unwilling
to accept their failure, they will frantically carry out disruptive activities and wage a deathbed struggle. Class struggle in
society will inevitably be reflected in the Party. The struggle
between the two lines is protracted and complex. We must always maintain a high degree of revolutionary vigilance. We
must never be bookish and take a simple view of the complicated class struggle.

The road of the revolutionary will be long, and its test will
also be protracted. Communist Party members who vow to
devote their life to the struggle for the cause of communism
must impose strict demands on themselves, in accordance with
the five requirements. They must persist in fighting self-
interest and criticizing revisionism, strengthen the Party spirit
of the proletariat, and strive to raise the consciousness of
class struggle, the struggle between the two lines, and the need
for continuous revolution. They must closely follow the great
leader Chairman Mao, advance boldly along the line of unity
for victory set by the Ninth National Party Congress, and carry
out to the end the great cause of continuous revolution under
the proletarian dictatorship.

15

IMPORTANT TEACHING MATERIALS FOR
EDUCATION IN IDEOLOGY AND POLITICAL LINE*

Red Flag

The two revolutionary songs "The Internationale" and "The
Three Main Rules of Discipline and the Eight Points for Attention"** that we carry in this issue have recently been sung
widely by the people throughout the country. In the present
excellent situation at home and abroad, it is of great significance to organize the workers, peasants, and soldiers to do
still better in learning and singing these two revolutionary
songs well, to grasp their content and put their ideas into practice, to study conscientiously the article "Eugene Pottier,"
written by Lenin in commemoration of the author of the words
of "The Internationale," and to study conscientiously "On the
Reissue of the Three Main Rules of Discipline and the Eight
Points for Attention — Instruction of the General Headquarters
of the Chinese People's Liberation Army," written by Chairman Mao. This is of great significance in carrying out education

*"Chin-hsing ssu-hsiang ho cheng-chih lu-hsien chiao-yü
ti chung-yao chiao-ts'ai." Hung-ch'i, No. 12 (November 1, 1971),
7-11. This is a "short commentary" by Hung-ch'i, the theoretical journal of the Party Central Committee. This translation is taken from the New China News Agency English re-
lease of November 10, 1971.
**Words and music for these two songs may be found in
Hung-ch'i, No. 12 (November 1, 1971), 10-11; translation is avail-

in ideology and political line, inspiring our revolutionary fighting will, and fulfilling our tasks at home and abroad still better.

"The Internationale" was born in the struggle of the vanguard fighters of the Paris Commune for the establishment of the first state power of the proletariat in history. Both "The Internationale" and Lenin's article embody the basic standpoint and views of Marxism, epitomize the historical mission of the proletariat and the orientation and aim of its struggle, and express its dauntless spirit of struggle to liberate the whole of mankind. Over the past century, the inspiring, powerful, and majestically sonorous song "The Internationale" has spread the revolutionary truth of the proletariat to all corners of the globe and has become "the worldwide song of the proletariat"; and "it is now more alive than ever before."

"The Internationale" says: "We want no condescending saviors to rule us from their judgement hall"; "Toilers from shops and fields united, we are the union of all who work." This is the historical materialist concept that the slaves make history, a concept propagated over and over again since the birth of Marxism. It is diametrically opposed to the historical idealist

---

able in Selections from China Mainland Magazines, No. 717 (November 29, 1971), 7-8.

The three main rules of discipline are:
1) Obey orders in all your actions;
2) Do not take a single needle or piece of thread from the masses;
3) Turn in everything captured.
The eight points for attention are:
1) Speak politely;
2) Pay fairly for what you buy;
3) Return everything you borrow;
4) Pay for anything you damage;
5) Do not hit or swear at people;
6) Do not damage crops;
7) Do not take liberties with women;
8) Do not mistreat captives. — Editor.

concept that heroes make history, namely, a few emperors, princes, generals, ministers, sages, and prophets make history, a concept propagated over and over again by the landlord and capitalist classes. "The Internationale" also says: "We workers ask not for their favors; let us consult for all"; "Let each stand in his place! The internationale shall be the human race." That means that the historical mission of the proletariat is to overthrow the rule of the bourgeoisie and all other exploiting classes, establish the dictatorship of the proletariat in place of the dictatorship of the bourgeoisie, ensure the triumph of socialism over capitalism, and fulfill the great task of liberating the whole of mankind and ultimately realizing communism. In achieving this lofty ideal, the proletariat must rely on its own unity and struggle and must have the leadership of its vanguard — a Marxist-Leninist political party. Under Party leadership, we should strengthen our revolutionary unity, closely unite with the proletariat and oppressed people and nations throughout the world, support one another in struggle, and unite with all forces that can be united in a joint struggle. This stands in opposition to the modern revisionist line which betrays the dictatorship of the proletariat, pushes social-imperialism, and splits the militant unity of the revolutionary people of the world. "The Internationale" is imbued with the revolutionary optimism of the proletariat, cherishing firm confidence in the inevitable victory of the cause of communism, the coming of the day when "the golden sunlight still will stay," and the complete elimination by the revolutionary people of all monsters and demons who try to reverse the wheel of history and make the earth stop revolving. It stands diametrically opposed to the absurd attempt of "mayflies lightly plotting to topple the giant tree" and the pessimism of all decadent classes. "The four seas are rising, clouds and waters raging, the five continents are rocking, wind and thunder roaring." The countries want independence, the nations want liberation, and the people want revolution — this has now become a mighty, irresistible trend of history. "No more tradition's chains shall bind us." The recent disastrous defeat of U. S. imperialism in the United

Nations made the people of the world still more elated and confident. At such a moment, when we sing "The Internationale," this song of unity for struggle of the world's proletariat warms our hearts.

"The Three Main Rules of Discipline and the Eight Points for Attention" was the Red Army song based on "The Three Main Rules of Discipline and the Eight Points for Attention" formulated for the army by Chairman Mao during the Second Revolutionary Civil War. It embodies Chairman Mao's line on army-building and the glorious tradition of the Chinese People's Liberation Army; it is a powerful weapon encouraging the whole Party, the whole army, and the people throughout the country to observe discipline, implement policies, and unite and fight to achieve the revolutionary aim of the proletariat; and it is a powerful weapon for carrying out the Marxist-Leninist line "unite to win still greater victories" set forth by the Ninth Party Congress. Conscientiously abiding by the three main rules of discipline and the eight points for attention will make our country more vigorous and full of vitality, and the whole Party, the whole army, and the revolutionary people will be more united to "defend the motherland and continue to advance" along Chairman Mao's revolutionary line.

The first of the three main rules of discipline says: "obey orders in all your actions, for only by marching in step can we win victories." This is a summation of the historical experience of the Chinese revolution: the whole Party, the whole army, and the people of the whole country march in step to implement Chairman Mao's proletarian revolutionary line and policies and attain unity in thinking, policy, plan, command, and action on the basis of Chairman Mao's instructions; and they unite in a common struggle against the enemy — this is our basic guarantee for continuous new victories for our revolutionary cause. In studying the second and third rules, we should strive to carry forward the revolutionary tradition of hard struggle and building the country through diligence and frugality, treasure the property of the state and the people, (even a needle, a piece of thread, a brick, or a tile), and combat

the extravagance, waste, corruption, and degeneration characteristic of the exploiting classes. The first of the eight points for
attention says "to speak politely and respect the masses of the
people and not to be arrogant." Revolutionary cadres and Party
members must firmly bear this point in mind. They must have
faith in the masses, rely on them, fight self and criticize revisionism, combat arrogance and conceit, and persist in continuing the revolution under the dictatorship of the proletariat. The
fifth point says that we must strengthen ideological and political
education among the masses in all the work we do, and that compulsion and commandism are not allowed. The way to settle
ideological questions among the people is to present the facts
and reason things out so as to arrive at the correct recognition.
"Everyone must be conscious in observing discipline." Revolutionary discipline is established on the basis of the consciousness
of the proletarian fighters. Chairman Mao teaches: "Increase
the sense of discipline, and the revolution will be ever victorious." Under the guidance of Chairman Mao's correct line,
conscious observation of revolutionary discipline guarantees unity
in thinking and actions within the revolutionary ranks and assures
that any sabotage or disturbance by the class enemy is smashed and
victory won. In the past decades we have won great victories in the
democratic revolution and socialist revolution, precisely because
we have kept to and carried forward this glorious tradition under
the guidance of Chairman Mao's proletarian revolutionary line.

The songs "The Internationale" and "The Three Main Rules
of Discipline and the Eight Points for Attention" are important
teaching materials for education in ideology and political line.
Let us study Marxism-Leninism-Mao Tse-tung Thought hard,
learn and sing the two revolutionary songs well, heighten our
consciousness of class struggle and the struggle between the
two lines and of continuing the revolution under the dictatorship
of the proletariat, raise our ability to distinguish between true
and sham Marxism, conscientiously carry out the principle
"grasp revolution, promote production and other work and preparedness against war," closely follow our great leader Chairman Mao, and march ahead courageously!

16

BE OPEN AND ABOVEBOARD, AND
DO NOT INTRIGUE AND CONSPIRE*

Hsiao Pin

Summing up the historical experience of the struggle between
the two lines within the Party, the great leader Chairman Mao
put forth to the whole Party the basic principles for strengthening the Party's ideological and organizational construction:
"Practice Marxism, and not revisionism; unite, and don't split;
be open and aboveboard, and don't intrigue and conspire."
These three principles are an important content of the education
in ideology and political line in progress at present. We should
grasp them deeply and enforce them resolutely.

To be open and aboveboard or to intrigue and conspire is not
an ordinary question of work style but a question of principle
directly related to class struggle and the line struggle, and it
is a demarcation line between the proletarian revolutionary and
the bourgeois careerist. The history of the struggle between
the two lines within the Party over the past few decades shows
that the fundamental problem of inner-Party struggle is whether
to practice Marxism or revisionism. In order to oppose Chairman Mao's Marxist-Leninist line and advance the revisionist
line, all bourgeois agents who sneaked into the Party would invariably practice splittism organizationally and play intrigue
and conspiracy tactically. On the other hand, for the purpose

---

*Hsiao Pin, "Yao kuang-ming cheng-ta, pu-yao kao yin-mou
kuei-chi," Hung-ch'i [Red Flag], No. 3 (March 1, 1972), 31-35.

of upholding Chairman Mao's Marxist-Leninist line and opposing the revisionist line, all proletarian revolutionaries and
Communists are bound to uphold revolutionary unity and insist
on being open and aboveboard. Practice Marxism, unite, and
be open and aboveboard — these are our Party's political and
organizational lines, and both are consistent with each other.
Practice revisionism, practice splittism, and play intrigue and
conspiracy — these are the political program and action plan of
all anti-Party cliques, and both are also consistent with each
other. Therefore, only from the perspective of class struggle
and the struggle between the two lines in dealing with problems
shall we be able to understand better the profound meaning of
"Be open and aboveboard, and don't intrigue and conspire."

To be open and aboveboard is not an "inborn" quality of certain people. It is an embodiment of the proletarian Party spirit.
To play at intrigue and conspiracy is not a unique characteristic of some individual reactionaries, but is a special feature of
the bourgeois class. They reflect two basically opposite world
outlooks and have deep-seated and different class roots.

The proletariat is the greatest class in the history of mankind. It is the most far-sighted, impartial, and selfless, and it
is the most thoroughly revolutionary. On the very day of its
establishment, the proletarian political party — the Communist
Party — declared publicly to the whole world its purpose: "Dis-
dain to conceal its views" ("The Communist Manifesto"). "We
must firmly uphold the truth, and truth requires a clear-cut
stand. We Communists have always disdained to conceal our
views" ("A Talk to the Editorial Staff of the Shansi-Suiyuan
Daily"). Our Party has always publicly stated its fighting tasks
and basic line in different periods of the revolution, as well as
its strategy and tactics used for implementing these tasks. It
called on and mobilized the masses of the people to struggle
resolutely to carry them out. Our Party has openly declared
that the basic program of the Chinese Communist Party is to
overthrow completely the bourgeoisie and all exploiting classes, to replace the dictatorship of the bourgeoisie with the
dictatorship of the proletariat, and to use socialism to defeat

capitalism; and it has said that its ultimate aim is the realization of communism. On the other hand, the bourgeoisie and its
political party have always disguised the interests of the exploiting classes as the interests of the whole of mankind and
have never dared to state publicly their real intent of exploiting
and oppressing the proletariat and the laboring people. Even
when they are engaged in counterrevolutionary work every day,
superficially and verbally they always preach compassion and
morality to cheat the laboring people. It is precisely by relying on disguise, fraud, intrigue, and conspiracy that they conceal the essence of their bourgeois dictatorship and maintain
their reactionary rule.

Chairman Mao points out: "For the proletariat, the sharpest and most effective weapon is a serious and militant scientific attitude" ("Oppose Stereotyped Party Writing"). The
political party of the proletariat represents the fundamental
interests of the proletariat and the laboring people. In struggling for the seizure and consolidation of political power, it
relies on the correctness of its political line, the strong unity
of the Party, and the conscious revolutionary action of the
millions of the masses of the people. Nurtured with the thought
of Mao Tse-tung, the Chinese Communists have fine revolutionary traditions of doing mass work. In the course of the
prolonged democratic revolution and socialist revolution, our
Party has openly carried out ideological and political work
among the masses of the people, armed the heads of the masses
with Marxism-Leninism-Mao Tse-tung Thought, handed the
Party's line, principles, and policies to the masses, raised
their political consciousness to make them rise and strive
consciously for their own emancipation, and led them to struggle to fulfill the historical mission of the proletariat. Yet the
bourgeoisie and its agents, the revisionists in the Communist
Party, serve the interests of a handful of exploiters; and they
are opposed by the broad masses of the people. They can never accomplish their reactionary political aims without employing such means as fraud, conspiracy, speculation, and double-
dealing. Moreover, the exploiting classes and the revisionist

cliques are full of struggles for power and profit, tricks and plots. Their reactionary class nature and their counterrevolutionary political aims determine the viciousness and baseness of the patterns of their activities. In this sense, bourgeois politics and revisionist politics are precisely politics of intrigue and conspiracy.

Under the conditions of proletarian dictatorship, the struggle between the proletariat and the bourgeoisie and the struggle between the Marxist and the revisionist lines are still very acute, complex, and violent. But the ratio of class forces and the situation of class struggle have undergone revolutionary changes more favorable to the proletariat and unfavorable to the bourgeoisie. In our state of proletarian dictatorship, our Party is the core force leading our cause, and Marxism-Leninism-Mao Tse-tung Thought is the theoretical basis guiding our thinking. The close integration of the Party's strong leadership, Marxism-Leninism-Mao Tse-tung Thought, and the millions of the masses of the people has created a tremendous material force that enables the proletarian dictatorship to grow more consolidated and stronger day by day. Under these circumstances, it becomes more difficult for the class enemies at home, who were overthrown but have not yet been totally eliminated, and their representatives in the Party to subvert the proletarian dictatorship and restore capitalism by relying on overt counterrevolutionary sabotage activities. As a result, they have to pin greater hopes on intrigue and conspiracy in attaining their counterrevolutionary aims. Therefore, intrigue and conspiracy have become common tactics of opposition to the proletariat and the revolutionary people employed by landlords, rich peasants, counterrevolutionaries, bad elements, and rightists who have not been successfully remolded, as well as by class enemies who have wormed their way into the Party. They reflect a special characteristic of class struggle under the proletarian dictatorship.

Looking back on the history of proletarian dictatorship in the international Communist movement, we see clearly that in the Soviet Union the notorious Trotsky, Bukharin, and company

went all out to play vicious double-dealing in order to oppose
Marxism-Leninism. By the 1930s, as the socialist revolution
became deep-rooted, they eventually degenerated entirely into
secret agents who assassinated the leaders of the Party and
the people and who betrayed their motherland. They became
a counterrevolutionary clique of murderers. Khrushchev, the
No. 1 representative of modern revisionism, was known by all
as an old hand at intrigue, conspiracy, and counterrevolutionary
double-dealing. He adopted mean, shameless, and vicious tactics to disguise himself so as to win others' trust in him.
Once the opportunity ripened, he staged a counterrevolutionary
coup d'etat, usurped the leadership of the Soviet Communist
Party and the state, and restored capitalism. Khrushchev's
successor, Brezhnev, also used intrigue and conspiracy to
oust his predecessor from power, and has been practicing
Khrushchevism without Khrushchev. He has become an ambitious new tsar of the contemporary era. Clowns like Khrushchev
and Brezhnev have turned the first great socialist state founded
by Lenin into an aggressive social-imperialist power. This
historical lesson profoundly tells us that we must maintain
high vigilance against the intrigue and conspiracy of the small
handful of class enemies who wormed their way into the Party.
    Since the dictatorship of the proletariat was established in
our country, the bourgeoisie and its agents in the Party have
time and again used intrigue and conspiracy in a vain attempt
to realize their fond dream of restoring capitalism. This was
true for the Kao Kang and Jao Shu-shih anti-Party alliance and
the P'eng Te-huai anti-Party clique, and was even more true
for Liu Shao-ch'i and other swindlers like him who were exposed during the Great Proletarian Cultural Revolution. A
common trick used by these counterrevolutionary revisionist
chieftains in carrying out intrigue and conspiracy was to engage
in counterrevolutionary double-dealings. Chairman Mao once
pointed out incisively: "Feigning compliance while acting in
opposition, saying one thing while meaning another, and talking
nicely before other people while making trouble behind their
back — these are expressions of double-dealings." The

historical experience of class struggle at home and abroad
shows that these counterrevolutionary doubledealers are
vicious enemies of proletarian dictatorship.

On the basis of the historical experience of class struggle
at home and abroad and of the laws of class contradictions and
class struggle in socialist society, Chairman Mao points out
clearly: "Conspirators exist objectively, and this is not a
question of whether we like it or not." Chairman Mao teaches
us time and again that we must be particularly vigilant against
the bourgeois conspirators and careerists who worm their way
into the Party to stage a counterrevolutionary comeback. As
early as on the eve of the victory of the democratic revolution,
Chairman Mao stated at the Second Plenary Session of the
Seventh Party Central Committee that we must learn to wage
both overt and covert struggle against the enemies at home
and abroad. "We should be ready to deal lucidly with the tactics the other side will adopt, the tactics of Monkey, who gets
into the stomach of the Princess of the Iron Fan to play the
devil." In 1955, after the Kao Kang and Jao Shu-shih anti-
Party alliance was smashed, Chairman Mao again taught us
that we should be open and aboveboard in politics and that we
should never learn to play those tricks of Kao Kang and Jao
Shu-shih. In that same year, Chairman Mao, in his preface
and main notes to "The Materials on the Hu Feng Counterrevolutionary Clique," made a penetrating analysis and exposure
of a whole set of counterrevolutionary doubledealings adopted
by the Hu Feng clique. He asked the whole Party to "maintain
high vigilance in its various departments of work and to distinguish clearly the elements who feigned support of the revolution while actually opposing the revolution." In 1964, Chairman Mao, in his famous talk on the question of successors to
the proletarian revolution, stressed: "They must especially
watch out for careerists and conspirators like Khrushchev and
prevent such bad elements from usurping the leadership of the
Party and the state at any level." During the Great Proletarian
Cultural Revolution, Chairman Mao reminded us many times
to be vigilant against the intrigue and sabotage of the class

enemies at home and abroad, and called on us to "read and study seriously and have a good grasp of Marxism," and to see through and resist the evil wind and deceitful tactics of Liu Shao-ch'i and other swindlers in opposing the Party and the people. It is precisely due to Chairman Mao's wise leadership that the various intrigues and conspiracies of these bourgeois conspirators and careerists who frenziedly attempt to restore capitalism in China have been smashed one by one. Those who are versed in conspiracies and intrigues have also been put on the dock one by one to be judged by history.

We must maintain high vigilance against, and also pay attention to, the intrigues and conspiracies of all bourgeois representatives and all class enemies. This is because these counterrevolutionary doubledealers may sneak into our "stomach" to play the devil, and their sinister tactics of disguise and deceit may temporarily hoodwink a section of people. At the same time, we must despise them, because they run counter to the objective laws governing the advance of history and to the will of the millions upon millions of the people. They are feeble and powerless and are destined for total destruction. Chairman Mao points out: "All sly people, all those who do not have a scientific attitude in their work, fancy themselves resourceful and clever; but in fact they are most stupid and will come to no good" ("Rectify the Party's Style of Work"). The experience of class struggle tells us: No disguised enemy can hoodwink the revolutionary people for long. Since they have to do bad things and make trouble, they must show their true features in certain ways. To prepare public opinion for their counterrevolutionary activities, they will invariably try to sabotage the Party's line and policies, distort Marxism-Leninism-Mao Tse-tung Thought, and disguise idealism as materialism and metaphysics as dialectics. These things contradict their lip service to Marxism-Leninism-Mao Tse-tung Thought. As long as we uphold the proletarian Party spirit and Chairman Mao's proletarian revolutionary line and policies and raise our level of Marxism and class vigilance, we can see through the sinister activities of the counterrevolutionary double-dealers, and we can defend the correct line of Chairman Mao.

When opposing Bakunin's sabotage activities against the International Workers' Association, Marx and Engels emphatically pointed out: "In dealing with all these intrigues and conspiracies, there is only one method, only one with destructive power, that is, to make them public. When these intrigues and conspiracies are thoroughly exposed, they are deprived of any power" ("The Socialist Democratic League and the International Workers' Association"). All intrigues or conspiracies cannot stand the sunlight. Once they are uncovered, they show the abominable features of the plot originators. Hence, to continue to uncover and criticize penetratingly the counterrevolutionary revisionist line pushed by Liu Shao-ch'i and other swindlers like him and to expose thoroughly their intrigues and conspiracies are important ways of raising our consciousness of the line struggle, sharpening our revolutionary vigilance, and increasing our ability to distinguish between genuine and sham Marxism.

"Be open and aboveboard, and don't intrigue and conspire." This is our sharp ideological weapon for uncovering and beating the bourgeois conspirators and careerists. Since a handful of class enemies at home and abroad take intrigue and conspiracy as an important means of subverting the dictatorship of the proletariat, we must wage a tit-for-tat struggle against them by teaching the whole Party and the people of the whole country to be open and aboveboard. In this way, deprived of any opportunity, the class enemies will be effectively exposed, isolated, and overcome. Our Party will become more united and vigorous under the leadership of Chairman Mao and the Party Central Committee. And our great socialist revolution and socialist construction will flourish still further.

"The role of Communists as the vanguard and model is very important." Communists fighting on various fronts must consciously make themselves models of being open and aboveboard and become vanguards who fight resolutely against the bourgeois conspirators and careerists. Having dedicated their lives

to the fight for the emancipation of mankind and for the realization of communism, Communists have no personal interests
and aims other than those of the proletarian revolution and
those of the masses of the people, and no ulterior motives that
cannot be discussed. That is why they can be open and aboveboard, state their political views publicly at any time, and express their attitude of approval or objection on any important
political issue. If they say one thing in appearance and do another thing in practice, they will lose their Party spirit and
the required qualities of Communists.

Daring to uphold truth and to correct mistakes is an expression of a Communist being open and aboveboard. "Communists
must be ready at all times to stand up for the truth, because
truth is in the interests of the people" ("On Coalition Government"). Communists must fearlessly oppose all deeds which
are against the truth and harmful to the cause of proletarian
revolution, even if this means they themselves will be isolated
and temporarily attacked. At the same time, "Communists
must be ready at all times to correct their mistakes, because
mistakes are against the interests of the people" ("On Coalition
Government"). Communists must unswervingly and sternly
overcome all ideas and deeds which are incompatible with the
interests of the people. They should not, like the intriguers
and conspirators, feign self-examination in appearance while
secretly making trouble.

Communists must not only be open and aboveboard politically,
they must also be broad-minded and frank in their relationship
with comrades and in work style. They should not go in for the
bourgeois politicians' tactics of pulling and pushing. Liu Shao-
ch'i and other swindlers like him are good at playing such
tricks. They cater to the tastes of some people, indulge in
mutual flattery, promise official posts, and cultivate private
ties in order to serve the realization of their sinister aims.
Every Communist must understand their tactics and insist on
being open and aboveboard in all respects so as to resist and
uncover their intrigues and conspiracies and defeat them
thoroughly. If we can maintain high vigilance against the

intrigues and conspiracies of the enemy, and if we are open and aboveboard politically, organizationally, and in work style, then it will be possible that we will not be cheated or used by the enemy. No man is free from the slightest mistake, but it is possible for him not to make a mistake in line and not to be used by any bad element. The "theory that the line struggle is unknowable" and the "theory that it is impossible to avoid being cheated" are groundless.

Under the dictatorship of the proletariat and in the struggle between the two classes and between the two lines, whether or not we can be open and aboveboard is a critical test for the stand and world outlook of vast numbers of Party members. All Communist Party members, particularly the Party's high-level cadres, must follow Chairman Mao's teaching "Read and study seriously and have a good grasp of Marxism." They must make efforts to transform their world outlook, resolutely overcome all nonproletarian ideas, and consciously resist erosion by bourgeois ideas and styles. They must uphold Marxism and Party unity and be open and aboveboard. They must combat revisionism, splittist activities, intrigues, and conspiracies. They must always forge ahead vigorously along Chairman Mao's revolutionary line of continuous revolution.

17

GRASP MILITARY TRAINING ACCORDING TO
CHAIRMAN MAO'S LINE OF ARMY-BUILDING*

Party Committee of a Certain PLA
Regiment Stationed in Peking

The great leader Chairman Mao instructs us: "The whole
Party must pay attention to war and study military affairs" and
"Improve the military art." A series of instructions by Chairman Mao on strengthening military training are an important
component of Chairman Mao's line of army-building and a
fundamental guideline for improvement of military training and
for overall improvement of the fighting strength of the armed
forces. Only by carrying out strict training and setting strict
demands on the basis of Chairman Mao's army-building line
can we improve the political and military qualities of our army.
Chairman Mao has always emphasized the importance of
strengthening our army's ideological and political work, while
at the same time he has placed great stress on firmly grasping
military training under the command of politics. As early as
the time when our army was first founded, despite very difficult
circumstances and frequent battles, Chairman Mao still pointed
out that it was necessary to "try to avoid some battles in order
to find time for training." During the War of Resistance Against

---

*Chung-kuo jen-min chieh-fang-chün Pei-ching pu-tui mou
t'uan tang wei-hui, "An-chao Mao-chu-hsi chien-chün lu-hsien
chua-chin chün-shih hsün-lien." Hung-ch'i [Red Flag], No. 5
(May 1, 1972), 32-34.

Japan, Chairman Mao called on the whole Party to "pay attention to the study of military problems" and to "seek improvement in politics, organization, armament, technique, tactics,
and discipline." He stated: "Military consolidation and training
and political consolidation and training should be given equal
emphasis, and the two should be integrated." During the War
of Liberation, Chairman Mao again stressed: "Emphasis should
be put on military training during breaks in the fighting." After
the founding [of the Chinese People's Republic], Chairman
Mao again pointed out many times that only by undergoing strict
training and setting strict demands could the army fight. In
the past several decades, our armed forces have, in accordance
with Chairman Mao's teachings, strengthened political education, raised the consciousness of the line, firmly grasped military training, and improved the military art. [Because of this,
we have] succeeded in strengthening the overall fighting strength
of the armed forces, defeated vicious enemies of all kinds, and
fulfilled various fighting tasks entrusted to us by the Party and
the people.

Our army is armed with Marxism-Leninism-Mao Tse-tung
Thought, and is a people's army led by Chairman Mao and
the Communist Party. It has a high level of consciousness
of class struggle, of the line struggle, and of continuing the
revolution under the proletarian dictatorship. It has the brave,
self-sacrificial spirit of fearing neither hardship nor death.
This is the decisive factor for the strong fighting power of our
army. Meanwhile, a fine military art is also one of the important factors for our army's fighting power. We must understand and master Chairman Mao's principles of strategy and
tactics, handle skillfully the weapons in our hands, flexibly apply various techniques, and be good both in offense and in defense, in marching and in fighting. [Only by doing so] can we
score a big victory at a small cost in battle. Strenuously opposing Chairman Mao's army-building line, Liu Shao-ch'i and
swindlers like him said such absurd things as: It was not so
serious to have a lower standard of military training; military
techniques should not be studied exclusively, for they could be

picked up quickly when they are needed; and so on. This is
naked resistance and betrayal of Chairman Mao's instruction
on strengthening military training. They attempted in vain to
negate the importance of military training, abolish military
training, and weaken our army's fighting strength. If these
fallacies were not criticized, they would interfere with the overall implementation of preparation against war. After our Party
committee has conscientiously studied Chairman Mao's series
of directives on strengthening political and military work,
it will understand that politics must be in command of and lead
military affairs, but it cannot replace military affairs. Preparation against war and training must absolutely not be based
on the standpoint of a "lower standard," but should be based on
that of "early preparation" and "incessant quest for perfection."
Improvement of military techniques is absolutely not given by
heaven; it can only be developed and cultivated from the practice of political and military training guided by the thought of
Mao Tse-tung. Therefore, military training cannot be relaxed,
but should be grasped and intensified persistently. With Chairman Mao's teachings as the weapon, we have criticized the
various fallacies spread by Liu Shao-ch'i and swindlers like
him. Under the guidance of Chairman Mao's proletarian line
of army-building, we have not only seriously conducted political
education but also seriously carried out military training.

In order to raise awareness of proper military training on
the part of the broad masses of cadres and fighters, we continue to conduct education in Chairman Mao's proletarian line
of army-building to deal with some comrades' muddled ideas.
In the course of training, we pay attention to drawing the following lines of distinction. One is the line between revolutionary
heroism and championism. In military training, to work hard
to acquire the techniques for annihilating the enemy, to improve
the military quality of the armed forces, and to achieve good
records — all this should be encouraged and promoted. But
cultivating "superskills" for personal fame and material gain
should be opposed. If the idea of revolutionary heroism is also
opposed, the masses' activism for drilling will be undermined.

The second line is that between the preservation of necessary systems and formats and the promotion of "frills" and other formalistic things. All systems and formats that are compatible with actual war needs are summed up from practice and serve the content of training; they are indispensable. Those systems and formats which have been tested and found useful must not only be upheld but must also be firmly implemented repeatedly, while formalistic things incompatible with actual war needs must be criticized and eliminated. The third line is between the proper handling of advanced models and the haphazard presentation of "pacesetters." In the course of training, to grope for laws and to sum up and exchange experiences as a guide to overall training, we identify some advanced models, engage in needed evaluation and comparison, and make on-the-spot visits. This is a correct method of leadership. By emphasizing proper models, we can "light a lamp to illuminate a wide stretch" and provide cadres and fighters with an orientation for study and with an objective to achieve. This is fundamentally different from the practice of faking things, haphazardly summoning "pacesetters," and seeking "sensational surprises." The clarification of these demarcation lines will help cadres and fighters see clearly in training what is compatible with Chairman Mao's army-building line, and they should be upheld firmly. What runs counter to Chairman Mao's army-building line should be opposed in order to raise continuously their consciousness of good military training under the command of politics.

Chairman Mao has set up a series of guidelines, principles, and methods for our army's military training. They represent the scientific summing up of our army's combat and training experience over the past several decades. To train the army according to these guidelines, principles, and methods will enable us to improve the political and military quality of the armed forces. Liu Shao-ch'i and swindlers like him opposed Chairman Mao's guidelines, principles, and methods, undermined the glorious traditions of our military training, and interfered with and thwarted the firm implementation of Chairman

Mao's army-building line. In the course of intensifying military training, we have criticized black trash pushed by Liu Shao-ch'i and swindlers like him and trained the army strictly according to the guidelines, principles, and methods specified by Chairman Mao. We determine the content of a training program on the basis of actual war needs and teach cadres and fighters to "give first priority to improvement of the level of such techniques as shooting, bayonet charge, and hand-grenade throwing, and secondary priority to raising the level of tactics." Emphasis is placed on training in close combat and night fighting, swimming, and camping exercises; and the necessary time is set aside for systematic instruction ranging from single-soldier training to whole-battalion training. Concerning the methods of drilling, we follow Chairman Mao's teachings and widely promote military democracy by "unfolding a mass training movement where officers teach men, men teach officers, and men teach men." In every lesson of training, it is essential to arouse the masses to hold discussions in order to make everyone understand what and how to train and stick to the practice of "from the masses and to the masses" as a means of pooling the wisdom of the masses and improving the quality of training. We also pay attention to permeating the whole process of military training with Chairman Mao's military thinking, applying Chairman Mao's strategic and tactical principles to every military subject, combining learning with drilling, and deepening the understanding of Chairman Mao's military thinking through practice. For instance, when organizing companies to stage tactical exercises, we took them to Hsin-pao-an, the battlefield where the Thirty-Fifth Army of the Kuomintang was annihilated during the War of Liberation. There we conscientiously studied Chairman Mao's thesis: "Concentrate a superior force and annihilate the enemies one by one"; "select a relatively weak point (not two points) of the various battle positions of enemy troops and launch a fierce attack to conquer it without fail"; and so on. Leading comrades who had participated in that war were invited to recount the battle history, how our army applied Chairman Mao's strategic and tactical principles to wiping out the enemy, and how their own units, in accordance with Chairman Mao's teachings, chose the attack spots and concentrated superior forces to launch a violent attack on the enemy and win the victory. Later, we organized the unit to stage tactical exercises in light of the combat conditions in those years. Through the study of battles and on-the-spot exercises, everyone acquired a deeper understanding of Chairman Mao's strategic and tactical principles about concentration of superior forces in fighting battles of annihilation, and both cadres and fighters have raised their strategic and tactical levels.

In doing military training well in accordance with Chairman Mao's army-building line, we must carry out strict training and strict demands. Military affairs are a science. "There is no flat and broad path in science." We must be prepared to overcome great difficulties and work arduously. If we do not experience strict training and strict demands and just try to avoid work and find an easy way out, no real skills can be acquired. In time of war, fighting between the enemy and ourselves is very severe and complicated, and it becomes an overall test for the political and military quality of our army. If we are a bit lax in peacetime training, then in fighting we cannot cope well with various complicated situations and will muddle important things and will suffer a great deal. Only by imposing on ourselves strict training and strict demands without any compromise can we really master military science and improve our skills for defeating all enemies. In order to train our army rigorously, we persist in training it in accordance with how battles should be fought. Every crucial lesson of combat techniques required by actual war needs must be practiced repeatedly. Conditions likely to appear in war should be perceived in a more complicated way, so that more training and exercises can be carried out for each situation and every kind of terrain. For instance, once during a winter field-camping exercise, the weather suddenly changed. Snow fell heavily and the air temperature dropped to over thirty degrees below zero. We took this as a very good opportunity for rigorous training of our army, and we decided to organize the unit to make a long-distance "raid." We also arranged a training program in line with actual war needs. Fully equipped, the cadres and fighters of the whole regiment braved wind and snow and marched 160 li nonstop for a day and night on a plateau 1,000-odd meters above sea level. During the march, various tactical and technical maneuvers were attempted. Thus, the unit not only trained in the revolutionary spirit of fearing neither hardship nor death but also raised the level of its military techniques. The comrades said: "Though this kind of training is a bit tiring, we have received a rigorous tempering."

To grasp well military training in compliance with Chairman Mao's army-building line is an important task of the Party committee. "The Party should give military work positive attention and discussions." If a perfunctory attitude is taken toward military training, the Party actually abandons its leadership over military work. We demand that every Party committee member concern himself with military work, share his labor but not his household belongings, grasp military and political affairs simultaneously, and strengthen energetically ideological and political work in the course of military training. To guarantee implementation of military training, our Party committee should make overall plans and unified arrangements for all items of work and make military training an important part of the Party committee's work plan, so as to ensure effective leadership of the Party over military work. By doing so, we have [specific] arrangements for each plan, safeguards for its timetable, and personnel in charge of organization. [Work is] constantly studied and examined to make sure military training is effectively carried out. In the final analysis, whether or not military training is well grasped is a question of consciousness of the line. Only by raising consciousness of implementing Chairman Mao's proletarian line of army-building can we distinguish between right and wrong, eliminate interference from the "Left" or the Right, and consciously grasp military training for the consolidation of the proletarian dictatorship. We must firmly grasp the line as the key link and, through "reading and studying conscientiously and mastering Marxism-Leninism," we must strengthen education in ideology and the political line, incessantly raise the consciousness of the line struggle, do well in military training, and fight for the overall improvement of the fighting power of the armed forces.

18

THE MASSES ARE THE MAKERS OF HISTORY*

Tien Chih-sung

Who makes history? The heroes or the slaves? This is a basic question underlying the long-continued struggle between the idealist and the materialist conceptions of history.

To preserve their reactionary rule, the exploiting classes have for thousands of years invariably resorted to reversing history by propagating the idealist conception of history, the conception that history is made by heroes. A few heroes belonging to the exploiting classes have been referred to by them as "talents by natural endowment," or identified with "god's will" and as makers of history. On the other hand, the masses have been branded the "mob," who can only put themselves at the mercy of the heroes, or worse still, "inert matter" holding back historical progress.

From this reactionary fallacy it follows that in a society under the dictatorship of the exploiting classes, the development of history is decided by the will of a handful of rulers representing the interests of the exploiting classes, whereas the exploited and oppressed working masses must succumb to the rulers, put up with slavery, and do nothing but appeal to heaven and look forward to the advent of the "savior." This idealist conception of history is the very spiritual shackle that keeps the laboring people in bondage.

---

*Peking Review, No. 29 (July 21, 1972), 7-11.

Reversing the Reversal of History

The emergence of Marxism brought to light for the first time the objective laws governing the development of mankind's history; it scientifically proved the great truth that history is made by the slaves. Reversing the history the exploiting classes have reversed, Marxism thus brought about the utter bankruptcy of the idealist conception of history and uprooted the theoretical basis of thousands of years of reactionary rule by the exploiting classes. Chairman Mao, in leading the Chinese revolution, has from time to time educated all Party members and cadres, the proletariat, and other working people in the basic viewpoint of historical materialism, i.e., the masses are the makers of history. He has at the same time waged a protracted struggle against historical idealism of all descriptions. In addition to the mass line he has worked out for our Party, Chairman Mao's teachings that "the masses have boundless creative power," that "we must have faith in the masses and we must have faith in the Party," and that "the masses are the real heroes, while we ourselves are often childish and ignorant" are all pointed criticisms of the idealist conception of history, which the slave-owner class, the landlord class, and the capitalist class have long spread to deny the fact that history is made by slaves.

All exploiting classes, however, will by no means make their exit from the stage of history of their own accord. Nor will they easily give up their reactionary theories after being overthrown by the revolutionary people. That Liu Shao-ch'i and other political swindlers like him have used idealist apriorism as their anti-Party theoretical program and propagated the idealist conception of history, the conception that history is made by heroes, is yet another clear reflection of the struggle between the two classes and the two lines in the course of China's socialist revolution. And when this fallacy was mercilessly exposed and forcefully repudiated by the people throughout the country, they again produced another fallacy that "history is made jointly by both heroes and slaves." Their vain attempt was to use dualist sophistry to negate the basic principle of Marxism.

In philosophy, dualism postulates that spirit and matter are two independent and parallel principles of the universe; the "theory of history being made jointly by both heroes and slaves," which Liu Shao-ch'i and his kind propounded, regards heroes and masses as two independent and parallel motive forces in the making of history.

But does this mean that this so-called "theory" really acknowledges the role of the masses in the making of history? Not at all. In the eyes of Liu Shao-ch'i and those like him, the common people are only concerned about "getting rich and leading a happy life," and all the workers want is to "work less and earn more." As they see it, the masses are just money-hungry rabble who have nothing to do with the making of history. The representatives of the exploiting classes, on the other hand, are said to be "men with foresight and prescience"; and, so they say, a nation "owes its existence, its revival after decline, and its rebirth after ruin to them." Comparing their praise of the representatives of the exploiting classes and slander of the masses, one can see clearly that the preposterous theory of "history being made jointly by both heroes and slaves" is only the idealist conception of history in disguise.

If one denies that slaves or the masses are the makers of history, one inevitably acknowledges that heroes make history. But Liu Shao-ch'i and his like, in trumpeting the "theory of history being made jointly by both heroes and slaves," reconciled the two diametrically opposed viewpoints to each other so that there are both heroes and masses in the making of history. It sounds most impartial. Characteristic of all political swindlers, it is, however, plausible sophistry.

Ever since the dissolution of the primeval communal ownership of land, as Engels pointed out, all history has been a history of class struggle, "of struggles between exploited and exploiting, between dominated and dominating classes at various stages of social development" (Manifesto of the Communist Party, "Preface to the German Edition of 1883"). The mode of production of the social material means is the material basis for historical development. In all societies, the contradiction between the forces of production and the relations of production is the fundamental contradiction. The development of the productive forces brings about a change in the relations of production, advancing the replacement of one mode of production by another and the development of a social system from lower to higher stages.

"The greatest productive power is the revolutionary class itself" (Karl Marx, The Poverty of Philosophy). In class society, the contradiction between the productive forces and the relations of production is manifested in the struggle between the revolutionary classes standing for the development of the social productive forces and the reactionary classes which want to preserve the old relations of production; here, the masses are the decisive force in the class struggle. All social change is the outcome of revolutionary struggles by the masses. All advanced thinking and theories are the epitome of these struggles and mirror the revolutionary will of the masses; all science and technology are the crystallization of the practical experience of the masses; all progressive culture and art stem from the life of the people, which is full of struggle. Without the masses' struggle for production, a society cannot possibly exist, still less can history develop. In class society, without the class struggle of the masses, the development of history is also out of the question. "The people, and the people alone, are the motive force in the making of world history." This is an irrefutable truth.

The Role of Heroes

What, then, should be the proper approach to the role of heroes? Can it be that historical materialism negates their role in history? Absolutely not. Marxism has never denied this. On the contrary, it holds that their role is quite a big one. The crux of the matter is: What is meant by heroes? How to assess their role in its true light? And what should be

the approach in handling the relationship between the role of
heroes and the masses who make history? It is these questions on which we fundamentally differ from Liu Shao-ch'i and
his ilk, and where an acute struggle exists.

In class society, heroes have a nature pertaining to their
own class; there is no such thing as a hero who transcends
classes. Each class has its own conception of heroes. To the
proletariat and other working masses, heroes are outstanding
figures who can only emerge from the people's revolutionary
struggles, who represent the interests of the masses, and
who, in line with the direction in which history develops, help
propel history forward. The emergence of such heroes is exactly a manifestation of the making of history by the masses.
In contrast, the exploiting classes regard those exponents who
can best preserve the interests of their own classes and the
system of exploitation as "heroes." The reactionary ruling
classes certainly do not recognize the heroes of the proletariat.
And the proletariat and the masses certainly do not accept the
exponents of the reactionary ruling classes as heroes. For
instance, in modern Chinese history, Hung Hsiu-ch'üan, a leader of the Revolutionary Movement of the Taiping Heavenly
Kingdom who fought imperialist aggression and Ch'ing dynasty
feudal rule, is acknowledged as a hero by the proletariat and
other working people. But the reactionary ruling classes curse
him, calling him a "traitor." At the same time, they laud Tseng
Kuo-fan, who, in collaboration with imperialism, suppressed the
Revolutionary Movement of the Taiping Heavenly Kingdom, as
a "hero." But the proletariat and the masses take him for what
he was: a lackey, a traitor who was dead set on preserving the
reactionary rule of the landlord class.

In the opinion of the proletariat, as Chairman Mao has said:
"To die for the people is weightier than Mount Tai, but to work
for the fascists and die for the exploiters and oppressors is
lighter than a feather." This fundamental opposition between
conceptions about heroes is determined by the fundamental
opposition of interests between the exploiting and exploited
classes. An exploiting class has its periods of ebb and flow;

because its place in history varies in different periods, the role in history of its exponents in different periods is also not the same.

Heroes do not come from nowhere; they are the outcome of history in progress, of class struggle. Marx pointed out: "Every social epoch needs its great men, and when it does not find them, it invents them, as Helvetius says" (The Class Struggles in France 1848-1850). The history of mankind has fully borne out this scientific thesis. Hailed by Karl Marx as the most spectacular man in ancient history, Spartacus of ancient Rome was an ordinary slave by origin. The revolutionary storm of the slave-insurgents, however, made him a hero, who, with thousands of men under his command, made an onslaught against the slave system. At the close of the Ch'in dynasty, Chen Sheng and Wu Kuang came from the ranks of ordinary peasants. But aggravated class contradictions and large-scale peasant uprisings compelled them to rise in rebellion, and thus they became leaders of these uprisings.

Even in bourgeois revolutions, there were quite a few outstanding persons who came from the masses. Many talented generals of the French Revolution were, before the revolution, ordinary men — an actor, a typesetter, a barber, a dyer, a peddler, a subaltern — all of whom were looked down upon. But for the revolution, how could such people turn out to be outstanding military commanders? "A sympton of every real revolution," Lenin said, "is a rapid, tenfold, and even hundredfold increase in the number of the toiling and oppressed masses . . . who are capable of waging the political struggle" ("Left-wing" Communism, an Infantile Disorder). This kind of thing is even more common and more obvious in a proletarian revolution. All this testifies to the fact that heroes in various periods are those who come to the fore to answer the needs of the struggles of the masses; that every time history presents a new task of struggle, heroes who lead the masses in it are bound to emerge.

Heroes Are Born of the Masses

Marxism holds that the reason why heroes can play an

important part in history is that, in the last analysis, they represent the interests of the revolutionary classes and the progressive forces, because they mirror the people's demands and,
therefore, have their support. Whoever he is, any hero or
great man draws his strength only from the masses. He who
fails to reflect the demands of the masses gets nowhere. "It
is man's social being," said Chairman Mao, "that determines
his thinking. Once the correct ideas characteristic of the advanced class are grasped by the masses, these ideas turn into
a material force which changes society and changes the world."

It is imperative that a hero should represent the advanced
class, rightly reflect the objective demands of social development, and engage in the concrete revolutionary practice of
transforming society and the world. This is at the core of the
question. The fallacy that "history is made jointly by both
heroes and slaves," however, denies this fundamental question
of principle, the question of which class is to be represented.
This is, of course, idealist sophistry vainly trying to combine
the two classes, the revolutionary class and the reactionary
class, into one.

Heroes of the proletariat and the revolutionary masses are
founders of revolutionary ideas or their disseminators; they
are also organizers of revolutionary struggles. Compared
with the rank and file, they aim higher and are more far-
sighted. Whether they are able to concentrate the wisdom of
the masses or not and whether their leadership is correct or
not have much to do with the success or failure of their struggles. As has often been the case in history, although there is
every possibility of a struggle succeeding and winning victory,
it fails in the end because its leaders are not good at making
use of these possibilities. This shows that heroes exert a
considerable influence on quickening or slowing down the making of history by the masses. However, they can only affect
the tempo but not change the direction of historical progress.
Heroes are born of revolutionary struggles and can play their
roles only when they are with the masses. Advanced ideas
and theories are a reflection of the demand of the masses for

revolution and an epitome of their experience in struggle; they will become a material force advancing history only when they are grasped by the masses.

In his article "The Bankruptcy of the Idealist Conception of History," Chairman Mao pointed out with penetrating insight: "The reason why Marxism-Leninism has played such a great role in China since its introduction is that China's social conditions call for it, that it has been linked with the actual practice of the Chinese people's revolution, and that the Chinese people have grasped it. Any ideology — even the very best, even Marxism-Leninism itself — is ineffective unless it is linked with objective realities, meets objectively existing needs, and has been grasped by the masses of the people. We are historical materialists, opposed to historical idealism." These words have completely exploded the idealist conception of history.

There have been many heroes in history who at first made revolution and indeed became quite influential; they later became divorced from the masses and eventually suffered defeat or lapsed, only to be forsaken and forgotten by the masses.

Among the bourgeois revolutionaries, such heroes are quite many. During the French Revolution, Robespierre was in the limelight for a time. The Jacobins he represented, with a view to rallying the strength of the masses for their own use, tried at the beginning of the revolution somewhat firmly to satisfy some popular demands (the peasants' demand for land, for instance). They were thus able to enlist popular support and, with revolutionary spirit, sent Louis XVI to the guillotine. But Robespierre was, after all, a bourgeois revolutionary. No sooner was the revolution won, than he started to ignore the interests of the masses, and even worse, he suppressed them. The result was he lost their support and became powerless to withstand the forces of reaction that struck back. He himself was finally sent to the guillotine by the reactionary forces. Then there was Chang Tai-yen. During the Chinese Revolution of 1911, he was hunted down seven times and thrice thrown into prison, but his revolutionary will never subsided. For a time he was able to play a big role in the revolution, having a strong influence among the people. But, after the revolution, he secluded himself from the times and the people, lost his revolutionary vitality, and soon faded out of the memory of the majority of the people.

This characteristic of bourgeois revolutionaries is determined by their class nature. Even during the period of struggle against feudalism, although the bourgeoisie were at one, in part and temporarily, with the working masses in opposing the feudal system, the two basically opposed each other as far as their class interests were concerned. In the course of revolution, bourgeois revolutionaries, confined to their narrow class interests, are afraid of the masses; they often waver, appease the enemy, and even betray the people. Their antagonism to the masses, which is fundamental, becomes obvious daily after the seizure of political power. This accounts for the fact that although the bourgeois revolutions in the eighteenth and nineteenth centuries were led by representatives of the bourgeoisie, the masses remained the principal forces of the revolution.

If the task of the bourgeois democratic revolution is to be fulfilled relatively completely, it is necessary to rely on the masses to overcome its leaders' proneness to conciliation which is reactionary in nature; it is also necessary to rely on the masses to wage repeated struggles and frustrate the attacks and attempts at a comeback by the reactionary forces. In the course of proletarian revolution there are also many fellow travellers who, when the revolution develops to a certain stage, draw to a halt, drop out of the revolution, and even become turncoats. These people are in essence bourgeois revolutionaries. As to those reactionary ringleaders who act counter to the historical current and set themselves against the people, they are obstacles to the progress of history. The masses will have to topple them if history is to continue its advance.

All this speaks well for the fact that it is not the heroes who make history but the other way round, and that history, instead

of being "made jointly by both heroes and slaves," is made by
the slaves alone.

The Role of Proletarian Leaders

Proletarian leaders represent mankind's most revolutionary
and most advanced class. There is a difference in principle
between them and the outstanding historical figures of other
classes. Representing the fundamental interest of the proletariat and other working people, they consistently maintain the
closest ties with the broad masses and penetratingly sum up
the experience of the masses in struggle. Proficient in the
laws of historical development, they have mastered the science
of Marxism and applied it in revolutionary practice. They
therefore are most far-sighted and most thoroughgoing in
revolution, and do not have the kind of class limitations which
the outstanding historical figures of other classes cannot overcome. Proletarian leaders, for these reasons, are able to
bring into play, to the greatest extent possible, the role of the
masses as the makers of history. They enjoy high prestige
among the masses, prestige built up in prolonged revolutionary struggles. This big historical role of proletarian heroes
makes all heroes of the past pale beside them.

Is it correct then to come to the conclusion that, in the period of proletarian revolution, "history is made jointly by
both heroes and slaves"? The answer is still no. Proletarian
leaders are leaders and organizers of the activities of the proletariat and the masses in the making of history. Their emergence and the establishment of their thought constitute a very
important part of the process of history-making by the proletariat and the masses, and are the product of that process
having developed to a certain stage, not something isolated
from that process. Chairman Mao has pointed out explicitly
in "On Practice" that Marxist theory of revolution was created
at a time when practice in revolutionary struggle by the proletariat had developed into its second period, "the period of
conscious and organized economic and political struggles."

The Marxist viewpoint that the masses are the motive force in the making of history has, therefore, fully confirmed the great historical role of the revolutionary leaders as representatives of the advanced class. Liu Shao-ch'i and his like, in propounding the fallacy that "history is made jointly by both heroes and slaves," regard "heroes" as something outside and above "the people" so as to distort and degrade the leaders of the proletariat and build up their own image. Herein lies the essential difference between the two.

Marxism holds that the masses are the makers of history. This does not imply in the least the cult of the spontaneity of mass movements. Liu Shao-ch'i and his like, while propagating the idealist conception of history, the conception that history is made by heroes, also propagated the fallacy that any mass movement is "naturally rational." This is a variation of the "theory of spontaneity" which Marxism strongly repudiated long ago. It has nothing in common with the historical materialist principle that history is made by the masses. Any mass struggle, without correct leadership and a correct line to follow, can neither last long nor achieve any result. The proletarian revolution is a great earthshaking revolution aimed at wiping out the system of exploitation. No revolution in the past can be compared with this revolutionary struggle in depth and extent. Thus it needs all the more to be armed by advanced thinking and the strong leadership of its own leaders and vanguard organization; guidance by a correct line also becomes more important. The correctness or incorrectness of the ideological and political line decides everything. The history of the Chinese revolution is a history showing how Chairman Mao's correct line has struggled against and defeated the "left" and right opportunist lines at different times. Without the correct line which Chairman Mao has worked out for us, there can be no victory for the Chinese revolution. To propagate the "theory of spontaneity" during the period of proletarian revolution is to oppose directly Marxist leadership over the mass movement and to deny the decisive importance of a correct ideological and political line for the success of the revolutionary cause; it is only an attempt to lead the mass movement astray.

* * *

In making history, the masses have traversed a course of gradually developing from being unaware to being aware. The founding of the Marxist materialist conception of history showed the objective laws of the development of society and history, bringing the role of the masses in making history to a new stage and opening up a broad avenue for mankind to leave the realm of necessity in which man is blindly at the disposal of history and to enter the realm of freedom in which man will consciously handle history. As Chairman Mao has put it, "The epoch of world communism will be reached when all mankind voluntarily and consciously changes itself and the world." So that this day will come, the proletariat and revolutionary people still need to go through arduous and tortuous struggles, which must be led by a proletarian political party if it is to win victory. The mass line formulated by Chairman Mao for our Party requires us to have faith in the masses, to rely on them, respect their initiative, learn wholeheartedly from them, and, at the same time, to indefatigably educate them in Marxism-Leninism, steadily raise their level of political consciousness, and lead them to forge ahead. Lenin said: "A party is the vanguard of a class, and its duty is to lead the masses and not merely to reflect the average political level of the masses" ("The Extraordinary All-Russia Congress of Soviets of Peasants' Deputies"). Uphold the Marxist principle that the masses are the makers of history and adhere to the Party leadership — this is the only way to ensure that our revolutionary cause will continue to move ahead victoriously along the correct path.

IV From the "Criticize Lin Piao" to the "Criticize Lin Piao and Confucius" Campaigns

19

SPEECH AT THE CONCLUSION OF THE STUDY CLASS
FOR CADRES OF THE YUNNAN PROVINCIAL PARTY
COMMITTEE AND THE KUNMING MILITARY
REGION PARTY COMMITTEE (February 6, 1972)

Wang Pi-ch'eng

Absolutely Secret
(Based on Minutes)

Comrades:

The study class for cadres organized by our Provincial Committee and the Military Region Party Committee is coming to its conclusion today after ten days' work that began on January 28. Among a total of 1,851 participants, 841 are from the military system and 1,010 from the local civilian sector. This study class has conscientiously transmitted and discussed Central Committee Document No. 4 personally authorized for issuance by Chairman Mao and has conducted a thorough criticism of the counterrevolutionary program "Outline of

---

*"Wang Pi-ch'eng t'ung-chih tsai Yün-nan sheng-wei ho K'un-ming chün-ch'ü tang-wei kan-pu hsüeh-hsi pan chieh-shu shih ti chiang-hua." A Xerox copy of this document is available at the Gardner Collection of the Brown University Library. The speaker is commander of the Kunming Military Region and concurrently second secretary of the Provincial Party Committee and first vice chairman of the Provincial Revolutionary Committee.

'Project 571'" concocted by Lin Piao and his followers. At
the beginning of the study class, Comrade Chou Hsing read and
explained Central Committee Document No. 4 on behalf of
the Provincial Party Committee and the Military Region Party
Committee and criticized Lin Piao's counterrevolutionary program, thereby taking the lead in and preparing the ground for
our study. During the study period all participants repeatedly
and earnestly discussed Central Committee Document No. 4.
With an intense proletarian indignation, and using Marxism-
Leninism-Mao Tse-tung Thought as the weapon, they criticized
Lin Piao's counterrevolutionary program point by point and
paragraph by paragraph and denounced it in general meetings.
The comrades participating in the study class have taken a
serious attitude and concentrated their efforts on studying and
analyzing the document conscientiously; they have actively
thrown themselves into the battle of great criticism and have
produced good results. Through study and criticism all participating comrades have further enhanced their levels of political consciousness and political sensitivity. They have also
studied the specific arrangements for transmitting and discussing Central Committee Document No. 4 and summed up the
experience of the great criticism, thus laying a solid foundation
for all army units in the region and the entire province in transmitting the document, in criticizing bandit Lin Piao's counterrevolutionary program, and in cultivating and training backbone
cadres. In the following, I shall talk about three issues.

I. A Basic Evaluation of the Study Class

Based on the general reaction of the participants, the study
class is a success. Although its time period is relatively short,
the results have been very impressive. An in-depth education
in ideological and political line has been carried out, and the
consciousness of class struggle, struggle between lines, and
continuous revolution under the proletarian dictatorship has
been elevated.

1) The class hatred toward bandit Lin and his followers has

been further aroused and the proletarian affection for our great leader Chairman Mao deepened. Through study and criticism everybody has seen all the more clearly the counterrevolutionary, heinous features of the careerist, conspirator, renegade, and traitor Lin Piao. All participants have said: "Lin Piao's counterrevolutionary program is a violence-charged, blood-dripping fascist program, a full record of his scheme to overturn heaven and earth by the landlords, rich peasants, reactionaries, bad elements and Rightists, and ironclad proof of their collusion with foreign powers to sell out their own country for personal glory." Lin Piao and his followers viciously attacked and slandered our great leader Chairman Mao, used the utterly inhuman Gestapo techniques of fascism, and plotted in dark corners to assassinate our great leader Chairman Mao and overthrow the Party Central authority led by Chairman Mao. This is indeed a monstrous crime that cannot be redeemed even by his death. By reviewing the history of our Party's revolutionary struggle over the last fifty years, through a comparison and contrast between the old society before the liberation and the new society it has brought about, and by way of underscoring the superiority of the socialist system under the proletarian dictatorship in our country, all participants have further deepend their realization that Chairman Mao's leadership is the greatest blessing to the whole Party, the whole army, and all the people, that Chairman Mao's leadership and the direction of his revolutionary line are the fundamental guarantees for making progress in our various enterprises and for winning victories at all times, and that Lin Piao and his followers who had rabidly defamed and cursed our great leader Chairman Mao were no other than our sworn enemies. We must show a still greater love for Chairman Mao, defend Chairman Mao with concrete actions, defend the Party Central authorities headed by Chairman Mao, defend Chairman Mao's proletarian revolutionary line, and wage a resolute struggle against the Lin-Ch'en anti-Party clique to the end.

2) A better understanding has been acquired of the substance and great significance of the struggle against the Lin-Ch'en

anti-Party clique. As a result, the determination and confidence
of all in carrying this struggle through to the very end has been
further solidified. By criticizing the counterrevolutionary
program of Lin Piao and company, as well as their ten major
crimes for implementing this program, all participants have
realized that the criminal objective of Lin Piao and his followers in staging a counterrevolutionary coup d'etat was to subvert the proletarian dictatorship and restore capitalism. The
struggle to smash the Lin-Ch'en anti-Party clique is a major
task that affects the destiny and future of our Party and state.
It thus carries a far-reaching significance in propelling forward
the socialist revolution and socialist construction. As our comrades have said, Lin Piao and his followers represented the
rotten and decaying reactionaries. Although they attempted in
vain to turn back the wheel of history, they turned out to be a
mantis trying to stop a cart; they invited their own destruction.
All participants have expressed their resolve to transmit successfully Central Committee Document No. 4, to thoroughly
mobilize the masses, and to develop the great criticism campaign in a deep-going way. All are determined to fight this
battle well and criticize deeply and penetratingly Lin Piao and
his followers' counterrevolutionary program of coup d'etat.

3) The capacity for identifying counterrevolutionary double-
dealers has been further enhanced. In the course of criticism,
comrades compared and contrasted Lin Piao's public speeches
and conduct in the past, on the one hand, with his counterrevolutionary coup plan, on the other. As a result, they have seen
all the more clearly Lin Piao's ugly features as a counterrevolutionary double-dealer. This fellow Lin Piao, who glibly
shouted such phrases as "hold high," "follow closely," and "be
most loyal," turned out to be a hypocrite with honey dripping
from his tongue but daggers concealed in his heart, a careerist
with a smile dipped in treachery. He was a renegade and traitor who raised the flag of support for the Chairman and held
up the signboard of the Communist Party but in fact harbored
extreme hatred for Chairman Mao, the Communist Party and
the socialist system under the proletarian dictatorship in our

country. Everybody has deeply recognized that guarding against capitalist conspirators and careerists and identifying counterrevolutionary double-dealers under the conditions of the proletarian dictatorship is a very important problem. To solve this problem, it is imperative to follow the teaching of Chairman Mao "Read and study conscientiously and have a good grasp of Marxism" and to improve the ability to distinguish genuine from sham Marxism. It is also imperative to carry out in earnest Chairman Mao's important instructions on the "three dos and three don'ts," to persevere in Marxism and oppose revisionism, to persevere in unity and oppose splittism, and to persevere in being open and aboveboard and in opposing intrigues and conspiracies, so as to smash resolutely the counterrevolutionary conspiratorial activities of the Lin-Ch'en anti-Party clique, to grasp firmly class struggle, and to solidify the proletarian dictatorship.

4) The conscious implementation and defense of Chairman Mao's revolutionary line has been further enhanced. Through study and criticism everybody has come to the understanding that the ringleaders of all opportunist lines always attempt to substitute their revisionist line for the Party's correct line in order to change the proletarian character of the Party. Lin Piao and his followers were no exceptions. Through the criticism of Lin Piao's counterrevolutionary program and his slanders and assaults in the three areas of situation, line, and policy, we have deepend our realization that the central issue of the struggle is the question of line. Everybody has come to appreciate that the excellent situation is the result of implementing the correct line and that Party policies are the concrete expressions of the revolutionary line. The correctness or incorrectness of the ideological and political line decides everything. As repeatedly proved by the historical experience of our Party during the last half century, Chairman Mao's revolutionary line reflects the objective laws of historical development, represents the fundamental interests of the proletariat and the masses of the laboring people. It is the lifeline of the

whole Party, army, and people. All participants have expressed their earnest desire to raise their "three types of consciousness" through the education in ideological and political line and to march daringly forward along Chairman Mao's revolutionary line.

Although this study class has accomplished these things, owing to the shortage of time, the study made of Central Committee Document No. 4 and the criticism of bandit Lin's counterrevolutionary program are only a beginning. Now that this study session has been concluded, we must continue our study and criticism together with the vast masses, and we must do a good job of transmitting and discussing Central Committee Document No. 4, in order to score still greater victories in the struggle to smash the Lin-Ch'en anti-Party clique.

II. Deepen Our Understanding of the Great Significance of Transmitting and Discussing Central Committee Document No. 4 and Be Resolute in Criticizing Deeply and Thoroughly Lin Piao's Counterrevolutionary Program

Central Committee Document No. 4, personally authorized for issuance by our great leader Chairman Mao, is an extremely important document. With a mass of facts the document has fully exposed Lin Piao and company's heinous crime of conspiring to stage a counterrevolutionary armed coup d'etat. Using Marxism-Leninism-Mao Tse-tung Thought as the weapon, it criticizes thoroughly the counterrevolutionary program "Outline of 'Project 571'" concocted by Lin Piao and his followers, and it points out clearly the direction to follow while also raising new and greater demands for developing a step further the great criticism of the Lin-Ch'en anti-Party clique by the whole Party, army, and people. Earnestly transmitting and discussing Central Committee Document No. 4 and thoroughly criticizing Lin Piao's counterrevolutionary program is a continuation and deepening of the study of Central Committee Documents Nos. 68 and 77. It is another important battle in the struggle to smash the Lin-Ch'en anti-Party clique.

Serious and effective implementation of the transmission and
discussion will have an important and far-reaching impact on
repudiating thoroughly the counterrevolutionary revisionist
line of the Lin-Ch'en anti-Party clique, on heightening the consciousness of the commanders and fighters of all army units
of the region and the masses of the people of all nationalities
in the province concerning class struggle, struggle between
lines, and continuing the revolution under the proletarian dictatorship, and on solidifying the proletarian dictatorship itself
and forestalling the restoration of capitalism.

Based on the experience of this study class, to successfully
transmit and discuss Central Committee Document No. 4 and
to criticize deeply and penetratingly Lin Piao's counterrevolutionary program, it is necessary to grasp firmly the issue
of comprehension. In other words, we must fully understand
that to mobilize the whole Party, army, and people to deepen
the criticism of Lin Piao's counterrevolutionary program is a
great strategic arrangement of Chairman Mao. It fully reflects
Chairman Mao's confidence in and concern for the vast masses
of workers, peasants, and soldiers, and it fully attests to the
greatness, splendor and correctness of our Party.

A Marxist always values the usefulness of negative educational materials. In their struggle against their enemies,
Marx, Engels, Lenin, and Stalin always used public criticism
of such educational materials in educating the Party, the proletariat, and the vast laboring masses and in elevating the level
of Marxist-Leninist consciousness of the vast numbers of
Party members and the masses. Such was the case when Marx
and Engels struggled against such sham socialists and opportunists as Proudon, Lassalle, Dühring, and Bakunin. This was
also what Lenin and Stalin did in their struggle against old
revisionists and renegades of the proletariat such as Bernstein, Kautsky, Plekhanov, Trotsky, and Bukharin. In the
course of criticizing the renegade Kautsky, Lenin heard people say that in Berlin almost nobody was aware of Kautsky's
little pamphlet entitled The Dictatorship of the Proletariat.
Then Lenin said:

> I would like to suggest that our ambassadors in Germany
> and Switzerland try to purchase a copy of his book, even
> at a great cost, and pass it to conscious workers as a gift,
> so that they could repudiate this "Europeanized" (should
> read: "imperialist and reformist") social-democrat who
> has long since turned into a "stinking corpse."

In leading us to struggle against domestic and foreign class
enemies, our great leader Chairman Mao has particularly
valued teachers by negative example, and he is very capable
of grasping negative materials to expose the enemies and educate the masses. In 1955 a large quantity of materials on the
Hu Feng counterrevolutionary clique were published during
the campaign against it. Chairman Mao himself wrote a preface entitled, "Materials Pertaining to the Hu Feng Counterrevolutionary Clique," as well as the major comments, thus
pointing out the direction the great mass movement should follow to sweep clean the hidden counterrevolutionaries and providing us with an effective weapon for identifying and uncovering all counterrevolutionary double-dealers. In 1957, to
counter the feverish assault launched by the bourgeois Rightists against the Party, negative materials were also first published in the newspapers to expose the reactionary features of
the bourgeois Rightists in broad daylight, before the masses
were mobilized to launch the counterattack, thus enabling the
masses to receive a socialist education in an extremely deepgoing way. In the great struggle against the contemporary re-
visionist-renegade clique of Khrushchev and Brezhnev, negative materials are also made public repeatedly before a
thorough criticism is launched, thus forcefully educating the
people of our country and of the world. Specifically, we have
even published a collection of "Khrushchev's Speeches."
Chairman Mao again personally wrote the publisher's note in
which he pointed out penetratingly:

> A revolutionary Party and a revolutionary people must
> always and repeatedly be educated in both positive and

negative ways. Only through comparison and contrast can they be steeled to maturity; only thus can there be guarantees for scoring victories. He who belittles the usefulness of teachers by negative example is not a full-fledged dialectical materialist.

Chairman Mao has persistently taught us that Japanese imperialism, American imperialism, Chiang Kai-shek, Khrushchev, and the leaders of the opportunist line in various periods of the Party are all very good teachers by negative example. Had there been only teachers by positive example and none by negative example, the Chinese revolution would not have been victorious. This time, again, Chairman Mao is grasping Lin Piao as an excellent teacher by negative example. Not only have Lin and company's counterrevolutionary crimes been announced to the masses but also their counterrevolutionary materials have been published in full, in spite of the most atrocious language used for cursing the revolution and slandering our leader. This has been done so that all the people of the whole country, with the exception of the landlords, rich peasants, reactionaries, bad elements, Rightists and reactionary capitalists, can criticize them. This has fully attested to the great valor of a proletarian revolutionary leader. Lin Piao's counterrevolutionary program is bound to serve as another round of negative education for the vast masses and therefore arouse the intense proletarian indignation of the whole Party, army, and people. It will greatly raise the level of their political consciousness and political sensitivity, and it will build a still higher fighting morale for carrying the struggle to smash the Lin-Ch'en anti-Party clique through to the end.

A few comrades underestimated the consciousness and wisdom of the vast numbers of Party members and the masses of workers, peasants, and soldiers. Therefore they displayed some fear and hesitation in criticizing Lin Piao's counterrevolutionary program. On the one hand, they were worried about their own "low levels," which they feared would make some issues "difficult to explain" and "hard to criticize." On

the other hand, they were worried about the "low level of consciousness" of the masses, which would make it difficult for
them to "draw a clear demarcation line" on some issues and
which could even "produce side-effects." These concerns have
turned out to be totally groundless. We should recognize thoroughly that the Lin-Ch'en anti-Party clique represented the
rotten, decaying imperialists, revisionists, reactionaries, and
the already overthrown landlord class. They attempted to go
against the tide of history and violated in a fundamental way
the laws of historical development, as well as to defy the will
and desires of the people of our country. "Yet we are the new
emerging force; the truth is on our side. To them, we have
always been invincible." This counterrevolutionary program
of Lin Piao's is so reactionary and feeble, the whole thing is so
glutted with rumors and slanders; what is there in it that cannot be criticized? In particular, we should go a step further
and fully realize that this counterrevolutionary program of
Lin Piao's is characterized by extreme sharpness and vivid-
ness since it has stripped Lin Piao of all his masks and laid
bare his heinous features as a renegade and traitor. Once
handed over to the masses, this counterrevolutionary program
devised by Lin and his followers is bound to be subjected to
indignant repudiation and thorough criticism by the vast
masses. This has been proved by our earlier experience in
studying Central Committee Documents Nos. 68 and 77, as
well as in studying Central Committee Document No. 4 at
various test points. The vast masses of workers, peasants,
and soldiers are steadfast in their standpoint, unequivocal in
displaying their love and hatred, and possessed of a high level
of political consciousness and a rich reservoir of wisdom.
They have carried out the criticism very effectively and with
a high standard. If only we show full trust in the masses,
fight a people's war, and unite the leadership with the masses,
we can be certain that Lin Piao's counterrevolutionary program will be criticized deeply and penetratingly, that the ability of the vast masses to discriminate in the course of struggle
will be elevated, and that their ideological level of Marxism-

Leninism-Mao Tse-tung Thought will be raised.

There are also a few comrades who have underestimated the painstaking nature of criticizing deeply and thoroughly this counterrevolutionary program of Lin Piao's, and entertained an oversimplified view of things. In the course of criticism they did not make a serious effort or work hard enough, holding point after point as not worth refuting. Rather, they were content to discuss things divorced from personalities and to make only generalized criticism. We must fully recognize that in order to fight well this battle of great criticism it is imperative that we have full confidence in our victory, devote all our strength to the battle, and guard against oversimplification of matters. Lin Piao's counterrevolutionary program is a collection of all sorts of reactionary viewpoints expressed over many years by the imperialists, revisionists, counter-revolutionaries, landlords, rich peasants, reactionaries, bad elements, and Rightists to oppose China, communism and the people. Only by using Marxism-Leninism-Mao Tse-tung Thought as the weapon to launch a thorough criticism of them, by drawing a demarcation line between them and ourselves and sweeping clean their evil influence, and by elevating the line consciousness of the vast masses can the poisonous weeds be turned into fertilizer and the potential usefulness of teachers by negative example be fully tapped. In the discussion our comrades put it well: "With regard to bandit Lin's counter-revolutionary program, we must, on the one hand, realize its feebleness and, on the other hand, also recognize its provocative nature. If we do not criticize it in a serious and earnest manner, the objective consequence would be tantamount to helping spread the poison." In my opinion, these are very perceptive words. We must nurture an intense proletarian indignation and plunge ourselves actively and daringly into the battle of criticizing Lin Piao's counterrevolutionary program. It should be recognized that whether or not we seriously and earnestly criticize this counterrevolutionary program is a question of what attitude and affection we have toward our great leader Chairman Mao, toward Chairman Mao's revolution-

ary line and policies, and toward the socialist system under
the proletarian dictatorship. We must have a firm grasp of
this great criticism campaign and must not make our criticism
lukewarm or irrelevant.

There are also a few comrades who have not adequately ap-
preciated the prolonged nature of the struggle to smash the
Lin-Ch'en anti-Party clique. They felt that since bandit Lin
and his son had already died, with their bodies crushed to
pieces, and their sworn followers had all been caught, it appeared to be time to conclude the struggle and there was not
much to be gained from the great criticism. In the course of
transmitting Central Committee Documents Nos. 68 and 77 at
an earlier time, some units also had a similar experience and
learned the lesson. In transmitting Document No. 68, the general situation was under firm control, and the results were
also good. But when it came to the transmission of Document
No. 77, a few units showed laxity in mood, and the results of
the study were not as good. It should be recognized that under
the wise leadership of the Party Central Committee led by
Chairman Mao, and under the direction of Chairman Mao's
revolutionary line and policies, our struggle against the Lin-
Ch'en anti-Party clique has scored great victories. However,
the struggle between the two lines has not because of that come
to an end; to thoroughly repudiate Lin Piao's counterrevolutionary line and to sweep clean its evil influence from all
realms of life remain a long-term combat task. In such a
struggle, there must be no laxity in mood at any time. At
present, the transmission and discussion of Central Committee
Document No. 4 is aimed at deepening the criticism of Lin
Piao's counterrevolutionary program and developing a new upsurge of exposing and criticizing the Lin-Ch'en anti-Party
clique by the army units of the entire region and the people of
the entire province.

To sum up, in order to carry out successfully the transmission and the discussion, as well as the great criticism, it is
imperative to go a step further to understand the essence of
the struggle against the Lin-Ch'en anti-Party clique. It is

necessary to clearly perceive that the struggle to smash the counterrevolutionary conspiracy of coup d'etat is a vehement class struggle. This struggle is a continuation of the struggle between two classes, two roads, and two lines since the Ninth Party Congress, especially after the Second Plenum of the Ninth Party Central Committee. It is a continuation of the struggle between the proletarian headquarters headed by Chairman Mao and the bourgeois headquarters with Lin Piao at its head. By criticizing Lin Piao's counterrevolutionary program, we will come to perceive more clearly that the essence of Lin Piao and company's plan to stage a counterrevolutionary coup is to oppose the Party's line set forth by the Ninth Party Congress, to change the fundamental line and policies of the Party in the entire historical period of socialism, and to change the socialist system of proletarian dictatorship. Chairman Mao teaches us: "Practice Marxism, and not revisionism; unite, and don't split; be open and aboveboard, and don't intrigue and conspire." The Lin-Ch'en anti-Party clique was precisely practicing revisionism, going in for splittism, and going in for intrigues and conspiracies. In a word, we want to go the socialist road; they wanted to restore capitalism. Here is the fundamental distinction between the two lines. Chairman Mao's proletarian revolutionary line represents the interests of the proletariat and the vast laboring masses. It reflects the objective laws of social development and is therefore the lifeline of the whole Party, army, and people. The counterrevolutionary revisionist line of the Lin-Ch'en anti-Party clique sums up in a concentrated way the wishes of the already overthrown landlord-bourgeois class in our country, as well as of the imperialists, revisionists, and reactionaries, to restore capitalism. Had their scheme been realized, the proletarian dictatorship would have been turned into a dictatorship of the landlord-comprador-bourgeois class, and our country would have become a colony of Soviet revisionist social imperialism. However, such were only their wishful thinking and cherished dreams. The leading cadres and Party committees at various levels must understand thoroughly the great significance of the struggle against the Lin-Ch'en anti-Party clique on the plane of struggle between two classes, two roads, and two lines. They must fully mobilize the masses and hold line struggle as the key link in order to conduct well the great revolutionary criticism and thoroughly wipe out the evil influence of the Lin-Ch'en anti-Party revisionist line in all realms of life. We should resolutely defend the great leader Chairman Mao, defend the Party Central Committee headed by Chairman Mao, defend Chairman Mao's proletarian revolutionary line and policies, defend the proletarian socialist system of our country, and "unite to win still greater victories."

III. Party Committees at All Levels Must Strengthen Their Leadership and Must Have a Firm, Fine and Successful Grasp of the Task of Transmitting and Discussing Central Committee Document No. 4

The Provincial Party Committee and the Military Region Party Committee have both made their own specific plans concerning the transmission and discussion of Central Committee Document No. 4, so I will not comment further. The following are my few suggestions primarily on how to organize and lead successfully the transmission and discussion as well as the great criticism:

1) The Party committees at all levels should grasp the task of transmitting and discussing Central Committee Document No. 4 as their first business of paramount importance. Chairman Mao teaches us: "The line is the key link; once it is grasped, everything falls into place." In order to grasp the key link of line, we should now grasp effectively the transmission and discussion of Central Committee Document No. 4 and the criticism of Lin Piao's counterrevolutionary program. In order to have a firm grasp of the key link, the crucial task is to have the leading cadres take the lead in studying well. The leading cadres at various levels must all conscientiously study and analyze Central Committee Document No. 4 and understand its spirit and substance. They should earnestly study

the relevant teachings of Marx and Lenin as well as the series
of important directives issued by Chairman Mao on smashing
the Lin-Ch'en anti-Party clique. Marxism-Leninism-Mao Tse-
tung Thought should be used as the weapon to deepen the criticism of Lin Piao's counterrevolutionary program and raise
our own ideological consciousness and political level. Only by
so doing can the work of transmission and discussion be done
properly, and only by so doing can we lead the vast numbers
of cadres and the masses to study well and criticize well. In
the struggle of criticizing Lin Piao's counterrevolutionary
program, the Party committees at all levels, especially the
leading cadres at the hsien or regiment level and above, should
take the lead in exposition and criticism and be fighters who
break through the enemy lines. At the same time, they should
be present at the front line to organize the masses in a concrete manner for combat and be good commanders as well.

2) When criticizing Lin Piao's counterrevolutionary program, it is imperative to grasp the central issue and identify
the focus. The central issue is the issue of line, and the focus
is the slanders and attacks launched by Lin Piao and his followers against us in matters concerning situation, line, and policy.

With respect to the question of situation, we should severely
criticize such reactionary fallacies as "the political situation
is not stable," "the national economy is stagnant," and "the
living standard [of the masses] is declining," advanced by Lin
Piao and his followers to denegrate the excellent domestic
situation. Such criticism will make it clear that in depicting
the situation as pitch-black and hopeless, Lin Piao and company were manufacturing public opinion in support of their
counterrevolutionary coup d'etat, vainly trying to negate in one
stroke the great victories won by the people of the whole country after a prolonged and daring struggle, and to nullify Chairman Mao's proletarian revolutionary line. It will also enable
us to recognize the excellent situation at home and abroad at
the present time and understand that the emergence of such an
excellent situation is a result of adhering faithfully to Chairman Mao's revolutionary line. It will further reinforce our

confidence of victory and strengthen our revolutionary fighting will, thereby making us more resolute in thoroughly carrying out Chairman Mao's revolutionary line, further developing this excellent situation, and winning still greater victories. As for the reaction of some comrades who feel that we still have some shortcomings in the process of making progress and that in some places small numbers of the masses still face certain practical difficulties in life, we certainly should specifically analyze these matters so that concrete solutions can be found. However, all this must be distinguished from the vicious attacks launched by Lin Piao and his followers. What they vainly attempted was to subvert the proletarian dictatorship and restore capitalism. Thus they depicted us as good for nothing and depicted the situation as pitch-black. We must recognize that we are undertaking great enterprises that have never been attempted before by our forefathers; hence it is not surprising that there should emerge certain shortcomings and certain difficulties. Yet these should by no means be considered as having negated the excellent situation. We should lead the masses to distinguish the mainstream from the tributary, to fully appreciate the excellent situation, and to repudiate thoroughly the counterrevolutionary fallacies advanced by Lin Piao and his followers.

Concerning the issue of line: (a) We should severely criticize Lin Piao and company's slanders and attacks against our great leader Chairman Mao. This is the central issue of Lin Piao's counterrevolutionary program. Our great leader Chairman Mao is the great contemporary banner-bearer of Marxism-Leninism and the representative of the correct line of our Party. In their attempt to change the Party's correct line, all opportunists have always concentrated their efforts on attacking our great leader. In order to defend Chairman Mao's proletarian revolutionary line, we must thoroughly repudiate Lin Piao and his followers' slanders and assaults against Chairman Mao. (b) We should severely criticize Lin Piao and his followers for their crimes of trying vainly to distort and vilify the revolutionary history of our Party led by Chairman

Mao during the last half-century, especially the history of
struggle between two lines, and to reverse the verdicts pronounced on a small handful of evil spirits and wicked devils,
as well as followers of opportunist lines in various periods of
history. They held the ridiculous view that our socialist system under the proletarian dictatorship is a "social feudalism."
Is this not nullifying completely the revolutionary history of
our Party for the past fifty years? Is this not saying that not
only have we not undergone a socialist revolution but that we
have not even had a democratic revolution? Is this not totally
refuting Chairman Mao's revolutionary line? As a matter of
fact, it is no other than Lin Piao and his followers who tried
in vain to overthrow the proletarian dictatorship in order to
institute a fascist dictatorship of the landlord-bourgeois class
and to establish a feudal dynasty of the Lin family. They also
advanced the nonsense that inner-Party struggle is "using one
force to attack another force," "a small handful today, and a
small handful tomorrow, which add up to a large group"; and
they clamored for "giving political liberation to all" the so-
called "oppressed" people, and so forth and so on. All this is
a slander against the history of the struggle between lines in
our Party and thus fully exposes their intense hatred of the
correct line represented by Chairman Mao and proves that
they were jackals from the same lair as the leaders of opportunist lines in various periods of history. (c) We should severely criticize the slanders and attacks made by Lin Piao
and company against the fundamental line of the Party in the
historical period of socialism. Chairman Mao has mapped out
this fundamental line for our Party, and its essence is to persevere in the proletarian dictatorship and persevere in continuous revolution under the proletarian dictatorship. Lin Piao
and his followers vilified the state machinery of our proletarian dictatorship as a "meat grinder designed for mutual
killing and constant strife," and as "social fascism." This
fully reflected their intense hatred toward the proletarian
dictatorship and exposed their reactionary nature as members
of the landlord-bourgeois class. Lin Piao and his followers

denegrated the great theory of continuous revolution as
"Trotsky's theory of uninterrupted revolution." This is pure,
shameless defamation. The criminal intent of this slander
was to negate in a fundamental way the theoretical foundation
of the Party's basic line. Lin Piao and company's assault on
the Great Cultural Revolution was an attack on the great implementation of the theory of continuous revolution, and the intent
was the same: nullification of the Party's basic line. (d) We
should severely criticize Lin Piao and his followers for their
crime of opposing the Party's line laid down by the Ninth Party
Congress and of vainly attempting to split both the Party and
the army. Lin Piao was the greatest separatist. He always
ganged up in mountain stronghold, practiced factionalism, advocated the policy of punishment, and engaged in ruthless
struggle and merciless blows. Sometimes he also deceived
people with words such as "unity," but since he said nothing
about principles or struggles, it was still meant to serve his
counterrevolutionary revisionist line. Our comrades in the
army should in particular criticize such shameless lies per-
petuated by Lin Piao and his followers as "the army is being
oppressed," "the pen oppresses the gun," and so on. What they
meant by "the army is being oppressed" was that Lin and his
chief lieutenants and a small handful of sworn followers were
being exposed and criticized. What they meant by "the pen"
was no other than the proletarian headquarters headed by
Chairman Mao which they wanted to attack. We should expose
their criminal scheme of attempting to incite the army and
sow discord in the relationship between the army and the Party,
so as to strengthen further our Party consciousness, to persist in the absolute leadership of the army by the Party, to
solidify the internal and external unity of the army, and to
implement still more consciously Chairman Mao's proletarian
line of army-building. (e) We should severely criticize Lin
Piao and company's idealist concept of world outlook. Bourgeois idealism is the theoretical foundation of their counterrevolutionary revisionist line. We should continue to criticize
the idealist theory of genius expounded by Lin Piao and his

followers, with the realization that their purpose in clamoring
for "genius" and going all out to laud Lin Piao and Lin Li-kuo
as "geniuses" was to prepare counterrevolutionary public
opinion so that Lin Piao and his son could institute their feudal-
fascist dynasty. We should go a step further to identify what
materialist empiricism [wei-wu-lun ti fan-ying-lun] and idealist apriorism are and heighten our ability to distinguish genuine from sham Marxism.

In short, through criticism made in the five areas discussed
above, we will be able to clearly identify Chairman Mao's
Marxist-Leninist line, on the one hand, and the Lin-Ch'en
counterrevolutionary revisionist line, on the other, and to perceive the true character of Lin Piao's counterrevolutionary
program, thereby enhancing our own consciousness of line
struggle. We will also acquire a deeper understanding of the
fact that Chairman Mao's leadership is the greatest blessing
of the whole Party, army, and people, and that Chairman Mao's
proletarian revolutionary line is the lifeline of the whole Party,
army, and people.

As regards the issue of policy, we should severely criticize
the landlord-bourgeois counterrevolutionary slogan of the so-
called "rich people and strong nation" propagated by Lin Piao
and his followers. We should repudiate such counterrevolutionary fallacies disseminated by them as "rich nation but poor
people," the peasants "being short of food and clothing," the
workers "being exploited in a disguised form," and so on. We
should fully apply the method of "remembrance and comparison," keep in touch with the concrete conditions, and always
speak of the happiness under Chairman Mao's leadership and
of the superiority of the socialist system, in order to enable
all to understand the criminal objective of Lin Piao and his
followers in inflaming people and sowing discord among
them. We should severely criticize their crime of attacking
the Party's cadre policy and slandering the cadres' attending
the May 7th Cadre Schools as a "disguised form of unemployment," in a vain attempt to sow discord in the Party-cadres
relationship. We should severely criticize their crime of

attacking the Party's policy toward the intellectuals and slandering young intellectuals' going to mountains and rural areas as "a disguised form of reform through forced labor," in a vain attempt to sow discord in the Party-intellectuals relationship. All this will enable the vast numbers of youths to further strengthen their determination to go the road of uniting with the workers and the peasants and to realize more clearly that the Party and Chairman Mao are most concerned about and have the greatest affection for the young generation. The vicious fomentation carried out by Lin Piao and company was designed to corrupt the youths with bourgeois ideology and lead them astray. We should severely criticize their counterrevolutionary fallacies such as "the Red Guards have been deceived and used in the early period" and "suppressed and made scapegoats in the later period," so as to enable all to see clearly that it was Lin Piao who had been the ringleader responsible for subverting the Red Guard movement. Their wild attempt to turn black into white and to sow discord in the relationship between the Red Guards and the Party could never have been successful. Through criticism, we will recognize that Lin Piao and his followers' vicious attack on the Party's various policies was a vain attempt to change the Party's policies and line. We will realize that the so-called "to ally with all forces that can be allied with," which they had advanced, meant no more than to ally with the landlords, rich peasants, reactionaries, bad elements, and Rightists, and to ally with the Soviet Union and the United States to oppose China, Communism, and revolution and to restore capitalism.

3) Attention should be given to applying the experience gained in transmitting Central Committee Documents Nos. 68 and 77, in order to link up with current realities and to strengthen the concrete work of organization and leadership in transmitting and discussing Central Committee Document No. 4. We should have a good grasp of the task of cultivating backbone personnel (i.e., cadres, propagandists, interpreters, etc.), do a good job first at test points and make good preparations for the transmission and discussion. In the course of

transmission and discussion, emphasis should be placed on seeing to it that the cadres study the document well, in order to fully develop their backbone functions in taking the lead in the great criticism. When the vast masses of workers, peasants, and soldiers are involved in the transmission and discussion, a specific direction should be stressed, so that each phase of the study and criticism will have its own clear purpose and demands, as well as its own emphasis. We should keep track of the ideological conditions of the masses at all times and do a good job of the ideological mobilization work and do it repeatedly, in order to ensure that the great criticism will be carried on in an atmosphere of combat, as well as in a solidly planned manner.

4) We should have a firm hold of the general direction of the struggle, with its spearhead always pointing at the Lin-Ch'en anti-Party clique. We should strictly differentiate the two types of contradictions. In developing criticism, we must never confuse certain misunderstandings and erroneous opinions held among the people with the counterrevolutionary fallacies professed by Lin Piao and his followers, so as not to harm the masses and the cadres. With respect to certain ideological problems reflected in a few cadres and the masses, we should try to awaken their self-awareness through the great criticism of the Lin-Ch'en anti-Party clique, and to solve these problems through exchange of views and feelings, by maintaining close contact with reality and learning from experience and past lessons, and through the technique of self-education. Key units and units with more problems than others should maintain close links with the concrete conditions and expose and criticize the counterrevolutionary crimes of Lin Piao and company in a deepgoing way, in order to discover all wrongdoings and individuals in their units connected with the Lin-Ch'en anti-Party clique.

5) We should conscientiously control the direction of the proletarian struggle and fully anticipate that the imprecations on revolution contained in Lin Piao's counterrevolutionary program and his counterrevolutionary strategy are bound to

arouse the intense proletarian indignation of the whole Party, army, and people. But these imprecations are also bound to strike a responsive cord among a small handful of counter-revolutionaries. Party organizations at all levels should keep a close eye on the movements of enemies, take effective measures against them, strengthen their security work, and step up the suppression and reform of the landlords, rich peasants, reactionaries, bad elements, and Rightists. In border provinces, mountainous areas, and inland regions where work tends to be slack, able cadres should be dispatched to help them do a good job of the transmission and discussion. As for existing sabotage activities of the enemies, especially those who took advantage of the traitorous Lin-Ch'en anti-Party affair to carry out counterrevolutionary activities, we should resolutely deal them blows.

All army units in this region must sharpen their vigilance and strengthen their preparedness for war. During the Spring Festival and the periods immediately before and following Nixon's visit to China, all army units, especially the border defense units, should keep a close watch on enemy movements both inside and across the border, in order to guard against enemy sabotage and attack.

Both the army units and the civilian organizations should continue to earnestly do a good job of security work. Lately, bandit-agents sent by the Americans and Chiang Kai-shek have made it a top priority task to collect documents on the Lin-Ch'en anti-Party clique; they were ordered to obtain such documents in a given time period and by any means. We must heighten our vigilance. This time the document has been widely distributed, down to the production brigade in rural areas and to the squads and groups in factories and mines. All units must faithfully adhere to the regulations on the safe-keeping of documents. A team of two persons should be assigned to safeguard each copy of the document, and neither copying nor carrying on the person of individuals should be permitted, in order to prevent theft or loss.

6) We should firmly grasp the revolution and rush to

promote production. Party committees at various levels must
have a good grasp of the line as the key link and coordinate
the criticism of the Lin-Ch'en anti-Party clique with the study
of Marxism-Leninism-Mao Tse-tung Thought, as well as with
the grasping of revolution and the promotion of production.
We should make the great criticism a powerful stimulus that
will further strengthen our fighting will and solidify the revolutionary unity. Positive factors of all kinds should be mobilized and the struggle-criticism-transformation process
deepened, in order to promote a great leap in both industry
and agriculture, advance the development of the army units,
and do a better job in all work.

The situation in our province is as excellent as that in the
whole country. Since the formation of the provincial revolutionary committee, the national economy in our province has
indeed made great accomplishments. However, when compared with our fellow provinces and municipalities, there still
remains a considerable disparity. We must go a step further
to muster all our revolutionary enthusiasm, to aim high, to
rely on ourselves, and to wage arduous struggle, in order to
achieve still greater progress for the national economy in our
province and make a greater contribution to the state.

This province of Yunnan is a border province, and we must
carry out Chairman Mao's instructions concerning the anti-
revisionist struggle in border areas, that is "production should
make greater progress every year, the economy should be
more prosperous every year, and the living standard of the
people should be better every year." We should criticize the
sabotage and troublemaking of Lin Piao and his followers in
the border work of our province. They talked glibly about the
so-called "political border defense," while actually trying to
purvey their landlord-capitalist politics. They violated the
nationalities policy and subverted economic construction in
the border areas in a vain attempt to create trouble in the
border regions and undermine our proletarian dictatorship.
We must continue to expose and criticize in order to sweep
their evil influence into oblivion. We must follow Chairman

Mao's consistent teachings to proceed from the realities of
the border areas, keep close links with their specific conditions, and thoroughly carry out the principles and policies of
the Party, in order to do a better job in our border work.

In accordance with the spirit of the National Planning Conference, we should first strengthen the centralized leadership
of the Party in order to do a good job in economic work. The
leading comrades of the Central Committee have pointed out
emphatically that this is a very important problem. Chairman
Mao has also given instructions on strengthening the centralized leadership of the Party and authorized the issuance of the
minutes of the work conference of the Canton Military Region
on political-ideological work involved in the "three supports
and two militaries." The Chairman said that this report had
identified problems but did not solve them completely. So, in
order to draw the attention of all areas the Chairman made
the comment "Study conscientiously." The Chairman said that
it would be turning things upside down if matters already decided by a local Party committee were again submitted to the
Party committee of the corresponding military unit for delib-
eration. Leading comrades of the Central authorities said
that the three supports and two militaries had made great
achievements, but centralized leadership of the Party should
be implemented under the local Party committee once it had
been set up. Military cadres should unite with local cadres
to bring the role of both military and local cadres into full
play and faithfully strengthen the centralized leadership of the
Party, in order to promote our economic work and various
other types of work.

We should follow Chairman Mao's glorious thinking on agriculture, light industry, and heavy industry and conscientiously
study the problem of proper proportions and relations among
agriculture, light industry, and heavy industry, in order to ensure faster development of agriculture and light industry and
thereby also promote a faster development of heavy industry.
So far as our province is concerned, we should promote agriculture in particular. Once agriculture has taken off, the

initiative will be in our hands. Agriculture is the foundation
of the national economy. We must adhere faithfully to the
principle of "taking grain as the key link and ensuring an all-
round development" and correctly handle the ordering of the
twelve characters representing grain, cotton, edible oil, flax,
silk, tea, sugar, vegetables, tobacco, fruits, medical herbs,
and the miscellaneous ones, as well as the relationships among
agriculture, forestry, animal husbandry, sideline production,
and fisheries. Only after we have developed agriculture will
light industry have an adequate supply of raw materials; and
only when agriculture and light industry are well developed
can the market be prosperous; and only then, moreover, can
more capital be accumulated and a larger market be ensured
for the development of heavy industry. Therefore we should
have a firm grasp of agriculture and strive to increase its
productivity at a rate still higher than that of last year. While
firmly grasping grain production, we should simultaneously
get a firm hold of industrial crops. The state has demanded
that our province make a greater contribution in producing
tobacco and sugar; we must fulfill this assigned task. At
present we should firmly grasp the capital construction work
in agriculture and irrigation, improve the processing and
handling of seedlings, complete the planting of early-ripening
rice in time, and make good preparations for the late spring
plowing, in order to lay the foundation for an all-round bumper
harvest in agriculture this year. To develop agriculture successfully, the key is to grasp the line, on the one hand, and to
adhere to the principle "in agriculture, learn from Tachai,"
on the other. The chief task is to ensure good leadership in
rural areas and at the basic levels. At the same time, we
should increase industry's support of agriculture in order to
truly make work in the industrial sector rely on agriculture
as its foundation.

    In industry, we should further develop the mass movement
"in industry, learn from Tach'ing." We should strengthen the
unity and balance among various sectors, pay close attention
to the weak links, improve industrial management, promote

production, practice frugality, greatly increase the productivity
of labor, ensure "all redness" for the first quarter of this year,
and be resolute in fulfilling and overfulfilling the state plan.
At the same time, there should also be new developments on
the various battle fronts such as finance, trade, culture, education, and health.

To develop agricultural and industrial production well, one
very important task is to earnestly carry out the Party's policies in accordance with the spirit of the National Planning
Conference, especially in regard to cadres, intellectuals, and
veteran workers, as well as to distribution in rural areas.
Earlier on, in the course of implementing Central Committee
Document No. 82 (on the problem of distribution in rural
areas), whenever the policies of the Central authorities had
been introduced to the masses, the reaction was generally
very good; as a result, the activism of the masses was mobilized and production further developed. Many poor and lower-
middle peasants said: "We have poured out our hearts, just as
if Chairman Mao had personally come to our place for an investigation and study trip." Concerning the question of policies, the major task at present remains that of promoting understanding and facilitating implementation. By criticizing
the Lin-Ch'en anti-Party clique, we should further enhance
our understanding of the importance of carrying out Chairman
Mao's proletarian policies and strengthen our policy consciousness. Investigations of the actual steps taken for implementat-
ing policies should be conducted, and the phenomenon of policy
violations should be resolutely rectified.

Comrades, to develop economic work successfully in accordance with Chairman Mao's instructions is not merely an
economic task but also a political task. Lin Piao and his followers and the Soviet revisionist renegade clique made vicious
slanders and attacks against us in a wild attempt to negate our
excellent situation, but all their efforts were to no avail. They
can only arouse all the more our most intense indignation. We
must have great ambitions and set our hearts on performing
great deeds, wage arduous struggle, and strive to uplift

ourselves. We must strike a telling blow at the Lin-Ch'en anti-Party clique, as well as at the imperialists, revisionists and reactionaries, with concrete actions such as doing good revolutionary work and production work, improving the work of war preparation, and strengthening the construction work of the army units. All nationalities in our province and the commanders and fighters of all units in our region must unite more closely than ever around our great leader Chairman Mao and the Party Central Committee headed by Chairman Mao, follow Chairman Mao's proletarian revolutionary line, and win still greater victories.

20

REPORT TO THE TENTH NATIONAL CONGRESS
OF THE COMMUNIST PARTY OF CHINA*
(Delivered on August 24 and Adopted on August 28, 1973)

Chou En-lai

Comrades!

The Tenth National Congress of the Communist Party of China is convened at a time when the Lin Piao anti-Party clique has been smashed, the line of the Party's Ninth National Congress has won great victories, and the situation both at home and abroad is excellent.

On behalf of the Central Committee, I am making this report to the Tenth National Congress. The main subjects are: On the line of the Ninth National Congress, on the victory of smashing the Lin Piao anti-Party clique, and on the situation and our tasks.

On the Line of the Ninth National Congress

The Party's Ninth Congress was held when great victories had been won in the Great Proletarian Cultural Revolution personally initiated and led by Chairman Mao.

---

*Chou En-lai, "Tsai Chung-kuo kung-ch'an-tang ti-shih-tz'u ch'üan-kuo tai-piao ta-hui shang ti pao-kao." Jen-min jih-pao [People's Daily], September 1, 1973. This translation is taken, with minor editorial revisions, from Peking Review, Nos. 35-36 (September 7, 1973), 17-25.

In accordance with the theory of Marxism-Leninism-Mao Tse-tung Thought on continuing the revolution under the dictatorship of the proletariat, the Ninth Congress summed up the experience of history as well as the new experience of the Great Proletarian Cultural Revolution, criticized Liu Shao-chi's revisionist line, and reaffirmed the basic line and policies of the Party for the entire historical period of socialism. As comrades may recall, when the Ninth Congress opened on April 1, 1969, Chairman Mao issued the great call, "Unite to win still greater victories." At the First Plenary Session of the Ninth Central Committee on April 28 of the same year, Chairman Mao once again clearly stated: "Unite for one purpose, that is, the consolidation of the dictatorship of the proletariat." "We must ensure that the people throughout the country are united to win victory under the leadership of the proletariat." In addition he predicted: "Probably another revolution will have to be carried out after several years." Chairman Mao's speeches and the political report of the Central Committee adopted at the congress formulated a Marxist-Leninist line for our Party.

As we all know, the political report to the Ninth Congress was drawn up under Chairman Mao's personal guidance. Prior to the congress, Lin Piao had produced a draft political report in collaboration with Ch'en Po-ta. They were opposed to continuing the revolution under the dictatorship of the proletariat, contending that the main task after the Ninth Congress was to develop production. This was a refurbished version under new conditions of the same revisionist trash that Liu Shao-ch'i and Ch'en Po-ta had smuggled into the resolution of the Eighth Congress, which alleged that the major contradiction in our country was not the contradiction between the proletariat and the bourgeoisie, but that "between the advanced socialist system and the backward productive forces of society." Naturally, this draft by Lin Piao and Ch'en Po-ta was rejected by the Central Committee. Lin Piao secretly supported Ch'en Po-ta in the latter's open opposition to the political report drawn up under Chairman Mao's guidance, and it was only after his attempts were frustrated that Lin Piao grudgingly accepted the political

line of the Central Committee and read its political report to
the congress. However, during and after the Ninth Congress,
Lin Piao continued with his conspiracy and sabotage in spite of
the admonishments, rebuffs and efforts to save him by Chairman Mao and the Party's Central Committee. He went further
to start a counterrevolutionary coup d'etat, which was aborted,
at the Second Plenary Session of the Ninth Central Committee
in August 1970, then in March 1971 he drew up the plan for an
armed counterrevolutionary coup d'etat entitled "Outline of
Project '571,'" and on September 8, he launched the coup in a
wild attempt to assassinate our great leader Chairman Mao and
set up a rival central committee. On September 13, after his
conspiracy had collapsed, Lin Piao surreptitiously boarded a
plane, fled as a defector to the Soviet revisionists in betrayal
of the Party and country, and died in a crash at Undur Khan in
the People's Republic of Mongolia.

The shattering of the Lin Piao anti-Party clique is our Party's
greatest victory since the Ninth Congress and a heavy blow
dealt to enemies at home and abroad. After the September 13th
incident, the whole Party, the whole Army, and the hundreds of
millions of people of all nationalities in our country seriously
discussed the matter and expressed their intense proletarian
indignation at the bourgeois careerist, conspirator, double-
dealer, renegade and traitor Lin Piao and his sworn followers,
and pledged resolute support for our great leader Chairman
Mao and the Party's Central Committee which he headed. A
movement to criticize Lin Piao and rectify style of work has
been launched throughout the country. The whole Party, Army
and people have been conscientiously studying Marxism-
Leninism-Mao Tse-tung Thought, conducting revolutionary mass
criticism of Lin Piao and other swindlers like him, and settling
accounts with the counterrevolutionary crimes of these swindlers ideologically, politically and organizationally, and have
raised their own ability to distinguish genuine from sham Marxism. As facts showed, the Lin Piao anti-Party clique was only
a tiny group which was extremely isolated in the midst of the
whole Party, Army and people and could not affect the situation

as a whole. The Lin Piao anti-Party clique has not stemmed, nor could it possibly have stemmed the rolling torrent of the Chinese people's revolution. On the contrary, what it did further aroused the whole Party, Army and people to "unite to win still greater victories."

Thanks to the movement to criticize Lin Piao and rectify style of work, the line of the Ninth Congress is more deeply rooted among the people. The line of the Ninth Congress and the proletarian policies of the Party have been implemented better than before. New achievements have been made in struggle-criticism-transformation in all realms of the super-structure. The working style of seeking truth from facts and following the mass line and the glorious tradition of modesty, prudence and hard work, which were for a time impaired by Lin Piao, have been further developed. The Chinese People's Liberation Army, which won fresh merit in the Great Proletarian Cultural Revolution, has made new contributions in strengthening the preparations against war and in taking part in revolution and construction together with the people. The great revolutionary unity of the people of all nationalities led by the proletariat and based on the worker-peasant alliance is stronger than ever. Having rid itself of the stale and taken in the fresh, our Party, with a membership of twenty-eight million, is now an even more vigorous vanguard of the proletariat.

Spurred by the movement to criticize Lin Piao and rectify style of work, the people of our country overcame the sabotage by the Lin Piao anti-Party clique, surmounted serious natural disasters, and scored new victories in socialist construction. Our country's industry, agriculture, transportation, finance and trade are doing well. We have neither external nor internal debts. Prices are stable and the market is flourishing. There are many new achievements in culture, education, public health, science and technology.

In the international sphere our Party and Government have firmly implemented the foreign policy laid down by the Ninth Congress. Our revolutionary friendship with fraternal socialist countries and with the genuine Marxist-Leninist parties and

organizations of various countries and our cooperation with
friendly countries have been further strengthened. Our country has established diplomatic relations with an increasing number of countries on the basis of the Five Principles of Peaceful Coexistence. The legitimate status of our country in the
United Nations has been restored. The policy of isolating China
has gone bankrupt; Sino-U.S. relations have been improved to
some extent. China and Japan have normalized their relations.
Friendly contacts between our people and the people of other
countries are more extensive than ever; we assist and support
each other, impelling the world situation to continue to develop
in the direction favorable to the people of all countries.

Revolutionary practice since the Ninth Congress and chiefly
the practice of the struggle against the Lin Piao anti-Party
clique have proved that the political and organizational lines
of the Ninth Congress are both correct and that the leadership
given by the Party's Central Committee headed by Chairman
Mao is correct.

On the Victory of Smashing the
Lin Piao Anti-Party Clique

The course of the struggle to smash the Lin Piao anti-Party
clique and the crimes of the clique are already known to the
whole Party, Army and people. So, there is no need to dwell
on it here.

Marxism-Leninism holds that inner-Party struggle is the
reflection within the Party of class struggle in society. The
Liu Shao-ch'i renegade clique collapsed and the Lin Piao anti-
Party clique sprang out to continue the trial of strength with
the proletariat. This was an acute expression of the intense
domestic and international class struggles.

As early as January 13, 1967, when the Great Proletarian
Cultural Revolution was at high tide, Brezhnev, the chief of the
Soviet revisionist renegade clique, frantically attacked China's
Great Proletarian Cultural Revolution in his speech at a mass
rally in Gorky Region and openly declared that they stood on

the side of the Liu Shao-ch'i renegade clique, saying that the downfall of this clique was "a big tragedy for all real communists in China, and we express our deep sympathy to them." At the same time, Brezhnev publicly announced continuation of the policy of subverting the leadership of the Chinese Communist Party, and ranted about "struggling. . . for bringing it back to the road of internationalism" (Pravda, January 14, 1967). In March 1967 another chief of the Soviet revisionists said even more brazenly at mass rallies in Moscow that "sooner or later the healthy forces expressing the true interests of China will have their decisive say," "and achieve the victory of Marxist-Leninist ideas in their great country" (Pravda, March 4 and 10, 1967). What they called "healthy forces" are nothing but the decadent forces representing the interests of social-imperialism and all the exploiting classes; what they meant by "their decisive say" is the usurpation of the supreme power of the Party and the state; what they meant by "victory of ideas" is the reign of sham Marxism-Leninism and real revisionism over China; and what they meant by the "road of internationalism" is the road of reducing China to a colony of Soviet revisionist social-imperialism. The Brezhnev renegade clique has impetuously voiced the common wish of the reactionaries and blurted out the ultra-Rightist nature of the Lin Piao anti-Party clique.

Lin Piao and his handful of sworn followers were a counter-revolutionary conspiratorial clique "who never showed up without a copy of Quotations in hand and never opened their mouths without shouting 'Long Live' and who spoke nice things to your face but stabbed you in the back." The essence of the counter-revolutionary revisionist line they pursued and the criminal aim of the counterrevolutionary armed coup d'etat they launched were to usurp the supreme power of the Party and the state, thoroughly betray the line of the Ninth Congress, radically change the Party's basic line and policies for the entire historical period of socialism, turn the Marxist-Leninist Chinese Communist Party into a revisionist, fascist party, subvert the dictatorship of the proletariat and restore capitalism. Inside China, they wanted to reinstate the landlord and bourgeois classes, which our Party, Army and people had overthrown with their own hands under the leadership of Chairman Mao, and to institute a feudal-comprador-fascist dictatorship. Internationally, they wanted to capitulate to Soviet revisionist social-imperialism and ally themselves with imperialism, revisionism and reaction to oppose China, communism and revolution.

Lin Piao, this bourgeois careerist, conspirator and double-dealer, engaged in machinations within our Party not just for one decade but for several decades. On his part there was a process of development and self-exposure, and on our part there was also a process of getting to know him. Marx and Engels said in the Manifesto of the Communist Party that "all previous historical movements were movements of minorities, or in the interest of minorities. The proletarian movement is the self-conscious, independent movement of the immense majority, in the interest of the immense majority." Chairman Mao has made "working for the interests of the vast majority of people of China and the world" one of the principal requirements for successors to the cause of the proletarian revolution, and it has been written into our Party Constitution. To build a party for the interests of the vast majority or for the interests of the minority? This is the watershed between proletarian and bourgeois political parties and the touchstone for distinguishing true Communists from false. Lin Piao joined the Communist Party in the early days of China's new-democratic revolution. Even at that time he was pessimistic about the future of the Chinese revolution. Right after the Kutien Meeting [December 1929], Chairman Mao wrote a long letter "A Single Spark Can Start a Prairie Fire" to Lin Piao, trying seriously and patiently to educate him. But, as the facts later proved, Lin Piao's bourgeois idealist world outlook was not at all remolded. At important junctures of the revolution he invariably committed Right opportunist errors and invariably played double-faced tricks, putting up a false front to deceive the Party and the people. However, as the Chinese revolution developed further and especially when it turned socialist in nature and became more and more thoroughgoing, aiming at the complete overthrow of the bourgeoisie and all other exploiting classes, the establishment of the dictatorship of the proletariat in place of the dictatorship of the bourgeoisie and the triumph of socialism over capitalism, Lin Piao and his like, who were capitalist-roaders in power working only for the interests of the minority and whose ambition grew with the rise of their positions, overestimating their own strength and underestimating the strength of the people, could no longer remain under cover and therefore sprang out for a trial of strength with the proletariat. When under the baton of Soviet revisionism he attempted to have his "decisive say" in order to serve the needs of domestic and foreign class enemies, his exposure and bankruptcy became complete.

Engels rightly said, "The development of the proletariat proceeds everywhere amidst internal struggles.... And when, like Marx and myself, one has fought harder all one's life long against the alleged socialists than against anyone else (for we only regarded the bourgeoisie as a class and hardly ever involved ourselves in conflicts with individual bourgeois), one cannot greatly grieve that the inevitable struggle has broken out..." (Friedrich Engels' letter to August Bebel, October 28, 1882).

Comrades!

In the last fifty years our Party has gone through ten major struggles between the two lines. The collapse of the Lin Piao anti-Party clique does not mean the end of the two-line struggle within the Party. Enemies at home and abroad all understand that the easiest way to capture a fortress is from within. It is much more convenient to have the capitalist-roaders in power who have sneaked into the Party do the job of subverting the dictatorship of the proletariat than for the landlords and capitalists to come to the fore themselves; this is especially true when the landlords and capitalists are already quite odious in society. In the future, even after classes have disappeared, there will still be contradictions between the superstructure and the economic base and between the relations of production and the productive forces. And there will still be two-line struggles reflecting these contradictions, i.e., struggles between the advanced and the backward and between the correct and the erroneous. Moreover, socialist society covers a considerably long historical period. Throughout this historical period, there are classes, class contradictions and class struggle, there is the struggle between the socialist road and the capitalist road, there is the danger of capitalist restoration, and there is the threat of subversion and aggression by imperialism and social-imperialism. For a long time to come, there will still be two-line struggles within the Party, reflecting these contradictions, and such struggles will occur ten, twenty or thirty times. Lin Piaos will appear again and so will persons like Wang Ming, Liu Shao-ch'i, P'eng Te-huai and Kao Kang. This is something independent of man's will. Therefore, all comrades in our Party must be fully prepared mentally for the struggles in the long years to come and be able to make the best use of the situation and guide the struggle to victory for the proletariat, no matter how the class enemy may change his tactics.

Chairman Mao teaches us that "the correctness or incorrectness of the ideological and political line decides everything." If one's line is incorrect, one's downfall is inevitable, even with the control of the central, local and army leadership. If one's line is correct, even if one has not a single soldier at first, there will be soldiers, and even if there is no political power, political power will be gained. This is borne out by the historical experience of our Party and by that of the international communist movement since the time of Marx. Lin Piao wanted to "have everything under his command and everything at his disposal," but he ended up in having nothing under his command and nothing at his disposal. The crux of the matter is line. This is an irrefutable truth.

Chairman Mao has laid down for our Party the basic line and policies for the entire historical period of socialism and also specific lines and policies for specific work. We should attach importance not only to the Party's lines and policies for specific

work but, in particular, to its basic line and policies. This is
the fundamental guarantee of greater victories for our Party.

Having summed up the experience gained in the ten struggles
between the two lines within the Party and particularly the experience acquired in the struggle to smash the Lin Piao anti-
Party clique, Chairman Mao calls on the whole Party: "Practice Marxism, and not revisionism; unite, and don't split; be
open and aboveboard, and don't intrigue and conspire." He thus
puts forward the criterion for distinguishing the correct line
from the erroneous line, and gives the three basic principles
every Party member must observe. Every one of our comrades must keep these three principles firmly in mind, uphold
them and energetically and correctly carry on the two-line
struggle within the Party.

Chairman Mao has constantly taught us: It is imperative to
note that one tendency covers another. The opposition to Ch'en
Tu-hsiu's Right opportunism which advocated "all alliance, no
struggle" covered Wang Ming's "Left" opportunism which advocated "all struggle, no alliance." The rectification of Wang
Ming's "Left" deviation covered Wang Ming's Right deviation.
The struggle against Liu Shao-ch'i's revisionism covered Lin
Piao's revisionism. There were many instances in the past
where one tendency covered another and when a tide came, the
majority went along with it, while only a few withstood it. Today, in both international and domestic struggles, tendencies
may still occur similar to those of the past, namely, when there
was an alliance with the bourgeoisie, necessary struggles were
forgotten, and when there was a split with the bourgeoisie, the
possibility of an alliance under given conditions was forgotten.
It is required of us to do our best to discern and rectify such
tendencies in time. And when a wrong tendency surges toward
us like a rising tide, we must not fear isolation and must dare
to go against the tide and brave it through. Chairman Mao
states, "Going against the tide is a Marxist-Leninist principle."
In daring to go against the tide and adhere to the correct line
in the ten struggles between the two lines within the Party,
Chairman Mao is our example and teacher. Every one of our

comrades should learn well from Chairman Mao and hold to this principle.

Under the guidance of the correct line represented by Chairman Mao, the great, glorious and correct Communist Party of China has had prolonged trials of strength with the class enemies both inside and outside the Party, at home and abroad, armed and unarmed, overt and covert. Our Party has not been divided or crushed. On the contrary, Chairman Mao's Marxist-Leninist line has further developed and our Party grown ever stronger. Historical experience convinces us that "this Party of ours has a bright future." Just as Chairman Mao predicted in 1966, "If the Right stage an anti-Communist coup d'etat in China, I am sure they will know no peace either and their rule will most probably be short-lived, because it will not be tolerated by the revolutionaries, who represent the interests of the people making up more than 90 percent of the population." So long as our whole Party bears in mind historical experience, and upholds Chairman Mao's correct line, all the schemes of the bourgeoisie for restoration are bound to fail. No matter how many more major struggles between the two lines may occur, the laws of history will not change, and the revolution in China and the world will eventually triumph.

On the Situation and Our Tasks

Chairman Mao has often taught us: We are still in the era of imperialism and the proletarian revolution. On the basis of fundamental Marxist principle, Lenin made a scientific analysis of imperialism and defined "imperialism as the highest stage of capitalism." Lenin pointed out that imperialism is monopolistic capitalism, parasitic or decaying capitalism, moribund capitalism. He also said that imperialism intensifies all the contradictions of capitalism to the extreme. He therefore concluded that "imperialism is the eve of the social revolution of the proletariat," and put forward the theories and tactics of the proletarian revolution in the era of imperialism. Stalin said, "Leninism is Marxism of the era of imperialism and the proletarian revolution." This is entirely correct. Since Lenin's death, the world situation has undergone great changes. But the era has not changed. The fundamental principles of Leninism are not outdated; they remain the theoretical basis guiding our thinking today.

The present international situation is one characterized by great disorder on the earth. "The wind sweeping through the tower heralds a rising storm in the mountains." This aptly depicts how the basic world contradictions as analyzed by Lenin show themselves today. Relaxation is a temporary and superficial phenomenon, and great disorder will continue. Such great disorder is a good thing for the people, not a bad thing. It throws the enemies into confusion and causes division among them, while it arouses and tempers the people, thus helping the international situation develop further in the direction favorable to the people and unfavorable to imperialism, modern revisionism and all reaction.

The awakening and growth of the Third World is a major event in contemporary international relations. The Third World has strengthened its unity in the struggle against hegemonism and power politics of the superpowers and is playing an ever more significant role in international affairs. The great victories won by the people of Vietnam, Laos and Cambodia in their war against U.S. aggression and for national salvation have strongly encouraged the people of the world in their revolutionary struggles against imperialism and colonialism. A new situation has emerged in the Korean people's struggle for the independent and peaceful reunification of their fatherland. The struggles of the Palestinian and other Arab peoples against aggression by Israeli Zionism, the African peoples' struggles against colonialism and racial discrimination, and the Latin American peoples' struggles for maintaining 200-nautical-mile territorial waters or economic zones all continue to forge ahead. The struggles of the Asian, African and Latin American peoples to win and defend national independence and safeguard state sovereignty and national resources have further deepened and broadened. The just struggles of the Third World as well as of the people of Europe, North America and Oceania support and encourage each other. Countries want independence, nations want liberation, and the people want revolution — this has become an irresistible historical trend.

Lenin said that "an essential feature of imperialism is the rivalry between several Great Powers in the striving for hegemony." Today, it is mainly the two nuclear superpowers — the U.S. and the USSR — that are contending for hegemony. While hawking disarmament, they are actually expanding their armaments every day. Their purpose is to contend for world hegemony. They contend as well as collude with each other. Their collusion serves the purpose of more intensified contention. Contention is absolute and protracted, whereas collusion is relative and temporary. The declaration of this year as the "year of Europe" and the convocation of the European Security Conference indicate that strategically the key point of their contention is Europe. The West always wants to urge the Soviet revisionists eastward to divert the peril toward China, and it would be fine so long as all is quiet in the West. China is an attractive piece of meat coveted by all. But this piece of meat is very tough, and for years no one has been able to bite into it. It is even more difficult now that Lin Piao the "super-spy" has fallen. At present, the Soviet revisionists are "making a feint to the east while attacking in the west," and stepping up their contention in Europe and their expansion in the Mediterranean, the Indian Ocean and every place their hands can reach. The U.S.-Soviet contention for hegemony is the cause of world intranquillity. It cannot be covered up by any false appearances they create and is already perceived by an increasing number of people and countries. It has met with strong resistance from the Third World and has caused resentment on the part of Japan and West European countries. Beset with troubles internally and externally, the two hegemonic powers — the U.S. and the USSR — find the going tougher and tougher. As the verse goes, "Flowers fall off, do what one may," they are in a sorry plight indeed. This has been further proved by the U.S.-Soviet talks last June and the subsequent course of events.

"The people, and the people alone, are the motive force in the making of world history." The ambitions of the two hegemonic powers — the U.S. and the USSR — are one thing, but whether they can achieve them is quite another. They want to devour China, but find it too tough even to bite. Europe and Japan are also hard to bite, not to speak of the vast Third World. U.S. imperialism started to go downhill after its defeat in the war of aggression against Korea. It has openly admitted that it is increasingly on the decline; it could not but pull out of Vietnam. Over the last two decades, the Soviet revisionist ruling clique, from Khrushchev to Brezhnev, has made a socialist country degenerate into a social-imperialist country. Internally, it has restored capitalism, enforced a fascist dictatorship and enslaved the people of all nationalities, thus deepening the political and economic contradictions as well as contradictions among nationalities. Externally, it has invaded and occupied Czechoslovakia, massed its troops along the Chinese border, sent troops into the People's Republic of Mongolia, supported the traitorous Lon Nol clique, suppressed the Polish workers' rebellion, intervened in Egypt, causing the expulsion of the Soviet experts, dismembered Pakistan and carried out subversive activities in many Asian and African countries. This series of facts has profoundly exposed its ugly features as the new Czar and its reactionary nature, namely, "socialism in words, imperialism in deeds." The more evil and foul things it does, the sooner the time when Soviet revisionism will be relegated to the historical museum by the people of the Soviet Union and the rest of the world.

Recently, the Brezhnev renegade clique has talked a lot of nonsense on Sino-Soviet relations. It alleges that China is against relaxation of world tension and unwilling to improve Sino-Soviet relations, etc. These words are directed to the Soviet people and the people of other countries in a vain attempt to alienate their friendly feelings for the Chinese people and disguise the true features of the new Czar. These words are above all meant for the monopoly capitalists in the hope of getting more money in reward for services in opposing China and communism. This was an old trick of Hitler's, only Brezhnev is playing it more clumsily. If you are so anxious to relax world tension, why don't you show your good faith by doing a thing or two — for instance, withdraw your armed forces from Czechoslovakia or the People's Republic of Mongolia and return the four northern islands to Japan? China has not occupied any foreign countries' territory. Must China give away all the territory north of the Great Wall to the Soviet revisionists in order to show that we favor relaxation of world tension and are willing to improve Sino-Soviet relations? The Chinese people are not to be deceived or cowed. The Sino-Soviet controversy on matters of principle should not hinder the normalization of relations between the two states on the basis of the Five Principles of Peaceful Coexistence. The Sino-Soviet boundary question should be settled peacefully through negotiations free from any threat. "We will not attack unless we are attacked; if we are attacked, we will certainly counterattack" — this is our consistent principle. And we mean what we say.

We should point out here that necessary compromises between revolutionary countries and imperialist countries must be distinguished from collusion and compromise between Soviet revisionism and U.S. imperialism. Lenin put it well: "There are compromises and compromises. One must be able to analyze the situation and the concrete conditions of each compromise, or of each variety of compromise. One must learn to distinguish between a man who gave the bandits money and firearms in order to lessen the damage they can do and facilitate their capture and execution, and a man who gives bandits money and firearms in order to share in the loot" ("Left-Wing" Communism, an Infantile Disorder). The Brest-Litovsk Treaty concluded by Lenin with German imperialism comes under the former category; and the doings of Khrushchev and Brezhnev, both betrayers of Lenin, fall under the latter.

Lenin pointed out repeatedly that imperialism means aggression and war. Chairman Mao pointed out in his statement of May 20, 1970: "The danger of a new world war still exists, and the people of all countries must get prepared. But revolution is the main trend in the world today." It will be possible to prevent such a war, so long as the peoples, who are becoming more and more awakened, keep the orientation clearly in sight, heighten their vigilance, strengthen unity and persevere in struggle. Should the imperialists be bent on unleashing such a war, it will inevitably give rise to greater revolutions on a worldwide scale and hasten their doom.

In the excellent situation now prevailing at home and abroad, it is most important for us to run China's affairs well. Therefore, on the international front, our Party must uphold proletarian internationalism, uphold the Party's consistent policies, strengthen our unity with the proletariat and the oppressed people and nations of the whole world and with all countries subjected to imperialist aggression, subversion, interference, control or bullying, and form the broadest united front against imperialism, colonialism and neocolonialism, and in particular, against the hegemonism of the two superpowers — the U.S. and the USSR. We must unite will all genuine Marxist-Leninist Parties and organizations the world over, and carry the struggle against modern revisionism through to the end. On the domestic front, we must pursue our Party's basic line and policies for the entire historical period of socialism, persevere in continuing the revolution under the dictatorship of the proletariat, unite with all the forces that can be united and work hard to build our country into a powerful socialist state, so as to make a greater contribution to mankind.

We must uphold Chairman Mao's teachings that we should "be prepared against war, be prepared against natural disasters, and do everything for the people" and should "dig tunnels deep, store grain everywhere, and never seek hegemony," maintain high vigilance and be fully prepared against any war of aggression that imperialism may launch and particularly against surprise attack on our country by Soviet revisionist social-imperialism. Our heroic People's Liberation Army and our vast militia must be prepared at all times to wipe out any enemy that may invade.

Taiwan Province is our motherland's sacred territory, and

the people in Taiwan are our kith and kin. We have infinite concern for our compatriots in Taiwan, who love and long for the motherland. Our compatriots in Taiwan can have a bright future only by returning to the embrace of the motherland. Taiwan must be liberated. Our great motherland must be unified. This is the common aspiration and sacred duty of the people of all nationalities of the country, including our compatriots in Taiwan. Let us strive together to attain this goal.

Comrades!

We must be aware that although we have achieved great successes in socialist revolution and socialist construction, we are always lagging behind the needs of the objective situation. We still face very heavy tasks in our socialist revolution. The tasks of struggle-criticism-transformation in the Great Proletarian Cultural Revolution need to be carried on in a thoroughgoing way on all fronts. More efforts are required to overcome the shortcomings, mistakes and certain unhealthy tendencies in our work. Our whole Party must make good use of the present opportune time to consolidate and carry forward the achievements of the Great Proletarian Cultural Revolution and work well in all fields.

First of all, we should continue to do a good job of criticizing Lin Piao and rectifying style of work. We should make full use of that teacher by negative example, the Lin Piao anti-Party clique, to educate the whole Party, Army and the people of all nationalities of our country in class struggle and two-line struggle, and criticize revisionism and the bourgeois world outlook so that the masses will be able to draw on the historical experience of the ten struggles between the two lines in our Party, acquire a deeper understanding of the characteristics and laws of class struggle and two-line struggle in the period of socialist revolution in our country, and raise their ability to distinguish genuine from sham Marxism.

All Party members should conscientiously study works by Marx, Engels, Lenin and Stalin and by Chairman Mao, adhere to dialectical materialism and historical materialism, combat idealism and metaphysics and remold their world outlook.

Senior cadres, in particular, should make greater efforts to "read and study conscientiously and have a good grasp of Marxism," try their best to master the basic theories of Marxism, learn the history of the struggles of Marxism against old and new revisionism and opportunism of all descriptions, and understand how Chairman Mao has inherited, defended and developed Marxism-Leninism in the course of integrating the universal truth of Marxism-Leninism with the concrete practice of revolution. We hope that through sustained efforts "the vast numbers of our cadres and the people will be able to arm themselves with the basic theories of Marxism."

We should attach importance to the class struggle in the superstructure, including all spheres of culture, and transform all parts of the superstructure which do not conform to the economic base. We should handle correctly the two types of contradictions of different nature. We should continue to carry out in earnest all of Chairman Mao's proletarian policies. We should continue to carry out well the revolution in literature and art, the revolution in education and the revolution in public health, and the work with regard to the educated youth who go to mountainous and other rural areas, run the May 7 cadres schools well and support all the newly emerging things of socialism.

Economically ours is still a poor and developing country. We should thoroughly carry out the General Line of going all out, aiming high and achieving greater, faster, better and more economical results in building socialism, grasp revolution and promote production. We should continue to implement the principle of "taking agriculture as the foundation and industry as the leading factor" and the series of policies of walking on two legs, and build our country independently and with the initiative in our own hands, through self-reliance, hard struggle, diligence and frugality. Marx pointed out that "the greatest productive power is the revolutionary class itself." One basic experience from our socialist construction over more than two decades is to rely on the masses. In order to learn from Tach'ing in industry and to learn from Tachai in agriculture.

we must persist in putting proletarian politics in command, vigorously launch mass movements, and give full scope to the enthusiasm, wisdom and creativeness of the masses. On this basis, planning and coordination must be strengthened, rational rules and regulations improved, and both central and local initiative further brought into full play. Party organizations should pay close attention to questions of economic policy, concern themselves with the well-being of the masses, do a good job of investigation and study, and strive effectively to fulfill or over-fulfill the state plans for developing the national economy so that our socialist economy will make still greater progress.

We should further strengthen the centralized leadership of the Party. Of the seven sectors — industry, agriculture, commerce, culture and education, the Army, the government and the Party — it is the Party that exercises overall leadership. Party committees at all levels should study "On Strengthening the Party Committee System," "Methods of Work of Party Committees" and other writings by Chairman Mao, sum up their experience and further strengthen the centralized leadership of the Party ideologically, organizationally as well as through rules and regulations. At the same time, the role of revolutionary committees and mass organizations should be brought into full play. We should strengthen the leadership given to primary organizations in order to ensure that leadership there is truly in the hands of Marxists and in the hands of workers, poor and lower-middle peasants and other working people, and that the task of consolidating the dictatorship of the proletariat is fulfilled in every primary organization. Party committees at all levels should apply democratic centralism better and improve their art of leadership. It should be emphatically pointed out that quite a few Party committees are engrossed in daily routines and minor matters, paying no attention to major issues. This is very dangerous. If they do not change, they will inevitably step onto the road of revisionism. It is hoped that comrades throughout the Party, leading comrades in particular, will guard against such a tendency and earnestly change such a style of work.

The experience with regard to combining the old, the middle-aged and the young in the leadership, which the masses created during the Great Proletarian Cultural Revolution, has provided us with favorable conditions for training millions of successors to the revolutionary cause of the proletariat in accordance with the five requirements put forward by Chairman Mao. Party organizations at all levels should keep on the agenda this fundamental task which is crucial for generations to come. Chairman Mao says: "Revolutionary successors of the proletariat are invariably brought up in great storms." They must be tempered in class struggle and two-line struggle and educated by both positive and negative experience. Therefore, a genuine Communist must be ready to accept a higher or lower post and be able to stand the test of going up or stepping down many times. All cadres, veteran and new alike, must maintain close ties with the masses, be modest and prudent, guard against arrogance and impetuosity, go to any post as required by the Party and the people, and firmly carry out Chairman Mao's revolutionary line and policies under every circumstance.

Comrades! The Tenth National Congress of the Party will have a far-reaching influence on the course of our Party's development. We will soon convene the Fourth National People's Congress. Our people and the revolutionary people of all countries place great hopes on our Party and our country. We are confident that our Party, under the leadership of Chairman Mao, will uphold his proletarian revolutionary line, do our work well, and live up to the expectations of our people and the people throughout the world!

The future is bright, the road is tortuous. Let our whole Party unite, let our people of all nationalities unite, be resolute, fear no sacrifice, and surmount every difficulty to win victory!

Long live the great, glorious and correct Communist Party of China!

Long live Marxism-Leninism-Mao Tse-tung Thought!

Long live Chairman Mao! A long, long life to Chairman Mao!

21

THE FALLACIES ADVANCED BY THE
LIN PIAO ANTI-PARTY CLIQUE*

Wen-hui Daily

I. Various Manifestations of Apriorism

The idealist apriorism Lin Piao expounded was to serve as
the theoretical principle for opposing the Party. Such apriorism
has the following various manifestations.

1. "Revolution Explodes Deep in the Heart"

On the question of transforming one's world outlook, Lin Piao
advocated the so-called "revolution explodes deep in the heart."
According to this erroneous view, to transform one's world
outlook requires no participation in social practice, or study
of Marxism-Leninism-Mao Tse-tung Thought. The only thing
needed is to experience an "explosion deep in the heart," and
then everything will be in order. This is a new version of the
black "self-cultivation" theory. It is idealist apriorism.

---

*"Lin Piao fan-tang chi-t'uan ti miao-lun." Wen-hui pao,
November 8, 11, 15, 18, 22, and 25, 1973. This series of materials, compiled by Wen-hui Daily, the leading Chinese Communist newspaper in Hong Kong, are intended for use as accom-
panying study materials for the "campaign to study the documents of the Tenth Party Congress."

2. Solving Ideological Problems Through "Blitz-like Action"

On solving ideological problems, Lin Piao propagated "blitz-like action" and expected solutions to be "once and for all." He opposed conducting in-depth investigation and research to verify the nature of problems and refused to work on minute details. Therefore, he violated in a fundamental way the theory of knowledge of dialectical materialism, that is, "practice, knowledge, again practice, and again knowledge," in a vain attempt to lead ideological and political work astray.

3. "To Learn One Thing Once Is to Have Learned Everything" and "Once Is for All"

On the question of study, Lin Piao blatantly propagated the absurd view of "once is for all," and erroneously held that one need only study one thing once, since "to learn one thing once is to have learned everything." Moreover, there was even no need to study the works of Marx, Lenin, and Chairman Mao. Nor was there any need to make efforts to conduct work of investigation and research. Such a "once is for all" theory is a product of pure idealist apriorism. It is in fact dialectical sophistry that opposes both study and practice.

4. "From the Subjective to the Objective"

On the issue of work and production, Lin Piao advocated the method of the so-called "from the subjective to the objective." This turned upside down the relationship between knowledge and practice and was also a product of idealist apriorism. According to Lin Piao's theory, one would be able to construct a whole chariot behind closed doors or deal with things using only one's intuition. This completely violates the Marxist view of giving priority to practice.

5. "Inspirationism"

"Inspirationism" was the main argument of the literary

fallacy pushed by the Lin Piao counterrevolutionary revisionism. He refused to recognize the life of the people as the only
source of literature and art, but propagated the utmost importance of "inspiration," insisting that literary and artistic works
must depend on momentary flashes of inspiration. This is an
out-and-out fallacy of idealist apriorism.

6. "Naturally Endowed Talent" Alone Is Sufficient

According to Lin Piao's view of things, it would seem that
there is no need to take part in social practice or rely on the
masses of the people. Once a person has naturally endowed
"talent," he is able to know and understand everything. What
incredible nonsense!

Lin Piao expounded idealist apriorism with a sinister purpose.
It was to oppose socialist revolution and sabotage socialist construction in a vain attempt to restore capitalism.

7. The Theory of Genius

The Lin Piao anti-Party clique trumpeted the theory of
"genius," advocating that "history is made by heroes." They
shamelessly exalted Lin Piao as the "extraordinary genius,"
and the "brilliant leader who has always been right." They
frenziedly shouted: "We must recognize the genius, learn
from the genius, publicize the genius, and protect the genius."
Their aim was, on the one hand, to negate the determining role
of the masses of the people in the making of history, to deceive
and mislead the masses, and to suffocate the talents and wisdom of the masses, so that the masses would be left powerless
and forever at their mercy. On the other hand, they attempted
to make the masses believe in them as "geniuses" and "heroes"
and therefore willingly delegate to them the power to rule the
world and govern all mankind. In short, they wanted to have
complete domination over the masses of the people in order to
accomplish their sinister goal of subverting the proletarian
dictatorship and restoring capitalism.

II. The "Class Struggle Is Out" Theory

1. The Theory That Only Productivity Counts

Lin Piao and his like expounded the counterrevolutionary
view that only productivity counts. They considered the main
task after the Ninth Party Congress to be the development of
production and attempted in vain to alter the basic line of the
Party in the historical stage of socialism, to oppose continuous
revolution, to sabotage the proletarian dictatorship, and to
restore capitalism.

2. "The Working Class Is the Producing Class"

Lin Piao advocated the nonsense that "the working class is
the producing class." This is a reproduction of the "class
struggle is out" theory. Like his predecessors Bernstein,
Kautsky, and Liu Shao-ch'i, Lin Piao went all out to oppose the
class struggle of the working class against the bourgeoisie.
His design was to reverse the correct direction of the worker
movement, sabotage the movement itself, and attempt to use
trade unions as an instrument of carrying out the revisionist
line and restoring capitalism.

Ever since it came into existence, the working class has been
the adversary of the bourgeoisie. The economic status of the
working class determines its most thorough going revolutionary
character and its sense of organization and discipline. These
qualities have made the working class the gravedigger of the
bourgeoisie. In the process of waging struggles, the working
class in particular has developed its own revolutionary theory,
Marxism, and created its own revolutionary party. Therefore,
the working class has shouldered the great historical mission
of destroying the system of exploitation, eliminating classes,
and liberating all mankind. The history of the working class
is a history of struggles waged against the bourgeoisie. Thus,
how can it be said that the working class is merely a "producing class"?

3. "Politics Is to Get the Peasants to Do Good Farm Work
   and the Workers to Do Good Factory Work"

Politics is a struggle by one class against another. By no
means can farm work and factory work alone represent politics.
The so-called "politics is to get the peasants to do good farm
work and the workers to do good factory work" is sinister sophistry designed by Lin Piao to deceive the peasants and the
workers into being concerned only with farm work and factory
work, without concerning themselves with proletarian politics
and line, or waging class struggle, or carrying out the affairs
of the nation. In so doing, they themselves — the careerists
and conspirators — would be free to subvert the proletarian
dictatorship and proceed to restore capitalism.

III. Slandering the Great Accomplishments of Our Nation

The Lin Piao anti-Party clique conspired to subvert the proletarian dictatorship, slandered the accomplishments made by
our nation after the proletarian dictatorship had assumed
leadership, and engaged in sinister agitation and sowed seeds
of discord among the masses of the people. All this represents
a shameless onslaught against Chairman Mao's revolutionary
line and policies.

1. Sneering at the Excellent Situation

The Lin Piao anti-Party clique violently sneered at and distorted the revolutionary situation, spreading such counterrevolutionary fallacies as "the national economy is stagnant," "the
peasants lack food and are short of clothing," the people's "living
standard is falling," and so on. They negated the glorious achievements made on the various fronts of socialist construction.

2. The "Theory of Disguised Exploitation"

The Lin Piao anti-Party clique confused right and wrong,

turned black into white, and held the absurd view that the
workers were subjected to "disguised exploitation." This is
a vicious slander of the socialist system, with the counterrevolutionary intent of inciting the workers to demand higher
wages and better treatment. They deliberately placed in antagonism the interests of the state and the interests of the people,
the immediate interests of the masses and their long-range
interests, and the development of production and the improvement of livelihood. They vainly attempted to distribute all
national income, eliminate socialist accumulation, and thereby
destroy the economic base of the proletarian dictatorship, in
order to achieve their goal of usurping the Party and seizing
power.

3. The "Theory of Disguised Reform through Labor"

Lin Piao maliciously sneered at the policy of sending educated
youths up into the mountains and down into the countryside and
equated it with "disguised reform through labor." He attempted
in vain to alter the orientation of the youth movement, to win
over the support of the younger generation from the proletariat,
and to cultivate successors from among the landlord and bourgeois classes according to his counterrevolutionary revisionist
line.

4. The "Theory of Disguised Unemployment"

Lin Piao viciously attacked the "May 7" cadre schools, holding the erroneous view that cadres sent to the "May 7" cadre
schools "had practically lost their jobs." He attempted in vain
to stir up discontent among cadres sent down to lower levels to
practice manual labor and to lure the cadres onto the revisionist
road by turning the proletarian cadres at the service of the
people into revisionist "mandarins" with high salaries and
luxurious living conditions. The Lin Piao anti-Party clique's
blatant slander of the great victories won in the socialist enterprises of our nation and its attack on Chairman Mao's revolu-

tionary line and policies had their sinister purpose. It was to restore capitalism in our nation, to pull the socialist new China back to the rotton, backward, and dark old China, and to push the people of our nation once again into the miserable abyss of exploitation and enslavement.

5. The So-Called "Rich People and Strong Nation"

The Lin Piao anti-Party clique openly repudiated the fundamental differences between the socialist system and the capitalist system and put forth the counterrevolutionary principle of "rich people and strong nation," which had been used many times during the period under the dictatorship of the landlord-bourgeois class. They opposed the socialist principle of distribution, the socialist system of ownership, and the dictatorship of the proletariat, and in so doing fabricated public opinion for the restoration of capitalism.

During the last two decades or so, under the leadership of Chairman Mao and the Party Central Committee, the industrial and agricultural production of our nation has progressed at a speed unparalleled in any period of old society. The proletarian class and the laboring people have become the owner of the means of production; the roots of poverty have been removed; and material and cultural life has been steadily uplifted and improved. A poverty-stricken, backward, and semifeudal and semicolonial old China has been transformed into a prospering and vigorous socialist new China.

The Lin Piao anti-Party clique sneered at the great accomplishments of our nation and attacked the socialist system. His program of so-called "rich people and strong nation" was actually designed to overthrow our socialist nation under the proletarian dictatorship. The so-called "rich people and strong nation" propagated by Lin Piao and his kind was aimed at making the landlord-bourgeois class "rich" and the Lin Piao anti-Party clique "strong." It was to push the proletarian class and the laboring people back into the dark old society.

6. "Questioning Everything and Overthrowing Everything"

Lin Piao and company once propagated the seemingly "Left" but actually "Right" slogan of "questioning everything and overthrowing everything." The facts are crystal clear — they did not really intend to overthrow everything. What they did want to "overthrow" was the socialist system under the proletarian dictatorship, the proletarian revolutionary line of Chairman Mao, and all those who held fast to the correct line of Chairman Mao. By no means did Lin Piao and his kind repudiate all systems of government. They had long dreamed of acquiring the "power of suppression" and attempted in vain to seize it through conspiratorial means in order to establish a government under the dictatorship of the landlord-compradorbourgeois class and exercise a fascist dictatorship over the people.

7. "Politics Can Stimulate Other Things"

Lin Piao spread the fallacy that "politics can stimulate other things." This is also a tactic of using an extremely "Left" slogan to cover his extreme "Right" deeds. The kind of "politics" Lin Piao had in mind was by no means the politics that is "overstressed." Nor was it "armchair politics." It was out-and-out counterrevolutionary politics of the landlord-bourgeois class. Look what Lin Piao and his like were doing: ganging up together, staging the counterrevolutionary coup, surrendering to the enemy and betraying the nation, and thereby turning themselves into traitors and renegades. All these are excellent, ironclad proof. They deliberately abstracted politics to avoid the class content of politics and distorted the commanding-commanded relationship between proletarian politics and various other work into one of "stimulating" and "stimulated," thereby actually negating the commanding role of proletarian politics. They furiously attacked and undermined the Marxist principle of dialectical unity between politics and economy in order to create confusion. They attempted vainly to substitute bourgeois politics for proletarian politics and to use bourgeois politics to

smash the economic base of socialism and the various enterprises of the proletarian class, so as to achieve their sinister
aim of total restoration of capitalism.

8. The So-Called "Equal Attention to Both Ends"

Lin Piao also advanced such nonsense as, in matters of politics, "revolution comes first," but in matters of production,
"production remains first," thus advocating "equal attention to
both ends." Lin Piao put politics in opposition to technical
work and equated the two things with the two ends of a weighing
scale which should be balanced. This negated the commanding
role of politics vis-à-vis technical work and provided a pretext
for pursuing his revisionist line.

IV. Opposing the Strategic Principles of Chairman Mao

During the various periods of the new democratic revolution
and socialist revolution, Lin Piao used his erroneous military
ideas to oppose the great military thinking and principles of
Chairman Mao.

1. Prior to the War of Resistance Against Japan

During the second revolutionary civil war, Lin Piao took an
opportunistic stand to oppose Chairman Mao's thesis of establishing revolutionary bases and advocated the practice of roving
rebel bands. In his article "A Single Spark Can Start a Prairie
Fire," Chairman Mao severely criticized this erroneous idea.
During the second half of the second revolutionary civil war,
Lin Piao went all out to trumpet the so-called "quick and brief
sneak attack" and thus rendered service to Wang Ming's "Left"
opportunist line.

2. The Period of the War of Resistance Against Japan

At the outset of the War of Resistance Against Japan, Lin Piao
followed again Wang Ming's right opportunist line of capitulationism and opposed Chairman Mao's strategic principle of
maintaining independence and initiative and waging guerrilla
warfare in the mountains. Instead, he advocated fighting large

and regular battles in cooperation with the Kuomintang. At that
time Japanese imperialism was launching a furious attack on
North China, and the Kuomintang forces were losing one battle
after another. The Kuomintang thus could not be relied on to
fight major battles. The only effective way of blunting the
fierce spearhead of the enemy and gradually turning the tide of
the war was to mobilize the masses on a large scale. Time
and again Chairman Mao criticized the mistaken idea of relying on the Kuomintang and concentrating military power to
fight major battles. He repeatedly and clearly pointed out to
the whole Party that all the work in North China should be
based on guerrilla warefare and that this was the only correct
policy to follow. However, Lin Piao went so far as to disregard
the repeated instructions of Chairman Mao and adamantly advocated the waging of positional warfare and a war of attrition
against the Japenese forces. As a matter of fact, under the
circumstances prevailing then, fighting large battles not only
could not succeed in halting the advance of the Japanese forces
but also would obstruct the strategic task of sparing troops for
mobilizing the masses, developing guerrilla warfare, and establishing base areas, thereby directly impeding and undermining the
thorough implementation of Chairman Mao's strategic principles.

Many times Lin Piao mentioned the limited space, manpower,
and food supplies in the mountainous areas as a pretext to oppose Chairman Mao's repeated instructions on establishing base
areas in the mountains. This fully exposed his unwillingness
to do the hard work of setting up guerrilla bases and his true
capitulationist stand of relying solely on the Kuomintang to
fight major battles.

3. The Period of the War of Liberation

During the period of the War of Liberation, Lin Piao took an
opposite stand to Chairman Mao's strategic and tactical thought.
He put forth a series of subjective and metaphysical "principles
of tactics" to rival Chairman Mao's ten major military principles. Only after Lin Piao's erroneous ideas had been defeated by Chairman Mao's correct military line did the War of
Liberation gain a speedy victory.

4. Erroneously Discrediting the Militia as "Outdated"

During the period of socialist revolution, Lin Piao and company went so far as to attack the militia as "outdated."

Chairman Mao's thesis of the people's war is the indispensable weapon for defeating the enemy and assuring victory.
Lin Piao even went so far as to oppose the people's war and ferociously sabotage the development of the militia.

5. Blatantly Exalting Confucius

Lin Piao and other swindlers like him were by nature schemers and conspirators who did not read books or newspapers and had no knowledge at all. Yet they spread freely the ideology of slave-owners and feudal lords. Lin Piao exalted Confucius but scorned Ch'in Shih Huang-ti for his "burning of the books and burying scholars alive." He openly advocated the need to learn from Chu Hsi's philosophy of "dealing with people." Lin Piao and company attempted in vain to borrow weapons from the reactionaries of the past to attack the proletarian class and to call on the spirits of historical figures to render service to their counterrevolutionary restoration and subversive conspiracy.

V. The Fallacy of Considering the History of Mankind as a History of Political Coups

Lin Piao and other swindlers like him started from the idealist conception of history and talked freely about palace coups. They believed that the history of mankind is one of political coups and that only a few daring men are needed for shaking heaven and earth and making history, and other such nonsense.

Ever since the period of slavery the history of mankind has been a history of class struggle. By distorting it into a history of coups, Lin Piao revealed his sinister wild scheme to subvert the proletarian dictatorship.

1. The So-Called "One Blow to Eliminate All" Class Enemies

Lin Piao trumpeted the view that after the Great Cultural

Revolution had been underway for more than two years, not only had all the "renegades, spies, capitalist-roaders been eliminated with one blow" but also "the influences of century-old capitalism and thousand-year-old feudalism" were also wiped out entirely. This is another lie. Lin Piao's purpose in advancing these fallacies was to blur people's concept of class struggle, to paralyze people's revolutionary fighting will, and to cover his own vicious scheme of plotting for a counterrevolutionary coup and restoring capitalism.

The facts have made it clear to all that the destruction of one or two anti-Party cliques in no way means the complete elimination of all class enemies. A few rounds of revolutionary criticism movements can in no way wipe out once and for all the ideology of the exploiting class. The bourgeoisie always seeks to strike back against the proletariat; they apply their ideological influences and constantly change their techniques. Once there is an opportunity, the submerged dregs surface again. Therefore we must never slacken our vigilance against them.

2. Agitating for "Redistribution of Power"

Lin Piao and his kind violated the line set forth by the Ninth Party Congress and vainly attempted to split the Party and the revolutionary ranks. They set up mountaintop strongholds, promoted sectarianism, cultivated private ties, pursued personal interests, developed counterrevolutionary influences, and organized the bourgeois headquarters. They "drew a self-centered dividing line," appointed only "men with personal ties," and advanced the reactionary bourgeois line of "attacking a great many in order to protect a handful," in a conspiracy for endangering comrades who were steadfast in carrying out Chairman Mao's revolutionary line. They blatantly fabricated counterrevolutionary public opinion, shamelessly engaged in self-glorification, erected monuments and decreed literary works in their own honor, and agitated for "redistribution of power" in order to "seize the power of leadership." All this finally led to a counterrevolutionary coup in a vain attempt to murder the great leader Chairman Mao, to set up a rival Party Central Committee, and to surrender to Soviet socialist imperialism.

3. "United Effort Without Unity of Minds"

Lin Piao propagated the fallacy of "united effort without unity of minds."

Without unity of knowledge, it is impossible to have unity of action; without unity of hearts or a common ideological basis, it is impossible to speak of unity, let alone united effort.

In order to cover up his subversive activities of undermining revolutionary unity and splitting the Party, Lin Piao spread the fallacy of the so-called "united effort without unity of minds." His aim was to subvert the common ideological basis of revolutionary unity, negate the class substance of such unity, and eliminate class distinction, in a wild attempt to deceive the people and make them follow him.

VI. Betraying the Marxist-Leninist Theory of Party-Building

The Lin Piao anti-Party clique in a fundamental way betrayed the Marxist-Leninist theory of proletarian dictatorship and party-building. Their revisionist line of party-building was designed to corrode Party cadres and members, to alter the proletarian character of the Party through dissemination of reactionary bourgeois ideas and conspiratorial activities, and to split the Party itself, thereby turning the Party into their instrument for restoring capitalism and subverting the proletarian dictatorship. To be sure, such were the wild dreams and wishful thinking of only a small handful of counterrevolutionary elements, and their schemes could never be realized.

1. Building the Party for Capitalism and Private Interests

In order to carry out anti-Party conspiratorial activities and practice revisionism, Lin Piao fanned up ill winds and wicked influences and attempted vainly to lure Communist Party members to become philistines and politicians by such nasty means as making promotions and promises, giving parties and feasts, and handing out gifts. The criminal conduct of this small handful of diehards has fully revealed that they were building the Party for capitalism and for private interests.

2. The Theory That "Small Matters Are Harmless"

Lin Piao was the agent of the bourgeoisie within the Party spreading the rotton ideology and work style of the exploiting class. He and his like went all out to introduce the corrupt and dirty ill winds and wicked influences of the exploiting class into the Party in order to promote their counterrevolutionary revisionist line and subvert the proletarian dictatorship. In order to carry on counterrevolutionary conspiratory activities, they went so far as to put forth the so-called "small matters are harmless" theory. In fact, they were for revisionism, for splittism, and for conspiracy and intrigue. The so-called "harmless" fallacies were advanced only for the defense of their criminal conduct.

3. The So-Called "Naturally Rational"

Lin Piao and company tried by every means to obstruct and sabotage the correct implementation of the Party's line and policies, and they opposed the Party's leadership in the mass movement. On the one hand, they propagated the theory that "history is made by heroes," thereby attempting to restrain and suppress the masses from the "Right" standpoint. On the other hand, they presented themselves in an extreme "Left" posture and asserted erroneously that all views from among the masses were "naturally rational" and therefore entirely correct, and that there was no need to do the painstaking work of making analysis and general deductions. On the surface, it appears that they trusted and respected the masses. But in fact,

this was not true at all. The reactionary fallacy advanced by
them truly belongs to the opportunistic theory of "spontaneity."
It is a reproduction in a new situation of the fallacy that "whatever the masses want will be satisfied." It has nothing in common with the principle of historical materialism that considers
the masses of the people as the makers of history.

To propagate the theory of spontaneity during the period of
proletarian revolution is to directly oppose the leadership of
Marxism in the mass movement, to negate the decisive role
that a correct ideological and political line plays upon the outcome of revolutionary enterprises, and to attempt to lead the
mass movement astray.

VII. Advocating "Serving All Kinds of People"

On the development of light industry production, Lin Piao
once advocated that "whatever is profitable will be pursued"
and emphasized "serving all kinds of people," in a vain attempt
to lure the production of light industrial goods onto the rotten
road of capitalism. The slogan "serving all kinds of people"
expounded by him and his kind was in fact designed to revive
capitalist liberalization, to promote the life-style of the bourgeoisie, and to fill the market with feudalist-capitalist-revision-
ist merchandise, thereby providing service to the landlord-
bourgeois class.

1. "Techniques Come First" and "Techniques Are Useless"

Lin Piao pitted politics against techniques, advocating "techniques come first" at one time and "techniques are useless" at
another. In essence, both arguments were aimed at seizing the
leadership over techniques from the proletariat and placing it
in the hands of the bourgeoisie. To trumpet "techniques come
first" is to negate the leading role and commanding status of
proletarian politics by placing techniques above politics or at
least on the same level as politics. To advocate "techniques
are useless" is to discard techniques as an instrument of serv-

ing proletarian politics, to downgrade techniques, to give up leadership over techniques, and to foresake the important task of developing a proletarian technical force. Lin Piao's aim in advancing such fallacies was to sabotage the proletarian revolution and construction enterprises.

2. Negating the Importance of Military Training

Lin Piao and company spared no effort in opposing Chairman Mao's line of army-building. Alternately they asserted that "military affairs are the fullest expression of politics" and that "politics can stimulate other things." They pushed the absurd views such as to have a lower standard of military training is not too serious and that to learn military techniques does not require full-time effort, for they could be picked up very quickly when needed. This is in outright opposition to and a blatant betrayal of Chairman Mao's directives on strengthening military training. They attempted in vain to repudiate the importance of military training, to abolish military training, thereby to weaken the combat strength of our army.

3. Trumpeting "Recreation Comes First"

Regarding the development of literary, artistic, and athletic activities, Lin Piao propagated the fallacy of so-called "recreation comes first." His aim was to oppose and abolish the function of such activities in promoting revolutionary education, and to corrupt youths by emphasizing "recreation comes first," thereby making literary-artistic and athletic activities serve the purpose of implementing his revisionist line.

4. Advancing the "Theory of Child-Centeredness"

On the question of ideological education among young children, Lin Piao and his like played many tricks. At first they adopted the capitalist trash theory of "child-centeredness" and pushed the view that educational programs must follow the spontaneity

and interests of the child, thereby obstructing the carrying
on of proletarian ideological education among young children.
When this erroneous view had been criticized, they again presented themselves in an extreme "Left" posture by disregard-
ing the difference between young children and adults and by
practicing subjectivism on a large scale, in a vain attempt to
torpedo the effectiveness of ideological education conducted by
the proletariat among young children.

VIII. Sabotaging the Educational Revolution

In 1958 the vast masses responded to the call of Chairman
Mao and developed a high tide of educational revolution. At the
time when many revolutionary new events were developing
vigorously despite the suppression and sabotage by Liu Shao-
ch'i's revisionist line, Lin Piao jumped out to sneer at the revolution as "chaotic, bad, and deviated," in a vain attempt to
smother new developments of this kind.

During the Great Proletarian Cultural Revolution, the vast
masses stood up to rebel against the old educational system.
Lin Piao again brought forth idealism and metaphysics and
spared no efforts in obstructing and sabotaging the criticism
of the revisionist educational line. In so doing he again reck-
lessly trampled the revolutionary new developments. Lin Piao
and his like maliciously distorted and violated the path pointed
out by Chairman Mao's "May 7 Directive," the principle of
integrating theory with practice, the dialectic relationship between politics and technical work, and so on. His aim was to
lead educational revolution astray and prevent the workers,
peasants, and soldiers from learning knowledge useful to the
revolution, thereby destroying talented people who were both
red and expert and undermining the development of scientific
and cultural enterprises of socialism.

1. Agitating for "Memorizing Everything Mechanically" and "Seeking Big Profits from Small Investments"

The so-called "policy" of study advanced by Lin Piao did not deal with conscientiously studying the standpoint, views, and methods of Marxism. Nor did it mention the necessity of uniting the study of Marxism with revolutionary practice. Thus, in essence, it destroyed the unity between theory and practice, repudiated the indefinite cyclical process of practice, knowledge, again practice, and again knowledge. It was entirely a product of idealism and metaphysics.

Lin Piao further propagated the fallacy that "memorizing everything mechanically" alone is sufficient, which is diametrically opposed to the attitude toward study persistently advocated by Chairman Mao.

Lin Piao asserted blatantly that it was possible in study to seek "big profits from small investments." This view exemplifies his policy of studying only words and sentences and memorizing everything mechanically. "Seeking big profits from small investments" is a term used by the exploiting class and a business cliché of the bourgeoisie. Its adoption by Lin Piao thus reveals in one phrase his sinister design of using study as an opportunistic trade for decorative purposes, for gaining political capital, and for serving his revisionist line.

Lin Piao's policy of "seeking big profits from small investments" on the question of study was a malicious slander of Marxism-Leninism-Mao Tse-tung Thought. It was a most serious defamation of the vast masses of Party members, cadres, workers, peasants, and soldiers.

2. Advocating "Take a Shortcut"

Lin Piao stubbornly insisted that in study one can always "take a shortcut." This is unscientific and incompatible with the learning attitude of Marxism-Leninism. It causes one to slip onto the dangerous road of idealism and metaphysics. Lenin once said, "He who is unwilling to make a serious effort cannot find the truth." Chairman Mao also says, "As for learning materialism and dialectics, one must make an effort," since "without making an effort, one would slip into the spheres of idealism and metaphysics."

3. "Studying to Become a Mandarin" and "Studying Is Useless"

To suit the requirements of their plot to restore capitalism, the Lin Piao anti-Party clique sometimes propagated the idea of "studying to become a mandarin." They used the feudal concept that "everything is lowly except for studying, which is noble," to lure young students into the pursuit of pure expertise. Sometimes, however, they also spread the idea that "studying is useless" and "doing manual labour makes studying unnecessary," and therefore rejected the importance of studying the works of Marx, Lenin, and Mao Tse-tung, as well as the cultural knowledge of socialism. The first view was intended to repudiate manual labor by emphasizing studying. The second view was intended to repudiate studying by emphasizing manual labor. The common aim shared by both views was to pit studying against doing manual labor and to deceive the young students.

IX. Marxism-Leninism Is Too Distant

Lin Piao advanced the nonsense that "Marxism-Leninism is too distant from us" and therefore opposed the study of the works of Marx and Lenin. This too was to oppose the masses grasping Marxism-Leninism-Mao Tse-tung Thought so that his aim of restoring capitalism could be realized.

1. The Theory of "Two Levels" — the Top and the Bottom

Lin Piao erroneously maintained that "party spirit is on the top and materialism is at the bottom," insisting that party spirit and materialism were two separate, totally unrelated elements, with one always on the "top" and the other always at the "bottom." At the "bottom" there is only materialism, but not party spirit, while on the "top" there is only party spirit, but not materialism.

Can materialism exist without the party spirit? Absolutely not. All philosophies have their party spirit. Not only does materialism have its party spirit but idealism too has its party spirit. The difference lies only in the character of such party spirit.

Let us take at look at Ch'en Tu-hsiu, Wang Ming, Liu Shao-ch'i, and Lin Piao. It is not true that all of these people have at one time or another usurped the top position in the Party or the state? It is not true that all of them have been on the "top"? Yet what party spirit did anyone of them possess? All of them were representatives of the landlord-bourgeois class who sneaked into the Party. What they did have was the party spirit of the landlord-bourgeois class. In contrast, those hundreds of thousands of revolutionary fighters working on the front lines of the Three Great Revolutionary Movements have all displayed a proletarian party spirit, despite the fact that their positions are at the "bottom." This fact tells us that whether a person possesses the party spirit is not to be judged by whether he is on the "top," but by whether in the class struggle and the struggle between different lines he will unswervingly side with the proletariat, side with Marxism-Leninism, and steadfastly carry out the revolutionary line of Marxism-Leninism.

Lin Piao's fallacious view that party spirit exists only on the "top" has its origin in his idealist conception of history that "history is made by heroes." According to him, the masses at the "bottom" are all without a party spirit, that is, without a class stand of their own. As a result, whether they should follow one road or another, and whether they should do one thing or another, are all to be determined by those "on the top," since such decisions involve the question of party spirit and need not and must not be interfered in by those "at the bottom." It becomes clear, therefore, that the party spirit which Lin Piao and his like desire is something lofty, something high above the proletariat and the masses of the people. To be sure, such a party spirit far beyond the reach of the masses does exist, but it is by no means the party spirit of the proletariat. It can only be the spirit of the parties organized by the landlord-bourgeois class and the fascists. This is because only when a small handful of exploiters organize a party in their own interest will they always look down upon the masses of the people as a "mob" and glorify themselves as "heroes" high above the masses.

2. The So-Called "New Age" and the "Theory of Outdatedness"

Lin Piao erroneously asserted that the times in which we live are already "different" from Lenin's, maintaining that "during the last fifty years ... world history has moved into a brand-new age." The proclamation of the so-called "new age" by Lin Piao is diametrically opposed to Chairman Mao's teaching that we are still in an age of imperialism and proletarian revolution, and therefore negates the fundamental contradictions in the age of imperialism. By altering the definition of eras, the Lin Piao anti-Party clique repudiated the basic principles of Marxism-Leninism. Their fantastic logic was that with the changing times Marxism-Leninism would be outdated. Their true intent in advancing such a fallacy was to have everybody "store away" Marxism-Leninism-Mao Tse-tung Thought so that they could freely temper with the fundamental line and policies of the Party, restore capitalism, and place the Chinese people once again under the reactionary rule of the miserable old society.

The so-called "new age" and the "theory of outdatedness" put forth by Lin Piao were not novel things. The revisionists of the Second Comintern also once created the so-called theory of "postimperialism," proclaiming that Marxism was "insufficient" and "outdated." Khrushchev, Breshnev and other people like them have also slandered Marxism as "outdated" on the pretext that the historical conditions have changed. It is thus clear that Lin Piao was none other than a revisionist just like Kautsky, Khrushchev, and their kind.

3. The "Theory of Inner-Party Peace"

To suit the needs of their counterrevolutionary designs, Lin Piao and company — like Wang Ming and Liu Shao-ch'i — went all out to propagate the theory of "inner-Party peace" and tried

by all means to oppose the intensive ideological struggle within
the Party. By way of insinuation they discredited inner-Party
struggle as something that could be manufactured at will for
the sole purpose of "searching for targets of struggle," thereby
entirely wiping out the objective fact that inner-Party struggle
is a mere reflection of class struggle in society. In so doing,
they exposed themselves as the vicious enemy of Marxism-
Leninism-Mao Tse-tung Thought. In fact, did they really desire "inner-Party peace"? Absolutely not. They did not care
for peace at all. This can be seen in the "fierce struggles"
and "merciless attacks" they launched against the vast masses
of cadres and Party members who opposed their counterrevolutionary revisionist line. The so-called "inner-Party peace"
was merely a smoke screen they created for making a ferocious
onslaught against the proletarian class.

X. Is Lin Piao a "Leftist" or a "Rightist"?

Is the line followed by Lin Piao "Left" opportunism or
"Right" opportunism? In two different ways, both "Left" and
"Right" opportunists violate the periodicity of the development
of things and are divorced from social practice. The "Left"
opportunists are those "whose thinking outstrips a given stage
of development of the objective process. Some regard their
fantasies as truth, while others strain themself to realize in
the present an ideal which can only be realized in the future."
In their actions, they commit adventurism. The Right opportunists are "people whose thinking fails to advance with changing objective conditions," and who "fail to see that while the
struggle of opposites has already pushed the objective process
forward, their knowledge stops at the old stage." "They only
know how to trail behind the chariot, grumbling that it goes too
fast and trying to drag it back or turn it in the opposite direction." They are the diehards in the revolutionary ranks.
Lin Piao stood for revisionism, not Marxism; for splittism,
not unity; and for intrigue and conspiracy, not openness and
honesty. The counterrevolutionary principles he formulated

and the counterrevolutionary armed coup he staged were aimed
at seizing the highest power of the Party and the state, at altering in a fundamental manner the basic policies and line of the
Party, at subverting the dictatorship of the proletariat, and at
restoring capitalism. Internally, he intended to revive the
landlord-bourgeois class in order to exercise a feudal-comprador-fascist dictatorship. Externally, he intended to surrender to Soviet revisionism and collude with imperialism, revisionism, and counterrevolutionaries to oppose China, oppose
Communism, and oppose revolution.

The criminal conduct of the Lin Piao anti-Party clique has
fully exposed their sinister plot to halt the forward-moving
wheel of history and even turn it in the opposite direction.
The line they followed was in essence Right opportunism.
Lin Piao spoke like a "Leftist" but was a "Rightist" to the core.
He was a big Rightist in every sense of the word.

22

LIN PIAO AND THE DOCTRINE OF
CONFUCIUS AND MENCIUS*

Mass Criticism Group of Peking University
and Tsinghua University

Inspired by the spirit of the Tenth National Congress of the
Communist Party of China, the movement to criticize Lin Piao
and Confucius is developing in depth. Lenin pointed out that in
the acute struggle between the proletariat and the exploiting
classes, "the more varied the exploiters' attempts to uphold
the old, the sooner will the proletariat learn to ferret out its
enemies from their last nook and corner, to pull up the roots
of their domination." The current vigorous struggle to criticize
Confucius is a component part of the criticism of Lin Piao and
is precisely a battle to pull up the roots of Lin Piao's counterrevolutionary revisionist line. Lin Piao's hideout was flooded
with the trash of Confucian ideology and stank of putrid
Confucianism. More and more facts show that the reactionary
doctrine of Confucius and Mencius was an important source of
Lin Piao's revisionism. Lin Piao and company resorted to this
reactionary doctrine for restoring capitalism politically, tam-
pering with the Party's theoretical basis ideologically, muster-
ing ranks of counterrevolutionaries by recruiting deserters and

*Pei-ching ta-hsüeh Ch'ing-hua ta-hsüeh ta p'i-p'an tsu, "Lin
Piao yü K'ung Meng chih tao," Hung-ch'i [Red Flag], No. 2
(February 1, 1974), 8-15. This translation is taken, with minor
editorial revisions, from Peking Review, No. 7 (February 15,
1974), 6-12. Explanatory notes are from Peking Review.

renegades for a diehard clique organizationally, playing counter-revolutionary double-dealing tricks and engaging in intrigues and conspiracies tactically. Once Lin Piao's disguise was stripped off, he was exposed for what he was — an out-and-out devout disciple of Confucius.

Lin Piao Followed Confucius in Advocating "Self-Restraint and Restoration of the Rites" in His Attempt to Restore Capitalism

Lin Piao's political line was a counterrevolutionary revisionist line, an ultra-Rightist line of restoration and retrogression. In his own words, it was "restraining oneself and restoring the rites." In less than three months, between October 1969 and January 1970, Lin Piao and his diehard conspirator wrote four scrolls reading: "Of all things, this is the most important: To restrain oneself and restore the rites." "Restraining oneself and restoring the rites" was the reactionary program Confucius put forward in order to restore the slave system. In regarding "restraining oneself and restoring the rites" as the most important of all his affairs, Lin Piao revealed his impatience and wolfish ambition to subvert the dictatorship of the proletariat and restore capitalism.

The latter part of the Spring and Autumn period (770-476 B.C.) was a period of tremendous social changes in Chinese history, one of transition from the slave system to feudalism. At that time China was in great disorder. The slaves frequently rose in rebellion. The newly emerging landlords vigorously advocated reforms and waged struggles to seize power from the slave-owners. All this brought the old slave-owning order of the "rule of rites" to the brink of total collapse. Taking the stand of the declining slave-owning class, Confucius slandered the excellent situation in which "the rites were lost and music was ruined" as "absence of right principles throughout the country" and put forward his reactionary political program of "restraining oneself and restoring the rites." By "restoring the rites," he meant suppression of the slave uprisings, opposition to the reform line of the Legalist school representing the newly rising landlord class, and the pulling of society backward. He wanted to restore the rule of the slave-owning society of the Western Chou dynasty (c. 1066-771 B.C.) in accordance with the rites of the Chou dynasty, and the dictatorship of the slave-owners in line with the principle that "ceremonies, music, and punitive military expeditions proceed from the son of heaven." He meant to "revive states that were extinct, restore families whose line of succession had been broken, and call to office those who had fallen into obscurity," and to reinstate the over-thrown regime of slave-owners and the slave-owning aristocrats who had been deprived of their privileged status, so as to seize back power from the newly rising landlord class. In a nutshell, Confucius' "restoration of the rites" meant restoration of the old order. Lin Piao also attempted a restoration. They had the same counterrevolutionary nature and political needs. That was why Lin Piao grasped at "restraining oneself and restoring the rites" and considered it "most important." His counter-revolutionary coup d'etat and "Outline of Project '571'" are the best explanations of his clamors for the "restoration of the rites."

Lin Piao's "restoring the rites" meant subverting the dicta-torship of the proletariat. Lin Piao and his gang rabidly hated this dictatorship and the Great Proletarian Cultural Revolution. They slandered the dictatorship of the proletariat, which pro-tects the people and suppresses their enemies, as "enforcing the laws of Chin Shih Huang," and attacked continuing the revo-lution under the dictatorship of the proletariat as "creating con-tradictions." They did their utmost to smear and negate the tre-mendous achievements of the Great Proletarian Cultural Revo-lution and wantonly vilified the new things that have emerged during the Great Cultural Revolution. They slandered the ex-cellent situation and the thriving socialist cause since the start of the Great Cultural Revolution as "crisis-ridden" and "stag-nant," and described our state of the dictatorship of the prole-tariat as dark and dreary. In short, in their eyes, nothing in socialist New China was in keeping with their "rites." Like

Confucius, they were all reactionaries who extolled the past to negate the present and advocated retrogression.

Lin Piao's "restoring the rites" was a bid to usurp supreme power in the Party and the state and restore the dictatorship of the landlords and comprador-bourgeoisie. In October 1969, when Lin Piao wrote "restraining oneself and restoring the rites" on a scroll, he echoed Mencius and counseled his sworn followers that "this is most urgent." What did "most urgent" mean in fact? Let us look at the following:

In the winter of 1969, Lin Piao hung on the wall near his bed a scroll in his handwriting: "No ruler of a dynasty can surpass King Wen of Chou...." He styled himself a "sovereign" and alluded to himself as "King Wen." He was impatient to realize his dream of becoming an emperor.

In 1970 Lin Piao resisted Chairman Mao's instructions again and again and produced his anti-Party political program, clamoring that "if the state has no head, there will be no right titles and words will not be proper." He was desperately anxious to become "head of the state," and conspired to usurp Party leadership and seize state power. Following that, he launched an abortive counterrevolutionary coup d'etat at the Second Plenary Session of the Party's Ninth Central Committee.

In 1971 Lin Piao and company concocted a plan for a counterrevolutionary armed coup d'etat entitled "Outline of Project '571.'" They were impatient to "seize political power throughout the country" and launched the coup in September of that year.

These facts prove that the prime purpose of the Lin Piao anti-Party clique's "restoring the rites" was to seize supreme power of the Party and the state. This was the "most urgent" of their counterrevolutionary strategies.

The class content of Lin Piao's "restoring the rites" was to establish in China a feudal-comprador-fascist dynasty of the Lin family. Confucius shouted that he wanted to "revive states that were extinct, restore families whose line of succession had been broken, and call to office those who had fallen into obscurity." Internally, Lin Piao picked up this Confucian rubbish, carried out counterrevolutionary activities for a restoration,

and rabidly shouted that they wanted to "give political liberation
to all" enemies of the dictatorship of the proletariat in an attempt to reinstate the landlord and capitalist classes, which
were overthrown by our Party, army, and people under the
leadership of Chairman Mao, and to restore capitalism. If that
should happen, big and small despotic landlords such as Huang
Shih-jen and the Tyrant of the South (villains in the modern revolutionary ballets The White-Haired Girl and the Red Detach-
ment of Women respectively — translator) would once again
ride roughshod over the people, and the renegade, enemy agent,
and traitor Wang Ming and others like him would swaggeringly
come back to power and become "guests of honor" of the Lin
dynasty. And thousands upon thousands of revolutionaries would
fall victim to the counterrevolutionary butcher's knife, while
millions upon millions of workers and peasants would once again
be plunged into misery. Internationally, Lin Piao and company
acted according to the motto they had taken over from Mencius —
"the small states regarded the large as masters" — and engaged
in capitulationist, traitorous, counterrevolutionary activities,
trying to seek the patronage of Soviet revisionist social-
imperialism and alignment with imperialism, revisionism and
reaction against China, against communism, and against revolution. If the plot of Lin Piao, the "super spy," had succeeded,
the beautiful land of China would have been trampled upon by
the tanks of Soviet revisionism, the social-imperialist gangsters
would have run amuck in China, and the Chinese people would
have been subjugated and enslaved.

In a word, by picking up and waving the tattered banner of
Confucius' "restraining oneself and restoring the rites," Lin
Piao attempted to change fundamentally the Party's basic line
and China's socialist system, subvert the dictatorship of the
proletariat and restore capitalism. However, all this was no
more than an idiot's daydream.

Chairman Mao has said: " 'Lifting a rock only to drop it on
one's own feet' is a Chinese folk saying to describe the behavior of certain fools. The reactionaries in all countries are fools
of this kind." And Lin Piao was a reactionary of this kind. He

intended to ascend the throne as a vassal-king under the "nuclear umbrella" of his master — Soviet revisionism — but
crashed to death in the desert. Holding the broken banner of "restraining oneself and restoring the rites," he traversed the road
"Make trouble, fail, make trouble again, fail again...till their
doom," came to a dead end and went to meet Confucius.

Using the Reactionary Philosophy of Confucius and Mencius in Opposing Dialectical and Historical Materialism

In an attempt to restore capitalism, Lin Piao had not only a
counterrevolutionary political line but a counterrevolutionary
ideological line that served it. The reactionary philosophy of
Confucius and Mencius was a major source of this ideological
line. Lin Piao opposed materialism with the Confucian theory
of "heaven's will" and theory of "innate genius," opposed materialist dialectics with the doctrine of the mean, opposed the
Marxist theory of classes with the Confucian concept of "virtue,
benevolence and righteousness, loyalty and forbearance," and
launched an all-out attack on dialectical and historical materialism.

Confucius preached "heaven's will," alleging that there was
a supreme god called t'ien [heaven] who created man and all
things on earth and controlled everything in nature and the
world of man. His will was irresistible. The slave-owners,
like King Wen of the Chou dynasty, had the power to rule the
people because they had a heavenly mandate. Likewise, Duke
Chou* and Confucius had heavenly mandates so that they possessed "virtue" and became "sages" to "enlighten" the people.
This religious and theological idealist theory was invented solely

---

*Duke Chou, whose name was Tan, was a younger brother of
King Wu who founded the Western Chou dynasty. After the death
of King Wu, Duke Chou became the regent as King Cheng was
still too young. He instituted the rules and systems upholding
the dictatorship of the slave-owners of the Chou dynasty.

for the purpose of preserving the dictatorship of the slave-owners. From this reactionary theory of "heaven's will" Confucius derived his apriorism that some people were "born with knowledge" and his idealist conception of history that heroes were the makers of history. Lin Piao seized the idealist trash of Confucius as treasures in his bid to usurp power and restore capitalism. He wrote a scroll with the words "The heavenly horse flies through the skies, free and alone" and hung it in the center of the wall by the head of his bed, comparing himself to a heavenly horse, describing himself as a dragon-like and exceptionally endowed person, a superman and a genius that heaven had sent to the world of man. In an inscription he wrote to his diehard conspirator, he described the "virtues," which he and his band claimed to have, as "qualities from Heaven." Isn't this the same as Confucius' statement that "Heaven endows me with virtue"? For many years, Lin Piao and his diehard conspirators tried in a hundred and one ways by lies and sophistry to palm off the theory of "innate genius" as Marxism. But this is futile. "Qualities from Heaven," these characters in his own handwriting, showed that his theory of "innate genius" was a replica of Confucius' theory of "heaven's will." In clinging to the theory of "innate genius" which was his anti-Party theoretical program, he was trying to prove that he was a supreme ruler with a mandate "from Heaven."

Lin Piao argued that "chung yung" [the doctrine of the mean] was "rational." This exposed his true nature — opposing the revolution and dialectics. By "chung yung" Confucius and Mencius meant that everything should be done according to the "rites"; being neither excessive nor deficient was "chung," and maintaining normalcy and constancy was "yung." In a word, the doctrine of the mean required that everything should be done according to the old rules of the slave system, and the least deviation or change was impermissible. This is a metaphysical theory that reactionary classes use to defend the old system and oppose any changes. Lin Piao lauded this theory to the skies and said it was "rational." Proceeding from this "rationality," Lin Piao viciously cursed that the struggle by the proletarian

revolutionary line against the revisionist line "has been excessive" and "entirely leftist," "has gone to the extreme," "has
been carried out to extreme," and "has created a mess." What
a heap of labels! This, however, cannot in any way tarnish the
brilliance of Chairman Mao's revolutionary line. It only serves
to show that what Lin Piao upheld was an ultra-Rightist line
aimed at preserving the old system and order and turning back
the wheel of history. When talking about "being excessive," Lin
Piao was opposing the revolution with the Confucian doctrine of
the mean. Chairman Mao refuted this fallacy long ago, pointing
out that "a revolution is not a dinner party," and that "proper
limits have to be exceeded in order to right a wrong, or else
the wrong cannot be righted." Lin Piao cried about "creating a
mess." Well, it is only the order of the bourgeoisie and revisionism that has been disrupted. Without disrupting that order,
we cannot destroy the old world and create the new. Does it
scare the bunch of you that your order is disrupted? Well, this
is just the beginning, and much remains to be done before eliminating all exploiting classes in the world. The world outlook of
the proletariat is materialist dialectics which "is in its essence
critical and revolutionary" (Marx, "Afterword to the Second
German Edition of Capital"). Whether we foster new things to
defeat old ones or use every means to prevent the old things
from dying is a major issue in the struggle between the two
lines. Theoretically, this struggle is bound to appear as one
between materialist dialectics and metaphysics. Lin Piao used
Confucius and Mencius' doctrine of the mean to oppose dialectics. This is an ideological root cause for his pushing an ultra-
Rightist line.

Lin Piao said that the "virtue, benevolence and righteousness,
loyalty and forbearance" advocated by Confucianism were the
principles for "human relations," that this was "historical materialism." He also said that "loyalty, which means treating
people with benevolence and love, and forbearance, which means
tolerance and forgiveness — these are Confucian principles."
He talked about "benevolence and love," entirely removing the
class character, and talked about "human relations" while

negating class antagonism. He thus used the reactionary theory of human nature of Confucius and Mencius to tamper with and negate the theory of class of historical materialism.

The theory of human nature as preached by the Confucian school is a hypocritical idealist theory. It advocates an apriorist and supraclass human nature. Confucius alleged that "benevolence" meant "to love all men," and Mencius said that man was born in possession of "benevolence" and that "man is born good." Did they love all men irrespective of classes? Not in the least. When the State of Cheng* killed all the rebelling slaves, did not Confucius commend the slaughter and say "excellent"? Did not Mencius theorize the exploitation of and rule over the slaves and laborers as "a universal principle"? Neither did they love the newly emerging landlord class. As soon as he took office as acting prime minister of the State of Lu**, Confucius killed Shao-cheng Mou, a representative of the reformers. Confucius promptly expelled his disciple Jan Chiu, broke off their relation of teacher and student, and instigated his other disciples to attack him because he served the newly emerging landlord class. These proved that the "human love" irrespective of classes, "benevolence" by birth and other notions advocated by Confucius and Mencius were all trash designed to fool the people. In fact those they loved were the handful of slave-owners of the exploiting classes and the reactionary slave system. While talking about "benevolence and love," Lin Piao, in his plan for a counterrevolutionary armed coup d'etat, the "Outline of Project '571,'" viciously plotted to "devour" the proletariat at a mouthful, to assassinate the great leader of the proletariat, overthrow the working people who are now masters of the country, and institute a fascist dictatorship. Those they

---

*A state under the slave system in the Spring and Autumn Period, Cheng was in the southern part of the present Honan Province.

**A state under the slave system in the Spring and Autumn Period, Lu was in the southern part of the present Shantung Province.

loved were actually the handful of class enemies whom we have overthrown. This is Lin Piao's "human nature," also the human nature of the landlord and capitalist classes. A chieftain of the Chiang Kai-shek gang said mournfully two years after Lin Piao's death: "Lin Piao...had relatively more human nature. This is evidence of the Confucian ethics lying deep in men's hearts." This praise by the Chiang Kai-shek gang best explains what Lin Piao's human nature really was.

Doing their utmost to advocate the theory of human nature, the reactionary classes dress themselves up as "virtuous sovereigns" who care for the people so as to hide their man-eating features. On the other hand, they hoist the banner of "benevolence, righteousness and virtue" to denounce the revolutionary violence of the progressive classes. Did not Confucius curse the newly emerging landlord class as "rebels with courage but without righteousness" and the insurgent slaves as "robbers with courage but without righteousness"? Mencius went even further. He hurled abuses at revolutionary violence, saying "they slaughter men till the fields are filled with bodies," and "they slaughter men till a city is filled with bodies," and they "devour human flesh." He said they should be given capital punishment, crying: "Death is not enough for such a crime." Lin Piao took over the mantle of Confucius and Mencius. With the reactionary theory of human nature as his theoretical basis, he cried: "Those who rely on virtue will thrive, and those who rely on force will perish." He accused the dictatorship of the proletariat as "not benevolent." "'You are not benevolent!' Quite so. We definitely do not apply a policy of benevolence to the reactionaries and towards the reactionary activities of the reactionary classes." The proletariat must resolutely and mercilessly suppress all reactionary elements of the reactionary classes who dare to resist. Otherwise we shall lose our state power, and the landlord and capitalist classes will come back to power. Did not Lin Piao, under the camouflage of sham benevolence and righteousness, attempt to use counterrevolutionary violence to overthrow the dictatorship of the proletariat? In dealing with the counterrevolutionary violence of the reactionaries, we have no alternative but, as the saying goes, to deal with a man as he deals with you, namely, use revolutionary violence to suppress counterrevolutionary violence. We must uphold the Marxist theory of class struggle and dictatorship of the proletariat and persist in the Party's basic line so as to continuously consolidate and strengthen the proletarian dictatorship. This is our conclusion.

Resorting to Expediency of the Confucian School, Forming a Clique for Selfish Purposes, Engaging in Intrigues and Conspiracy

Lin Piao's political line and ideological line were revisionist. This inevitably led him organizationally to carry out splitting activities and form a clique to pursue his selfish interests, and tactically to resort to double-dealing and engage in intrigues and conspiracy. In order to entrench himself in the Party and to pull together his counterrevolutionary ranks, waiting for the opportunity to achieve his ambition of "restoring the rites," Lin Piao directed his sworn followers and others to comb through the Four Books and Five Classics*, histories of China and other

---

*The Four Books — four "classical canons" of the Confucians — include the Great Learning, the Doctrine of the Mean, the Analects of Confucius, and Mencius.

The Five Classics refer to the following five Confucian "classics" — the Book of Songs, the Book of History, the Book of Rites, the Book of Change, and the Spring and Autumn Annals. Feudal rulers after the Han dynasty called them the Five Classics, using them as an ideological tool to control the people.

The Book of Songs is China's earliest collection of songs. It was said that Confucius deleted certain songs in this book.

The Book of History, also known as the Shang shu, is a collection of political documents and records of history prior to the Spring and Autumn period and the Warring States period.

The Book of Rites contains the Rites of Chou, the Book of Ceremony, and the Records of Rites. The Rites of Chou records

countries, and even novels and proverbs for material to help him find ways and means for carrying out his counterrevolutionary conspiracies. All the tricks the slave-owning class and the feudal landlord class had accumulated for their reactionary rule and their double-dealing tactics became his important ideological weapons for carrying out splitting activities and conspiracies.

In an effort to preserve the dying slave system, Confucius said that "a prince should employ his ministers according to propriety, and ministers should serve their prince with loyalty," using this as the criterion in handling relations within the ruling clique of slave-owning nobility. That was precisely what Lin Piao practiced in his anti-Party clique.

Lin Piao made use of Confucius' trash that "a prince should employ his ministers according to propriety"; but this was only a hypocritical gesture. An out-and-out fascist dictator, Lin Piao made stupendous efforts to establish his "absolute authority." He drew a line between those he favored and those he disfavored according to the attitudes shown toward him, and followed the principle that "those who are obedient shall thrive and those who resist shall perish." Yet he played the tune of "employing ministers according to propriety" and put up the signboard of "seeking wise men." The fact is that the "propriety" he talked about meant handing out official posts and making promises and granting special favors, inviting guests and giving

---

the stipulations for government offices and functions of officials of the Chou dynasty. The Book of Ceremony records the ceremonies for marriage, funeral, sacrifices and social intercourse during the Chou dynasty. The Records of Rites contains essays on rites by Confucians before the Chin and Han dynasties.

The Book of Change, also known as the Chou Yi, is a book for fortune-telling in ancient China.

The Spring and Autumn Annals were the annals recording contemporary history written by the State of Lu in the Spring and Autumn period. Deletions and alterations were made by Confucius to safeguard the slave system.

them presents, wining and dining, and trafficking in mutual flattery and commendation. In short, it meant using personal fame, gains and position as lures to buy over and draw together a group of people to serve his undertaking for a counterrevolutionary restoration. When his sworn followers were exposed by the masses, he used his position and power to shield and protect them and help them slip away unpunished. By "seeking wise men," he meant recruiting deserters, renegades and monsters, organizing a bourgeois headquarters, and rigging up big and small counterrevolutionary "fleets" (Lin Piao's secret agencies — translator) to meet the needs of capitalist restoration.

By preaching that "a prince should employ his ministers according to propriety," Lin Piao wanted his sworn followers to act as "ministers serving their prince with loyalty." Like all previous reactionary rulers, Lin Piao used the idea of "loyalty to the prince" as the ideological pillar to maintain his rule in the ranks of counterrevolutionaries. He lauded Confucius and Mencius for their preachings of the concept of "loyalty and filial piety" which meant "respect for superiors" and "obedience," and advocated absolute obedience. He forced members of his secret agencies to swear allegiance and pledge "eternal loyalty" to the Lin family, father and son. Even when the downfall of Lin Piao's anti-Party clique was imminent, he issued the counterrevolutionary order of "success or death," vainly calling on members of his counterrevolutionary "fleets" to die as funerary objects for the "Lin dynasty." These facts show that an important organizational principle of the Lin Piao anti-Party clique was the moral obligations and preachings of Confucius and Mencius.

Lin Piao set great store by Confucius' saying: "Want of patience in small matters confounds big plans." He copied it and hung it on the wall as a counterrevolutionary maxim. Toward the many painstaking criticisms and education given him by Chairman Mao and the Party Central Committee, he nursed his hatred and waited for an opportunity to counterattack. Plotting to usurp Party leadership and state power, he repeatedly reminded himself "to have patience" so as not to permit the "foolhardiness of common men" to confound his big plan of "re-storing the rites" and "spoil one's great plan of a lifetime." Be-hind the "patience," Lin Piao gritted his teeth, sharpened his knife and watched how the wind blew to achieve his aim. This was actually a repeat performance of the counterrevolutionary trick of "seeking survival in forbearance" of Hu Feng.*

Lin Piao highly valued the "stratagem of tao-hui (conceal-ment)" in order to "seek survival in forbearance" and realize his "big plan." In March 1970 when the Lin Piao anti-Party clique was busy drawing up its scheme to usurp Party leader-ship and state power, Lin Piao directed his diehard conspirator to write the words "tao-hui" in one of the notebooks, and per-sonally copied a poem from the Romance of the Three Kingdoms that praises Liu Pei for having deceived Ts'ao Ts'ao** by the "stratagem of tao-hui": "Constrained to lodge for a time in the tiger's lair, the hero was alarmed when his ambitions were laid bare. Using the thunderclap to cover up his panic, he rose to the occasion, clever and quick." Here Lin Piao maligned the proletarian headquarters as the "tiger's lair" and compared himself to a "hero" who "lodges for a time in the tiger's lair."

---

*Hu Feng was the ringleader of the Hu Feng counterrevolutionary clique. Under the leadership of the Party Central Committee headed by Comrade Mao Tse-tung, the people of the whole coun-try in 1955 exposed and waged struggles against this counter-revolutionary clique hidden in the revolutionary ranks.

**The Romance of the Three Kingdoms, a long Chinese his-torical novel, takes its material from the history between the latter years of the Eastern Han dynasty and Three Kingdoms (184-280). The author is Lo Kuan-chung who lived in the four-teenth century.

Liu Pei (161-223) was the founder of the Kingdom of Han (Shu) in the period of the Three Kingdoms. Ts'ao Ts'ao (155-220) was the prime minister in the latter years of the Eastern Han dy-nasty and father of Ts'ao Pi who founded the Kingdom of Wei in the period of Three Kingdoms. Ts'ao Ts'ao was posthumously given the title Emperor Wu of Wei.

This shows that he was a bourgeois careerist and conspirator who nestled beside us. This also shows his ferocious features in using double-dealing tactics to disguise himself and cover up his counterrevolutionary aims and waiting for an opportune moment to execute his murderous plan against the proletarian headquarters.

In order to disguise his real self, he was quick to change to suit the occasion, and he secretly formulated a series of counterrevolutionary double-dealing tactics in line with the admonition of Confucius and Mencius, which said: "To love those others hate and to hate those others love.... Calamities will certainly come down on him who does so." "A great man may not be true to his words or consistent in his action," "one cannot accomplish great things without telling lies" and "keep a smile on the face" — all these, without adding a single word, are sufficient to vividly expose Lin Piao as a counterrevolutionary double-dealer who "never showed up without a copy of Quotations in hand and never opened his mouth without shouting 'Long Live' and who spoke nice things to your face but stabbed you in the back."

Why Did the Revisionist Chieftain Lin Piao Seek Help from Confucius and Mencius?

Like chieftains of opportunist lines in the past, Lin Piao was a representative of the bourgeoisie within our Party, a devout worshiper of Confucius. People will naturally ask: Why did a representative of the bourgeoisie seek ideological weapons from the slave-owning and feudal landlord classes? And why do all the revisionist chieftains within the Party invariably seek help from the doctrine of Confucius and Mencius? This is a question worthy of attention.

That the revisionist chieftain Lin Piao and his like worshiped Confucius was not strange at all. It has deep class and historical roots.

In the first place, it should be pointed out that the devotion of Lin Piao and company to Confucius was closely linked to the

historical characteristics and class status of the Chinese bourgeoisie and especially the big bourgeoisie, which they represented. The world entered the era of imperialism and proletarian revolution in the late nineteenth and early twentieth centuries. The Chinese bourgeoisie, which then lived in a semicolonial, semifeudal society, had its class character formed
right from its inception. The Chinese bourgeoisie was very
weak economically and politically, and in the ideological and
cultural sphere it was incapable of establishing an ideological
system powerful enough to replace feudal culture. The big
bourgeoisie, which held the dominant position in old China, grew
out of a combination of imperialism and feudalism, and its fundamental character was comprador and feudal in nature. The
big bourgeoisie all along stubbornly supported and enthusiastically hawked the imperialist philosophy of enslavement and the
feudal culture characterized by the worship of Confucius and the
study of Confucian classics. In the period of the socialist revolution when the contradiction between the proletariat and the
bourgeoisie has become the principal internal contradiction in
China, whoever dreams of restoring capitalism in China must
politically exercise a feudal, comprador and fascist dictatorship, and in the ideological and cultural sphere, seek weapons
from imperialism and feudalism. Ch'en Tu-hsiu, Wang Ming,
Liu Shao-ch'i, Lin Piao and company, who represented the interests of the bourgeoisie, invariably reflected this class character in practicing revisionism and resorting to the doctrine of
Confucius and Mencius. This was especially true of Lin Piao
who came from a landlord-capitalist family and who all along
refused to remold his world outlook.

Second, from the point of view of history, the doctrine of Confucius and Mencius was the ideology of the declining slave-
owning class, a highly deceptive ideological system of the exploiting classes. Essentially it stands for retrogression and
against progress, for conservatism and against reform, for
restoration of the old order and against revolution. It is a doctrine of exploitation and oppression, of staging a counterrevolutionary comeback. It was later utilized by the decadent

landlord class and the big bourgeoisie as well as by the imperialists who tried to vanquish China, and it became the dominant
ideology in China's feudal society and semicolonial, semifeudal
society of the past 2,000 years and more, the spiritual fetters
used by all the past reactionary rulers to enslave the working
people, and the ideological weapon of all reactionaries who conspire for a comeback and oppose communism. Because all the
past reactionary rulers energetically advocated and forcibly
pushed the doctrine of Confucius and Mencius, this doctrine became an age-old, traditional concept that had penetrated into
every sphere of social life in old China. All reactionaries who
advocated retrogression invariably took up the tattered banner
of worshiping Confucius and used the doctrine of Confucius and
Mencius in every possible way to deceive the masses with
demagogy. Therefore it is not surprising that all the chieftains
of opportunist lines in our Party who opposed the revolution and
advocated retrogression should worship Confucius. The revisionist chieftain Lin Piao was a big Party tyrant and big warlord who did not read books, newspapers, and documents and
who had no learning at all. But he tirelessly collected quotations from Confucius and Mencius and preached their doctrine,
because his reactionary thought was the same as that of Confucius and Mencius, his counterrevolutionary nature was to bring
about a capitalist restoration, and his vicious desire was to use
reactionary traditional ideas in an effort to subvert the dictatorship of the proletariat and restore capitalism.

With the deepening of the movement to criticize Lin Piao and
rectify the style of work, it is quite natural that we criticize the
doctrine of Confucius and Mencius and the notion of exalting
Confucianism and opposing the Legalist school. The current
struggle to criticize Lin Piao and Confucius is a life-and-death
struggle between the two classes and the two lines and an event
of paramount importance for the entire Party, the entire army,
and the people of the whole country. Not to criticize Confucius
and the idea of exalting Confucianism and opposing the Legalist
school is, in effect, not to criticize Lin Piao. A deep criticism
of the doctrine of Confucius and Mencius and the idea of exalting

Confucianism and opposing the Legalist school is of great significance in thoroughly exposing and criticizing the ultra-Rightist nature of Lin Piao's revisionist line, strengthening education in ideological and political line, consolidating and expanding the achievements of the Great Proletarian Cultural Revolution, and doing a good job in the revolution in the superstructure. Under the leadership of Chairman Mao and the Party Central Committee, we must develop the thoroughgoing revolutionary spirit of the proletariat and win new victories in the struggle to criticize Lin Piao and Confucius!

V Lin Piao in Self-Defense: Speeches, Writings, and Instructions, 1965-1970

23

LONG LIVE THE VICTORY OF PEOPLE'S WAR!*
(September 1965)

In Commemoration of the Twentieth
Anniversary of Victory in the Chinese
People's War of Resistance Against Japan

Full twenty years have elapsed since our victory in the great
War of Resistance Against Japan.

After a long period of heroic struggle, the Chinese people,
under the leadership of the Communist Party of China and Comrade Mao Tse-tung, won final victory two decades ago in their
war against the Japanese imperialists who had attempted to sub-
jugate China and swallow up the whole of Asia.

The Chinese people's War of Resistance was an important
part of the world war against German, Japanese, and Italian
fascism. The Chinese people received support from the people
and the anti-fascist forces all over the world. And in their turn,
the Chinese people made an important contribution to victory in
the Anti-Fascist War as a whole.

Of the innumerable anti-imperialist wars waged by the Chinese people in the past hundred years, the War of Resistance
Against Japan was the first to end in complete victory. It occu-
pies an extremely important place in the annals of war, in the
annals of both the revolutionary wars of the Chinese people and
the wars of the oppressed nations of the world against imperialist aggression.

---

*"Jen-min chan-cheng sheng-li wan-sui." Hung-ch'i [Red
Flag], No. 10 (September 3, 1965), 1-28. This translation is
taken, with minor editorial revisions, from Peking Review,
No. 36 (September 3, 1965), 9-30.

It was a war in which a weak semicolonial and semifeudal
country triumphed over a strong imperialist country. For a
long period after the invasion of China's northeastern provinces
by the Japanese imperialists, the Kuomintang followed a policy
of nonresistance. In the early stage of the War of Resistance,
the Japanese imperialists exploited their military superiority
to drive deep into China and occupy half her territory. In the
face of the massive attacks of the aggressors and the anti-
Japanese upsurge of the people throughout the country, the Kuomintang was compelled to take part in the War of Resistance,
but soon afterward it adopted the policy of passive resistance
to Japan and active opposition to the Communist Party. The
heavy responsibility of combating Japanese imperialism thus
fell on the shoulders of the Eighth Route Army, the New Fourth
Army, and the people of the Liberated Areas, all led by the
Communist Party. At the outbreak of the war, the Eighth Route
and New Fourth Armies had only a few tens of thousands of men
and suffered from extreme inferiority in both arms and equipment, and for a long time they were under the crossfire of the
Japanese imperialists on the one hand and the Kuomintang troops on
the other. But they grew stronger and stronger in the course of the
war and became the main force in defeating Japanese imperialism.

How was it possible for a weak country finally to defeat a
strong country? How was it possible for a seemingly weak
army to become the main force in the war?

The basic reasons were that the War of Resistance Against
Japan was a genuine people's war led by the Communist Party
of China and Comrade Mao Tse-tung, a war in which the correct
Marxist-Leninist political and military lines were put into effect,
and that the Eighth Route and New Fourth Armies were genuine
people's armies which applied the whole range of strategy and
tactics of people's war as formulated by Comrade Mao Tse-tung.

Comrade Mao Tse-tung's theory of and policies for people's
war have creatively enriched and developed Marxism-Leninism.
The Chinese people's victory in the anti-Japanese war was a
victory for people's war, for Marxism-Leninism and the thought
of Mao Tse-tung.

Prior to the war against Japan, the Communist Party of China had gone through the First Revolutionary Civil War of 1924-1927 and the Second Revolutionary Civil War of 1927-1936 and summed up the experience and lessons of the successes and failures in those wars, and the leading role of Mao Tse-tung's thought had become established within the Party. This was the fundamental guarantee of the Party's ability to lead the Chinese people to victory in the War of Resistance.

The Chinese people's victory in the War of Resistance paved the way for their seizure of state power throughout the country. When the Kuomintang reactionaries, backed by the U.S. imperialists, launched a nationwide civil war in 1946, the Communist Party of China and Comrade Mao Tse-tung further developed the theory of people's war, led the Chinese people in waging a people's war on a still larger scale, and in the space of a little over three years the great victory of the People's Liberation War was won, the rule of imperialism, feudalism and bureaucrat-capitalism in our country ended, and the People's Republic of China founded.

The victory of the Chinese people's revolutionary war breached the imperialist front in the East, wrought a great change in the world balance of forces, and accelerated the revolutionary movement among the people of all countries. From then on, the national-liberation movement in Asia, Africa, and Latin America entered a new historical period.

Today, the U.S. imperialists are repeating on a world-wide scale the past actions of the Japanese imperialists in China and other parts of Asia. It has become an urgent necessity for the people in many countries to master and use people's war as a weapon against U.S. imperialism and its lackeys. In every conceivable way U.S. imperialism and its lackeys are trying to extinguish the revolutionary flames of people's war. The Khrushchev revisionists, fearing people's war like the plague, are heaping abuse on it. The two are colluding to prevent and sabotage people's war. In these circumstances it is of vital practical importance to review the historical experience of the great victory of the people's war in China and to recapitulate Comrade

Mao Tse-tung's theory of people's war.

The Principal Contradiction in the Period of the War of Resistance Against Japan and the Line of the Communist Party of China

The Communist Party of China and Comrade Mao Tse-tung were able to lead the Chinese people to victory in the War of Resistance Against Japan primarily because they formulated and applied a Marxist-Leninist line.

Basing himself on the fundamental tenets of Marxism-Leninism and applying the method of class analysis, Comrade Mao Tse-tung analyzed: first, the mutual transformation of China's principal and nonprincipal contradictions following the invasion of China by Japanese imperialism; second, the consequent changes in class relations within China and in international relations, and, third, the balance of forces as between China and Japan. This analysis provided the scientific basis upon which the political and military lines of the War of Resistance were formulated.

There had long been two basic contradictions in China — the contradiction between imperialism and the Chinese nation, and the contradiction between feudalism and the masses of the people. For ten years before the outbreak of the War of Resistance, the Kuomintang reactionary clique, which represented the interests of imperialism, the big landlords and the big bourgeoisie, had waged civil war against the Communist Party of China and the Communist-led Workers and Peasants' Red Army, which represented the interests of the Chinese people. In 1931 Japanese imperialism invaded and occupied northeastern China. Subsequently, and especially after 1935, it stepped up and expanded its aggression against China, penetrating deeper and deeper into our territory. As a result of its invasion, Japanese imperialism sharpened its contradiction with the Chinese nation to an extreme degree and brought about changes in class relations within China. To end the civil war and to unite against Japanese aggression became the pressing nationwide demand of the people.

Changes of varying degrees also occurred in the political attitudes of the national bourgeoisie and the various factions within the Kuomintang. And the Sian Incident (1) of 1936 was the best case in point.

How was one to assess the changes in China's political situation, and what conclusion was to be drawn? This question had a direct bearing on the very survival of the Chinese nation.

For a period prior to the outbreak of the War of Resistance, the "Left" opportunists represented by Wang Ming within the Chinese Communist Party were blind to the important changes in China's political situation caused by Japanese aggression since 1931 and denied the sharpening of the Sino-Japanese national contradiction and the demands of various social strata for a war of resistance; instead, they stressed that all the counter-revolutionary factions and intermediate forces in China and all the imperialist countries were a monolithic bloc. They persisted in their line of "closed-doorism" and continued to advocate "Down with the whole lot."

Comrade Mao Tse-tung resolutely fought the "Left" opportunist errors and penetratingly analyzed the new situation in the Chinese revolution.

He pointed out that the Japanese imperialist attempt to reduce China to a Japanese colony heightened the contradiction between China and Japan and made it the principal contradiction; that China's internal class contradictions — such as those between the masses of the people and feudalism, between the peasantry and the landlord class, between the proletariat and the bourgeoisie, and between the peasantry and urban petty bourgeoisie on the one hand and the bourgeoisie on the other — still remained, but that they had all been relegated to a secondary or subordinate position as a result of the war of aggression unleashed by Japan; and that throughout China opposition to Japanese imperialism had become the common demand of the people of all classes and strata, except for a handful of pro-Japanese traitors among the big landlords and the big bourgeoisie.

As the contradiction between China and Japan ascended and became the principal one, the contradiction between China and

imperialist countries such as Britain and the United States de-
scended to a secondary or subordinate position. The rift between
Japan and the other imperialist countries had widened as a result of Japanese imperialism's attempt to turn China into its
own exclusive colony. This rendered it possible for China to
make use of these contradictions to isolate and oppose Japanese
imperialism.

In the face of Japanese imperialist aggression was the Party
to continue with the civil war and the Agrarian Revolution? Or
was it to hold aloft the banner of national liberation, unite with
all the forces that could be united to form a broad national
united front and concentrate on fighting the Japanese aggressors?
This was the problem sharply confronting our Party.

The Communist Party of China and Comrade Mao Tse-tung
formulated the line of the Anti-Japanese National United Front
on the basis of their analysis of the new situation. Holding aloft
the banner of national liberation, our Party issued the call for
national unity and united resistance to Japanese imperialism, a
call which won fervent support from the people of the whole
country. Thanks to the common efforts of our Party and of
China's patriotic armies and people, the Kuomintang ruling
clique was eventually compelled to stop the civil war, and a new
situation with Kuomintang-Communist cooperation for joint resistance to Japan was brought about.

In the summer of 1937 Japanese imperialism unleashed its
all-out war of aggression against China. The nationwide War of
Resistance thus broke out.

Could the War of Resistance be victorious? And how was victory to be won? These were the questions to which all the Chinese people demanded immediate answers.

The defeatists came forward with the assertion that China was
no match for Japan and that the nation was bound to be subjugated. The blind optimists came forward with the assertion that
China could win very quickly, without much effort.

Basing himself on a concrete analysis of the Chinese nation
and of Japanese imperialism — the two aspects of the principal
contradiction — Comrade Mao Tse-tung showed that while the

"theory of national subjugation" was wrong, the "theory of quick victory" was untenable, and he concluded that the War of Resistance would be a protracted one in which China would finally be victorious.

In his celebrated work On Protracted War, Comrade Mao Tsetung pointed out the contrasting features of China and Japan, the two sides in the war. Japan was a powerful imperialist country. But Japanese imperialism was in its era of decline and doom. The war it had unleashed was a war of aggression, a war that was retrogressive and barbarous; it was deficient in manpower and material resources and could not stand a protracted war; it was engaged in an unjust cause and therefore had meager support internationally. China, on the other hand, was a weak semicolonial and semifeudal country. But she was in her era of progress. She was fighting a war against aggression, a war that was progressive and just; she had sufficient manpower and material resources to sustain a protracted war; internationally, China enjoyed extensive sympathy and support. These were all the basic factors in the Sino-Japanese war.

He went on to show how these factors would influence the course of the war. Japan's advantage was temporary and would gradually diminish as a result of our efforts. Her disadvantages were fundamental; they could not be overcome and would gradually grow in the course of the war. China's disadvantage was temporary and could be gradually overcome. China's advantages were fundamental and would play an increasingly positive role in the course of the war. Japan's advantage and China's disadvantage determined the impossibility of quick victory for China. China's advantages and Japan's disadvantages determined the inevitability of Japan's defeat and China's ultimate victory.

On the basis of this analysis, Comrade Mao Tse-tung formulated the strategy for a protracted war. China's War of Resistance would be protracted, and prolonged efforts would be needed gradually to weaken the enemy's forces and expand our own, so that the enemy would change from being strong to being weak and we would change from being weak to being strong and accumulate sufficient strength finally to defeat him. Comrade Mao

Tse-tung pointed out that with the change in the balance of forces between the enemy and ourselves the War of Resistance would pass through three stages, namely, the strategic defensive, the strategic stalemate, and the strategic offensive. The protracted war was also a process of mobilizing, organizing, and arming the people. It was only by mobilizing the entire people to fight a people's war that the War of Resistance could be persevered in and the Japanese aggressors defeated.

In order to turn the anti-Japanese war into a genuine people's war, our Party firmly relied on the broadest masses of the people, united with all the anti-Japanese forces that could be united, and consolidated and expanded the Anti-Japanese National United Front. The basic line of our Party was: boldly to arouse the masses of the people and expand the people's forces so that, under the leadership of the Party, they could defeat the aggressors and build a new China.

The War of Resistance Against Japan constituted a historical stage in China's new-democratic revolution. The line of our Party during the War of Resistance aimed not only at winning victory in the war but also at laying the foundations for the nationwide victory of the new-democratic revolution. Only the accomplishment of the new-democratic revolution makes it possible to carry out a socialist revolution. With respect to the relations between the democratic and the socialist revolutions, Comrade Mao Tse-tung said: "In the writing of an article the second half can be written only after the first half is finished. Resolute leadership of the democratic revolution is the prerequisite for the victory of socialism." (2)

The concrete analysis of concrete conditions and the concrete resolution of concrete contradictions are the living soul of Marxism-Leninism. Comrade Mao Tse-tung has invariably been able to single out the principal contradiction from among a complexity of contradictions, analyze the two aspects of this principal contradiction concretely and, "pressing on irresistibly from this commanding height," successfully solve the problem of understanding and handling the various contradictions.

It was precisely on the basis of such scientific analysis that

Comrade Mao Tse-tung correctly formulated the political and military lines for the people's war during the War of Resistance Against Japan, developed his thought on the establishment of rural base areas and the use of the countryside to encircle the cities and finally capture them, and formulated a whole range of principles and policies, strategy and tactics in the political, military, economic and cultural fields for the carrying out of the people's war. It was this that ensured victory in the War of Resistance and created the conditions for the nationwide victory of the new-democratic revolution.

Correctly Apply the Line and Policy of the United Front

In order to win a people's war, it is imperative to build the broadest possible united front and formulate a series of policies which will ensure the fullest mobilization of the basic masses as well as the unity of all the forces that can be united.

The Anti-Japanese National United Front embraced all the anti-Japanese classes and strata. These classes and strata shared a common interest in fighting Japan, an interest which formed the basis of their unity. But they differed in the degree of their firmness in resisting Japan, and there were class contradictions and conflicts of interest among them. Hence the inevitable class struggle within the united front.

In formulating the Party's line of the Anti-Japanese National United Front, Comrade Mao Tse-tung made the following class analysis of Chinese society:

The workers, the peasants, and the urban petty bourgeoisie firmly demanded that the War of Resistance should be carried through to the end; they were the main force in the fight against Japanese aggression and constituted the basic masses who demanded unity and progress.

The bourgeoisie was divided into the national and the comprador bourgeoisie. The national bourgeoisie formed the majority of the bourgeoisie; it was rather flabby, often vacillated, and had contradictions with the workers, but it also had a certain

degree of readiness to oppose imperialism and was one of our
allies in the War of Resistance. The comprador bourgeoisie
was the bureaucrat-capitalist class, which was very small in
number but occupied the ruling position in China. Its members
attached themselves to different imperialist powers, some of
them being pro-Japanese and others pro-British and pro-
American. The pro-Japanese section of the comprador bourgeoisie were the capitulators, the overt and covert traitors. The
pro-British and pro-American section of this class favored resistance to Japan to a certain extent, but they were not firm in
their resistance and very much wished to compromise with
Japan, and by their nature they were opposed to the Communist
Party and the people.

The landlords fell into different categories: there were the
big, the middle, and the small landlords. Some of the big landlords became traitors, while others favored resistance but vacillated a great deal. Many of the middle and small landlords had
the desire to resist, but there were contradictions between them
and the peasants.

In the face of these complicated class relationships, our
Party's policy regarding work within the united front was one
of both alliance and struggle. That is to say, its policy was to
unite with all the anti-Japanese classes and strata, try to win
over even those who could be only vacillating and temporary
allies, and adopt appropriate policies to adjust the relations
among these classes and strata so that they all served the general cause of resisting Japan. At the same time, we had to
maintain our Party's principle of independence and initiative,
make the bold arousing of the masses and expansion of the people's forces the center of gravity in our work, and wage the necessary struggles against all activities harmful to resistance,
unity, and progress.

Our Party's Anti-Japanese National United Front policy was
different both from Ch'en Tu-hsiu's Right opportunist policy of
all alliance and no struggle, and from Wang Ming's "Left" opportunist policy of all struggle and no alliance. Our Party
summed up the lessons of the Right and "Left" opportunist

errors and formulated the policy of both alliance and struggle.

Our Party made a series of adjustments in its policies in or-der to unite all the anti-Japanese parties and groups, including the Kuomintang, and all the anti-Japanese strata in a joint fight against the foe. We pledged ourselves to fight for the complete realization of Dr. Sun Yat-sen's revolutionary Three People's Principles. The government of the Shensi-Kansu-Ningsia revo-lutionary base area was renamed the Government of the Shensi-Kansu-Ningsia Special Region of the Republic of China. Our Workers and Peasants' Red Army was redesignated the Eighth Route Army and the New Fourth Army of the National Revolu-tionary Army. Our land policy, the policy of confiscating the land of the landlords, was changed to one of reducing rent and interest. In our own base areas we carried out the "three-thirds system" (3) in our organs of political power, drawing in those representatives of the petty bourgeoisie, the national bourgeoi-sie, and the enlightened gentry and those members of the Kuo-mintang who stood for resistance to Japan and did not oppose the Communist Party. In accordance with the principles of the Anti-Japanese National United Front, we also made necessary and appropriate changes in our policies relating to the economy, taxation, labor and wages, antiespionage, people's rights, cul-ture and education, etc.

While making these policy adjustments, we maintained the in-dependence of the Communist Party, the people's army and the base areas. We also insisted that the Kuomintang should insti-tute a general mobilization, reform the government apparatus, introduce democracy, improve the people's livelihood, arm the people, and carry out a total war of resistance. We waged a resolute struggle against the Kuomintang's passive resistance to Japan and active opposition to the Communist Party, against its suppression of the people's resistance movement and its treacherous activities for compromise and capitulation.

Past experience had taught us that "Left" errors were liable to crop up after our Party had corrected Right errors, and that Right errors were liable to crop up after it had corrected "Left" errors. "Left" errors were liable to occur when we broke with the Kuomintang ruling clique, and Right errors were liable to occur when we united with it.

After the overcoming of "Left" opportunism and the formation of the Anti-Japanese National United Front, the main danger in our Party was Right opportunism or capitulationism.

Wang Ming, the exponent of "Left" opportunism during the Second Revolutionary Civil War, went to the other extreme in the early days of the War of Resistance Against Japan and became the exponent of Right opportunism, i.e., capitulationism. He countered Comrade Mao Tse-tung's correct line and policies with an out-and-out capitulationist line of his own and a series of ultra-Right policies. He voluntarily abandoned proletarian leadership in the Anti-Japanese National United Front and willingly handed leadership to the Kuomintang. By his advocacy of "everything through the united front" or "everything to be submitted to the united front," he was in effect advocating that everything should go through or be submitted to Chiang Kai-shek and the Kuomintang. He opposed the bold mobilization of the masses, the carrying out of democratic reforms, and the improvement of the livelihood of the workers and peasants, and wanted to undermine the worker-peasant alliance which was the foundation of the united front. He did not want the Communist-led base areas of the people's revolutionary forces but wanted to cut off the people's revolutionary forces from their roots. He rejected a people's army led by the Communist Party and wanted to hand over the people's armed forces to Chiang Kai-shek, which would have meant handing over everything the people had. He did not want the leadership of the Party and advocated an alliance between the youth of the Kuomintang and that of the Communist Party to suit Chiang Kai-shek's design of corroding the Communist Party. He decked himself out and presented himself to Chiang Kai-shek, hoping to be given some official appointment. All this was revisionism, pure and simple. If we had acted on Wang Ming's revisionist line and his set of policies, the Chinese people would have been unable to win the War of Resistance Against Japan, still less the subsequent nationwide victory.

For a time during the War of Resistance, Wang Ming's revisionist line caused harm to the Chinese people's revolutionary cause. But the leading role of Comrade Mao Tse-tung had already been established in the Central Committee of our Party. Under his leadership, all the Marxist-Leninists in the Party carried out a resolute struggle against Wang Ming's errors and rectified them in time. It was this struggle that prevented Wang Ming's erroneous line from doing greater and more lasting damage to the cause of the Party.

Chiang Kai-shek, our teacher by negative example, helped us to correct Wang Ming's mistakes. He repeatedly lectured us with cannons and machine-guns. The gravest lesson was the Southern Anhwei Incident which took place in January 1941. Because some leaders of the New Fourth Army disobeyed the directives of the Central Committee of the Party and followed Wang Ming's revisionist line, its units in southern Anhwei suffered disastrous losses in the surprise attack launched by Chiang Kai-shek and many heroic revolutionary fighters were slaughtered by the Kuomintang reactionaries. The lessons learned at the cost of blood helped to sober many of our comrades and increase their ability to distinguish the correct from the erroneous line.

Comrade Mao Tse-tung constantly summed up the experience gained by the whole Party in implementing the line of the Anti-Japanese National United Front and worked out a whole set of policies in good time. They were mainly as follows:

1) All people favoring resistance (that is, all the anti-Japanese workers, peasants, soldiers, students and intellectuals, and businessmen) were to unite and form the Anti-Japanese National United Front.

2) Within the united front, our policy was to be one of independence and initiative, i.e., both unity and independence were necessary.

3) As far as military strategy was concerned, our policy was to be guerrilla warfare waged independently and with the initiative in our own hands, within the framework of a unified strategy; guerrilla warfare was to be basic, but no chance of waging

mobile warfare was to be lost when the conditions were favorable.

4) In the struggle against the anti-Communist diehards headed by Chiang Kai-shek, our policy was to make use of contradictions, win over the many, oppose the few, and destroy our enemies one by one, and to wage struggles on just grounds, to our advantage, and with restraint.

5) In the Japanese-occupied and Kuomintang areas our policy was, on the one hand, to develop the united front to the greatest possible extent and, on the other, to have selected cadres working underground. With regard to the forms of organization and struggle, our policy was to assign selected cadres to work under cover for a long period, so as to accumulate strength and bide our time.

6) As regards the alignment of the various classes within the country, our basic policy was to develop the progressive forces, win over the middle forces, and isolate the anti-Communist diehard forces.

7) As for the anti-Communist die-hards, we followed a revolutionary dual policy of uniting with them, insofar as they were still capable of bringing themselves to resist Japan, and of struggling against and isolating them, insofar as they were determined to oppose the Communist Party.

8) With respect to the landlords and the bourgeoisie — even the big landlords and big bourgeoisie — it was necessary to analyze each case and draw distinctions. On the basis of these distinctions we were to formulate different policies so as to achieve our aim of uniting with all the forces that could be united.

The line and the various policies of the Anti-Japanese National United Front formulated by Comrade Mao Tse-tung stood the test of the War of Resistance and proved to be entirely correct.

History shows that when confronted by ruthless imperialist aggression, a Communist Party must hold aloft the national banner and, using the weapon of the united front, rally around itself the masses and the patriotic and anti-imperialist people who

form more than 90 percent of a country's population, so as to
mobilize all positive factors, unite with all the forces that can
be united and isolate to the maximum the common enemy of the
whole nation. If we abandon the national banner, adopt a line of
"closed-doorism" and thus isolate ourselves, it is out of the
question to exercise leadership and develop the people's revolutionary cause, and this in reality amounts to helping the enemy and bringing defeat on ourselves.

History shows that within the united front the Communist
Party must maintain its ideological, political and organizational
independence, adhere to the principle of independence and initiative, and insist on its leading role. Since there are class differences among the various classes in the united front, the Party
must have a correct policy in order to develop the progressive
forces, win over the middle forces, and oppose the die-hard
forces. The Party's work must center on developing the progressive forces and expanding the people's revolutionary forces.
This is the only way to maintain and strengthen the united front.
"If unity is sought through struggle, it will live; if unity is
sought through yielding, it will perish." (4) This is the chief
experience gained in our struggle against the die-hard forces.

History shows that during the national-democratic revolution
there must be two kinds of alliance within this united front, first,
the worker-peasant alliance and, second, the alliance of the
working people with the bourgeoisie and other nonworking people. The worker-peasant alliance is an alliance of the working
class with the peasants and all other working people in town and
country. It is the foundation of the united front. Whether the
working class can gain leadership of the national-democratic
revolution depends on whether it can lead the broad masses of
the peasants in struggle and rally them around itself. Only when
the working class gains leadership of the peasants, and only on
the basis of the worker-peasant alliance, is it possible to establish the second alliance, form a broad united front, and
wage a people's war victoriously. Otherwise, everything that
is done is unreliable, like castles in the air or so much
empty talk.

Rely on the Peasants and Establish
Rural Base Areas

The peasantry constituted more than 80 percent of the entire population of semicolonial and semifeudal China. They were subjected to threefold oppression and exploitation by imperialism, feudalism, and bureaucrat-capitalism, and they were eager for resistance against Japan and for revolution. It was essential to rely mainly on the peasants if the people's war was to be won.

But at the outset not all comrades in our Party saw this point. The history of our Party shows that in the period of the First Revolutionary Civil War, one of the major errors of the Right opportunists, represented by Ch'en Tu-hsiu, was their failure to recognize the importance of the peasant question and their opposition to arousing and arming the peasants. In the period of the Second Revolutionary Civil War, one of the major errors of the "Left" opportunists, represented by Wang Ming, was likewise their failure to recognize the importance of the peasant question. They did not realize that it was essential to undertake long-term and painstaking work among the peasants and establish revolutionary base areas in the countryside; they were under the illusion that they could rapidly seize the big cities and quickly win nationwide victory in the revolution. The errors of both the Right and the "Left" opportunists brought serious setbacks and defeats to the Chinese revolution.

As far back as the period of the First Revolutionary Civil War, Comrade Mao Tse-tung had pointed out that the peasant question occupied an extremely important position in the Chinese revolution, that the bourgeois-democratic revolution against imperialism and feudalism was in essence a peasant revolution, and that the basic task of the Chinese proletariat in the bourgeois-democratic revolution was to give leadership to the peasants' struggle.

In the period of the War of Resistance Against Japan, Comrade Mao Tse-tung again stressed that the peasants were the most reliable and the most numerous ally of the proletariat and constituted the main force in the War of Resistance. The peasants

were the main source of manpower for China's armies. The
funds and the supplies needed for a protracted war came chiefly
from the peasants. In the anti-Japanese war it was imperative
to rely mainly on the peasants and to arouse them to participate
in the war on the broadest scale.

The War of Resistance Against Japan was in essence a peasant revolutionary war led by our Party. By arousing and organizing the peasant masses and integrating them with the proletariat, our Party created a powerful force capable of defeating
the strongest enemy.

To rely on the peasants, build rural base areas, and use the
countryside to encircle and finally capture the cities — such
was the way to victory in the Chinese revolution.

Basing himself on the characteristics of the Chinese revolution, Comrade Mao Tse-tung pointed out the importance of
building rural revolutionary base areas.

> Since China's key cities have long been occupied by the
> powerful imperialists and their reactionary Chinese allies,
> it is imperative for the revolutionary ranks to turn the
> backward villages into advanced, consolidated base areas,
> into great military, political, economic, and cultural bas-
> tions of the revolution from which to fight their vicious en-
> emies who are using the cities for attacks on the rural dis-
> tricts, and in this way gradually to achieve the complete
> victory of the revolution through protracted fighting; it is
> imperative for them to do so if they do not wish to com-
> promise with imperialism and its lackeys but are deter-
> mined to fight on, and if they intend to build up and temper
> their forces, and avoid decisive battles with a powerful en-
> emy while their own strength is inadequate. (5)

Experience in the period of the Second Revolutionary Civil
War showed that when this strategic concept of Comrade Mao
Tse-tung's was applied, there was an immense growth in the
revolutionary forces and one Red base area after another was
built. Conversely, when it was violated and the nonsense of the

"Left" opportunists was applied, the revolutionary forces suffered severe damage, with losses of nearly 100 percent in the
cities and 90 percent in the rural areas.

During the War of Resistance Against Japan, the Japanese
imperialist forces occupied many of China's big cities and the
main lines of communication, but owing to the shortage of troops
they were unable to occupy the vast countryside, which remained
the vulnerable sector of the enemy's rule. Consequently, the
possibility of building rural base areas became even greater.
Shortly after the beginning of the War of Resistance, when the
Japanese forces surged into China's hinterland and the Kuomintang forces crumbled and fled in one defeat after another, the
Eighth Route and New Fourth Armies led by our Party followed
the wise policy laid down by Comrade Mao Tse-tung and boldly
drove into the areas behind the enemy lines in small contingents
and established base areas throughout the countryside. During
the eight years of the war, we established nineteen anti-Japanese
base areas in northern, central, and southern China. With the
exception of the big cities and the main lines of communication,
the vast territory in the enemy's rear was in the hands of the
people.

In the anti-Japanese base areas, we carried out democratic
reforms, improved the livelihood of the people, and mobilized
and organized the peasant masses. Organs of anti-Japanese
democratic political power were established on an extensive
scale, and the masses of the people enjoyed the democratic
right to run their own affairs; at the same time, we carried out
the policies of "a reasonable burden" and "the reduction of rent
and interest," which weakened the feudal system of exploitation
and improved the people's livelihood. As a result, the enthusiasm of the peasant masses was deeply aroused, while the various anti-Japanese strata were given due consideration and were
thus united. In formulating our policies for the base areas, we
also took care that these policies should facilitate our work in
the enemy-occupied areas.

In the enemy-occupied cities and villages, we combined legal
with illegal struggle, united the basic masses and all patriots,

and divided and disintegrated the political power of the enemy
and his puppets so as to prepare ourselves to attack the enemy
from within in coordination with operations from without when
conditions were ripe.

The base areas established by our Party became the center
of gravity in the Chinese people's struggle to resist Japan and
save the country. Relying on these bases, our Party expanded
and strengthened the people's revolutionary forces, persevered
in the protracted war and eventually won the War of Resistance
Against Japan.

Naturally, it was impossible for the development of the revolutionary base areas to be plain sailing all the time. They constituted a tremendous threat to the enemy and were bound to be
attacked. Therefore, their development was a tortuous process
of expansion, contraction and then renewed expansion. Between
1937 and 1940 the population in the anti-Japanese base areas
grew to 100 million. But in 1941-42 the Japanese imperialists
used the major part of their invading forces to launch frantic
attacks on our base areas and to wreak havoc. Meanwhile, the
Kuomintang, too, encircled these base areas, blockaded them,
and went so far as to attack them. So by 1942 the anti-Japanese
base areas had contracted and their population was down to less
than 50 million. Placing complete reliance on the masses, our
Party resolutely adopted a series of correct policies and measures, with the result that the base areas were able to hold out
under extremely difficult circumstances. After this setback,
the army and the people in the base areas were tempered, and
grew stronger. From 1943 onward, our base areas were gradually restored and expanded, and by 1945 the population had
grown to 160 million. Taking the entire course of the Chinese
revolution into account, our revolutionary base areas went
through even more ups and downs, and they weathered a great
many tests before the small, separate base areas, expanding in
a series of waves, gradually developed into extensive and con-
tiguous base areas.

At the same time, the work of building the revolutionary base
areas was a grand rehearsal in preparation for nationwide victory.

In these base areas, we built the Party, ran the organs of state power, built the people's armed forces, and set up mass organizations; we engaged in industry and agriculture and operated cultural, educational, and all other undertakings necessary for the independent existence of a separate region. Our base areas were in fact a state in miniature. And with the steady expansion of our work in the base areas, our Party established a powerful people's army, trained cadres for various kinds of work, accumulated experience in many fields, and built up both the material and the moral strength that provided favorable conditions for nationwide victory.

The revolutionary base areas established in the War of Resistance later became the springboards for the People's War of Liberation, in which the Chinese people defeated the Kuomintang reactionaries. In the War of Liberation we continued the policy of first encircling the cities from the countryside and then capturing the cities, and thus won nationwide victory.

Build a People's Army of a New Type

"Without a people's army the people have nothing." (6) This is the conclusion drawn by Comrade Mao Tse-tung from the Chinese people's experience in their long years of revolutionary struggle, experience that was bought in blood. This is a universal truth of Marxism-Leninism.

The special feature of the Chinese revolution was armed revolution against armed counterrevolution. The main form of struggle was war, and the main form of organization was the army which was under the absolute leadership of the Chinese Communist Party, while all the other forms of organization and struggle led by our Party were coordinated, directly or indirectly, with the war.

During the First Revolutionary Civil War, many fine Party comrades took an active part in the armed revolutionary struggle. But our Party was then still in its infancy and did not have a clear understanding of this special feature of the Chinese revolution. It was only after the First Revolutionary Civil War,

only after the Kuomintang had betrayed the revolution, massa-
cred large numbers of Communists, and destroyed all the revolutionary mass organizations, that our Party reached a clearer
understanding of the supreme importance of organizing revolutionary armed forces and of studying the strategy and tactics of
revolutionary war, and created the Workers and Peasants' Red
Army, the first people's army under the leadership of the Communist Party of China.

During the Second Revolutionary Civil War, the Workers and
Peasants' Red Army created by Comrade Mao Tse-tung grew
considerably and at one time reached a total of 300,000 men.
But it later lost nine-tenths of its forces as a result of the
wrong political and military lines followed by the "Left" opportunist leadership.

At the start of the War of Resistance Against Japan, the people's army led by the Chinese Communist Party had only a little
over 40,000 men. The Kuomintang reactionaries attempted to
restrict, weaken, and destroy this people's army in every conceivable way. Comrade Mao Tse-tung pointed out that in these
circumstances, in order to sustain the War of Resistance and
defeat the Japanese aggressors, it was imperative greatly to
expand and consolidate the Eighth Route and New Fourth Armies
and all the guerrilla units led by our Party. The whole Party
should give close attention to war and study military affairs.
Every Party member should be ready at all times to take up
arms and go to the front.

Comrade Mao Tse-tung also incisively stated that Communists do not fight for personal military power but must fight for
military power for the Party and for the people.

Guided by the Party's correct line of expanding the revolutionary armed forces, the Communist-led Eighth Route and New
Fourth Armies and anti-Japanese guerrilla units promptly went
to the forefront at the very beginning of the war. We spread the
seeds of the people's armed forces in the vast areas behind the
enemy lines and kindled the flames of guerrilla warfare everywhere. Our people's army steadily expanded in the struggle, so
that by the end of the war it was already a million strong, and

there was also a militia of over two million. That was why we were able to engage nearly two-thirds of the Japanese forces of aggression and 95 percent of the puppet troops and to become the main force in the War of Resistance Against Japan. While resisting the Japanese invading forces, we repulsed three large-scale anti-Communist onslaughts launched by the Kuomintang reactionaries in 1939, 1941 and 1943, and smashed their countless "friction-mongering" activities.

Why were the Eighth Route and New Fourth Armies able to grow big and strong from being small and weak and to score such great victories in the War of Resistance Against Japan?

The fundamental reason was that the Eighth Route and New Fourth Armies were founded on Comrade Mao Tse-tung's theory of army-building. They were armies of a new type, a people's army which wholeheartedly serves the interests of the people.

Guided by Comrade Mao Tse-tung's theory on building a people's army, our army was under the absolute leadership of the Chinese Communist Party and most loyally carried out the Party's Marxist-Leninist line and policies. It had a high degree of conscious discipline and was heroically inspired to destroy all enemies and conquer all difficulties. Internally there was full unity between cadres and fighters, between those in higher and those in lower positions of responsibility, between the different departments, and between the various fraternal army units. Externally, there was similarly full unity between the army and the people and between the army and the local government.

During the anti-Japanese war our army staunchly performed the three tasks set by Comrade Mao Tse-tung, namely, fighting, mass work, and production, and it was at the same time a fighting force, a political work force, and a production corps. Everywhere it went it did propaganda work among the masses, organized and armed them, and helped them set up revolutionary political power. Our armymen strictly observed the Three Main Rules of Discipline and the Eight Points for Attention (7), carried out campaigns to "support the government and cherish the people," and did good deeds for the people everywhere. They also made use of every possibility to engage in production themselves so as to overcome economic difficulties, better their own livelihood, and lighten the people's burden. By their exemplary conduct they won the wholehearted support of the masses, who affectionately called them "our own boys."

Our army consisted of local forces as well as of regular forces; moreover, it energetically built and developed the militia, thus practicing the system of combining the three military formations, i.e., the regular forces, the local forces, and the militia.

Our army also pursued correct policies in winning over enemy officers and men and in giving lenient treatment to prisoners of war. During the anti-Japanese war we not only brought about the revolt and surrender of large numbers of puppet troops, but succeeded in converting not a few Japanese prisoners, who had been badly poisoned by fascist ideology. After they were politically awakened, they organized themselves into anti-war organizations such as the League for the Liberation of the Japanese People, the Anti-War League of the Japanese in China and the League of Awakened Japanese, helped us to disintegrate the Japanese army, and cooperated with us in opposing Japanese militarism. Comrade Sanzo Nosaka, the leader of the Japanese Communist Party, who was then in Yenan, gave us great help in this work.

The essence of Comrade Mao Tse-tung's theory of army-building is that in building a people's army prominence must be given to politics, i.e., the army must first and foremost be built on a political basis. Politics is the commander; politics is the soul of everything. Political work is the lifeline of our army. True, a people's army must pay attention to the constant improvement of its weapons and equipment and its military technique, but in its fighting it does not rely purely on weapons and technique; it relies mainly on politics, on the proletarian revolutionary consciousness and courage of the commanders and fighters, on the support and backing of the masses.

Owing to the application of Comrade Mao Tse-tung's line on

army-building, there has prevailed in our army at all times a high level of proletarian political consciousness, an atmosphere of keenness to study the thought of Mao Tse-tung, an excellent morale, a solid unity, and a deep hatred for the enemy, and thus a gigantic moral force has been brought into being. In battle it has feared neither hardships nor death, it has been able to charge or hold its ground as the conditions require. One man can play the role of several, dozens or even hundreds, and miracles can be performed.

All this makes the people's army led by the Chinese Communist Party fundamentally different from any bourgeois army, and from all the armies of the old type which served the exploiting classes and were driven and utilized by a handful of people. The experience of the people's war in China shows that a people's army created in accordance with Comrade Mao Tsetung's theory of army-building is incomparably strong and invincible.

Carry Out the Strategy and Tactics of People's War

Engels said, "The emancipation of the proletariat, in its turn, will have its specific expression in military affairs and create its specific, new military method." (8) Engels' profound prediction has been fulfilled in the revolutionary wars waged by the Chinese people under the leadership of the Chinese Communist Party. In the course of protracted armed struggle, we have created a whole range of strategy and tactics of people's war by which we have been able to utilize our strong points to attack the enemy at his weak points.

During the War of Resistance Against Japan, on the basis of his comprehensive analysis of the enemy and ourselves, Comrade Mao Tse-tung laid down the following strategic principle for the Communist-led Eighth Route and New Fourth Armies: "Guerrilla warfare is basic, but lose no chance for mobile warfare under favorable conditions." (9) He raised guerrilla warfare to the level of strategy, because, if they are to defeat a

formidable enemy, revolutionary armed forces should not fight
with a reckless disregard for the consequences when there is a
great disparity between their own strength and the enemy's. If
they do, they will suffer serious losses and bring heavy setbacks
to the revolution. Guerrilla warfare is the only way to mobilize
and apply the whole strength of the people against the enemy,
the only way to expand our forces in the course of the war, de-
plete and weaken the enemy, gradually change the balance of
forces between the enemy and ourselves, switch from guerrilla
to mobile warfare, and finally defeat the enemy.

In the initial period of the Second Revolutionary Civil War,
Comrade Mao Tse-tung enumerated the basic tactics of guerrilla warfare as follows: "The enemy advances, we retreat; the
enemy camps, we harass; the enemy tires, we attack; the enemy retreats, we pursue." (10) Guerrilla war tactics were further developed during the War of Resistance Against Japan. In
the base areas behind the enemy lines, everybody joined in the
fighting — the troops and the civilian population, men and women,
old and young; every single village fought. Various ingenious
methods of fighting were devised, including "sparrow warfare," (11), land-mine warfare, tunnel warfare, sabotage warfare, and guerrilla warfare on lakes and rivers.

In the later period of the War of Resistance Against Japan
and during the Third Revolutionary Civil War, we switched our
strategy from that of guerrilla warfare as the primary form of
fighting to that of mobile warfare in the light of the changes in
the balance of forces between the enemy and ourselves. By the
middle, and especially the later, period of the Third Revolutionary Civil War, our operations had developed into large-scale
mobile warfare, including the storming of big cities.

War of annihilation is the fundamental guiding principle of
our military operations. This guiding principle should be put
into effect regardless of whether mobile or guerrilla warfare
is the primary form of fighting. It is true that in guerrilla warfare much should be done to disrupt and harass the enemy, but
it is still necessary actively to advocate and fight battles of annihilation whenever conditions are favorable. In mobile warfare

superior forces must be concentrated in every battle so that
the enemy forces can be wiped out one by one. Comrade Mao
Tse-tung has pointed out:

> A battle in which the enemy is routed is not basically de-
> cisive in a contest with a foe of great strength. A battle of
> annihilation, on the other hand, produces a great and imme-
> diate impact on any enemy. Injuring all of a man's ten fin-
> gers is not as effective as chopping off one, and routing ten
> enemy divisions is not as effective as annihilating one of
> them. (12)

Battles of annihilation are the most effective way of hitting the
enemy; each time one of his brigades or regiments is wiped out,
he will have one brigade or one regiment less, and the enemy
forces will be demoralized and will disintegrate. By fighting
battles of annihilation, our army is able to take prisoners of
war or capture weapons from the enemy in every battle, and the
morale of our army rises, our army units get bigger, our weapons become better, and our combat effectiveness continually
increases.

In his celebrated ten cardinal military principles Comrade
Mao Tse-tung pointed out:

> In every battle, concentrate an absolutely superior force
> (two, three, four and sometimes even five or six times the
> enemy's strength), encircle the enemy forces completely,
> strive to wipe them out thoroughly and do not let any escape
> from the net. In special circumstances, use the method of
> dealing crushing blows to the enemy, that is, concentrate
> all our strength to make a frontal attack and also to attack
> one or both of his flanks, with the aim of wiping out one
> part and routing another so that our army can swiftly move
> its troops to smash other enemy forces. Strive to avoid
> battles of attrition in which we lose more than we gain or
> only break even. In this way, although we are inferior as
> a whole (in terms of numbers), we are absolutely superior

in every part and every specific campaign, and this ensures
victory in the campaign. As time goes on, we shall become
superior as a whole and eventually wipe out all the enemy. (13)

At the same time, he said that we should first attack dispersed
or isolated enemy forces and only attack concentrated and strong
enemy forces later; that we should strive to wipe out the enemy
through mobile warfare; that we should fight no battle unprepared and fight no battle we are not sure of winning; and that in
any battle we fight we should develop our army's strong points
and its excellent style of fighting. These are the major principles of fighting a war of annihilation.

In order to annihilate the enemy, we must adopt the policy of
luring him in deep and abandon some cities and districts of our
own accord in a planned way, so as to let him in. It is only after letting the enemy in that the people can take part in the war
in various ways and that the power of a people's war can be
fully exerted. It is only after letting the enemy in that he can
be compelled to divide up his forces, take on heavy burdens,
and commit mistakes. In other words, we must let the enemy
become elated, stretch out all his ten fingers, and become
hopelessly bogged down. Thus we can concentrate superior
forces to destroy the enemy forces one by one, to eat them up
mouthful by mouthful. Only by wiping out the enemy's effective
strength can cities and localities be finally held or seized. We
are firmly against dividing up our forces to defend all positions
and putting up resistance at every place for fear that our territory might be lost and our pots and pans smashed, since this
can neither wipe out the enemy forces not hold cities or localities.

Comrade Mao Tse-tung has provided a masterly summary of
the strategy and tactics of people's war: You fight in your way
and we fight in ours; we fight when we can win and move away
when we can't.

In other words, you rely on modern weapons, and we rely on
highly conscious revolutionary people; you give full play to your
superiority, and we give full play to ours; you have your way of

fighting, and we have ours. When you want to fight us, we don't let you, and you can't even find us. But when we want to fight you, we make sure that you can't get away, and we hit you squarely on the chin and wipe you out. When we are able to wipe you out, we do so with a vengeance; when we can't, we see to it that you don't wipe us out. It is opportunism if one won't fight when one can win. It is adventurism if one insists on fighting when one can't win. Fighting is the pivot of all our strategy and tactics. It is because of the necessity of fighting that we admit the necessity of moving away. The sole purpose of moving away is to fight and bring about the final and complete destruction of the enemy. This strategy and these tactics can be applied only when one relies on the broad masses of the people, and such application brings the superiority of people's war into full play. However superior he may be in technical equipment and whatever tricks he may resort to, the enemy will find himself in the passive position of having to receive blows, and the initiative will always be in our hands.

We grew from a small and weak to a large and strong force and finally defeated formidable enemies at home and abroad because we carried out the strategy and tactics of people's war. During the eight years of the War of Resistance Against Japan, the people's army led by the Chinese Communist Party fought more than 125,000 engagements with the enemy and put out of action more than 1.7 million Japanese and puppet troops. In the three years of the War of Liberation, we put eight million of the Kuomintang's reactionary troops out of action and won the great victory of the people's revolution.

Adhere to the Policy of Self-Reliance

The Chinese people's War of Resistance Against Japan was an important part of the Anti-Fascist World War. The victory of the Anti-Fascist War as a whole was the result of the common struggle of the people of the world. By its participation in the war against Japan at the final stage, the Soviet army under the leadership of the Communist Party of the Soviet Union headed by Stalin played a significant part in bringing about the defeat of Japanese imperialism. Great contributions were made by the peoples of Korea, Vietnam, Mongolia, Laos, Cambodia, Indonesia, Burma, India, Pakistan, Malaya, the Philippines, Thailand and certain other Asian countries. The people of the Americas, Oceania, Europe, and Africa also made their contribution.

Under extremely difficult circumstances, the Communist Party of Japan and the revolutionary forces of the Japanese people kept up their valiant and staunch struggle and played their part in the defeat of Japanese fascism.

The common victory was won by all the peoples, who gave one another support and encouragement. Yet each country was, above all, liberated as a result of its own people's efforts.

The Chinese people enjoyed the support of other peoples in winning both the War of Resistance Against Japan and the People's Liberation War, and yet victory was mainly the result of the Chinese people's own efforts. Certain people assert that China's victory in the War of Resistance was due entirely to foreign assistance. This absurd assertion is in tune with that of the Japanese militarists.

The liberation of the masses is accomplished by the masses themselves — this is a basic principle of Marxism-Leninism. Revolution or people's war in any country is the business of the masses in that country and should be carried out primarily by their own efforts; there is no other way.

During the War of Resistance Against Japan, our Party maintained that China should rely mainly on her own strength while at the same time trying to get as much foreign assistance as possible. We firmly opposed the Kuomintang ruling clique's policy of exclusive reliance on foreign aid. In the eyes of the Kuomintang and Chiang Kai-shek, China's industry and agriculture were no good, her weapons and equipment were no good, nothing in China was any good, so that if she wanted to defeat Japan she had to depend on other countries, and particularly on the U.S.-British imperialists. This was completely slavish thinking. Our policy was diametrically opposed to that of the

Kuomintang. Our Party held that it was possible to exploit the contradictions between U.S.-British imperialism and Japanese imperialism, but that no reliance could be placed on the former. In fact, the U.S.-British imperialists repeatedly plotted to bring about a "Far Eastern Munich" in order to arrive at a compromise with Japanese imperialism at China's expense, and for a considerable period of time they provided the Japanese aggressors with war matériel. In helping China during that period, the U.S. imperialists harbored the sinister design of turning China into a colony of their own.

Comrade Mao Tse-tung said: "China has to rely mainly on her own efforts in the War of Resistance." (14) He added, "We hope for foreign aid but cannot be dependent on it; we depend on our own efforts, on the creative power of the whole army and the entire people." (15)

Self-reliance was especially important for the people's armed forces and the Liberated Areas led by our Party.

The Kuomintang government gave the Eighth Route and New Fourth Armies some small allowances in the initial stage of the anti-Japanese war, but gave them not a single penny later. The Liberated Areas faced great difficulties as a result of the Japanese imperialists' savage attacks and brutal "mopping-up" campaigns, of the Kuomintang's military encirclement and economic blockade and of natural calamities. The difficulties were particularly great in the years 1941 and 1942, when we were very short of food and clothing.

What were we to do? Comrade Mao Tse-tung asked: How has mankind managed to keep alive from time immemorial? Has it not been by men using their hands to provide for themselves? Why should we, their latter-day descendants, be devoid of this tiny bit of wisdom? Why can't we use our own hands?

The Central Committee of the Party and Comrade Mao Tse-tung put forward the policies of "ample food and clothing through self-reliance" and "develop the economy and ensure supplies," and the army and the people of the Liberated Areas accordingly launched an extensive production campaign, with the main emphasis on agriculture.

Difficulties are not invincible monsters. If everyone cooperates and fights them, they will be overcome. The Kuomintang reactionaries thought that it could starve us to death by cutting off allowances and imposing an economic blockade, but in fact it helped us by stimulating us to rely on our own efforts to surmount our difficulties. While launching the great campaign for production, we applied the policy of "better troops and simpler administration" and economized in the use of manpower and material resources; thus we not only surmounted the severe material difficulties and successfully met the crisis, but lightened the people's burden, improved their livelihood, and laid the material foundations for victory in the anti-Japanese war.

The problem of military equipment was solved mainly by relying on the capture of arms from the enemy, though we did turn out some weapons too. Chiang Kai-shek, the Japanese imperialists, and the U.S. imperialists have all been our "chiefs of transportation corps." The arsenals of the imperialists always provide the oppressed peoples and nations with arms.

The people's armed forces led by our Party independently waged people's war on a large scale and won great victories without any material aid from outside, both during the more than eight years of the anti-Japanese war and during the more than three years of the People's War of Liberation.

Comrade Mao Tse-tung has said that our fundamental policy should rest on the foundation of our own strength. Only by relying on our own efforts can we in all circumstances remain invincible.

The peoples of the world invariably support each other in their struggles against imperialism and its lackeys. Those countries which have won victory are duty bound to support and aid the peoples who have not yet done so. Nevertheless, foreign aid can only play a supplementary role.

In order to make a revolution and to fight a people's war and be victorious, it is imperative to adhere to the policy of self-reliance, rely on the strength of the masses in one's own country, and prepare to carry on the fight independently even when all material aid from outside is cut off. If one does not operate

296 THE LIN PIAO AFFAIR

by one's own efforts, does not independently ponder and solve
the problems of the revolution in one's own country, and does
not rely on the strength of the masses, but leans wholly on foreign aid — even though this be aid from socialist countries
which persist in revolution — no victory can be won, or be consolidated even if it is won.

The International Significance of Comrade Mao Tse-tung's Theory of People's War

The Chinese revolution is a continuation of the Great October
Revolution. The road of the October Revolution is the common
road for all people's revolutions. The Chinese revolution and
the October Revolution have in common the following basic
characteristics: (1) Both were led by the working class with a
Marxist-Leninist party as its nucleus. (2) Both were based on
the worker-peasant alliance. (3) In both cases state power was
seized through violent revolution and the dictatorship of the
proletariat was established. (4) In both cases the socialist system was built after victory in the revolution. (5) Both were
component parts of the proletarian world revolution.

Naturally, the Chinese revolution had its own peculiar characteristics. The October Revolution took place in imperialist
Russia, but the Chinese revolution broke out in a semicolonial
and semifeudal country. The former was a proletarian socialist
revolution, while the latter developed into a socialist revolution
after the complete victory of the new-democratic revolution.
The October Revolution began with armed uprisings in the cities
and then spread to the countryside, while the Chinese revolution
won nationwide victory through the encirclement of the cities
from the rural areas and the final capture of the cities.

Comrade Mao Tse-tung's great merit lies in the fact that he
has succeeded in integrating the universal truth of Marxism-
Leninism with the concrete practice of the Chinese revolution
and has enriched and developed Marxism-Leninism by his masterly generalization and summation of the experience gained
during the Chinese people's protracted revolutionary struggle.

Comrade Mao Tse-tung's theory of people's war has been proved by the long practice of the Chinese revolution to be in accord with the objective laws of such wars and to be invincible. It has not only been valid for China, it is a great contribution to the revolutionary struggles of the oppressed nations and peoples throughout the world.

The people's war led by the Chinese Communist Party, comprising the War of Resistance and the Revolutionary Civil Wars, lasted for twenty-two years. It constitutes the most drawn-out and most complex people's war led by the proletariat in modern history, and it has been the richest in experience.

In the last analysis, the Marxist-Leninist theory of proletarian revolution is the theory of the seizure of state power by revolutionary violence, the theory of countering war against the people by people's war. As Marx so aptly put it, "Force is the midwife of every old society pregnant with a new one." (16)

It was on the basis of the lessons derived from the people's wars in China that Comrade Mao Tse-tung, using the simplest and the most vivid language, advanced the famous thesis that "political power grows out of the barrel of a gun." (17)

He clearly pointed out:

> The seizure of power by armed force, the settlement of the issue by war, is the central task and the highest form of revolution. This Marxist-Leninist principle of revolution holds good universally, for China and for all other countries. (18)

War is the product of imperialism and the system of exploitation of man by man. Lenin said that "war is always and everywhere begun by the exploiters themselves, by the ruling and oppressing classes." (19) So long as imperialism and the system of exploitation of man by man exist, the imperialists and reactionaries will invariably rely on armed force to maintain their reactionary rule and impose war on the oppressed nations and peoples. This is an objective law independent of man's will.

In the world today, all the imperialists headed by the United

States and their lackeys, without exception, are strengthening their state machinery, and especially their armed forces. U.S. imperialism, in particular, is carrying out armed aggression and suppression everywhere.

What should the oppressed nations and the oppressed people do in the face of wars of aggression and armed suppression by the imperialists and their lackeys? Should they submit and remain slaves in perpetuity? Or should they rise in resistance and fight for their liberation?

Comrade Mao Tse-tung answered this question in vivid terms. He said that after long investigation and study the Chinese people discovered that all the imperialists and their lackeys "have swords in their hands and are out to kill. The people have come to understand this and so act after the same fashion." (20) This is called doing unto them what they do unto us.

In the last analysis, whether one dares to wage a tit-for-tat struggle against armed aggression and suppression by the imperialists and their lackeys, whether one dares to fight a people's war against them, is tantamount to whether one dares to embark on revolution. This is the most effective touchstone for distinguishing genuine from fake revolutionaries and Marxist-Leninists.

In view of the fact that some people were afflicted with the fear of the imperialists and reactionaries, Comrade Mao Tse-tung put forward his famous thesis that "the imperialists and all reactionaries are paper tigers." He said,

> All reactionaries are paper tigers. In appearance, the reactionaries are terrifying, but in reality they are not so powerful. From a long-term point of view, it is not the reactionaries but the people who are really powerful. (21)

The history of people's war in China and other countries provides conclusive evidence that the growth of the people's revolutionary forces from weak and small beginnings into strong and large forces is a universal law of development of class struggle, a universal law of development of people's war.

A people's war inevitably meets with many difficulties, with ups and downs and setbacks in the course of its development, but no force can alter its general trend toward inevitable triumph.

Comrade Mao Tse-tung points out that we must despise the enemy strategically and take full account of him tactically.

To despise the enemy strategically is an elementary requirement for a revolutionary. Without the courage to despise the enemy and without daring to win, it will be simply impossible to make revolution and wage a people's war, let alone to achieve victory.

It is also very important for revolutionaries to take full account of the enemy tactically. It is likewise impossible to win victory in a people's war without taking full account of the enemy tactically, and without examining the concrete conditions, without being prudent and giving great attention to the study of the art of struggle, and without adopting appropriate forms of struggle in the concrete practice of the revolution in each country and with regard to each concrete problem of struggle.

Dialectical and historical materialism teaches us that what is important primarily is not that which at the given moment seems to be durable and yet is already beginning to die away, but that which is arising and developing, even though at the given moment it may not appear to be durable, for only that which is arising and developing is invincible.

Why can the apparently weak new-born forces always triumph over the decadent forces which appear so powerful? The reason is that truth is on their side and that the masses are on their side, while the reactionary classes are always divorced from the masses and set themselves against the masses.

This has been borne out by the victory of the Chinese revolution, by the history of all revolutions, the whole history of class struggle and the entire history of mankind.

The imperialists are extremely afraid of Comrade Mao Tsetung's thesis that "imperialism and all reactionaries are paper tigers," and the revisionists are extremely hostile to it. They all oppose and attack this thesis and the philistines follow suit by ridiculing it. But all this cannot in the least diminish its importance. The light of truth cannot be dimmed by anybody.

Comrade Mao Tse-tung's theory of people's war solves not only the problem of daring to fight a people's war, but also that of how to wage it.

Comrade Mao Tse-tung is a great statesman and military scientist, proficient at directing war in accordance with its laws. By the line and policies, the strategy and tactics he formulated for the people's war, he led the Chinese people in steering the ship of the people's war past all hidden reefs to the shores of victory in most complicated and difficult conditions.

It must be emphasized that Comrade Mao Tse-tung's theory of the establishment of rural revolutionary base areas and the encirclement of the cities from the countryside is of outstanding and universal practical importance for the present revolutionary struggles of all the oppressed nations and peoples, and particularly for the revolutionary struggles of the oppressed nations and peoples in Asia, Africa, and Latin America against imperialism and its lackeys.

Many countries and peoples in Asia, Africa, and Latin America are now being subjected to aggression and enslavement on a serious scale by the imperialists headed by the United States and their lackeys. The basic political and economic conditions in many of these countries have many similarities to those that prevailed in old China. As in China, the peasant question is extremely important in these regions. The peasants constitute the main force of the national-democratic revolution against the imperialists and their lackeys. In committing aggression against these countries, the imperialists usually begin by seizing the big cities and the main lines of communication, but they are unable to bring the vast countryside completely under their control. The countryside, and the countryside alone, can provide the broad areas in which the revolutionaries can maneuver freely. The countryside, and the countryside alone, can provide the revolutionary bases from which the revolutionaries can go forward to final victory. Precisely for this reason, Comrade Mao Tse-tung's theory of establishing revolutionary base areas in the rural districts and encircling the cities from the countryside is attracting more and more attention among the people in these regions.

Taking the entire globe, if North America and Western Europe can be called "the cities of the world," then Asia, Africa, and Latin America constitute "the rural areas of the world." Since World War II, the proletarian revolutionary movement has for various reasons been temporarily held back in the North American and West European capitalist countries, while the people's revolutionary movement in Asia, Africa, and Latin America has been growing vigorously. In a sense, the contemporary world revolution also presents a picture of the encirclement of cities by the rural areas. In the final analysis, the whole cause of world revolution hinges on the revolutionary struggles of the Asian, African, and Latin American peoples who make up the overwhelming majority of the world's population. The socialist countries should regard it as their internationalist duty to support the people's revolutionary struggles in Asia, Africa, and Latin America.

The October Revolution opened up a new era in the revolution of the oppressed nations. The victory of the October Revolution built a bridge between the socialist revolution of the proletariat of the West and the national-democratic revolution of the colonial and semicolonial countries of the East. The Chinese revolution has successfully solved the problem of how to link up the national-democratic with the socialist revolution in the colonial and semicolonial countries.

Comrade Mao Tse-tung has pointed out that in the epoch since the October Revolution, anti-imperialist revolution in any colonial or semicolonial country is no longer part of the old bourgeois or capitalist world revolution, but is part of the new world revolution, the proletarian-socialist world revolution.

Comrade Mao Tse-tung has formulated a complete theory of the new-democratic revolution. He indicated that this revolution, which is different from all others, can only be, nay must be, a revolution against imperialism, feudalism, and bureaucrat-capitalism waged by the broad masses of the people under the leadership of the proletariat.

This means that the revolution can only be, nay must be, led by the proletariat and the genuinely revolutionary party armed with Marxism-Leninism, and by no other class or party.

This means that the revolution embraces in its ranks not only the workers, the peasants, and the urban petty bourgeoisie, but also the national bourgeoisie and other patriotic and anti-imperialist democrats.

This means, finally, that the revolution is directed against imperialism, feudalism, and bureaucrat-capitalism.

The new-democratic revolution leads to socialism, and not to capitalism.

Comrade Mao Tse-tung's theory of the new-democratic revolution is the Marxist-Leninist theory of revolution by stages as well as the Marxist-Leninist theory of uninterrupted revolution.

Comrade Mao Tse-tung made a correct distinction between the two revolutionary stages, i.e., the national-democratic and the socialist revolutions; at the same time, he correctly and closely linked the two. The national-democratic revolution is the necessary preparation for the socialist revolution, and the socialist revolution is the inevitable sequel to the national-democratic revolution. There is no Great Wall between the two revolutionary stages. But the socialist revolution is only possible after the completion of the national-democratic revolution. The more thorough the national-democratic revolution, the better the conditions for the socialist revolution.

The experience of the Chinese revolution shows that the tasks of the national-democratic revolution can be fulfilled only through long and tortuous struggles. In this stage of revolution, imperialism and its lackeys are the principal enemy. In the struggle against imperialism and its lackeys, it is necessary to rally all anti-imperialist patriotic forces, including the national bourgeoisie and all patriotic personages. All those patriotic personages from among the bourgeoisie and other exploiting classes who join the anti-imperialist struggle play a progressive historical role; they are not tolerated by imperialism but welcomed by the proletariat.

It is very harmful to confuse the two stages, that is, the

national-democratic and the socialist revolutions. Comrade
Mao Tse-tung criticized the wrong idea of "accomplishing both
at one stroke," and pointed out that this utopian idea could only
weaken the struggle against imperialism and its lackeys, the
most urgent task at that time. The Kuomintang reactionaries
and the Trotskyites they hired during the War of Resistance deliberately confused these two stages of the Chinese revolution,
proclaiming the "theory of a single revolution" and preaching
so-called "socialism" without any Communist Party. With this
preposterous theory they attempted to swallow up the Communist Party, wipe out any revolution, and prevent the advance of
the national-democratic revolution, and they used it as a pretext for their nonresistance and capitulation to imperialism.
This reactionary theory was buried long ago by the history of
the Chinese revolution.

The Khrushchev revisionists are now actively preaching that
socialism can be built without the proletariat and without a genuinely revolutionary party armed with the advanced proletarian
ideology, and they have cast the fundamental tenets of Marxism-
Leninism to the four winds. The revisionists' purpose is solely
to divert the oppressed nations from their struggle against imperialism and sabotage their national-democratic revolution,
all in the service of imperialism.

The Chinese revolution provides a successful lesson for making a thoroughgoing national-democratic revolution under the
leadership of the proletariat; it likewise provides a successful
lesson for the timely transition from the national-democratic
revolution to the socialist revolution under the leadership of
the proletariat.

Mao Tse-tung's thought has been the guide to the victory of
the Chinese revolution. It has integrated the universal truth of
Marxism-Leninism with the concrete practice of the Chinese
revolution and creatively developed Marxism-Leninism, thus
adding new weapons to the arsenal of Marxism-Leninism.

Ours is the epoch in which world capitalism and imperialism
are heading for their doom and socialism and communism are
marching to victory. Comrade Mao Tse-tung's theory of people's

war is not only a product of the Chinese revolution, but has also
the characteristics of our epoch. The new experience gained in
the people's revolutionary struggles in various countries since
World War II has provided continuous evidence that Mao Tse-
tung's thought is a common asset of the revolutionary people of
the whole world. This is the great international significance of
the thought of Mao Tse-tung.

Defeat U.S. Imperialism and Its
Lackeys by People's War

Since World War II, U.S. imperialism has stepped into the
shoes of German, Japanese, and Italian fascism and has been
trying to build a great American empire by dominating and enslaving the whole world. It is actively fostering Japanese and
West German militarism as its chief accomplices in unleashing
a world war. Like a vicious wolf, it is bullying and enslaving
various peoples, plundering their wealth, encroaching upon their
countries' sovereignty and interfering in their internal affairs.
It is the most rabid aggressor in human history and the most
ferocious common enemy of the people of the world. Every people or country in the world that wants revolution, independence,
and peace cannot but direct the spearhead of its struggle against
U.S. imperialism.

Just as the Japanese imperialists' policy of subjugating China
made it possible for the Chinese people to form the broadest
possible united front against them, so the U.S. imperialists'
policy of seeking world domination makes it possible for the
people throughout the world to unite all the forces that can be
united and form the broadest possible united front for a con-
verging attack on U.S. imperialism.

At present, the main battlefield of the fierce struggle between
the people of the world on the one side and U.S. imperialism and
its lackeys on the other is the vast area of Asia, Africa, and
Latin America. In the world as a whole, this is the area where
the people suffer worst from imperialist oppression and where
imperialist rule is most vulnerable. Since World War II,

revolutionary storms have been rising in this area, and today they have become the most important force directly pounding U.S. imperialism. The contradiction between the revolutionary peoples of Asia, Africa, and Latin America and the imperialists headed by the United States is the principal contradiction in the contemporary world. The development of this contradiction is promoting the struggle of the people of the whole world against U.S. imperialism and its lackeys.

Since World War II, people's war has increasingly demonstrated its power in Asia, Africa, and Latin America. The peoples of China, Korea, Vietnam, Laos, Cuba, Indonesia, Algeria, and other countries have waged people's wars against the imperialists and their lackeys and won great victories. The classes leading these people's wars may vary, and so may the breadth and depth of mass mobilization and the extent of victory, but the victories in these people's wars have very much weakened and pinned down the forces of imperialism, upset the U.S. imperialist plan to launch a world war, and become mighty factors defending world peace.

Today, the conditions are more favorable than ever before for the waging of people's wars by the revolutionary peoples of Asia, Africa, and Latin America against U.S. imperialism and its lackeys.

Since World War II and the succeeding years of revolutionary upsurge, there has been a great rise in the level of political consciousness and the degree of organization of the people in all countries, and the resources available to them for mutual support and aid have greatly increased. The whole capitalist-imperialist system has become drastically weaker and is in the process of increasing convulsion and disintegration. After World War I, the imperialists lacked the power to destroy the new-born socialist Soviet state, but they were still able to suppress the people's revolutionary movements in some countries in the parts of the world under their own rule and so maintain a short period of comparative stability. Since World War II, however, not only have they been unable to stop a number of countries from taking the socialist road, but they are no longer

capable of holding back the surging tide of the people's revolutionary movements in the areas under their own rule.

U.S. imperialism is stronger, but also more vulnerable, than
any imperialism of the past. It sets itself against the people of
the whole world, including the people of the United States. Its
human, military, material, and financial resources are far from
sufficient for the realization of its ambition of dominating the
whole world. U.S. imperialism has further weakened itself by
occupying so many places in the world, overreaching itself,
stretching its fingers out wide and dispersing its strength, with
its rear so far away and its supply lines so long. As Comrade
Mao Tse-tung has said, "Wherever it commits aggression, it
puts a new noose around its neck. It is besieged ring upon ring
by the people of the whole world." (22)

When committing aggression in a foreign country, U.S. imperialism can only employ part of its forces, which are sent to
fight an unjust war far from their native land and therefore have
a low morale, and so U.S. imperialism is beset with great difficulties. The people subjected to its aggression are having a
trial of strength with U.S. imperialism neither in Washington
nor New York, neither in Honolulu nor Florida, but are fighting
for independence and freedom on their own soil. Once they are
mobilized on a broad scale, they will have inexhaustible strength.
Thus superiority will belong not to the United States but to the
people subjected to its aggression. The latter, though apparently
weak and small, are really more powerful than U.S. imperialism.

The struggles waged by the different peoples against U.S. imperialism reinforce each other and merge into a torrential
worldwide tide of opposition to U.S. imperialism. The more
successful the development of people's war in a given region,
the larger the number of U.S. imperialist forces that can be
pinned down and depleted there. When the U.S. aggressors are
hard pressed in one place, they have no alternative but to loosen
their grip on others. Therefore the conditions become more favorable for the people elsewhere to wage struggles against U.S.
imperialism and its lackeys.

Everything is divisible. And so is this colossus of U.S.

imperialism. It can be split up and defeated. The peoples of Asia, Africa, Latin America, and other regions can destroy it piece by piece, some striking at its head and others at its feet. That is why the greatest fear of U.S. imperialism is that people's wars will be launched in different parts of the world, and particularly in Asia, Africa, and Latin America, and why it regards people's war as a mortal danger.

U.S. imperialism relies solely on its nuclear weapons to intimidate people. But these weapons cannot save U.S. imperialism from its doom. Nuclear weapons cannot be used lightly. U.S. imperialism has been condemned by the people of the whole world for its towering crime of dropping two atom bombs on Japan. If it uses nuclear weapons again, it will become isolated in the extreme. Moreover, the U.S. monopoly of nuclear weapons has long been broken; U.S. imperialism has these weapons, but others have them too. If it threatens other countries with nuclear weapons, U.S. imperialism will expose its own country to the same threat. For this reason, it will meet with strong opposition not only from the people elsewhere but also inevitably from the people in its own country. Even if U.S. imperialism brazenly uses nuclear weapons, it cannot conquer the people, who are indomitable.

However highly developed modern weapons and technical equipment may be and however complicated the methods of modern warfare, in the final analysis the outcome of a war will be decided by the sustained fighting of the ground forces, by the fighting at close quarters on battlefields, by the political consciousness of the men, by their courage and spirit of sacrifice. Here the weak points of U.S. imperialism will be completely laid bare, while the superiority of the revolutionary people will be brought into full play. The reactionary troops of U.S. imperialism cannot possibly be endowed with the courage and the spirit of sacrifice possessed by the revolutionary people. The spiritual atom bomb which the revolutionary people possess is a far more powerful and useful weapon than the physical atom bomb.

Vietnam is the most convincing current example of a victim

of aggression defeating U.S. imperialism by a people's war.
The United States has made south Vietnam a testing ground for
the suppression of people's war. It has carried on this experiment for many years, and everybody can now see that the U.S.
aggressors are unable to find a way of coping with people's war.
On the other hand, the Vietnamese people have brought the
power of people's war into full play in their struggle against
the U.S. aggressors. The U.S. aggressors are in danger of being swamped in the people's war in Vietnam. They are deeply
worried that their defeat in Vietnam will lead to a chain reaction. They are expanding the war in an attempt to save themselves from defeat. But the more they expand the war, the
greater will be the chain reaction. The more they escalate the
war, the heavier will be their fall and the more disastrous their
defeat. The people in other parts of the world will see still
more clearly that U.S. imperialism can be defeated, and that
what the Vietnamese people can do, they can do too.

History has proved and will go on proving that people's war
is the most effective weapon against U.S. imperialism and its
lackeys. All revolutionary people will learn to wage people's
war against U.S. imperialism and its lackeys. They will take
up arms, learn to fight battles and become skilled in waging
people's war, though they have not done so before. U.S. imperialism, like a mad bull dashing from place to place, will finally be burned to ashes in the blazing fires of the people's
wars it has provoked by its own actions.

The Khrushchev Revisionists Are Betrayers
of People's War

The Khrushchev revisionists have come to the rescue of U.S.
imperialism just when it is most panic-stricken and helpless in
its efforts to cope with people's war. Working hand in glove
with the U.S. imperialists, they are doing their utmost to spread
all kinds of arguments against people's war and, wherever they
can, they are scheming to undermine it by overt or covert
means.

The fundamental reason why the Khrushchev revisionists are opposed to people's war is that they have no faith in the masses and are afraid of U.S. imperialism, of war and of revolution. Like all other opportunists, they are blind to the power of the masses and do not believe that the revolutionary people are capable of defeating imperialism. They submit to the nuclear blackmail of the U.S. imperialists and are afraid that if the oppressed peoples and nations rise up to fight people's wars or the people of socialist countries repulse U.S. imperialist aggression, U.S. imperialism will become incensed, they themselves will become involved, and their fond dream of Soviet-U.S. cooperation to dominate the world will be spoiled.

Ever since Lenin led the Great October Revolution to victory, the experience of innumerable revolutionary wars has borne out the truth that a revolutionary people who rise up with only their bare hands at the outset finally succeed in defeating the ruling classes who are armed to the teeth. The poorly armed have defeated the better armed. People's armed forces, beginning with only primitive swords, spears, rifles, and hand-grenades, have in the end defeated the imperialist forces armed with modern airplanes, tanks, heavy artillery, and atom bombs. Guerrilla forces have ultimately defeated regular armies. "Amateurs" who were never trained in any military schools have eventually defeated "professionals" graduated from military academies. And so on and so forth. Things stubbornly develop in a way that runs counter to the assertions of the revisionists, and facts are slapping them in the face.

The Khrushchev revisionists insist that a nation without nuclear weapons is incapable of defeating an enemy with nuclear weapons, whatever methods of fighting it may adopt. This is tantamount to saying that anyone without nuclear weapons is destined to come to grief, destined to be bullied and annihilated, and must either capitulate to the enemy when confronted with his nuclear weapons or come under the "protection" of some other nuclear power and submit to its beck and call. Isn't this the jungle law of survival par excellence? Isn't this helping the imperialists in their nuclear blackmail? Isn't this openly forbidding people to make revolution?

The Khrushchev revisionists assert that nuclear weapons and strategic rocket units are decisive while conventional forces are insignificant, and that a militia is just a heap of human flesh. For ridiculous reasons such as these, they oppose the mobilization of and reliance on the masses in the socialist countries to get prepared to use people's war against imperialist aggression. They have staked the whole future of their country on nuclear weapons and are engaged in a nuclear gamble with U.S. imperialism, with which they are trying to strike a political deal. Their theory of military strategy is the theory that nuclear weapons decide everything. Their line in army-building is the bourgeois line which ignores the human factor and sees only the material factor and which regards technique as everything and politics as nothing.

The Khrushchev revisionists maintain that a single spark in any part of the globe may touch off a world nuclear conflagration and bring destruction to mankind. If this were true, our planet would have been destroyed time and time again. There have been wars of national liberation throughout the twenty years since World War II. But has any single one of them developed into a world war? Isn't it true that the U.S. imperialists' plans for a world war have been upset precisely thanks to the wars of national liberation in Asia, Africa, and Latin America? By contrast, those who have done their utmost to stamp out the "sparks" of people's war have in fact encouraged U.S. imperialism in its aggressions and wars.

The Khrushchev revisionists claim that if their general line of "peaceful coexistence, peaceful transition, and peaceful competition" is followed, the oppressed will be liberated and "a world without weapons, without armed forces, and without wars" will come into being. But the inexorable fact is that imperialism and reaction headed by the United States are zealously priming their war machine and are daily engaged in sanguinary suppression of the revolutionary peoples and in the threat and use of armed force against independent countries. The kind of rubbish peddled by the Khrushchev revisionists has already taken a great toll of lives in a number of countries. Are these painful lessons, paid for in blood, still insufficient? The essence of the general line of the Khrushchev revisionists is nothing other than the demand that all the oppressed peoples and nations and all the countries which have won independence should lay down their arms and place themselves at the mercy of the U.S. imperialists and their lackeys who are armed to the teeth.

"While magistrates are allowed to burn down houses, the common people are forbidden even to light lamps." Such is the way of the imperialists and reactionaries. Subscribing to this imperialist philosophy, the Khrushchev revisionists shout at the Chinese people standing in the forefront of the fight for world peace: "You are bellicose!" Gentlemen, your abuse adds to our credit. It is this very "bellicosity" of ours that helps to prevent imperialism from unleashing a world war. The people are "bellicose" because they have to defend themselves and because the imperialists and reactionaries force them to be so. It is also the imperialists and reactionaries who have taught the people the arts of war. We are simply using revolutionary "bellicosity" to cope with counterrevolutionary bellicosity. How can it be argued that the imperialists and their lackeys may kill people everywhere, while the people must not strike back in self-defense or help one another? What kind of logic is this? The Khrushchev revisionists regard imperialists like Kennedy and Johnson as "sensible" and describe us together with all those who dare to carry out armed defense against imperialist aggression as "bellicose." This has revealed the Khrushchev revisionists in their true colors as the accomplices of imperialist gangsters.

We know that war brings destruction, sacrifice, and suffering on the people. But the destruction, sacrifice, and suffering will be much greater if no resistance is offered to imperialist armed aggression and the people become willing slaves. The sacrifice of a small number of people in revolutionary wars is repaid by security for whole nations, whole countries, and even the whole of mankind; temporary suffering is repaid by lasting or even perpetual peace and happiness. War can temper the people and push history forward. In this sense, war is a great school.

When discussing World War I, Lenin said,

> The war has brought hunger to the most civilized countries, to those most culturally developed. On the other hand, the war, as a tremendous historical process, has accelerated social development to an unheard-of degree. (23)

He added,

> War has shaken up the masses, its untold horrors and suffering have awakened them. War has given history momentum and it is now flying with locomotive speed. (24)

If the arguments of the Khrushchev revisionists are to be believed, would not that make Lenin the worst of all "bellicose elements"?

In diametrical opposition to the Khrushchev revisionists, the Marxist-Leninists and revolutionary people never take a gloomy view of war. Our attitude towards imperialist wars of aggression has always been clear-cut. First, we are against them, and second, we are not afraid of them. We will destroy whoever attacks us. As for revolutionary wars waged by the oppressed nations and peoples, far from opposing them, we invariably give them firm support and active aid. It has been so in the past, it remains so in the present and, when we grow in strength as time goes on, we will give them still more support and aid in the future. It is sheer daydreaming for anyone to think that since our revolution has been victorious, our national construction is forging ahead, our national wealth is increasing, and our living conditions are improving, we too will lose our revolutionary fighting will, abandon the cause of world revolution, and discard Marxism-Leninism and proletarian internationalism. Of course, every revolution in a country stems from the demands of its own people. Only when the people in a country are awakened, mobilized, organized, and armed can they overthrow the reactionary

rule of imperialism and its lackeys through struggle; their role
cannot be replaced or taken over by any people from outside. In
this sense, revolution cannot be imported. But this does not ex-
clude mutual sympathy and support on the part of revolutionary
peoples in their struggles against the imperialists and their
lackeys. Our support and aid to other revolutionary peoples
serves precisely to help their self-reliant struggle.

The propaganda of the Khrushchev revisionists against people's war and the publicity they give to defeatism and capitulationism tend to demoralize and spiritually disarm revolutionary
people everywhere. These revisionists are doing what the U.S.
imperialists are unable to do themselves and are rendering
them great service. They have greatly encouraged U.S. imperialism in its war adventures. They have completely betrayed
the Marxist-Leninist revolutionary theory of war and have become betrayers of people's war.

To win the struggle against U.S. imperialism and carry people's wars to victory, the Marxist-Leninists and revolutionary
people throughout the world must resolutely oppose Khrushchev
revisionism.

Today, Khrushchev revisionism has a dwindling audience
among the revolutionary people of the world. Wherever there
is armed aggression and suppression by imperialism and its
lackeys, there are bound to be people's wars against aggression
and oppression. It is certain that such wars will develop vigorously. This is an objective law independent of the will of either
the U.S. imperialists or the Khrushchev revisionists. The revolutionary people of the world will sweep away everything that
stands in the way of their advance. Khrushchev is finished. And
the successors to Khrushchev revisionism will fare no better.
The imperialists, the reactionaries, and the Khrushchev revisionists, who have all set themselves against people's war, will
be swept like dust from the stage of history by the mighty broom
of the revolutionary people.

*   *   *

Great changes have taken place in China and the world in the twenty years since the victory of the War of Resistance Against Japan, changes that have made the situation more favorable than ever for the revolutionary people of the world and more unfavorable than ever for imperialism and its lackeys.

When Japanese imperialism launched its war of aggression against China, the Chinese people had only a very small people's army and a very small revolutionary base area, and they were up against the biggest military despot of the East. Yet even then, Comrade Mao Tse-tung said that the Chinese people's war could be won and that Japanese imperialism could be defeated. Today, the revolutionary base areas of the peoples of world have grown to unprecedented proportions, their revolutionary movement is surging as never before, imperialism is weaker than ever, and U.S. imperialism, the chieftain of world imperialism, is suffering one defeat after another. We can say with even greater confidence that the people's wars can be won and U.S. imperialism can be defeated in all countries.

The peoples of the world now have the lessons of the October Revolution, the Anti-Fascist War, the Chinese people's War of Resistance and War of Liberation, the Korean people's War of Resistance to U.S. Aggression, the Vietnamese people's War of Liberation and their War of Resistance to U.S. Aggression, and the people's revolutionary armed struggles in many other countries. Provided each people studies these lessons well and creatively integrates them with the concrete practice of revolution in their own country, there is no doubt that the revolutionary peoples of the world will stage still more powerful and splendid dramas in the theater of people's war in their countries and that they will wipe off the earth once and for all the common enemy of all the peoples, U.S. imperialism, and its lackeys.

The struggle of the Vietnamese people against U.S. aggression and for national salvation is now the focus of the struggle of the people of the world against U.S. aggression. The determination of the Chinese people to support and aid the Vietnamese people in their struggle against U.S. aggression and for national salvation is unshakable. No matter what U.S. imperialism may do to

expand its war adventure, the Chinese people will do everything
in their power to support the Vietnamese people until every single one of the U.S. aggressors is driven out of Vietnam.

The U.S. imperialists are now clamoring for another trial of
strength with the Chinese people, for another large-scale ground
war on the Asian mainland. If they insist on following in the
footsteps of the Japanese fascists, well then, they may do so,
if they please. The Chinese people definitely have ways of their
own for coping with a U.S. imperialist war of aggression. Our
methods are no secret. The most important one is still mobilization of the people, reliance on the people, making everyone a
soldier and waging a people's war.

We want to tell the U.S. imperialists once again that the vast
ocean of several hundred million Chinese people in arms will
be more than enough to submerge your few million aggressor
troops. If you dare to impose war on us, we shall gain freedom
of action. It will then not be up to you to decide how the war
will be fought. We shall fight in the ways most advantageous to
us to destroy the enemy and wherever the enemy can be most
easily destroyed. Since the Chinese people were able to destroy
the Japanese aggressors twenty years ago, they are certainly
still more capable of finishing off the U.S. aggressors today.
The naval and air superiority you boast about cannot intimidate
the Chinese people, and neither can the atom bomb you brandish
at us. If you want to send troops, go ahead, the more the better.
We will annihilate as many as you can send, and can even give
you receipts. The Chinese people are a great, valiant people.
We have the courage to shoulder the heavy burden of combating
U.S. imperialism and to contribute our share in the struggle for
final victory over this most ferocious enemy of the people of
the world.

It must be pointed out in all seriousness that after the victory
of the War of Resistance Taiwan was returned to China. The
occupation of Taiwan by U.S. imperialism is absolutely unjusti-
fied. Taiwan Province is an inalienable part of Chinese territory. The U.S. imperialists must get out of Taiwan. The Chinese people are determined to liberate Taiwan.

In commemorating the twentieth anniversary of victory in the War of Resistance Against Japan, we must also point out in all solemnity that the Japanese militarists fostered by U.S. imperialism will certainly receive still severer punishment if they ignore the firm opposition of the Japanese people and the people of Asia, again indulge in their pipe dreams, and resume their old road of aggression in Asia.

U.S. imperialism is preparing a world war. But can this save it from its doom? World War I was followed by the birth of the socialist Soviet Union. World War II was followed by the emergence of a series of socialist countries and many nationally independent countries. If the U.S. imperialists should insist on launching a third world war, it can be stated categorically that many more hundreds of millions of people will turn to socialism; the imperialists will then have little room left on the globe; and it is possible that the whole structure of imperialism will collapse.

We are optimistic about the future of the world. We are confident that the people will bring to an end the epoch of wars in human history. Comrade Mao Tse-tung pointed out long ago that war, this monster, "will be finally eliminated by the progress of human society, and in the not too distant future too. But there is only one way to eliminate it and that is to oppose war with war, to oppose counterrevolutionary war with revolutionary war." (25)

All peoples suffering from U.S. imperialist aggression, oppression and plunder, unite! Hold aloft the just banner of people's war and fight for the cause of world peace, national liberation, people's democracy, and socialism! Victory will certainly go to the people of the world!

Long live the victory of people's war!

Notes

1) Under the influence of the Chinese Workers and Peasants' Red Army and the people's anti-Japanese movement, the Kuomintang Northeastern Army under Chang Hsüeh-liang and the

Kuomintang 17th Route Army under Yang Hu-cheng agreed to
the anti-Japanese national united front proposed by the Communist Party of China and demanded that Chiang Kai-shek should
stop the civil war and unite with the Communist Party to resist
Japan. Chiang Kai-shek refused. On December 12, 1936, Chang
Hsüeh-liang and Yang Hu-cheng arrested him in Sian. Proceeding from the interest of the entire nation, the Chinese Communist Party offered mediation and Chiang Kai-shek was compelled to accept the terms of unity with the Communist Party
and resistance to Japan.

2) Mao Tse-tung, "Win the Masses in Their Millions for the
Anti-Japanese National United Front," Selected Works, English
ed., Foreign Languages Press, Peking, 1965, Vol. I, p. 290.

3) The "three-thirds system" refers to the organs of the political power which were established according to the principle
of the Anti-Japanese National United Front and in which the
members of the Communist Party, non-Party progressives and
the middle elements each occupied one-third of the places.

4) Mao Tse-tung, "Current Problems of Tactics in the Anti-
Japanese United Front," Selected Works, Vol. II.

5) Mao Tse-tung, "The Chinese Revolution and the Chinese
Communist Party," Selected Works, Vol. II.

6) Mao Tse-tung, "On Coalition Government," Selected
Works, Vol. III.

7) The Three Main Rules of Discipline and the Eight Points
for Attention were drawn up by Comrade Mao Tse-tung for the
Chinese Workers and Peasants' Red Army during the Agrarian
Revolutionary War and were later adopted as rules of discipline
by the Eighth Route Army and the New Fourth Army and the
present People's Liberation Army. As these rules varied
slightly in content in the army units of different areas, the General Headquarters of the Chinese People's Liberation Army in
October 1947 issued a standard version as follows:

The Three Main Rules of Discipline:

　(1) Obey orders in all your actions.

　(2) Do not take a single needle or piece of thread from the
　　　masses.

(3) Turn in everything captured.

The Eight Points for Attention:

(1) Speak politely.

(2) Pay fairly for what you buy.

(3) Return everything you borrow.

(4) Pay for anything you damage.

(5) Do not hit or swear at people.

(6) Do not damage crops.

(7) Do not take liberties with women.

(8) Do not ill-treat captives.

8) Friedrich Engels, "Possibilities and Perspectives of the War of the Holy Alliance Against France in 1852," Collected Works of Marx and Engels, Russian ed., Moscow, 1956, Vol. VII, p. 509.

9) Mao Tse-tung, "On Protracted War," Selected Works, Vol. II.

10) Mao Tse-tung, "A Single Spark Can Start a Prairie Fire," Selected Works, English ed., FLP, Peking, 1965, Vol. I, p. 124.

11) Sparrow warfare is a popular method of fighting created by the Communist-led anti-Japanese guerrilla units and militia behind the enemy lines. It was called sparrow warfare because, first, it was used diffusely, like the flight of sparrows in the sky; and because, second, it was used flexibly by guerrillas or militiamen, operating in threes or fives, appearing and disappearing unexpectedly and wounding, killing, depleting and wearing out the enemy forces.

12) Mao Tse-tung, "Problems of Strategy in China's Revolutionary War," Selected Works, English ed., FLP, Peking, 1965, Vol. I, p. 248.

13) Mao Tse-tung, "The Present Situation and Our Tasks," Selected Works, English ed., FLP, Peking, 1961, Vol. IV, p. 161.

14) Mao Tse-tung, "Interview with Three Correspondents from the Central News Agency, the Sao Tang Pao and the Hsin Min Pao," Selected Works, Vol. II.

15) Mao Tse-tung, "We Must Learn to Do Economic Work," Selected Works, Vol. III.

16) Karl Marx, Capital, English ed., Foreign Languages

Publishing House, Moscow, 1954, Vol. I, p. 751.

17) Mao Tse-tung, "Problems of War and Strategy," Selected Works, Vol. II.

18) Ibid.

19) V. I. Lenin, "The Revolutionary Army and the Revolutionary Government," Collected Works, English ed., FLPH, Moscow, 1962, Vol. VIII, p. 565.

20) Mao Tse-tung, "The Situation and Our Policy After the Victory in the War of Resistance Against Japan," Selected Works, English ed., FLP, Peking, 1961, Vol. IV, pp. 14-15.

21) Mao Tse-tung, "Talk with the American Correspondent Anna Louise Strong," Selected Works, English ed., FLP, Peking, 1961, Vol. IV, p. 100.

22) The Statement of Chairman Mao Tse-tung in Support of the People of the Congo (Leopoldville) Against U.S. Aggression, November 28, 1964.

23) V. I. Lenin, "For Bread and Peace," Collected Works, English ed., Progress Publishers, Moscow, 1964, Vol. XXVI, p. 386.

24) V. I. Lenin, "The Chief Task of Our Day," Collected Works, English ed., Progress Publishers, Moscow, 1965, Vol. XXVII, p. 162.

25) Mao Tse-tung, "Problems of Strategy in China's Revolutionary War," Selected Works, English ed., FLP, Peking, 1965, Vol. I, p. 182.

24

[QUOTATIONS FROM THE] REPORT TO THE
ARMY-WIDE POLITICAL WORK CONFERENCE*
(January 1966)

Giving prominence to politics is not a random policy. It is
not something that may be done either this way or that way. It
is a fundamental measure based upon the laws of development
in the socialist society and its economic structure. Not giving
prominence to politics, therefore, violates the laws of development in the socialist society....

Mao Tse-tung thought is the apex of Marxism-Leninism in
the contemporary era. It is Marxism-Leninism at its highest
and liveliest. Chairman Mao's books are the supreme instruction for all types of work in our whole army. Chairman Mao's
words have the highest quality and prestige and the greatest
power. Every sentence he says is truth in itself, and each sentence is worth ten thousand sentences.

---

*Lin Piao yü-lu [Quotations from Lin Piao] (Kunming:
Hsin-i-chung ko-ming tsao-fan ping-t'uan cheng-chih pu,
1967), p. 3.

25

LETTER ON LIVING STUDY AND APPLICATION OF
CHAIRMAN MAO TSE-TUNG'S WORKS ON THE
INDUSTRIAL AND COMMUNICATIONS FRONT*
(March 11, 1966)

The industrial and communications system emphasizes putting
politics in command and giving prominence to politics — it is
excellent to do so. It is greatly beneficial for raising the political consciousness of the proletariat and strengthening socialist construction in our country. Doing so will further strength-
en the activism and creativeness of the proletariat and make
our socialist cause more prosperous. It is excellent that
you are giving top priority to active study of Chairman Mao's
works in the entire work and policies for the industrial and
communications system.

Our country is a great socialist state of proletarian dictatorship, and it has a population of 700 million. It requires a unified
ideology, a revolutionary ideology, and a correct ideology —
the thought of Mao Tse-tung. Only with this thought can a vigor-

---

*"Chiu kung-yeh chiao-t'ung chan-hsien huo-hsüeh huo-yung
Mao Tse-tung chu-tso hsieh-ti i-feng hsin." Jen-min jih-pao
[People's Daily], June 19, 1966; reprinted in Lin Piao chuan-
chi [A Special Collection on Lin Piao] (Hong Kong: Tzu-lien,
1970), pp. 65-66. An English translation entitled "Chairman
Mao Has Elevated Marxism-Leninism to a Completely New
Stage With Great Talent" is published in Peking Review, No. 26
(June 26, 1966), 6. A Japanese translation may be found in
Chūgoku kenkyū geppō [Monthly Research Report on China,
Tokyo], No. 262 (December 1969), 1.

ous revolutionary fervor be maintained and a firm, correct political orientation be upheld.

The thought of Mao Tse-tung reflects the objective laws of class struggle at home and abroad and the basic interests of the proletariat and the working people. The thought of Mao Tse-tung is not developed spontaneously from among the working people. It is the Marxist-Leninist ideology inherited and developed by the genius of Chairman Mao on the basis of the great revolutionary practice. It has synthesized the new experience of the international Communist movement and has brought Marxism-Leninism to a higher and completely new stage.

Therefore, it is necessary to instill Chairman Mao's ideology into the workers and peasants through the living study and application of his works. Only by so doing can the working people's spiritual outlook be reformed and the spiritual strength transformed into an enormous material strength.

The industrial and communications system has in the past several years started working in this way. During this current conference of the industrial and communications system, we have further summed up experiences and put forth new methods. This will certainly bring about more achievements.

Lin Piao

26

LETTER TO MEMBERS OF THE STANDING
COMMITTEE OF THE MILITARY CONTROL COMMISSION
OF THE PARTY CENTRAL COMMITTEE*
(March 22, 1966)

Comrades of the Standing Committee,

I am herewith sending you for your attention the Summary
of the Forum on the Work in Literature and Art in the Armed
Forces which Comrade Chiang Ch'ing convened. The Summary,
which has been repeatedly gone over by the comrades attending
the forum and has been personally examined and revised by the
Chairman three times, is an excellent document. It applies
Mao Tse-tung thought to answer many important questions
concerning the cultural revolution in the period of socialism.
It is of both extremely great practical and far-reaching historic significance.

The last sixteen years have witnessed sharp class struggle
on the front of literature and art, and the question of who will
win out has not yet been settled. If the proletariat does not occupy the positions in literature and art, the bourgeoisie certainly will. This struggle is inevitable. And it represents an

---

*"Lin Piao t'ung-chih kei chung-yang chün-wei ch'ang-wei
ti hsin." Hung-ch'i [Red Flag], No. 9 (May 27, 1967), 10. This
translation is taken, with minor editorial revisions, from Peking
Review, No. 23 (June 2, 1967), 9. The complete text of "The
Summary of the Forum on the Work in Literature and Art in
the Armed Forces with which Comrade Lin Piao Entrusted
Comrade Chiang Ch'ing" may be found in Peking Review,
No. 23 (June 2, 1967), 10-16.

extremely broad and deep socialist revolution in the realm of ideology. If things are not done properly, revisionism will prevail. We must hold high the great red banner of Mao Tsetung thought and unswervingly carry this revolution through to the end.

The problems and the ideas raised in the Summary correspond fully with the realities in the work of literature and art in the armed forces, and the ideas must be resolutely carried out so as to enable this work in the armed forces to play an important role in keeping politics in the forefront and in promoting the revolutionization of people's thinking.

Please let me know your opinions on the Summary before it is submitted to the Central Committee for examination and approval.

With greetings,

Lin Piao

27

QUOTATION FROM A SPEECH BEFORE
THE MILITARY ACADEMIES*
(April 18, 1966)

The thought of Mao Tse-tung is the highest level of Marxism-Leninism. We must raise high the great red banner of the thought of Mao Tse-tung. We must use the thought of Mao Tse-tung to unify the ideologies of the entire Party and the entire army. We must further promote the ideological revolutionization of the people, and we must dig out the roots of the capitalist ideologies and prevent revisionism.

---

*"Tsai chün-shih yüan-hsiao ti chiang-hua." In Mao chu-hsi wen-hsüan [Selected Writings of Chairman Mao, 1959-1967] (n.d., n.p., a Red Guard publication), p. 91.

28

ADDRESS TO THE ENLARGED SESSION OF
THE POLITBURO OF THE CENTRAL COMMITTEE*
(May 18, 1966)

It would be better if other members of the Standing Committee made their speeches first. Since I am asked to speak first,
I am going to say something. Since I don't have a prepared
text, I shall speak without one. At times, I may read some
materials.

This is the enlarged session of the Politburo. Not long ago
the enlarged session convened by Mao Tse-tung concentrated
on and took the initiative in the solution of the P'eng Chen problem. Now we will continue our efforts to solve this problem.
The Lo Jui-ch'ing problem has already been solved. The problem of Lu Ting-i and Yang Shang-k'un was exposed during the
investigation of underground activities and has been fermenting
for some time. Now we are going to solve it. The problems
of these four are interconnected and bear certain similarities.
The worst is the P'eng Chen problem; the other problems are
less important. The exposure and solution of these problems
are of grave concern to the whole Party; they are closely related to ensuring the continual development of revolution, the
prevention of capitalist restoration, of revisionist usurpation
of political power, of a counterrevolutionary coup d'etat, and
of subversion. It is an important measure of China's advancement. It is also Mao Tse-tung's wise and resolute decision.

The greatest problem here is the prevention of a counter-

*"Tsai Chung-kung chung-yang cheng-chih-chü k'uo-ta hui-i
shang ti chiang-hua." Reprinted in Chung-kung nien-pao [Yearbook on Chinese Communism], 1970, Section VII, pp. 50-56.

revolutionary coup d'etat, the prevention of subversion, and the prevention of revisionist usurpation of political power.

The fundamental problem of revolution is the problem of political power. Once they obtain political power, the proletariat and the laboring people will have everything. Once they lose it, they will lose all. Production is certainly the basis; however, it relies on the change, consolidation, and development resulting from the seizure of political power. Otherwise, it will become mere economism, beggarism, and the importuning of favors. When the proletariat obtains political power, the millionaires, billionaires, and multibillionaires can be overthrown with one stroke, and everything will return to the proletarian class. Therefore, no matter how complicated matters become, never forget orientation and center. In other words, never forget political power — always have it in mind. Once you forget political power, you forget politics and the fundamental views of Marxism. Consequently, you swerve toward economism, anarchism, and daydreaming. It is just like a fool who has lost his head and does not know what to do.

Among the areas of the superstructure — ideology, religion, arts, law, and political power — the last is the very center. What is political power? Sun Yat-sen believed it to be the management of the affairs of the masses. But he did not understand that political power is an instrument by which one class oppresses another. Revolution and counterrevolution are the same in this regard. I would put it this way: Political power is the power to suppress. Of course, suppression is not the only function of political power. The political power of the proletariat should also reform the peasants and small property owners, enhance economic reconstruction, and resist foreign aggression. Suppression is the most essential of these many functions. Reactionaries in the society and representatives of the exploiting class who have infiltrated into the Party should be suppressed. Some should be sentenced to death, some should be imprisoned, some should be controlled through labor reform, some should be expelled from the Party, and some should be dismissed from public office. If it were otherwise, it would mean that we don't understand the fundamental views of Marxism regarding political power, that we would lose political power and become fools.

In recent years, especially last year, Chairman Mao has reminded us of the problem of preventing revisionism inside and outside the Party, on every front, in every area, and at high and low levels. I understand that he refers chiefly to the leading organs. In recent months Chairman Mao has paid particular attention to the adoption of many measures toward preventing a counterrevolutionary coup d'etat. After the Lo Jui-ch'ing problem, he talked about it. Now that the P'eng Chen problem has been exposed, he has again summoned several persons and talked about it, dispatched personnel and had them stationed in the radio broadcasting stations, the armed forces, and the public security systems in order to prevent a counterrevolutionary coup d'etat and the occupation of our crucial points. This is the "article" Chairman Mao has been writing in recent months. This is the "article" he has not quite finished and printed, and because of this, Chairman Mao has not slept well for many days. It is a very profound and serious problem. This is the endeavor of Chairman Mao that we ought to learn from.

Today coups d'etat have become a fad. Generally speaking, change of political power results from either people's revolution, which starts from below — such as Ch'en Sheng's and Wu Kuang's rebellion (in the Ch'in dynasty), the T'ai P'ing Rebellion (in the Ch'ing dynasty), and the communist revolution of our Party — or counterrevolutionary coups d'etat, which include court coups d'etat, internal coups d'etat, collusion of the high and the low, collusion with the subversive activities of foreign enemies or with armed invasion, and combination with natural calamities. This has been so both historically, and it is true in the present.

Concerning coups d'etat in the world, we may put aside those in the distant past. According to incomplete statistics, there have been sixty-one coups d'etat in the capitalist countries of Asia, Africa, and Latin America since 1960. Of the sixty-one coups d'etat, fifty-six were successful. Eight chiefs of state

were beheaded, seven were kept on as puppets, and eleven
were deposed. These statistics were compiled before the
coups in Ghana, Indonesia, and Syria. During the course of
these six years, there has been an average of eleven coups
per year.

Marxists are materialists who always put emphasis on reality. We cannot hear of and witness this phenomenon without
feeling. If we make issues of other things and forget this, we
don't see the essential problems and are fools. Without vigilance, great trouble will come.

In the decades before liberation we wanted to accomplish
the seizure of political power. After the victory of the revolution we seized political power, and many comrades then neglected the problem of political power. They concentrated on
reconstruction, education, and dealing with Chiang Kai-shek
and the U.S. They don't know that political power, once seized,
can be lost again and that the dictatorship of the proletariat
can be turned into dictatorship of the capitalist class. Regarding this negative aspect, we, at least I, have not thought much
about this problem, but have thought more about war and the
problems that arise when war breaks out. Taking all of this
into account, we should make a great effort to prevent internal
subversion and counterrevolutionary coups d'etat. The reason
is very simple. We have deep impressions and know many
things through evidence. The law of human knowledge is that
it goes from perception to rationality.

Now let us examine the problem from the standpoint of our
national history. There are many examples of political power
lost through coups d'etat before a dynasty was in existence for
ten, twenty, thirty, or fifty years.

Rebellions broke out soon after the establishment of the
Chou dynasty. In the Spring and Autumn period and the Warring States period, great disturbances never ceased. "There
were no righteous wars in the Spring and Autumn period."
The states conducted subversive activities against each other.
And within a single state, men killed one another. Shang Chen,
son of Emperor Chen of the state of Ch'u, encircled the palace

of his father with guards to compel Emperor Chen to commit suicide. Emperor Chen liked eating bear's paws very much and pleaded for his favorite dish before his suicide in order to delay his death and wait for outside help. His plea was turned down, for bear's paws could not be easily cooked. Emperor Chen was forced to kill himself at once. The Prince of Wu sent Chuan Chu to murder Wang Liao and thus acquired political power. Before Prince Hsien of Chin and Princes Huang and Yi of Ch'i came into power, there were many coups d'etat and many victims. There were too many incidents like these in those periods, and I don't want to give more examples. Besides assassinations, other forms of treachery were used in the seizure of political power. For example, Lü Pu-wei presented Prince Chuan Hsiang of Ch'in his pregnant concubine Chao, who gave birth to Ch'in Shih Huang. During the early rule of Ch'in Shih Huang, political power was actually in the hands of Lü Pu-wei.

The three emperors of the Ch'in dynasty ruled the country for fifteen years. Ch'in Shih Huang died after twelve years of rule. Chao Kao put the Second Emperor on the throne and had him kill twenty-six of his brothers and sisters.

Liu Pang of the Han dynasty ruled for twelve years. Empress Lü seized political power from the Liu family. Soon afterward Chou Po and Chen Ping colluded to overthrow the Lü family.

Ssu-ma Yin of the Chin dynasty ruled for twenty-five years, and thereafter civil wars broke out among the eight princes, who mercilessly killed each other off.

There were more merciless killings resulting from the seizure of political power in the period of the Northern and Southern dynasties.

Emperor Wen of the Sui dynasty ruled for twenty-four years and was killed by his son, later known as Emperor Yang. There is a play called "Bridge over Royal River," which relates Yang Kuang's assassination of his father and his brother, Yang Yung.

In the T'ang dynasty, brothers killed each other for the throne. Li Shih-min killed his elder brother Chien Chen and

younger brother Yuan Chi. This was the "Rebellion of Hsuan-
wu Gate."

Chao Kuang-yin of the Sung dynasty ruled for seventeen
years and was killed by his brother Chao Kuang-i. "Candle-
shadow, axe-sound: mystery of antiquity." This incident was
depicted in a Peking opera called "Congratulating the Queen
and Chiding the Court."

Kublai Khan of the Yuan dynasty ruled China for sixteen
years, and his son Timur [Tamerlane] ruled for thirteen years.
Thereafter a power-seizure war broke out between the queen
and her grandson, resulting in violent disturbances and massacre.

Chu Yüan-chang of the Ming dynasty stayed in power for
thirty-one years. His fourth son, Prince Yen (later Emperor
Ch'eng-tsu), started a war against the heir apparent, the Chien-
wen Emperor, and burned the palace. It was a mystery as to
whether or not the Chien-wen Emperor was burned with the
royal palace. Emperor Ch'eng-tsu later sent envoys abroad
in search of the lost king.

During the last years of the K'ang-hsi Emperor's rule, not
long after the establishment of the Ch'ing dynasty, one court
intrigue after another resulted from power-seizure struggles.
It was said that the K'ang-hsi Emperor appointed his fourteenth
son as his successor in his will, but the Yung-cheng Emperor
changed it for his own benefit, and the K'ang-hsi Emperor died
after drinking ginsen soup prepared by the Yung-cheng Emperor. After his accession, the Yung-cheng Emperor killed
all his brothers.

The Republican Revolution of 1911 made Sun Yat-sen president of China. Three months later, Yüan Shih-k'ai seized political power from him. After another four years, Yüan was
also overthrown. Then came a period of over a decade of civil
wars among the warlords: two Hopei-Manchu wars and one
Hopei-Anhwei war.

These reactionary coups d'etat should have terrified us and
heightened our vigilance.

Our seizure of political power has already lasted sixteen

years. Will this regime of the proletariat be overthrown and usurped? If we are not careful enough, we shall lose our political power. Soviet Russia was overthrown by Khrushchev. Yugoslavia was changed long ago. Hungary suffered a great deal for more than ten days through the appearance of Imre Nagy; this was again subversion. There are too many examples like these to be listed. Now Chairman Mao has noticed this problem to which we have seldom paid attention. Several times he has summoned responsible comrades to discuss the problem of preventing a counterrevolutionary coup d'etat. Did he do this without reason? No, there are many clear indications that confirm it. "The wind blows all over the tower before the mountain rain comes." "On Distinguishing the Traitor," an essay in an anthology of ancient Chinese prose, Ku-wen kuan-chih, says, "When we see the slightest sign, then we know with clarity." A Chinese proverb says, "A halo round the moon means wind; a damp base of a pillar means rain." Bad things are always revealed by some sign beforehand. All substance is revealed through phenomena. Many recent ghostly events and ghostly phenomena have attracted our attention. There is a likelihood of a counterrevolutionary coup d'etat, killings, seizure of political power, capitalist restoration, and the doing away with all those associated with socialism. I am not going to talk in detail of these phenomena and their origins. After experiencing the anti-Lo Jui-ch'ing, anti-P'eng Chen, anti-Lu Ting-i and his wife, and anti-Yang Shang-k'un campaigns, you may have smelled it — gunpowder. Representatives of the capitalist class infiltrated our Party and the Party's leadership organs, became the power faction, and took control of the government machinery, political power, military power, and the headquarters of the ideological-war front. They united to undertake subversive activities and caused much trouble.

Lo Jui-ch'ing was the one who controlled military power. P'eng Chen controlled the General Secretariat. Commander-in-chief of the war on the cultural and ideological front was Lu Ting-i. Confidential affairs, intelligence, and liaison were in the hands of Yang Shang-k'un. There are two prerequisites for a coup d'etat. One is propaganda organs — newspapers, broadcasting stations, literature, cinema, and publications — related to ideological work. The subversive activities of the capitalist class needed ideological leadership in order to create confusion in the people's ideology. The other prerequisite is military work to control the armed forces. When the civilian and the military are coordinated, and public opinion and rifles are in their hands, then a counterrevolutionary coup d'etat can occur at any time. If a general election is needed, people can be called to cast ballots. If armed uprising is needed, the armed forces can be dispatched immediately. Whether it is a parliamentary coup d'etat or a military coup d'etat, they can accomplish it. There were many Teng T'os, Wu Hans, and Liao Mo-shas. Chairman Mao said that we have not occupied the ideological front for the past sixteen years. If we allow this to continue, people will elect them instead of us and Chairman Mao. When war breaks out, the armed forces will follow them and fight against us. Seizure of political power depends on rifles and inkwells. These deserve our attention. Therefore we should not be paralyzed ideologically; we must take concrete actions in order to prevent it from coming into being and to discover and dig up representatives of the capitalist class, time bombs, and land mines. Otherwise, once the opportune time comes, a counterrevolutionary coup d'etat will occur; once we have a natural calamity, or once a war breaks out, or Chairman Mao dies, this political crisis will come, and this vast country of 700 million people will be in disorder and chaos.

Of course, there are two other possible prospects. Their conspiracy may not be able to win a victory or even be realized because our Party has a revolutionary experience of several decades under Chairman Mao and is a party armed with Marxism-Leninism-Mao Tse-tung Thought. It is not juvenile; it is mature. Our Party has always firmly grasped the gun barrels and has never for a moment been separated from them. Unlike the European (communist) parties, our Party has never advocated parliamentary activity. Our Party is

closely connected with the broad laboring masses. It has a
long revolutionary tradition and abundant revolutionary experience.

The overall situation is very fine, the world situation is fine,
and the China situation is also fine. It is not easy for them to
realize their conspiracy. They may win and they may also
lose. If we don't pay attention to it and we act like fools, then
they will win. If we are vigilant, they will not win. They want
to cut off our heads, but they may not succeed. If they initiate
a counterrevolutionary coup d'etat, we are going to cut off
their heads.

At all times, no matter how fine the situation is, things always have a dark side. We should be able to see the dark side
when the situation is fine. If there is no bad side, it cannot be
called good. The good can be good only because there is a bad
side; the bad can be bad only because there is a good side.

Chairman Mao still lives, so we can enjoy the shade under
so big a tree. Chairman Mao is now over seventy and very
healthy, and he can live to over one hundred.

We cannot be paralyzed just because of the fine situation;
we have to take action to prevent a counterrevolutionary coup
d'etat. Some people may create trouble, and some people are
creating trouble. There are many ambitious conspirators.
They are representatives of the capitalist class eager to overthrow the political power of our proletarian class. We shall
never let them succeed. These sons of bitches want to take
chances and are just waiting for the right opportunity. They
want to kill us, and we have to suppress them. They are
pseudorevolutionaries, pseudo-Marxists, and pseudobelievers
in Mao Tse-tung thought — they are traitors. They rebel even
when Chairman Mao lives. They obey nominally while actually
rebelling. They are ambitious conspirators who create trouble
and want to kill by any means. Lu Ting-i is one, and his wife
is another. He said he didn't know about his wife's affairs,
but how could he not know? Lo Jui-ch'ing is another. The
methods of P'eng Chen were even more inconspicuous and
crafty. It was not easy to uncover him. He appeared to be a

supporter of Chairman Mao, but in the Shansi-Chahar-Hopei
area he entirely practiced the Wang Ming line, in fact out-Wang
Minging Wang Ming. In 1938, when the Sixth Plenary Session
of the Sixth National Congress criticized the Wang Ming line,
P'eng participated in the session, and afterward he praised
Chiang Kai-shek as a man of political vision and advocated
earnest and sincere support for Generalissimo Chiang. He
said: "The most solid center of the War of Resistance is Generalissimo Chiang." He also remarked: "Between the KMT
and the CCP, there should be mutual help, mutual love, and
mutual forebearance. I opposed the employment of creating
difficulties to upset the [KMT] government." He pretended to
adhere to the anti-Wang Ming line in Yenan, but practiced the
Wang Ming line in the Northeast. P'eng Chen refused to implement the instructions of the Party Central Committee and
Chairman Mao in the Northeast. Amid the sounds of guns and
cries of war, he daydreamed about peace negotiations with
Chiang Kai-shek of the KMT, and victory over the negotiation
table without any war preparations. He was not in the least
Marxist-Leninist; nor was he a follower of Mao Tse-tung
thought, and he didn't implement class struggle. He didn't put
emphasis on the villages; nor did he build up headquarters in
the villages with cadres and main forces. He never forgot the
city and was unwilling to leave the city. When he had to withdraw from Shenyang, he lingered on in the suburbs. He moved
his headquarters to Pen-hsi, Fushun, and Meichiangkou. He
didn't want to settle in the village. He didn't want to fight. He
wanted peace. In the Northeast he staked all the main forces
on one single throw and fought a life-or-death battle against
the enemy. He used military adventurism to conceal political
capitulationism. He cultivated his personal sphere of influence
under the pretext of taking care of the mountaintop. He didn't
care for the supply and reinforcement of the main forces, but
gathered some deserters and built up some local troops who
later deserted us and became "separate mountaintops." His
opposition to mountaintopism was in reality the building-up of
his own "mountaintop," gathering capitulationists and traitors,

trying to found his own army, forming small circles, and allying himself with others of his kind in everlasting bonds. The Peking Municipal Government became a place from which no water could leak and which no needle could penetrate. He created a party within the Party and a faction within the Party. Chairman Mao, Premier Chou, and other comrades had sensed it, and I too had sensed it.

There are quite a few who held high the banners of Marxism and Mao Tse-tung thought only to oppose Marxism and Mao Tse-tung thought. Quite a few anticommunist elements bore the banner of Communist Party membership. The present exposure is a great victory of the Party; if it were otherwise, the situation would be very dangerous. If they were allowed to continue, it would not be their exposure by the Party, but their trial of the Party.

Our society is still built on the foundation of class antagonisms. The capitalist class, the landlord class, and all the exploiting classes were overthrown, but not eliminated. We confiscated their properties, but not their reactionary thoughts. We cannot confiscate "their heads" even if we imprison them. They are but a small minority in proportion to the whole population, but their political influence is great, and their power to resist is all out of proportion. The self-made influence of the petty bourgeoisie in the cities and villages, the ever-growing new capitalist class, the infiltration of the complicated elements into the working class, the corrupted elements of the Party and government machinery, and the encirclement by and subversive activities of imperialism and modern revisionism brought our country face to face with the danger of capitalist restoration. This danger is comprehensive — all the reactionary forces are closely related and coordinated. The danger is within the country and without; the danger within is the chief one. There is danger within the Party and outside of the Party, and the danger within is the chief one. There is danger at the upper and lower levels, and the danger at the upper level is the chief one. Danger comes from the upper level — Khrushchev changed the color of Soviet Russia.

The exploiting classes have been overthrown for sixteen
years; but they still live and their hope still exists. Many landlords secretly keep their deeds for land. The overthrown landlords and capitalist class always dream of the recovery of
their lost paradise. Their gun barrels were taken away and
their emblem of power was confiscated. But they still occupied an advantageous position in the ideological and cultural
fronts and used this advantage to spread poison and create public opinion for capitalist restoration. The Great Proletarian
Cultural Revolution is the sharp struggle between the capitalist
restoration and the proletarian class's efforts to oppose the
capitalist restoration. This struggle is of primary importance
to the fate and the future state of the country and the Party; it
is also of primary importance to world revolution.

We should seriously take note of this important problem of
capitalist revolution and never forget it. We should never forget class struggle and the dictatorship of the proletariat, and
we should give prominence to politics and hold high the great
red banner of Mao Tse-tung thought; otherwise, we are but
fools. Never lose vigilance in the midst of a busy schedule
and complicated routine; otherwise, they will start killing overnight, many will be beheaded, the national system will be
changed, political power will change color, and production relations will change from advance to retreat.

It is anti-Marxist and not in accord with dialectics to say
that contradiction does not exist in socialist society. How can
there be no contradiction? Contradiction exists through a hundred years, a thousand years, and a hundred million years.
Contradiction exists in the universe till the earth perishes and
the sun dies. Not long ago the Hsingtai area suffered from an
earthquake, and Premier Chou personally went to handle the
natural calamity, which means that struggle exists even in
nature. When sunspots increase to a certain level, they render radio communications impossible at times. Everything
exists in contradiction, struggle, and change — this is the view
of the Marxists. From a grain of sand to the sun, no matter
whether it is as big as the Milky Way or as small as a tiny

atom, whether macrocosm or microcosm, contradiction exists.
The nature of Marxism is critical and revolutionary. Its starting point is criticism, struggle, and revolution. Only by criticism, struggle, and revolution can the proletarian class seize
and keep the political power and push forward our enterprises.
Therefore we should promote our vigilance and struggle; the
illusion of peace cannot be allowed to exist. Struggle is life —
if you don't struggle against them, they will struggle against
you; if you don't fight against them, they will fight against you;
and if you don't kill them, they will kill you. If we lose this
vigilance, and if we are not united in struggle, we are not Marxists. The more solidly our Party is united, the better. The
more struggles, the greater our fighting capabilities. However,
we should not unite with the anti-Party elements; on the contrary, we should criticize and expose them until they are expelled from the Party. Unity is not absolute, but relative; it is
the unity to criticize and expose the anti-Party elements.

In short, we should struggle. This time we struggled against
P'eng Chen, Lo Jui-ch'ing, Lu Ting-i and his wife, and Yang
Shang-k'un. This was an act of Marxism and dialectical materialism, an important political measure and a measure to
prevent counterrevolutionary subversion. Otherwise, we would
have gained the country and then quickly lost it; we would have
created an enterprise but would not have been able to keep it;
the efforts of numerous martyrs who have shed their blood in
sacrifice for the revolution in the past hundred years and in
the past decades would have been in vain; and we would become
sinners and opportunists in history.

We should struggle against them and at the same time unite
ourselves, taking Chairman Mao and Mao Tse-tung thought as
the center. These people have something in common — anti-
Chairman Mao and anti-Mao Tse-tung thought. It is alike with
P'eng Chen, Lo Jui-ch'ing, Lu Ting-i, and Yang Shang-k'un,
as well as with Teng T'o, Wu Han, and Liao Mo-sha. The materials against them are too numerous to be listed. They either
ostensibly or by insinuation maliciously opposed Chairman
Mao and Mao Tse-tung thought in different languages with

different styles and different methods.

Chairman Mao is the founder of our Party and of our nation's revolution, the great leader of our Party and nation, and the greatest contemporary Marxist-Leninist. Chairman Mao has ingeniously, creatively, and thoroughly inherited, guarded, and glorified Marxism-Leninism, promoting it to a brand new stage. Mao Tse-tung thought is Marxism-Leninism in an age when imperialism moves toward total collapse and socialism moves toward world victory. Mao Tse-tung thought is the guideline of all works of the Party and the nation. We should unfold Mao Tse-tung thought before the eyes of the people of the entire nation; let it be seen more broadly by the people of the entire nation, let it be united more broadly with the people of the entire nation; let Mao Tse-tung thought be planted more deeply in the hearts of the people to further revolutionize the ideology of the people of the entire nation. We should use Mao Tse-tung thought as a weapon to criticize and expose all kinds of revisionism and representatives of the capitalist class on every front and in every field of capitalist ideology paving the way for capitalist restoration, and to push the Great Proletarian Cultural Revolution and socialist revolution to a successful end. Thus we can assuredly prevent revisionism and avoid capitalist restoration. This is the most basic and central problem. Many bad elements opposed the study of Chairman Mao's works, and these are anti-Party elements. The Ministry of Propaganda of the Central Committee, controlled by Lu Ting-i, opposed the study of Chairman Mao's works, saying contemptuously that they are elementary, vulgar, and pragmatic. They propagated no Mao Tse-tung thought, but capitalist ideology, no revolutionary thought, but reactionary thought; they did not push revolution forward, but dragged it backward. When others propagated Mao Tse-tung thought, they laughed and sneered and suppressed, attacked, and opposed them by all means.

Marxists should at least know that existence determines consciousness, material is primary and spirit secondary, and consciousness has a great pushing capability. Material and spirit can be exchanged. Chairman Mao said: "Where does the

correct thought of mankind come from? Is it dropped from
the sky? No. Is it inborn in man's head? No. The correct
thought of mankind comes from the threefold practice of production struggle, class struggle, and scientific experimenta-
tion. Human existence in society determines human thought.
Correct thought, represented by the advanced classes, once
grasped by the masses can become a material force to reform
society and the world." This is the viewpoint of the Marxist-
Leninist and Comrade Mao Tse-tung's theory of knowledge. If
we can make good use of Mao Tse-tung thought, then we'll be
able to make striking progress. Spirit has great potentiality.

For several decades Chairman Mao has constantly expounded
the dialectical relationship between the spiritual and the material. The nucleus of Marxism is dialectics. Chairman Mao
uses dialectics with great ease, applying it to everything and
applying the proletarian philosophical basis of dialectical materialism to every problem — Chairman Mao has thoroughly
and creatively developed the dialectics of Marxism.

Chairman Mao has experienced much more than Marx, Engels, and Lenin. Of course, Marx, Engels, and Lenin were
great figures. Marx lived sixty-four years, Engels, seventy-
five years. They possessed abundant vision, inherited the advanced ideology of mankind, and predicted the development of
human society. Unlike Chairman Mao, they did not have the
experience of personal leadership in proletarian revolution,
personally commanding so many political battles and, especially, military battles. Lenin lived only fifty-four years and
died in the sixth year after the victory of the October Revolution. He never experienced so many long-term, complicated,
violent, and many-sided struggles as Chairman Mao has experienced. The population of China is ten times greater than
that of Germany and three times greater than that of Soviet
Russia. China's rich revolutionary experience cannot be ex-
celled. Chairman Mao commands the highest prestige in the
nation and the whole world, and he is the most outstanding and
the greatest figure. Chairman Mao's sayings, works, and revolutionary practice have shown that he is a great proletarian

genius. Some people don't admit genius, but this is not Marxist. Engels said that Hegel and St. Simon were the geniuses of
the eighteenth century and Marx was the genius of the nineteenth century. He said that Marx stood higher than all others;
he could see further than others, and his observation was rich-
er and keener; therefore, he was a genius. Lenin also accepted
genius; he said there had to be more than ten leaders of genius,
and then Russia could be led to win victory in the revolution.
Chairman Mao is a genius. What is the difference between him
and us? We undertook struggle together — some are senior
to him in age. We are not as old as he, but we have as much
experience. We also read books, but we understand either
nothing at all or don't understand fully; but Chairman Mao understands. I saw many people make small circles and dots on
the books they read — sometimes a book was full of such circles and dots; these betrayed that the reader did not understand
them, not knowing the center or the main or secondary points.
Decades ago, Chairman Mao understood the nucleus of dialectics, but even now we don't; he not only understands it, he can
also utilize it skillfully. There is an immeasurable distance
between comprehension and utilization. One may be able to
understand something, but one may not be able to use it. You
know the rules of the game of table tennis, but you cannot defeat Chuang Tse-tung and Hsü Yin-sheng. You may acquire
some bookish military knowledge, but you may not necessarily
be able to win a battle. Dialectical materialism pervades Mao
Tse-tung thought, and Chairman Mao has liberally applied and
developed Marxism-Leninism; he is unparalled in the present
world. Marx and Engels were geniuses of the nineteenth century; Lenin and Comrade Mao Tse-tung are the geniuses of
the twentieth century. Don't be obstinate — no good is no good.
If we don't admit it, we shall commit great faults. If we don't
see it, we don't know that we should select such a great genius
of the proletarian class as our leader.

The difference between man and beast is that man can manufacture tools. In the process of labor, man develops his brain
and causes it to think. Thought is the greatest characteristic

of man. Under given conditions, thought has a decisive function.
We should cherish the function of advanced thought, advanced
thought in the socialist age, and Mao Tse-tung thought. Neglect
of the function of thought is vulgar and mechanical materialism.
In the socialist age, with the common ownership of property,
it is dangerous and impossible to neglect the function of advanced thought while advocating material incentives. The difference between us and the revisionists is that, unlike us, they
rely too much on material incentives. We should never take
the path of the material incentives of the capitalist class. We
should use Mao Tse-tung thought and the great righteous enterprises to arouse people's enthusiasm and make them open their
eyes for the future, move forward steadfastly, and shake off
the influences of the tradition of all exploiting classes and the
habitual forces handed down for thousands of years. Liberation from these narrow influences will give rise to enormous
force and generate great utility.

   The cultural and ideological fronts were controlled by the
bad elements. The Ministry of Propaganda of the Central
Committee, controlled by P'eng Chen and Lu Ting-i, was the
propaganda ministry serving the interests of the capitalist
class. The Ministry of Culture, controlled by them, was the
ministry of culture serving the interests of the capitalist class.
They hated Mao Tse-tung thought and obstructed the propagation of Mao Tse-tung thought. Mao Tse-tung thought should be
laid before the broad masses, otherwise, the appearance of
our country cannot be changed. We should make Mao Tse-tung
thought penetrate deeply into the masses. Changes in every
respect will occur when Mao Tse-tung thought is tied to the
masses.

   Mao Tse-tung thought is the concentrated expression of proletarian ideology, fundamentally opposed to the private ownership system and the ideology of the exploiting class. We oppose the private ownership system and the idea of self, which
are the essential factors in the emergence of revisionism.
These factors are quite widespread. In a village there are
private plots and collective plots. There is a struggle over

whether a basket of dung should be sent to a private plot first
or to a collective plot first. This is the psychology and ideology of two classes, the expression of two roads, and the manifestation of class struggle. If we don't fight with Marxism-
Leninism-Mao Tse-tung Thought, the capitalist ideology
will occupy the battlefield, cause a qualitative change, and
make trouble. Didn't Hungary have the academic lords of the
Petöfi Club? Through their encouragement 200,000 people encircled the parliament, demanding that Nagy take over political
power. These bad fellows of our Party are Nagys. Once there
is trouble, many people will respond to their call. Luckily, we
have defeated in the past years our group of Nagys — Kao Kang,
P'eng Te-huai, and Chang Wen-t'ien. This time we defeated
another group of Nagys, a group of Khrushchev revisionists.

After this struggle you should not have any thoughts about
peace. The ideas of self and of exploiting class have taken
deep root in some people's hearts and infiltrated into their
every cell. They will again create trouble; we should encourage vigilance.

The human mind is a reflection of existence. It has contradictions and class characteristics. Our socialist society is no
exception. Take the revolutionary ranks for example. In their
minds there is contradiction between right and wrong thoughts,
between proletarian and capitalist ideologies, within collectiv-
ism, between communism and individualism, between genuine
Marxism and false Marxism, and between pro-mass line and
anti-mass line. This series of contradictions produces struggles in their minds — either this one conquers that one or is
conquered by that one.

There is contradiction between revolutionary and counterrevolutionary thoughts in some people's heads. They should
always struggle to eliminate the hidden counterrevolutionary
ideas.

We should be aware of the fact that the earth moves and
everything develops, and we should also have a clear vision of
the rules of the development of history; we should not do anything to obstruct the advancement of history. Such things are

harmful to others as well as to oneself and will result in destruction of body and bankruptcy of reputation. This is Chairman Mao's call for maintenance of integrity at the time of a proletarian's advanced age. The old comrades should strictly train and sincerely reform themselves in accordance with the five requirements for the revolutionary successors given by Chairman Mao. If we don't see this situation clearly and care only for self-interests, we shall inevitably commit grievous mistakes and even shamelessly join the conspiratorial anti-Party group.

We support Chairman Mao now and will support him even after he dies. Mao Tse-tung thought shall be handed down from generation to generation. Mao Tse-tung thought is genuine Marxism-Leninism. It is Marxism-Leninism combined with reality. It is the ideological basis of the unity and revolution of the nation's labors, and the guideline for the actions of the nation's people. Mao Tse-tung thought is the lighthouse of mankind; it is the sharpest weapon of world revolution and universal truth. Mao Tse-tung thought can change the appearance of human ideology and the appearance of our mother country, make the Chinese people stand up straight before the world forever, and make the oppressed and exploited peoples of the world stand up straight forever. No matter how long Chairman Mao lives — ninety or over one hundred years — he is forever the supreme leader of our Party, and his words will be the guideline for our actions. Whoever is against him shall be punished by the entire Party and the whole country. Whoever makes a secret report after his death, as Khrushchev did [after Stalin's], must be an ambitious conspirator and a good-for-nothing and shall be punished by the entire Party and the whole country.

Mao Tse-tung thought is an everlasting universal truth, an everlasting guideline for our actions, the common property of the Chinese people and the revolutionary people of the world — it is always resplendent. It was not just meritorious but a "must" that the PLA should take Chairman Mao's works as the textbook for cadres and fighters. The use of Mao Tse-tung thought to unite the armed forces and the entire Party can solve any problem. Every sentence of Chairman Mao's works is a truth; one single sentence of his surpasses ten thousand of ours. I have not read Chairman Mao's works enough and will study harder from now on.

We should grasp politics and the creative study and application of Chairman Mao's works. We should never let them go. This is to meet the needs of the revolution, of the situation, of the struggle against the enemy, of war preparation, of gaining a thorough victory for the Great Proletarian Cultural Revolution, of preventing and opposing revisionism, and of preventing capitalist restoration. Those good-for-nothings attacked us by saying that we implemented pragmatism. It was not true; this is the effective, practical, and objective truth. What is pragmatism? It is the subjective idealism of the capitalist class. In their view, whatever is in concert with their interests is the truth, and whatever is against their interests is not the truth. Our expertise at giving prominence to politics and creative study and application of Chairman Mao's works is in concert with the truths of the law of social development of socialism, of the law of development of the natural world, and of the needs of proletarian revolution. If our actions are not supervised by the needs of revolution, we will certainly commit grievous mistakes and are doomed to failure.

29

SPEECH AT THE ELEVENTH PLENUM
OF THE EIGHTH CENTRAL COMMITTEE*
(August 1, 1966)

There are two kinds of people with respect to the study of
Mao Tse-tung thought. One kind of people make great efforts to study Mao Tse-tung thought. Some of them studied
it well but were subject to attacks because the Lu Ting-i gang
of the Central Committee's Propaganda Department was the
highest organ in charge of ideology. Opposing the thought of
Mao Tse-tung, they slandered Mao's works as "Hsüan-wei ham"
— if one eats it every day, one would get sick of it. They slan-
derously distorted the concept of "setting up a pole to see its
shadow" by saying that without the sun there would be no shadow. They even maliciously attacked those who are now studying
Mao's works, saying that in the future, when war comes, they are
likely to be traitors and turncoats. These black gangsters are
full of hatred against the thought of Mao Tse-tung. The other
kind of people do not study Mao's works, and they are in a
backward or intermediate state.

There are also two kinds of people with respect to political
and ideological work. One kind of people give serious attention
to political and ideological work, while the other kind of people
do not pay serious attention to it and may even try to disrupt it.
In the matter of handling work, our cadres are also of two kinds.

*"Lin Piao t'ung-chih tsai pa-chieh shih-i chung-ch'üan-hui
shang ti chiang-hua." In Mao chu-hsi wen-hsüan [Selected Writings of Chairman Mao, 1959-1967] (n.d., n.p., a Red Guard publication), pp. 95-97.

One kind of cadres are enthusiastic about work and have achieved good results, but they are impatient and offend many people. In the movement they are attacked by the largest number of big-character posters, and their dismissal from office is demanded. The other kind of cadres are good fellows; they do nothing and take part in nothing. They offend no one and have good relations with all. They are capable of winning votes at elections and are attacked in few big-character posters in the movement.

Therefore, we demand an overall examination and overall readjustment of cadres. In this connection, in the light of the five requirements for the cultivation of successors to the cause of proletarian revolution set forth by Chairman Mao, we have proposed three criteria, to which the Chairman has agreed:

1) Do they hold high the red banner of Mao Tse-tung thought? Those who fail to do so shall be dismissed from office.

2) Do they engage in political and ideological work? Those who disrupt it and the Great Cultural Revolution are to be dismissed.

3) Are they enthusiastic about the revolution? Those who are entirely devoid of such enthusiasm are to be dismissed.

These three criteria are consistent with the five requirements set forth by the Chairman. We must select, promote, and employ cadres in accordance with Chairman Mao's five requirements and these three criteria, especially the first one.

This time a group of people is to be dismissed, another group of people is to be promoted, and still another group of people is to be retained in their posts. Organizationally there should be an overall adjustment of those who have made mistakes and those who have made serious mistakes. If they accept education and resolutely repent, they will be allowed to continue to be tested in future work. As for those who are incorrigible, they should be dismissed firmly. Unless this is done, the stalemate cannot be broken. It is they who will carry out subversive activities once trouble flares up.

My heart has been quite heavy recently. My ability does not
measure up to my work. I expect to make mistakes, but I will
do my best to reduce my mistakes to a minimum. I will rely
on the Chairman, on the whole body of comrades of the Standing Committee, and on the comrades of the Cultural Revolution
Group. Chairman Mao is the axle; we are the wheel. We must
do everything according to Mao Tse-tung thought and not by
any other method. We should not be two headquarters opposing
each other. We should be united following the Chairman. He
gives overall consideration to problems; he is farsighted. What
is more, he has ideas, many of which we do not understand. We
must resolutely carry out Chairman Mao's instructions, whether
we understand them or not. I have no talent; I rely on the wisdom of the masses and do everything according to the Chairman's directives. I do not interfere with him on major problems; nor do I trouble him with small matters. Sometimes I
cannot avoid making mistakes and fail to keep pace with the
Chairman's thinking. What should I do then? The solution is
to change at an appropriate time and not to persist in mistakes —
be prepared at any time to correct them. The Chairman is the
genius of the world revolution. There is a great distance between him and us, and we must quickly rectify the mistakes we
have made. The Central Committee has given me work, and I
know that my level and ability are not good enough. I have
thought of it many times. But since the Chairman and the Central Committee have made their decision, I can only obey and
try my best. In the meantime, I am prepared to hand it over
to a more suitable comrade.

(Turning to the Central Committee Cultural Revolution Group)*

Your work was beset with difficulties. The movement was
started in a vigorous manner, but cold water was poured then

---

*This section is based on a more complete version of the
original which appeared as "Tui chung-yang wen ko ti chiang-
hua." Chung-kung nien-pao [Yearbook on Chinese Commu-
nism], 1972, Section IV., pp. 29-30. The date in this source
is given as August 8, 1966. — Editor.

on it. The Chairman has reversed the situation; if he had not done so, the Great Cultural Revolution would have been cut short, the bourgeoisie would have gained the upper hand, and we would have suffered defeat. To eliminate bourgeois ideology and establish proletarian ideology, to transform man's soul and wipe out old ideas, we must not proceed with ideology alone: We must proceed with material things by developing production and improving technology, on the one hand, and proceed with the spiritual aspect by transforming man's ideology, on the other. The important factor of productivity is man, and we must develop the human factor, change ideas and concepts, and raise our sense of responsibility to society. This is easier said than done. In practice there will be reversals and numerous struggles. We can reform man only through criticism and recognition by waging major struggles on the entire ideological front. Struggles will advance from many lower stages to higher stages on the two fronts, the material front and the spiritual front. Our Cultural Revolution is devoted to the spiritual front. We are progressing on both fronts and Mao Tse-tung thought is the general locomotive that pulls us forward on both fronts. We must advance like a train along two tracks. We must not promote material incentives, as the revisionists did; we would be bound to move backward, and capitalism would be restored and revisionism would be bound to appear. In doing everything we must let Mao Tse-tung thought take the lead and we must firmly grasp Mao Tse-tung thought as a spiritual weapon and fight this battle through to the end. We shall win the war against material incentives in our minds. This is not a minor task; it is a major task. You comrades have played a positive role in the recent several months. From now on I hope you will play a bigger role. Of course, if anyone pours cold water, the Chairman will see that the situation is reversed. Otherwise, nobody will be able to resist great pressures from the top, and big rocks would be in our way.

The Great Cultural Revolution is an undertaking that has never been attempted before. Soviet Union did not have it, so revisionism was inevitable.

Now fish eyes are mixed with pearls, and we must separate them. We must hand the pearls over to the masses of workers and peasants so that the people can have culture and see the bright future before them. When fish eyes are mixed with pearls and we choose the pearls for ourselves, there will be difficulties. We must now tell them that Mao Tse-tung thought is the pearls and we must all share responsibilities.

30

ON THE QUESTION OF THE CADRE LINE*
(August 10, 1966)

On the morning of August 10 Vice Chairman Lin said:

Among army cadres some are too backward and have not
corrected their errors. They should be discharged. We cannot afford to have a corrupt cadre policy.

In judging cadres we first of all want to see whether they
support or oppose Chairman Mao, whether they emphasize politics, and whether their revolutionary vigor is high. We look
at their main current and tributaries.

Be sure not to lose the political direction. To support the
Chairman and give prominence to politics is the very best; to
do otherwise is the very worst. In other things, good or bad
is a matter of degree. In the final analysis, which line should
be in first place and which in second place — this is the question of two kinds of cadre policy. One kind gives attention to
petty details but not to major principles; the other kind also
pays attention to small details but primarily heeds key principles. Some cadres have small problems: their living style,

*"Kuan-yü kan-pu lu-hsien wen-t'i." Published by Pei-ching
ti-chih hsüeh-yüan Mao Tse-tung ssu-hsiang ch'ih-wei-tui
[The Mao Tse-tung Thought Red Guard Group of Peking Geol-
ogy College], December 3, 1966. A copy of the original Chinese text was obtained from Taiwan sources. The title also appears differently as "Lin Piao fu-chu-hsi pa-yüeh shih-jih
chih-shih chi-yao" [Excerpts of Instructions by Vice Chairman
Lin Piao on August 10].

relations with the opposite sex, work attitude, and work methods have shortcomings. However, they support the Chairman and give prominence to politics, and their revolutionary vigor is high. Cadres of another kind do not have petty shortcomings or trouble with the opposite sex, and they are popular, get along well with everyone, and commit no petty theft. However, they oppose the Chairman and oppose giving prominence to politics. If we employ the second kind of cadres our army will become revisionist. Our cadre policy must stress the main principles.

The cadre policy has no room for men of peace and harmony. Popular persons are afraid of offending people in their work. We cannot choose this kind of cadre. We must select those cadres who support the Chairman, give prominence to politics, and have revolutionary vigor. This is a question of orientation. To act in this way is to give our army a certain outlook; otherwise it will turn into a different kind.

In order to use the person who has committed errors on small matters, we must criticize and help him. If jade is not polished, it will not serve its purpose. If he can conscientiously reform himself, he is to be warmly welcomed. We must act in accordance with the Chairman's five requirements. To use a person we must criticize him; this shows confidence in him. If we really use a person he will definitely want to reform. If he does not, there is no way to use him. Good persons and able persons must be recruited into the leadership organs.

Our cadre policy from now on should be that whoever opposes Chairman Mao will be discharged. Whoever does not give prominence to politics will be discharged. It does not matter how much ability he may have. This is my opinion; please report to the Standing Committee of the Military Commission to see what their opinion is. This question must be discussed with comrades in military units. This is a question of orientation, and the spirit should be thoroughly transmitted downward.

Two policies and two lines. One is to raise high the great red banner of Mao Tse-tung thought, to give prominence to politics, and to exhibit revolutionary zeal. The other is not to raise high the great red banner of Mao Tse-tung thought and

not give prominence to politics. It represents the purely military viewpoint, the technical viewpoint, and emphasis on the
petty and small. We do not want to transform our military
forces into a spiritually corrupt army; we do not want our
army to wither and stop developing. We should educate and
struggle against the cadres in error whenever possible. Those
who are incurable should be dismissed.

Attention must be given to the cadre policy. I would like
Comrade Yang Ch'eng-wu to pay attention to this question. I
would like Comrade Liu Chih-chien to discuss this with Comrade
Chiang Ch'ing. At present our Liberation Army's position is
very high, and the cadres should manifest no more disorder.
It would be a great humiliation if opposition to Chairman Mao
should again crop up among army cadres. You should all act
resolutely in accordance with the five requirements for successors
set forth by Chairman Mao and the concrete opinions which I
have expressed here today.

I am entrusting Comrade Liu Chih-chien to handle well the
Liberation Army Daily [Chieh-fang-chün pao]. If it is handled
correctly, the military units will give politics prominence. If
this link is handled correctly, work in all areas will advance,
and Chairman Mao's thought will take command.

Last winter, when I put forward the five criteria for
giving prominence to politics, Liang Pi-yeh had a few things to
say. He indicated that an emphasis on politics meant a falling
behind in military preparations. This is erroneous. Military
preparations and politics should not be discussed together in
that way.

On the afternoon of August 10 Vice Chairman Lin said:

There are several kinds of cadres. One kind hold high the
great red banner of Mao Tse-tung thought, support Chairman
Mao, give prominence to politics, and have revolutionary zeal.
But they may have shortcomings in minor details. Another
kind do not stress politics and do not have revolutionary zeal;
but they do not have any particular problems in small matters.
Which kind should we use? We must use the first kind, not the

second. If we cannot save the second kind through education, they must be dismissed once and for all. This will ensure our army's high morale and great combat strength. We cannot allow our army to become a corrupt, depraved army or a Peiyang warlord army. Of course, we should criticize and correct the small shortcomings among the first kind. To criticize them is to use them and trust them.

There is another type of cadres who are perfect; they are correct both on the main principles and on small details. This is very good, but of course there are not many such cadres.

Through this campaign we can evaluate cadres comprehensively. Those who should be promoted must be promoted; those who should be dismissed must be dismissed. It will be a great insult if persons opposed to Chairman Mao still emerge from among our army cadres.

31

ON THE QUESTION OF THE CULTURAL REVOLUTION
IN UNITS AT THE ARMY LEVEL AND ABOVE*
(August 10, 1966)

Vice Chairman Lin said that army units should, in accordance
with the Sixteen-Article Resolution on the Great Cultural Revolution issued by the Party Central Committee, conduct a thorough rectification in organs at the levels of army and military
region, in organs of the various services and department headquarters, and in various military academies and schools. We
should rely on the momentum unleashed by the Resolution of
the Party center to conduct a thorough rectification of all organs. The work of rectifying organs scheduled for the next
Spring Festival should be conducted ahead of schedule in the
coming September and October. We should promote great contending and great blooming, big character posters, big debates,
and thorough democracy. A big fire should be boldly lighted to
burn things in a big way. We should do it seriously and thoroughly, not in a routine fashion. (Units below the division level
should carry out positive education in accordance with the directives of the Military Affairs Commission and the General
Political Department.) Cadres must be examined in all aspects.
The "four olds," should be demolished and the "four news" set
up. All organs must be simplified and bureaucratic organs and
the bureaucratic work-style should be thoroughly rectified.
This campaign of thorough rectification of organs should last

*"Kuan-yü chün i-shang chi-kuan wen-hua ta ko-ming wen-
t'i." Chung-kung nien-pao [Yearbook on Chinese Communism],
1972, Section VI, p. 31.

for two to three months for the entire army. The various units
of the army may make arrangements and preparations according to the concrete conditions of each unit. In general, the campaign should be started in September.

The primary purposes of such a thorough rectification of organs are to examine: (1) whether or not the great banner of the
thought of Mao Tse-tung is being raised high, and whether or
not support is being given to Chairman Mao; (2) whether politics is being put to the fore or the purely military viewpoints
are adhered to; and (3) whether or not the revolutionary work
spirit has prevailed (and also the work style).

Through this campaign of the Great Cultural Revolution, organs are to be thoroughly rectified and thought is to be reformed, so that the ideology in the organs can be revolutionized, the "four olds" destroyed, and the "four news" set up.
Cadres should be examined in all aspects, and organizational
structures simplified.

This campaign should be combined with criticism of the mistakes committed by the anti-Party clique of P'eng Chen, Lo Jui-
ch'ing, Lu Ting-i, and Yang Shang-k'un in order to wipe out
their evil influences and carry out the Sixteen-Article Resolution of the Central Committee on the Great Cultural Revolution.
Promotions and demotions should be determined in accordance
with the findings of the campaign. Those who deserve promotion should be promoted, and those who deserve demotion should
be demoted. We should boldly promote a lot, and also demote
a lot.

32

SPEECH AT PEKING MASS RALLY CELEBRATING
THE GREAT PROLETARIAN CULTURAL REVOLUTION*
(August 18,1966)

Comrades, Students:

First of all, on behalf of our great leader Chairman Mao and
on behalf of the Party's Central Committee, I give you greetings!

We firmly support your proletarian revolutionary spirit of
daring to break through, to act, to make revolution, and to rise
up in rebellion!

Our Chairman Mao is the highest commander of this Great
Proletarian Cultural Revolution. Chairman Mao is the supreme
commander, and faithfully following the instructions of our supreme commander — Chairman Mao — we will certainly carry
the Great Cultural Revolution forward triumphantly and win a
great victory!

The Great Proletarian Cultural Revolution initiated by Chairman Mao is a great creation in the communist movement, a
great creation in the socialist revolution!

The Great Proletarian Cultural Revolution is aimed precisely
at eliminating bourgeois ideology, establishing proletarian ideology, remolding people's souls, revolutionizing their ideology,
digging out the roots of revisionism, and consolidating and developing the socialist system.

We will strike down those in authority who are taking the

*"Tsai ch'ing-chu wu-ch'an chieh-chi wen-hua ta-ko-ming
ch'ün-chung ta-hui-shang ti chiang-hua." Jen-min jih-pao
[People's Daily], August 19, 1966. This translation is taken,
with minor editorial revisions, from Peking Review, No. 35
(August 26, 1966), 8-9.

capitalist road, strike down the reactionary bourgeois authorities, strike down all bourgeois royalists, oppose any act to suppress the revolution, and strike down all ghosts and monsters.

We will energetically eradicate all the old ideas, old culture,
old customs, and old habits of the exploiting classes, and transform all those parts of the superstructure that do not correspond to the socialist economic base. We will sweep out all the
vermin and clear away all obstacles!

We will make vigorous efforts to establish proletarian authorities and the new ideas, new culture, new customs, and new
habits of the proletariat. In a word, we will work with great
energy so that Mao Tse-tung's thought achieves complete as-
cendancy. We will enable hundreds of millions of people to
grasp Mao Tse-tung's thought, ensure that it seizes all ideological positions, apply it in transforming the mental outlook
of the whole of society, and enable Mao Tse-tung's thought,
this great spiritual force, to transform into a great material
force!

The current Great Cultural Revolution is a tremendous event
affecting the destiny and the future of our Party and our country!

On what do we rely to make this Great Cultural Revolution
successful? We rely on the great thought of Mao Tse-tung as
well as on the wisdom and strength of the masses!

Chairman Mao is the most outstanding leader of the proletariat in the present era and the greatest genius in the present
era. Chairman Mao has the strongest faith in the masses. He
pays the greatest attention to them. He gives the strongest
support to the revolutionary movement of the masses. His
heart is one with the hearts of the revolutionary masses!

Mao Tse-tung's thought marks a completely new stage in the
development of Marxism-Leninism. It is the Marxism-Leninism
at the highest level in the present era. It is Marxism-Leninism
of the present era for remolding the souls of the people. It is
the most powerful ideological weapon of the proletariat.

The masses are the makers of history. Once they master
Mao Tse-tung's thought they will become the wisest and most
courageous people, capable of exerting inexhaustible strength!

With the brilliant leadership of Chairman Mao and having
mastered Mao Tse-tung's thought which is the keenest weapon,
we will be invincible and all-conquering and will achieve
complete victory in the Great Proletarian Cultural Revolution!

The Decision Concerning the Great Proletarian Cultural
Revolution recently promulgated by the Party's Central Committee was drawn up under the personal direction of the great
leader Chairman Mao. It is the magnificent program of the
Great Proletarian Cultural Revolution and the latest embodiment of Mao Tse-tung's thought. It is imperative to act resolutely in accordance with this decision, to arouse the masses
boldly, resolutely to oppose monopolizing things which should
be done by the masses themselves, rely firmly on the revolutionary Left, win over the middle and unite with the great majority, concentrate all forces to strike at the handful of ultra-
reactionary Rightists, and thus carry the Great Proletarian
Cultural Revolution through to the end!

The Great Cultural Revolution is a long-term task. In between there are big campaigns and small campaigns. It will
last a very long time. So long as bourgeois ideology exists,
we will fight on to the end!

The present campaign is a big one; it is a general attack on
the ideas of the bourgeoisie and all other exploiting classes.
Under the leadership of Chairman Mao, we must launch fierce
attacks on bourgeois ideology, old customs and old forces of
habit! We must thoroughly topple, smash and discredit the
counterrevolutionary revisionists, bourgeois Rightists, and
reactionary bourgeois authorities, and they must never be
allowed to rise again!

Long live the Great Proletarian Cultural Revolution!
Long live the great Chinese people!
Long live the great Communist Party of China!
Long live the great thought of Mao Tse-tung!
Long live the great leader Chairman Mao! Long live, long
live Chairman Mao!

33

SPEECH AT PEKING RALLY TO RECEIVE
REVOLUTIONARY TEACHERS AND STUDENTS
FROM ALL PARTS OF CHINA*
(August 31, 1966)

Comrades, Students, Red Guard Fighters:
On behalf of our great teacher, great leader, great supreme
commander, and great helmsman Chairman Mao, I extend
greetings to you students coming from all parts of the country;
greetings to you all! On behalf of the Central Committee of the
Party, I greet you all!
Students! You have come to Peking and have been exchang-
ing experience in the Great Cultural Revolution with the revolutionary teachers and students of Peking. You have traveled
a long way and worked hard! We are confident that after your
return, you will work even better, in accordance with Chairman
Mao's instructions and the Party Central Committee's sixteen-
point decision, to smash all resistance, overcome all difficulties, and develop the Great Proletarian Cultural Revolution with
even greater vigor and vitality!
The present situation in the Great Proletarian Culture Revolution is very fine!
The Red Guards and other revolutionary organizations of the
young people have been springing up like bamboo shoots after
the spring rain. They take to the streets to sweep away the

_____

*"Tsai chieh-chien wai-ti lai Ching ko-ming shih-sheng
ta-hui-shang ti chiang-hua." Jen-min jih-pao [People's Daily]
September 1, 1966. The official English translation that appears
here is taken, with minor editorial revisions, from Peking Review,
No. 37 (September 9, 1966), 10-11.

"four olds" [old ideas, culture, customs, and habits]. The
Great Cultural Revolution has already touched on politics
and on economics. The struggle [against and crushing of those
persons in authority who are taking the capitalist road], the
criticism and repudiation [of the reactionary bourgeois academic "authorities" and the ideology of the bourgeoisie and
all other exploiting classes] and the transformation [of education, literature and art and all other parts of the superstructure that do not correspond to the socialist economic base]*
in the schools have been extended to the whole of society. The
revolutionary torrents of the masses are washing away all the
sludge and filth left over from the old society, and are transforming the whole face of society in our country.

Young revolutionary fighters! Chairman Mao and the Party's
Central Committee warmly acclaim your proletarian revolutionary spirit of daring to think, to speak, to act, to break through,
and to make revolution. You have done many good things. You
have put forward many good proposals. We are greatly elated,
and we warmly support you! Firmly oppose any attempt that is
made to suppress you. Your revolutionary actions are very
fine! We hail you and salute you!

Comrades, students!

We must act in accordance with Chairman Mao's teachings;
dare to struggle and dare to make revolution and be good at
waging struggles and at making revolution. We must take Mao
Tse-tung's thought as our compass in the Great Proletarian
Cultural Revolution and carry out the sixteen-point decision
seriously, fully, thoroughly, and without reservation.

We must, in accordance with Chairman Mao's teachings,
distinguish who are our enemies and who are our friends.
Attention must be paid to uniting with the great majority and
concentrating forces to strike at the handful of bourgeois
Rightists. The main target of the attack is those persons in
authority who have wormed their way into the Party and are

---

*All bracketed notes from the Peking Review translation. —
Editor.

taking the capitalist road. It is essential to hold fast to this
main orientation in the struggle.

We must act in accordance with the teachings of Chairman
Mao, and carry out the struggle by reasoning and not by coercion or force. Don't hit people. This applies also to the struggle against those persons in authority who are taking the capitalist road as well as to the struggle against landlords, rich
peasants, counterrevolutionaries, bad elements, and Rightists.
Coercion or force in the struggle against them can only touch
their skins. Only by reasoning is it possible to touch their
souls. Only by reasoning, by exposing them fully and criticizing them profoundly, is it possible to expose their counterrevolutionary features thoroughly, isolate them to the fullest
extent, discredit them, pull them down, and smash them.

The Red Guards and other revolutionary organizations of
the young people in the colleges and middle schools are the
shock force fighting in the van in the Great Cultural Revolution
and a powerful reserve force of the People's Liberation Army.

Students and Red Guard fighters! Always be loyal to the
Party, to the people, to Chairman Mao, and to Mao Tse-tung's
thought. Work hard to study and apply Chairman Mao's works
creatively; make big efforts to apply what you study. Serve the
people wholeheartedly, keep in close contact with the masses,
be exemplary in carrying out the Party's policies, safeguard
the interests of the people, protect state property, and abide by
the Three Main Rules of Discipline and the Eight Points for
Attention.

Students! Provided we earnestly study Chairman Mao's works,
follow his teachings and act in accordance with his instructions,
the Great Proletarian Cultural Revolution can certainly achieve
great victories! Let imperialism, modern revisionism, and all
reactionaries tremble before our victories!

Long live the Great Proletarian Cultural Revolution!

Long live the Communist Party of China!

Long live the invincible thought of Mao Tse-tung!

Long live the great leader, Chairman Mao! Long live, long
live Chairman Mao!

34

SPEECH AT PEKING RALLY TO RECEIVE
REVOLUTIONARY TEACHERS AND STUDENTS
FROM ALL PARTS OF CHINA*
(September 15, 1966)

Comrades, Students, Red Guard Fighters:
In order to carry out the Great Proletarian Cultural Revolution well, you have come from all parts of the country to Peking,
and are here by the side of our great leader Chairman Mao.
You have traveled a long way and worked hard! I greet you on
behalf of Chairman Mao and the Central Committee of the Party.
We extend you a warm welcome!
Led by Chairman Mao, and guided by the sixteen-point deci-
sion drawn up under his leadership, the Great Proletarian
Cultural Revolution in our country is advancing triumphantly
on a nationwide scale. The situation is very fine! It is getting
finer every day.
Red Guard fighters, revolutionary students, the general ori-
entation of your struggle has always been correct. Chairman
Mao and the Party's Central Committee firmly support you!
So do the broad masses of workers, peasants, and soldiers!
Your revolutionary actions have shaken the whole of society and
given a blow to the dregs and left-over evils from the old world.
You have scored brilliant successes in the vigorous fight to
destroy the "four olds" [old ideas, old culture, old customs, and

---

*"Tsai chieh-chien ch'üan-kuo ko-ti lai Ching ko-ming
shih-sheng ta-hui-shang ti chiang-hua." Jen-min jih-pao
[People's Daily], September 16, 1966. This translation is
taken, with minor editorial revisions, from Peking Review,
No. 39 (September 23, 1966), 10-11.

old habits] and foster the "four news" [new ideas, new culture, new customs, and new habits]. You have created utter consternation among those in power who are taking the capitalist road, the reactionary bourgeois "authorities," and bloodsuckers and parasites. You have acted correctly and done well!

Chairman Mao teaches us that the fundamental contradiction to be solved by the Great Proletarian Cultural Revolution is the contradiction between the two classes, the proletariat and the bourgeoisie, and between the two roads, the socialist and the capitalist. The main target of attack in the present movement is those in the Party who are in power and are taking the capitalist road. To bombard the headquarters is to bombard the handful of persons in power who are taking the capitalist road. Ours is a socialist country under the dictatorship of the proletariat. The leadership of our country is in the hands of the proletariat. It is precisely for the purpose of consolidating and strengthening our dictatorship of the proletariat that we must struggle against and overthrow the handful of persons in power who are taking the capitalist road. Quite clearly, the handful of reactionary bourgeois elements, and those belonging to the five categories of landlords, rich peasants, counterrevolutionaries, bad elements, and Rightists who have not really turned over a new leaf, are different from us. They oppose the dictatorship exercised over them by the broad masses of revolutionary people headed by the proletariat, and they are trying to bombard our headquarters of the proletarian revolution. Can we tolerate these actions? No, we must smash the plots of these ghosts and monsters, we must see through them, we must not let their schemes succeed. They are only a small handful, but they can deceive some good people at times. We must keep firmly to the general orientation of our struggle. Any deviation from this general orientation will lead us astray.

In the Great Proletarian Cultural Revolution, the broad masses of workers, peasants, and soldiers and the revolutionary students have a common aim and their orientation is the same. All of them must unite and go forward hand in hand under the banner of Mao Tse-tung's thought!

Some people are now going against Chairman Mao's instructions and the sixteen-point decision. By exploiting the profound
class feelings of the masses of workers and peasants for the
Party and Chairman Mao, they are creating antagonism between
the masses of workers and peasants and the revolutionary
students and are inciting the former to struggle against the
latter. Under no circumstances must we let them hoodwink us!

The masses of workers, peasants, and soldiers, under the
leadership of the Chinese Communist Party headed by Chairman
Mao, have always been the main force of the revolution in our
country. Today, they are the main force of the socialist revolution and socialist construction in our country and also the
main force in the country's Great Proletarian Cultural Revolution.

Our masses of workers, peasants, and soldiers must follow
Chairman Mao's teachings and stand fast at their posts in production and combat stations. They must stand firmly on the
side of the revolutionary students, support their revolutionary
actions and give them powerful backing.

The Red Guards and all revolutionary youth are good sons
and daughters of the Chinese people. You must learn from the
workers, peasants, and soldiers. Learn from them their extremely firm revolutionary stand and their most thoroughgoing
revolutionary spirit. Learn from them their high sense of
organization and discipline and all their other fine qualities.
Like the workers, peasants, and soldiers, be forever loyal
to Chairman Mao, to Mao Tse-tung's thought, to the Party and
to the people, and temper yourselves in the great storm of the
revolutionary struggle to become successors to the proletarian
revolutionary cause.

Under the leadership of Chairman Mao, our great leader,
great teacher, great supreme commander, and great helmsman,
and under the banner of Mao-Tse-tung's thought, let the masses
of workers, peasants, and soldiers and the revolutionary students
unite, let all revolutionary comrades unite, and carry the Great
Proletarian Cultural Revolution through the end.

Long live the Great Proletarian Cultural Revolution!

Long live the great Communist Party of China!
Long live the ever-triumphant thought of Mao Tse-tung!
Long live the great leader Chairman Mao! Long live, long
live Chairman Mao!

35

INSTRUCTION ON RAISING THE STUDY OF
CHAIRMAN MAO'S WRITINGS TO A NEW STAGE*
(September 18, 1966)

The kind of attitude one maintains with respect to the thought
of Mao Tse-tung is a very important question. We must therefore grasp the question of attitude toward Chairman Mao and
toward the thought of Mao Tse-tung. The political colleges in
particular must be sure to conduct themselves in this manner.
The other colleges, schools, and all educational offices must
also do things in the same manner.

The thought of Mao Tse-tung is a program of unified action
for the entire Party, the entire army, and the people of the
whole country. Nothing in the world can replace the thought of
Mao Tse-tung. Such people as Reed, Konstantinov, and Yudin

---

*"Kuan-yü hsüeh-hsi Mao chu-hsi chu-tso t'i-kao tao i-ko
hsin chieh-tuan ti chih-shih." In Mao chu-hsi wen-hsüan [Se-
lected Writings of Chairman Mao, 1959-1967] (n.d., n.p., a Red
Guard publication), pp. 99-102; reprinted in Kung-fei wen-hua
ta-ke-ming chung-yao wen-chien hsü-pien [Supplement to Important Documents of the Cultural Revolution of the Communist
Bandits] (Taipei: Kuo-fang-pu ch'ing-pao-chü, 1969), pp. 173-
176. The speech was given at a reception held for responsible
cadres from the higher military academies, political institutes,
and the Propaganda Office of the General Political Departments.
Some of the instructions were transmitted by Hsiao Hua to an
Air Force cadre conference and were reported in Chieh-fang-
chün pao [Liberation Army Daily], October 10, 1966. See Mao
chu-hsi wen-hsüan, pp. 91-94.

will not do. How can their writings even compare with Chairman Mao's? Right now, in all of China and in the entire world, there is nothing that can unify the thoughts of men like his works can. The writings of Marx and Lenin are too numerous; they cannot be finished. Moreover they are too far removed from us. In the classical works of Marxism-Leninism, we must devote ninety-nine percent of our efforts to the study of Chairman Mao's works; they are our revolutionary textbooks. The thought of Mao Tse-tung must be completely adhered to by the entire Party, the entire army, and all of the people in the country. We must use the thought of Mao Tse-tung to unify our thinking. At present the entire country is learning from the PLA and studying the works of Chairman Mao. The conditions now are different from the past, and the situation has changed. Our military forces are the main pillar of the proletariat; they have to study well. The troops must participate in many things, such as the "four clean-ups," the Great Cultural Revolution, production, and mass work. Also many cadres are constantly being transferred to work at the local level. Because of this, the armed forces should truly become a great school of the thought of Mao Tse-tung. This has to be fully carried out, and ideology has to be corrected. If the cadres are studying, then they must do a good job. They must not act perfunctorily; they should truly grasp the thought of Mao Tse-tung.

The thought of Mao Tse-tung is the science of revolution. It is the supreme truth of the proletarian tested by the experience of protracted revolutionary struggles; it represents the most realistic Marxism-Leninism. Chairman Mao's theory is the summation of decades of revolutionary practice. Once the thought of Mao Tse-tung is mastered, the cadre's political level will be raised and his revolutionary spirit bolstered. He can then carry out the thought of Mao Tse-tung and the Party's line and policy.

Now the whole country is engaged in the Great Cultural Revolution. The Eleventh Plenum of the Eighth Central Committee raised still higher the great red banner of the thought of Mao Tse-tung and proposed that the entire Party and the entire

nation study the works of Chairman Mao and raise the study to
a new stage. In studying Chairman Mao's works the army units
must reconsider the new situation. They must adjust themselves to the new conditions of the Great Proletarian Cultural
Revolution. They must make a maximum effort to truly master
and grasp the thought of Mao Tse-tung. There are three months
before your schools recruit new students for the next year. It
is necessary to carry out the Cultural Revolution well this
year. Through the Cultural Revolution, we can simplify and
streamline organizations and offices. We would rather have a
fewer people than have bad sorts. To put organizations in good
order and strengthen the teaching faculty are matters of extreme importance. If the organizations are not correctly
strengthened and the ideology not unified, and there are even
bad people in the organizations, how can we do a good job? It
is necessary to improve our understanding of the thought of
Mao Tse-tung and to sternly criticize the tendency toward
underestimating the thought of Mao Tse-tung.

Some people show a blind faith in foreign dogmas. They always feel that the Soviet Union is better than we are. Things
far away are better than those close to home. They say such
things as that Marxism-Leninism cannot emerge from mountain ditches. How can their doctrines be compared with the
thought of Mao Tse-tung? Chairman Mao stands much higher
than Marx, Engels, Lenin, or Stalin. There is no one in the
world today who has reached the level of Chairman Mao. Some
people say that Capital is the basis of all theories. In fact, it
only sets forth the laws and problems of capitalist societies.
In our country we have already overthrown capitalism; we are
now setting forth the laws and problems of a socialist society.
To oppose imperialism, modern revisionism, and the reactionaries in various countries and to build socialism, we must rely
upon the thought of Mao Tse-tung. The thought of Mao Tse-
tung is Marxism-Leninism at its highest level. We must raise
high the great red banner of the thought of Mao Tse-tung. We
must use the thought of Mao Tse-tung to unify the thinking of
the entire Party and the entire nation, to further revolutionize

the thoughts of the people, to dig out the roots of capitalism, and to prevent revisionism. The Eleventh Plenum of the Eighth Central Committee placed strong emphasis on studying Chairman Mao's works. Now the study of Chairman Mao's works by the entire Party and the entire nation has entered a new stage, and a new posture and a new situation has emerged.

We must destroy the racial inferiority complex which holds that foreigners are better than Chinese. A racial inferiority complex undermines our revolutionary will. Some people say that the foreign moon is better than the Chinese moon and that we cannot be compared with foreigners. Actually, when Chinese go abroad the people there regard us as foreigners. Some Chinese abroad are even more "foreign" than the foreigners themselves — they are very learned. The viewpoints of foreign dogmatism and of local dogmatism are all contrary to the thought of Mao Tse-tung. Among foreigners or the ancients is there one higher than Chairman Mao? Is there anybody with such mature thinking? A genius like Chairman Mao emerges only once in several hundred years in the world and in several thousand years in China. Chairman Mao is the greatest genius in the world.

All in all, the present movement to study the works of Chairman Mao in the entire Party and throughout the country has entered a new stage of development and brought forth a new situation. The armed forces must grasp this even more firmly and seek to implement this further. They must raise the great red banner of the thought of Mao Tse-tung even higher than in the past. It is very possible that there are some people in the military units who feel that we have done about enough during these past few years — if we do it for too long, we will become numb. If we feel this way, then we will easily relax, study inadequately, and implement insufficiently; then we will not be able to maintain the high morale as in the past.

Our military forces have always relied on the political consciousness and bravery of the people in fighting. This requires political education — using the thought of Mao Tse-tung to educate the troops. The level of the troop's fighting ability depends on political work, on whether or not political education is firmly grasped. Of the numerous methods which may be used to promote discipline and the correct work style, to produce cadres and good people and good deeds, the number one method is to educate people in Mao Tse-tung's thought. When a person's consciousness is raised, then his courage, enthusiam, creativity, organizational discipline, and revolutionary spirit of enduring hardship will all become manifest. Despite the fact that the working conditions of the whole army are very complex, and there are different kinds of situations, on this one point complexities and differences do not matter. Everything must be united by the thought of Mao Tse-tung.

How will this be handled next year? Propaganda offices under the General Political Department and various schools and colleges must study. The study of Chairman Mao's works by the entire Party and the entire nation has created a new situation. Our military forces must move the study of Chairman Mao's works to a new stage and develop a new situation to meet the new conditions of the Cultural Revolution. As to the contents of study, the methods of study, and the amount of time for study, you must look into them.

Cadres must study the works of Chairman Mao. There are some cadres in the army units who attend to matters of an administrative nature. They are busy all day long. How can they have much time to study? The reason why they are in school is to allow them to sit down and study. If they do not study Chairman Mao's writings, they will become divorced from theory and the basic orientation. As for the specific ways of handling these matters, you work them out yourselves. You can organize training classes for a number of months — ten months or eight months will suffice.

You must also study to determine which approaches are better for the higher military academies and political institutes.

I have said in the past that with respect to studying Chairman Mao's works the army units can study in connection with whatever they are doing. Schools and units are not the same. The former have a longer time for study, and the contents of their study can therefore be more. General studies and selective studies can be combined, and general studies and special topical studies can also be integrated. There are three methods: One is to study according to special subjects; another is to follow the order of materials as prearranged; and the third is to combine special topical studies with general studies. When there is plenty of time available, the combination of general and special studies should be adopted. When time is short, general study should not be used. However, partial general study may be used, that is, to select and study some works of Chairman Mao which are closely related to current situation and concrete needs of the units. The decision on the method to be used must be based on the amount of time available for study. In any case, do not do it superficially. A two- or four-month class should not give general study; but a seven- or eight-month class may include general study. A long-term class which conducts general study should place the main emphasis on special subjects. There should be main emphases. Do not follow equalitarianism. Equalitarianism has no place in work and in study. Equalitarianism is not compatible with dialectics. We must stress results, and not formalism. We should sum up the experiences of the past few years in order to find out how to study properly and to truly understand and skillfully apply Mao Tse-tung's thought. Whichever style or method that yields the best results should be adopted. Now the question is not whether or not to study Chairman Mao's thought; it is rather whether or not his thought has really been mastered and whether or not we know how to apply it.

How can we resolve the relationship between general study and selective study? The long-term classes may give general study with emphasis on selective study. Equalitarianism is no good. Some people have high reading ability and have good study habits, and they also have the time. They should be allowed to do general study; otherwise, they will be uneasy and afraid that they may miss something.

Some special subjects must be selected for emphasis. Some documents, like combat orders, can be read over quickly, but

key documents must be read repeatedly. Chairman Mao's
philosophical works have to be studied many times before they
can be understood.

In army units study must be combined with practice. By
studying this article today and that article tomorrow, we can
come close to achieving general study after a long period of
time. Some works must be read over and over again. Some
need to be read only a few times. Also, study in connection
with whatever you are doing. Study with a purpose and integrate study with your own work. Studies which can be applied
are easy to understand and easy to remember. For example,
if those who are engaged in finance and trade study Chairman
Mao's works on finance and economy, they can understand, remember, and apply them better. If practice is not integrated,
the study will not be easy to understand, remember, and apply.
The fundamental principle is to combine theory with practice.
In sum, the main emphasis is to integrate practice with selective studies, while at the same time engaging in general studies. It is all the more important for the companies to combine
practice with selective studies. They must deal with concrete
problems in their study and conduct living study and application. It is permissible for individuals to engage in general
studies if they so wish, but no rigid rule shall be imposed.

Although the "three constantly read articles" are required
study for fighters, cadres must also study them. The "three
constantly read articles" are the easiest to understand; but
they are the most difficult to carry out. The "three constantly
read articles" must become the motto for study. They must be
studied at all levels, including ours here. From the vice chairmen of the Central Committee down to each Party member in
each branch, we all must study them. Once we study them, we
have to apply them so as to revolutionize our thought. The
study of ideological methods and policies is also very important.

We must control well the Liberation Army Daily [Chieh-
fang-chün pao] to give prominence to the thought of Mao Tse-
tung and combine it with practice in the army units. To lead

the troops to study Chairman Mao's works requires repeated
education and propaganda. It looks as if our troops are not
changing; but in actuality the cadres and fighters are changing
every day. Repeated propaganda must be integrated with new
situations and conducted in new words so that it will not become dull and monotonous. In the final analysis, the principles
of Marxism-Leninism are the proletarian standpoint, the theory
of dialectical materialism, and the theory of historical materialism. Once they are combined with practice, they will not
be redundant. This type of propaganda will not be repetitive in
style, but will stress the same content. Only through repeated
emphasis can a better understanding be achieved.

You will go back and study the problems I have raised today.
A new situation of the Cultural Revolution has emerged in the
nation, and the study of the works of Chairman Mao by the entire Party and the entire nation has entered a new stage. In order to meet the new situation and the new stage of development,
the troops in particular must engage in study. The troops must
adhere consistently to the thought of Mao Tse-tung and resist
the thoughts of revisionism and the ideology of all exploiting
classes. They must strengthen their revolutionization, raise
their political consciousness, and improve the level of their
policy comprehension and ideological methods.

One Hundred Quotations from Chairman Mao [Mao chu-hsi
yü-lu i-pai lu], compiled by the Propaganda Office of the General Political Department for fighters to study and memorize,
may be promoted. This is also a form of selective study with
special topical emphasis. However, such special emphasis
should be given even greater prominence and should be studied
even more thoroughly.

The Great Proletarian Cultural Revolution is a political
class outside the classroom. It is a test without formal examination. The mass movement is politics. It is the best political
class. These words were said by Chairman Mao. I have also
said similar words.

I will end my discussion here today. In a month or two we
can have another discussion.

36

SPEECH AT RALLY CELEBRATING THE
SEVENTEENTH ANNIVERSARY OF THE FOUNDING
OF THE PEOPLE'S REPUBLIC OF CHINA*
(October 1, 1966)

Comrades and Friends,
Today is the great festival of the seventeenth anniversary of
the founding of the People's Republic of China. On behalf of our
great leader Chairman Mao, the Central Committee of the
Party, and the Government of the People's Republic of China,
I most warmly salute the workers, peasants, and soldiers, the
revolutionary teachers and students, the revolutionary Red
Guards and other militant youth organizations, the revolutionary
people of all nationalities, and the revolutionary cadres throughout the country, and extend a hearty welcome to our friends
from different countries of the world!
The seventeen years that have elapsed since the founding of
the People's Republic of China have been no ordinary years.
They are years which have witnessed earthshaking changes in
China. They are years which have witnessed earthshaking
changes in the world as well.
Comrade Mao Tse-tung led the Chinese people in carrying
out the revolution, and they traversed a tortuous path beset

---

*"Tsai Chung-Hua jen-min kung-ho-kuo ch'eng-li shih-ch'i
chou-nien ch'ing-chu ta-hui-shang ti chiang-hua." Jen-min jih-
pao, [People's Daily], October 2, 1966; also Hung-ch'i [Red
Flag], No. 13 (October 1, 1966), 2-4. This translation is taken,
with minor editorial revisions, from Peking Review, No. 41
(October 7, 1966), 10-11.

with all kinds of hardships. Our domestic and foreign enemies were strong, but in the end they were overthrown and driven out by the Chinese people. The imperialists headed by the United States, all the reactionaries and the modern revisionists — all these paper tigers have been punctured by the Chinese people and all the revolutionary people of the world.

In the short space of seventeen years, the Chinese people have completely changed the face of old China. This is a highly meritorious deed performed by the masses of the Chinese people under the leadership of Comrade Mao Tse-tung. We are convinced that all the oppressed peoples and oppressed nations of the world will take their own paths in the light of their own countries' conditions and seize final victory as the Chinese people did.

Today we are celebrating this great festival amidst the upsurge of the Great Proletarian Cultural Revolution. This revolution is a great revolution, an entirely new and creative revolution, carried out after the seizure of political power by the proletariat. It is to overthrow through struggle the small handful of persons within the Party who have been in authority and have taken the capitalist road, to sweep away all ghosts and monsters in our society, and to break the old ideas, culture, customs, and habits of the exploiting classes and foster the new ideas, culture, customs, and habits of the proletariat, with a view to further consolidating the dictatorship of the proletariat and developing the socialist system. The historical experience of the dictatorship of the proletariat in the world teaches us that if we fail to do so, the rule of revisionism will come about and the restoration of capitalism will take place. Should this come to pass in our country, China would go back to its former colonial and semicolonial, feudal and semifeudal road, and the imperialists and reactionaries would again ride roughshod over the people. The importance of our Great Cultural Revolution is therefore perfectly clear.

At present, hundreds of millions of people have been aroused. The revolutionary people feel proud and elated, while the reactionary bourgeoisie has been completely discredited. We are forging ahead. We have already laid the cornerstone of great victory.

The Great Proletarian Cultural Revolution is promoting the revolutionization of people's minds and has thus become a powerful motive force for the development of socialist production in our country. This year is the first year of our Third Five-Year Plan. The plan for this year's industrial production is expected to be overfulfilled, and as for agriculture another good harvest is to be reaped. New heights are being scaled in China's science and technology. Our great motherland has never been so prosperous and so full of vigor. Our national defense has never been so strong.

Chairman Mao long ago pointed out that the class struggle between the proletariat and the bourgeoisie and the struggle between the roads of socialism and capitalism exist throughout the historical period of socialism. The Great Proletarian Cultural Revolution constitutes a new stage in the struggle between the two classes and between the two roads. In the course of this revolution, the struggle is still going on between the revolutionary proletarian line represented by Chairman Mao and the bourgeois line of opposing revolution. Those who cling to the erroneous line are only a small handful of persons who divorce themselves from the people, oppose the people, and oppose Mao Tse-tung's thought, and this spells their certain failure.

Comrades and friends! At present, an excellent situation prevails in the world. The great upheavals of the past few years in the world show that the days of imperialism headed by the United States, modern revisionism, and all reaction are numbered.

U.S. imperialism is trying hard to find a way out by launching a world war. We must take this seriously. The focal point of the present struggle lies in Vietnam. We have made every preparation. Not flinching from maximum national sacrifices, we are determined to give firm support to the fraternal Vietnamese people in carrying the war of resistance against U.S. aggression and for national salvation through to the end. Imperialism

headed by the United States and modern revisionism with the
leadership of the CPSU as its center are colluding and actively
plotting peace talk swindles for the purpose of stamping out the
raging flames of the Vietnamese people's national revolutionary
war against U.S. aggression, of the national revolutionary struggles in Asian, African, and Latin American countries and of the
world revolution. They will not succeed in their schemes so
long as the people of the whole world keep their eyes wide open.
Twenty years ago Chairman Mao said that the people of the
whole world must form a united front against U.S. imperialism
so as to defeat it. The revolutionary people of all countries
are now advancing along this road.

Chairman Mao has said, "People of the world, be courageous,
dare to fight, defy difficulties, and advance wave upon wave.
Then the whole world will belong to the people. Monsters of
all kinds shall be destroyed." Such is the inevitable future of
the world.

The Chinese people will continue to hold high the banner of
Marxism-Leninism and the banner of proletarian internationalism and, together with the Marxist-Leninists of the whole world
and the revolutionary people of all countries, carry the struggle against U.S. imperialism and its lackeys and the struggle
against modern revisionism with the leadership of the CPSU
as its center through to the end!

Comrades and friends!

All our achievements and successes have been scored under
the wise leadership of Chairman Mao and represent the victory
of Mao Tse-tung's thought. We must use Mao Tse-tung's
thought to unify the thinking of the whole Party and the thinking
of the people of the whole country. We must hold high the great
red banner of Mao Tse-tung's thought and further unfold the
mass movement for the creative study and application of Chairman Mao's works throughout the country. We must turn the
whole country into a great school of Mao Tse-tung's thought.
We must build our great motherland into a still more powerful
and prosperous country. This is the demand of the Chinese people as well as the hope placed in us by the people of all countries.

Long live the people of all the nationalities in China!
Long live the great unity of the people of the world!
Long live the People's Republic of China!
Long live the Communist Party of China!
Long live the ever-victorious thought of Mao Tse-tung!
Long live our great leader Chairman Mao! Long life, long, long life to him!

37

REMARKS AT A SMALL GROUP MEETING*
(October 12, 1966)

1. With respect to the great role the Red Guards play, Comrade Lin Piao remarked: "With regard to the Red Guards, now foreigners are clear-minded, while Chinese are not; and the masses are clear-minded, while the leadership is not."

2. With respect to the brilliant combat achievements of the Red Guards, Comrade Lin Piao said: "The situation, whether it is good or bad, should be analyzed, and problems should be explained with facts. Red Guards should be organized in every place, and exhibitions of the achievements of rebels should be held in all areas to educate our cadres to discard the word 'fear.' "

3. Concerning the fundamental problem in the current campaign, Comrade Lin Piao pointed out: "The fundamental problem now is that there is too much 'fear' and too little 'dare.' We should present facts to educate everybody. Since the liberation, public security work is at its best when it follows the mass line in the purge of counterrevolutionaries. We should convince others with facts and reasons. All that we fear now should be aired and analyzed to reach a conclusion. The disadvantages of 'fear,' the advantages of 'dare,' and their results should all be clearly discussed."

Chou commented: "There must be a cause for all the chaos."

4. Regarding the struggle among the masses, Comrade Lin

---

*"Tsai hsiao-tsu hui-i shang ti fa-yen." In Mao chu-hsi wen-hsüan [Selected Writings of Chairman Mao] (n.d., n.p., a Red Guard publication), pp. 104-105.

Piao explained: "The masses are highly dialectical in observing problems. Of struggles between one group of the masses against another, some are spontaneous and others are illegal. Even in illegal struggles there are some which are centrally organized and others which receive support from the leadership. When the main current in a problem is unclear, it is necessary to refer to facts and to adhere to reason. Some persons merely say that they have no fear, but actually they do in their thinking. When a mass movement is started, leaders should advance themselves forward, rather than hiding and dodging the issue."

5. On the question of class background, Comrade Lin Piao cautioned: "Among the five red elements, there are some who are not red; among the five black elements, there are also some who are not black. Do not rely solely on the class background, it is better to differentiate among the left, the middle, and the right."

6. Talking about the important significance of the Great Cultural Revolution, Comrade Lin Piao recalled: "A good number of achievements may be listed as follows:

"1) The campaign to study Mao's works has reached a high tide.

"2) A group of anti-Party elements has been dragged out.

"3) We have identified a group of Party persons in power taking the capitalist road as well as a group of people who committed mistakes in political orientation.

"4) The four bad elements have been severely attacked.

"5) The pompous air of bureaucrats and overlords has been destroyed.

"6) We have begun to get the feel for mass democracy.

"7) It has been a great purification of the Party and society.

"8) It has been good exercise for war preparations.

"9) It is going to promote ideological revolutionization of men, and at the same time promote production and work.

"10) We have cultivated a large group of revolutionary successors who dare to act, fight, and develop themselves through struggle.

"However, some people now fail to see the major current

mentioned above. They see only bad phenomena in isolated cases, and even exaggerate them everywhere. This is an attempt to downgrade the Great Cultural Revolution and to calumniate the Chairman. They support Chairman Mao's Great Cultural Revolution only in words, not in deeds. Some even oppose it, because they have become the objects for revolution. They do not want to attack themselves, so they have to sing the opposite tune. Now we should expand propaganda on the great achievements of the Cultural Revolution."

38

TALK AT THE CENTRAL WORK CONFERENCE*
(October 25, 1966)

Primarily I want to speak on two problems: one is the necessity of cultural revolution, and the other is how to engage in
cultural revolution. [In other words, I shall pose] the questions
of whether it is necessary to launch cultural revolution and how
it is going to be launched. In fact, they are interlinked. My
emphasis will be on the necessity of cultural revolution.

This conference has been held for seventeen days and has
been very successful. From the very beginning this conference
has been led by Chairman Mao personally. It is, in point of
fact, the continuation of the Eleventh Plenary Session of the
Central Committee in which the problem of two lines has been
clarified.

During the last several months the condition of the Great
Cultural Revolution has been that while there was great enthusiasm at both ends, it was not enthusiastic enough in between,
during which time there were even some setbacks. At one time
the situation was rather tense. After seeing this situation,
Chairman Mao suggested that everybody be invited to a discussion meeting. It was originally planned for three days, but then
it continued for seven days, and by now some two weeks have
elapsed. Following the clarification of conditions, ideology has
been further clarified. It is now possible to grasp Chairman
Mao's line and to persist in this line. Thus, this is a very
necessary conference. There has been great enthusiasm at

---

*"Chung-yang kung-tso hui-i-shang ti chiang-hua." Reprinted
in Chung-kung nien-pao [Yearbook on Chinese Communism],
1970, Section VII, pp. 56-62.

both ends in that one end was personally led by Chairman Mao and at the other end were the masses.

The broad masses, who were most exuberant, have exerted great influence: from school to society and from the cultural sphere to the spheres of the economy, politics, and society. In each of these areas, considerable results have been achieved. This is especially so in politics. A number of people in authority taking the capitalist road have been ferreted out from within the Party. Many reactionary bourgeois authorities in society have been reduced to a state of odium. It has also become possible to discover a number of counterrevolutionaries and undesirable elements. Many counterrevolutionary cases have been exposed, including [some involving] arms, radio stations, and gold. What is most important is that ideologically it has truly touched people's souls by massively shattering the old ideology and establishing the new ideology. This is a very profound, great revolution. Drastic changes have been brought about in social outlook and in the spiritual outlook of the people. In this movement Chairman Mao's thought has been extensively disseminated and popularized. It has become deeply engraved in the minds of people and has been a tremendous education for youth and for society in general. After this movement it has become possible for a great many youth to be nurtured to become dependable successors of the revolution.

During the period of the Great Cultural Revolution, our social production has not been undermined, as certain comrades had feared. On the contrary, production has increased. It stands to reason that the Cultural Revolution should accelerate production, and this has also been borne out by the facts. This movement has set an unprecedented example in the world. In regard to antirevisionism, this kind of method on the part of China is replete with demonstrative characteristics.

We can all see clearly that above us is Chairman Mao. Throughout, this movement has been unleashed and led by the Chairman. With tremendous energy and resolve, Chairman Mao undertook this task; he mobilized a mammoth mass movement to undertake it. It is impossible for the leader of an

ordinary working class party to have such great energy and
resolve. Only Chairman Mao, who is such a great Marxist-
Leninist, has extremely rich experiences of struggle and is
steeped in the wisdom of Marxism-Leninism; only he dares to
unleash such a revolutionary mass movement that has resoundingly shaken the entire nation and world. Some comrades under
Chairman Mao's leadership have also been most effective in
consistently supporting and implementing Chairman Mao's line.
. . . [Half-paragraph illegible.]
In the last two days it has become evident that there are two
causes for such conditions in various places. On the one hand,
they stem from local causes and ideological causes. But what
is more important is that there are some leadership comrades
in the Central Committee — said to be Comrades Liu Shao-
ch'i and Teng Hsiao-p'ing — who have been engaged in another
line that is contrary to Chairman Mao's line. The Liu-Teng
line, as has been said in Chairman Mao's wall poster, takes
the reactionary bourgeois stand and implements bourgeois dictatorship. It tries to beat down the Great Cultural Revolution
movement so resoundingly launched by the proletariat; it distorts truth and falsehood, besieges the revolutionaries, represses dissident views, practices white terror, and considers
it natural to strengthen the prestige of the bourgeoisie and
dampen the morale of the proletariat. How poisonous is their
intention! After the last few days, comrades have learned more
about this source.

Generally speaking, ideology, social consciousness, world
outlook, customs and habits, political views, legal views, artistic views, motion pictures and drama in the arts, plastic
art, literature, the educational system, etc., are what we call
culture. Why do we have to launch this Cultural Revolution?
The decisive factor [impelling] us to launch a revolution in the
sphere of social consciousness is that basic changes have occurred in the economic base of our society.

Where does ideology emanate? Marxism and Chairman Mao
Tse-tung have consistently held the view that ideology comes
from matter, that social consciousness stems from the

existence of society, and that the economic basis of society is derived from the system of social ownership. Since national liberation, the proletariat has controlled political power, and there has been a fundamental change in the ownership system of Chinese society. We have confiscated the farmlands belonging to landlords and turned them over to the peasants and later collectivized them. These are the two changes undergone by the system of agricultural ownership. The system of landlord ownership has been changed to individual ownership of peasants and later to the collective ownership of peasants. The system of bourgeois ownership has undergone diverse transitional stages to become socialist public ownership. Now preparations are under way to abolish fixed interest. Since changes have occurred in the economic basis, this superstructure of our social consciousness must also change and catch up. Unless we catch up, we will be hampered in solidifying the system of socialist ownership and slacken our progress. This will also make it impossible for the new social productive forces to develop; it will make it impossible to solidify the fruits of revolution. This will also lead to the restoration of capitalism, thus subverting the people's democratic dictatorship which protects the public ownership system of society. Consequently, China will be dominated by revisionism and retrogress to a semifeudal and semicolonial status. Thus, whether the Great Cultural Revolution is launched or not is an important problem involving whether the proletarian regime can be solidified and the fruits of revolution can be developed; it is a political problem involving the success or failure of the revolution.

There are three facets in the proletarian revolution and in the class struggle undertaken by the proletariat: one facet is politics, the second is economics, and the third is consciousness and form.

To overthrow a regime by means of war is a violent and brutal action. We succeeded in routing the Kuomintang during the period of 1946-1949 (naturally, we spent many years before that). We achieved victory and seized political power, thus establishing our own state and setting up the state of proletarian

dictatorship. In regard to the revolution of two kinds of ownership system — namely, the revolution to overthrow the feudal
ownership system and the bourgeois ownership system — it
took a shorter period of time. On the other hand, there is
another front which needs even more time and a more devious
struggle. This is the struggle in the ideological sphere, which
must take a longer time than the gaining of political power and
the changing of ownership systems. Next year will mark the
fiftieth anniversary of the Soviet Union's revolutionary victory.
Nonetheless, how much bourgeois ideology has been eliminated
and how much proletarian ideology has been augmented? One
result after these fifty years is that after Stalin's death, instead
of forging ahead, the Soviet Union has retrogressed by heading
toward revisionism, toward the restoration of new forms
adopted by the bourgeoisie, and toward the capitalist system
which is being manifested in forms of varying degrees. Yugoslavia was the first country to launch a restoration. In addition, there is not only the Soviet Union but also a number of
"socialist" countries which have been victorious for one or
two decades, but because they failed to grasp this facet of the
struggle, revolution has stagnated and retreated, and signs of
restoration have emerged. If we do not grasp this point, we
will be faced with the same conditions as occurred in the Soviet Union and Yugoslavia. The Soviet Union has been in existence for fifty years, but it is now ruled by revisionism. Unless we grasp the Great Proletarian Cultural Revolution
consistently, the same result will ensue. Thus Chairman Mao
proposed: "If you are truly concerned with the affairs of state,
you must then push the Great Proletarian Cultural Revolution
to the end."

Chairman Mao regards the Great Cultural Revolution as an
important matter of the state and as politics. In revising the
"Excerpts of the Army Units Literature and Art Work Forum"
in March this year, Chairman Mao agreed to write down that
all class struggles are political struggle, thereby reiterating
this classic viewpoint of Marxism-Leninism by regarding it as
an important matter of the state and as a political problem.

Unless we grasp the Great Cultural Revolution firmly and unless we push the Great Proletarian Cultural Revolution to the end, then we will also change our color midway.

That we have firmly grasped economic construction regularly is good. Nonetheless, with regard to cultural destruction and construction and with regard to destruction and construction in the ideological sphere, not all comrades have grasped the situation as firmly and emphasized these tasks as strongly as Chairman Mao. There are people who feel that this is an extra burden. They feel that since everything is all right, why must we then undertake the Great Cultural Revolution? In fact, since we have gained political power, on the one hand, it is necessary to undertake economic construction; but on the other hand, from the standpoint of long-range significance, it is even more important to undertake ideological construction. Ideology has tremendous functions of motivation in social, political, and economic development. Old ideology serves the old economic base and reflects the demands of reactionary classes, thus obstructing the development of society; new ideology serves the new economic base and reflects the demands of progressive classes, thus exercising accelerative and promotive functions in the development of society.

Once ideology is clarified, it will become a tremendous material force which accelerates social development. This is why we should massively (not just slightly or moderately) destroy the old ideology and establish the new ideology on a mass scale. Whatever represents new ideology, whatever represents people's ideology, whatever represents proletarian ideology, whatever represents communist ideology, whatever represents the ideology of Marxism-Leninism, and whatever can resist the old ideology — this is the ideology of our Chairman Mao. It is therefore necessary to massively establish this kind of ideology. Many comrades have failed to grasp this point firmly; they have failed to grasp on a massive scale what should be destroyed and what should be established. Among the comrades who work in the Central Committee, all have known in the last few days what Liu and Teng have done in propagating

Chairman Mao's thought and what attitude they have taken. We also know the attitude adopted by Lu Ting-i in the former Ministry of Propaganda, an attitude which is most exacerbating and intolerable.

After seizing political power, from the standpoint of domestic tasks, we must undertake cultural construction apart from suppressing the opposition of the exploiters and engaging in economic construction. As regards what to destroy and what to establish culturally, not only should we do this but almost all ruling classes in history have done the same as well. There is no state and no ruling class that would allow the propagation of an ideology that is opposed to its class stand. It must insist on its own ideology in order to consolidate its political and economic systems. Though the ruling ideology of each epoch in history would appear as if it represented the outlook of the entire society, in point of fact it represented only the interests of the exploitative class which enjoyed a ruling status. The ruling class ideology of each epoch represented only the ideology of the interests of that ruling class. In the past the ideology of the laboring people did not occupy a ruling status; moreover, most of them have been fooled and deceived consistently.

Our Party is one of Marxism-Leninism-Mao Tse-tung Thought. Based on the theories of Marxism and Mao Tse-tung thought, we must thoroughly break away from the old systems of ownership and from old traditional concepts. It is necessary and right that we establish our proletarian rule ideologically.

Although we have by now achieved a ruling status, both economically and politically, we have not yet completely attained a ruling status ideologically. We have overthrown the old classes economically and politically; but in the sphere of ideology the ways of the old class still predominate. Consequently, it is necessary for us to develop this struggle on the ideological front unrelentingly and persistently. After many decades Stalin still did not resolve this struggle problem. Chairman Mao has made a timely presentation of this problem and has asked us to resolve it. This is not only our fortune but also a very glorious and great task.

It would seem that instead of a few decades it might take a century or even centuries to eliminate the old ideology. Naturally, antagonism between old things and new things will prevail in future society, and this antagonism will persist in two hundred years, three hundred years, four hundred years, one thousand years, and even ten thousand years. Thus there is bound to be struggle in the ideological sphere in which the new will oppose the old and the old will try to preserve itself and refuse to be withdrawn from the stage of history. Though there may be some distinction between that condition and the kind of class struggle we are waging today, nonetheless there is this common point in that the new must vanquish the old.

It is conceivable that there will be ideological contradictions and struggles in the future. Thus, this struggle in culture and in the sphere of ideology is a protracted struggle. It is by no means a simple and easy matter. The method of our struggle has sometimes been one of criticism in newspapers and magazines. For instance, we have criticized Wu Hsün chuan [The Biography of Wu Hsün], and Hung lou meng yen-chiu [A Study of Dream of the Red Chamber], we have criticized the reactionary ideology of Hu Shih and Hu Feng, we have criticized Yang Hsien-chen, and then Wu Han, Teng T'o, Chien Po-tsan, Chou Yang, etc. All of these movements have been led by Chairman Mao personally and have had far-reaching significance. However, after the movement has been developed to a certain stage, it should take the form of massive sweeping away and massive destruction in the entire society, as has happened in the last five months. After having been launched for six months or a year, this kind of movement and this kind of campaign should have laid a solid foundation. The function of this kind of movement can by no means be replaced by criticisms in newspapers and periodicals, but it has its extraordinary functions as well as prowess. This movement is a great innovation, although both big and small campaigns can be launched alternately.

What is the substance of old culture and old ideology? We may use a great variety of semantics to express it, such as old culture, old ideology, poisonous weed, bull-ghost and snake-god, reactionary authority, old scholarship, old morality, old art, old laws, old educational system, old world outlook, etc. These things are inherently old in that they pertain to the old private ownership system. In short, they are old because they are "szu" [private, selfish]. What then is new in new things and new ideology? In a word, they are new because they are "kung" [public].

Prehistoric human society lasted a long time, at least half a million years. It has been said by scientists that the formation of the globe has taken six billion years. Nonetheless in the several millennia when there was culture in human society, there were only class societies, such as slave society, feudal society, and capitalist society. What was common in these societies? The private ownership system, which has had a history of several millennia. While the diverse ideologies of the exploitative class may be divided into eight, ten or even twenty patterns, nevertheless they all amounted to private ownership.

Our present society is one of a socialist public ownership system in which everything belongs to the public, be it land, factories, or means of production. Under these circumstances, in order to solidify this system it is necessary to extirpate the old culture of the bourgeoisie and other exploitative classes. We must destroy the various old consciousnesses and forms used to uphold and revive the private ownership system. The existence and effects of exploitative consciousness and forms are bound to restore and uphold the old regime of private ownership. Those who are opposed to the destruction of old culture and old consciousness and forms are bound to suppress revolution and repress the masses. If we want to solidify the socialist system, its economic system and political system, we must then advocate the concept of public-mindedness — that is to say, we must foster a new man to construct a new society, a man with the spirit of communism. What is the man steeped in communist spirit? He is people like Chang Szu-te, [Norman] Bethune, Liu Hu-lan, and Lei Feng, who have been praised by Chairman Mao. Other such men are Ou-yang

Hai, Ch'iao Yu-lu, Wang Chieh, and Liu Ying-chun, all of whom
are men of communism and a new type of man. Our new society needs this kind of man, and we must also gradually
transform the people of society into this type of man.

What is communism? In a certain sense, communism is for
the public, and it may be called the doctrine of "public property";
it is for the public. The kind of people we wish to foster are
what Chairman Mao calls people who are divested of low interests and are men of morality. We must foster this kind of men
who have new morality and, as Chairman Mao has said, are
wholeheartedly devoted to the people. This type of person is a
person of communism. On the contrary, there is the kung
[self-centered] person, who is interested only in his own fame,
profit, power, status, and glamour. Such a person is egocen-
tric and is oblivious of the masses and the laboring people. In
short, he is only mindful of himself. In a class society, each
person belongs to a specific class, belonging either to this society and a certain stratum and group of this society, or to
another class and a certain stratum and group of that society.
There is no such thing as an abstractly independent individual.
He only remembers himself, and this is a purely bourgeois
world outlook. Bourgeois individualism is what is detrimental
to others but profitable to oneself. In order to make money,
they will not care if thousands and tens of thousands of people
have to become bankrupt. To look at the world with a selfish
viewpoint is to look at the world from a bourgeois standpoint;
it is not to look at the world from a proletarian standpoint.

What we need now is to foster people dedicated to the public.
There are different class characteristics even in public interest. The public we have in mind is the public of the people, the
public of the proletariat, and the public of socialism and communism. Since the founding of our Party, there have been a
great many public-minded people of this type, and now we have
more of them. Where Chairman Mao's thought has been further intensified and propagated, the number of this kind of people has risen tremendously. Since the workers, peasants,
soldiers, and intellectual youth have begun to study Chairman

Mao's works on a wide scale, innumerable good people and good events have emerged.

In constructing our country, two lines may be followed. One is like the one that has happened in the Soviet Union, which has unilaterally emphasized the material, machinery, mechanization, and even material incentives. The other line is the one which Chairman Mao has led us to follow.

Chairman Mao has led us to create a new type of nation which, besides being engaged in mechanization, is engaged more importantly in revolutionization; and revolutionization is used to lead mechanization. In comparing machinery with man, the human being is naturally more important. Chairman Mao says that man is the most precious thing in the world. Militarily, weapons are important, but they are not the decisive factor. The decisive factor is man. This is a Marxist viewpoint, the truly Marxist viewpoint. Machinery can be transformed into productive force only through human efforts; an isolated machine can only be a heap of iron. Machinery is created and used by man; apart from man, there would be no machinery, and even with machinery there could be no production. Machinery is a feasible productive force, but it is only when man and machinery are coordinated that it can be transformed into practical productive force.

Machinery is nothing but an artificial organ. Unlike other animals, man is an instrument of our liberation. There are diverse kinds of machinery which, in fact, are merely organs to substitute for our productive labor, thus replacing, helping, and strengthening our hands. Thus all kinds of machinery are for the purpose of strengthening our organs. They are, as a matter of fact, used to strengthen human ability and are therefore centered around man. To neglect man is to neglect the greatest productive force. Politically, ...[line illegible] this is to neglect the strength of revolution.

[Paragraph illegible.]

The question may be put as follows: In what position should the Great Proletarian Cultural Revolution be placed? Is there any necessity to undertake it? Is it an extra burden, or is it

something within our duties ? If it is within our duties, then
not to undertake it is tantamount to neglecting our duty. The
state of the dictatorship of the proletariat has three great
tasks: political construction, economic construction, and ideological construction. In the past we have carried out the first
two great constructions, but there is another one — ideological
construction, which is also cultural revolution — which has not
yet been comprehensively developed. It must be realized that
without successful development of the cultural revolution and
ideological construction, the fruits we have gained from the
first two great constructions will be negated. Thus, it is incumbent on us to emulate Chairman Mao's massive launching
of cultural revolution.

Chairman Mao's thesis is to be found in his works. His
books provide the basis for what we must study. There are
also a great many writings of Chairman Mao that cannot be
found in books, and they are also what we must study. We
should do as Chairman Mao does. In both theory and practice,
and both in Marxist theory or in his personal talents, Chairman
Mao is not only superior to us in all respects, but he is also
the greatest contemporary Marxist-Leninist in the world. We
must use Chairman Mao's example to measure ourselves, to
catch up with him, to emulate and study him. We must also
put the Great Cultural Revolution in an important position and
regard it as an important matter of the state, a political problem, an important part of the class struggle, and an important
front. This is the only suitable way.

Because cultural revolution is a political struggle between
the proletariat and the bourgeoisie, a struggle between two
lines is bound to arise. As regards this two-way struggle, we
have seen clearly during the past two days that one line, represented by Liu and Teng, represses the masses and opposes
revolution. The other line, boldly advocated by Chairman Mao,
trusts the masses and mobilizes the masses. This is also the
mass line of the Party and the proletarian revolutionary line.
It will be seen that while one is a mass line, the other is an
anti-mass line. This then is the sharp antagonism between the

two lines within our Party. Within a short period the line of
Liu and Teng almost achieved a dominant position, and it was
implemented throughout the nation. Nevertheless, in the final
analysis, Chairman Mao's line will eventually triumph because
this is the truth.

Chairman Mao has said: "People, and the people alone, form
the motive power in creating world history." This sentence is
classic, being the most succinct and essential of the Marxist
theory of historical materialism. The theory of historical materialism is primarily to prove that the history of people and
masses develops forward; it is the forward development of live
productive forces; only thus will there be social revolution;
only thus can changes in the system of ownership be induced
and changes be brought about in production. Thus the masses
are the progressive motive force, the most basic force, as
well as the most consistent force in each historic stage. The
masses are strong because they are numerous and have more
wisdom. With more people, there is also greater resourceful-
ness, and so they can create.

Any revolutionary mass movement is bound to be rational.
While there may be individual segments and persons among
the masses, and there may be such deviations as being
"Left" or Right, the mainstream of mass movement is
always rational and suitable for social development. Consequently, we must trust the masses and rely on their creativity.
At the beginning of this movement we did not make many regulations. Chairman Mao has said time and again that we did not
create the Red Guards but that they have been created by the
masses, and thereafter became a nationwide movement. Many
things are started by the masses. First, we make ourselves
pupils of the masses, study from them, distill their views, then
promote them, and make ourselves teachers. To come from
the masses and to implement among the masses has been
Chairman Mao's consistent thinking and methodology. The
youth of this generation are children we have fostered during
the seventeen years since our revolutionary victory. By now
they are about twenty years old, and most of them are

ideologically aware. Nurtured by Mao Tse-tung thought and under the leadership of a correct revolutionary line, they are comparatively receptive to the new, proletarian world outlook. In our Cultural Revolution, we must have confidence in this group of young friends. They are small rampaging generals whose rampaging spirit is most precious. What we cannot think is that, no matter how difficult and unsolvable the problem, by means of their rampage a matter can be clarified immediately and one can stiffen one's resolve. There are still a considerable number of comrades who are afraid of the students and the masses, and they have this or that kind of fear. Since Comrade [Ch'en] Po-ta has already enumerated them, I need not repeat. The resolution of the Eleventh Plenary Session of the Central Committee on the Great Proletarian Cultural Revolution states that the responsible persons of a great many units are afraid of troubles. In fact, such troubles trouble the enemy, not ourselves. Sometimes we may also create some small troubles for ourselves.

Chairman Mao said long ago that troubles have a dual character. There is a good side and also a bad side. We must not notice only the bad side and ignore the good side. Moreover, what is bad can also be transmuted into the good side.

There can be no great troubles in the general direction. Our army is highly solidified, and our production has risen time and again. What troubles can some students and youth make in launching the Cultural Revolution? It is impossible to have big troubles. This is our view concerning the problem of trouble, our outlook regarding trouble.

Chairman Mao says: In making revolution, one cannot be so meticulous, unhurried, gracious, or so mild, respectful and modest, because it is unlike inviting guests to a dinner, or writing an essay, or painting and embroidering.... There are bound to be deviations, perhaps few, perhaps many. Nevertheless, if the mainstream is good, one need not be afraid. If you should now worry about some trouble, there would be even greater troubles in the future when the bull-ghosts and snake-gods would rebel against the proletariat and against us. This time I have asked Comrade Hsieh Fu-chih to prepare some materials that could illustrate the accomplishments of the Red Guards, and I have also sent some people to make observations. In fact, people were prepared to rebel against us, and they have even made every preparation for the "change of weather." Some of them would regard their old land deeds as their life roots, pasting them up if they were torn, photographing them and preserving them. Why should they want these things? The reason why they kept them so secretively is none other than that when the Kuomintang and imperialism returned, they could say that this house belonged to them or that land belonged to them. This is their wishful thinking on the change of weather. Although the exploitative class has been overthrown, these people are still alive; what they think is reactionary, and they are fraught with hatred toward the people. There are also many in our Party who wish for a change of weather. Such chaps as P'eng [Chen], Lo [Jui-ch'ing], Yang [Shang-k'un], and Lu [Ting-i] all cherish the thought of a change of weather and are bent on launching a counterrevolutionary coup. If we do not undertake this Cultural Revolution or if we do not bother them, they will come to attack us. There are now current a number of rumors, reactionary handbills, and anonymous reactionary letters which spread hate against revolution. These are all indications of their illusions of a change of weather. Whenever the opportunity arises, these undesirable elements will come out to stir up troubles and rebel against the people. Some of them would take advantage of the organizational principle that "the lower echelon obeys the superior one" to give orders to usurp political power and to change our social system. In fact, they have been attacking us. Thus we cannot but attack them, and if we do not overthrow them, they will overthrow us. This is why we say that there are great lurking perils. The Soviet Union had been in existence for forty years; but with the emergence of Khrushchev the entire country has changed color.

We must not fear trouble. We must be daring, unafraid. Otherwise, we would commit errors, great political errors. To distrust the masses is a great error. The Liu-Teng line is based on distrust of the masses; at the same time it is also distrustful of Chairman Mao. Instead of trusting the masses, they believe only in themselves, in those who have the same ideology, in the bourgeois world outlook, and in the bourgeois line.

Did not Chairman Mao raise the problem of the preservation of the old virtues of the proletariat? There is no other means of preserving such old virtues than these: one is to trust Chairman Mao, the second is to trust the masses, and the third is to treat oneself correctly. In so doing, one is, in effect, observing what Chairman Mao has mentioned as the five requirements of the successor. Chairman Mao has said that the first requirement of the proletarian revolutionary successor is to believe in Marxism-Leninism, which is to believe in Chairman Mao, and to believe in Mao Tse-tung thought. Mao Tse-tung thought and Marxism-Leninism are unified things in which there is only a difference of epoch. The former is even more superior and is the more developed Marxism-Leninism.

The second requirement of the proletarian successor, according to Chairman Mao, is to serve the people. The third requirement is to rally with the great majority. The fourth requirement is the system of democratic centralism. All these deal with the problem of having faith in the masses. Since the masses are the creators of history, we must not think that we are superior to them. In fact, what we may claim is only that we may be senior in background. In regard to either wisdom or moral character, it thus becomes doubtful whether we can catch up with a Lei Feng, a Chang Szu-te, or some of the other heroes. Consequently, though some of the comrades may be exalted in status and senior in qualifications, this does not imply that their ideology and talents are better than others. It may be said that the wisdom of the masses is indeed tremendous. I have seen some students who are no older than twenty or so, but they are resourceful and they can say what old folks of sixty, seventy, or eighty cannot.

Chairman Mao has said that the fifth requirement of the proletarian revolutionary successor is the problem of treating

oneself correctly. What kind of approach should one take in
regard to himself? One should divide one into two. There
may be some merits, but certainly there must be shortcomings.
In regard to one's merits, one should develop them fully in
order to make contributions to the revolution. In regard to
one's shortcomings, it is necessary to struggle continuously
in order to adapt to the needs of revolution. It is incumbent
on us to consider ourselves as a part of a revolutionary force.
In the meantime we must also make ourselves the objects of
revolution. In making revolution, one must revolt against oneself; otherwise the revolution will not be successful. First of
all, one must be detached [from personal concerns] and not
only be conscious of oneself alone. When one sees only oneself,
it implies that there is a certain limitation. The Marxist-
Leninist must be able to transcend this kind of limitation. When
I am part of a certain mountain, my concern is for that mountain and not others. This is also a kind of limitation. A seg-
ment of our comrades are interested only in their own units,
but are oblivious of the 700 million people [in China] or several billion people [of the world]. This is also a kind of limitation. Nor should we feel that we are special just because our
present status is higher. It behooves us to be liberated from
the word "I" and from the limitation of the small unit. We
must concern ourselves with the great unit and the whole.
Chairman Mao says that the proletariat must not only liberate
their own class, but also all of mankind. Unless all of mankind is liberated, it will be impossible for the proletariat to
achieve complete liberation. Consequently, we must endeavor
to break the various limitations. As regards the question of
preserving the old virtues of proletarian revolution, the most
important thing is that we must implement the five prerequisites prescribed by Chairman Mao. In a word, this means that
we must believe in Chairman Mao and the masses, and we must
handle ourselves correctly.

Chairman Mao says that we should have faith in the masses
and in the Party. These are two basic principles. This must
be so now; we must believe Chairman Mao and believe the

masses, for otherwise nothing will be consummated. To preserve the old virtues is indeed a serious problem. It is sometimes impossible to preserve them. There are people who
have engaged in revolution for thirty, forty, or fifty years, and
they have reached the ages of fifty, sixty, seventy, or even
eighty. It is still questionable whether they will be able to
preserve their old virtues to the end. There are many who
have slipped in the last few years, having failed to preserve
their old virtues. It is incumbent upon us to carefully and
meticulously preserve this old virtue in order to set an example for posterity. If we do not trust Chairman Mao and the
masses, and if we are overly self-confident, then we will not
be able to preserve the old virtues. The erroneous line in this
cultural revolutionary movement has been primarily [? (word
unclear)] initiated by Liu and Teng, but it has been implemented
in many places. Comrades are concerned with this problem,
though naturally this should be dealt with discriminatingly.
There is a difference between initiation and implementation,
and between what is serious and what is light. The general
appraisal is that the majority of comrades are not self-
conscious and they did not purposely resist Chairman Mao's
line. In most cases it is a question of understanding, but not
a question of being anti-Party, antisocialism, or anti-Mao
Tse-tung thought. I am very aware of this. Among the secretaries of the Central Committee Politburo, provincial committees, and municipal committees, there are many good fellows and some bad ones individually, but the majority are good.
Of course, you should also have your responsibilities. There
are varying degrees of implementing the erroneous line in different areas; hence your responsibilities also vary. However,
where it is an individual problem, we must handle it properly,
without either magnifying or minimizing the case. People usually are prone to forget that quantitative change can cause qualitative change when different quantities are regarded as an
equal quantity and different qualities are regarded as the same
quality. For instance, water freezes at zero degree; it changes
into water when the temperature rises above zero, and into

steam when the temperature reaches 100 degrees or more. This is due to the difference of temperature. Thus we should accord differential treatment to cadres of various levels instead of treating them uniformly. There are some serious cases and some light ones, but on the whole it is largely a question of understanding. There is only a handful who have opposed Chairman Mao's correct line.

If our comrades would endeavor to grasp Mao Tse-tung thought, study the policy of the Party Central Committee, have confidence in the masses, and correctly deal with the deviations and errors that have arisen in their own work, it will then be possible to rectify these shortcomings [? (word unclear)] and do the work well and in a relaxed and happy manner, thus enabling the entire Party to become further solidified under the banner of Mao Tse-tung thought.

39

INSTRUCTION OF VICE CHAIRMAN LIN PIAO*
(October 1966)

This directive of Chairman Mao's is very important. If you
will resolutely implement this directive, and satisfactorily fulfill this important political mission, it will have political and
military significance. In carrying out this mission, you must
pay special attention to the cultivation of the habit of studying
more of Chairman Mao's works.

In accordance with this supreme directive we have formulated a political training program for revolutionary teachers
and students coming to Peking from other parts of the country.
Our military training plan has already been issued. Each unit
is expected to carry out the directive.

(The directive of Mao's to which Lin refers in his instruction
reads as follows: The armed forces will be responsible for the
organization of revolutionary teachers and students from other
areas of the country who are coming to Peking into squads,
platoons, companies, battalions, regiments, and divisions as
prescribed in the table of organization of the PLA. After they
have been so organized, they will take up training, study politics, study the People's Liberation Army, study the speeches
of Comrade Lin Piao and Premier Chou En-lai, study the Three
Main Rules of Discipline and the Eight Points for Attention, study
the three-eight work style of the PLA, study the formations of
their unit, study the basic tasks of their unit, and practice

---

*"Lin fu chu-hsi ti chih-shih." In Mao chu-hsi wen-hsüan
[Selected Writings of Chairman Mao, 1959-1967] (n.d., n.p., a
Red Guard publication), p. 50.

marching. Each individual must study the song "The Three Main Points of Discipline and the Eight Points for Attention" so that the revolutionary teachers and students will be orderly when they march in review. Mao Tse-tung, October 1966)

40

SPEECH AT PEKING MASS RALLY*
(November 3, 1966)

Students, Comrades, and Red Guard Fighters:

With boundless love and infinite loyalty for our great leader Chairman Mao, you have come to Peking in the new nationwide upsurge of the Great Proletarian Cultural Revolution to see Chairman Mao and to exchange revolutionary experience. On behalf of Chairman Mao and the Central Committee of the Party, I extend my warmest welcome to you!

Chairman Mao is extremely happy to receive you today. This is the sixth time in two months or more, including National Day, that Chairman Mao has received revolutionary students and teachers and Red Guards from all over the country. Chairman Mao is the greatest proletarian revolutionary; he is always with the masses, has full confidence in them, shares weal and woe with them, and wholeheartedly supports the revolutionary mass movement. Chairman Mao has set the most glorious example for all comrades in our Party and for the younger generation.

The present situation of the Great Proletarian Cultural Revolution is excellent! The gigantic, vigorous mass movement is developing in depth with each passing day. A tremendous change

---

*"Tsai chieh-chien ch'üan-kuo ko-ti lai Ching ko-ming shih-sheng ta-hui-shang ti chiang-hua." Jen-min jih-pao [People's Daily], November 4, 1966; Hung-ch'i [Red Flag], No. 15 (December 13, 1966), 3-4. This English translation is taken, with minor editorial revisions, from Peking Review, No. 46 (November 11, 1966), 11-12.

has taken place over the whole face of society and in the mental outlook of the people. The great thought of Mao Tse-tung has become more extensively disseminated and has gone deeper into the hearts of the people. As a result of Chairman Mao's call "to take a firm hold of the revolution and promote production," the Great Cultural Revolution has promoted the revolutionization of people's thinking and spurred extremely rapid development in industrial and agricultural production and in science and technology. The recent successful guided missile-nuclear weapon test is a great victory for Mao Tse-tung's thought and a great victory for the Proletarian Cultural Revolution!

The Eleventh Plenary Session of the Eighth Central Committee of the Chinese Communist Party announced the victory of the proletarian revolutionary line represented by Chairman Mao and the bankruptcy of the bourgeois reactionary line. In the past two months and more, the correct line of Chairman Mao has been put before the broad masses and has been grasped by them, and criticisms have been made of the erroneous line. The broad masses have really translated into action Chairman Mao's call to "concern yourselves with affairs of the state." This is an extremely fine thing. It is an important guarantee that the Great Proletarian Cultural Revolution will be carried through to the end.

Chairman Mao's line is one of letting the masses educate and emancipate themselves. It is the line of putting "daring" above everything else and of daring to trust the masses, daring to rely on them, and daring to arouse them boldly. It is the application and a new development of the Party's mass line in the Great Cultural Revolution. It is the line of the Great Proletarian Cultural Revolution.

The bourgeois line is one of opposing the mass line, of opposing the education and emancipation of the masses by themselves, of repressing the masses and opposing the revolution. This bourgeois reactionary line directs the spearhead of struggle against the revolutionary masses, and not against the handful of persons within the Party who are in authority and are taking the capitalist road, and all the ghosts and monsters in

society. It uses various ways and means to incite one group
among the masses to struggle against another group, and one
section of students to struggle against another section.

The proletarian revolutionary line of Chairman Mao is as incompatible with the bourgeois reactionary line as fire is to
water. Only by thoroughly criticizing and repudiating the bourgeois reactionary line and eradicating its influence can the line
of Chairman Mao be carried out correctly, completely, and
thoroughly.

Under the guidance of Chairman Mao's correct line, the
broad revolutionary masses of our country have created the
new experience of developing extensive democracy under the
dictatorship of the proletariat. By this extensive democracy,
the Party is fearlessly permitting the broad masses to use the
media of free airing of views, big-character posters, great debates, and extensive exchange of revolutionary experience to
criticize and supervise the Party and government leading institutions and leaders at all levels. At the same time, the people's democratic rights are being fully realized in accordance
with the principles of the Paris Commune. Without such extensive democracy, it would be impossible to initiate a genuine
Great Proletarian Cultural Revolution, stage a great revolution
in the depths of people's souls, carry out the Great Proletarian
Cultural Revolution thoroughly and completely, eradicate the
roots of revisionism, consolidate the dictatorship of the proletariat, and guarantee the advance of our country along the road
of socialism and communism. This extensive democracy is a
new form of integrating Mao Tse-tung's thought with the broad
masses, a new form of mass self-education. It is a new contribution by Chairman Mao to the Marxist-Leninist theory on
proletarian revolution and proletarian dictatorship.

International historical experience of the dictatorship of the
proletariat has demonstrated that without carrying out a
thoroughgoing Great Proletarian Cultural Revolution of this
kind and without practicing such extensive democracy, the dictatorship of the proletariat will be weakened and will change in
essence, while capitalism will use various ways to stage a

comeback and the exploiting classes will once again ride on the backs of the people.

Such extensive democracy must be thoroughly practiced not only between the leadership and the masses; it is also absolutely necessary to carry it out thoroughly among the masses themselves and between all sections of the masses. Unless there is such extensive democracy among the masses themselves and unless they are good at mutual consultation, at listening to dissenting views, at presenting facts and reasoning things out, at using their brains to ponder problems, they cannot possibly educate and emancipate themselves, achieve the purpose of developing the ranks of the Left, uniting the great majority and isolating the handful of bourgeois Rightists, and fully carry out the line of the Great Proletarian Cultural Revolution put forward by our great teacher Chairman Mao.

Chairman Mao supports you comrades traveling on foot to exchange revolutionary experience, the advantages of which are widespread contact with the masses, contact with all aspects of the life of society, and a deeper understanding of class struggle in socialist society. It provides better opportunities to learn from the workers and the peasants and to propagate Mao Tse-tung's thought on an even broader scale. All this is very useful for the revolutionary teachers and students to have a better understanding of Mao Tse-tung's thought and the correct line of Chairman Mao. Of course, this kind of traveling on foot for the exchange of revolutionary experience must be undertaken in a planned and organized way and must be well prepared.

The Central Committee of the Party is convinced that with the experience gained in the last few months, the Great Proletarian Cultural Revolution will in the days to come make still better progress and attain still greater success!

March forward under the great banner of Mao Tse-tung's thought!

Long live the victory of the line of Chairman Mao!

Long live the victory of the Great Proletarian Cultural Revolution!

Long live the Chinese Communist Party!

Long live Chairman Mao! Long life, long, long life to him!

41

FOREWORD TO SECOND EDITION OF
QUOTATIONS FROM CHAIRMAN MAO TSE-TUNG*
(December 16, 1966)

Comrade Mao Tse-tung is the greatest Marxist-Leninist of
our era. Comrade Mao Tse-tung has, with genius, creatively,
and in an all-round way, inherited, defended, and developed
Marxism-Leninism, advancing it to a completely new stage.

Mao Tse-tung's thought is Marxism-Leninism of the era in
which imperialism is heading for total collapse and socialism
is advancing toward worldwide victory. It is a powerful ideological weapon for opposing imperialism and a powerful ideological weapon for opposing revisionism and dogmatism. Mao
Tse-tung's thought is the guiding principle for all the work of
the whole Party, the whole army, and the whole country.

Therefore, the most fundamental task in our Party's political
and ideological work should be always to hold high the great
red banner of Mao Tse-tung's thought, to arm the minds of the
people throughout the country with it, and to persevere in putting it in command of all work. The broad masses of the workers, peasants, and soldiers and the broad ranks of the revolutionary cadres and the intellectuals should all really master
Mao Tse-tung's thought; they should all study Chairman Mao's
writings, follow his teachings, act according to his instructions,
and become Chairman Mao's good fighters.

---

*"Mao chu-hsi yü-lu tsai-pan ch'ien-yen." The text in Chi-
nese is also available in Jen-min jih-pao [People's Daily], December 17, 1966; Hung-ch'i [Red Flag], No. 1 (January 1967).
This translation is taken, with minor editorial revisions, from
Peking Review, No. 52 (December 23, 1966), 7.

In studying the works of Chairman Mao, one should do so
with specific problems in mind, study and apply his works in
a creative way, combine study with practice, study first what
is urgently needed so as to get quick results, and make great
efforts to apply what one studies. In order really to master
Mao Tse-tung's thought, it is necessary to study many of Chairman Mao's basic concepts over and over again, and it is best
to memorize some of his important passages and study and apply them repeatedly. The newspapers should frequently carry
quotations from Chairman Mao in connection with the actual
situation for readers to study and apply. The experience of the
broad masses in their creative study and application of Chairman Mao's works in the past few years has proved that to study
selected quotations from Chairman Mao with specific problems
in mind is a good method for learning Mao Tse-tung's thought,
a method conducive to quick results.

We have selected and compiled the Quotations from Chairman Mao Tse-tung with the purpose of helping the broad
masses learn Mao Tse-tung's thought more effectively. In organizing study, different units should select passages for study
that are relevant to the situation, the tasks, the current thinking of the masses, and the state of their work.

A new era is emerging in our great motherland in which the
workers, peasants, and soldiers are mastering Marxism-
Leninism-Mao Tse-tung Thought. Once Mao Tse-tung's
thought is grasped by the broad masses, it will become an inexhaustible source of strength and an infinitely powerful spiritual atom bomb. The mass publication of the Quotations from
Chairman Mao Tse-tung is an extremely important measure
for the broad masses to grasp Mao Tse-tung's thought and for
promoting the revolutionization of the thinking of our people.
It is our hope that all comrades will study seriously and diligently, and bring about a new high tide in the creative study
and application of Chairman Mao's works throughout the country and, under the great red banner of Mao Tse-tung's thought,
strive to build our country into a great socialist country with a
modern agriculture, modern industry, modern science and culture, and modern national defense!

42

[REMARKS TRANSMITTED BY HSIAO HUA]*
(1966 ?)

Comrade Lin Piao said: "The thought of Mao Tse-tung is the zenith of Marxism-Leninism in the contemporary era; it is the highest and most creative form of Marxism-Leninism." He also said: "Chairman Mao's writings are the highest directives for all of the work of the entire army. Chairman Mao's words bear the highest standard, his prestige is the highest, and his ability is the greatest. Everything he says is truth, and every phrase he utters is worth ten thousand phrases."

---

*Mao chu-hsi wen-hsüan [Selected Writings of Chairman Mao] (n.d., n.p., a Red Guard publication), p. 87. The title in English is added; the remarks were transmitted in January 1966 at an All-Army Political Work Conference.

43

CRITICISM OF P'ENG TE-HUAI*
(? 1966)

P'eng Te-huai has always made alliances here and alliances
there, committed this mistake and that mistake, all due to his
ambition. Right-wing opportunist elements must be thoroughly
exposed and the struggle against them carried through to the
end; there is no other way than to make your crimes notorious.
This way of proceeding will benefit both you and the Party;
only in this way can you reform; otherwise it is impossible.
The exposure and solution of this problem by the Lushan Plenum was a great victory which eliminated the greatest hidden
danger within the Party. The several recent instances in which
the Chairman mentioned the possibility of split within the Party
are in fact references to P'eng Te-huai.... At the Lushan
Plenum he was thinking whether or not this hidden danger had
been thoroughly exposed and eliminated, for otherwise it would
continue to develop and, per chance the Chairman should pass
away, would be an even greater problem. The interests of the
whole Party, the whole army, and all of the people lie in immediately exposing it and struggling against it, in guarding the
General Line and educating the whole Party, and in consolidating
the Party's Central Committee headed by Chairman Mao. We
must expose and carry the struggle through to the end. You
can reform or not, but of course we hope you will.

*"Lin Piao tui P'eng Te-huai ti p'i-p'an." Chung-kung nien-
pao [Yearbook on Chinese Communism] , 1969, Part VII, p. 75.

44

ON "BIG CRITICISM"*
(? 1966)

The Great Cultural Revolution in the industrial and communications enterprises is very important; if it is handled well,
they can become great schools of Mao Tse-tung thought; but if
it is handled poorly, they can become important pillars of revisionism. The majority of the leading members of revisionist
countries are organizational and enterprise cadres.

In the industrial and communications enterprises there is a
struggle between two lines, between two roads. Without recog-
nizing this problem, there will be no Great Cultural Revolution
in the enterprises to speak of — all that will happen is the
adoption of an attitude of formalism and expediency.

We must use the Great Cultural Revolution to develop the
forces of production, to liquidate the influence of capitalism
and revisionism and the influence of Liu, Teng, and P'eng, for
theirs is the bourgeoise line, not the proletarian line. The problem of Liu and Teng is not a matter of ninety days, but of ten
or twenty years. During the period in which they were in control, never did they raise high the great red banner of Mao Tse-
tung thought, but rather followed their own set of policies which

*"Lun 'ta-p'i-p'an.'" In Kung-fei wen-hua ta-ko-ming chung-
yao wen-chien hsü-pien [Supplement to Important Documents
on the Great Cultural Revolution of the Communist Bandits]
(Taipei: Kuo-fang-pu ch'ing-pao-chü, 1969), pp. 170-172. These
are excerpts of a speech given by Lin Piao at a Cultural Revolution meeting for the central industrial and communications
departments.

greatly conflicted with Mao Tse-tung thought.

The core of Marxism-Leninism-Mao Tse-tung Thought is head-to-head struggle; it is destructive, revolutionary, unmasking, and critical; only in this way can it spur society's advance and effect the transition to socialism and communism. The Liu-Teng line is fundamentally opposed to Marxism-Leninism-Mao Tse-tung Thought; it is a bourgeois line, not a revolutionary one. P'eng and Po [I-po] are even worse — they use two-faced methods which are even more evil. They have had a profound influence toward us and, in the same way, toward industrial and communications enterprises. The hidden and concealed changes over the past ten or twenty years have been profound, and they have greatly interferred with Mao Tse-tung thought. Industry and communications do not lack for needed reforms, for they have been profoundly influenced by capitalism, revisionism, Liu, Teng, P'eng, and Po. Class struggle should be taken very seriously and an attitude of dauntless courage adopted for great destruction and great construction. Under the influence of capitalism and revisionism, Mao Tse-tung thought can be firmly established only through great destruction and great construction. Only in this way can a new posture emerge and new results occur. In producing a greater and even longer-lasting leap forward, the Great Cultural Revolution is the most important link in the proletarian revolution.

This Great Cultural Revolution of ours, daring as it does to give free rein to the masses and to be fully democratic, is something unknown in the past or present, in China or abroad. No country dares do this; only our great Chairman Mao dares to show this kind of resolution, to exhibit courage this great. Chairman Mao places his highest confidence in the masses. The reason that the masses must be given such free rein and things handled so democratically is due to the profound and deeply-rooted influence of the thousands-of-years old system of ownership and the concept of private ownership; the profound influence of capitalism and revisionism; and the profound influence and fettering effect of the many errors in our own minds — without this great emphasis on democracy they could not be

blasted out and no solution would be possible. The reason that
so many socialist nations have become revisionist is because
they could not blast out this kind of influence and the concept
of private ownership — without great destruction and construction, no solution is possible.... If we continue to do things according to the ideas of Liu and Teng, we too will become revisionist. If China becomes revisionist, then world revolution
will be set back countless years. The Chairman's great emphasis on democracy has great strategic insight and inestima-
bly great significance.

At first the Great Cultural Revolution was intellectual criticism, but then it extended to the schools, and now it has
reached factories and villages; it has penetrated society,
gripped the whole country, and startled the whole world....
If the Great Cultural Revolution is to permeate every realm,
change the outlook of society and promote its advance, it must
replace the old with the new, put the dialectic into practice,
and carry the struggle against the old through to the end.
Marxism-Leninism must be revolutionary and critical. The
line which slights or forgets ideological revolution opposes
Mao Tse-tung thought, opposes Marxism-Leninism. If attention is paid only to other fronts, and the ideological front is
overlooked, in the future all of our accomplishments will come
to nought.

The Great Cultural Revolution is the most important link in
the proletarian revolution. The seizure of political power and
changing of the system of ownership were two great victories.
If we only have these two victories but do not carry the ideological, cultural revolution through to the end, we cannot defeat the bourgeoisie and raise up the proletariat. If the positive
nature of people is not brought into play, political power and
the socialist system of ownership cannot be consolidated. Therefore this battle must be fought well. Many socialist countries
have become revisionist precisely because this battle was not
fought well. We are presently faced with two restorations: the
military aggression of American imperialism — this we do not
fear, for we are prepared; but peaceful evolution is the greatest

danger — many socialist countries have suffered peaceful evolution. We must use our greatest strength to resist it. For this reason we must carry the Great Cultural Revolution (in industry and communications) through to the end.

(From a speech by Lin Piao at a Cultural Revolution meeting for central authorities in industry and communications.)

Note: These are portions of a speech by Lin Piao at a Cultural Revolution meeting for CCP Ministries of Industry and Communications.

45

ON IDEOLOGICAL STRUGGLE*
(1966 ?)

Our Communist Party is governed by a principle, namely, contradiction. Contradiction can be resolved only through struggle. The philosophy of our Communist Party is dialectics; it is the struggle of opposites. When we change a thing, we have to rely on struggle. Our Communist Party is a proletarian political party. The reason why it is vigorous, incorruptible, and resistant to decay is because our ideological method is that of struggle. Our philosophy stresses struggle. Our philosophy is one that emphasizes struggle. Chairman Mao made this judgment in an article of his. This philosophy of struggle is one that guarantees our uninterrupted advance, one that safeguards our continuous dynamism. Otherwise there will be decay, demoralization, and opportunism. The Second International, for instance, did not advocate struggle.

Relying on the fundamental principles of Marxism-Leninism, the Chinese Communist Party adopts this policy of struggle. Whenever there are shortcomings, we struggle with them. The principle of our Party life is that whenever contradictions emerge, struggles should be launched. Struggle is the only way to correct mistakes. First, reduce the market of a person [who makes mistakes], so that he will not be able to influence others. Second, make him come to his senses.

---

*"Lun ssu-hsiang tou-cheng." A speech delivered by Lin Piao, published in Mao chu-hsi wen-hsüan [Selected Writings of Chairman Mao, 1959-1967] (n.d., n.p., a Red Guard publication), pp. 118-119.

Our comrades, therefore, should not fear struggle. But fear still persists in military units at present. No matter whether it is in a military district, a military service, an army, a division, a regiment, a battalion, a company, or a company [Party] branch, we must adhere consistently to this principle of life. When there are errors, we must not shirk our duties or take an attitude of liberalism; we must wage a fearless and courageous struggle.

Some people are often worried that struggle will create problems. The truth is that not only will struggle not bring problems, it can resolve problems. If we do not struggle, then there will indeed be problems. Everyone should read carefully what Chairman Mao has written about his opposition to liberalism. Liberalism in all its varieties does not want struggle; it tolerates the continued existence of bad thoughts. This causes our Party to degenerate and is not consistent with Marxism-Leninism and dialectics. This is a kind of philistine thought.

Opposite ideas may be expressed. Once they are expressed, then we have an opposite. This will facilitate the execution of struggle and education. We must have this kind of work style at all levels. It is a democratic work style. It permits people to speak out on both sides of an issue — the positive and the negative side. Positive ideas may be accepted; negative ideas must be refuted. To allow an idea to speak out and to allow it to exist are two separate matters, and they must not be confused. To allow it to speak out does not mean that it is allowed to exist — it must be refuted. We must maintain the democratic work style and allow both positive and negative ideas to speak out. Do not deny the negative idea opportunities to speak out just because we are in struggle. If it is not allowed to do so, positive ideas will have no chance to be aired, and the life of our Party will not be vigorous. So, from now on we will continue to rely upon the old rule which Chairman Mao advocates, that is, daring to think and daring to speak.

Our army is one that has been nurtured by Chairman Mao and one that has Party spirit. It is a good thing that we understand what Party spirit is and what factional spirit is. It should be our tradition. In other words, do not confuse the public with the private domain, or political relationships among comrades with personal friendship among individuals. They are not the same thing, and must be clearly differentiated. Personal friendship is just that. Political matters, Party affairs, and matters concerning the people and revolution cannot be confused with personal friendship among individuals. When matters concerning the Party and the ideological line develop deviations, we must resolutely stand on the side of the Party and the revolution, we must not indulge in sentimentalism and factional viewpoints. In this way will we be able to guarantee our Party unity.

46

STATEMENTS CONCERNING CHU TE*
(1966 ?)

1. P'eng Te-huai has made many mistakes, one after another, tying up with this force and that, and this all resulted from his ambition. These right-wing opportunist elements must be thoroughly exposed, and they must be fought against, to the very last. To do so will be in your own [Chu Te's] interest and good for the Party too. Only in this way can you be perfectly reformed.

2. It was a very great victory that this problem was exposed and settled at the Lushan Conference. In this way the biggest root of disease within the Party was wiped out. Chairman Mao stated a number of times that there is a possibility of a split arising in the Party. As a matter of fact he was referring to P'eng Te-huai and Chu Te. The merits and the disadvantages of thorough exposure at the Lushan Conference were weighed, and it was finally decided that they will be exposed resolutely and that the root of disease will be thus wiped out. Otherwise, there was a possibility of the disease spreading further and creating bigger problems.

3. The purpose of the struggle now being developed is to defend the general policy line, educate the whole Party, and

---

*Originally posted in the wall-newspaper of the Second Battalion of the Peking Commune of the Chinese People's University on February 8, 1967, and reported in Mainichi Shimbun [Daily News, Tokyo], February 9, 1967. This translation is taken, with minor editorial revisions, from Daily Summary of the Japanese Press, February 9, 1967, p. 1.

strengthen the Party Center, headed by Chairman Mao, and the interests of the whole Party, the whole army, and the entire people are staked on it.

4. Exposure struggles must be carried out thoroughly. You can reform or not reform. We desire that you reform.

5. Chu Te, you are very ambitious. Your self-criticism is extremely inadequate. Some people think that he made self-criticism voluntarily. That is not so. It was because the Party Center decided that he should "strip himself naked."

6. You probably do not know, but [Foreign Minister] Ch'en I's criticizing Chu Te was not going to excess. Chu Te is not obeying Chairman Mao. He tried to become the leader himself. At the time of the Kao Kang Incident, he advocated the idea of becoming chairman in turn. Does he have such real power?

7. Your self-criticism is not sincere. You have never been a "commander-in-chief" even for one day. At the time of the Nanchang Uprising, the situation became completely anarchic and chaotic. It was Ch'en I who led the troops and took them to Chingkangshan. It was Tsao Te [German military officer Litov] who commanded the Army before the Tsunyi Conference. In the days of the War of Resistance Against Japan, it was "X X X" [the original text uses "X" and does not give the real name] who took command at the front. In the Liberation War Chairman Mao took command.

8. You are no longer of any use. You may think that you can still manage somehow, but you became separated from Chairman Mao's command, and at Chingkangshan you lost two of the three battalions when you moved south to launch an attack. Chairman Mao himself sallied forth and had to bring you back.

(Wall-Newspaper's Note: It can be seen from Vice Chairman Lin's statements that Chu Te is definitely not a proletarian class militarist, but a revisionist element with big ambitions, and that he belongs to the bourgeois power faction in the army. We must thoroughly expose the real nature of this big fool, Chu Te, through this Great Cultural Revolution, and criticize and fight against him in a thoroughgoing manner.)

47

ON CRITICISM*
(? 1966)

Some people feel that if they commit no mistakes there is no
need for criticism. According to Lenin, there is nobody who
does not make mistakes. This is a scientific appraisal. Refusing to acknowledge it does not accord with Marxism-Leninism.
Comrade Mao Tse-tung has said, "Who does not make mistakes? Even in writing one makes revisions several times,
and each time mistakes are corrected." An intelligent man is
merely one who is quick to correct his own mistakes, and that
is all there is to it. If a person has made mistakes, and still
pretends to be faultless, sticks to his mistakes to the end, seeks
ways of explaining them away, and insists that he is right where
he has in fact been wrong, then he is the biggest fool. An intelligent man quickly casts away all pretensions and tells no lies.
Nobody can get away with lies, because nobody can cover up the
sky with his hands. When an intelligent man makes a mistake,
he will have it corrected in a few days or even in a few hours.
But a fool makes a mistake without being able to correct it for
a half-year, or even for several years. An intelligent man is
quick to correct his mistakes; thus, we call him a good man because he is quick to find out what is wrong. Otherwise he would
be a fool and coward who dares not admit his own mistakes.
There are big and small mistakes, with different degrees of
bad effect. The earlier they are corrected, the better. Those
who consider that they have no mistakes to be criticized are

_____
*"P'i-p'an." Shou-tu hung-wei ping [Capital Red Guards,
Peking], December 2, 1966.

in fact afraid of criticism.

There is a very vulgar type of person who always lavishes flattering words upon others, and does not utter a word when he sees others commit mistakes. This is extremely damaging and has hurt many cadres. To engage in personal smuggling at the expense of the interest of revolution by lavishing praise on somebody who has committed mistakes, rather than helping him correct them, is the worst possible thing to do. Such is called liberalism and toadyism, and it is detrimental to the interest of the revolution.

Party members have the right to criticize. It is not merely a small matter of right, but more importantly a duty to fulfill. Without criticism one will be hurt badly. Every Party member has the duty to conduct criticism and self-criticism. Whether or not one has a sense of responsibility toward the revolution is judged by whether or not one will criticize bad conduct. Mistakes are unavoidable. The more criticism we have, the better are the chances that mistakes will be corrected. An organization that does not practice criticism is doomed to fall apart.

ON THE GREAT PROLETARIAN
CULTURAL REVOLUTION*
(March 19, 1967)

This is a great civil struggle without guns that encompasses
the whole country. But never regard lightly enemies without
guns, for they can overthrow the dictatorship of the proletariat.
Enemies without guns can become enemies with guns, and struggle without arms can become struggle with arms. If this change
occurs, the cost will be great. By carrying on this Great Proletarian Cultural Revolution we can avoid armed conflict; we can
avoid a great historic detour, a great retracing of steps, and great
destruction; and we can avoid a great loss of property which sus-
tains the life of the people. Therefore the victory of the Great Proletarian Cultural Revolution is very great and plays an important
role in avoiding the fate of Yugoslavia and the Soviet Union. It not
only secures the great achievements in the victorious advance of
our people along the path of socialism and communism, but it
also has far-reaching strategic significance.

---

*"T'an wu-ch'an chieh-chi wen-hua ta-ko-ming." Kung-fei
wen-hua ta-ko-ming chung-yao wen-chien hsü-pien [Supple-
ment to Important Documents on the Great Cultural Revolution
of the Communist Bandits] (Taipei: Kuo-fang-pu ch'ing-pao-
chü, 1969), p. 166. This is a passage from a speech delivered
at a conference of cadres at the army level and above. A
shorter version of this remark may be found in Mao chu-hsi
wen-hsüan [Selected Writings of Chairman Mao, 1957-1967]
(n.d., n.p., a Red Guard publication), p. 120.

SPEECH AT MEETING OF CADRES
AT THE ARMY LEVEL AND ABOVE*
(March 20, 1967)

I want to talk about three things today. The first is about
the question of classes, class struggle, and class viewpoint....
Several years ago Chairman Mao raised the question of class
struggle in socialist society. The class struggle and the dictatorship of the proletariat are basic questions in Marxism-
Leninism. But under the conditions of socialism the question
of the class struggle is apparently easily neglected; it is as
though there might be no class struggle. Our Chairman Mao
has especially stressed class struggle under conditions of the
dictatorship of the proletariat and socialism. This point has
not been heeded by some Marxist-Leninists, not to mention the
Khrushchev-style revisionists. Concerning this question, Chairman Mao has greatly developed Marxism-Leninism.

Chairman Mao said: "Classes struggle; some classes triumph; others are eliminated. Such is history; such is the history of civilization for thousands of years. To interpret history
from this viewpoint is historical materialism; standing in opposition to this viewpoint is historical idealism." Marx and
Engels said long ago that history since mankind became liter-
ate is the history of class struggle. From the time that the
primitive communal societies collapsed, the history of mankind has been a history of class struggle. Lenin went even

---

*"Tsai chün i-shang kan-pu hui-i shang ti chiang-hua." In
Chung-kung nien-pao [Yearbook on Chinese Communism],
1971, Section VII, pp. 25-28.

further in emphasizing that after the proletariat has seized political power, there will still be acute class struggle.

In the article "Congratulations to the Hungarian Workers," Lenin said: "To obliterate classes will mean a protracted, difficult, and stubborn class struggle. After overthrowing the political power of the bourgeoisie, after destroying the bourgeois countries, after establishing the dictatorship of the proletariat, class struggle still will not have disappeared (as imagined by the lackeys of the old socialist and old social democratic parties). It will simply have changed its form, and in many aspects will be even more cruel."

Lenin stressed in his work "Left-Wing" Communism, An Infantile Disorder: "The dictatorship of the proletariat is the spearhead by which the new class engages in fearless, ruthless struggle against a relatively strong enemy — the bourgeoisie. The resistance of the bourgeoisie, because it has been overthrown (even if it happens in only one country), is ten times more fierce. Its strength resides not only in the forces of international capitalism, not only in the solidarity of its international unity, but also in the force of custom and habit, in the forces of small production. Because of this it is regrettable that in the world today there are many, many small producers; and the small producers are constantly, day in and day out, spontaneously and to a great extent creating capitalism and the bourgeoisie."

In antiquity and the present, in China and abroad, in the social realm where classes exist, the basic question influencing all others is that of class struggle. It is exactly as our great leader Chairman Mao has taught us: "In class society everyone lives in a certain class position; the imprint of class is on every type of thought." Ideologically everyone has a class imprint. There is no one who does not belong to a specific class; all are subordinated to definite social relationships, a specific class. This type of social class is a phenomenon produced by mankind in certain historical stages. It is different from the primitive communist society; it is also different from the high-level communist society of the future. The fact of this class existence has passed down through history for thousands of years and permeates every aspect of society. The existence of this class struggle comes from a definite economic foundation and is reflected in the superstructure. It forms cleavages in line in politics, law, culture, religion, ethics, and political parties; it develops the differences in policies and divergences in social customs and habits. These divergencies and distinctions all bear the class imprint; all have their origin in classes and class struggle.

Class and class struggle thus constitute the basic general source of all phenomena in class society. If we observe social phenomena apart from this basic source, we will not be perceptive and we will observe things incorrectly. It is an objective existence. It is not the case that this objective existence has no influence on our thinking. Consciously or unconsciously it influcences our thought. Our Communist Party should use Marxism-Leninism-Mao Tse-tung Thought to influence our thinking in a conscious way. They should consciously guide our thinking, our line, our policies. If we depart from this standpoint, we will make mistakes in our line and policies. If we do not consciously emphasize classes, class struggle, and the class viewpoint, if we do not pay attention to class analysis, we will fall into objectivism. And objectivism is an ideological system of the bourgeoisie. The ideology of objectivism superficially denies class. However, in actuality it employs this form to conceal its class outlook, its class aspirations, policies, and behavior. All this is done to facilitate their deception of the masses.

For several thousand years all of society has existed in a class environment and class struggle. Class struggle ordinarily takes three forms: One is on the ideological front; another is on the political front; and the third is on the economic front. These three are not isolated, but rather mutually interwoven. Sometimes one is predominant and sometimes another, but whichever it is it is never unrelated to the others. Thus these three aspects are really united.

Owing to the emergence of different classes, the class

struggle in each stage has taken different forms of class resistance. It is just as Marx said in his Communist "Manifesto": There are slave-owners and slaves, landlords and peasants, the bourgeoisie and the proletariat. Of course, the stages of development of every country are different, and in different stages every country will have two primary opposing classes. However, there will always be remnants of other classes and the sprouts of new classes.

As Chairman Mao has pointed out, our country started to enter into the socialist era after 1949. Chairman Mao said: "After the Chinese revolution has been triumphant and has solved the question of land, two types of basic contradictions will still exist. The first type is internal, that is, the contradiction between the workers and the bourgeoisie. The second type is outside the country, that is, the contradiction between China and the imperialist countries." The contradiction, opposition, resistance, and struggle between the proletariat and the bourgeoisie form the general source of our entire political and social life. If we do not view every type of social phenomenon as that of the class struggle, we will confuse things, substitute wrong for right. This would be a return to the concept of all people, to view people as isolated individuals. No man is an independent individual; he is always a social being. Just as when doctors examine our blood, they draw out a drop of blood and can discern red and white cells, acidity and alkalinity in the whole body. This drop of blood represents your whole body. Your individual actions are a manifestation of the entire class body.

Therefore, without this kind of proletarian viewpoint we will perceive an individual incorrectly and deviate from the proper evaluation and handling of problems. For example, our view of old cadres might be that they are all very good. In reality we must make a class analysis of old cadres. Many old cadres preserve the original proletarian revolutionary traditions. But some, on encountering the socialist period, have not kept pace, have not become fighters for the socialist revolution, but rather have come to rest in the stage of the old democratic revolution.

Some have changed their nature and become capitalists and new capitalists. How did this happen? Is it good or bad? We must use the proletarian viewpoint to view them. It would not be that they have become complete capitalists, or complete proletarian revolutionaries. Our view of young people is similar to this: We may say that they are all bad when they clash with our units or, from another viewpoint, say that they are all good. In reality, in society today with classes still existing, many persons stand on the side of the proletariat. But there certainly still are those who side with the bourgeoisie, landlords, rich peasants, counterrevolutionaries, bad elements, and Rightists. The offspring of cadres are also like this: Some are of the proletariat; some have changed their nature and become bourgeois elements.

Without the proletarian viewpoint, we cannot view clearly the question of the so-called "disorder." In reality, there have been two kinds of disorder this time. One is of the primary kind: the thorough beating administered to the enemy, to the top Party persons taking the capitalist road, to the bourgeois chiefs within the Party, and to the bourgeois chiefs on the top of society. They have been thrown into confusion. This kind of disorder has been a victory for the Great Proletarian Cultural Revolution; this is a very good thing. Of course, in the struggle of the two opposing sides there have been defects on the proletarian side; there have been defects among cadres. But this has been the exception, and this can be handled.

Without the proletarian viewpoint we cannot have a proper evaluation of culture. It is only with the proletarian viewpoint that we can distinguish what is good and what is bad; we cannot do without it.

The significance of the Great Proletarian Cultural Revolution rests on its being an unusually severe, penetrating class struggle. This struggle was first initiated by the bourgeoisie, and afterward the proletariat counterattacked. First of all it was ideological struggle, and then it gradually became a struggle for political power and economic power. Many, many complex things emerged in the course of the struggle, but the question of which things could be adopted or shunned, which were right or wrong, could only be made clear from the viewpoint of classes and class struggle, that is, from the general basis of classes and class struggle.

In our Party Chairman Mao is most correct and revolutionary; he represents the proletariat. Liu and Teng are in error; they are reactionary and represent the bourgeoisie. One wants to take the socialist road; the other wants to take the capitalist road. Therefore a sharp struggle has developed between the two lines.

This class struggle after the proletariat seized political power is not a short-term, but rather a long-term struggle. In his work "On the Correct Handling of Contradictions Among the People" — a work which demarcates eras — Chairman Mao pointed out: In China "the class struggle between the proletariat and the bourgeoisie, among the various political forces, and on the ideological front is still protracted, still twisting and turning, and sometimes even violent." Chairman Mao also pointed out: "The struggle for victory or defeat on the ideological front between socialism and capitalism in China will still require a rather long time to be resolved. This is because the influence of the bourgeoisie and the intellectuals from the old society will still exist for a long time, and their ideology will also continue for a long time. If we are not sufficiently aware of this situation, or fail to recognize it altogether, we will commit gross errors and neglect the necessary ideological struggle."

To varying degrees many people still have bourgeois tendencies and proletarian tendencies. Only people with Chairman Mao's highest standards of Marxism-Leninism can reject, conquer, and eradicate the bourgeois side. If the level of Marxism-Leninism is slightly lower, the struggle between these two sides will continue in one's mind. The overthrow of the bourgeoisie and the destruction of its class political power can be completed in a relatively short time. The overthrow of its system of ownership can also be complete within a short time. But overthrowing the ideological bases of the exploiting classes and the bourgeoisie is no simple task; it will take a long time. Moreover, if we do not fight for a final victory on this front, then the victories in political power and economics may slip away. The accomplishments brought forth in past revolutions, the fruits of revolution, the revolutionary goals struggled for by the masses may all be stolen away bit by bit by the bour- geoisie. They may be seized secretly, or violently in broad daylight.

Therefore we should open up a violent struggle on the ideo- logical front and carry on a protracted struggle. Only in this way can we guarantee the consolidation of proletarian political power, ensure consolidation of the socialist system of owner- ship, and move forward. Otherwise political power will slowly change color or develop into a violent counterrevolution- ary coup, the capitalist system of ownership will come to re- place the socialist system, and the ownership system of the landlords and rich peasants will come to replace the system of the people's communes. Therefore, victory or defeat in this struggle will determine China's direction and destiny. It will also influence the destiny of all mankind. With regard to the present period, China may be said to be playing a decisive role in the world. With regard to the revolution as it affects world revolution, China today is a decisive factor. If we make a com- parison on this point, no country has as great a role as China's. As long as China does not falter or change its nature, the world has hope. Many areas have fallen, have become black; our in- fluence can still make them bright again, make them go from black to red. Many places in the world have revolutionary forces which have already risen, or are just beginning to rise; the majority always want revolution, and they look to us for support. Consequently, the Great Proletarian Cultural Revolu- tion is a very important matter, an event which concerns the fate of many countries. This is a question of the proletariat's engaging in an unusually severe class struggle, of one class overcoming another class, or being overcome. Therefore we must especially strengthen our class viewpoint, our concept of class struggle; only then can we vigorously engage in the

Cultural Revolution; only then can we catch up with the great spirit and courage of Chairman Mao in the Cultural Revolution. Otherwise, we will never catch up and will always commit errors. Ordinarily this was a question often debated by old students. But under new conditions, a renewal of emphasis has its role. Do we not put up the mottos we write at one place day and night so that we can recite them by heart? But it is always better to take a look frequently, and all the more so today. Actually, the ideological movement and living ideas today, from top to bottom, and from bottom to top, all have this kind of problem. Therefore we need to raise this question again, and this is the first point I want to discuss today....

50

INSTRUCTION ON THE CULTURAL REVOLUTION*
(August 9, 1967)

You have talked about a variety of situations, and I am not as familiar with them as you are. The condition is tense in all regions and areas. Specific problems should be resolved by the premier and the Cultural Revolution Group of the Central Committee. They are working day and night. Different methods should be applied for the solution of specific problems in different areas. Concerning the problem of Wuhan, I have asked Chairman Mao for instructions and have no specific measures in mind myself. The instructions of Chairman Mao should be followed resolutely in dealing with it.

According to the directive given to us by Chairman Mao, a bad situation can, under certain circumstances, turn into a good situation. The Wuhan Incident was an extremely bad event, but it has given great impetus to every part of the whole nation, and its educational significance has been great. At this time it has thoroughly exposed the reactionary line of Ch'en Tsai-tao, exposed counterrevolution, and exposed the acute and compli-

---

"Tui wen-ko ti chih-shih." Chu-ying tung-fang-hung [East Is Red, Pearl River Studio, Canton], September 13, 1967; reprinted in Lin Piao chuan-chi [Special Collection on Lin Piao] (Hong Kong: Chung-kuo wen-t'i yen-chiu chung-hsin, 1970), pp. 104-110; and under the different title of "Important Speech of August 9" ["Pa-chiu" chung-yao chiang-hua], in Kung-fei wen-hua ta-ko-ming chung-yao wen-chien hui-pien [Collection of Important Documents on the Great Cultural Revolution of the Communist Bandits] (Taipei: Kuo-fang-pu, ch'ing-pao-chü, 1969), pp. 214-219.

cated nature of class struggle.

Of all the great military regions of the country, there were two about which we were uneasy. One was Peking, the other was Wuhan; there was no way for us to hold them. The Great Cultural Revolution has solved this problem. The law of events says that when a thing has reached its nadir, it will then turn for the better. Chairman Mao says that once an infection has burst, it will quickly heal. The forces of revolution are always advancing; the forces of reaction will always be defeated. Ch'en Tsai-tao, no matter how reactionary, could not go against the revolutionary current. For something to be latent is not as good as for it to be exposed; thus the exposure of bad men and bad things is good. Chairman Mao has instructed us that when an infection has burst, then it will quickly heal; something that does not hurt and does not itch can dig in; if the problem is not solved and is not completely exposed, there will be no reason to strike it down.

The situation of the Great Cultural Revolution is excellent; it has already achieved great and splendid victories. We relied on two conditions to launch the Great Cultural Revolution: the first was the thought of Chairman Mao and his lofty prestige; the second was the strength of the People's Liberation Army. Only under these two conditions did we dare fully to mobilize the masses. With these two conditions, bad things could be changed into good. Without these two conditions, especially without the brilliant leadership of Chairman Mao and the absolute authority of the thought of Mao tse-tung, it could not have been done. Only because we have Chairman Mao can we have courage and spirit. Today we have Chairman Mao, in excellent health, personally leading us and personally taking the helm. During the Great Cultural Revolution he has let all kinds of bad things be exposed fully; he has drawn out hidden calamities and caused them to turn into things that are beneficial to the proletariat, to turn into good things; he has made our government even more stable, and he has gotten rid of an old stage and turned it into a new and victorious stage.

The victory of the Great Cultural Revolution has been very great. The cost has been very slight, very slight indeed; the victory has been very great, very great indeed. On the surface things have seemed confused, but this confusion has been the result of creating confusion in the reactionary line, of creating confusion among the reactionary classes, of exposing all of them, and of causing the downfall of the small group in power who were taking the capitalist road. This confusion is necessary and normal; if there were no confusion, then reactionary things could not be exposed. That we have dared to act in this manner is precisely because of the lofty prestige of Chairman Mao and the strength of the People's Liberation Army. Given these conditions, if we did not let things be exposed now, then when could they be exposed? Under Chairman Mao's leadership, confusion is not to be feared.

Confusion occurs under four circumstances: (1) Good men struggle against bad men. (2) Bad men struggle against bad men. This is a force that we can indirectly use to our own benefit. (3) Bad men struggle against good men, such as in the cases of the Peking Military Region, the Navy, the Air Force, the Headquarters of the General Staff, and the General Logistics Department; good men have suffered rectification [at the hands of bad men]; they have eaten bitterness, but now they have tasted sweetness. (4) Good men struggle against good men, which is of course not good and does much damage; but this is an internal contradiction and can easily be resolved. Only in the third circumstance did bad men struggle against good men and did good men suffer rectification. Comrade Ch'iu Hui-tso [head of the General Logistics Department] underwent this for more than a month. Li Tso-p'eng, Wang Hung-k'un, and Chang Hsiu-ch'uan were also rectified. Wu Fa-hsien's case was also similar. In the past you have eaten bitterness, but now you have tasted sweetness. If bad men are rectifying good men, then there is nothing to fear, for at worst it will be like the experiences of Ch'iu Hui-tso, Li, Wang, Chang, and Wu Fa-hsien; you must be patient and calm. See how favorable the situation is to us; this is a policy unequaled in a hundred years, in a thousand years. We have our great leader Chairman Mao in excellent health; as long as we have the two conditions of Chairman Mao's lofty prestige and the strength of the People's Liberation Army,

then we shall not be afraid, for bad men certainly will be criticized and repudiated, and they will be punished. Even someone
who kicks over Heaven can still be put down. [At this point
this version of the Chinese text omits a paragraph on Hsü Shih-
yu, commander of the Nanking Military Region.]

Every military region has comrades who have made mistakes.
Now a Ch'en Tsai-tao has emerged; we do not want to go on to
produce a Li Tsai-tao or a Chang Tsai-tao; those who still can
be saved from this should be saved. At present none of us has
collapsed, nor do we expect to, but each of us should resolve
to correct our mistakes. If we do not resolve to correct our
mistakes, then we are certain of going along the road to
destruction, and there will be nothing to prevent it. If we do not
want to collapse, then there are three conditions to be observed:

1. You should firmly grasp the situation below; you should
carry on investigation of the Leftists, the Rightists, and the
various mass organizations in order to understand the situation.
Chairman Mao has said that investigation and study are basic
tasks. Only if you firmly grasp the true situation can you bring
up questions and the methods of their solution.

2. Closely follow the Central Committee. Ask for instructions and report to Chairman Mao, the Central Committee, and
the Cultural Revolution Group. You should not think that you
understand the matter yourself and therefore not report to the
Central Committee; you should not consider something a petty
matter and hence try to handle it yourself; you should not consider yourself so intelligent that you need not ask for instructions and make reports; and you should not be afraid of bother-
ing the Central Committee. No matter whether it is a large or
a small matter, you should always ask for instructions and
make reports. The premier and the comrades of the Cultural
Revolution Group are at work day and night. You can send tele-
grams or make phone calls. If you make a phone call few people will see it and communication will be slow, but if you send
a telegram everyone will see it. You could also come by plane
and arrive in an hour or two. You yourself should not take
things for granted, you should not act cleverly, you should not
advocate something on your own initiative. I want to stress

this; of the three conditions, this one is the most important.

3. One year of the Great Cultural Revolution has passed, and now the ranks of the Leftists and Rightists are clearly distinguishable. You absolutely cannot use whether or not they have attacked military regions as a criterion for delineating Leftists and Rightists. As a basis for delineating Leftists and Rightists you should take whether they support or oppose this Great Cultural Revolution launched by Chairman Mao himself, and whether they defend or oppose Chairman Mao. You should stand firmly beside Chairman Mao, stand beside the Leftists, and stand beside the masses. You should not consider merely whether class origins are pure of whether Party members or cadres are numerous when you divide people into Leftists and Rightists or when you look at problems. Class origins should be looked at, of course, but you should not only look at class origins; the most important thing is to realize on what party line these people stand. As for the treatment of the conservative faction, you must fully carry out political thought work; you must carry out the work of striving to break them up; you must not let them stand against us for any period; you must strive for those greatly hoodwinked masses and make them stand on the side of our revolutionary faction. As for the heads of the conservative faction, you should proceed according to the spirit of Chairman Mao's directive and let the masses seize them. You should also determinedly support the Leftists and strive to win over those of the masses who have been hoodwinked. Leftists themselves have problems, and you should stress joining together and advise them to avoid internal fighting; they should not take up departmentalism, showing off, or petty organizationism, for these are of no benefit to the Leftists, but are of benefit to the Rightists. You must not oppress the masses and thus produce problems and bad conditions; you must ask for instructions and report to the Central Committee; you should not be frantic, but slowly resolve things step by step, as in "four fasts and one slow"; you should make conditions clear to all, then report and ask instructions from the Central Committee, wait for approval, and then act. This is the consistent work-style of Chairman Mao.

Speaking honestly, I am worried about the comrades who take
up this kind of heavy responsibility and make mistakes that will
not be of benefit to the Great Cultural Revolution. At present
we rely on the army; if the army makes no mistakes, then all
will be well. If you do not want to make mistakes, then you
should rely on the Leftists and rely on the masses, and, most
important, you should ask the Central Committee and the Cultural Revolution Group for instructions. If you make mistakes
you should improve your attitude and as soon as possible recognize and examine your mistakes, for the faster you correct
them, the better — and the masses will be satisfied and will
understand. To make mistakes and yet not recognize them as
mistakes, to dodge and dissemble and hem and haw is not good;
to stoutly refuse to correct mistakes is dangerous; an obstinate
method will not work. Those of our ranks who have joined the
Great Cultural Revolution have rushed off to the front at great
speed, and those who do not understand the circumstances inevitably make mistakes; those who make mistakes but do not
admit it will be grabbed by the queue; those who make mistakes
but correct them will be able to gain the full understanding of
the masses. This ought to be the style of a member of the
Communist Party.

In past revolutions people have also rushed off to the front.
The Agrarian Revolution, the Autumn Harvest Uprisings, fighting local bullies, fighting Chiang Kai-shek, fighting the Japanese — all these events made people rush off to the front. After
several decades, the conditions of the agricultural villages
were already familiar to us, and all those problems had become
clear; after the revolution triumphed we entered a new stage,
a new process, which in turn produced new conditions. Socialist revolutionary theory, line, direction, policy — we had studied none of them; in thought and theory we were unprepared.
In the past, the three great mountains were overthrown, but
what were carried out were bourgeois-democratic revolutions;
all were democratic revolutions of a bourgeois nature. After
they were successful, things changed, and the mandate of the
bourgeoisie was changed. The present revolution is to change
the mandate of some of the people who were part of the revolu-

tion that we originally carried out. For this sort of revolution we had no preparation; nor were we familiar with it. Only the level of Chairman Mao's theory was sufficiently high. In theoretical line, thought, direction, and policy he was farsighted, for he had the idea in mind long before this and had made preparations. Comrades whose level of theory was also high were also prepared, but most of the rest of us did not have ideological preparation. Formerly we were familiar with the rural Agrarian Revolution, but we were not familiar with capitalism. In the United States, England, France, Japan, and other countries, capitalism was fully developed, and its exploitation and aggression were clearly visible to the ordinary worker. But Chinese capitalism was not fully developed, and moreover we had been in the rural villages and had not seen any capitalism, and our understanding of the laws of capitalist development was scant. For instance, if we use bourgeois-democratic ideology to view today's revolution, then mistakes will be unavoidable and we will not be able to understand the present Great Cultural Revolution. If we simply take the old methods of fighting local bullies, Chiang Kai-shek, or the Japanese and move them up intact to the present, then mistakes will be unavoidable. There are two kinds of people who make mistakes: one kind is willing to reform and the other is unwilling; those who are unwilling to reform are the more injurious to the Party. The questions discussed by Chairman Mao at the Second Plenum of the Seventh Congress Central Committee have great significance for the socialist revolution and are the highest development of Marxism. But what we have failed to realize is that when we do new work, our brains are still full of the old. Our Party is the political party of the proletariat, but of the leadership group of the past, only the very core of leaders were authentic Marxist-Leninists and, except for this backbone, quite a few of them had a bourgeois ideology, and some were bourgeois elements. So we absolutely must correct any mistakes we have made, for if we do not correct them, they could make us go down the capitalist road, and the whole nation would then change its color, and individuals could form into a small group in authority taking the capitalist road. This Great Cultural Revolution in

reality proceeds through a political revolution; if there were
no political revolution, then there would be capitalism. The
Great Cultural Revolution is a revolution in socialist political
thought; if there is no revolution in political thought, then there
can be no socialist society. In theory and ideology, we do not
know what is capitalism or what is socialism; what is correct
and what is mistaken is not clear to us; only if we thoroughly
study the theories of Chairman Mao can we clear this up. Only
when the acceptance of the thought of Chairman Mao has been
achieved fully can we proceed to socialism. Today, under the
leadership of Chairman Mao, we must carefully study and reform our world view, or else we will make mistakes; only if
we study and comprehend the thought of Chairman Mao will we
understand Marxism-Leninism, and only then will we be free
from mistakes.

In making the Great Cultural Revolution a success we must
rely on the People's Liberation Army built by Chairman Mao,
we must avoid making mistakes, and we must frequently ask
for instructions from the Central Committee and the Cultural
Revolution Group. Moreover, on another front, we must intensify political thought work in the ranks, we must put politics in
command, we must study the works of Chairman Mao, we must
have the thought of Chairman Mao direct everything, and we
must make ourselves face and develop in the socialist direction
indicated by Chairman Mao; we must not develop toward capitalism. We must put Chairman Mao's thought in command. Work
in the ranks will have many ramifications; if we grasp and
study the works of Chairman Mao, make a living studying and
a living application of them, then we can easily handle all problems. But if we do not do this, then we would be oppressing
the people, just as happened in Inner Mongolia. The General
Political Department of the Army, after its antiextravagance
policy [fan-t'an cheng], will then be able to grasp and study
the works of Chairman Mao for an uninterrupted period; but,
in the midst of the Great Cultural Revolution, such an opportunity is lacking, and there are those who have not kept up with
the situation. Leading cadres have continually made mistakes,
and we must certainly prevent them from collapsing; at present

we should still be thinking of ways to get them to carry things through to a successful conclusion. In studying the works of Chairman Mao it is most important to rely on each of the great military regions, armies, divisions, regiments, battalions, and companies; firmly grasping and studying the works of Chairman Mao is a great doctrine. In work, the two most important things are relying on the great military regions and firmly grasping the works of Chairman Mao and studying them; these two educational lines teach the army ranks to correctly handle the Leftists, the little generals of the Red Guards, and the revolutionary masses. Now we must grasp the tool of criticism and criticize the reactionary bourgeois line and criticize those in power taking the capitalist road. Only if we hold well to political thought work, clear the heads of cadres and fighters, and arm ourselves with the thought of Mao Tse-tung — only then will we be able to fulfill our duty of "three supports" and "two mobilizations." Some cadres should take part in three-in-one work, while others should pay more attention to local work. The basic problem of the revolution is the question of political power. But there are many people who are insufficiently aware of the nature of this question, or of the important nature of political power, or of the important nature of the leadership group; their minds must be made clear on these points. For the last eighteen years the capitalist-roaders have held some of the organs of the Party and the government. Since the Great Cultural Revolution began, some of these groups have been overthrown; now we must establish a new state apparatus. The leadership group is very important. The leadership group is the regime; it is the state apparatus. The former leadership group of the clique that was in power was not able to constitute a state apparatus and has collapsed, and the army has taken charge of the situation. In our state apparatus there were many things that were capitalist and revisionist, so there is nothing wrong with their collapse — if they have collapsed, then let them. Our leadership group should be made up of people who are always loyal to Chairman Mao, and who are always taking the revolutionary road of Chairman Mao. With the army now in charge, we do not want to make any mistakes, and if we do make mistakes we must immediately correct them, depending on the teachings and leadership of Chairman Mao. Cadres of the military regions, the provincial military regions, and the military personnel bureau who have made mistakes should come forth to be admonished in accordance with the directive of Chairman Mao; they should let the revolutionary rebels be their teachers and let their own mistakes serve as teaching materials, and they should come forth to receive the teachings of experience. Those past Party and government officials whose thought was illogical also ought to undergo education. For those whose thought is illogical to undergo education and be transformed is a good thing, and we welcome those who return to the revolutionary line of Chairman Mao. We must teach these cadres according to the teaching of Chairman Mao: "Take warning from the past in order to be careful for the future, treat the illness to save the man." That is to say, men who have temporarily toppled, once reeducated, are good. The majority of cadres can be won over; those whose thought is illogical can also be won over — we can make new men of them. Once they have corrected their mistakes they can still work; those whose thoughts are still illogical can be changed; if it is possible to avoid knocking them down, then we should avoid it, while even those we knock down can be reeducated. The leadership group is the state apparatus, and it must be a group that is in accord with the thought of Chairman Mao, one which stands on the revolutionary line of Chairman Mao; if it does not, then it must be removed, but we must not punish the members without educating them.

Once again I want to speak of the three conditions, especially the second, for I am afraid you may make mistakes. In your work it is best to be a little slower and consider matters a little more; there is not need to be frantic; let things be drawn out over a few days' time — the sky will not fall. The premier and Comrades Ch'en Po-ta and Chiang Ch'ing are working day and night. I hope that everyone, in positions high and low, will pay attention to asking for instructions and making reports.

51

SPEECH AT RALLY CELEBRATING THE
EIGHTEENTH ANNIVERSARY OF THE FOUNDING
OF THE PEOPLE'S REPUBLIC OF CHINA*
(October 1, 1967)

Comrades and Friends:

Today is the eighteenth anniversary of the founding of the
People's Republic of China. On this glorious festive occasion,
on behalf of our great leader Chairman Mao, the Central Committee of the Party, the Government of the People's Republic
of China, the Military Commission of the Party's Central Committee, and the Cultural Revolution Group under the Party's
Central Committee, I most warmly salute the workers, peasants, commanders, and fighters of the People's Liberation
Army, the Red Guards, the revolutionary cadres and revolutionary intellectuals and the people of all nationalities throughout the country, and extend a hearty welcome to our comrades
and friends who have come from different parts of the world!

We are celebrating the eighteenth anniversary of the founding
of the People's Republic of China at a time when tremendous
victories have been won in the Great Proletarian Cultural Revolution and an excellent situation prevails both in China and in
the whole world.

---

*"Tsai Chung-Hua jen-min kung-ho-kuo ch'eng-li shih-pa
chou-nien ch'ing-chu ta-hui-shang ti chiang-hua." Hung-ch'i
[Red Flag], No. 15 (October 6, 1967), 5-7; Jen-min jih-pao
[People's Daily], October 2, 1967. This translation is taken,
with minor editorial revisions, from Peking Review, No. 41
(October 6, 1967), 9-10.

The Great Proletarian Cultural Revolution movement initiated and led personally by Chairman Mao has spread to the whole of China. Hundreds of millions of people have been aroused. From the capital to the border regions, from the cities to the country-side, and from factory workshops to workers' homes, everyone, from teenagers to grey-haired old folk, concerns himself with state affairs and with the consolidation and strengthening of the dictatorship of the proletariat. Never before has a mass move-ment been so extensive and deep-going as the present one. The broad masses of workers and peasants, commanders and fight-ers of the People's Liberation Army, Red Guards, revolution-ary cadres and revolutionary intellectuals, gradually uniting themselves through their struggles in the past year, have formed a mighty revolutionary army. Under the leadership of the Party's Central Committee headed by Chairman Mao, they have badly routed the handful of Party persons in authority tak-ing the capitalist road headed by China's Khrushchev, who have collapsed on all fronts.

Frightened out of their wits by China's Great Proletarian Cultural Revolution, U.S. imperialism, Soviet revisionism, and all reaction hoped that this great revolution would upset our national economy. The facts have turned out to be exactly the opposite of the wishes of these overlords. The Great Proletar-ian Cultural Revolution has further liberated the productive forces. Glad tidings about the successes in our industrial pro-duction keep on coming in. In agriculture, we are reaping a good harvest for the sixth consecutive year. Our markets are thriving and the prices are stable. The successful explosion of China's hydrogen bomb indicates a new level in the develop-ment of science and technology. What is even more important, the Great Cultural Revolution has educated the masses and the youth, greatly promoted the revolutionization of the thinking of the entire Chinese people, enhanced the great unity of the peo-ple of all nationalities, and tempered our cadres and all the PLA commanders and fighters. Our great motherland has never been so powerful as it is today.

China's Great Proletarian Cultural Revolution has won

decisive victory. In the history of the international communist movement, this is the first great revolution launched by the proletariat itself in a country under the dictatorship of the proletariat. It is an epoch-making new development of Marxism-Leninism which Chairman Mao has effected with genius and in a creative way.

In response to the great call of Chairman Mao, we must not only thoroughly destroy the bourgeois headquarters organizationally, but must also carry out more extensive and penetrating revolutionary mass criticism and repudiation so that the handful of Party persons in authority taking the capitalist road headed by China's Khrushchev will be completely overthrown and discredited politically, ideologically, and theoretically and will never be able to rise again. Such mass criticism and repudiation should be combined with the struggle-criticism-transformation in the respective units so that the great red banner of Mao Tse-tung's thought will fly over all fronts.

At present, the most important task before us is, in accordance with Chairman Mao's teachings and his theory, line, principles and policy for making revolution under the dictatorship of the proletariat, to hold fast to the general orientation of the revolutionary struggle pointed out by Chairman Mao, to closely follow his strategic plan and, through the revolutionary mass criticism and repudiation combined with the struggle-criticism-transformation in the respective units, to consolidate and develop the revolutionary great alliance and revolutionary "three-way combination" and make a success of the struggle-criticism-transformation in these units, thus carrying the Great Proletarian Cultural Revolution through to the end.

Chairman Mao has recently instructed us that "it is imperative to combat selfishness and criticize and repudiate revisionism." By combating selfishness, we mean to use Marxism-Leninism-Mao Tse-tung Thought to fight selfish ideas in one's own mind. By criticizing and repudiating revisionism, we mean to use Marxism-Leninism-Mao Tse-tung thought to combat revisionism and struggle against the handful of Party persons in authority taking the capitalist road. These two tasks are interrelated. Only when we have done a good job of eradicating self-ish ideas can we better carry on the struggle against revisionism through to the end. We must respond to the great call of Chairman Mao and, with the instruction "combat selfishness and criticize and repudiate revisionism" as the guiding principle, strengthen the ideological education of the army and civilian cadres and of the Red Guards. Various kinds of study classes should be organized both at the central and local levels and can also be run by the revolutionary mass organizations, so that the whole country will be turned into a great school of Mao Tse-tung's thought. These studies will help our veteran and new cadres and young revolutionary fighters to study and apply Mao Tse-tung's thought in a creative way, liquidate all sorts of nonproletarian ideas in their minds, raise their ideological and political level, and perform new meritorious deeds for the people.

We must respond to the great call of Chairman Mao and "take firm hold of the revolution and promote production," energetically promote the development of our industrial and agricultural production, and rapidly raise our scientific and technological level.

We must respond to the great call of Chairman Mao and unfold a movement of "supporting the army and cherishing the people." We must strengthen the dictatorship of the proletariat and resolutely suppress the sabotaging activities by class enemies, domestic and foreign.

The Great Proletarian Cultural Revolution is a movement that integrates Mao Tse-tung's thought with the broad masses of the people. Once Mao Tse-tung's thought is grasped by hundreds of millions of people, it turns into an invincible material force, ensuring that the dictatorship of the proletariat in our country will never change its color and enabling our socialist revolution and socialist construction to advance victoriously along the road of Mao Tse-tung's thought!

Proletarian revolutionaries, unite, hold high the great red banner of Mao Tse-tung's thought and carry the Great Proletarian Cultural Revolution through to the end!

Workers of all countries, unite; workers of the world, unite with the oppressed peoples and oppressed nations!

Down with imperialism headed by the United States!

Down with modern revisionism with the Soviet revisionist leading clique as its center!

Resolute support to the Vietnamese people in their great war against U.S. aggression and for national salvation!

Resolute support to the revolutionary struggles of the peoples of Asia, Africa, and Latin America!

Resolute support to the revolutionary struggles of all peoples!

We are determined to liberate Taiwan!

Long live the great unity of the people of all nationalities of China!

Long live the People's Republic of China!

Long live the great, glorious and correct Communist Party of China!

Long live great Marxism-Leninism!

Long live the ever-victorious thought of Mao Tse-tung!

Long live Chairman Mao, our great teacher, great leader, great supreme commander and great helmsman! A long life, and long, long life to him!

52

SPEECH AT PEKING RALLY COMMEMORATING
THE FIFTIETH ANNIVERSARY OF THE
OCTOBER REVOLUTION*
(November 6, 1967)

Comrades, Young Red Guard Fighters, and Friends:

Today the Chinese people join the proletarians and revolutionary people throughout the world in grand and solemn commemoration of the fiftieth anniversary of the Great October Socialist Revolution.

The October Revolution led by the great Lenin was a turning point in human history.

The victory of the October Revolution broke through the dark rule of capitalism, established the first state of the dictatorship of the proletariat in the world, and opened a new era of the world proletarian revolution.

For more than one hundred years since Marx and Engels formulated the theory of scientific socialism, the international proletariat, advancing wave upon wave and making heroic sacrifices, has been waging arduous struggles for the great ideal of communism and has performed immortal exploits in the cause of the emancipation of mankind.

In his struggle against the revisionism of the Second

---

*"Tsai shou-tu jen-min chi-nien shih-yüeh ke-ming wu-shih chou-nien ta-hui shang ti chiang-hua." Jen-min jih-pao [People's Daily], November 7, 1967; Hung-ch'i [Red Flag], No. 16 (November 23, 1967), 7-10. This translation is taken, with minor editorial revisions, from Peking Review, No. 46 (November 10, 1967), 5-8.

International and in the great practice of leading the October
Socialist Revolution, Lenin solved a series of problems of the
proletarian revolution and the dictatorship of the proletariat
as well as the problem of victory for socialism in one country,
thus developing Marxism to the stage of Leninism. Leninism
is Marxism in the era of imperialism and proletarian revolution. The salvoes of the October Revolution brought Leninism
to all countries, so that the world took on an entirely new look.

In the last fifty years, following the road of the October Revolution under the banner of Marxism-Leninism, the proletariat
and revolutionary people of the world have carried world history forward to another entirely new era, the era in which imperialism is heading for total collapse and socialism is advancing to worldwide victory. It is a great new era in which
the proletariat and the bourgeoisie are locked in the decisive
battle on a worldwide scale.

Led by the great leader Chairman Mao, the Chinese people
have followed up their victory in the national-democratic revolution with great victories in the socialist revolution and socialist construction. Socialist China has become the mighty
bulwark of world revolution. Adhering to the road of the October Revolution, the heroic people of Albania have raised a
bright red banner in Europe. By their war against U.S. imperialist aggression and for national salvation, the Vietnamese
people have set a brilliant example of struggle against imperialism for the people of the whole world. The movement of
national-democratic revolution in Asia, Africa, and Latin
America is developing vigorously. The ranks of the Marxist-
Leninists are growing steadily, and a new situation has emerged
in the international communist movement.

Compared with half a century ago, the world proletarian revolution today is far deeper in content, far broader in scope, and
far sharper in its struggle. The new historical era has posed a
series of important new problems for Marxist-Leninists. However, in the final analysis, the most fundamental problem remains that of seizing and consolidating political power.

Chairman Mao says: "The aim of every revolutionary

struggle in the world is the seizure and consolidation of political power." This is a great Marxist-Leninist truth.

The struggle between the Marxist-Leninists and the revisionists always focuses on this fundamental issue. The modern revisionists, represented by Khrushchev and his successors, Brezhnev, Kosygin, and company, are wildly opposing the revolution of the people of the world and have openly abandoned the dictatorship of the proletariat and brought about an all-round capitalist restoration in the Soviet Union. This is a monstrous betrayal of the October Revolution. It is a monstrous betrayal of Marxism-Leninism. It is a monstrous betrayal of the great Soviet people and the people of the world. Therefore, if the proletariat fails to smash the wanton attacks of the modern revisionists, if it does not firmly defend the road of the October Revolution opened up by the great Lenin, continue to advance along this road under the new historical conditions and thoroughly solve the question of how to seize and consolidate political power, it will not be able to win final victory, or will probably lose political power even after seizing it, and, like the Soviet people, will come under the rule of a new privileged bourgeois stratum.

It is our good fortune that because Comrade Mao Tse-tung has comprehensively inherited and developed the teachings of Marx, Engels, Lenin, and Stalin on proletarian revolution and the dictatorship of the proletariat, the most fundamental issue of the world proletarian revolution, that is, the road to the seizure and consolidation of political power, has been brought to a higher stage in theory and in practice. Our great leader Chairman Mao has developed Marxism-Leninism and raised it to an entirely new peak. The ever-victorious thought of Mao Tse-tung is Marxism-Leninism in the era in which imperialism is heading for total collapse and socialism is advancing to worldwide victory.

In the course of leading the great struggle of the Chinese revolution, Chairman Mao has with genius solved a whole series of complicated problems concerning the seizure of political power by force of arms. Under his leadership, the Chinese people went through the most protracted, fierce, arduous, and complex people's revolutionary war in the history of the world proletarian revolution and founded the red political power, the dictatorship of the proletariat.

The way the Chinese people seized political power by force of arms under Chairman Mao's leadership may be summarized as follows: Under the leadership of the political party of the proletariat, to arouse the peasant masses in the countryside to wage guerrilla war, unfold an agrarian revolution, build rural base areas, use the countryside to encircle the cities, and finally capture the cities. This is a great new development of the road to the seizure of political power by force of arms indicated by the October Revolution.

Chairman Mao has said: "As a rule, revolution starts, grows and triumphs first in those places in which the counterrevolutionary forces are comparatively weak." Since in our time all the reactionary ruling classes have a tight grip on the main cities, it is necessary for a revolutionary political party to utilize the vulnerable links and areas of reactionary rule, fully arouse the masses, conduct guerrilla warfare, establish stable revolutionary bases and so build up and temper their own forces and, through prolonged fighting, strive step by step for complete victory in the revolution. Hence, reliance on the masses to build rural revolutionary base areas and use the countryside to encircle the cities is a historic task which the oppressed nations and peoples in the world today must seriously study and tackle in their fight to seize political power by force of arms.

Not only has Comrade Mao Tse-tung creatively developed Leninism on the question of seizure of political power by the proletariat, he has made an epoch-making creative development of Leninism on the most important question of our time — the question of consolidating the dictatorship of the proletariat and preventing the restoration of capitalism.

From the first day of the victory of the October Revolution, Lenin paid close attention to the consolidation of the new-born Soviet state power. He recognized the sharp and protracted nature of the class struggle under the dictatorship of the proletariat, pointing out that "the transition from capitalism to communism takes an entire historical epoch. Until this epoch is over, the exploiters inevitably cherish the hope of restoration, and this hope turns into attempts at restoration."

The biggest lesson in the history of the international communist movement in the last fifty years is the restoration of capitalism in the Soviet Union and other socialist countries. This harsh fact has strikingly brought the Marxist-Leninists of the world face to face with the question of how to consolidate the dictatorship of the proletariat and prevent the restoration of capitalism.

It is Comrade Mao Tse-tung, the great teacher of the world proletariat of our time, who in the new historical conditions, has systematically summed up the historical experience of the dictatorship of the proletariat in the world, scientifically analyzed the contradictions in socialist society, profoundly shown the laws of class struggle in socialist society and put forward a whole set of theory, line, principles, methods and policies for the continuation of the revolution under the dictatorship of the proletariat. With supreme courage and wisdom, Chairman Mao has successfully led the first Great Proletarian Cultural Revolution in history. This is an extremely important landmark, demonstrating that Marxism-Leninism has developed to the stage of Mao Tse-tung's thought.

The victory of the Great Proletarian Cultural Revolution has opened up in China, which has a quarter of the world's population, a bright path for consolidating the dictatorship of the proletariat and for carrying the socialist revolution through to the end. The proletariat and the revolutionary people of the world who are fighting imperialism, modern revisionism, and all reaction resolutely support our Great Proletarian Cultural Revolution. They find in the victory of this revolution tremendous inspiration, bright prospects, and greater confidence in victory.

The imperialists headed by the United States and their lackeys, the modern revisionists and all the reactionaries, have taken great pains to curse and vilify our Great Proletarian Cultural Revolution. This proves by negative example that our victory has dealt the enemy a very heavy blow and that they are nothing but a bunch of vampires that are bound to be destroyed.

The world is moving forward. And theory, which reflects the laws of the world, is likewise developing continuously.

Mao Tse-tung's thought is the banner of our era.

Once Mao Tse-tung's thought — Marxism-Leninism at its highest in the present era — is grasped, the oppressed nations and peoples will, through their own struggles, be able to win liberation.

Once Mao Tse-tung's thought — Marxism-Leninism at its highest in the present era — is grasped, the countries that have already established the dictatorship of the proletariat will, through their own struggles, be able to prevent the restoration of capitalism.

Once Mao Tse-tung's thought — Marxism-Leninism at its highest in the present era — is grasped, the people of those countries where political power has been usurped by the revisionists will, through their own struggles, be able to overthrow the rule of revisionism and reestablish the dictatorship of the proletariat.

Once Marxism-Leninism-Mao Tse-tung Thought is integrated with the revolutionary practice of the people of all countries, the entire old world will be shattered to smithereens.

Comrades, young Red Guard fighters, and friends:

The fifty years since the October Revolution have been years of fierce struggle between socialism and capitalism and between Marxism-Leninism and modern revisionism, with the former winning one victory after another. The imperialist system resembles a dying person who is sinking fast, like the sun setting beyond the Western Hills. The emergence of Khrushchev revisionism is a product of imperialist policy and reflects the deathbed struggle of imperialism. Although imperialism and revisionism will go on making trouble in collusion with each other, the reactionary adverse current can, after all, never become the main current. The dialectics of history is irresistible. Henceforth, the proletariat and the revolutionary people of the world will raise still higher the great red banner of Marxism-Leninism-Mao Tse-tung Thought, and march forward in giant strides along the road opened up by the October Revolution!

Those who betray the October Revolution can never escape the punishment of history. Khrushchev has long since fallen. In redoubling its efforts to pursue the policy of betrayal, the Brezhnev-Kosygin clique will not last long either. The proletariat and the working people of the Soviet Union, with their glorious tradition of revolution, will never forget the teachings of the great Lenin and Stalin. They are sure to rise in revolution under the banner of Leninism, overthrow the rule of the reactionary revisionist clique, and bring the Soviet Union back into the orbit of socialism.

Comrades, young Red Guard fighters, and friends!

The situation in our great motherland is excellent. Under the guidance of the latest instructions of the great leader Chairmao Mao, the Great Proletarian Cultural Revolution is forging ahead victoriously.

We must raise still higher the great banner of the October Revolution and the great banner of Marxism-Leninism-Mao Tse-tung Thought, and carry the Great Proletarian Cultural Revolution through to the end.

We must build our great motherland into a still more powerful base for world revolution.

We must give ever more vigorous support to the revolutionary struggles of the proletariat and people of all countries.

We must, together with the revolutionary people everywhere, carry through to the end the struggle against U.S.-led imperialism and against modern revisionism with the Soviet revisionist renegade clique as its center.

We must intensify our efforts in studying and mastering Mao Tse-tung thought and disseminate it still more widely throughout the world.

These are glorious tasks entrusted to the people of our country by history, and they are our incumbent internationalist duty.

Our great leader Chairman Mao has given the call: "Let the Marxist-Leninists of all countries unite, let the revolutionary people of the whole world unite and overthrow imperialism, modern revisionism, and all reaction. A new world without imperialism, without capitalism, and without exploitation of man by man will surely be built."

Let us fight with courage for the realization of this great call of Chairman Mao's!

Long live the Great October Socialist Revolution!

Long live the Great Proletarian Cultural Revolution!

Workers of all countries, unite!

Workers of all countries, unite with the oppressed peoples and oppressed nations!

Long live the invincible Marxism-Leninism-Mao Tse-tung Thought!

Long live the great teacher, great leader, great supreme commander, great helmsman Chairman Mao! A long, long life to him!

53

ON THE QUESTION OF "GIVING
PROMINENCE TO POLITICS"*
(November 1967)

Today I, the premier, and comrades from the Central Cultural Revolution Group are meeting with the Political Work
Group, the Literature and Art Group, and the Military Newspaper Group. All these three Groups are involved with political
and ideological work. Political work concerns ideology, concerns the essence, concerns revolutionization — it is the controlling factor in every undertaking. Political and ideological
work controls everything. Our army has up to now relied on
political ideology, relied on the thought of Mao Tse-tung. If we
stray from this, the Liberation Army will lose that which makes
it the Liberation Army; it will become an army of oppression.
If it is not a Marxist-Leninist army, not a proletarian army,
but rather a bourgeois army, then victory over our enemies
will be impossible.

The main task of our army is to fight, and also to join in
mass work, production, work projects, etc. There have in the
past been two theories about war: One asserts that if fighting

_____

*"'T'an 't'u-ch'u cheng-chih wen-t'i.'" Kung-fei wen-hua ta-
ko-ming chung-yao wen-chien hsü-pien [Supplement to Important Documents on the Great Cultural Revolution of the Communist Bandits] (Taipei: Kuo-fang-pu ch'ing-pao-chü, 1969), pp.
167-170. The three Groups referred to in the speech were reported to have been organized in August 1967 to take over the
functions of the General Political Department.

skills are well developed, then the soldiers' courage will be
great; the other asserts that if the soldiers' courage is great,
fighting skills will result. Fighting depends mainly on courage,
on not fearing death. Now, of course technique, weapons, and
strategy are relevant to overall strength, but the most important thing is not to fear death. Otherwise, things that are handled well in normal times, when they are needed on the battlefield, will collapse, and the fighting task will not be accomplished. It is a serious problem if, when one sees the fierce-
ness of the enemy's firepower and the strength of his fortifica-
tions, he refuses to continue fighting and just falls apart. To
revolutionize ideology with Mao Tse-tung thought in command
is crucial to the survival of the nation, the Party, and our political power — this determines whether the people will gain
all or lose all. This is the central political question, the essence of essences, the core of cores. Without an army there
is no political power, and without political power, there is
nothing. In other words, without an army, there is nothing. An
army depends on politics taking command, depends on the revolution of ideology. A vital army must be guided by progressive
ideology. Progressive ideology is not produced spontaneously
by the workers and peasants, but is the ideology of Chairman Mao.

Chairman Mao has incorporated progressive ideology from
abroad, such as the theories of Marx, Engels, Lenin, Stalin,
and others, as well as the progressive ideology of ancient China.
He has incorporated it judiciously, so it is the concentrated representation of the most progressive ideology of mankind. Today, the chief task for the army and the nation is to rely on
Mao Tse-tung thought to transform the face of China and of the
world, and to continue to transform them.

The struggle in our army is between the line which gives
prominence to military affairs and the line that gives prominence to politics. We must resolutely follow the line of giving
prominence to politics, but by no means discard military affairs — they are under the command of politics. Facts prove
that if political work is done well, training, production, work
projects, internal solidarity, discipline, and the relations between

army and people will also be done well, and wars will be fought
well. Everything is many-faceted, so essentials must be
grasped; when this is done, everything else will fall into place.
If all facets are grasped at once, and this is seen as one task
among others or neglected altogether, a mess will result; the
fundamental thing must be grasped, that is, politics must be
grasped. Mao Tse-tung thought must be used to lead the troops.
Armies have weapons and material, but people are most important. People are living weapons, living fighting strength. Without people, weapons become scrap metal. If we want to do things
even better, we can do so only by placing political work ahead
of all other work; it cannot be placed second or third; nor can
it be seen as equal to other work.

The Political Work, the Literature and Art, and the Military
Newspaper Groups should note and understand the situation at
the bottom, and should solicit instructions and report at any
time to the Chairman, the Central Committee, the premier, the
Central Cultural Revolution Group, and the Staff Group of the
Military Affairs Commission; and should discover problems
through attention and investigation, put forth opinions, and ask
instructions of relevant departments. These three groups must
all exhibit revolutionary fervor. The Military Newspaper Group
should seek out Comrades Ch'en Po-ta and Yao Wen-yüan; the
Literature and Art Group should seek out Comrades Chiang
Ch'ing and X X X; and the Political Work Group should seek out
the Staff Group of the Military Affairs Commission. These
three groups cannot work at cross-purposes, but must pull together and do their jobs well. Do not add personnel; just concentrate your strength and grasp the essential problems. Do
not grasp this and then that; but grasp what is essential, and it
won't be necessary to have many people. The General Political
Department can perhaps absorb a few people, but not too many.
We must follow the central instruction and streamline the organization — it must not become too large. If there are too
many people, it will be like three monks with no water to drink.
As mentioned above, both ends must be firmly grasped, living
ideology must be firmly grasped. Work should be organized

according to the tasks set out by the top and the situation at
the bottom; as the living ideology continuously changes at the
bottom, new tasks will continuously be put forward. If both
ends are not firmly grasped, nothing will be done well.

It is my opinion that you cannot take charge of everything.
Most important is first to take charge of study, and second to
grasp control of cadres. Actually, one is an ideological problem, and the other is an organizational problem. In studying
the works of Chairman Mao attention now is given to memorization, and some emphasize application. There must be some
memorization, but I think the main thing is to emphasize application. Factionalism must be overcome — support the Left but
do not support any factions. Just talk and no reform will not
work. Stress application. It is impossible to be familiar with
all of the cadres. Start with cadres at the army level and above,
and then at the division level. In the past, cadres were controlled by Hsiao Hua, and they did not ask instructions or report. We have had "three-eight cadres" in our army for over
thirty years; we have had "liberation cadres" for thirty years
too, and even forty years. Our army has plenty of cadres, and
many are talented, but we have not discovered which ones
should be promoted and which should not; which ones can be
used and which ones cannot. We are unsure how to deploy them,
how to fill in for those whom the Central Committee moves
around — we should all study and understand this better. We
must understand the political attitude and political behavior of
cadres. Everything must be done in accordance with the instructions of Chairman Mao.

Putting forward ideas and making use of people — one is an
ideological matter and the other is an organizational matter.
Revolutionize ideology well, and organize the work team well —
the concrete tasks are manifold. If you try to do this and do
that, you'll never finish, so the main thing is to grasp political
and ideological work. During these past few years (Lo Hsün-
ch'u: since Vice Chairman Lin has been directing our work) the
army's main task has been to grasp the living study and application of the works of Chairman Mao (the premier: this has

been grasped well). The next step is to organize work teams with careful investigation. No matter which "mountaintops" they are from, those who opposed Chairman Mao should not be used. Those who support Chairman Mao, give prominence to politics, exhibit revolutionary fervor, follow the Chairman's five requirements for revolutionary successors, and grasp the essentials will succeed.

Any place that does political work well can produce cadres — cadres like Lei Feng, Ts'ai Yung-hsiang, Wang Chieh, and Li Wen-chung, all of whom used Mao Tse-tung thought to lead the troops. If a unit's atmosphere is permeated with politics, there will be fewer transgressions (the premier: Truly spoken). That is right. You in the Political Work Group should grasp this main point. Some can come up with new things; and some cannot; so they still grab firmly the old methods. Don't be like Lo Jui-ch'ing and just put up an empty show. When the fighting starts, those who have practiced formalism will run to the back. The Political Work, Literature and Art, and Military Newspaper Groups must strengthen the ideological revolutionization of men.

54

INSTRUCTION ON THE PROBLEM
OF THE THREE-WAY ALLIANCE*
(1967 ?)

Without this campaign, this dynamic Great Cultural Revolution, many good people would be overlooked, successors would be overlooked, and new sprouts would be left undiscovered. In the course of this struggle, bad people will be exposed, pulled down, discredited, and destroyed; good people will come to the fore. This will guarantee our great plans for the next hundred years. Many good people, many proletarian revolutionaries, will come to the fore. Otherwise, they would remain buried in hell, suppressed and unable to rise. We will smash the bad people and discover the good ones. Without this revolution, the bad people could not be smashed, and the good ones could not be discovered; leadership would probably fall into the hands of the bad people.

It is not necessarily true that we must wait until all the members of a standing committee are liberated before a three-way alliance is formed. The participants in the alliance should be those who can carry on business; otherwise, you will have to continue to handle things. At the same time, if you do not take part in struggle, but just put in an appearance, that will not do. You must go through the ordeal of struggle. The participants in the alliance need a considerably long period of time to establish their authority among the masses.

---

*"Kuan-yü san-chieh-ho wen-t'i ti chih-shih." Lin Piao chuan-chi [A Special Collection on Lin Piao] (Hong Kong: Tzu-lien, 1970), pp. 124-125.

The number of cadres in units which have forged a three-way alliance should be kept as small as possible; they should be divided into several groups. Except those who are in charge of an office, students should return to school, workers should return to work. Otherwise, the situation will just revert to what it was before very quickly, so this habit should be cultivated from the beginning. Great alliances and three-way alliances cannot always match up to the ideal of purity; these people who can be helped should be helped as much as possible. As for the so-called "mixed pot," it includes those who have no leadership ability; those who have some should not be in the "mixed pot."

Things will be difficult for those rebels who do not rely on the army. The masses know the importance of weapons. If they seize power without the support of weapons, they will not rest easy, for there is no such thing as political power without weapons.

If they do not trust the army and do not trust revolutionary leadership cadres — meeting these two criteria — they should be reorganized. If they do not trust the representatives of mass organizations — thus meeting all three of the criteria — then they must be liquidated. It must be made clear to everyone that revolutionary committees are temporary organs of power, and for them to be perfect is impossible. Continuous adjustment must go on; absorb good people, and weed out those who are bad. In one sense they represent political power today; in another they make preparations for transition to more formal structures.

55

ON THE SOCIAL FOUNDATION
OF REVISIONISM*
(1967 ?)

To fight revisionism and to prevent its emergence is the
main task of the Great Cultural Revolution. The main foundation of Soviet revisionism is the privileged stratum. To prevent revisionism, it is imperative to stamp out this privileged
stratum, to stamp out all the roots of such a privileged stratum.

The Party-building line headed by Liu-Teng is a revisionist
one; it is the root of a privileged stratum in our country. This
line opposes the use of Mao Tse-tung's thought to unify the
whole Party and establishes authorities at high and low levels.
It permits the people at the subordinate level only to follow orders, but does not allow them to use the thought of Mao Tse-
tung as the supreme directive to command everything. It promotes the organizational principle of slavishness and the political privileges of the leadership, but boycotts the leadership
of Chairman Mao. It promotes an independent small kingdom
and the establishment of a royalist party.

This line opposes Chairman Mao's directives and disallows
the cadres to participate in labor and to mingle with the masses.

---

*"Hsiu-cheng chu-i ti she-hui chi-ch'u." Hung-ch'i p'iao-
p'iao [Red Flags Wave, a Red Guard publication in Canton],
No. 4 (January 1968). This translation is taken, with minor editorial revisions, from Survey of China Mainland Press (Hong
Kong), No. 4155 (February 9, 1968), 3-4. A Japanese version
of this document may be found in Chūgoku kenkyū geppō [Monthly
Research Report on China, Tokyo], December 1969, 13-14.

It undermines the glorious traditions of our Party and our
army in leading a hard and frugal life and in maintaining solidarity at the higher and lower levels. It promotes economic
privileges of cadres, raising their salaries and giving them
special material treatment. It enlarges the differences between
worker and peasant. In short, this line opposes Chairman Mao's
cadre policy, which looks upon a cadre as a servant of the people.

In the final analysis it inherits the bureaucratic system of
the exploiting classes. In the last analysis it aims at protecting the system of exploitation. This line leads to a decline in
the fighting will of the cadres, causing them to chase after
comfort and leisure, to seek no further progress but be content
with the status quo. Inflating their conceit, it corrupts many
cadres and veterans, making them divorce themselves from
the masses. Their feelings changed, they are unable to follow
Chairman Mao. A few have degenerated. A few have been
poisoned. By accepting and executing this bourgeois reactionary line, they have committed errors without knowing them.

This line, in fact, is the historical origin and social foundation of the reactionary [revisionist] line. This line has buried
some cadres, undermined the Party's style of work, and also
buried the children of some cadres. It creates in them a desire
for personal privileges, making them conceited and egoistic. It
breeds a sense of superiority in them, making them give up
thought reform, lead a life of laxity, and divorce themselves
from the masses.

At the present time many who side with the conservatives
have erred, and if they do not alert themselves, they will surely
go revisionist. If we build our Party and our state according
to this line, then the Party will be a revisionist party and the
state will be a revisionist state. And the people we train will
be revisionist bureaucrats. The successors we cultivate will
be revisionist successors. In this way, a privileged stratum
can most easily be formed. If we do not get rid of it, we shall
see our Party and state perish, and our heads will roll.

For a long time the broad masses of Party members and

cadres have been consistently resisting this line and perservering in Chairman Mao's Party-building line. Now is the time to settle the Liu-Teng line thoroughly. The Great Proletarian Cultural Revolution is aimed at eliminating ideas of privileges, fostering proletarian ideas, transforming man's soul, realizing revolutionization of man, digging up the roots of revisionism, and consolidating and developing the socialist system.

TEN GREAT ACHIEVEMENTS OF THE
CULTURAL REVOLUTION*
(1967 ?)

1. The study of Chairman Mao's writings has been raised still higher.
2. A group of counterrevolutionary elements have been exposed.
3. A handful of people in authority who took the capitalist road have been exposed; people who were misled have been liberated.
4. The four bad elements (including a small number of anti-Party, antisocialist Rightists) have received a great blow.
5. A big blow to those who acted like overlords and mandarins.
6. The taste of great democracy has been spread.
7. The Party and society have been greatly revigorated.
8. An excellent exercise for war preparedness.
9. While strengthening the ideological revolutionization of men, production and construction have also been promoted.
10. A large number of revolutionary successors have been cultivated. These little generals, having grown up through struggles, dare to challenge and dare to act.

---

*"Wen-hua ta-ko-ming ti shih-ta ch'eng-chiu." Hsiang Pei-ching t'ung-hsün [Report to Peking, Canton], No. 1 (October 20, 1967), 1; a Japanese version may be found in "Bunka daikakumei no jūdai seika," Chūgoku kenkyū geppō [Monthly Research Report on China], December 1969, p. 14.

CRITERIA FOR EVALUATING LEFTISTS*
(1967 ?)

1. In terms of the general orientation, perceive whether they are against the capitalist-roaders within the Party and the bourgeois reactionary line, and perceive their attitude toward the Party and Chairman Mao. Regarding the above point, discern whether it is a question of understanding or a matter of persistent viewpoint.

2. With respect to organizational purity, first of all, [pay attention to] the purity of the leading members. They must not be landlords, rich peasants, counterrevolutionaries, bad elements, or rightists. See whether there are any capitalist-roaders and backstage bosses.

3. Examine views of the masses toward the organization involved.

4. Evaluation must be made on the basis of political principle. There may be sectarian sentiments.

---

*"Heng-liang tso-p'ai piao-chun." In Mao chu-hsi wen-hsüan [Selected Writings of Chairman Mao, 1959-1967] (n.d., n.p., a Red Guard publication), p. 120. These are excerpts of Lin's talks at an enlarged meeting of the Military Affairs Commission.

NINE-POINT INSTRUCTION TO THE
AIR FORCE PARTY COMMITTEE*
(1967 ?)

1. The general situation of the Great Proletarian Cultural
Revolution is very good. We must be resolute and firm; there
will be twists and reversals, but the great alliance is sound,
so do not fear some splits.

2. Do not fear disorder, for complete disorder will turn out
to be good. Disorder is a process through which everyone can
struggle against selfishness and criticize revisionism.

3. The sky will not fall. Even if it does, with our great
leader Chairman Mao and ever-victorious Mao Tse-tung thought
we can make it through, can remedy our deficiencies. In reporting the situation, use the four fasts and one slow.

4. Pay attention to the mainstream, not tributaries. Investigate and study, but do not be too rigid or guarantee anything.
Some organizations, even though their overall direction is correct, will suffer defeat because their policies and tactics are
wrong — the Nanchang Uprising was also like this.

5. Distinguish the enemy with a clear mind and steady eye,
and do not overestimate him; have faith that the masses are
the majority.

6. Support of the Left is support of Mao Tse-tung thought.

_____

*"Tui k'ung-chün tang-wei ti chiu-tien chih-shih." Published
in Kang chiu-i-san chien-hsün [Bulletin of Unit 913 of Steel
Works] (1967?); reprinted in Kung-fei wen-hua ta-ko-ming
chung-yao wen-chien hsü-pien [Supplement to Important Documents on the Cultural Revolution of the Communist Bandits]
(Taipei: Kuo-fang-pu ch'ing-pao-chü, 1969), p. 172.

Support the Left but do not support any factions. Support those who are in harmony with Mao Tse-tung thought, and do not support those who are not. Support the Left and do not engage in petty squabbles. Do not support one faction attacking another.

7. Your reports of the situation must be accurate. Do not make things up. Be comprehensive and objective.

8. Strive to be active and positive. Do not fear suffering what you must. If you are mistaken, conscientiously examine yourself and fundamentally reform your world view.

9. Protect against both "Leftism" and Rightism; that is, protect against meddling with Mao Tse-tung thought, meddling with Chairman Mao's latest instructions. Stand firmly on the side of Chairman Mao. Protecting against the Right is protecting against the old conservatives making troubles.

59

INSTRUCTION TO THE THREE SERVICES*
(1967 ?)

1. Do not separate the "5.13" [May 13 ?] Group into revolutionaries and conservatives.

2. Among those who are attacking the "5.13" Group are also leftist organizations (referring to those in the military).

3. The "three services" must not put too much pressure on the clashing factions; they must not interfere excessively with the Great Cultural Revolution in military academies.

---

*"Tui san-chün ti chih-shih." In Mao chu-hsi wen-hsüan [Selected Writings of Chairman Mao, 1959-1967] (n.d., n.p., a Red Guard publication), p. 119.

60

ON EDUCATIONAL REFORM*
(1967 ?)

The content of education should be streamlined and abbreviated. Things of secondary importance should be axed; questions of secondary importance must be pared away. The result of trying to study everything is that nothing is studied well. In warfare one's forces should be concentrated to destroy one point; do not open your mouth too wide. One only uses small forces for points of secondary importance; this is the dialectical method. Everything has many aspects, essential aspects and secondary aspects. When the essentials have been solved, the secondary aspects can be handled with a quick stroke. The basic principles of military affairs, politics, and philosophy are few in number; when they are mastered, you can apply them easily. Everything is like this — the crucial aspects must be grasped. What are the crucial aspects? They must be carefully selected — for example, in warfare the crucial aspects are the concentration of forces, the main direction of attack, and the time of general attack. There are always those who want to do more and as a result go backward. The more they do, the more excesses they commit; as a result the things they actually learn are fewer — this is also the dialectic. Lao-tzu meant this when he said, "Simplicity prospers, multiplicity confuses." With many subjects, teachers and students are much too busy; when one's head is crammed full of all this stuff, con-

---

*"T'an chiao-yü kai-ko." Chung-hsüeh hung-wei-ping [Middle School Red Guards, Canton], November 6, 1967.

cepts become unclear, and one cannot be skilled in technical work. Students come to school, get exhausted, study a bunch of things without any order, not to speak of not being able to apply them confidently — this is not in the spirit of more, faster, better, and more economically. In order to identify the crucial aspects correctly, we must rely on everyone truly penetrating the subject, grasping it correctly, and applying the proper perspective.

Care must be taken with regard to teaching methods; bourgeois methods cannot be used. The bourgeoisie approach education as an undertaking in itself, and therefore create mysteries, extend the time needed, and raise the cost of it all. Our educational content must be simple and easy to understand; educational methods must be many and varied to enable everyone to truly learn something. Formalism and triviality we do not need.

61

ON WRITING
(1967?)

[Reported by Lin Tou-tou]

After I started working for the newspaper, my father occasionally gave me advice on problems concerning the writing
of articles. I tried to recall as much as possible what he had
told me and wrote it down in my notebook. Some comrades
found my notes most helpful and wanted to read them over and
over again. Recently the leadership of the newspaper asked
me to organize these notes for use as internal study materials.
As my comprehension ability is low and my memory may not
be accurate, I am sure there are many errors, omissions, and
inaccuracies. Because these materials deal specifically with
my personal situation, they may not be fit for use by other
comrades. Particularly because they have not been read by
my father, I feel unsure of them. They are only for the reference of comrades of the Air Force Journal [K'ung-chün pao],

*Lin Tou-tou chi-shu, "Lun hsieh-tso." Huo-chü t'ung-hsün
[Torch Bulletin, a Red Guard publication in Canton], No. 1
(July 1968); reprinted in Kung-fei wen-hua ta-ko-ming chung-
yao wen-chien hsü-pien [Supplement to Important Documents
on the Great Cultural Revolution of the Communist Bandits]
(Taipei: Kuo-fang-pu ch'ing-pao-chü, 1969), pp. 159-166.
Lin Tou-tou is Lin Piao's daughter who, according to Peking's
official account, revealed to Chou En-lai her father's escape
attempt on September 12, 1971, the day it actually took place.

and it is hoped that they will not be circulated externally.

First let's talk about the writing of short essays. Recently, after reading my two short articles "Towering Determination" [Chuang-chih ling-yün] and "Only Deep Roots Can Give Luxuriant Foliage" [Ken-sheng ts'ai-neng yeh-mao], published in the May 27 and July 6 issues of the Air Force Journal, my father felt very pleased and put them specially under the plate glass on his desk. Because the print on the journal is very small, he asked someone to read them for him. He frequently telephoned me from out of town to encourage me, saying: "These articles are quite well written. They are free from the rigid frame of stereotyped Party writing, they are short and to the point, and they are novel and lively. The first article has been reprinted by the Liberation Army Daily [Chieh-fang-chün pao] with the title changed to 'Heroes of This Kind Are Most Revered' [Che-chung ying-hsiung tsui-ko-ching], which is well changed." He also said: "I rejoice to see the next generation growing up. Although this is but the first step in the long march of ten thousand li, it is a good beginning and the direction is correct."

Father said: "Short commentaries and random notes are good forms of writing. From now on make greater use of them. They are powerful weapons for criticizing erroneous ideas, propagating new ideas and publicizing heroes. Don't write those stinking, lengthy, and dry articles. They are like machine products, devoid of sentiment and uninteresting. When complicated and important problems cannot be clearly explained in a short article, a longer one can be written. Articles devoid of content are bad, be they long or short. You must pay special attention to studying Chairman Mao's 'Oppose Stereotyped Party Writing.' This is of great advantage not only to raising your thought but also to the writing of good articles — especially good short essays."

On the structure and style of articles, Father had this to say: "You are young, and have little experience. Besides, your health is not very good, so don't try to write a long novel, much less entertain the thought of becoming a famous writer. You

should, as you are doing now, write some short essays and
prose regularly, and some report literature [pao-kao wen-
hsüeh] as well. Report literature is a style of writing that
combines the functions of both novel and essay. It is more
closely linked with political life. It is inspiring and serves
the function of giving pragmatic education to the people.

"In writing essays, one must have one's own style. But as a
beginner at writing, you may learn all kinds of style and structure. I mean not learning indiscriminately but learning selec-
tively. Speaking of content, the main thing is to learn what is
positive. It is especially necessary to get hold of a better work,
a better style, and a better article, and study it again and again.
Read intensively and practice to write more often, and fight a
battle of annihilation with concentrated strength. Try to make
a breakthrough on a particular style of writing in a given period of time, and the effort will yield results. Study and practice
writing articles of various styles, and in due course you will
find out the way to gradually develop your own style. However,
when studying works of others, especially the works of some
old writers, you must adopt an analytical attitude. As taught
by Chairman Mao, you must 'discard the dregs and absorb the
essence.' The old writers were incorrect in thought and feeling, they took the bourgeois or petty-bourgeois stand. 'Deep in
their soul is a kingdom of the petty-bourgeois intellectuals.'
Their writings that gave expression to their personal feelings
which are decadent and depressed must never be studied. The
style you must gradually form should be full of revolutionary
enthusiasm, extremely political, and striking a high note. This
is the style of revolutionary literature.

"There are many articles and works in the world, too many
to be packed in a train. Every article is different, and there
are no fixed rules on the method of writing. Unlike mathemat-
ics, physics and chemistry, which have but one answer to each
question, literary works vary from people to people. Therefore,
don't put blind faith in any conventional forms. You must dare
to create. In accordance with the needs of the revolutionary
struggle and the livelihood of the masses, you must form your

own unique style through constant practice and continuous improvement. Like learning calligraphy with a brush, you must
first rely on copying. Later, you can slowly develop your own
characteristics. It is neither possible to make an exact copy
from a copybook, nor is it beautiful to look at. Calligraphers
of all ages each had his own style. In writing, therefore, while
it is necessary to learn from other people, don't try to imitate
them. When you write more often you will become skillful.
Practice creates talents, and when talents bear blossom, your
own style will come into being. Don't despise your own style
and discard it lightly. You should consciously consolidate it,
and temper and improve it continuously through practice."

Concerning basic skills, Father said: "To write articles one
must pass 'three difficult tests.' First, one must pass the test
of ideology, but this cannot be achieved at one stroke. One must
rely on studying Chairman Mao's writing as long as one lives
and steel one's own ability of observation and judgment through
protracted and complex political life and class struggle. For
determining whether an article is good or bad, the political
criterion is the first yardstick. Therefore, it is necessary
forever to persist in the correct line of Mao Tse-tung thought
and to hand the red flag of Mao Tse-tung thought from generation to generation. It is necessary forever to take the stand of the
proletariat and the masses of the people. 'As far as members
of the Communist Party are concerned, this also means taking
the stand of the Party, of Party spirit, and of Party policy.'"
Father put great emphasis on these two phrases in Chairman
Mao's "Talks at the Yenan Forum on Literature and Art." When
I was leaving for my work post, he especially wrote an inscription of this teaching for me and asked me to hang it on the wall
and regard it as a motto in my work. "One must closely rely
on the Party organization, praise the new society, deal blows
at the reactionaries. The thematic thought of each article
should be clearcut to show what you support or oppose, love
or hate. In this way you can show you have a soul. Support
what is good to the Party, and oppose what is bad to the Party.

"It should also be clear that your works and articles are to

serve the people and to serve the workers, peasants and soldiers, are closely linked with the current struggle, and are
meeting the needs of the current struggle. Works and articles
are for the education of the people and for the remolding of man. Because of this, you must first reform your
own thought well and revolutionize yourself ideologically.
Chairman Mao said: "Today, those writers who persist
in the individualistic stand of the petty bourgeoisie cannot genuinely serve the revolutionary masses of workers,
peasants, and soldiers.' How can people soaked with bourgeois
ideas write works which are filled with revolutionary thought
and feelings? As a common saying goes: 'How can a person
who is not correct himself correct other people?' That is why
we advocate that the educator must first be educated and that
the engineer in charge of the remolding of the soul must first
have a pure proletarian soul. Being a creative writer is arduous. Aside from taking the proletarian stand and adopting the
feelings of a revolutionary, he must take part in a great deal
of labor before he can write good works. Never in his lifetime
can a lazy man write anything of value. This reasoning is not
easy to understand, and is even more difficult to carry out.
You must study well Chairman Mao's 'Talks on the Yenan
Forum on Literature and Art.' It is a basic lesson, and you
must carry it with you at all times. You must read it again
and again, read it intensively, and when you come across questions, you must make investigations. You must forever carry
out Chairman Mao's instructions and temper and improve yourself through practice in life.

"To pass the hard test of life, you must unconditionally integrate with the workers, peasants, and soldiers. Chairman
Mao said: 'The laboratory of the school of arts lies in society.'
You must regard society as the laboratory. Go deep into practice, unite yourself with the masses, and develop an affection
for the laboring people. You must especially play an active
role in the socialist education movement in the city and countryside, grow deep roots among the masses, and develop a broad
base of life. You can achieve only in this way. You must not

long for the academic life which is divorced from reality. The
life of the masses is the fountainhead of creativity. Think,
which successful modern works and articles are not created by
going deep into practice? Take what you have written yourself,
for example. 'Uncle Tung' (published in the Liberation Army
Literature and Art [Chieh-fang-chün wen-i], January 1967),
'In Memory of My Respected and Beloved Uncle Liu Ya-lou'
(published in the People's Daily [Jen-min jih-pao], May 12,
1965), and 'Yangchow After the Rains' are the better ones.
Could they have been written without a direct experience with
life? This point must be grasped and must be insisted on.
However, not everyone who has practice in life can discover
problems, think of ways to deal with them, and write creatively.
One must have the habit of using one's brain diligently. Just
as in making investigations it won't do to investigate things
without studying them. One also must have the ability to see
things in the abstract and to generalize and improve them.
Investigation and research must have a goal to accomplish.
Investigation must be made with problems in mind, but must
not be carried out with the conclusion already drawn. There
must be nothing to confine oneself and tie down one's thought
in advance, and in this way new things can be absorbed. When
you go deep into life, you must also learn to observe life and
associate ideas and give more thought to the important affairs
of the state, the Party, the class struggle, and the world revolution. In this way you will stand high, become broad-minded,
and be spirited, and you will not be so shortsighted and narrow-
minded as to confine yourself to the trivialities of life.

"When writing a newsletter, a feature story, or report, the
chief thing is to write about people and their thoughts. One
cannot have eyes only for things and not for people. The reader
tends to forget articles without leading figures soon after reading them. Although 'Yangchow After the Rains' is quite well
written, because it has no leading figure, people are not deeply
impressed by it. The reason you were unable to write anything
in the past was because you were shy and tried to avoid people.
In order to write good works, you must not only come into con-

tact with people but must also be able to understand their psychology and feelings and acquaint yourself with their movements
and language. Only in this way can you portray their character,
forcefully praise the heroes, arouse the response of the reader,
attract the attention of the masses, and achieve the purposes of
propaganda and education. This also means the human factor
first and living ideas first. Therefore you must pay attention
regularly to contact with all kinds of people in society in order
to enrich your emotions and knowledge. By conversing with
people you often can discover very important problems. By
conversing, you can associate your ideas with problems, develop your thought. This is of great advantage to writing. Novel analogies and flashes of thought — so-called inspiration —
must be firmly grasped. You must 'think uninterruptedly,' as
if condensing your thought into raindrops. Once you have gone
deep into life, you will continuously receive sparks of thought
which constitute the 'spare parts' of thought. Good ideas often
flash and disappear like lightning. Therefore, they must be
opportunely grasped so that these 'spare parts' may gradually
be assembled to form a whole which can be gradually made
perfect. Like other kinds of work, writing is only for those
who have determination.

"One must also pass the difficult test of skill. One important
aspect of this is to have a firm grasp of vocabulary. You must
pay attention to studying all kinds of vocabulary, idioms, proverbs, and anecdotes. All things originating from the masses,
from folklore, from classic works, and from foreign countries
must be studied, but the chief thing is to study the language of
the masses. Language gives shape to thought and is an important instrument for expressing thought. With a good vocabulary,
your articles will be vivid and succinct, will be three dimen-
sional, will have strong artistic expression, and will make a
deeper impression on people. An article devoid of good vocabulary is like a cup of plain water. In his article 'Oppose Stereotyped Party Writing,' Chairman Mao declared the poverty of
language and vocabulary the fourth indictment and criticized it
by saying: 'It is because many of us have not mastered language

that our articles and speeches contain few vigorous, vivid and effective expressions and resemble not a hale and healthy person, but an emaciated piehsan, a mere bag of bones.'

"All the accomplished classic writers in ancient and modern times, in China and abroad, paid attention to their vocabulary. It was said that Tolstoy, a great Russian writer of the nineteenth century, mastered more than 10,000 expressions, and that after having sent off the manuscript of his representative work, Anna Karenina, for the sake of changing an expression, several times that night he rushed back to the post office twenty or thirty li away to get the manuscript back. Although he was not a proletarian writer, his spirit of using words with care deserves to be studied. Again, our revolutionary writer Lu Hsün was also known for his rich vocabulary and care in the use of words. It was said when he was engaged in the translation of foreign works he often felt restless in sleeping or eating when he could not find a suitable expression, and once he found the expression, he would leap with joy. Moreover, he never coined any adjective which only he himself could understand. Chairman Mao also mentioned this spirit of Lu Hsün in his article 'Oppose Stereotyped Party Writing.'

"Our great leader Chairman Mao's articles are not only the strongest in ideological character and the best in literary style, they also are the most brilliant models in the use of words and idioms. Take for example the 'three constantly read articles' which you often read. In the article 'In Memory of Norman Bethune' he used the terms 'constantly perfecting his skill' and 'changing their work the moment they see something different'; in the article 'Serve the People' he quoted from Ssu-ma Ch'ien: 'Though death befalls all men alike, it may be heavier than Mount Tai or lighter then a feather'; and in the article 'The Foolish Old Man Who Removed the Mountains' he cited an anecdote from the 'T'ang Wen' chapter in the Lieh Tzu. All these are used in the most natural, proper, and pertinent way. Such articles are imbued with life, are interesting to read, and are able to impress people deeply.

"It takes painful efforts to master vocabulary. As to the

method of building a vocabulary, one way is to build a vocabulary according to the problem you are studying or the kind of
article you are writing — like studying Mao's works with problems in mind. Another way is to carry with you a notebook,
'make use of your eyes, ears, hands and mind,' and take notes
of everything you see and hear. You must also constantly refer
to such notes, continuously associate your thoughts with them,
and develop the habit of using your brain diligently. You should
learn from your mother. Although she is advanced in age and
is preoccupied with work, she still constantly accumulates and
stores up vocabulary. Whenever we discover a good term that
can express a thought or explain a rule of life, we always feel
we have found something extremely valuable and quickly note
it down. You ought to copy down the idioms, allusions, and good
terms of expression in Chairman Mao's works, and organize
them into a card index to facilitate your studies. You make a
great effort to learn English. You should also learn Chinese
in the fundamental way you learn English. Good terms of expression, idioms, and examples must be borne in mind and
even memorized. You should make as much effort in learning
your vocabulary as you do in your study of English and classical
Chinese. You cannot learn words from a dictionary, however;
no matter how hard you try, you cannot remember them. Only
through learning with your ears, through reading, writing articles, editing contributions from the fighters can you associate
individual words with a story or an article and remember them.
By consciously studying persistently in this way over a long
period of time, you can gradually build up a big vocabulary, and
by continuously making use of it, you can make it your own.
You have seen the Soochow embroidery, haven't you? Why is
it so beautiful? Because it uses a great variety of silk thread.
It is said there are as many as 4,800 kinds. There are 20 or
30 kinds of red thread alone. Because of the great variety of
colors, the finished product is very fine looking and very real.
This is also true with the writing of articles. Vocabulary is
like a thread. The greater the vocabulary you are able to master, the more freedom you will have in the use of words and

phrases with endless variations, and you can easily choose the correct colors to 'weave out' the best works. Of course, in writing an article, the chief thing to consider is thought and not vocabulary. You must accumulate your vocabulary mainly at ordinary times. When you have built up a big vocabulary, you will be able to use words and phrases freely; and when you write an article, good words and phrases will pop up one after another to form sentences. The words used must be selected with care. You must make proper use of them in a natural way, and must not use the hackneyed phrases which are lifeless and dead. Nor must you deliberately play with words and pile up phrase after phrase. The use of too many phrases in an article will make it look bulky and repetetive and damage the ideas you want to express.

"Episodes are one of the elements which makes an article lively. Why do report literature, novels, and plays attract the interest of their readers? Because they have good episodes. They are colorless if everything is described with straightforwardness. Herein lies the method of dialectics: The development of a story is often beyond the imagination of the reader, and the end is always perfect. This is the unity of opposites. Why do we say 'add some salt to make things sweet' or 'at times it is better to keep quiet than make noise'? This is the reason. To write ordinary articles, there should be more imaginative and abstract thinking. It is a good method to write articles by means of 'narration and discussion.' Purely descriptive articles will not do in this age of ours. In narrating facts, key features should be discussed, sentiments expressed, and truths explained. Only articles of this kind have ideological and militant character, sinews and bones, blood and flesh, spirit and stance.

"In writing theoretical essays, it is necessary to 'quote classics and cite examples.' We should give a new definition to the quoting of classics and examples. By 'classics' we mean works of a theoretical nature, such as those of Marxism-Leninism-Mao Tse-tung Thought. What we call 'examples' are typical cases. In other words, these are facts. Having both things and integrating them well, we can write good essays.

"As to the style of essays, do not pursue it too far. The style is determined by the content. The main thing is to have ideas established first. After that we should get the ideas organized in our head or write an outline before we start to draft the article at one stretch. Finally, the draft should be revised again and again and carefully polished. With good ideas established, an article is half done. The remaining question is the use of various means to express the theme and to perfect it. Only by so doing can a work sound in both political content and art form be created. This is also true with music. Once the key and melody are created, the song has its soul. The construction of an article is easier to handle. These things are not lifeless. We can learn from others or courageously create new things.

"If a writer is able to pass the hard test in these three areas, his competence will be high; using the same style, he can write articles one level higher than others. This is like making candy: the basic raw materials used are generally nothing more than sugar, eggs and milk, but the pattern and variety of products can be rich and colorful."

Concerning the quality of literature and the question of studying it, father told me: "Literature possesses class character, serves politics, and belongs to the superstructure. It is not simply for providing people with the pleasure of art, but is principally for the purpose of educating people ideologically. Proletarian literature is an important instrument for the imaginative and popular propagation of Marxism-Leninism-Mao Tse-tung Thought, a creative tool for influencing and educating people. Proletarian literature is an integral part of the whole revolutionary undertaking of the proletariat. The creation of literary works is an extremely solemn political task entrusted to you by the Party. Literature is very strong in political character. There are all kinds of literature in the world. That of imperialism and revisionism is deceptive and corrupt, while ours awakens people and raises the quality of man. Theirs is narcotic, while our revolutionary literature stimulates con-

ciousness. Theirs is opiate, while ours is coffee that inspires
the fighting spirit. Therefore, a writer must possess the political brain of the proletariat and a steadfast and correct political
orientation, and he must adopt an extremely sober and cautious
attitude toward writing. There is no ambiguity whatsoever on
this point. As far as you children of revolutionary cadres are
concerned, no matter what work you may do, you have an un-
shirkable obligation to socialism. You should forever cherish
the Party and Chairman Mao, arm yourselves with the thought
of Mao Tse-tung, and forever serve proletarian politics. Your
ideological level should be very high, and you should set strict
standards for yourselves. In the course of building socialism
and in the practice of the Three Great Revolutionary Movements,
your contributions to the Party should be greater than those of
the children of ordinary people. The way you behave is not the
problem of an individual, but a political problem of great importance. In the eyes of the ordinary people your behavior has
a political significance."

With regard to some of my problems in ideological understanding, father pointed out specifically: "Don't be afraid of
creating problems and making mistakes in dealing with literature and art. So long as you exert yourself in study, hold high
the great red banner of Mao Tse-tung thought, carry out work
according to Chairman Mao's teachings on every occasion, and
conduct yourself in a correct political manner, you will make no
mistake. It is inevitable that one will make minor mistakes in
work; so don't be afraid of making mistakes. Aren't we taught
by Chairman Mao that we must dare to think and to act? You
are still young, but you will become mature gradually through
practice in the future. Don't belittle literature, because a
good essay can give the masses great education and inspiration.
It is good for you to do newspaper work, and you must work
conscientiously and learn humbly.

"You must read books. Learn whatever you need. Those who
do not read books have only blind faith but no consciousness.
But you cannot read too many books. There are so many books
in the world that they are like goods in a department store.

Can you buy all of them? You must choose the best and most useful ones for repeated study and application. You also must learn humbly from other people. I've heard that some comrades in your newspaper office are well steeled in practical work although they have not read many books. They are all your teachers and are of great help to you, and you should learn well from them. The chief thing is to learn through practical work. A newspaper can link you extensively with the masses and reality and is the best school. Working for a newspaper gives you a lot of opportunities to practice writing and go to the grassroots level. It may be regarded as a small society and a small world; it can also serve the function of dissecting a sparrow. In the future, you must go to various departments of the Air Force and move among various trades and professions, so as to enrich your life and broaden your vision. Work first in the newspaper office, and then in the Political Department. Work first within the army, and then elsewhere outside the army. You must especially respond to the calls of the Party Central Committee, Chairman Mao, and the Party Committee of the Air Force and take an active part in the socialist education movement in the localities. This is a living classroom for political education. Especially for those of you who are brought up in the new society and who have not gone through great storms and directly experienced class exploitation and class oppression, this is an indispensable basic course. I hope that all of you will temper and reform yourselves through practice in life and in the heat of class struggle, and become thoroughgoing revolutionaries forever."

62

[ON MAO TSE-TUNG THOUGHT]*
(1967?)

Mao Tse-tung thought must be taken as the yardstick for
everything. In Chairman Mao's thought and instructions, we
must have strong faith without any doubt whatsoever at all
times and on all questions.

---

*[English title added]. Quoted in "Wei-ta ti hua-shih-tai ti
hui-i" [A Great, Epoch-Making Conference], editorial, Chieh-
fang-chün pao [Liberation Army Daily], August 12, 1967; and
Lin Piao yü-lu [Quotations from Lin Piao] (Kunming: Hsin-i-
chung ko-ming tsao-fan ping-t'uan cheng-chih pu, 1967), p. 9;
also quoted in Selection 1 of this volume.

63

INSTRUCTIONS TO HUANG YUNG-SHENG
AND LIU HSING-YÜAN*
(?1967)

(Transmitted by the Canton Military Region)

1. Concerning the problems of conducting study classes successfully: Vice Chairman Lin said, "In order to grasp well the
study classes, we must grasp well the various levels, closely
adhere to Chairman Mao's strategical arrangements, and first
resolve the problems of having the cadres step out from among
the ranks. At present cadres across the country hesitate to
step out, and this is a very big problem." Political Commissar
Liu reported to the Central authorities about the plan for organizing collective study for bureau and commission heads in
Kwangtung Province. After listening to it, Vice Chairman Lin
said that it was a good way to do it.

2. (Omitted)

3. (Omitted)

4. When cadres supporting the Left hold divergent views,
they must reconcile such divergences among themselves. This
has been pointed out by the Chairman many times. In the conversation, Vice Chairman Lin repeatedly emphasized that such
differing views should not surface in society at large. The Liberation Army should not allow its units to give support to any
factions they please. Rather, every region should have one

_____

*"Lin Piao fu chu-hsi chieh-chien Huang Yung-sheng, Liu
Hsing-yüan shih ti chih-shih." Hung-ssu tsao-fan-che t'ung-
hsün [Bulletin of the Red Rebels, Canton], December 4, 1967.

unified attitude. The internal problems of the Liberation Army must be resolved first. Chairman Mao, Vice Chairman Lin, Premier Chou, and the Central Cultural Revolution Group have all emphasized that in supporting the Left the Liberation Army must act as one man. The most recent instructions of Chairman Mao should be communicated to the lower levels and carried out faithfully, and all levels should conduct study seriously and not make troubles for each other.

5. Vice Chairman Lin said that there would be more upheavals in the Cultural Revolution. The army must control its temper and not suppress others on the pretext of executing the September 5 Order. In dealing with mass organizations, it must not use the suppressive methods, but rely on political and ideological work. The Chairman is very concerned about those cadres who have committed mistakes. On releasing Ch'en Tsai-tao for collective training, the Chairman uttered four sentences: (1) welcome, (2) study well, (3) wage revolution anew, and (4) Ch'en Tsai-tao is also a "model soldier."

Moreover, the Red Revolutionary League (the rebel faction) and the Red Defense League (the conservative faction) in Hangchow have established an overall alliance. The Red Revolutionary League displayed a high character. Even after the Red Defense League had lost, some positions were still reserved for its members. The Chairman was very much pleased with this event.

Hunan may send 200 men to Peking for study. As to how to get them there, authorities in Peking are to be consulted.

64

SPEECH AT A MEETING OF ARMY CADRES*
(March 24, 1968)

Comrades:

The meeting is now open.

The purpose of this meeting today is to announce to you an important recent decision of the Central Committee.

Recently some new problems have again appeared in the life of our Party; some new contradictions have appeared, a new situation with regard to class struggle has appeared. Although these problems are not as big as those concerning Liu [Shao-ch'i], Teng [Hsiao-p'ing], T'ao [Chu], P'eng [Te-huai], Lu [Ting-i], Lo [Jui-ch'ing], and Yang [Ch'eng-wu], they are still more important than other general problems. The Chairman has said that this problem is not a big one, yet not a small one either. It concerns Yang Ch'eng-wu's collusion with Yü Li-chin to usurp leadership of the Air Force and depose Wu Fa-hsien. Yang Ch'eng-wu has also colluded with Fu Ch'ung-pi to depose Hsieh Fu-chih. The personal ambition of Yang Ch'eng-wu has also led him to consider ousting Hsü Shih-yu, Han Hsien-ch'u, Huang Yung-sheng, and others at his level of status.

The Central Committee has met with the Chairman repeatedly,

---

*"Tsai chieh-chien chün-tui kan-pu shih ti chiang-hua." Kung-jen lien-ch'ou [Workers' Joint Planning, Canton], April 15, 1968; reprinted in Chung-kuo wen-t'i yen-chiu chung-hsin, comp., Lin Piao chuan-chi [A Special Collection on Lin Piao] (Hong Kong: Tzu-lien, 1970), pp. 127-136. In this speech Lin criticized mistakes committed by Acting Chief of Staff Yang Ch'eng-wu and explained why Yang had been purged.

altogether four times, and it has reached the following decisions:
to revoke Yang Ch'eng-wu's position as acting chief of staff, to
arrest and prosecute Yü Li-chin, to revoke Fu Ch'ung-pi's position as commander of the garrison district, to appoint Comrade
Huang Yung-sheng as chief of staff, and finally to appoint Wen
Yü-ch'eng as deputy chief of staff and commander of the Peking
Garrison District.

Comrades, life is contradiction; life is struggle. Progress is
always forward development through contradiction and struggle.
Contradiction is solved through struggle. Therefore, what we see
now is by no means rare. Of course we hope that there will be no
contradiction, but it exists objectively; it is an objective law of
things. In the past, in the present, and in the future there has
never been and will never be a time without contradiction. However, we can of course try as hard as possible to prevent contradictions from becoming serious contradictions, try as hard
as possible to prevent comrades from making mistakes, or prevent them from making many mistakes, and try as hard as possible to make comrades do their work well. This expectation
is one which Chairman Mao has held in the past and now; it is
Chairman Mao's constant concern regarding all cadres. All of
us Central Committee comrades feel this way — all hope that
nothing happens, or that things seldom happen, or that when
something does happen it is not of great consequence. This is
our feeling, our expectation. But objectively speaking, things
will always happen, for our wills are not supreme. We can only
face reality, expose contradictions and solve them. The pus
has to come out of the abscess, just as paper cannot contain a
fire. Thus we can only confront contradictions and solve them.

First, Yang Ch'eng-wu's principal error is mountaintopism,
double-dealing, and distortion of Marxism. Mountaintopism,
sectarianism, cliqueism, individualism, and factionalism all
belong to the same category. The names are different; they
differ slightly in meaning and scope; but their basic nature is
the same. They do not express a proletarian ideology, but
rather express that of the exploiting class, the bourgeoisie.
All of them are incompatible with Party spirit and Party

solidarity. They are anti-Communist, anti-Party, and destructive of solidarity. When this kind of thinking extends itself one
inch, Party solidarity recedes one inch. We must strengthen
Party solidarity and oppose mountaintopism, sectarianism,
cliqueism, individualism, and factionalism. (Comrade [Yao]
Wen-yüan shouts a slogan: "Smash plotters and those with individual ambition!") The communist ideology is sharply and
directly opposed to this kind of backward ideology. When this
kind of backward thinking extends itself an inch, progressive
thinking recedes an inch, and our cause loses an inch. Communism can be summed up as destroying selfishness and developing
dedication to the public; the theories of communism are many,
but basically they can be summed up this way. Mountaintopism
is a betrayal of communism. This kind of thinking is bound to
evoke all kinds of bad behavior. This kind of backward thinking
can evoke traitorous behavior — some of this has already become a reality, while some is still hidden.

Yang Ch'eng-wu only trusted that small gang of his, those who
were most intimate with him, and did not trust others. This is
at odds with the historical facts of the victory of the Chinese
revolution. The total military victory was achieved by the First,
Second, Third, and Fourth Field Armies. The Shansi-Chahar-
Hopeh area was only a part of the four field armies, and Yang
Ch'eng-wu was only in charge of one district within that area —
there were three other districts. This district was controlled
by cadres of the 115th Division, and only one-fourth of them
were there — three-fourths were elsewhere. He now relies on
just that small gang, and tries to oust everybody else. If things
proceeded according to his ideas, Wu Fa-hsien and Hsieh Fu-
chih would be removed, and then Hsü Shih-yu, Han Hsien-ch'u,
Huang Yung-sheng, Ch'en Hsi-lien, and Yang Te-chih would also
be removed. Therefore, we cannot follow his methods, because
first, he is wrong, and second, he is in the minority. We weighed
the two sides and decided not to smash the others, but to smash
them.

Sectarianism and mountaintopism have historically harmed
our Party's cause. When they rear their heads, our endeavors

suffer losses. In opposing these things, prominence must be given to Marxism-Leninism-Mao Tse-tung Thought, for then our fighting forces will be strengthened, our power will increase. In order to safeguard our Party's cause, in the interests of the Party, we must resolutely oppose this kind of thinking, oppose this kind of backward ideology. All who have had this kind of thinking and behavior have fallen ignominiously. Wang Ming, Chang Kuo-t'ao, Liu Shao-ch'i's traitorous clique, and Ho Lung have all collapsed. Teng Hsiao-p'ing and his plan to make the Secretariat he controlled into an independent kingdom also collapsed. P'eng Chen and the impregnable Peking Municipal Committee which he controlled also collapsed. All of those who practiced mountaintopism met bad ends. Mountaintopism does not help the revolution, and it brings a bad end to those who practice it. The reason is that communism, public-spiritedness, and Party spirit are all part of the proletarian ideology, are proletarian virtues, are unique political characteristics possessed only by the proletariat and not by any other class. We are a proletarian Party, the representatives of communism; communism is the end for which we struggle. Thus, we cannot adopt this kind of backward ideology. Therefore our Chairman has opposed it all along. In point of fact, this mountaintopism is enlarged individualism, inflated individualism. Superficially it is for the whole gang, but in fact it is for the individual and merely uses the gang. Mountaintopism would turn our Party's political power, our class's political power into political power of the individual, political power of the faction, political power of the bourgeoisie, political power which oppresses the proletariat. Therefore we must be extremely vigilant and avoid this error. (Comrade Chiang Ch'ing shouts a slogan: "Smash those with individual ambition! Smash the double-dealers!")

One the one hand we must oppose the mountaintopism of Yang Ch'eng-wu; but on the other we must remember:

First, just because we oppose Yang Ch'eng-wu, we should not oppose those under him, those who knew him, and those who supported him. These relationships were determined by historical circumstances, not by the choice of individuals. Because

Yang Ch'eng-wu invoked the name of the Communist Party, invoked the name of Chairman Mao, he fooled people, and his true face of one filled with personal ambition was not perceived. Therefore we must have faith in all those cadres who worked under him, except for those who even after this whole affair has been brought to light still do not disassociate themselves and continue to follow him — these kind of people we cannot use. To have been warned and still not disassociate oneself from him cannot be permitted. But anyone who, after having it all explained, stands on the side of Chairman Mao's line, will be fully trusted. (Comrade Chiang Ch'ing shouts a slogan: "Learn from the PLA! Salute the PLA!")

Second, those on the General Staff or those outside of it who in the past were opposed by Yang Ch'eng-wu, like Wang Shang-jung, Lei Ying-fu, Chang Ai-p'ing, etc., had their own accounts. At that time, to oppose them and overthrow them was correct; it was led by the Party and approved by the Central Committee; it was correct. Wang Shang-jung and Lei Ying-fu were Ho Lung's men and were part of Ho Lung's comprehensive scheme to seize military power, to seize power in the General Staff and in the Navy. That struggle was a correct struggle to expose Ho Lung's ambition to control the military, to cover his claws and teeth. The overall judgment of these men cannot be overturned just because they opposed Yang Ch'eng-wu, just as revoking Wang [Li], Kuan [Feng], and Ch'i [Pen-yü]'s position did not mean we could overturn the whole judgment on the February Adverse Current. The struggle against the February Adverse Current was a correct struggle. Smashing the evil general of the February Adverse Current, T'an Chen-lin, and others was necessary, was correct. (Comrade Chiang Ch'ing shouts a slogan: "Smash the evil general of the February Adverse Current, T'an Chen-lin!" Deputy Premier Hsieh shouts a slogan: "Swear to defend Chairman Mao to the death! Swear to defend the Party's Central Committee to the death! Swear to defend the Central Cultural Revolution Group to the death!")

This is the first point I wanted to make. The next is that Yang Ch'eng-wu's political character is evil. He is a two-faced,

three-sworded man just like the one Chairman Mao had in mind
when he said: "In struggling against deviation, opposition to the
behavior of double-dealers is worthy of the most serious attention, for the greatest danger of double-dealers is that they will
probably develop activities in small groups; the history of
Chang Kuo-t'ao is proof of this. They will support you by day
but betray you at night, say this but think that, say nice things
to your face but stir up trouble behind your back — all of these
are manifestations of the behavior of double-dealers. Only by
making cadres and Party members more aware of the behavior
of double-dealers can Party discipline be consolidated." (Comrade Yao Wen-yüan shouts a slogan: "Smash those with personal
ambition! Smash all plotters!")

Chairman Mao has said: "A serious and nearly pervasive
tendency which today still exists in our Party is the one toward
blind mountaintopism. For example, differences exist in experience of struggle, in regions of work (differences between
base areas, differences between regions controlled by the enemy,
by the KMT, and revolutionary base areas), and in work department (differences between this part of the army and that, between this kind of work and that) — these differences result in
a lack of mutual understanding, respect, and solidarity among
comrades. These seem to . . . [editor's note: the original document has three characters which are unclear] in fact, they
seriously obstruct the growth of Party unity and the Party's
fighting spirit." "Internally, the tendency to sectarianism produces . . . [two characters unclear] and obstructs Party unity
and solidarity; externally, sectarianism produces exclusivism,
which obstructs the efforts of the Party to ally with all of the
people of the country. Only by digging out the root of these two
tragedies can the Party be enabled to happily complete without
obstacle its great task of uniting all Party comrades and allying
with all of the people in the country."

Everyone thought that Yang Ch'eng-wu opposed Lo Jui-ch'ing,
but in fact he was a Lo Jui-ch'ing element — he followed closely
behind Lo. On the surface he opposed Lo Jui-ch'ing, but actually
he was a Lo Jui-ch'ing element. He took part in the struggle

against P'eng Chen, but actually he supported P'eng Chen. So his behavior appeared to be one thing but was in fact the opposite; at night he acted one way, in the daylight another. He would do things and then not admit them. For example, Fu Ch'ung-p'i's driving several fully armed cars and forcing his way into the compound of the Central Cultural Revolution Group to arrest people was in fact directed by Yang Ch'eng-wu, but he wouldn't admit it. He and several others went to see Nieh Yüan-tzu, where they said wrong things and some very bad things, but afterwards he lied and would not admit it. At the General Staff Department, he asked not to give her [Nieh Yüan-tzu] publicity, but clandestinely he promoted her. All of this illustrates his two-faced methods. He opposed Ho Lung and P'eng Chen's firing officials and grabbing power, but he himself did it. Originally the Air Force had no one from the Shansi-Chahar-Hopeh forces, but then he became cozy with Yü Li-chin, very cozy indeed, and used the attraction between the sexes to accomplish his ends. There was a secretary in the Air Force who was having an affair with him. When his wife wanted to bring suit, and the secretary wanted him to get a divorce, Wu Fa-hsien separated this comrade. This was just thoughtfulness on his part aimed at protecting the face of Yang Ch'eng-wu and his daughter, but Yang Ch'eng-wu insisted on branding several comrades who conferred on the matter as counterrevolutionaries and demanded that Wu Fa-hsien admit his error. This was totally unreasonable, just a ploy to smash Wu Fa-hsien.

The Central Committee originally stipulated that there was to be no spying within the Party, but Yang Ch'eng-wu spied on Wu Fa-hsien. He kept track of when Wu's car went out, where it went, and when it came back. He even went so far as to spy on the activity of comrades in the Central Cultural Revolution Group and on the premier.

When Lo Jui-ch'ing was being struggled against, Yang wouldn't agree to the conclusion that Lo was a capitalist-roader; on the surface he opposed Lo Jui-ch'ing, but in fact he protected him. At the Enlarged Meeting of the Military Affairs Commission he opposed Lo Jui-ch'ing, but when he saw that the remarks of

Teng Hsiao-p'ing and P'eng Chen shielded Lo Jui-ch'ing, he
withdrew his own remarks. He did not allow mention of the relationship between Lo Jui-ch'ing and Yang Shang-k'un. He colluded
with Wang, Kuan, and Ch'i; many of the evil deeds of Wang,
Kuan and Ch'i were his doing, so he really worked behind the
scenes for Wang, Kuan, and Ch'i. He is a truly typical double-
dealer and careerist with a bad political quality.

On the surface he supported Chairman Mao, but in fact he was
disloyal to him and to the Central Cultural Revolution Group;
moreover, he used secret agent tactics to spy on the activity of
Chairman Mao and Comrade Chiang Ch'ing. Last spring Chairman Mao asked him to go to Peitaiho to discuss the problem of
Wang, Kuan, and Ch'i with me because at that time I was in poor
health and living at Peitaiho; he wouldn't go. He only went after
repeated urgings. So pay no attention to his superficial support
of Chairman Mao, for in fact he did not support him. In the past
I used a common phrase to express the idea that Chairman
Mao's good health brought us all good fortune: It is good to enjoy the cool breeze under a tall tree. But some people opposed
this phrase. Yang Ch'eng-wu, attempting to shield those who
opposed that phrase, said, "This is nothing." From this it can
be seen that he does not have a very high estimate of the great
role Chairman Mao plays with regard to the whole Party, the
whole country, and the people all over the world.

On the surface he supported Comrade Chiang Ch'ing, but in
fact he was dissatisfied with her. When she was sick, as early
as last spring he, along with Ch'i Pen-yü, collected black material on her and established a special dossier. (The premier
shouts a slogan: "Smash whoever opposes Comrade Chiang
Ch'ing!" Comrade Yeh Ch'ün shouts a slogan: "He can't escape
the responsibility for collecting black material on Comrade
Chiang Ch'ing!") It was evident that he was persecuting Comrade Chiang Ch'ing. She is one of the outstanding female comrades in our Party and is also one of our outstanding cadres.
She is an extremely enthusiastic revolutionary and, at the same
time, she is resourceful, very sensitive to things, and very good
at discovering problems. Moreover, when necessary, she can

take very decisive measures. In the past, people didn't understand her very well because she was in ill health. In this great
Cultural Revolution, one can see her great role. On the one
hand, she loyally executed Chairman Mao's instructions, and on
the other, she has been very creative herself, and during the
Great Cultural Revolution she has made great accomplishments.
Under the perspicacious leadership of Chairman Mao and the
efforts of comrades in the Central Cultural Revolution Group,
she has played a unique role in the great successes won by the
Great Cultural Revolution. She has stood from beginning to end
in the forefront of the campaign.

On the surface it appears that Yang Ch'eng-wu has no ambition, but in fact he is an ambitious man. After the Eleventh
Plenum of the Eighth Central Committee he wanted to remove
the word "acting" from acting chief of staff. Chairman Mao and
the Central Committee noticed this right away, but since he
was not an appropriate choice, the Chairman said: "Let's see
how it goes, for we really have no assurance." Looking at it
now, the Chairman was right, but Yang Ch'eng-wu had no self-
perception; he still felt uncomfortable about that word "acting,"
and wanted to remove it.

He wanted to establish his absolute authority in the General
Staff Department; on the surface he didn't want to assert himself, but in fact he struggled to do so with all his might. There
is a female comrade in the General Staff Department who didn't
agree with Yang Ch'eng-wu's attempt to establish his absolute
authority. He isolated her and wanted her to examine herself,
and he sent three people to keep an eye on her. Recently, the
three services had some material that normally would not be
his concern, but he put his name to it, and turned it into the
"Vigorously Establish" article of his and used all his strength
to get it published. He wasn't even satisfied to have it on the
second page. That day all the papers had Chairman Mao's instructions on educational reform on the first page, and he wanted
it ahead of Chairman Mao's article. After it was published, he
even ordered the whole army to study it. Wu Fa-hsien rescinded
this order, but Yang used the telephone to circulate it.

Many things can be said of him; manifestations of his mountaintopism and double-dealing are legion. At meetings during
these two days I have heard here and there many stories; what
I have heard is not complete, and also not accurate. I also
can't remember them all too clearly, but from just these facts
one can see his political character.

Third, concerning the question of an article of his. Today
Chairman Mao said to me that in addition to mountaintopism
and double-dealing I should also talk about Marxism-Leninism.
This article of Yang Ch'eng-wu's is anti-Marxist. We must
clarify the question of absolute and relative. Chairman Mao
does not agree with his way of bringing up absolute authority.
Originally this was brought up by an ordinary soldier and later
published in the People's Daily. It is all right to use it as a
romantic idiom to express the soldier's love for Chairman Mao,
but to use it as scientific, philosophical language is incorrect.
But Yang Ch'eng-wu thought it also made sense philosophically,
and this was incorrect, a departure from Marxism-Leninism.
In his criticism last December, Chairman Mao said, "This way
of bringing up absolute authority is not proper, for never has
there been separate, absolute authority. All authority is relative; all absolute things exist within relative things, just as
absolute truth is the sum of innumerable relative truths, that
is, absolute truth only exists among individual relative
truths." This was Chairman Mao's conception of the problem.
Relative and absolute are categories frequently used in the
question of truth, categories expressing the unity of opposites.
Marxism does not recognize isolated absolutes. Absolutes can
only exist among relatives; they are always combined with
relatives. We feel that a step forward is a step closer to absolute truth, but absolutes cannot exist by themselves, cannot
become an entity in themselves; just as abstract concepts cannot be separated from concrete things, the general cannot be
separated from the particular, and commonality cannot be separated from individuality. We recognize that there are absolutes,
but they can only exist among relatives. Our knowledge is always relative; it is always in a state of relativity. No matter

whether it is knowledge of nature, of society, or of a particular
ideological principle, it is always in a state of relativity. Only
by passing through numberless relative stages can our knowledge
approach absoluteness; but we can never exert enough strength.
Things are only absolute when they cease developing, but they
will always be developing. One can say that the dialectic is the
law of development, the law of movement, the law of change.
Things are always developing and are never unchanging. Therefore, we cannot view concepts as dead things, for they change
as things change — they are not unchanging. If we have an absolute concept, our thinking is frozen.

Of course, our knowledge of something under certain conditions has some reliability; if we do not recognize this point,
we will become relativists. However, to see things as absolute,
to see truth as absolute, will freeze the motion of things, freeze
our concepts, freeze our ideology. Natural science is also like
this. Its truths are conditional, temporary, relative, and not unchanging. For example, the fact that water above zero is a
liquid, above 100 degrees is a gas, and below zero is a solid is
also relative and conditional. If you take water to the top of a
high mountain, it will become a gas below 100 degrees because
the air pressure there is lower; under other conditions it will
not turn into a solid at zero. All the scientific truths of physics,
chemistry, and biology are true under certain conditions; they
are all in the process of developing and are thus conditional.
There are still today many things which are not known, and
those things which are known have many errors. Therefore all
of the natural science that has been included in books will continue to develop. Of the many things that are recognized as true
the world over, a good number contain errors. For instance,
many principles which are considered true are true only under
the conditions on earth; on the moon they would not hold true;
and on the sun, with its ten thousand degree temperature, they
would be even less true. Thus communist ideology is not conservative; it is never-stopping and developing, all according to
this relation between relative and absolute truth. Everything
that we know is both absolute and relative. Therefore anything

that we know has a double nature, not just a single nature. As
Lenin said, the relation between absolute and relative is also
relative. Only with this kind of guiding ideology can we see that
all things are in the process of changing, science included. This
pair of categories is one frequently used in epistemology and
discussions of truth. If our understanding of this problem is
erroneous and unclear, then we will stop developing and commit
the error of dogmatism, and our ideology will become frozen.
Marxism is correct, but Lenin developed it greatly. Many of
Marxism's conditional principles could not be used afterwards;
but many fundamental principles are still correct, are true.
When Marxism-Leninism entered the new stage of Mao Tse-
tung thought, Chairman Mao greatly developed it. Hasn't Chairman Mao solved things which Marxism-Leninism had not been
able to solve, and brought out things which it had not been able
to bring out? Isn't Chairman Mao still in the process of developing his own thought?

Therefore, seeing things as absolute is erroneous. Things —
such as a table, a teacup, a loudspeaker — are always concrete,
not abstract. The concept of a table can only exist among concrete tables; therefore, Chairman Mao teaches us to look for
the abstract in the concrete, to look for the particular in the
general. He teaches us to dissect sparrows [and see that they
contain everything], that is, to combine the absolute and the
relative, the general and the particular. Yang Ch'eng-wu's idea
is absurd; not only is it absurd philosophically, but it is also
mistaken politically. Historically, absolute authority has only
existed in slave societies. Legally, slaves were not people but
beasts, tools that could talk. Only at that time did absolute
authority exist; afterward, in feudal society and capitalist society, it did not exist; and this is even more the case in socialist and communist societies.

We can only see absolute authority as love of Chairman Mao,
as a figure of speech. Romantic language of this type can still
be used, but to use it in the philosophical, scientific, or political
sense is incorrect and anti-Marxist. It denies the development
of things, the development of ideology. Ideological errors must

lead to erroneous behavior, and thus this matter must be made clear.

What I have said has been rather random; I have heard this and that, and let it all come out. It is incomplete, and sometimes incorrect; I am just telling everyone of the Central Committee's decisions. Altogether I have talked about three problems: mountaintopism, double-dealing, and the question of absolute and relative. Let us shout a few slogans to end my talk:

Be ever loyal to Chairman Mao!

Be ever loyal to Mao Tse-tung thought!

Be ever loyal to Chairman Mao's revolutionary line!

Smash whoever opposes Chairman Mao! Smash whoever opposes the Party Central Committee!

Smash whoever opposes the Central Cultural Revolution Group! Smash Liu, Teng, and T'ao!

Smash P'eng Te-huai! Smash Ho Lung! Smash P'eng, Lo, Lu, Yang!

Smash Hsiao Hua! Smash the blackguard general of the February Adverse Current, T'an Chen-lin!

Oppose reopening the case of the February Adverse Current! Smash mountaintopism!

Smash sectarianism! Smash double-dealers! Smash bourgeois schemers!

Never forget class struggle, never forget the dictatorship of the proletariat, never forget to give prominence to politics, never forget to raise high the great red banner of Mao Tse-tung thought!

Long live the victory of the revolutionary line of Chairman Mao!

Long live the dictatorship of the proletariat!

Long live the great, glorious, correct Chinese Communist Party!

A long, long life to our great leader Chairman Mao!

65

IMPORTANT DIRECTIVES TO THE ARMY*
(April 6-9, 1968)

At four o'clock in the morning on April 14, Comrade Tseng
Wei-shan summoned the comrades who attended a plenary session of the Party committee of the Peking Military Region to
transmit to them the directives that Vice Chairman Lin and
other central officials issued when they received the comrades
from the 63rd and the 69th Armies.

Comrade Tseng Wei-shan's remarks: "Formerly I transmitted
to you only the general idea of the criticisms. In effect, Vice
Chairman Lin and other central officials have made stern criticisms of the army units stationed in Shansi, the provincial
military districts, and me.

"In the night on April 6, (Lin Piao) received (responsible men
of) the 63rd Army and issued his directives. On April 9, (Lin
Piao) received (responsible men of) the 69th Army — Comrade
Chang Jih-ching was present — and gave them the directives.
When greeting their visitors, the central officials and the comrades of the Military Commission of the Central Committee
shook hands with them, and inquired about their names, age, family
background, experience, and status. They talked seriously of
the Shansi problems with them. To us, their talking is of great
concern and a great education. I have rearranged these directives on some specific problems as follows":

*Originally published in Pei-hang hung-ch'i [Red Flag of
the Peking College of Aviation], No. 47. This translation
is taken, with minor editorial revisions, from Facts and Features, I:26 (October 16, 1968), 19-23.

1. The Problems of the Military Academy

Vice Chairman Lin asked Hsü Hsin: "You have studied in Soviet Russia. Did you learn very well? You remarked that it was so difficult for you to study because no interpreter helped you, and that none of you did very well."

Comrade Chiang Ch'ing: "It was fortunate that they did not learn very well, or it would have been a disaster for us."

Vice Chairman Lin inquired of the premier: "Do you happen to know anything about their studies in Soviet Russia?"

The premier: "I do. But I don't have any idea as to how many students went there."

Hsü Hsin: "None of those who returned wanted to go back again. But they had to, according to the agreement."

Comrade Chiang Ch'ing: "Like doing business, a contract couldn't be overlooked."

Vice Chairman Lin: "I didn't know anything about it. At the military academy Kuomintang officers were the instructors. How could they teach us? It was satiric indeed. Could you tolerate having those who had been defeated as your instructors? Should you have seriously learned from them, you would surely have lost in battle."

Comrade Chiang Ch'ing: "I want to be against them resolutely."

Vice Chairman Lin: "What we advocate is people's war. I am against the military academy and its supporters. You seem to have picked up horse dung and left the gold. It was said that you have written some 90,000 words of material. We can start a war merely by making a telephone call, and the three hours you spent on writing that could be used for marching 30 li."

Comrade Chiang Ch'ing: "Why did you want to learn from them? It was shameful indeed!"

Vice Chairman Lin: "During the first annihilation campaign by the Kuomintang at Kiangsi, Wang Chia-hsiang criticized us for 'practicing narrow experimentalism.' They held that only one who has experience can be regarded as a Marxist-Leninist, and vice versa. Theories are generally accumulated from experience. It is impossible to have theories without securing the experience first. People like Wang Chia-hsiang have neither experience nor the theories. They have nothing but foreign dogma."

Comrade Chiang Ch'ing: "The military academy is a higher educational institution. You, the cadres, are all great intellectuals and dogmatists. Dogmatism is revisionism. It is really harmful."

2. Politics Comes First

When receiving the responsible men of the 63rd Army, Vice Chairman Lin instructed that politics must be given the first priority.

Vice Chairman Lin: "Fighting will rely on politics, which thus deserves to be especially emphasized. If there is no politics, there will be no consciousness, no class passion, and no courage. In going to war, casualty, torture, and many other difficulties are impossible to avoid. You must remember this. When you happen to possess a political thought, there will be strong consolidation and good discipline. That is why Chairman Mao's troops have never been defeated."

3. The Problem of Learning from the Masses

Vice Chairman Lin: "Did you learn something from the masses? Did you accumulate any experience regarding overproduction? You should learn from the masses, and cadres and soldiers should participate in the movement of three-supports and two-militaries so as to unite a group of political cadres. In the past we never had such good conditions for training cadres."

4. Propaganda for Mao Tse-tung's Thought
Was Led the Wrong Way

Comrade Chiang Ch'ing: "Concerning 'quotations gymnastics,' do you have permission to do that? If not, how could you do it?

Remember, don't be a formalist! Mao Tse-tung's thought must not be disgraced."

Comrade Huang Yung-sheng: "The traffic police use Quotations from Mao Tse-tung as their billy club. How could this be allowed? It cannot be taken as words of command. Since the paper Chan-yu Pao has made it public, we have to investigate."

Vice Chairman Lin: "They use Quotations from Mao Tse-tung as the billy clubs? How could the precious book be used as a billy club?"

Comrade Chiang Ch'ing: "Quotations from Mao Tse-tung should not be used as a billy club, or as words of command, standing for 'one, two, three, four'. Since the paper reported it, we must have this matter investigated."

Comrade K'ang Sheng: "I heard that you would study Quotations from Mao Tse-tung while you were eating."

Vice Chairman Lin: "The Central Cultural Revolution Group, investigate this matter and issue a regulation."

5. Engineer Troops Make Good Examples

Vice Chairman Lin: "The engineer troops must have tough bodies and political training. The most hardworking troops are engineer troops. They are mountaineers and marchers. It is a good way to rotate the troops for construction, production, and training."

6. Senior Cadres Should Perform Self-Revolution

Vice Chairman Lin: "Having been in the army for several decades, the senior cadres have both political and military experience. Our troops indeed have a good foundation."

The premier: "Did you listen to the tape recording of Vice Chairman Lin's talk on the twenty-fourth?"

Vice Chairman Lin: "Our army is the Party's ranks. Our ranks always obey Chairman Mao. As long as the problem of Yang Ch'eng-wu was made clear, I believe the troops were no longer in doubt. Yang Ch'eng-wu changed gradually. Of those

senior cadres who followed him, some changed for the better,
some for the worse. One should remain unchanged even
after one is promoted or praised. But some really cannot do
that. It is very dangerous, for one who has once been promoted
begins to develop his personal ambition. The higher the position he achieves, the more accurate his ideology should be. It
would be wrong to think he can do anything he wishes as long
as the Party trusts him. We hate to see our cadres doing the
wrong thing or falling down. It will not only severely damage
the Party but make himself fall if he imitates bourgeois politics. Ideological work in the army should thus be strengthened.
You should explain the Yang Ch'eng-wu incident and follow Chairman Mao."

Comrade Chiang Ch'ing: "Yang Ch'eng-wu was a two-faced
factional element, and a plotter."

Vice Chairman Lin: "In the past we did not expose him, so
some people were kept in the dark. He himself developed in
recent years."

7. The Problem of Southeastern Shansi

The problem of southeastern Shansi is that (the Peking Military Region) asked the Party Center to give it the right to open
fire on the mass organizations.

Comrade Chiang Ch'ing: "The army troops were only temporarily transferred to Shansi from the Hopei Provincial Military District."

The premier: "Yangchuan is one of the bigger coal mines in
Shansi, so you may transfer X regiments from Hopei Provincial
Military District."

Comrade Chiang Ch'ing: "Comrade Cheng Wei-shan, from
your request for permission to open fire and to annihilate (the
mass organizations) we can clearly see the attitude of your
military region. You don't cherish the broad masses. You attacked me all of a sudden. You, Cheng Wei-shan, should do
self-criticism. Despite your propaganda of my 'September 5
talk,' you don't try to love the revolutionary 'young generals,'

the Red Guard. You should make a report of self-examination."

Comrade Ch'en Po-ta: "All of you should submit a report of self-examination."

Comrade Chiang Ch'ing: "I don't understand the situation too well. But from your request for the right to shoot and annihilate them, we can see your attitude toward the Great Cultural Revolution and the proletarian headquarters with Chairman Mao as its leader and Vice Chairman Lin as its second head. You should make an intensive examination. You have to review what you have really done in Shansi."

8. Problems of Supporting and Protecting
Revolutionary Committees

The premier: "Chang Jih-ching, you and Liu Ke-ping are of two factions. You have tried collecting material on Liu Ke-ping, haven't you?"

K'ang Sheng: "The army troops stationed in Shansi should concern themselves with the general situation, and protect the revolutionary committee."

Chiang Ch'ing: "The army is a strong faction. No one can be strong enough to resist when your attacks are aimed at him. However, when two factions struggle against each other with force, there must be a 'black hand' in control behind the scenes. Liu Ke-ping and Li Hsüeh-feng are political commissars in the Shansi Provincial Military District. The Party Center summoned you to inform you of Liu Ke-ping and Li Hsüeh-feng. Didn't the Party Center have them dismissed from their offices?"

Vice Chairman Lin: "Did you notify them all? I heard that there were two factions in Shansi. One faction supported the revolutionary committee, while the other opposed it."

Chiang Ch'ing: "You must be concerned for the masses. Looting of arms is not a serious matter. The problems would have been solved if you, Chang Jih-ching, had yielded even a little bit to the revolutionary committee. Shansi was a province where the revolutionary committee was established very early. However, there has always been a double leadership."

Vice Chairman Lin: "Whenever there is double leadership, civil war will surely happen. Chang Jih-ching, you should actively go over to cooperate with Liu Ke-ping and Chen Yung-kuei. Chen Yung-kuei is very correct because he always addresses himself to the general situation. It will be dangerous for one whose actions are not in accord with the movement of supporting the Party and cherishing the people. The PLA fighters opposing the broad masses will not be good 'sons or brothers' of the workers or the peasants. The army should support the Party and cherish the people. The disunion in Shansi will be attributed to the unsound functioning of your army units. What the Party Center anticipates is that you will give up the double leadership in Shansi and support the revolutionary committee regardless of whether it is perfect or not. The army must support the revolutionary committee. Your opposition to Liu Ke-ping and Chen Yung-kuei is in fact opposition to Chairman Mao and the Party Center. You must do something and hurriedly reconcile. It would be terribly wrong for you not to support Liu Ke-ping when the Party Center does support him, and not to support the Party and cherish the people when the Party Center does wish you to do so."

K'ang Sheng: "You must cooperate with Chen Yung-kuei."

Vice Chairman Lin: "It seems to us that the Shansi Provincial Military District will be held responsible for the errors; so will the Peking Military Region. Afterward, if you do what the Party Center wants you not to do, it will be considered as lagging behind."

Chiang Ch'ing: "The reason you have done so is largely that you don't quite understand the nature of the Great Cultural Revolution. You don't really want the revolutionary committee. There were only a few bad men, but it seemed to you that there were many of them."

K'ang Sheng: "You didn't struggle against such men as Tao Lu-chia, An Tzu-min, Wang Chien, Wang Ta-jen, Po I-po and Wang Shih-ying. Wang Shih-ying was a running dog of Liu Shao-ch'i. He once said to two young men, 'There is no hope for China.'"

Vice Chairman Lin: "The problem of Shansi should be
thoroughly studied, and the unfavorable situation should be improved quickly."

Kang Sheng: "In the beginning you wanted Chang Jih-ching
back. But I said that his return would make the factional struggle even worse."

Vice Chairman Lin: "The Peking Military Region, the Shansi
Provincial Military District, and the 69th Army should all be
asked to make self-criticisms and quickly correct their mistakes. The armed struggle in the army is due largely to the
wrong direction which they have taken. In the past the function
of the army was not so great as it is now. The army is now
playing a very important role. Whether or not you carry out
the line indicated by the Party Center will determine how effectively you control your army. A solution to the problem of
Shansi is directly connected with that to the problem of the
Peking Military Region. Of course I don't mean that you are
all wrong. However, I would like to remind you that your problem will surely affect those in Hopei and Inner Mongolia."

Yao Wen-yüan: "You'd better read the article 'The Revolutionary Committee Is Good.'"

When transmitting the aforementioned directive, Chen Kuang-
jui, deputy political commissar of the Peking Military Region,
also gave a three-point instruction: "(1) The directive given by
Vice Chairman Lin and the Central's highest officials on April 9
has now been truthfully transmitted to you. Afterward, what
you have to discuss is how to seriously carry it out. (2) Party
members in the army will make some measures to improve
the situation at once. (3) You should take action at once and
pass down your instructions after intensive discussion tonight."

66

INSTRUCTIONS CONCERNING SZECHWAN*
(May 27, 1968)

Essentials of Vice Chairman Lin's May 27 instructions to
Chang Kuo-hua and Liang Hsing-ch'u:

The X X Conference will carry out self-criticism; self-
criticism facilitates the solution of problems. Only by adopting
this method can unity be achieved, and only through unity can
we face the enemy together. Struggle between two factions
cannot go on forever. At the beginning a period of disorder is
necessary, for disorder disorganizes the enemy. When they
have been sufficiently disorganized, things are easy. The Great
Cultural Revolution is good because it has dug out all those
deeply hidden traitors, special agents, and pseudo-Communist
Party members. Liu Shao-ch'i is a big traitor who committed
treason four times, and he was also in league with the KMT and
America. Those cadres who are genuine traitors and rascals
cannot be used; but if the problem is only ideological, after
they have been educated they can be used. Broad dissemination
and thorough study of Mao Tse-tung thought can produce talented

---

*"Lin Piao tui Ssu-ch'uan ti chih-shih." Tzu-liao chuan-chi
[Special Collection of Materials], No. 1 (July 1968), issued by
Hung-ch'i t'ung-hsün [Red Flag Bulletin, a Red Guard Publi-
cation]; this translation is based on the text reprinted in
Chung-kuo wen-t'i yen-chiu chung-hsin, comp., Lin Piao chuan-
chi [A Special Collection on Lin Piao] (Hong Kong: Tzu-lien,
1970), pp. 127-128. The instructions were reported to have
been transmitted by P'ei Chou-yü.

men. Those of us who fought in the past didn't come out of any
school, but were tempered through struggle and practice, so
only broad dissemination and thorough study of Mao Tse-tung
thought is necessary to produce cadres. Szechuan is a kind of
lair; birds of a feather flock together, and people cluster according to groups. Li Ching-ch'üan is not a Party member but
wormed his way in. . . . Some people appear on the surface to
be Communist Party members, but in fact are KMT members;
P'eng Chen in Manchuria was this way. He did not supplement
the main fighting forces, but only directed local troops. Ho
Lung previously felt that he had a working-style problem; today
it seems that it was not merely a working-style problem, but
was a political problem. It is good to expose some evil characters, but to only attack those out in the open is not enough.
The hidden ones must also be dug out. Having the army participate in local work is beneficial, for it leads to advance; without courageous advance we cannot maintain ourselves. On the
other hand we must attend to politics and allow education in
Mao Tse-tung thought to produce good cadres. At present there
are some cadres who must be smashed, that is, those capitalist-
roaders, traitors, special agents — those who cling resolutely
to their errors and will not reform. Some people, however,
should just have their mistakes smashed, but can still be used.
We have a great need for cadres, and the army must become
a furnace for forging them.

67

SPEECH AT RALLY CELEBRATING THE
NINETEENTH ANNIVERSARY OF THE FOUNDING
OF THE PEOPLE'S REPUBLIC OF CHINA*
(October 1, 1968)

Comrades and Friends:

The great People's Republic of China, founded and led personally by our great leader Chairman Mao Tse-tung, has triumphantly traversed the broad road of socialism for nineteen years.

While celebrating this glorious festival, I would like, on behalf of our great leader Chairman Mao and on behalf of the Party's Central Committee, the Chinese Government, the Military Commission, and the Cultural Revolution Group under the Party's Central Committee, to extend the warmest greetings to the working class, the poor and lower-middle peasants, the People's Liberation Army, the young Red Guard fighters, the revolutionary cadres, and the revolutionary intellectuals, who have performed outstanding and meritorious deeds in the Great Proletarian Cultural Revolution, and to express the warmest welcome to our comrades and friends from different countries of the world!

Our Great Proletarian Cultural Revolution has now scored great victories. Revolutionary committees have been established in twenty-nine provinces, municipalities, and autonomous regions, that is, in the whole country except Taiwan

---

*Peking Review, No. 40 (October 4, 1968), 13-14; for the text in Chinese, see Jen-min jih-pao [People's Daily], October 2, 1968.

511

Province. Industry, agriculture, science and technology, and revolutionary literature and art are all thriving. The counter-revolutionary plot of China's Khrushchev and the handful of his agents in various places to restore capitalism has gone completely bankrupt. Tempered through nineteen years of class struggle, and particularly through the storm of this Great Proletarian Cultural Revolution, the dictatorship of the proletariat in our country has become more consolidated and powerful than ever.

All these victories and achievements are the fruits of the valiant struggles waged by the revolutionary masses of our country in their hundreds of millions under the brilliant leadership of our great leader Chairman Mao.

At present, the central task confronting us is to follow Chairman Mao's great teaching, that is, carry out the tasks of struggle-criticism-transformation conscientiously. That means to consolidate and develop the revolutionary committees, to do a good job of mass criticism and repudiation, of purifying the class ranks, of Party consolidation and Party-building, of the educational revolution, and of simplifying the administrative structure and to change irrational rules and regulations and grasp revolution and promote production and carry the Great Proletarian Cultural Revolution through to the end!

Chairman Mao points out: The working class must exercise leadership in everything. In accordance with Chairman Mao's instructions, tens of thousands of industrial workers throughout the country organized in worker Mao Tse-tung thought propaganda teams, in cooperation with Mao Tse-tung thought propaganda teams of the People's Liberation Army, have entered or are entering colleges, middle and primary schools, and all the other places where intellectuals are concentrated. They have thus stepped onto the political stage of struggle-criticism-transformation in all spheres of the superstructure. This is a great event of the sixties of the twentieth century. Although this has not been long yet, revolutionary practice has proved, and will continue to prove, that together with its staunch ally the poor and lower-middle peasants and together with the broad

revolutionary masses, the Chinese working class, long tested
in heroic battles, will certainly perform even more brilliant
feats under the leadership of the Chinese Communist Party
headed by Chairman Mao!

On behalf of the proletarian headquarters led by Chairman
Mao, I call on the proletarian revolutionaries throughout the
country to closely follow Chairman Mao's great strategic plan,
carry out his latest instructions in an all-round way, and continue to perform new meritorious deeds in the seizure of all-
round victory in the Great Proletarian Cultural Revolution. At
the same time, all commanders and fighters of the Chinese
People's Liberation Army must at all times remain vigilant,
enhance the preparedness against war, and defend the country,
the dictatorship of the proletariat, and the Great Proletarian
Cultural Revolution. We definitely will liberate Taiwan and
are ready at all times to wipe out all enemies who dare to invade us!

At present, the situation at home and abroad is excellent.
The struggles of the revolutionary people are surging all over
the world. The U.S. imperialists are finding it difficult to get
along, and so are the Soviet revisionists and the reactionaries
of all countries. Their counterrevolutionary rule will not last
long. Awaiting them are the total collapse of the old world of
capitalism and the winning of worldwide victory of the proletarian socialist revolution.

Workers of all countries, unite! Workers and oppressed
peoples and nations of the world, unite!

Down with U.S. imperialism!

Down with Soviet revisionism!

Down with the reactionaries of all countries!

Smash the scheme of collusion between U.S. imperialism
and Soviet revisionism to carve up the world!

Long live the all-round victory of the Great Proletarian
Cultural Revolution!

Long live the victory of Chairman Mao's proletarian revolutionary line!

Long live the dictatorship of the proletariat!

Long live the great People's Republic of China!
Long live the great Communist Party of China!
Long live ever victorious Marxism-Leninism-Mao Tse-tung Thought!
Long live our great leader Chairman Mao, a long, long life to him!

68

[INSTRUCTIONS TO CH'ENG SHIH-CH'ING]*
(1968?)

When Comrade Ch'eng Shih-ch'ing, chairman of the Kiangsi
Provincial Revolutionary Committee, went to Peking to make
reports, he was a houseguest at the home of Comrade Lin Piao,
close comrade-in-arms of our most respected and beloved
great leader Chairman Mao and our respected and beloved
deputy supreme commander.

Vice Chairman Lin's home was extraordinarily plain and
simple. The whole family lived in a very ordinary house in
which the steam heat was not turned on. [The rooms] were
heated with only a stove of burning coal balls. The vice chairman's bedroom and office are adjoining. In the rooms there
were one wooden chair for himself for work and several hard-
seat stools for his guests. On the bed were two old blankets
which were neatly folded up. His desk was very simple, with
no table lamp. There was only a ceiling lamp.

The things that caught one's eyes the most in Vice Chairman
Lin's room were the large number of books and quotations.
Chairman Mao's portrait and an inscription of Chairman's quo-
tations were hung on the wall. The bookshelves were stacked

---

*"Ch'eng Shih-ch'ing tsai Lin Piao chia-li tso-k'o" [Ch'eng
Shih-ch'ing Was a Houseguest at Lin Piao's Home] was the
original title under which this text was published, Huo-chü
t'ung-hsün [Torch Bulletin, Canton], No. 1 (July 1968). The
text is reprinted in Lin Piao chuan-chi [Special Collection on
Lin Piao] (Hong Kong: Chung-kuo wen-t'i yen-chiu chung-hsin,
1970), pp. 265-267.

with Chairman Mao's works, along with the writings of Marx, Engels, Lenin, Stalin, and other revolutionary teachers and leaders. On his desk were a big globe and a map.

In such an environment our respected and beloved Vice Chairman Lin studies the affairs of the whole country and the whole world everyday, and helps our great leader Chairman Mao command the nation's Great Proletarian Cultural Revolution and direct revolutionary struggles of the oppressed nations and peoples in Asia, Africa, and Latin America.

Vice Chairman Lin Piao is always very strict with himself; he doesn't even smoke.

Two of Vice Chairman Lin's children were at home, and when they learned that Comrade Ch'eng Shih-ch'ing had been Li Wen-chung's political commissar, they asked to enlist in the unit in which Li Wen-chung served when he was alive.

While Comrade Ch'eng Shih-ch'ing was received as a houseguest in Vice Chairman Lin's home, Vice Chairman Lin gave him important instructions.

Vice Chairman Lin said: "The present situation in Kiangsi is very good. In the past, things were very chaotic. The masses are good and reasonable. Once the masses are aroused, things are easy to handle.

"We must carry out political and ideological work. This is the most fundamental thing. Cadres in all professions and trades must carry out political and ideological work. Any bad people who want to fish in troubled waters must be exposed, and once they are exposed, everything will be all right."

Vice Chairman Lin went on to say: "Li Wen-chung was a great inspiration to the whole army. Once political work is done well in the army, other work can be done well also. To carry out political work is to carry out mass work. The main thing is to have faith in the masses, trust them and rely on them because they are reasonable."

On the study of the Chairman's works, Vice Chairman Lin pointed out emphatically: "The most fundamental thing — the thing at the core, the soul of everything — is to grasp the study of Chairman Mao's works, to promote the ideological revolutionization of man, and to give prominence to politics. The greatest attention must be paid to political and ideological work. The greatest energy must be devoted to the proper execution of the ideological revolutionization of man."

Vice Chairman Lin also discussed the question of cadres. He said: "A cadre must be tested as he works. For some cadres, it takes a very long time to determine what kind of people they are.

"Cadres selected must have the essence of workers and peasants. The criterion of giving prominence to politics must be upheld well. Once the ideological revolutionization of a man is successfully carried out, all other things can be set straight. Use the Chairman's thought to educate the troops and the rebels.

"Liu Shao-ch'i, Teng Hsiao-p'ing, An Tzu-wen, and others ousted the cadres of the Red Army everywhere and replaced them with traitors. They did not trust the veteran cadres of the Red Army. Of all things, the dragging out of the traitors this time is the greatest victory. The overthrow of them is the greatest victory. It doesn't make much difference if things are put a bit at the lower level. The most important thing is to strike down the traitors and secret agents."

Vice Chairman Lin also instructed: "It takes courage to acquire high skill. Work must be carried out like lightning striking and storms brewing. Business must be handled with speed and accuracy, and not procrastination.

"It is necessary to look for cadres from among the workers and peasants. They understand life best, and know the class struggle and production. Shanghai is the place where workers are the mainstay. It is necessary to follow the line of the workers and peasants. To carry out local work means to implement political and ideological work."

When the conversation came to an end, Comrade Ch'eng Shih-ch'ing said farewell to the beloved Vice Chairman Lin and left with the trust of Chairman Mao, Vice Chairman Lin and the Party Central Committee.

69

REPORT TO THE NINTH NATIONAL CONGRESS
OF THE COMMUNIST PARTY OF CHINA*
(Delivered on April 1 and Adopted on April 14, 1969)

Comrades!

The Ninth National Congress of the Communist Party of China
will be a congress with a far-reaching influence in the history
of our Party.

Our present congress is convened at a time when great victory has been won in the Great Proletarian Cultural Revolution
personally initiated and led by Chairman Mao. This great revolutionary storm has shattered the bourgeois headquarters headed
by the renegade, hidden traitor, and scab Liu Shao-ch'i, exposed
the handful of renegades, enemy agents, and absolutely unrepentant persons in power taking the capitalist road within the
Party, with Liu Shao-ch'i as their arch-representative, and
smashed their plot to restore capitalism; it has tremendously
strengthened the dictatorship of the proletariat of our country,
tremendously strengthened our Party and thus prepared ample
conditions for this congress politically, ideologically, and
organizationally.

I. On the Preparation for the Great Proletarian
Cultural Revolution

The Great Proletarian Cultural Revolution of our country is

---

*"Tsai Chung-kuo kung-ch'an-tang ti-chiu-tz'u ch'üan-kuo
tai-piao ta-hui shang ti pao-kao." Hung-ch'i [Red Flag], No. 5
(May 1, 1969), 7-48; this translation is taken, with minor editorial
revisions, from Peking Review, No. 18 (April 30, 1969), 16-35.

a genuine proletarian revolution on an immense scale.

Chairman Mao has explained the necessity of the current great revolution in concise terms: "The current Great Proletarian Cultural Revolution is absolutely necessary and most timely for consolidating the dictatorship of the proletariat, preventing capitalist restoration, and building socialism." In order to comprehend this scientific thesis of Chairman Mao's fully, we should have a deep understanding of his theory of continuing the revolution under the dictatorship of the proletariat.

In 1957, shortly after the conclusion of the Party's Eighth National Congress, Chairman Mao published his great work "On the Correct Handling of Contradictions Among the People," in which, following his "Report to the Second Plenary Session of the Seventh Central Committee of the Communist Party of China," he comprehensively set forth the existence of contradictions, classes, and class struggle under the conditions of the dictatorship of the proletariat, set forth the thesis of the existence of two different types of contradictions in socialist society, those between ourselves and the enemy and those among the people, and set forth the great theory of continuing the revolution under the dictatorship of the proletariat. Like a radiant beacon, this great work illuminates the course of China's socialist revolution and socialist construction and has laid the theoretical foundation for the current Great Proletarian Cultural Revolution.

In order to have a deeper understanding of Chairman Mao's great historic contribution, it is necessary briefly to review the historical experience of the international communist movement.

In 1852, Marx said: "Long before me bourgeois historians had described the historical development of this class struggle and bourgeois economists the economic anatomy of the classes. What I did that was new was to prove: 1) that the existence of classes is only bound up with particular historical phases in the development of production, 2) that the class struggle necessarily leads to the dictatorship of the proletariat, 3) that this dictatorship itself only constitutes the transition to the abolition of all classes and to a classless society" (Marx and Engels, Selected Correspondence, Chinese ed., p. 63). Marx's theory of the

dictatorship of the proletariat clearly distinguished scientific
socialism from utopian socialism and sham socialism of every
kind. Marx and Engels fought all their lives for this theory
and for its realization.

After the death of Marx and Engels, almost all the parties
of the Second International betrayed Marxism, with the exception of the Bolshevik Party led by Lenin. Lenin inherited, defended, and developed Marxism in the struggle against the revisionism of the Second International. The struggle focused on
the question of the dictatorship of the proletariat. In denouncing
the old revisionists, Lenin time and again stated: "Those who
recognize only the class struggle are not yet Marxists....
Only he is a Marxist who extends the recognition of the class
struggle to the recognition of the dictatorship of the proletariat"
(Lenin, Collected Works, Chinese ed., Vol. 25, p. 399).

Lenin led the proletariat of Russia in winning the victory of
the Great October Socialist Revolution and founding the first
socialist state. Through his great revolutionary practice in
leading the dictatorship of the proletariat, Lenin perceived the
danger of the restoration of capitalism and the protracted nature of class struggle: "The transition from capitalism to Communism represents an entire historical epoch. Until this epoch
has terminated, the exploiters inevitably cherish the hope of restoration, and this hope is converted into attempts at restoration"
(Lenin, Collected Works, Chinese ed., Vol. 28, p. 235).

Lenin stated: "...the bourgeoisie, whose resistance is increased tenfold by its overthrow (even if only in one country),
and whose power lies not only in the strength of international
capital, in the strength and durability of the international con-
nections of the bourgeoisie, but also in the force of habit in the
strength of small production. For, unfortunately, small production is still very, very widespread in the world, and small
production engenders capitalism and the bourgeoisie continuously, daily, hourly, spontaneously, and on a mass scale"
(Lenin, Collected Works, Chinese ed., Vol. 31, p. 6). His conclusion was: "For all these reasons the dictatorship of the
proletariat is essential" (Ibid.).

Lenin also stated that "the new bourgeoisie" was "arising from among our Soviet government employees" (Lenin, Collected Works, Chinese ed., Vol. 29, p. 162).

He pointed out that the danger of restoration also came from capitalist encirclement: The imperialist countries "will never miss an opportunity for military intervention, as they put it, i.e., to strangle Soviet power" (Lenin, Collected Works, Chinese ed., Vol. 31, p. 423).

The Soviet revisionist renegade clique has completely betrayed these brilliant teachings of Lenin's. From Khrushchev to Brezhnev and company, they are all persons in power taking the capitalist road, who have long concealed themselves in the Communist Party of the Soviet Union. As soon as they came to power, they turned the bourgeoisie's "hope of restoration" into "attempts at restoration," usurped the leadership of the Party of Lenin and Stalin and, through "peaceful evolution," turned the world's first state of the dictatorship of the proletariat into a dark fascist state of the dictatorship of the bourgeoisie.

Chairman Mao has waged a tit-for-tat struggle against modern revisionism with the Soviet revisionist renegade clique as its center and has inherited, defended, and developed the Marxist-Leninist theory of proletarian revolution and the dictatorship of the proletariat. Chairman Mao has comprehensively summed up the historical experience of the dictatorship of the proletariat both in the positive and negative aspects and, in order to prevent the restoration of capitalism, has put forward the theory of continuing the revolution under the dictatorship of the proletariat.

As early as March 1949, on the eve of the transition of the Chinese revolution from the new-democratic revolution to the socialist revolution, Chairman Mao explicitly pointed out in his report to the Second Plenary Session of the Seventh Central Committee of the Party: After the countrywide seizure of power by the proletariat, the principal internal contradiction is "the contradiction between the working class and the bourgeoisie." The heart of the struggle is still the question of state power.

Chairman Mao especially reminded us: "After the enemies
with guns have been wiped out, there will still be enemies without guns; they are bound to struggle desperately against us,
and we must never regard these enemies lightly. If we do not
now raise and understand the problem in this way, we shall commit the gravest mistakes." Having foreseen the protracted and
complex nature of the class struggle between the proletariat
and the bourgeoisie after the establishment of the dictatorship
of the proletariat, Chairman Mao set the whole Party the militant task of fighting imperialism, the Kuomintang, and the bourgeoisie in the political, ideological, economic, cultural, and
diplomatic spheres.

Our Party waged intense battles in accordance with the resolution of the Second Plenary Session of the Seventh Central
Committee and the Party's General Line for the transition
period formulated by Chairman Mao. In 1956 the socialist
transformation of the ownership of the means of production in
agriculture, handicrafts,and capitalist industry and commerce
was in the main completed. That was the crucial moment for
the question of whether the socialist revolution could continue
to advance. In view of the rampancy of revisionism in the international communist movement and the new trends of class
struggle in our country, Chairman Mao, in his great work "On
the Correct Handling of Contradictions Among the People,"
called the attention of the whole Party to the following fact:
"In China, although in the main socialist transformation has
been completed with respect to the system of ownership ...
there are still remnants of the overthrown landlord and comprador classes, there is still a bourgeoisie, and the remolding
of the petty bourgeoisie has only just started." Countering the
fallacy put forward by Liu Shao-ch'i in 1956 that "in China, the
question of which wins out, socialism or capitalism, is already
solved," Chairman Mao specifically pointed out:

"The question of which will win out, socialism or capitalism,
is still not really settled.

"The class struggle between the proletariat and the bourgeoisie, theclass struggle between the different political forces,

and the class struggle in the ideological field between the proletariat and the bourgeoisie will continue to be long and tortuous and at times will even become very acute."

Thus, for the first time in the theory and practice of the international communist movement, it was pointed out explicitly that classes and class struggle still exist after the socialist transformation of the ownership of the means of production has been in the main completed, and that the proletariat must continue the revolution.

The proletarian headquarters headed by Chairman Mao led the broad masses in carrying on the great struggle in the direction he indicated. From the struggle against the bourgeois Rightist in 1957 to the struggle to uncover P'eng Te-huai's anti-Party clique at the Lushan Meeting in 1959, from the great debate on the General Line of the Party in building socialism to the struggle between the two lines in the socialist education movement — the focus of the struggle was the question of whether to take the socialist road or to take the capitalist road, whether to uphold the dictatorship of the proletariat or to restore the dictatorship of the bourgeoisie.

Every single victory of Chairman Mao's proletarian revolutionary line, every victory in every major campaign launched by the Party against the bourgeoisie, was gained only after smashing the revisionist line represented by Liu Shao-ch'i, which either was Right or was "Left" in form but Right in essence.

Now it has been proved through investigation that as far back as the First Revolutionary Civil War period Liu Shao-ch'i betrayed the Party, capitulated to the enemy, and became a hidden traitor and scab, that he was a crime-steeped lackey of the imperialists, modern revisionists, and Kuomintang reactionaries, and that he was the arch-representative of the persons in power taking the capitalist road. He had a political line by which he vainly attempted to restore capitalism in China and turn her into an imperialist and revisionist colony. In addition, he had an organizational line to serve his counterrevolutionary political line. For many years, recruiting deserters and turncoats, Liu Shao-ch'i gathered together a gang of renegades, enemy agents,

and capitalist-roaders in power. They covered up their counterrevolutionary political records, shielded each other, colluded
in doing evil, usurped important Party and government posts,
and controlled the leadership in many central and local units,
thus forming an underground bourgeois headquarters in opposition to the proletarian headquarters headed by Chairman Mao.
They collaborated with the imperialists, modern revisionists,
and Kuomintang reactionaries and played the kind of disruptive
role that the U.S. imperialists, the Soviet revisionists, and the
reactionaries of various countries were not in a position to do.

In 1939, when the War of Resistance Against Japan and for
National Liberation led by Chairman Mao was vigorously surging forward, Liu Shao-ch'i dished up his sinister book Self-
Cultivation. The core of that book was the betrayal of the dictatorship of the proletariat. It did not touch at all upon the questions of defeating Japanese imperialism and of waging the struggle against the Kuomintang reactionaries; nor did it touch upon
the fundamental Marxist-Leninist principle of seizing state
power by armed force; on the contrary, it urged Communist
Party members to depart from the great practice of revolution
and indulge in idealistic "self-cultivation," which actually meant
that Communists should "cultivate" themselves into willing slaves
going down on their knees before the counterrevolutionary dictatorship of the imperialists and the Kuomintang reactionaries.

After the victory of the War of Resistance Against Japan,
when the U.S. imperialists were arming Chiang Kai-shek's
counterrevolutionary troops in preparation for launching an
all-out offensive against the liberated areas, Liu Shao-ch'i,
catering to the needs of the U.S.-Chiang reactionaries, dished
up the capitulationist line, alleging that "China has entered the
new stage of peace and democracy." It was designed to oppose
Chairman Mao's general line of "go all out to mobilize the
masses, expand the people's forces and, under the leadership
of our Party, defeat the aggressor and build a new China," and
to oppose Chairman Mao's policy of "give tit for tat and fight
for every inch of land," which was adopted to counter the offensive of the U.S.-Chiang reactionaries. Liu Shao-ch'i preached

that "at present the main form of the struggle of the Chinese revolution has changed from armed struggle to non-armed and mass parliamentary struggle." He tried to abolish the Party's leadership over the people's armed forces and to "unify" the Eighth Route Army and the New Fourth Army, predecessors of the People's Liberation Army, into Chiang Kai-shek's "national army" and to demobilize large numbers of worker and peasant soldiers led by the Party in a vain attempt to eradicate the people's armed forces, strangle the Chinese revolution, and hand over to the Kuomintang the fruits of victory which the Chinese people had won in blood.

In April 1949, on the eve of the countrywide victory of China's new-democratic revolution when the Chinese People's Liberation Army was preparing to cross the Yangtse River, Liu Shao-ch'i hurried to Tientsin and threw himself into the arms of the capitalists. He wildly opposed the policy of utilizing, restricting, and transforming private capitalist industry, a policy decided upon by the Second Plenary Session of the Seventh Central Committee of the Party which had just concluded. He clamored that "capitalism in China today is still in its youth," that it needed an unlimited "big expansion" and that "capitalist exploitation today is no crime, it is a merit." He shamelessly praised the capitalist class, saying that "the more they exploit, the greater their merit," and feverishly advertised the revisionist theory of productive forces. He did all this in his futile attempt to lead China onto the capitalist road.

In short, at the many important historical junctures of the new-democratic revolution and the socialist revolution, Liu Shao-ch'i and his gang always wantonly opposed Chairman Mao's proletarian revolutionary line and engaged in counterrevolutionary conspiratorial and disruptive activities. However, since they were counterrevolutionaries, their plots were bound to come to light. When Khrushchev came to power, and especially when the Soviet revisionists ganged up with the U.S. imperialists and the reactionaries of India and other countries in whipping up a large-scale anti-China campaign, Liu Shao-ch'i and his gang became all the more rabid.

Chairman Mao was the first to perceive the danger of the counterrevolutionary plots of Liu Shao-ch'i and his gang. At the working conference of the Central Committee in January 1962, Chairman Mao pointed out the necessity of guarding against the emergence of revisionism. At the working conference of the Central Committee at Peitaiho in August 1962 and at the Tenth Plenary Session of the Eighth Central Committee of the Party in September of the same year, Chairman Mao put forward more comprehensively the basic line of our Party for the whole historical period of socialism. Chairman Mao pointed out: "Socialist society covers a fairly long historical period. In the historical period of socialism, there are still classes, class contradictions and class struggle, there is the struggle between the socialist road and the capitalist road, and there is the danger of capitalist restoration. We must recognize the protracted and complex nature of this struggle. We must heighten our vigilance. We must conduct socialist education. We must correctly understand and handle class contradictions and class struggle, distinguish the contradictions between ourselves and the enemy from those among the people and handle them correctly. Otherwise a socialist country like ours will turn into its opposite and degenerate, and a capitalist restoration will take place. From now on we must remind ourselves of this every year, every month, and every day so that we can retain a rather sober understanding of this problem and have a Marxist-Leninist line." This Marxist-Leninist line advanced by Chairman Mao is the lifeline of our Party.

Following this, in May 1963, under the direction of Chairman Mao, the Draft Decision of the Central Committee of the Chinese Communist Party on Certain Problems in Our Present Rural Work (i.e., the Ten-Point Decision) was worked out, which laid down the line, principles, and policies of the Party for the socialist education movement. Chairman Mao again warned the whole Party: If classes and class struggle were forgotten and if the dictatorship of the proletariat were forgotten, "then it would not be long, perhaps only several years or a decade, or several decades at most, before a counterrevolutionary restoration on a national scale would inevitably occur, the Marxist-Leninist party would undoubtedly become a revisionist party or a fascist party, and the whole of China would change its color. Comrades, please think it over. What a dangerous situation this would be! " Thus Chairman Mao still more sharply showed the whole Party and the whole nation the danger of the restoration of capitalism.

All these warnings and struggles did not and could not in the least change the reactionary class nature of Liu Shao-ch'i and his gang. In 1964, in the great socialist education movement, Liu Shao-ch'i came out to repress the masses, shield the capitalist-roaders in power, and openly attack the Marxist scientific method of investigating and studying social conditions initiated by Chairman Mao, branding it as "outdated." He raved that whoever refused to carry out his line was "not qualified to hold a leading post." He and his gang were working against time to restore capitalism. At the end of 1964 Chairman Mao convened a working conference of the Central Committee and, under his direction, the document Some Current Problems Raised in the Socialist Education Movement in the Rural Areas (i.e., the Twenty-three-Point Document) was drawn up. He denounced Liu Shao-ch'i's bourgeois reactionary line which was "Left" in form but Right in essence and repudiated Liu Shao-ch'i's absurdities, such as "the intertwining of the contradictions inside and outside the Party" and "the contradiction between the 'four cleans' and the 'four uncleans.' " And for the first time Chairman Mao specifically indicated: "The main target of the present movement is those Party persons in power taking the capitalist road." This new conclusion drawn by Chairman Mao after summing up the historical experience of the dictatorship of the proletariat, domestic and international, set right the course of the socialist education movement and clearly showed the orientation for the approaching Great Proletarian Cultural Revolution.

Reviewing the history of this period, we can see that the current Great Proletarian Cultural Revolution, with the participation of hundreds of millions of revolutionary people, has by no

means occurred accidentally. It is the inevitable result of the
protracted and sharp struggle between the two classes, the two
roads, and the two lines in socialist society. The Great Proletarian Cultural Revolution is "a great political revolution carried out by the proletariat against the bourgeoisie and all other
exploiting classes; it is a continuation of the prolonged struggle
waged by the Chinese Communist Party and the masses of revolutionary people under its leadership against the Kuomintang
reactionaries, a continuation of the class struggle between the
proletariat and the bourgeoisie." The heroic Chinese proletariat, poor and lower-middle peasants, People's Liberation
Army, revolutionary cadres, and revolutionary intellectuals,
who were all determined to follow the great leader Chairman
Mao closely in taking the socialist road, could no longer tolerate the restoration activities of Liu Shao-ch'i and his gang,
and so a great class battle was unavoidable.

As Chairman Mao pointed out in his talk in February 1967:
"In the past we waged struggles in rural areas, in factories,
in the cultural field, and we carried out the socialist education
movement. But all this failed to solve the problem because
we did not find a form, a method, to arouse the broad masses
to expose our dark aspect openly, in an all-round way and from
below." Now we have found this form — it is the Great Proletarian Cultural Revolution. It is only by arousing the masses
in their hundreds of millions to air their views freely, write
big-character posters, and hold great debates that the renegades,
enemy agents, and capitalist-roaders in power who have wormed
their way into the Party can be exposed and their plots to restore capitalism smashed. It is precisely with the participation
of the broad masses in the examination of Liu Shao-ch'i's case
that his true features as an old-line counterrevolutionary, renegade, hidden traitor, and scab were brought to light. The Enlarged Twelfth Plenary Session of the Eighth Central Committee of the Party decided to dismiss Liu Shao-ch'i from all posts
both inside and outside the Party and to expel him from the
Party once and for all. This was a great victory for the hundreds of millions of the people. On the basis of the theory of

continuing the revolution under the dictatorship of the proletariat, our great teacher Chairman Mao has personally initiated
and led the Great Proletarian Cultural Revolution. This is indeed "absolutely necessary and most timely" and it is a new
and great contribution to the theory and practice of Marxism-
Leninism.

II. On the Course of the Great Proletarian
Cultural Revolution

The Great Proletarian Cultural Revolution is a great political
revolution personally initiated and led by our great leader
Chairman Mao under the conditions of the dictatorship of the
proletariat, a great revolution in the realm of the superstructure. Our aim is to smash revisionism, seize back that portion
of power usurped by the bourgeoisie, exercise all-round dictatorship of the proletariat in the superstructure, including all
spheres of culture, and strengthen and consolidate the economic
base of socialism so as to ensure that our country continues to
advance in giant strides along the road of socialism.

Back in 1962, at the Tenth Plenary Session of the Eighth
Central Committee of the Party, Chairman Mao pointed out:
"To overthrow a political power, it is always necessary first
of all to create public opinion, to do work in the ideological
sphere. This is true for the revolutionary class as well as for
the counterrevolutionary class." This statement of Chairman
Mao's hit the Liu Shao-ch'i counterrevolutionary revisionist
clique right on the head. It was solely for the purpose of creating public opinion to prepare for the overthrow of the dictatorship of the proletariat that they spared no effort in seizing
upon the field of ideology and the superstructure, violently
exercising counterrevolutionary dictatorship over the proletariat in the various departments they controlled and wildly
spreading poisonous weeds. To overthrow them politically,
we must likewise first vanquish their counterrevolutionary
public opinion by revolutionary public opinion.

Chairman Mao has always attached major importance to the

struggle in ideology. After the liberation of our country, he initiated on different occasions the criticism of the film The Life of Wu Hsun, the Hu Feng counterrevolutionary clique, Studies of "The Dream of the Red Chamber", etc. And this time it was Chairman Mao again who led the whole Party in launching the offensive on the bourgeois positions occupied by Liu Shao-ch'i and his gang. Chairman Mao wrote the celebrated essay "Where Do Correct Ideas Come From?" and other documents, in which he criticized Liu Shao-ch'i's bourgeois idealism and metaphysics, criticized the departments of literature and art under Liu Shao-ch'i's control as being "still dominated by 'the dead,'" criticized the Ministry of Culture by saying that "if it refuses to change, it should be renamed the Ministry of Emperors, Kings, Generals and Prime Ministers, the Ministry of Scholars and Beauties or the Ministry of Foreign Mummies," and said that the Ministry of Health should likewise be renamed the "Ministry of Health for Urban Overlords." At the call of Chairman Mao, the proletariat first launched a revolution in the spheres of Peking Opera, the ballet, and symphonic music, spheres that had been regarded as sacred and inviolable by the landlord and capitalist classes. It was a fight at close quarters. Despite every possible kind of resistance and sabotage by Liu Shao-ch'i and his gang, the proletariat finally scored important successes after arduous struggles. A number of splendid model revolutionary theatrical works came into being and the heroic images of the workers, peasants, and soldiers finally rose aloft on the stage. After that, Chairman Mao initiated the criticism of Hai Jui Dismissed From Office and other poisonous weeds, focusing the attack right on the den of the revisionist clique — that impenetrable and watertight "independent kingdom" under Liu Shao-ch'i's control, the old Peking Municipal Party Committee.

The Circular of May 16, 1966, worked out under Chairman Mao's personal guidance, laid down the theory, line, principles, and policies for the Great Proletarian Cultural Revolution and constituted the great program for the whole movement. The Circular thoroughly criticized the "February Outline" turned

out by Liu Shao-ch'i's bourgeois headquarters for the purpose
of suppressing this great revolution. It called upon the whole
Party and the whole nation to direct the spearhead of struggle
against the representatives of the bourgeoisie who had sneaked
into the Party and to pay special attention to unmasking "persons like Khrushchev ... who are still nestling beside us." This
was a great call mobilizing the people of the whole country to
unfold a great political revolution. The Cultural Revolution
Group Under the Central Committee, which was set up by decision of the Circular, has firmly carried out Chairman Mao's
proletarian revolutionary line.

Under the guidance of Chairman Mao's proletarian revolutionary line, the broad revolutionary masses plunged into the
fight. In Peking University a big-character poster was written
in response to the call of the Central Committee. And soon
big-character posters criticizing reactionary bourgeois ideas
mushroomed all over the country. Then Red Guards rose and
came forward in large numbers and revolutionary young people
became courageous and daring pathbreakers. Thrown into a
panic, the Liu Shao-ch'i clique hastily hurled forth the bourgeois reactionary line, cruelly suppressing the revolutionary
movement of the student youth. However, this did not win them
much time in their deathbed struggle. Chairman Mao called
and presided over the Eleventh Plenary Session of the Eighth
Central Committee of the Party. The Plenary Session adopted
the programmatic document, Decision of the Central Committee
of the Chinese Communist Party Concerning the Great Proletarian Cultural Revolution (i.e., the Sixteen-Point Decision).
Chairman Mao put up his big-character poster "Bombard the
Headquarters," thus taking the lid off Liu Shao-ch'i's bourgeois
headquarters. In his letter to the Red Guards, Chairman Mao
said that the revolutionary actions of the Red Guards "express
your wrath against and your denunciation of the landlord class,
the bourgeoisie, the imperialists, the revisionists and their
running dogs, all of whom exploit and oppress the workers,
peasants, revolutionary intellectuals, and revolutionary parties
and groups. They show that it is right to rebel against reaction-

aries. I warmly support you." Afterward, Chairman Mao received 13 million Red Guards and other revolutionary masses
from all parts of the country on eight occasions at Tien An Men
in the capital, which heightened the revolutionary fighting will
of the people of the whole country. The revolutionary movements of the workers, peasants, and revolutionary functionaries
developed rapidly. Increasing numbers of big-character posters
spread like raging prairie fire and roared like guns; the slogan
"It is right to rebel against reactionaries" resounded throughout
the land. And the battle of the hundreds of millions of the people to bombard Liu Shao-ch'i's bourgeois headquarters developed
vigorously.

No reactionary class will ever step down from the stage of
history of its own accord. When the revolution touched that
portion of power usurped by the bourgeoisie, the class struggle
became all the more acute. After Liu Shao-ch'i's downfall, his
revisionist clique and his agents in various places changed their
tactics time and again, putting forward slogans which were
"Left" in form but Right in essence, such as "suspecting all"
and "overthrowing all," in a futile attempt to go on hitting hard
at the many and protecting their own handful. Moreover, they
created splits among the revolutionary masses and manipulated
and hoodwinked a section of the masses so as to protect themselves. When these schemes were shattered by the proletarian
revolutionaries, they launched another frenzied counterattack,
and that was the adverse current lasting from the winter of
1966 to the spring of 1967.

This adverse current was directed against the proletarian
headquarters headed by Chairman Mao. Its general program
boiled down to this: overthrowing the decisions adopted by the
Eleventh Plenary Session of the Eighth Central Committee of
the Party, reversing the verdict on the overthrown bourgeois
headquarters headed by Liu Shao-ch'i, reversing the verdict on
the bourgeois reactionary line, which had already been thoroughly
repudiated and discredited by the broad masses, and repressing
and retaliating against the revolutionary mass movement. However, this adverse current was seriously criticized by Chairman

Mao and resisted by the broad revolutionary masses; it could
not prevent the main current of the revolutionary mass movement from surging forward.

The twists and reversals in the revolutionary movement further brought home to the broad masses the importance of political power: the main reason why Liu Shao-ch'i and his gang
could do evil was that they had usurped the power of the proletariat in many units and localities, and the main reason why
the revolutionary masses were repressed was that power was
not in the hands of the proletariat in those places. In some
units the socialist system of ownership existed only in form,
but in reality the leadership had been usurped by a handful of
renegades, enemy agents, and capitalist-roaders in power, or
it remained in the hands of former capitalists. Especially
when the capitalist-roaders in power whipped up the evil counterrevolutionary wind of economism after failing in their scheme
to suppress the revolution on the pretext of "grasping production," the broad masses came to understand still better that
only by recapturing the lost power was it possible for them to
defeat the capitalist-roaders in power completely. Under the
leadership and with the support of Chairman Mao and the proletarian headquarters headed by him, the working class in
Shanghai, with its revolutionary tradition, came forward courageously and, uniting with the broad revolutionary masses and
revolutionary cadres, seized power from below in January 1967
from the capitalist-roaders in power in the former Municipal
Party Committee and Municipal People's Council.

Chairman Mao summed up in good time the experience of
the January storm of revolution in Shanghai and issued his call
to the whole nation: "Proletarian revolutionaries, unite and
seize power from the handful of Party persons in power taking
the capitalist road." Following that, Chairman Mao gave the
instruction: "The People's Liberation Army should support
the broad masses of the Left." He went on to sum up the experience of Heilungkiang Province and other provinces and
municipalities and laid down the principles and policies for the
establishment of the revolutionary committee which embraces

representatives of the revolutionary cadres, representatives
of the People's Liberation Army, and representatives of the
revolutionary masses, constituting a revolutionary three-in-
one combination, thus pushing forward the nationwide struggle
for the seizure of power.

The struggle between the proletariat and the bourgeoisie for
the seizure and counterseizure of power was a life-and-death
struggle. During the one year and nine months from Shanghai's
January storm of revolution in 1967 to the establishment of
the revolutionary committees of Tibet and Sinkiang in September
1968, repeated trials of political strength took place between
the two classes and the two lines, fierce struggles went on between proletarian and nonproletarian ideas, and an extremely
complicated situation emerged. As Chairman Mao has said:
"In the past, we fought north and south; it was easy to fight
such wars. For the enemy was obvious. The present Great
Proletarian Cultural Revolution is much more difficult than
that kind of war.

"The problem is that those who commit ideological errors
are mixed up with those whose contradiction with us is one between ourselves and the enemy, and for a time it is hard to
sort them out."

Nevertheless, relying on the wise leadership of Chairman
Mao, we finally overcame this difficulty. In the summer of
1967, Chairman Mao made an inspection tour north and south
of the Yangtse River and issued extremely important instructions, guiding the broad revolutionary masses to distinguish
gradually the contradictions between ourselves and the enemy
from those among the people and to further bring about the
revolutionary great alliance and the revolutionary three-in-one
combination and guiding people with petty-bourgeois ideas onto
the path of the proletarian revolution. Consequently, it was
only the enemy who was thrown into disorder while the broad
masses were steeled in the course of the struggle.

The handful of renegades, enemy agents, unreformed landlords, rich peasants, counterrevolutionaries, bad elements and
rightists, active counterrevolutionaries, bourgeois careerists,

and double-dealers who had hidden themselves among the masses would not reveal their colors until the climate suited them. In the summer of 1967 and the spring of 1968, they again fanned up a reactionary evil wind to reverse correct verdicts both from the Right and the extreme "Left." They directed their spearhead against the proletarian headquarters headed by Chairman Mao, against the People's Liberation Army, and against the newborn revolutionary committees. In the meantime, they incited the masses to struggle against each other and organized counterrevolutionary conspiratorial cliques in a vain attempt to stage a counterseizure of power from the proletariat. However, like their chieftain, Liu Shao-ch'i, this handful of bad people was finally exposed. This was an important victory for the Great Proletarian Cultural Revolution.

III. On Carrying Out the Tasks of Struggle-Criticism-Transformation Conscientiously

As in all other revolutions, the fundamental question in the current great revolution in the realm of the superstructure is the question of political power, a question of which class holds leadership. The establishment of revolutionary committees in all provinces, municipalities, and autonomous regions throughout the country (with the exception of Taiwan Province) marks the great, decisive victory achieved by this revolution. However, the revolution is not yet over. The proletariat must continue to advance, "carry out the tasks of struggle-criticism-transformation conscientiously," and carry the socialist revolution in the realm of the superstructure through to the end.

Chairman Mao says: "Struggle-criticism-transformation in a factory, on the whole, goes through the following stages: establishing a three-in-one revolutionary committee; carrying out mass criticism and repudiation; purifying the class ranks; consolidating the Party organization; and simplifying the administrative structure, changing irrational rules and regulations, and sending office workers to the workshops." We must act on Chairman Mao's instruction and fulfill these tasks in every single factory, every single school, every single commune, and every single unit in a deepgoing, meticulous, down-to-earth, and appropriate way.

Confronted with a thousand and one tasks, a revolutionary committee must grasp the fundamental: it must put the living study and application of Mao Tse-tung thought above all work and place Mao Tse-tung thought in command of everything. For decades, Mao Tse-tung thought has been showing the orientation of the revolution to the whole Party and the whole nation. However, as Liu Shao-ch'i and his gang of counterrevolutionary revisionists blocked Chairman Mao's instructions, the broad revolutionary masses could hardly hear Chairman Mao's voice directly. The storm of the present great revolution has destroyed the "palaces of hell-rulers," big and small, and has made it possible for Mao Tse-tung thought to reach the broad revolutionary masses directly. This is a great victory. This wide dissemination of Mao Tse-tung thought in a big country with a population of 700 million is the most significant achievement of the Great Proletarian Cultural Revolution. In this revolution, hundreds of millions of people always carry with them Quotations from Chairman Mao Tse-tung, which they study and apply conscientiously. As soon as a new instruction of Chairman Mao's is issued, they propagate it and go into action. This most valuable practice must be maintained and persevered in. We should carry on in a deepgoing way the mass movement for the living study and application of Mao Tse-tung thought, continue to run well the Mao Tse-tung thought study classes of all types and, in the light of Chairman Mao's "May 7 Directive" of 1966, truly turn the whole country into a great school of Mao Tse-tung thought.

All revolutionary comrades must be clearly aware that class struggle will by no means cease in the ideological and political spheres. The struggle between the proletariat and the bourgeoisie by no means dies out with our seizure of power. We must continue to hold high the banner of revolutionary mass criticism and use Mao Tse-tung thought to criticize the bourgeoisie, to criticize revisionism and all kinds of Right or ex-

treme "Left" erroneous ideas which run counter to Chairman
Mao's proletarian revolutionary line, and to criticize bourgeois
individualism and the theory of "many centers," that is, the
theory of "no center." We must continue to criticize thoroughly
and discredit completely the stuff of the renegade, hidden traitor,
and scab Liu Shao-ch'i, such as the slavish comprador philosophy and the doctrine of trailing behind at a snail's pace, and
must firmly establish among the cadres and the masses of the
people Chairman Mao's concept of "maintaining independence
and keeping the initiative in our own hands and relying on our
own efforts," so as to ensure that our cause will continue to
advance in the direction indicated by Chairman Mao.

Chairman Mao points out: "The revolutionary committee
should exercise unified leadership, eliminate duplication in the
administrative structure, follow the policy of 'better troops
and simpler administration,' and organize itself into a revolutionized leading group which maintains close ties with the
masses." This is a basic principle which enables the superstructure to serve its socialist economic base still better. A
duplicate administrative structure divorced from the masses,
scholasticism which suppresses and binds their revolutionary
initiative, and a landlord and bourgeois style of formality and
ostentation — all these are destructive to the socialist economic
base, advantageous to capitalism and disadvantageous to socialism. In accordance with Chairman Mao's instructions, organs
of state power at all levels and other organizations must keep
close ties with the masses, first of all with the basic masses —
the working class and the poor and lower-middle peasants.
Cadres, old and new, must constantly sweep away the dust of
bureaucracy and must not catch the bad habit of "acting as
bureaucrats and overlords." They must keep on practicing
frugality in carrying out revolution, run all socialist undertakings industriously and thriftily, oppose extravagance and
waste, and guard against the bourgeois attacks with sugarcoated
bullets. They must maintain the system of cadre participation
in collective productive labor. They must be concerned with
the well-being of the masses. They must themselves make

investigation and study in accordance with Chairman Mao's teachings, dissect one or several "sparrows," and constantly sum up experiences. They must make criticism and self-criticism regularly and, in line with the five requirements for the successors to the revolution as set forth by Chairman Mao, "fight self, criticize revisionism," and conscientiously remold their world outlook.

The People's Liberation Army is the mighty pillar of the dictatorship of the proletariat. Chairman Mao has pointed out many times: From the Marxist point of view the main component of the state is the army. The Chinese People's Liberation Army personally founded and led by Chairman Mao is an army of the workers and peasants, an army of the proletariat. It has performed great historic feats in the struggle for overthrowing the three big mountains of imperialism, feudalism, and bureau-cratic-capitalism, and in the struggles for defending the mother-land, for resisting U.S. aggression and aiding Korea, and for smashing aggression by imperialism, revisionism, and the reaction-aries. In the Great Proletarian Cultural Revolution, large numbers of commanders and fighters have taken part in the work of "three supports and two militaries" (i.e., support in-dustry, support agriculture, support the broad masses of the Left, military control, political and military training) and rep-resentatives of the army have taken part in the three-in-one combination; they have tempered themselves in the class strug-gle, strengthened their ties with the masses, promoted the ideological revolutionization of the army, and made new contri-butions to the people. And this is also the best preparation against war. We must carry forward the glorious tradition of "supporting the government and cherishing the people," "sup-porting the army and cherishing the people," strengthen the unity between the army and the people, strengthen the building of the militia and of national defense, and do a still better job in all our work. For the past three years it is precisely be-cause the people have supported the army and the army has protected the people that renegades, enemy agents, absolutely unrepentant persons in power taking the capitalist road, and

counterrevolutionaries have failed in their attempts to undermine this great people's army of ours.

Departments of culture, art, education, the press, health, etc.,
occupy an extremely important position in the realm of the
superstructure. The line "We must wholeheartedly rely on the
working class" was decided upon at the Second Plenary Session
of the Seventh Central Committee. And now, at Chairman Mao's
call that "The working class must exercise leadership in everything," the working class, which is the main force in the proletarian revolution, and its staunch ally the poor and lower-
middle peasants have mounted the political stage of struggle-
criticism-transformation in the superstructure. From July 27,
1968, mighty contingents of the working class marched to places
long dominated by the persons in power taking the capitalist
road and to all places where intellectuals were predominant in
number. It was a great revolutionary action. Whether the proletariat is able to take firm root in the positions of culture and
education and transform them with Mao Tse-tung thought is the
key question in carrying the Great Proletarian Cultural Revolution through to the end. Chairman Mao has attached profound
importance to our work in this connection and personally
grasped typicals, thus setting us a brilliant example. We must
overcome the wrong tendency among some comrades who make
light of the ideological, cultural, and educational front; we must
closely follow Chairman Mao and consistently do arduous and
meticulous work. "On its part, the working class should always raise its political consciousness in the course of struggle,"
sum up the experience in leading the struggle-criticism-transformation in the superstructure, and win the battle on this front.

IV. On the Policies of the Great Proletarian
Cultural Revolution

In order to continue the revolution in the realm of the superstructure, it is imperative to carry out conscientiously all of
Chairman Mao's proletarian policies.

Policies for the Great Proletarian Cultural Revolution were

early explicitly stipulated in the Circular of May 16, 1966, and
the Sixteen-Point Decision of August 1966. The series of Chairman Mao's latest instructions, including "serious attention must
be paid to policy in the stage of struggle-criticism-transformation in the Great Proletarian Cultural Revolution," have further
specified the various policies.

The main question at present is to carry them out to the
letter.

The Party's policies, including those towards the intellectuals, the cadres, "the sons and daughters that can be educated"
[The sons and daughters of those who have committed crimes
or mistakes — trans.], the mass organizations, the struggle
against the enemy and the economic policy — all these policies
come under the general subject of the correct handling of the
two different types of contradictions, those between ourselves
and the enemy and those among the people.

The majority or the vast majority of the intellectuals trained
in the old type of schools and colleges are able or willing to
integrate themselves with the workers, peasants, and soldiers.
They should be "reeducated" by the workers, peasants, and
soldiers under the guidance of Chairman Mao's correct line,
and encouragement should be given to those who have done well
in the integration and to the Red Guards and educated young
people who are active in going to the countryside or mountainous
areas.

Chairman Mao has taught us many times: "Help more people
by educating them and narrow the target of attack" and "carry
out Marx's teaching that only by emancipating all mankind can
the proletariat achieve its own final emancipation." With regard to people who have made mistakes, stress must be laid
on giving them education and reeducation, doing patient and
careful ideological and political work, and truly acting "on the
principle of 'learning from past mistakes to avoid future ones'
and 'curing the sickness to save the patient,' in order to achieve
the twofold objective of clarity in ideology and unity among
comrades." With regard to good people who committed the
errors characteristic of the capitalist-roader in power but have

now raised their political consciousness and gained the understanding of the masses, they should be promptly "liberated,"
assigned to suitable work, and encouraged to go among the
masses of the workers and peasants to remold their world outlook. As for those who have made a little progress and become
to some extent awakened, we should continue to help them, proceeding from the viewpoint of unity. Chairman Mao has recently
pointed out: "The proletariat is the greatest class in the history
of mankind. It is the most powerful revolutionary class ideologically, politically, and in strength. It can and must unite the
overwhelming majority of people around itself so as to isolate
the handful of enemies to the maximum and attack them."

In the struggle against the enemy, we must carry out the
policy "make use of contradictions, win over the many, oppose
the few, and crush our enemies one by one" which Chairman
Mao has always advocated. "Stress should be laid on the weight
of evidence and on investigation and study, and it is strictly
forbidden to obtain confessions by compulsion and to give them
credence." We must implement Chairman Mao's policies of
"leniency towards those who confess their crimes and severe
punishment of those who refuse to do so" and of "giving a way
out." We rely mainly on the broad masses of the people in
exercising dictatorship over the enemy. As for bad people or
suspects ferreted out through investigation in the movement for
purifying the class ranks, the policy of "killing none and not
arresting most" should be applied to all except the active
counterrevolutionaries against whom there is conclusive evidence of crimes such as murder, arson, or poisoning, and who
should be dealt with in accordance with the law.

As for the bourgeois reactionary academic authorities, we
should either criticize them and see, or criticize them and give
them work to do, or criticize them and provide them with a
proper livelihood. In short, we should criticize their ideology
and at the same time give them a way out. To handle this part
of the contradictions between ourselves and the enemy in the
manner of handling contradictions among the people is beneficial to the consolidation of the dictatorship of the proletariat
and to the disintegration of the enemy ranks.

In carrying out the policies of the Party, it is necessary to study the specific conditions of the unit concerned. In places where the revolutionary great alliance has not yet been sufficiently consolidated, it is necessary to help the revolutionary masses bring about, in accordance with revolutionary principles, the revolutionary great alliance on the basis of different fields of work, trades, and school classes so that they will become united against the enemy. In units where the work of purifying the class ranks has not yet started or has only just started, it is imperative to grasp the work firmly and do it well in accordance with the Party's policies. In units where the purification of the class ranks is by and large completed, it is necessary to take firm hold of other tasks in keeping with Chairman Mao's instructions concerning the various stages of struggle-criticism-transformation. At the same time, it is necessary to pay close attention to new trends in the class struggle. What if the bad people go wild again? Chairman Mao has a well-known saying: "Thoroughgoing materialists are fearless." If the class enemies stir up trouble again, just arouse the masses and strike them down again.

As the Sixteen-Point Decision indicates, "The Great Proletarian Cultural Revolution is a powerful motive force for the development of the social productive forces in our country." Our country has seen good harvests in agricultural production for years running, and there is also a thriving situation in industrial production and science and technology. The enthusiasm of the broad masses of the working people both in revolution and production has soared to unprecedented heights. Many factories, mines and other enterprises have time and again topped their production records, creating all-time highs in production. The technical revolution is making constant progress. The market is flourishing and prices are stable. By the end of 1968 we had redeemed all the national bonds. Our country is now a socialist country with neither internal nor external debts.

"Grasp revolution, promote production" — this principle is absolutely correct. It correctly explains the relationship between revolution and production, between consciousness and matter, between the superstructure and the economic base, and between the relations of production and the productive forces. Chairman Mao always teaches us: "Political work is the life-blood of all economic work." Lenin denounced the opportunists who were opposed to approaching problems politically: "Politics cannot but have precedence over economics. To argue differently means forgetting the A B C of Marxism" (Lenin, Collected Works, Chinese ed., Vol. 32, p. 72). Lenin again stated: To put politics on a par with economics also means "forgetting the A B C of Marxism" (Ibid.). Politics is the concentrated expression of economics. If we fail to make revolution in the superstructure, fail to arouse the broad masses of the workers and peasants, fail to criticize the revisionist line, fail to expose the handful of renegades, enemy agents, capitalist-roaders in power and counterrevolutionaries, and fail to consolidate the leadership of the proletariat, how can we further consolidate the socialist economic base and further develop the socialist productive forces? This is not to replace production by revolution but to use revolution to command production, promote it and lead it forward. We must make investigation and study, and actively and properly solve the many problems of policy in struggle-criticism-transformation on the economic front in accordance with Chairman Mao's General Line of "Going all out, aiming high, and achieving greater, faster, better, and more economical results in building socialism" and in accordance with his great strategic concept "Be prepared against war, be prepared against natural disasters, and do everything for the people" and with the series of principles such as "take agriculture as the foundation and industry as the leading factor." We must bring the revolutionary initiative and creativeness of the people of all nationalities into full play, firmly grasp revolution, and energetically promote production and fulfill and overfulfill our plans for developing the national economy. It is certain that the great victory of the Great Proletarian Cultural Revolution will continue to bring about new leaps forward on the economic front and in our cause of socialist construction as a whole.

V. On the Final Victory of the Revolution in Our Country

The victory of the Great Proletarian Cultural Revolution of our country is very great indeed. But we must in no way think that we may sit back and relax. Chairman Mao pointed out in his talk in October 1968: "We have won great victory. But the defeated class will still struggle. These people are still around and this class still exists. Therefore, we cannot speak of final victory. Not even for decades. We must not lose our vigilance. According to the Leninist viewpoint, the final victory of a socialist country not only requires the efforts of the proletariat and the broad masses of the people at home, but also involves the victory of the world revolution and the abolition of the system of exploitation of man by man on the whole globe, upon which all mankind will be emancipated. Therefore, it is wrong to speak lightly of the final victory of the revolution in our country; it runs counter to Leninism and does not conform to facts." There will be reversals in the class struggle. We must never forget class struggle and never forget the dictatorship of the proletariat. In the course of carrying out our policies at present, there still exists the struggle between the two lines, and there is interference from the "Left" or the Right. It still calls for much effort to accomplish the tasks for all the stages of struggle-criticism-transformation. We must closely follow Chairman Mao and steadfastly rely on the broad revolutionary masses to surmount the difficulties and twists and turns on our way forward and seize still greater victories in the cause of socialism.

VI. On the Consolidation and Building of the Party

The victory of the Great Proletarian Cultural Revolution has provided us with valuable experience on how we should build the Party under the conditions of the dictatorship of the proletariat. As Chairman Mao has indicated to the whole Party, "The Party organization should be composed of the advanced elements of the proletariat; it should be a vigorous vanguard organization capable of leading the proletariat and the revolutionary masses in the fight against the class enemy." Chairman Mao's instruction has determined our political orientation for consolidating and building the Party.

The Communist Party of China has been nurtured and built up by our great leader Chairman Mao. Since its birth in 1921, our Party has gone through long years of struggle for the seizure of state power and the consolidation of the dictatorship of the proletariat by armed force. Led by Chairman Mao, our Party has always stood in the forefront of revolutionary wars and struggles. Under the guidance of Chairman Mao's correct line, our Party has, in the face of extremely strong domestic and foreign enemies and in the most complex circumstances, led the proletariat and the broad masses of the people of China in adhering to the principle of maintaining independence and keeping the initiative in our own hands and relying on our own efforts, in upholding proletarian internationalism, and in waging heroic struggles with one stepping into the breach as another fell, and it is only thus that our Party has grown from Communist groups with only a few dozen members at the outset into the great, glorious, and correct Party leading the powerful People's Republic of China today. We deeply understand that without the armed struggle of the people, there would not be the Communist Party of China today and there would not be the People's Republic of China today. We must forever bear in mind Chairman Mao's teaching: "Comrades throughout the Party must never forget this experience for which we have paid in blood."

The Communist Party of China owes all its achievements to the wise leadership of Chairman Mao, and these achievements constitute victories for Mao Tse-tung thought. For half a century now, in leading the great struggle of the people of all the nationalities of China for accomplishing the new-democratic revolution, in leading China's great struggle for socialist revolution and socialist construction, and in the great struggle of the contemporary international communist movement against imperialism, modern revisionism, and reactionaries of various countries, Chairman Mao has integrated the universal truth of Marxism-Leninism with the concrete practice of revolution, has inherited, defended, and developed Marxism-Leninism in the political, military, economic, cultural, and philosophical spheres, and has brought Marxism-Leninism to a higher and completely new stage. Mao Tse-tung thought is Marxism-Leninism of the era in which imperialism is heading for total collapse and socialism is advancing to worldwide victory. The entire history of our Party has borne out this truth: Departing from the leadership of Chairman Mao and Mao Tse-tung thought, our Party will suffer setbacks and defeats; following Chairman Mao closely and acting on Mao Tse-tung thought, our Party will advance and triumph. We must forever remember this lesson. Whoever opposes Chairman Mao, whoever opposes Mao Tse-tung thought, at any time or under any circumstances, will be condemned and punished by the whole Party and the whole nation.

Discussing the consolidation and building of the Party, Chairman Mao has said: "A human being has arteries and veins through which the heart makes the blood circulate, and he breathes with his lungs, exhaling carbon dioxide and inhaling fresh oxygen, that is, getting rid of the stale and taking in the fresh. A proletarian party must also get rid of the stale and take in the fresh, for only thus can it be full of vitality. Without eliminating waste matter and absorbing fresh blood the Party has no vigor." With this vivid analogy, Chairman Mao has expounded the dialectics of inner-Party contradiction. "The law of contradiction in things, that is, the law of the unity of opposites, is the basic law of materialist dialectics." Opposition and struggle between the two lines within the Party are a reflection inside the Party of contradictions between classes and between the new and the old in society. If there were no contradictions in the Party and no struggles to resolve them, and if the Party did not get rid of the stale and take in the fresh, the Party's life would come to an end. Chairman Mao's theory on inner-Party contradiction is and will be the fundamental guiding thinking for the consolidation and building of the Party.

The history of the Communist Party of China is one in which

Chairman Mao's Marxist-Leninist line combats the Right and
"Left" opportunist lines in the Party. Under the leadership of
Chairman Mao, our Party defeated Ch'en Tu-hsiu's Right opportunist line, defeated the "Left" opportunist lines of Ch'ü
Ch'iu-pai and Li Li-san, defeated Wang Ming's first "Left" and
then Right opportunist lines, defeated Chang Kuo-t'ao's line of
splitting the Red Army, defeated the Right opportunist anti-
Party bloc of P'eng Te-huai, Kao Kang, Jao Shu-shih, and others
and after long years of struggle, has shattered Liu Shao-ch'i's
counterrevolutionary revisionist line. Our Party has consolidated itself, developed and grown in strength precisely in the
struggle between the two lines, especially in the struggles to
defeat the three renegade cliques of Ch'en Tu-hsiu, Wang Ming,
and Liu Shao-ch'i, which did the gravest harm to the Party.

In the new historical period of the dictatorship of the proletariat, the proletariat enforces its dictatorship and exercises
its leadership in every field of work through its vanguard, the
Communist Party. Departing from the dictatorship of the proletariat and from continuing the revolution under the dictatorship
of the proletariat, it is impossible to solve correctly the question of Party-building, the question of building what kind of
Party and how to build it.

Liu Shao-ch'i's revisionist line on Party-building betrayed
the very essence of the Marxist-Leninist teaching on the dictatorship of the proletariat and of the Marxist-Leninist theory on
Party-building. At the crucial moment when China's socialist
revolution was deepening and the class struggle was extraordinarily acute, Liu Shao-ch'i had his sinister book Self-Cultivation
republished, and it was precisely his aim to overthrow the dictatorship of the proletariat in our country and restore the dictatorship of the bourgeoisie. When he copied the passage from
Lenin on the necessity of the dictatorship of the proletariat,
which we quoted earlier in this report, Liu Shao-ch'i once
again deliberately omitted the most important conclusion that
"the dictatorship of the proletariat is essential," thereby clearly
revealing his own counterrevolutionary features as a renegade
to the dictatorship of the proletariat. Moreover, Liu Shao-ch'i

went on spreading such reactionary fallacies as the theory of "the dying out of class struggle," the theory of "docile tools," the theory that "the masses are backward," the theory of "joining the Party in order to climb up," the theory of "inner-Party peace," and the theory of "merging private and public interests" (i.e., "losing a little to gain much"), in a vain attempt to corrupt and disintegrate our Party, so that the more the Party members "cultivated" themselves, the more revisionist they would become and so that the Marxist-Leninist Party would "evolve peacefully" into a revisionist party and the dictatorship of the proletariat into the dictatorship of the bourgeoisie. We should carry on revolutionary mass criticism and repudiation and thoroughly eliminate the pernicious influence of Liu Shao-ch'i's reactionary fallacies.

The Great Proletarian Cultural Revolution is the most broad and deepgoing movement for Party consolidation in the history of our Party. The Party organizations at various levels and the broad masses of Communists have experienced the acute struggle between the two lines, gone through the test in the large-scale class struggle, and undergone examination by the revolutionary masses both inside and outside the Party. In this way the Party members and cadres have faced the world and braved the storm and have raised their class consciousness and their consciousness of the struggle between the two lines. This great revolution tells us: Under the dictatorship of the proletariat, we must educate the masses of Party members on classes, on class struggle, on the struggle between the two lines, and on continuing the revolution. We must fight revisionism both inside and outside the Party, clear the Party of renegades, enemy agents, and other elements representing the interests of the exploiting classes, and admit into the Party the genuine advanced elements of the proletariat who have been tested in the great storm. We must strive to ensure that the leadership of the Party organizations at all levels is truly in the hands of Marxists. We must see to it that the Party members really integrate theory with practice, maintain close ties with the masses, and are bold in making criticism and self-criticism. We must see to it that the Party members will always keep to the style of being modest, prudent, and free from arrogance and rashness and to the style of arduous struggle and plain living. Only thus will the Party be able to lead the proletariat and the revolutionary masses in carrying the socialist revolution through to the end.

Chairman Mao teaches us: "Historical experience merits attention. A line or a viewpoint must be explained constantly and repeatedly. It won't do to explain them only to a few people; they must be made known to the broad revolutionary masses." The study and spread of the basic experience of the Great Proletarian Cultural Revolution, the study and spread of the history of the struggle between the two lines, and the study and spread of Chairman Mao's theory of continuing the revolution under the dictatorship of the proletariat must be conducted not just once but should be repeated every year, every month, every day. Only thus will it be possible for the masses of Party members and the people to criticize and resist erroneous lines and tendencies the moment they emerge, and will it be possible to guarantee that our Party will always forge ahead victoriously along the correct course charted by Chairman Mao.

The revision of the Party Constitution is an important item on the agenda of the Ninth National Congress of the Party. The Central Committee has submitted the draft Party Constitution to the congress for discussion. This draft was worked out jointly by the whole Party and the revolutionary masses throughout the country. Since November 1967, when Chairman Mao proposed that basic Party organizations take part in the revision of the Party Constitution, the Central Committee has received several thousand drafts. On this basis the Enlarged Twelfth Plenary Session of the Eighth Central Committee of the Party drew up the draft Party Constitution, upon which the whole Party, the whole army, and the revolutionary masses throughout the country once again held enthusiastic and earnest discussions. It may be said that the draft of the new Party Constitution is the product of the integration of the great leader Chairman Mao's wise leadership with the broad masses; it reflects the will of the whole Party, the whole army and the revolutionary masses throughout the country and gives a vivid demonstration of the democratic centralism and the mass line to which the Party has always adhered. Especially important is the fact that the draft Party Constitution has clearly reaffirmed that Marxism-Leninism-Mao Tse-tung Thought is the theoretical basis guiding the Party's thinking. This is a great victory for the Great Proletarian Cultural Revolution in smashing Liu Shao-ch'i's revisionist line on Party-building, a great victory for Marxism-Leninism-Mao Tse-tung Thought. The Central Committee is convinced that after the discussion and adoption of the new Party Constitution by the congress, our Party will, in accordance with its provisions, surely be built into a still greater, still more glorious, and still more correct Party.

VII. On China's Relations with Foreign Countries

Now we shall go on specifically to discuss China's relations with foreign countries.

The revolutionary struggles of the proletariat and the oppressed people and nations of the world always support each other. The Albanian Party of Labor and all other genuine fraternal Marxist-Leninist Parties and organizations, the broad masses of the proletariat, and revolutionary people throughout the world as well as many friendly countries, organizations, and personages have all warmly acclaimed and supported the Great Proletarian Cultural Revolution of our country. On behalf of the great leader Chairman Mao and the Ninth National Congress of the Party, I hereby express our heartfelt thanks to them. We firmly pledge that we the Communist Party of China and the Chinese people are determined to fulfill our proletarian internationalist duty and, together with them, carry through to the end the great struggle against imperialism, modern revisionism, and all reaction.

The general trend of the world today is still as Chairman Mao described it: "The enemy rots with every passing day, while

for us things are getting better daily." On the one hand, the
revolutionary movement of the proletariat of the world and of
the people of various countries is vigorously surging forward.
The armed struggles of the people of southern Vietnam, Laos,
Thailand, Burma, Malaya, Indonesia, India, Palestine, and other
countries and regions in Asia, Africa, and Latin America are
steadily growing in strength. The truth that "Political Power
grows out of the barrel of a gun" is being grasped by ever
broader masses of the oppressed people and nations. An unprecedentedly gigantic revolutionary mass movement has broken
out in Japan, Western Europe, and North America, the "heart-
lands" of capitalism. More and more people are awakening.
The genuine fraternal Marxist-Leninist parties and organizations are growing steadily in the course of integrating Marxism-
Leninism with the concrete practice of revolution in their own
countries. On the other hand, U.S. imperialism and Soviet revisionist social-imperialism are bogged down in political and
economic crises, beset with difficulties both at home and abroad,
and find themselves in an impasse. They collude and at the
same time contend with each other in a vain attempt to redivide
the world. They act in coordination and work hand in glove in
opposing China, opposing communism, and opposing the people,
in suppressing the national liberation movement and in launching
wars of aggression. They scheme against each other and get
locked in strife for raw materials, markets, dependencies, important strategic points, and spheres of influence. They are
both stepping up arms expansion and war preparations, each
trying to realize its own ambitions.

Lenin pointed out: Imperialism means war. "...imperialist
wars are absolutely inevitable under such an economic system,
as long as private property in the means of production exists"
(Lenin, Collected Works, Chinese ed., Vol. 22, p. 182). Lenin
further pointed out: "Imperialist war is the eve of socialist
revolution" (Lenin, Collected Works, Chinese ed., Vol. 25,
p. 349). These scientific theses of Lenin's are by no means
out of date.

Chairman Mao has recently pointed out, "With regard to the

question of world war, there are but two possibilities: One is
that the war will give rise to revolution, and the other is that
revolution will prevent the war." This is because there are
four major contradictions in the world today: The contradiction
between the oppressed nations on the one hand and imperialism
and social-imperialism on the other; the contradiction between
the proletariat and the bourgeoisie in the capitalist and revisionist countries; the contradiction between imperialist and
social-imperialist countries and among the imperialist countries; and the contradiction between socialist countries on the
one hand and imperialism and social-imperialism on the other.
The existence and development of these contradictions are
bound to give rise to revolution. According to the historical
experience of World War I and World War II, it can be said with
certainty that if the imperialists, revisionists, and reactionaries should impose a third world war on the people of the
world, it would only greatly accelerate the development of these
contradictions and help arouse the people of the world to rise
in revolution and send the whole pack of imperialists, revisionists, and reactionaries to their graves.

Chairman Mao teaches us: "All reactionaries are paper
tigers." "Strategically we should despise all our enemies, but
tactically we should take them all seriously." This great truth
enunciated by Chairman Mao heightens the revolutionary militancy of the people of the whole world and guides us from victory to victory in the struggle against imperialism, revisionism, and all reaction.

The nature of U.S. imperialism as a paper tiger has long
since been laid bare by the people throughout the world. U.S.
imperialism, the most ferocious enemy of the people of the
whole world, is going downhill more and more. Since he took
office, Nixon has been confronted with a hopeless mess and an
insoluble economic crisis, with the strong resistance of the
masses of the people at home and throughout the world and with
the predicament in which the imperialist countries are disinte-
grating and the baton of U.S. imperialism is getting less and
less effective. Unable to produce any solution to these problems,

Nixon, like his predecessors, cannot but continue to play the counterrevolutionary dual tactics, ostensibly assuming a "peace-loving" appearance while in fact engaging in arms expansion and war preparations on a still larger scale. The military expenditures of the United States have been increasing year by year. To date the U.S. imperialists still occupy our territory Taiwan. They have dispatched aggressor troops to many countries and have also set up hundreds upon hundreds of military bases and military installations in different parts of the world. They have made so many airplanes and guns, so many nuclear bombs and guided missiles. What is all this for? To frighten, suppress and slaughter the people and dominate the world. By doing so they make themselves the enemy of the people everywhere and find themselves besieged and battered by the broad masses of the proletariat and the people all over the world, and this will definitely lead to revolutions throughout the world on a still larger scale.

The Soviet revisionist renegade clique is a paper tiger, too. It has revealed its social-imperialist features more and more clearly. When Khrushchev revisionism was just beginning to emerge, our great leader Chairman Mao foresaw what serious harm modern revisionism would do to the cause of world revolution. Chairman Mao led the whole Party in waging resolute struggles in the ideological, theoretical, and political spheres, together with the Albanian Party of Labor headed by the great Marxist-Leninist Comrade Enver Hoxha and with the genuine Marxist-Leninists of the world, against modern revisionism with Soviet revisionism as its center. This has enabled the people all over the world to learn gradually in struggle how to distinguish genuine Marxism-Leninism from sham Marxism-Leninism and genuine socialism from sham socialism and brought about the bankruptcy of Khrushchev revisionism. At the same time, Chairman Mao led our Party in resolutely criticizing Liu Shao-ch'i's revisionist line of capitulation to imperialism, revisionism, and reaction and of suppression of revolutionary movements in various countries and in destroying Liu Shao-ch'i's counterrevolutionary revisionist clique. All this has been done in the fulfillment of our Party's proletarian internationalist duty.

Since Brezhnev came to power, with its baton becoming less and less effective and its difficulties at home and abroad growing more and more serious, the Soviet revisionist renegade clique has been practicing social-imperialism and social-fascism more frantically than ever. Internally, it has intensified its suppression of the Soviet people and speeded up the all-round restoration of capitalism. Externally, it has stepped up its collusion with U.S. imperialism and its suppression of the revolutionary struggles of the people of various countries, intensified its control over and its exploitation of various East European countries and the People's Republic of Mongolia, intensified its contention with U.S. imperialism over the Middle East and other regions, and intensified its threat of aggression against China. Its dispatch of hundreds of thousands of troops to occupy Czechoslovakia and its armed provocations against China on our territory Chenpao Island are two foul performances staged recently by Soviet revisionism. In order to justify its aggression and plunder, the Soviet revisionist renegade clique trumpets the so-called theory of "limited sovereignty," the theory of "international dictatorship," and the theory of "socialist community." What does all this stuff mean? It means that your sovereignty is "limited," while his is unlimited. You won't obey him? He will exercise "international dictatorship" over you — dictatorship over the people of other countries, in order to form the "socialist community" ruled by the new tsars, that is, colonies of social-imperialism, just like the "New Order of Europe" of Hitler, the "Greater East Asia Co-prosperity Sphere" of Japanese militarism, and the "Free World Community" of the United States. Lenin denounced the renegades of the Second International: "Socialism in words, imperialism in deeds, the growth of opportunism into imperialism" (Lenin, Collected Works, Chinese ed., Vol. 29, p. 458). This applies perfectly to the Soviet revisionist renegade clique of today which is composed of a handful of capitalist-roaders in power. We firmly believe that the proletariat and the broad

masses of the people in the Soviet Union with their glorious
revolutionary tradition will surely rise and overthrow this clique
consisting of a handful of renegades. As Chairman Mao points
out: "The Soviet Union was the first socialist state and the
Communist Party of the Soviet Union was created by Lenin. Although the leadership of the Soviet Party and state has now been
usurped by revisionists, I would advise comrades to remain
firm in the conviction that the masses of the Soviet people and
of Party members and cadres are good, that they desire revolution, and that revisionist rule will not last long."

Now that the Soviet government has created the incident of
armed encroachment on the Chinese territory Chenpao Island,
the Sino-Soviet boundary question has caught the attention of
the whole world. Like boundary questions between China and
some of her other neighboring countries, the Sino-Soviet boundary question is also one left over by history. As regards these
questions, our Party and government have consistently stood
for negotiations through diplomatic channels to reach a fair and
reasonable settlement. Pending a settlement, the status quo of
the boundary should be maintained and conflicts avoided. Proceeding from this stand, China has satisfactorily and succes-
sively settled boundary questions with neighboring countries
such as Burma, Nepal, Pakistan, the People's Republic of Mongolia, and Afghanistan. Only the boundary questions between
the Soviet Union and China and between India and China remain
unsettled to this day.

The Chinese Government held repeated negotiations with the
Indian government on the Sino-Indian boundary question. As
the reactionary Indian government had taken over the British
imperialist policy of aggression, it insisted that we recognize
the illegal "McMahon line" which even the reactionary governments of different periods in old China had not recognized,
and moreover, it went a step further and vainly attempted to
occupy the Aksai Chin area, which has always been under Chinese jurisdiction, thereby disrupting the Sino-Indian boundary
negotiations. This is known to all.

The Sino-Soviet boundary question is the product of tsarist

Russian imperialist aggression against China. In the latter half of the nineteenth century, when power was not in the hands of the Chinese and Russian people, the tsarist government took imperialist acts of aggression to carve up China, imposed a series of unequal treaties on her, annexed vast expanses of her territory and, moreover, crossed the boundary line stipulated by the unequal treaties, in many places, and occupied still more Chinese territory. This gangster behavior was indignantly condemned by Marx, Engels, and Lenin. On September 27, 1920, the Government of Soviets led by the great Lenin solemnly proclaimed: It "declares null and void all the treaties concluded with China by the former Governments of Russia, renounces all seizure of Chinese territory and all Russian concessions in China, and restores to China, without any compensation and forever, all that had been predatorily seized from her by the Tsar's Government and the Russian bourgeoisie" (See "Declaration of the Government of the Russian Socialist Federated Soviet Republic to the Chinese Government"). Owing to the historical conditions of the time, this proletarian policy of Lenin's was not realized.

As early as August 22 and September 21, 1960, the Chinese Government, proceeding from its consistent stand on boundary questions, twice took the initiative in proposing to the Soviet government that negotiations be held to settle the Sino-Soviet boundary question. In 1964 negotiations between the two sides started in Peking. The treaties relating to the present Sino-Soviet boundary are unequal treaties imposed on the Chinese people by the tsars, but out of the desire to safeguard the revolutionary friendship between the Chinese and Soviet people, we still maintained that these treaties be taken as the basis for the settlement of the boundary question. However, betraying Lenin's proletarian policy and clinging to its new-tsarist social-imperialist stand, the Soviet revisionist renegade clique refused to recognize these treaties as unequal and, moreover, it insisted that China recognize as belonging to the Soviet Union all the Chinese territory which they had occupied or attempted to occupy in violation of the treaties. This great-power chauvinist and social-imperialist stand of the Soviet government led to the disruption of the negotiations.

Since Brezhnev came to power, the Soviet revisionist renegade clique has frenziedly stepped up its disruption of the status quo of the boundary and repeatedly provoked border incidents, shooting and killing our unarmed fishermen and peasants and encroaching upon China's sovereignty. Recently it has gone further and made successive armed intrusions into our territory Chenpao Island. Driven beyond the limits of their forbearance, our frontier guards have fought back in self-defense, dealing the aggressors well-deserved blows and triumphantly safeguarding our sacred territory. In an effort to extricate them from their predicament, Kosygin asked on March 21 to communicate with our leaders by telephone. Immediately, on March 22, our government replied with a memorandum, in which it was made clear that, "In view of the present relations between China and the Soviet Union, it is unsuitable to communicate by telephone. If the Soviet government has anything to say, it is asked to put it forward officially to the Chinese Government through diplomatic channels." On March 29 the Soviet government issued a statement still clinging to its obstinate aggressor stand, while expressing willingness to resume "consultations." Our government is considering its reply to this.

The foreign policy of our Party and government is consistent. It is: To develop relations of friendship, mutual assistance, and cooperation with socialist countries on the principle of proletarian internationalism; to support and assist the revolutionary struggles of all the oppressed people and nations; to strive for peaceful coexistence with countries having different social systems on the basis of the Five Principles of mutual respect for territorial integrity and sovereignty, mutual nonaggression, noninterference in each other's internal affairs, equality and mutual benefit, and peaceful coexistence, and to oppose the imperialist policies of aggression and war. Our proletarian foreign policy is not based on expediency; it is a policy in which we have long persisted. This is what we did in the past and we will persist in doing the same in the future.

We have always held that the internal affairs of each country should be settled by its own people. The relations between all countries and between all parties, big or small, must be built on the principles of equality and noninterference in each other's internal affairs. To safeguard these Marxist-Leninist principles the Communist Party of China has waged a long struggle against the sinister great-power chauvinism of the Soviet revisionist renegade clique. This is a fact known to all. The Soviet revisionist renegade clique glibly talks of "fraternal parties" and "fraternal countries," but in fact it regards itself as the patriarchal party, and as the new tsar, who is free to invade and occupy the territory of other countries. They conduct sabotage and subversion against the Chinese Communist Party, the Albanian Party of Labor, and other genuine Marxist-Leninist parties. Moreover, when any party or any country in their so-called "socialist community" holds a slightly different view, they act ferociously and stop at nothing in suppressing, sabotaging, and subverting and even sending troops to invade and occupy their so-called "fraternal countries" and kidnapping members of their so-called "fraternal parties." These fascist piratical acts have sealed their doom.

U.S. imperialism and Soviet revisionism are always trying to "isolate" China; this is China's honor. Their rabid opposition to China cannot do us the slightest harm. On the contrary, it serves to further arouse our people's determination to maintain independence and keep the initiative in our own hands, rely on our own efforts, and work hard to make our country prosperous and powerful; it serves to prove to the whole world that China has drawn a clear line between herself on the one hand and U.S. imperialism and Soviet revisionism on the other. Today it is not imperialism, revisionism, and reaction but the proletariat and the revolutionary people of all countries that determine the destiny of the world. The genuine Marxist-Leninist parties and organizations of various countries, which are composed of the advanced elements of the proletariat, are a new rising force that has infinitely broad prospects. The Communist Party of China is determined to unite and fight together

with them. We firmly support the Albanian people in their
struggle against imperialism and revisionism; we firmly support the Vietnamese people in carrying their war of resistance
against U.S. aggression and for national salvation through to
the end; we firmly support the revolutionary struggles of the
people of Laos, Thailand, Burma, Malaya, Indonesia, India,
Palestine, and other countries and regions in Asia, Africa, and
Latin America; we firmly support the proletariat, the students
and youth, and the masses of the Black people of the United
States in their just struggle against the U.S. ruling clique; we
firmly support the proletariat and the laboring people of the
Soviet Union in their just struggle to overthrow the Soviet revisionist renegade clique; we firmly support the people of
Czechoslovakia and other countries in their just struggle against
Soviet revisionist social-imperialism; we firmly support the
revolutionary struggles of the people of Japan and the West
European and Oceanian countries; we firmly support the revolutionary struggles of the people of all countries; and we firmly
support all the just struggles of resistance against aggression
and oppression by U.S. imperialism and Soviet revisionism.
All countries and people subjected to aggression, control, intervention, or bullying by U.S. imperialism and Soviet revisionism,
unite and form the broadest possible united front and overthrow
our common enemies!

On no account must we relax our revolutionary vigilance because of victory or ignore the danger of U.S. imperialism and
Soviet revisionism launching a large-scale war of aggression.
We must make full preparations, preparations against their
launching a big war and against their launching a war at an
early date, preparations against their launching a conventional
war and against their launching a large-scale nuclear war. In
short, we must be prepared. Chairman Mao said long ago:
"We will not attack unless we are attacked; if we are attacked,
we will certainly counterattack." If they insist on fighting, we
will keep them company and fight to the finish. The Chinese
revolution won out on the battlefield. Armed with Mao Tse-tung
thought, tempered in the Great Proletarian Cultural Revolution,

and with full confidence in victory, the Chinese people in their
hundreds of millions, and the Chinese People's Liberation Army
are determined to liberate their sacred territory Taiwan and
resolutely, thoroughly, wholly, and completely wipe out all aggressors who dare to come!

Our great leader Chairman Mao points out: "Working hand
in glove, Soviet revisionism and U.S. imperialism have done
so many foul and evil things that the revolutionary people the
world over will not let them go unpunished. The people of all
countries are rising. A new historical period of opposing U.S.
imperialism and Soviet revisionism has begun." Whether the
war gives rise to revolution or revolution prevents the war,
U.S. imperialism and Soviet revisionism will not last long!
Workers of all countries, unite! Proletarians and oppressed
people and nations of the world, unite! Bury U.S. imperialism,
Soviet revisionism, and their lackeys!

VIII. The Whole Party, the Whole Nation Unite to Win Still Greater Victories

The Ninth National Congress of the Party is being held at an
important moment in the historical development of our Party,
at an important moment in the consolidation and development
of the dictatorship of the proletariat in our country, and at an
important moment in the development of the international communist movement and world revolution. Among the delegates
to the congress are proletarian revolutionaries of the older
generation and also a large number of fresh blood. In the previous congresses of our Party there have never been such
great numbers of delegates of Party members from among the
industrial workers, poor and lower-middle peasants, and of
women delegates. Among the delegates from the Party members in the People's Liberation Army, there are veteran Red
Army fighters as well as new fighters. The delegates of Party
members from among Red Guards are attending a national congress of the Party for the first time. The fact that so many
delegates have come to Peking from all corners of the country

and gathered around the great leader Chairman Mao to discuss and decide on the affairs of the Party and state signifies that our congress is a congress full of vitality, a congress of unity, and a congress of victory.

Chairman Mao teaches us: "The unification of our country, the unity of our people, and the unity of our various national- ities — these are the basic guarantees of the sure triumph of our cause." Through the Great Proletarian Cultural Revolution our motherland has become unprecedentedly unified and our people have achieved a great revolutionary unity on an extremely broad scale under the great red banner of Mao Tse-tung thought. This great unity is under the leadership of the proletariat and is based on the worker-peasant alliance; it embraces all the fraternal nationalities, the patriotic democrats who for a long time have done useful work for the cause of the revolution and construction of our motherland, the vast numbers of patriotic overseas Chinese and our patriotic compatriots in Hongkong and Macao, our patriotic compatriots in Taiwan who are op- pressed and exploited by the U.S.-Chiang reactionaries, and all those who support socialism and love our socialist mother- land. We are convinced that after the present national congress of our Party, the people of all the nationalities of our country will certainly unite still more closely under the leadership of the great leader Chairman Mao and win still greater victories in the struggle against our common enemy and in the cause of building our powerful socialist motherland.

Chairman Mao said in 1962: "The next fifty to one hundred years, beginning from now, will be a great era of radical change in the social system throughout the world, an earthshaking era with- out equal in any previous historical period. Living in such an era, we must be prepared to engage in great struggles which will have many features different in form from those of the past." This magnificent prospect farsightedly envisioned by Chairman Mao illuminates our path of advance in the days to come and inspires all genuine Marxist-Leninists to fight val- iantly for the realization of the grand ideal of communism.

Let the whole Party unite, let the whole nation unite, hold

high the great red banner of Mao Tse-tung thought, be resolute, fear no sacrifice, and surmount every difficulty to win victory!

Long live the great victory of the Great Proletarian Cultural Revolution!

Long live the dictatorship of the proletariat!

Long live the Ninth National Congress of the Party!

Long live the great, glorious, and correct Communist Party of China!

Long live great Marxism-Leninism-Mao Tse-tung Thought!

Long live our great leader Chairman Mao! A long, long life to Chairman Mao!

70

TALK AT THE RECEPTION FOR SOME OF THE
DELEGATES TO THE CCP NINTH NATIONAL
CONGRESS FROM YUNNAN, KWEICHOW, AND
SZECHWAN*
(May 2, 1969)

(At the reception, Vice Chairman Lin was accompanied by
Comrade Yeh Ch'ün. When we walked in, Vice Chairman Lin
stood up, asked our names, shook hands with us, and sat down.
Vice Chairman Lin said): The Congress is over and I want
to have a little chat with you. You (refers to Tan Fu-jen
[political commissar of Kunming Military Region and chairman of Yunnan Provincial Revolutionary Committee]) just went
to Yunnan and can be more impartial. It is best that there will
be no reversals in Yunnan. I hope that when you go back, you
will do more work on ideological reform. (Yeh Ch'ün emphasized: "It would be best if there are no further reversals in
Yunnan. Political Commissar Tan interrupted: "Are you
sure?" The masses answered: "Yes.") Chairman Mao Tse-
tung called for unity: without unity there can be no victory;
unity is the weapon by which the proletarian class defeats the

---

*This translation is taken, with permission, from Issues &
Studies, VI: 8 (May 1970), 110-113; The text in Chinese is re-
printed in "Lin fu-chu-hsi chieh-chien Yün Kuei Ch'uan san-
sheng i-pu-fen fu-tse t'ung-chih ti chung-yao chih-shih" [Vice
Chairman Lin's Important Instructions at Reception of Some
Responsible Comrades from Yunnan, Kweichow, and Szechwan],
Wen-hua ta ke-ming wen-chien hui-pien [Compendium of Docu-
ments on the Great Cultural Revolution], No. 3-4 (1970), pp. 1-5.

bourgeois class. This is a saying of Lenin. Marx urged unity
in his first manifesto. In the Ninth National Congress, Chairman Mao urged unity. By what can the proletarian class with
bare hands and empty fists defeat the bourgeois class? It is
unity. Some of you comrades present here today are united
with each other, others oppose each other and still others partly
oppose each other. It doesn't matter which is which. You can
and should be united with each other. During the War of Resistance Against Japan, you were united together. In the democratic Revolution against local bullies and bad gentry and the antifeudalism campaign, you were united together. In the campaigns against the bourgeois class and for the implementation
of socialist revolution you should unite yourselves together.
Anti-imperialism and antifeudalism are not the special features
of the Communist Party; doesn't the bourgeois class also oppose feudalism? The antifeudalism and anti-imperialism efforts of the Communist Party lay the foundation for the campaign against capitalism. We are proletarians, and our duty is
to oppose the bourgeois class. Communist Party members
should fight against capitalism, and this cannot be done individually. Some thought that when a leader is overthrown, victory
is assured and problems are solved. Lenin did not agree with
this view. His brother was arrested and killed when he failed
in an attempt to assassinate the Tsar. Lenin thought that this
view led to a blind alley. To unite the proletarian class to
defeat the bourgeois class is the only way. There is no substitute. If the proletarian class wants to resolve its contradiction with the bourgeois class, there is no way but unity. Not
all of us are manual workers; but when we join the Communist
Party and struggle for communism, our ideology is on the same
side with the proletarian class. To make decisions entirely in
accordance with one's professional background is not always
appropriate. Marx, Engels, and Lenin were not manual laborers; nor was Stalin. They were not proletarians at birth, but
their thought was with the proletarian class, and they served
the proletarian class and were determined to strive for the
aims of communism. They were the representatives of the

proletarian class. Therefore, we should judge someone according to his professional background but not entirely so. Both unity and disunity can be found within your ranks. On the major premise, you are united; you are united on many issues, and you differ on some others. This is quite natural. However, we are not naturalists and cannot let it take its own course. Unity is strength. Scientific Marxism-Leninism extols the united and eliminates the disunited. Revolution is elimination. The old things should be overthrown either by violence or nonviolence. Sometimes even certain human beings should be overthrown. It will never do without revolution. The whole history of mankind is a process in which the new replaces the old by means of revolution. It is by revolution that slave society and feudalistic society have progressed to the present society. This is also applicable to the whole universe. Revolution relies on unity. Unity is the weapon and unity is strength. What can one man do? Nothing. One of the important factors why the bourgeois class can rule the great majority of people with a small minority is that the proletarian class does not unite itself but rather is split among itself. If we do not unite ourselves, the imperialist countries will invade us. Disunity is harmful to the country, the people, and the proletarian class. Everything is the unity of opposites and there is unity in each of the opposites. The opposites are contrasted. The two feet of the human body point in different directions and so do the two thumbs. But opposites can be balanced. It is absolutely necessary to have contradiction. To desire no contradiction is not Marxist. Contradiction exists permanently. But we should settle contradiction. Otherwise things cannot progress. If there is revolution, there should be unity. Without unity there can be no revolution. To get rid of unity is to eliminate revolution and help the enemies. You are all united in the campaigns against capitalist-roaders and enemies. Weren't you united together during the War of Resistance Against Japan? Weren't you united together to fight against the American imperialists? Weren't you united together to fight against Chiang Kai-shek? To overthrow Liu Shao-ch'i and those rem-

nants left over by the Kuomintang who are still reactionary in
thought is the great strategic undertaking of Chairman Mao.
Otherwise, it will be disastrous. It is necessary to overthrow
these people. But be careful not to make yourselves confused.
Don't struggle against yourselves with the method by which you
struggle against enemies or fight against yourselves. Otherwise, the enemies, Chiang Kai-shek and the American imperialists, will happily witness it. Don't exaggerate trifles. Don't
solve problems according to your own interest. Be a little
negligent. We should be both negligent and not negligent. We should
not be negligent in significant matters. But we may be negligent in
small matters. Marx once said that a two-man society could not
exist if either would not give up some of his own sovereignty. Without social consciousness, we are but beasts. The ability to use tools
and to unite themselves distinguishes mankind from beasts. Without unity, we could not produce anything and live, and we would go
back to the conditions of thousands of years ago. Revolution needs
unity, and unity within the class should be achieved. Therefore,
you should by all means answer Chairman Mao's call. For
victory, you should unite yourselves on the basis of Mao Tse-
tung thought. You should unite yourselves. There is always
difference in thought, and different levels of human knowledge
and consciousness cannot make it unified. But we need unification. Mao Tse-tung thought can make it unified. Differences
always exist but can be solved by criticism and self-criticism.
You should not overdo it. In the initial phase of the Cultural
Revolution, it was necessary to overdo criticism and self-
criticism; otherwise, the capitalist-roaders could not have
been overthrown, and capitalism would have been restored.
Have we finished overthrowing the capitalist-roaders? Revolution should not cease. Some units at the basic level still have
problems and should continue revolution. Units at the basic
level should be built well; revolution is not yet finished. To
win an overall victory, revolution should be continued. Therefore, you should unite yourselves. Particularly, you, leaders
at higher levels, should do so. Without unity, you only pay lip
service to revolution; that is harmful to revolution and destroys

revolution. Which is better, unity or disunity? Is our country prosperous or not? Are you united or not? Of course, it is better that our country be prosperous and that you unite yourselves. The spirit of the proletarian party and the virtue of Communist Party members is manifested in internal unity. Those who pay no attention to internal unity are not in concert with party spirit and lack the virtue of a Communist. They may be able to drag on for the time being; but sooner or later they will go in opposite directions. Therefore, you should adhere to principle, revolution and unity.

Comrades, don't quarrel with each other, or find fault with each other, or stand in each other's way. You should help each other, respect each other, support each other and comfort each other, and be friends. To work with the same will and joint effort, revolution can be done well and production can be done well. If you cannot unite yourselves well, revolution cannot be done well, and enemies will be happy to see it. Enemies will be delighted to see our country weak. The stronger our country, the more displeasure enemies will feel. When we uprooted the capitalist-roaders and destroyed their conspiracy of restoring capitalism, the enemies were frightened. Those matters which make enemies unhappy and frighten them are good for us. We should be happy with them. Now we should not do things which make enemies happy. The enemies hope that the proletarian revolutionaries will split within our ranks. The enemies will be happy with that. If so, our country cannot become prosperous: when war comes, we'll be in trouble. We want to build up a strong nation, don't we? If we split among ourselves, our country cannot become strong. When we overthrew the capitalist-roaders, the enemies were frightened; when we are united, the enemies feel unhappy. Therefore, we should unite ourselves and make them unhappy. My points are clear enough. I hope that you will respond to Chairman Mao's call to make further efforts to unite yourselves solidly. Disunity will not do. It is neither contradiction between the bourgeois class and the proletarian class nor that between the Kuomintang and the CCP. It is but contradiction within the revolutionary ranks. The

fundamental way to settle contradiction within the revolutionary
ranks is Chairman Mao's teachings, criticism, and self-criticism.
However, criticism and self-criticism should begin with the
will of unity and then can achieve the purpose of unity. There
is nothing serious among you. The provinces (Yunnan, Szechwan,
and Kweichow) all have a population of several tens of millions.
How many people are there in Kweichow? (Li Tsai-han answered: "More than twenty million.") Kweichow is a bit small;
but its population is ten times that of Albania; it is by no means
small. You all have significant missions. Ours is the greatest
age in human history. Socialist revolution is of the greatest
importance in our age. Promote people's awareness and carry
out communism. Systems can be changed with one stroke. Of
course, ideological reform requires a longer amount of time.
The Soviet revolution has a history of half a century and is still
backward because capitalism was restored. Our revolution is
but twenty years old. Socialist revolution should destroy all
the old things left over by each age in history. Their common
points are the system and ideology of private property. Five
thousand years of class society is quite long but is short in comparison with the whole history of mankind. The three hundred
years' history of capitalism is much shorter. It is easy to
change the private-ownership system; but to destroy the concept of private property needs a hundred years, several hundreds, and even longer. You should have the spirit of communism. Communism, as I said before, is a public-ownership
system. To put it in a simpler way, it is public. Some people
talk about "public" but conceal self in their hearts. At last
these people will satisfy their private ends by utilizing public
means. They will have no good end. This is the touchstone to
test whether the virtue of a Communist is genuinely Marxist
or falsely Marxist, whether he really supports Chairman Mao
or not, and whether he speaks truth or falsehood. Be of the
same will and cooperate. If you are not of the same will, you
have to cooperate. I said before that you should regard yourselves as traveling on the same boat during a storm and help
each other to save yourselves.

Comrades, make up your mind, and don't be afraid of sacrifice. Unite yourselves to win victory. Don't play too much with
insignificant matters; that is not the manner of a Communist.
Be magnanimous. To struggle for Communism and for the
liberation of all mankind is the great and glorious enterprise.
I hope that you comrades make up your mind. Don't think that
you are the first in the world. Don't think that you are always
right and others are always wrong. Don't attack with all your
might when you find a tiny fault in others. One is one; two is
two. Don't take one as ten thousand. An ant is an ant; and elephant is an elephant. Don't regard an ant as an elephant. It is
wrong to say ten thousand when you only see one, because it is
not objective. And you should be objective. One of the characteristics of idealism is exaggeration. A small amount is exaggerated into a great quantity. I hope you don't do this. Don't
make a scene over small matters. Don't quarrel with each
other, but live in harmony. Do cooperate with each other, support each other, help each other with revolution. Don't take one
faction into your hands. Unity cannot be achieved without struggle. Now that the stage of struggle is over, you should unite
yourselves.

There are some old friends in this gathering: Chang Kuo-hua
[chairman of Szechwan Revolutionary Committee], Liang Hsing-
chu [vice chairman of Szechwan Revolutionary Committee], Tan
Fu-jen, Chen Kang [vice chairman of Yunnan Revolutionary
Committee], Tien Wei-yang [formerly deputy political commissar of Shenyang Military Region, director, General Political
Department]. I don't know the others or understand their concrete affairs. Therefore, I have spoken rather generally.

MESSAGE TO COMRADE BEQIR BALLUKU*
Most Warmly Greeting the Twenty-Sixth Anniversary
of the Founding of the Albanian People's Army
(July 9, 1969)

Tirana
Vice Chairman of the Council of Ministers and
   Minister of Defense of the People's Republic
   of Albania

Dear Comrade Beqir Balluku:

On the occasion of the twenty-sixth anniversary of the founding of the heroic Albanian People's Army, the Chinese people
and the Chinese People's Liberation Army, imbued with profound feelings of proletarian internationalism, extend their
warmest greetings to the fraternal Albanian people and the
Albanian People's Army.

The Albanian People's Army is a heroic army of the people.
In the past twenty-six years, under the wise leadership of the
Albanian Party of Labor headed by the great Marxist-Leninist
Comrade Enver Hoxha, the Albanian People's Army, uniting
closely with the Albanian people, holding high the great revolutionary banner of Marxism-Leninism and displaying the
thoroughgoing revolutionary spirit of the proletariat, has always advanced from one victory to another with dauntless
heroism and with head erect, whether in the struggle against

---

*"Lin Piao t'ung-chih chih-tien Pa-lu-ku t'ung-chih." Jen-
min jih-pao [People's Daily], July 10, 1969; this official translation is taken from Peking Review, No. 29 (July 18, 1969), 3-4.

the Italian and German fascist aggressors and the class enemy
at home or in the struggle against U.S. imperialism, Soviet revisionism and their lackeys. Together with the Albanian people, the Albanian People's Army has forged a red Albania in
the flames of revolutionary war and built the country into a red
bastion that can never be overwhelmed or destroyed, thus performing immortal meritorious deeds for the motherland and
people.

The Albanian People's Army is a revolutionary army with a
high level of political consciousness and a reliable pillar of the
dictatorship of the proletariat in Albania. In the course of the
vigorous revolutionization campaign of the Albanian people over
the past few years, the Albanian People's Army has resolutely
carried out a series of important directives issued by the Albanian Party of Labor and Comrade Enver Hoxha, adhered to the
proletarian line on army-building, given prominence to proletarian politics, strengthened the Party's leadership over the
army, enhanced ideological and political work, and forged
closer ties between officers and men as well as between the
army and the people. As a result, a vigorous revolutionary
atmosphere has prevailed throughout the army. As the great
leader of the Albanian people Comrade Enver Hoxha pointed
out, the Albanian People's Army "is one of the most important
weapons of the dictatorship of the proletariat, is the beloved
army of the workers and peasants, of all the working masses
of our country."

The great leader of the Chinese people Chairman Mao
pointed out: "The world revolution has entered a great new
era" and "a new historical period of struggle against U.S.
imperialism and Soviet revisionism has begun." Heavily battered by the surging revolutionary movements of the proletariat
and the peoples all over the world, U.S. imperialism and Soviet
revisionist social-imperialism are bogged down in political
and economic crises and beset with difficulties both at home
and abroad and find themselves in an impasse. They collabo-
rate as well as contend with each other and work hand in glove
in doing all kinds of foul and evil things. Last year, the Soviet

revisionist renegade clique dispatched several hundred thousand troops to occupy Czechoslovakia. And this year, it carried out armed provocations in China's Chenpao Island and other frontier areas of our country. Recently, the Soviet revisionist renegade clique single-handedly engineered a sinister meeting in Moscow against communism, the people and revolution, a meeting which was frantically directed against China and Albania. The Soviet revisionist chieftain Brezhnev made rabid war cries at this sinister meeting and so further revealed the hideous features of Soviet revisionist social-imperialism. U.S. imperialism, Soviet revisionism and all reaction in the world are paper tigers. No matter what counterrevolutionary trickery they are up to and no matter how desperately they struggle, they can never escape their doom. The revolutionary people of the world will never let them off. The torrents of revolution are surging forward. The scheme of U.S. imperialism and Soviet revisionism to work in collusion to redivide the world between themselves is bound to fail, and the revolutionary cause of the people of the world is sure to triumph.

The people of China and Albania and their armies have established a profound revolutionary friendship in their common struggle against U.S. imperialism, Soviet revisionism and all reaction. Tempered in the Great Proletarian Cultural Revolution and inspired by the spirit of the Ninth National Congress of our Party, the Chinese people and the Chinese People's Liberation Army will hold the great red banner of Marxism-Leninism-Mao Tse-tung Thought still higher and always unite with and fight alongside the Albanian people and the Albanian People's Army. They will support, encourage and learn from each other and struggle together to bury U.S. imperialism, Soviet revisionism and their running dogs once and for all. Victory definitely belongs to the world's revolutionary people.

> Lin Piao
> Vice-Premier of the State Council
> and Minister of National Defense of
> the People's Republic of China

72

SPEECH AT RALLY CELEBRATING THE TWENTIETH
ANNIVERSARY OF THE FOUNDING OF THE
PEOPLE'S REPUBLIC OF CHINA*
(October 1, 1969)

Comrades and Friends:
Today is the twentieth anniversary of the founding of the great
People's Republic of China. At this time when the people throughout the country are joyously celebrating this glorious festive
occasion, on behalf of our great leader Chairman Mao, the Central Committee of the Communist Party of China, and the Government of the People's Republic of China, I extend salute to
the working class, the poor and lower-middle peasants, the Red
Guards, the revolutionary cadres, and the revolutionary intellectuals of all nationalities of our country! Salute to the heroic
Chinese People's Liberation Army! Salute to all those people
and overseas Chinese who love our socialist motherland! Warm
welcome and greetings to our comrades and friends coming
from various countries of the world!
On the eve of the founding of the People's Republic of China,
our great leader Chairman Mao solemnly proclaimed to the
whole world: The Chinese people, comprising one quarter of
humanity, have now stood up. From the very day of its birth,
the great socialist new China, like the sun rising in the east,
illuminates every corner of the land with a brilliant flame.
From then on, the history of our country has entered a completely new era!

*Peking Review, No. 40 (October 1, 1969), 15-16; for the text in
Chinese, see Jen-min jih-pao [People's Daily], October 2, 1969.

573

In the past twenty years the entire Chinese people, under the brilliant leadership of our great leader Chairman Mao, following Chairman Mao's proletarian revolutionary line, maintaining independence and keeping the initiative in their own hands, relying on their own efforts, waging arduous struggles and working hard, have transformed a backward semifeudal and semicolonial old China into an advanced socialist New China. Our motherland has undergone earthshaking changes.

In the course of struggle over the past twenty years, we have consolidated the political power of the proletariat, victoriously smashed the subversive schemes and disruptive activities of the enemies at home and abroad, and achieved great successes in socialist revolution and socialist construction. While carrying out socialist revolution on the economic front, we have also carried out socialist revolution on the political, ideological, and cultural fronts. The Great Proletarian Cultural Revolution personally initiated and led by Chairman Mao has completely shattered the bourgeois headquarters headed by the renegade, hidden traitor, and scab Liu Shao-ch'i and smashed their plot to restore capitalism. The unprecedented wide dissemination of great Mao Tse-tung thought and its being grasped by hundreds of millions of people are changing enormously people's mental outlook and promoting the steady development of our cause of socialism. Our socialist motherland is thriving and growing ever more prosperous. The people of all nationalities of our country are more united than ever before. The dictatorship of the proletariat has become even more consolidated. The great socialist China, standing like a giant in the East, has become a powerful political force against imperialism and revisionism.

All our victories are victories of Mao Tse-tung thought and of Chairman Mao's proletarian revolutionary line. The practice of our socialist revolution proves that the theory, line, principles, and policies of continuing the revolution under the dictatorship of the proletariat advanced by our great leader Chairman Mao constitute most important new contributions to the theory and practice of Marxism-Leninism and have opened up

a brilliant road for consolidating the dictatorship of the proletariat, preventing capitalist restoration, and carrying the socialist revolution through to the end after the seizure of political
power by the proletariat. From their protracted struggles, the
people of the whole country have come to realize the truth:
Closely following our great leader Chairman Mao means victory.

At the Party's Ninth National Congress of far-reaching historical significance, Chairman Mao issued the great call "Unite
to win still greater victories," which has greatly inspired the
fighting will of the people throughout the country.

Now we must continue to hold aloft the banner of unity and
victory of the Party's Ninth Congress, carry out in an all-round
way the fighting tasks set forth by the Party's Ninth Congress,
and implement all Chairman Mao's proletarian policies. We
must carry on in a more extensive and deepgoing way the mass
movement for the living study and application of Mao Tse-tung
thought and do an even better job of ideological revolutionization.
We must firmly grasp revolutionary mass criticism, carry out
the tasks of struggle-criticism-transformation conscientiously,
carry the Great Proletarian Cultural Revolution through to the
end, and further consolidate the dictatorship of the proletariat.
We must resolutely carry out Chairman Mao's great strategic
policy "Be prepared against war, be prepared against natural
disasters, and do everything for the people"; grasp revolution,
promote production and other work, and preparedness against
war; go all out, aim high, and achieve greater, faster, better,
and more economical results in building socialism and unfold
a new upsurge in revolution and production.

Comrades! We must rally even more closely around the
Party's Central Committee headed by Chairman Mao and
strengthen the Party's centralized and unified leadership. We
must follow Chairman Mao's teachings, remain modest and
prudent and guard against arrogance and rashness, continue to
develop the vigorous proletarian revolutionary spirit, carry on
forever the glorious revolutionary tradition of hard struggle,
bring into full play the initiative and creativeness of the broad
masses, and build our socialist motherland into a more pros-

perous and powerful country and build up a more powerful national defense.

In the past twenty years most profound changes have taken
place in the international situation. The revolutionary movement of the people of various countries is surging to unprecedented heights, while U.S. imperialism and social-imperialism
are becoming more isolated than ever before. In order to extricate themselves from the predicament of being beset with
difficulties both at home and abroad, U.S. imperialism and
social-imperialism are colluding and at the same time contending with each other, carrying out arms expansion and war preparations and wildly attempting to engineer a war of aggression
against our country and flagrantly resorting to nuclear blackmail against us. In the relations between countries, China has
always upheld the Five Principles of Peaceful Coexistence. Our
stand is: <u>We will not attack unless we are attacked; if we are
attacked, we will certainly counterattack.</u> The people of the
whole country must heighten their vigilance, strengthen preparedness against war, and be ready at all times to wipe out
all the enemies who dare to invade us. We are determined to
liberate Taiwan. We warn U.S. imperialism and social-imperialism: The heroic Chinese people and Chinese People's
Liberation Army armed with Mao Tse-tung thought are invincible. Should you insist on imposing a war on the Chinese people, we will keep you company and resolutely fight to the finish!
On the vast land of China, wherever you go, there will be your
burial ground!

We will always uphold proletarian internationalism and firmly
support the heroic Albanian people in their struggle against
imperialism and revisionism; firmly support the heroic Vietnamese people in carrying their war against U.S. aggression
and for national salvation through to the end; firmly support
the Laotian people in their just struggle against the invasion of
Laos by U.S. imperialism and the reactionaries of Thailand;
firmly support the Palestinian people and the people of all Arab
countries in their just struggle against U.S. imperialism and
Zionism; and firmly support the revolutionary struggles of all

the oppressed nations and people of the five continents!

People of the world, unite and oppose the war of aggression launched by any imperialism or social-imperialism, especially one in which atom bombs are used as weapons! If such a war breaks out, the people of the world should use revolutionary war to eliminate the war of aggression, and preparations should be made right now!

Long live the great People's Republic of China!

Long live the great, glorious and correct Communist Party of China!

Long live the victory of Chairman Mao's proletarian revolutionary line!

Long live invincible Marxism-Leninism-Mao Tse-tung Thought!

Long live our great leader Chairman Mao! A long, long life to Chairman Mao!

73

SPEECH AT RALLY CELEBRATING THE
TWENTY-FIRST ANNIVERSARY OF THE
FOUNDING OF THE PEOPLE'S REPUBLIC OF CHINA*
(October 1, 1970)

Comrades and Friends:

Today we are greeting the glorious festival of the twenty-
first anniversary of the establishment of the People's Republic
of China, our socialist motherland founded by our great leader
Chairman Mao.

On behalf of our great leader Chairman Mao, the Central
Committee of the Communist Party of China, and the Government of the People's Republic of China, I extend salute to the
working class, the poor and lower-middle peasants, the Red
Guards, the revolutionary cadres, and the revolutionary intellectuals all over the country! Salute to the people of all nationalities of our country! Salute to the Chinese People's Liberation Army and the people's militia! Salute to all those people
and overseas Chinese who love our socialist motherland! Warm
welcome to our distinguished guests, friends, and comrades
from various countries of the world!

Holding aloft the great red banner of Mao Tse-tung thought
and guided by the line of unity and victory laid down at the
Party's Ninth National Congress, the people of the whole country have in the past year taken great strides forward and continuously won new victories on all fronts. The revolution continues to deepen on the political and ideological front, the cul-

---

*Peking Review, No. 41 (October 9, 1970), 14-15; for the Chi-
nese text, see Jen-min jih-pao [People's Daily], October 2, 1970.

tural and educational front, the economic front, and in all spheres of the superstructure. A new high tide is rising in the great socialist revolution and socialist construction. An invigorating and thriving atmosphere prevails in the fields of agriculture, industry, commerce, culture, education and public health, science and technology, etc. Our national defense has been greatly strengthened. The dictatorship of the proletariat in our country is more consolidated than ever.

On this glorious festive occasion, let us hail the great achievements scored in the mass movement of the people of the whole country for the living study and application of Mao Tse-tung thought, hail the great achievements obtained in the movement of struggle-criticism-transformation in the Great Proletarian Cultural Revolution, hail the great achievements won in the socialist revolution and socialist construction, hail the great achievements won by the People's Liberation Army, the broad masses of the people's militia, and the people of the whole country in enhancing preparedness against war and consolidating national defense!

A new upsurge in the struggle against U.S. imperialism is emerging in the world. As Chairman Mao pointed out in his solemn statement of May 20 this year, "The danger of a new world war still exists, and the people of all countries must get prepared. But revolution is the main trend in the world today." Throughout the world, the people's revolutionary struggles are developing vigorously, and the united front against U.S. imperialism is constantly expanding and growing in strength. U.S. imperialism and social-imperialism are most isolated and are having a very tough time. China's foreign relations are daily developing. We have friends all over the world.

In celebrating the first National Day of the 1970s, our whole Party, whole army and whole people must, in response to the call of the Second Plenary Session of the Ninth Central Committee of the Party, persist in continuing the revolution under the dictatorship of the proletariat, firmly adhere to Chairman Mao's proletarian revolutionary line and policies, and continue to fulfill the various fighting tasks set forth by the Ninth Party Congress.

We must continue to deepen the mass movement for the living study and application of Mao Tse-tung thought and use Marxism-Leninism-Mao Tse-tung Thought consciously to remold our world outlook, linking closely with practice in the Three Great Revolutionary Movements of class struggle, the struggle for production, and scientific experiment. We must conscientiously study Chairman Mao's philosophic works, uphold dialectical materialism and historical materialism, and oppose idealism and metaphysics. We must be good at making investigation and study, summing up experience, and analyzing the contradiction in things so as to know and change the world correctly.

We must continue to grasp firmly revolutionary mass criticism, sweep away the remnant pernicious influence of the counterrevolutionary revisionist line pushed by the renegade, hidden traitor, and scab Liu Shao-ch'i, and carry the movement of struggle-criticism-transformation through to the end.

We must grasp the struggle between the two classes, the two roads, and the two lines as the key and continue to push forward the new high tide in the socialist revolution and socialist construction and work hard to fulfill or overfulfill the National Economic Plan for 1970 and the Third Five-Year Plan and to lay the foundation for the Fourth Five-Year Plan.

We must conscientiously fulfill the task of consolidating and building the Party, strengthen the building of the Party ideologically and organizationally, and give further play to the leading role of the vanguard of the proletariat.

We must continue to strengthen the building of the People's Liberation Army and the people's militia, continue to grasp firmly and strengthen the work for preparedness against war, and heighten our vigilance, defend the motherland. We are determined to liberate Taiwan!

We must uphold proletarian internationalism; firmly support the Albanian people's struggle against imperialism and revisionism; firmly support the peoples of Vietnam, Cambodia, and Laos in their war against U.S. aggression and for national salvation; firmly support the peoples of Korea, Japan, Southeast Asia, and other Asian countries in their struggles against U.S.

imperialism and against the revival of Japanese militarism by the U.S. and Japanese reactionaries; firmly support the Palestinian and other Arab people in their struggle against U.S. imperialism and its collaborator and lackeys; firmly support the people of Africa in their struggle against colonialism and racial discrimination; firmly support the American people's revolutionary struggle; and firmly support the just struggles of the peoples of Asia, Africa, Latin America, Oceania, North America, and Europe. We must further strengthen our militant unity with the genuine Marxist-Leninist Parties and organizations throughout the world and further strengthen our militant unity with the proletariat, the oppressed people, and the oppressed nations of the world and carry the struggle against imperialism, revisionism, and the reactionaries through to the end!

Let us greet the convocation of the Fourth National People's Congress with new victories on all fronts!

People of all nationalities of the country, hold high the great red banner of Mao Tse-tung thought and unite to win still greater victories under the leadership of the Party's Central Committee headed by our great leader Chairman Mao!

Long live the great People's Republic of China!

Long live the great, glorious and correct Communist Party of China!

Long live great Marxism-Leninism-Mao Tse-tung Thought!

Long live our great leader Chairman Mao! A long, long life to Chairman Mao!

Selected bibliography

Arai, Takao. Rin Hyō jidai [The Era of Lin Piao]. Tokyo: Ajia hyoron-sha, 1970.

Asia Research Center, comp. The Great Cultural Revolution in China. Tokyo: Tuttle, 1968.

Barnett, A. Doak. Uncertain Passage. Washington, D.C.: The Brookings Institution, 1974.

Chang Tso-hua. K'ang-Jih chün-tui chung ti cheng-chih kung-tso [Political Work in the Resistance Army]. Hankow: Shang-hai tsa-chih, 1938.

Chang Yü-sheng. Kung-fei-kung-nung hung-chün chien-shih [A Concise History of the Red Army of Workers and Peasants of the Communist Bandits]. Taipei, 1962.

Ch'en Ch'eng, comp. Ch'ih-fei fan-tung wen-chien hui-pien [A Collection of Reactionary Documents of the Red Bandits]. Taipei: Chung-yang wen-wu, 1962.

Cheng, J. Chester, ed. The Politics of the Chinese Red Army. Stanford, Calif.: Hoover Institution, 1965.

Chiang I-shan. Chung-kung chün-shih wen-chien hui-pien [Source Book on Military Affairs in Communist China]. Hong Kong: Yu-lien, 1965.

Chou Ching-wen. Mao Tse-tung ti chün-tui [The Army of Mao Tse-tung]. Hong Kong: Shih-tai, 1964.

583

Chūgoku jimmin kaihōgun [The Chinese People's Liberation Army] Tokyo: Asahi shimbun sha, 1967.

Chūgoku kenkyū geppō [Monthly Research Report on China, Tokyo], Nos. 261-262 (November-December 1969). Special issues on writings of Lin Piao, Parts I-II.

Chün-shih wei-yüan-hui wei-yüan-chang Nan-ch'ang hsing-yin ti-ssu-t'ing, comp. Ch'ih-fei wen-chien hui-pien [A Collection of the Documents of the Red Bandits]. 11 Vols. N.p., 1933-1934.

Chung-kung nien-pao [Yearbook on Chinese Communism], 1966-1973.

Chung-kung wen-hua ta ko-ming chung-yao wen-chien hui-pien [Important Documents of the Great Cultural Revolution in Communist China]. Taipei: Chung-kung yen-chiu, 1973.

Domes, Jürgen. The Internal Politics of China, 1949-1972. New York: Praeger, 1973.

Ebon, Martin. Lin Piao: The Life and Writings of China's New Ruler. New York: Stein & Day, 1970.

Fan, K, ed. Mao Tse-tung and Lin Piao: Post Revolutionary Writings. Garden City, N.Y.: Anchor Books, 1972.

George, Alexander. The Chinese Communist Army in Action. New York: Columbia University Press, 1967.

Gittings, John. The Role of the Chinese Army. London: Oxford University Press, 1967.

Griffith, Samuel B. The Chinese People's Liberation Army. New York: McGraw-Hill, 1967.

Hatano Ken'ichi, comp. Chūgoku kyōsantō shi [History of the Chinese Communist Party]. 7 vols. Tokyo: Jiji tsūshin sha, 1961.

Hsieh, Alice L. Communist China's Military Doctrine and Strategy. Santa Monica, Calif.: Rand Corporation, 1963.

Hung-ch'i p'iao-p'iao pien-chi pu, comp. Chieh-fang chan-cheng hui-i-lu [Reminiscences of the War of Liberation]. Peking: Chung-kuo ch'ing-nien, 1961.

Important Documents on the Great Proletarian Cultural Revolution in China. Peking: Foreign Languages Press, 1970.

Jen-min chieh-fang-chün tsung-pu. Chung-kuo jen-min chieh-fang chan-cheng chün-shih wen-chi [A Collection of Military Documents on the Liberation War of the Chinese People]. 6 vols. N.p., 1951.

Jenner, William. Lin Piao on War and Revolution. New York: Harper & Row, 1973.

Joffe, Ellis. "The Chinese Army in the Cultural Revolution: The Politics of Intervention." Current Scene, VIII:18 (December 7, 1970).

————. Party and Army: Professionalism and Political Control in the Chinese Officer Corps, 1949-1964. Cambridge, Mass.: Harvard University Press, 1965.

Johnson, Chalmers. "Lin Piao's Army and Its Role in Chinese Society." Current Scene, IV:13-14 (July 1966).

Karnow, Stanley. Mao and China. New York: The Viking Press, 1972.

Kau, Ying-mao, ed. "The Case Against Lin Piao." Chinese
Law and Government, V:3-4 (Fall-Winter 1972-73).

————, ed. The People's Liberation Army and China's Nation-
Building. White Plains, N.Y.: International Arts and
Sciences Press, 1973.

————, et al. The Political Work System of the Chinese Communist Military. Providence: East Asia Language and
Area Center, Brown University, 1971.

Kung-fei "Min-ping she-hui chu-i chiao-yü chiao-ts'ai"
["Socialist Education Teaching Materials for the Militia"
of the Communist Bandits]. Taipei, 1964.

Kuo-min cheng-fu chün-shih wei-yüan-hui wei-yüan-chang Nan-
ch'ang hsing-ying ti-ssu-t'ing. Ch'ih-fei wen-chien hui-
pien [A Collection of Red Bandit Documents]. 11 vols.
N.p., 1934.

Lewis, John W. Leadership in Communist China. Ithaca, N.Y.:
Cornell University Press, 1963.

Li Tso-p'eng et al. Chi Lin Piao t'ung-chih [About Comrade
Lin Piao]. N.p., 1969.

Lien-tui cheng-chih kung-tso ching-yen [Political Work Experience in Company-Level Units]. Shanghai: Shanghai
jen-min, 1965.

Lin fu chu-hsi chün-shih chu-tso hsüan-tu [Selected Readings
on the Military Writings of Vice Chairman Lin]. N.p., n.d.

Lin Piao. Hold High the Red Flag of the Party's General Line
and Mao Tse-tung's Military Thinking and March Forward
in Mighty Strides. Peking: Foreign Languages Press, 1959.

————. Long Live the Victory of People's War. Peking: Foreign Languages Press, 1965.

"Lin Piao and the Cultural Revolution." Current Scene, VIII:14 (August 1, 1970).

Lin Piao chuan-chi [Special Collection on Lin Piao]. Hong Kong: Chung-kuo wen-t'i yen-chiu chung-hsin, 1970.

Lin Piao lun [On Lin Piao]. Hong Kong, n.d.

Lin Piao shih-chien chuan-chi [Special Collection on the Lin Piao Affair]. Taipei: Chung-kuo ta-lu yen-chiu-so, 1972.

Lin Piao chih-chien yen-hsi [Analysis of the Lin Piao Affair]. Taipei: Kuo-min-tang ti-liu-tsu, 1972.

Lin Piao t'ung-chih erh-shih-san lun [Twenty-three Quotations from Comrade Lin Piao]. Yunnan: Yün-nan ta-hsüeh, 1967.

Lin Piao yü-lu [Quotations from Lin Piao]. Hong Kong: Chung-kuo wen-t'i yen-chiu chung-hsin, 1969. Translated in China Problems Research Center, ed. Quotations from Lin Piao. Hong Kong: Chih Luen Press, 1971.

Lin Piao yü-lu [Quotations from Lin Piao]. Kunming: Hsin-i-chung ko-ming tsao-fan ping-t'uan cheng-chih pu, 1968.

Lin Piao yü-lu [Quotations from Lin Piao]. N.p.: Shou-to hung-tai-hui et al., 1967.

Liu, F. F. A Military History of Modern China, 1924-1949. Princeton, N.J.: Princeton University Press, 1956.

Lo Jui-ch'ing. K'ang-Jih chün-tui chung-ti cheng-chih kung-tso [Political Work in the Anti-Japanese Military Forces]. N.p.: Chung-kuo wen-hua she, 1939.

Mao Tse-tung. Chung-kuo kung-ch'an-tang hung-chün ti-ssu-
chün ti-chiu-tz'u tai-piao ta-hui chüeh-i-an [Resolution
of the Ninth Party Congress of the Fourth Army]. Hong
Kong: Hsin-min-chu, 1949.

————. [Collection of Statements by Mao Tse-tung, 1956-
1967; a Red Guard publication]. N.p., 1967.

Mao Tse-tung ssu-hsiang wan-sui [Long Live Mao Tse-tung
Thought]. N.p., 1967.

Mao Tse-tung ssu-hsiang wan-sui [Long Live Mao Tse-tung
Thought]. 2 vols. N.p., 1967-1969.

[Mao Tse-tung]. Mō Takutō bunken shiryō kenkyūkai, comp.,
Mō Takutō shū [Collected Writings of Mao Tse-tung].
10 vols. Tokyo: Hokubō sha, 1971-1972.

————. Selected Military Writings of Mao Tse-tung. Peking:
Foreign Languages Press, 1963.

————. Selected Readings of Mao Tse-tung. Peking: Foreign
Languages Press, 1967.

————. Selected Works of Mao Tse-tung. 4 vols. Peking:
Foreign Languages Press, 1961-1965.

Min-ping chün-shih hsün-lien shou-ts'e [Manual of the Military Training of the Militia]. Peking: Chung-kuo ch'ing-
nien, 1959.

Mozingo, David P., and T. W. Robinson. Lin Piao on "People's
War": China Takes a Second Look at Vietnam. Santa
Monica, Calif.: Rand Corporation, 1965.

Nippon kokusai mondai kenkyūjo, comp. Chūgoku kyōsanto shiryō-
shu [Collected Materials on the History of the Chinese Communist Party]. 12 vols. Tokyo: Keisō shobō, 1971-1973.

O'Ballance, Edgar. The Red Army of China. London: Faber
& Faber, 1962.

Powell, Ralph L. "Communist China's Mass Militia." Current
Scene, III:7-8 (November 15 and December 1, 1964).

————. The Rise of Chinese Military Power. Princeton, N.J.:
Princeton University Press, 1955.

Rhoads, Edward J. M., et al. The Chinese Red Army, 1927-
1963: An Annotated Bibliography. Cambridge, Mass.:
Harvard University Press, 1964.

Rice, Edward E. Mao's Way. Berkeley: University of
California Press, 1972.

Robinson, Thomas W., ed. The Cultural Revolution in China.
Berkeley: University of California Press, 1971.

————. A Politico-Military Biography of Lin Piao, Part I,
1907-1949. Santa Monica, Calif.: Rand Corporation, 1971.

San-pa tso-feng [Three-Eight Work Style]. Shanghai: Shanghai jen-min, 1965.

Shih Ch'eng-chih. Lun Chung-kung ti chün-shih fa-chan [On
the Development of the Chinese Communist Military].
Hong Kong: Yu-lien, 1952.

Snow, Edgar. Red Star Over China. New York: Random
House, 1938.

Solomon, Richard H. Mao's Revolution and the Chinese Political Culture. Berkeley: University of California Press,
1971.

Tai Fu. Jen-min ho chün-tui [The People and the Army].
Shanghai: Shang-hai tsa-chih, 1950.

Takada, Fusao. Rin Hyō [Lin Piao]. Tokyo: Shin jimbutsu, 1969.

Tang-tai Chung-kuo yen-chiu-so, comp. Chung-kung chung-yang cheng-chih tou-cheng shih-liao hui-chi [Compilation of Historical Materials on Political Struggle of the CCP Central Committee]. Vol. 1. Hong Kong: Tang-tai Chung-kuo yen-chiu-so, 1972.

Terao, Gorō. Rin Hyō no sakusen [Battles Fought by Lin Piao]. Tokyo: Tokuma, 1969.

Ti-shih-pa chi-t'uan-chün tsung-cheng-chih-pu hsuan-ch'uan-pu, comp. Chün-min kuan-hsi [Army-People Relations]. Shanghai: Shang-hai tsa-chih, 1949.

Thornton, Richard C. China: Struggle for Power, 1917-1972. Bloomington, Indiana: Indiana University Press, 1973.

Ting Wang, comp. Chung-kung wen-hua ta-ko-ming tzu-liao hui-pien [Compilation of Materials of the Cultural Revolution in Communist China]. 6 vols. Hong Kong: Ming pao, 1967-1972.

Tsou, Tang, and Ping-ti Ho, eds. China in Crisis. 2 vols. Chicago: University of Chicago Press, 1968.

Union Research Institute, comp. CCP Documents of the Great Proletarian Cultural Revolution, 1966-1967. Hong Kong: Union Research Institute, 1968.

Wang Chia-hsiang et al. Cheng-chih kung-tso lun-ts'ung [Discussions on Political Work]. N.p.: Pa-lu-chün chün-cheng tsa-chih-she, 1941.

Wang Chien-min. Chung-kuo kung-ch'an-tang shih-kao [History of the Chinese Communist Party]. 3 vols. Taipei: Hsien-ping yin-shua-ch'ang, 1965.

Wang Hsiang-li. Jen-min ti chün-tui [The People's Army].
    N.p.: Kuang-Hua shu-tien, 1948.
Whitson, William. The Chinese High Command: A History of
    Communist Military Politics, 1927-1971. New York:
    Praeger, 1973.

————. The Military and Political Power in China in the
    1970's. New York: Praeger, 1972.

Yamashita, Ryuzo. Chūgoku jimmin kaihōgun [The Chinese
    People's Liberation Army]. Tokyo: Keizai, 1969.